CW01572857

GLOBALISATION AND GOVERNANCE

While it might have been viable for states to isolate themselves from international politics in the nineteenth century, the intensity of economic and social globalisation in the twenty-first century has made this choice impossible. The contemporary world is an international world – a world of collective security systems and collective trade agreements.

What does this mean for the sovereign state and 'its' international legal order? Two alternative approaches to the problem of governance in the era of globalisation developed in the twentieth century: universal internationalism and regional supranationalism. The first approaches collective action problems from the perspective of the sovereign equality of all states; yet the consent requirement here typically settles for a governmental minimalism in which the unanimity rule translates into a 'tyranny against the majority'. A second approach to transnational governance has tried to remedy this by re-establishing majoritarian governmental structures on the regional scale. This regional approach promised to reduce collective action problems, and it did so by inviting states to share their internal sovereignty within a broader supranational 'union' of states.

This collection of essays aims to analyse – and contrast – the two types of normative and decisional solutions that have emerged as responses to the 'international' problems within our globalised world.

ROBERT SCHÜTZE is Professor of European Union Law and Co-Director of the Global Policy Institute, Durham University.

GLOBALISATION AND GOVERNANCE

International Problems, European Solutions

Edited by

ROBERT SCHÜTZE

Professor of European Law and Co-Director,
Global Policy Institute, Durham University

CAMBRIDGE
UNIVERSITY PRESS

University Printing House, Cambridge CB2 8BS, United Kingdom

One Liberty Plaza, 20th Floor, New York, NY 10006, USA

477 Williamstown Road, Port Melbourne, VIC 3207, Australia

314–321, 3rd Floor, Plot 3, Splendor Forum, Jasola District Centre, New Delhi – 110025, India

79 Anson Road, #06-04/06, Singapore 079906

Cambridge University Press is part of the University of Cambridge.

It furthers the University's mission by disseminating knowledge in the pursuit of education, learning, and research at the highest international levels of excellence.

www.cambridge.org
Information on this title: www.cambridge.org/9781107129900
DOI: 10.1017/9781316417027

First published 2018

Printed in the United Kingdom by Clays Ltd, Elcograf S.p.A.

A catalogue record for this publication is available from the British Library

Library of Congress Cataloging-in-Publication Data

Names: Schutze, Robert, editor.
Title: Globalisation and governance : international problems, European solutions / edited by Robert Schutze.
Other titles: Globalization and governance
Description: Cambridge [UK]; New York, NY: Cambridge University Press, 2018.
Identifiers: LCCN 2018031530 | ISBN 9781107129900 (hardback)
Subjects: LCSH: International law—European Union countries—Congresses. | International cooperation—Congresses. | International agencies—Law and legislation—European Union countries—Congresses. | International relations—Congresses. | European Union countries—Foreign relations—Law and legislation—Congresses. | Administrative law—European Union countries—Congresses. | Constitutional law--European Union countries—Congresses. | Globalization—Congresses. | LCGFT: Conference papers and proceedings.
Classification: LCC KJE5105.A8 G56 2018 | DDC 341.242/2—dc23
LC record available at https://lccn.loc.gov/2018031530

ISBN 978-1-107-12990-0 Hardback

TABLE OF CONTENTS

LIST OF CONTRIBUTORS

PHILIP ALLOTT is Professor Emeritus of International Public Law at Cambridge University, a Fellow of Trinity College Cambridge and a Fellow of the British Academy.

OLYMPIA BEKOU is Professor of Public International Law at the University of Nottingham School of Law and Head of the International Criminal Justice Unit of the Human Rights Law Centre.

JOCHEN VON BERNSTORFF is Professor of Constitutional Law, Public International Law and Human Rights Law at the University of Tübingen.

MARKUS W. GEHRING is a Lecturer in Law at the University of Cambridge and Arthur Watts Senior Research Fellow at the British Institute for International and Comparative Law. He is also a Fellow and Director of Studies at Hughes Hall, a Fellow of the Lauterpacht Centre for International Law and Lead Counsel for the Centre for International Sustainable Development Law.

KATARZYNA GRANAT is a Junior Research Fellow and a Marie Curie Fellow at Durham University School of Law.

DAVID HELD is Professor of Politics and International Relations at Durham University. He is Master of Durham University's University College, Co-Director of the Global Policy Institute and holds a Visiting Professorship at LUISS University.

ALICIA HINAREJOS is Senior Lecturer in Law at the Faculty of Law, University of Cambridge, and a Fellow of Downing College.

BERNARD M. HOEKMAN is Professor of Global Economics at the Robert Schuman Centre for Advanced Studies, European University Institute, where he is the Director of the 'Global Economics: Trade, Investment and Development' research area.

DIMITRY KOCHENOV is Professor of EU Constitutional Law at the Faculty of Law, University of Groningen.

MARTTI KOSKENNIEMI is Academy Professor of International Law at the University of Helsinki, and Director of the Erik Castrén Institute of International Law and Human Rights.

LUDWIG KRÄMER was a German judge and an official in the EU Commission's environmental department (since then retired from both functions). He is director of an environmental law consultancy in Madrid/ Spain.

PETROS C. MAVROIDIS is Edwin B. Parker Professor of Foreign and Comparative Law at Columbia Law School.

VALSAMIS MITSILEGAS is Head of the Law Department, Professor of European Criminal Law, and Dean for Research (Humanities and Social Sciences) at Queen Mary University of London. He is also Director of the Queen Mary Institute for the Humanities and Social Sciences, and the Queen Mary Criminal Justice Centre.

CHRISTOPH MÖLLERS is a Professor of Public Law and Jurisprudence at the Faculty of Law, Humboldt-University Berlin. He is a Permanent Fellow at the Institute for Advanced Study Berlin, and a member of the Board of Trustees at the Hertie School of Governance.

AOIFE O'DONOGHUE is Professor of International Law and Global Governance at Durham University School of Law, and is Co-Director of the Northern/Irish Feminist Judgments Project.

ROBERT SCHÜTZE is Professor of European Union Law at Durham University School of Law, and Co-Director of the Global Policy Institute. He holds Visiting Professorships at LUISS University and the College of Europe.

MARC WELLER is Professor of International Law and International Constitutional Studies at the University of Cambridge. He is a Fellow of the Chartered Institute of Arbitrators, and an Associate Tenant at Doughty Street Chambers.

RAMSES A. WESSEL is Professor of International and European Law and Governance at the University of Twente's Centre for European Studies.

BRUNO DE WITTE is Professor of European Union Law at Maastricht University, and Co-Director of the Maastricht Centre for European Law. He also holds a part-time professorship at the European University Institute.

ACKNOWLEDGEMENTS

This collection of essays originates in a conference organised by Cambridge and Durham Universities with the kind support of the European Research Council (EU Framework Programme 2007–13: ERC Grant Agreement No. 312 304) and the Durham Global Policy Institute. The conference, which took place in Cambridge in July 2014, brought together academics from international and European law to take stock and exchange views on the normative foundations, practical problems and solutions to governance issues beyond the state. Heartfelt thanks go to Dr Markus Gehring for his organisational wizardry and brilliant help during the first part of this academic enterprise and to Dr Thomas Sparks and María Pérez-Crespo for their assistance in the final stages of this book. Our contributors have been exemplary in their diligence and patience and the same holds true for Tom Randall of Cambridge University Press.

TABLE OF CASES

I International

II European Union I: European Court of Justice

III   European Union II: General Court

IV Council of Europe

TABLE OF INSTRUMENTS

I International

II   European Union

LIST OF ABBREVIATIONS

AG	Advocate General
AFSJ	Area of Freedom, Security and Justice
AJCL	*American Journal of Comparative Law*
AJIL	*American Journal of International Law*
APIC	Agreement on Privileges and Immunities
AU	African Union
AUILR	*American University International Law Review*
Bull. EC	Bulletin of the European Communities
CAP	Common Agricultural Policy
CCP	Common Commercial Policy
CDE	Cahiers de Droit Européen
CFI	Court of First Instance
CFR	Charter of Fundamental Rights of the Union
CFSP	Common Foreign and Security Policy
CITES	Convention on International Trade in Endangered Species
CJEL	*Columbia Journal of European Law*
CJEU	Court of Justice of the European Union
CLJ	*Cambridge Law Journal*
CML Rev	*Common Market Law Review*
CMO	Common Market Organisation
CoA	Court of Auditors
CoP	Conference of the Parties
CRTA	The Committee on Regional Trade Agreements
CT	Constitutional Treaty
CYELS	*Cambridge Yearbook of European Legal Studies*
DSU	Dispute Settlement Understanding
EC	European Community (Treaty)
ECA	Enhanced Cooperation Agreement
ECB	European Central Bank
ECHR	European Convention on Human Rights
ECOFIN	Council of Ministers for Economics and Finance
ECtHR	European Court of Human Rights

ECJ	European Court of Justice
ECLR	*European Constitutional Law Review*
ECR	European Court Reports
ECSC	European Coal and Steel Community
EDC	European Defence Community
EEA	European Economic Area
EEAS	European External Action Service
EEC	European Economic Community (Treaty)
EFSF	European Financial Stability Facility
EFTA	European Free Trade Association
EIO	European Investigation Order
EIT	European-Integration Theory
EJIL	*European Journal of International Law*
ELJ	*European Law Journal*
EL Rev	*European Law Review*
EMU	European Monetary Union
ENP	European Neighbourhood Policy
EP	European Parliament
EPC	European Political Cooperation
EPPO	European Public Prosecutor's Office
ESCB	European System of Central Banks
ESDP	European Security and Defence Policy
ESM	European Stabilisation Mechanism
EU (old)	European Union (Maastricht Treaty)
EWS	Early Warning System
FES	Forest Environmental Services
FIT	Feed-in Tariff
GATS	General Agreement on Trade in Services
GATT	General Agreement on Tariffs and Trade
GC	General Court
GLJ	*German Law Journal*
GMO	Genetically Modified Organism
GPA	Agreement on Government Procurement
HILJ	*Harvard International Law Journal*
HR	High Representative
ICC	International Criminal Court
ICJ	International Court of Justice
ICLQ	*International & Comparative Law Quarterly*
ICTR	International Criminal Tribunal for Rwanda
ICTY	International Criminal Tribunal for the former Yugoslavia
IGC	Intergovernmental Conference
ILC	International Law Commission

ILO	International Labour Organisation
IMF	International Monetary Fund
IO	*International Organisation*
IRENA	International Renewable Energy Agency
ITA	International Technology Agreement
ITLOS	International Tribunal for the Law of the Sea
JCMS	*Journal of Common Market Studies*
JEPP	*Journal of European Public Policy*
JHA	Justice and Home Affairs
JICJ	*Journal of International Criminal Justice*
JIEL	*Journal of International Economic Law*
JIL	*Journal of International Law*
LDC	Least Developed Country
LIEI	*Legal Issues of Economic Integration*
MBI	Market-Based Instrument
MEEQR	Measures having an Equivalent Effect to Quantitative Restrictions
MFN	Most Favoured Nation
MLR	*Modern Law Review*
NAFTA	North American Free Trade Agreement
NATO	North Atlantic Treaty Organisation
NGO	Non-Governmental Organisation
OECD	Organisation for Economic Cooperation and Development
OEEC	Organisation for European Economic Cooperation
OJ	Official Journal of the European Union
OJLS	*Oxford Journal of Legal Studies*
OMC	Open Method of Coordination
OMT	Outright Monetary Transactions
OTP	Office of the Prosecutor
PA	Plurilateral Agreement
PJCC	Police and Judicial Cooperation in Criminal Matters
PTA	Preferential Trade Agreement
QMV	Qualified Majority Voting
REDD	Reducing Emissions from Deforestation and Forest Degradation
RTDEur	*Revue trimestrielle de droit européen*
SCM	Subsidies and Countervailing Measures
SEA	Single European Act
SGP	Stability and Growth Pact
TA	Treaty of Amsterdam
TEU	Treaty on European Union (post Lisbon)
TFEU	Treaty on the Functioning of the European Union
TN	Treaty of Nice
TRIPS	Agreement on Trade-Related Aspects of Intellectual Property Rights

TPP	Trans-Pacific Partnership
TSCG	Treaty on Stability, Coordination and Governance
TTIP	Transatlantic Trade and Investment Partnership
TWAIL	Third World Approaches to International Law
UN	United Nations
UNEP	United Nations Programme for the Environment
UNGA	United Nations General Assembly
UNSC	United Nations Security Council
US	United States
VJICL	*Vienna Journal of International Constitutional Law*
WEU	Western European Union
WTO	World Trade Organization
YBIL	*Yearbook of International Law*
YEL	*Yearbook of European Law*
YJIL	*Yale Journal of International Law*
YLJ	*Yale Law Journal*
ZaöRV	*Zeitschrift für ausländisches öffentliches Recht und Völkerrecht*

Introduction

International Governance – Theory and Practice

ROBERT SCHÜTZE

While it might have been viable for states to isolate themselves from international politics in the nineteenth century,[1] the intensity of economic and social globalisation in the twenty-first century has made this choice impossible.[2] Not only have all major markets become 'internationalised', the ability of states unilaterally to guarantee internal or external peace have dramatically declined: 'Nation-states can no longer secure the boundaries of their own territories, the vital necessities of their populations, and the material preconditions for the reproduction of their societies by their own efforts.'[3] The contemporary world is an *international* world – a world of *collective* security systems and *collective* trade agreements.

What does this mean for the sovereign state and 'its' international legal order?[4] If each legal order tries to 'reflect the principles of the social order that it seeks to regulate',[5] what legal principles do or should govern the contemporary world? If the empirical conditions in which 'national' solutions were found to offer satisfactory regulatory responses are no longer with us,[6] is there not a postulate of practical reason that demands new

---

[1] On the US American policy of 'isolationism' until World War I, see G. C. Herring, *From Colony to Superpower: U.S. Foreign Relations since 1776* (Oxford University Press, 2011).

[2] On social and economic globalisation, see D. Held and A. McGrew (eds.), *The Global Transformations Reader: An Introduction to the Globalisation Debate* (Polity Press, 2003).

[3] J. Habermas, *The Divided West* (Polity, 2006), 176.

[4] On the dialectical relationship between the emergence of the modern state and modern international law, see W. G. Grewe, *The Epochs of International Law* (Walter de Gruyter, 2000), Parts III and IV.

[5] W. Friedmann, *The Changing Structure of International Law* (Columbia University Press, 1978), 3. For a similar point, albeit with a positivistic and conservative 'sting', see P. Weil, 'Towards Relative Normativity in International Law?' (1983) 77 *AJIL* 413.

[6] One illustration of this loss of 'boundary control' of most nation-states is the loss of 'public' power in the intense corporate tax competition that has resulted from globalisation and thereby weakened the modern welfare state (see D. Rodrik, *The Globalization*

normative solutions? In other words: if the problems within today's world are international problems, should the regulatory solutions not be 'international' or 'supranational' solutions?

Two alternative approaches to the problem of 'governance' in the era of 'globalisation' developed in the twentieth century: universal internationalism and regional supranationalism. Both were born in the shockwaves of two terrifying World (!) Wars, which profoundly questioned the stability and permanence of an international 'order' founded on the idea of sovereign nation states. The post-war period thus sees the creation of global institutions,[7] such as the 1945 United Nations (UN) and the 1947 General Agreement on Tariffs and Trade (GATT) to stabilise world peace and to liberalise the world economy.[8] Nevertheless, modern international law retained its adherence to the 'sovereign equality' of all states.[9] In theory, the 'spheres' of international and national law have indeed stayed divided;[10] and by allowing each state to sovereignly determine the status of international norms within its domestic legal order, the 'normativity' of international law has remained contested.[11] Practically, the tension

---

    Paradox (Oxford University Press, 2012), 193: 'There has been a remarkable reduction in corporate taxes around the world since the early 1980s. The average for the member countries of the OECD countries, excluding the United States, has fallen from around 50 per cent in 1981 to 30 per cent in 2009.').

[7] A. Verdross and B. Simma, *Universelles Völkerrecht. Theorie und Praxis* (Duncker & Humblot, 1976). On the relationship between these formal 'universal' institutions and US American hegemony, see only: G. J. Ikenberry, 'Globalization as American Hegemony' in D. Held and A. McGrew (eds.), *Globalization Theory* (Polity, 2007), 41; and on the 'hegemonic stability thesis' for international institutions more generally, see C. Kindleberger, *The World in Depression 1929–1939* (University of California Press, 1986).

[8] For a historical introduction to the United Nations Charter, see H. Kelsen, *The Law of the United Nations: A Critical Analysis of its Fundamental Problems* (Lawbook Exchange, 2011). On the origins and historical background of the GATT, see J. H. Jackson, *World Trade and The Law of the GATT* (Bobbs-Merrill, 1969).

[9] See Article 2(1) UN Charter: 'The Organization is based on the principle of the sovereign equality of all its Members.' On the need of a 'hegemonic' superpower to be more equal than all others, see however above n. 7.

[10] The classic dualism doctrine was based on the idea that international law and national law form 'two circles that may touch, but never overlap' (H. Triepel, *Völkerrecht und Landesrecht* (Scientia, 1958), 111); and while this idea has been softened around the edges in the past hundred years, it is still part and parcel of contemporary international law. See only Article 2(7) UN Charter: 'Nothing contained in the present Charter shall authorize the United Nations to intervene in matters which are essentially within the domestic jurisdiction of any state[.]'. This is also the case, mutatis mutandis, for the GATT.

[11] H. L. A. Hart, *The Concept of Law* (Oxford University Press, 1997), Chapter 10. See also: M. Koskenniemi, *From Apology to Utopia: The Structure of International Legal Argument* (Cambridge University Press, 2005).

between binding international norms and state sovereignty is however generally resolved by a voluntarist doctrine of consent. The consent requirement, despite its 'legitimacy' pretensions,[12] nevertheless means settling for a 'governmental' minimalism in which the unanimity rule translates into a 'tyranny against the majority'.[13]

A second approach to transnational 'governance' has tried to remedy these shortcomings by re-establishing majoritarian governmental structures at the regional scale. This regional approach promised to reduce collective action problems, and it did so by inviting a limited group of states to share their internal sovereignty within a broader supranational 'union' of states.[14] The best analysed example here is the European Union (EU).[15] From the very start, European integration contrasted with international 'coordination' in two essential ways. Normatively, the status of supranational law within the domestic legal orders would generally not depend on national law; and decisionally, the creation of supranational norms would, as a rule, not require unanimous consent.[16] In both respects, the European Treaties clearly 'broke' with 'ordinary' international law because they set up a government endowed with 'real powers stemming from a limitation of sovereignty or a transfer of powers from the States'.[17] But what kind of 'government' has the EU; and what governance solutions did it have to offer?

This collection of essays wishes to analyse – and contrast – the two types of normative and decisional answers that have emerged as responses to

---

[12] For the idea that only a (unanimous) consent may legitimise 'international' or 'supranational' law, see J. H. H. Weiler, 'The Transformation of Europe' (1991) 100 *YLJ* 2403, 2473.

[13] A. McNair, 'International Legislation' (1933–4) 19 *Iowa Law Review* 177 at 181 (quoting N. Politis, my translation).

[14] See only the 'Spaak Report' on the advantages of creating a European Economic Community (cf. R. Schulze and T. Hoeren, *Dokumente zum Europäischen Recht: Band 1: Gründungsverträge* (Springer 1999), 756 (my translation, emphasis added)): 'And even if we much desire a far-reaching liberalisation of world trade, for the reason set out above, *a true common market can only be created by a limited group of States* – although their number should be as big as the creation of such a common market would allow.'

[15] P. Pescatore, *The Law of Integration: Emergence of a new Phenomenon in International Relations, based on the Experience of the European Communities* (Sijthoff, 1974).

[16] This dual supranationalism formula formed part of the 1951 European Coal and Steel Community. Within the 1957 European Economic Community it was however questioned by the Luxembourg Compromise; yet after 1979 and *Cassis de Dijon*, the dual character of supranationalism was restored first by the judiciary, and after 1987 by the Member States through the Single European Act. For the – mistaken – idea that normative and decisional supranationalism are or were in a state of 'equilibrium' within the European integration project, see Weiler, 'The Transformation of Europe' (above n. 12).

[17] Case 6/64, *Costa* v. *ENEL* (1964) ECR 585, 593.

the 'international' problems within our globalised world: universal internationalism and European supranationalism. We have tried to chart this – enormous – intellectual terrain by dividing our analysis into two-times-two 'quarters'. The book is therefore divided into two parts – international and supranational – which are each further divided alongside a 'theoretical' (formal) and a 'practical' (substantive) dimension.

The theoretical dimension is to explore the 'formal foundations' of each legal order, that is: the normative 'resources' that were historically developed to 'explain' and 'justify' governance beyond the nation state. How has (inter)national legal theory justified the binding nature of norms adopted outside the state? How can a 'treaty' – a consensual instrument – be the fountain of *compulsory* international law; and 'how can one give meaning to concepts such as "crimes against humanity"'?[18] The discussion of the practical dimension is to complementarily offer an – impressionistic – arsenal of the substantive 'challenges' (and 'solutions') to the problems of our times; yet the book also hopes to show that the practical solutions are – of course – in a dialectic relationship with the theoretical 'superstructure' in which they are embedded. For us, the three 'common' concerns that pose the most pressing collective action problems today are: the maintenance of peace and security, the regulation of the economy (and finance), and the protection of the environment; and we have finally added 'criminal law' as this area of law traditionally enjoys strong 'emotive' associations with (national) 'communities'.

The central premise behind the book is as simple as it is (perhaps) uncontroversial: when contrasting internationalism with supranationalism, the 'formal' and 'substantive' tools offered by the latter to 'govern' collective transnational problems are distinctly firmer and sharper; and the contemporary solutions for global 'governance' problems therefore should lie – at least in the immediate future – in the creation of regional 'governments' beyond the nation state. The specific advantages of 'regionalism' in solving transnational problems are not new;[19] yet the rise of regionalism at the turn of the twenty-first century is impressive.[20] Offering a middle ground

---

[18] Cf. S. Benhabib, *Another Cosmopolitanism* (Oxford University Press, 2008), 20–1.

[19] For an excellent analysis here, see L. Fawcett and A. Hurrell (eds.), *Regionalism in World Politics: Regional Organization and International Order* (Oxford University Press, 1992), esp. Chapter 2; as well as: W. Mattli, *The Logic of Regional Integration: Europe and Beyond* (Cambridge University Press, 1999).

[20] For an overview of the 'new regionalism', see F. Söderbaum, *Rethinking Regionalism* (Palgrave, 2016); as well as: T. Börzel and T. Risse (eds.), *The Oxford Handbook of Comparative Regionalism* (Oxford University Press, 2016).

between 'cosmopolitanism' and 'nationalism', 'regionalism' promises to contain the – external – pressures of globalisation while it also represents an – internal – compromise that combines unity and diversity.[21] And as long as the realisation of the 'positive idea of a world republic' is 'utopian', the best 'practical' solution here undoubtedly remains its 'negative substitute' in the form of a (regional) federation of states.[22] Importantly, then: regional supranationalism is not an argument against international 'universalism'. The two approaches to govern transnationally can complement each other;[23] even if there are – of course – normative tensions between a 'particular' and the 'universal' approach; and these divergences have in the past resurfaced both in the context of the United Nations and the World Trade Organization.[24]

Having outlined the overall structure and argument of the collection, let me briefly introduce the diverse voices within it. Part I(A) begins with

---

[21] On this combination in the context of the European Union, see H. Wallace, 'Politics and Policy in the EU: The Challenge of Governance' in H. Wallace and W. Wallace (eds.), *Policy-Making in the European Union* (Oxford University Press, 1996), 16: 'European integration can be seen as a distinct West European effort to contain the consequences of globalisation. Rather than be forced to choose between the national polity for developing policies and the relative anarchy of the globe, west Europeans invented a form of regional governance with polity-like features to extend the state and harden the boundary between themselves and the rest of the world.'

[22] I. Kant, 'Perpetual Peace: A Philosophical Sketch' in *Political Writings* (Cambridge University Press, 1991), 105. For the view that no 'government' – neither universal nor regional – is needed, see A.-M. Slaughter, *A New World Order* (Princeton University Press, 2004). However, the view that 'global governance though national governments' (ibid., 32) is the solution to global problems is at best naïve and at worst hegemonic.

[23] For the United Nations, see only Article 52(1) UN Charter: 'Nothing in the present Charter precludes the existence of regional arrangements or agencies for dealing with such matters relating to the maintenance of international peace and security as are appropriate for regional action, provided that such arrangements or agencies and their activities are consistent with the Purposes and Principles of the United Nations.' For the GATT, see only Article XXIV(4): 'The contracting parties recognize the desirability of increasing freedom of trade by the development, through voluntary agreements, of closer integration between the economies of the countries parties to such agreements.'

[24] In the context of the United Nations, the best-known example is the 'Kadi Saga'. For a discussion of this famous 'divergence', see only: R. Schütze, *Foreign Affairs and the EU Constitution* (Cambridge University Press, 2014), 65–90. For a discussion of the increasing divergence between the WTO rules and EU internal market law, see R. Schütze, *Framing Dassonville: Text and Context in European Law* (Cambridge University Press, in preparation), esp. Chapter 6. For the – contrary and indefensible – idea that international and European trade law are converging and not diverging, see however J. H. H. Weiler, 'Epilogue: Towards a Common Law of International Trade' in J. H. H. Weiler (ed.), *The EU, The WTO and the NAFTA* (Oxford University Press, 2000), 201.

a historical exploration of the 'unsettled' formal foundations of international government in the eighteenth century, and here in particular the philosophy of Immanuel Kant (Robert Schütze). Leaping over the well-settled nineteenth century,[25] our second chapter then investigates the renaissance of 'objective' normativity at the beginning of the twentieth century through the work of Hans Kelsen (Jochen von Bernstorff). These historical pieces are complemented by two philosophical investigations on the normative structure of the contemporary world order seen through the prism of 'tyranny' (Aoife O'Donoghue) and the epistemological question of the relationship between a 'theory' of a 'new order' and the 'reality' of the 'new world' (Philip Allott).

How do these formal foundations translate into substantive international 'governance' solutions? Part I(B) offers a vision of a 'real utopia' through the 'international constitutionalisation and the use of force' (Marc Weller). It subsequently moves to an analysis of the changing legal structure of international trade law, where the world economy is less and less 'governed' by a universal World Trade Organization (WTO); and where the dramatic rise of 'regional' trade agreements or 'plurilateral agreements' has challenged and 'fragmented' global approaches within this area (Bernard Hoekman and Petros Mavroidis). The global environment and its governance problems is the subject of Chapter 7 (Markus Gehring), while the last chapter within this first part explores the theory and practice of international criminal law through the prisms of 'universalism' and 'pluralism' (Olympia Bekou).

What are the normative and decisional resources brought to transnational problems by the EU? The theoretical schism between the 'old' order of international law and the 'new' order of European law is the theme of Part II(A). For while there are excellent attempts to explain regional integration with the normative vocabulary of international law (Bruno de Witte), the EU has resolutely embraced a 'constitutional' paradigm in which it sees itself as exercising autonomous 'public' power – even if there remain significant 'governmental' deficits (Christoph Möllers). Based on the principle of subsidiarity, the Union conceives itself as a unity-in-diversity that aims to offer 'European' solutions only where the Member States are not themselves able to provide 'governmental' responses. The origins and components of the principle – as well as its shortcomings – will be analysed in Chapter 10 (Katarzyna Granat). European supranationalism

---

[25] For a wonderful discussion here, see M. Koskenniemi, *The Gentle Civilizer of Nations: The Rise and Fall of International Law 1870–1960* (Cambridge University Press, 2001).

also means dual citizenship in which citizens are members of two political orders. Far from being a 'cynical public relations exercise',[26] the EU citizenship provisions have had a 'constructive' function that has 'transformed' – at least to some extent – the 'logic' or 'mindset' of the European institutions (Dimitry Kochenov).

Have these – very – different normative foundations given rise to different substantive solutions in our four reference areas? Part II(B) begins to analyse this question by exploring the 'regional' approach that the EU has taken to foreign and security policy (Ramses Wessel). It is here argued that 'it is perhaps the best example of a combination of national, EU and international legal elements' that have been developed to cope with globalisation.[27] This hybridity, while no longer part of the internal market core, can also be found at the margins of European economic integration, where there has been a resurgence of intergovernmental techniques in the (executive) 'governance' of Economic and Monetary Union (Alicia Hinarejos). A much more 'positive' integration example however is, by contrast, offered in the subsequent chapters dealing with EU environmental law (Ludwig Krämer) and EU criminal law (Valsamis Mitsilegas). Especially the last chapter underlines the dialectical interplay between the theoretical foundations of an area and its practical challenges and solutions.

The 'European' solutions to the 'international' problems caused by globalisation are of course not meant to be 'universal'. They are 'particular' solutions generated within and for one particular region – Europe – and will neither necessarily nor directly offer substantive answers to different regions of the world.[28] Yet the European 'example' may be inspiring in at least one more general way: for it has shown a remarkable imagination and determination to go beyond the 'sovereigntist' thinking of the nation state era.[29] Indeed: the ability to formally imagine a European 'government' – not

---

[26] For this view, see J. H. H. Weiler, 'Citizenship and Human Rights' in J. A. Winter et al. (eds.), *Reforming the Treaty on European Union* (Kluwer Law International, 1996), 57, 68.

[27] For this point, see page 339 below.

[28] *Pace* neo-functionalists, there is indeed no universal logic of regional integration. For an excellent comparative analysis here, see only: L. Fioramonti (ed.), *Regionalism in a Changing World* (Routledge, 2013); and more recently: L. Fioramonti and F. Mattheis, 'Is Africa Following Europe? An Integrated Framework for Comparative Regionalism' (2016) 54 *JCMS* 674.

[29] See T. Börzel and T. Risse, 'Introduction' in T. Börzel and T. Risse (eds.), *The Oxford Handbook of Comparative Regionalism* (Oxford University Press, 2016), 3, 5: 'While the EU is the most developed regional organization and continues to be a model for comparison and emulation, we argue that it is not necessarily one of its kind, if it ever was. Systematic comparisons with regionalisms in other parts of the world deconstruct the allegedly sui generis "nature of the beast". For an interesting way to link 'European Studies' with

just informal 'governance' – in which (formal) 'legislation' is adopted by a 'bicameral legislature' that comprises a 'Parliament' that is 'democratically' elected testifies to a remarkable change in the normative 'mindset' brought to the solution of collective transnational problems.[30] And despite the sirens of decline and doom,[31] Europe's imagination and determination are not confined to a generation of messianic patriarchs; nor do the Union's normative resources or substantive solutions lie in its nation states' past.[32] The EU must – and will – evolve into a more perfect union that will further develop its own 'constitutionalism' within which international problems will find supranational solutions. But these – broader and controversial – matters shall all be returned to in the 'Conclusion' (Martti Koskenniemi), while an 'Epilogue' lays out elements of a theory of global governance (David Held).

'Regionalism Studies', see A. Warleigh-Lack and B. Rosamond, 'Across the EU Studies–New Regionalism Frontier: Invitation to a Dialogue' (2010) 48 *JCMS* 993.

[30] M. Koskenniemi, 'Constitutionalism as Mindset: Reflections on Kantian Themes about International Law and Globalisation' (2007) 8 *Theoretical Inquiries in Law* 9. And see also: P. Allott, Chapter 4 in this volume: 'It is the task of *philosophy* to provide the emerging international society with the self-consciousness of a true society.'

[31] See only: G. Majone, *Rethinking the Union of Europe Post-Crisis: Has Integration Gone Too Far?* (Cambridge University Press, 2014); as well as J. H. H. Weiler, 'In the Face of Crisis: Input Legitimacy, Output Legitimacy and the Political Messianism of European Integration' (2012) 34 *Journal of European Integration* 825.

[32] See especially: G. Majone, *Dilemmas of European Integration: The Ambiguities and Pitfalls of Integration by Stealth* (Oxford University Press, 2009), 188: 'the absolute primacy of the territorial state over all competing principles of social cohesion' as well as Weiler, 'In the Face of Crisis' (above n.31), 837: 'primacy of the national communities as the deepest source of legitimacy of the integration project'.

PART I

International Perspectives

A. *Formal Foundations*

1

The 'Unsettled' Eighteenth Century

Kant and his Predecessors

ROBERT SCHÜTZE

I Introduction

With the decline of the (inter)national idea of 'empire' in the early modern period,[1] the belief in a 'universal' law binding all humanity was gradually replaced by legal pluralism. The apostles of state sovereignty came to deny the very existence of supranational legal authority above the state and introduced a distinction that still structures our modern imagination: the distinction between national and international law. The former would be the sphere of subordination *within* a sovereign state; the latter became the sphere of coordination *between* sovereign states. International law is henceforth no longer the (cosmopolitan) *ius gentium* of mankind;[2] it is the *ius inter gentes* that regulates the formal interactions between sovereign states: war and peace.[3] From the perspective of modern international law, a 'civil law' between sovereigns leads to a contradiction: for if sovereignty

---

[1] On this point: J. N. Figgis, *Political Thought from Gerson to Grotius: 1414–1625* (Cambridge University Press, 2011) as well as R. Koebner, *Empire* (Cambridge University Press, 1966), esp. Chapter 2.

[2] In antiquity, the idea of 'international law' begins inside the history of the *ius gentium*. It is associated with 'natural law', that is: the law that is universally valid because it applies to all human beings. Roman legal theory conceptually contrasts it to the 'civil law'. The latter applies within particular civil societies, whereas the *ius gentium* applies to all societies as *ius commune* (Gaius, *The Institutes*, trans. W. M. Gordon and O. F. Robinson (Duckworth, 1988)). Unlike our modern understanding, the *ius gentium* is consequently *not* the law between civil societies (or states). The *ius gentium* is the common law of mankind that nonetheless steps into the background whenever a society has chosen 'its' domestic law. This conception of *ius gentium* identifies the latter with *private* international law; it is the law that applies to relations with foreign individuals (cf. P. Vinogradoff, *Historical Types of International Law* (Brill, 1923), 25).

[3] W. Grewe, *The Epochs of International Law* (De Gruyter, 2000), 25. See also R. Tuck, *The Rights of War and Peace* (Oxford University Press, 2001).

is the defining characteristic of the modern state, there could be no higher 'public' authority.

What then are the normative foundations of modern international law? How could international norms be 'laws' if there was no 'government' above the states? Could there be a 'positive' international law; or was the latter simply dissolved into natural law? These questions gained prominence in the seventeenth century,[4] and come to be heavily debated in the eighteenth century. The latter thereby represents a 'Sattelzeit': a time of semantic reformation in which many pre-modern concepts are redefined so as to receive their modern meaning.[5] Within that century, we thus find *both* older and newer conceptions of the normative foundations of international law coexisting (a coexistence that is lost in the nineteenth century).[6] This parallel existence of old and new ideas will be discussed in section II. It explores the ambivalent foundations of international law through three – contrasting – common topoi. The first reaches back to a (metaphysical) world republic that 'authorises' all positive international law; the second conception grounds international law solely in the consent of sovereign states, while a third conception defends the idea of 'civil law' between states through a federal foundation.

The most sophisticated combination of all three conceptions has emerged in the writings of Immanuel Kant. Originally disregarded as a legal philosopher, Kant's ideas on the foundations of (inter)national law have regained enormous importance in the twentieth century.[7] Section III explores his – changing – views, which in themselves reflect the unsettled nature of eighteenth-century thought. Originally endorsing the idea that world peace could only be achieved through the creation of a world

---

[4] H. Steiger, 'Völkerrecht' in O. Brunner et al. (eds.), *Geschichtliche Grundbegriffe: Historisches Lexikon zur politisch-sozialen Sprache in Deutschland*, 9 vols. (Klett-Cotta, 2004), VII, 97, 110: 'Das Verhältnis von "ius naturae" und "ius gentium" bleibt begrifflich-theoretisch letzten Endes offen. Weder den Spaniern noch Grotius gelingt eine endgültige Klärung. Sie geben dem Naturrecht eindeutig den Vorrang.' For the emergence and development of early modern natural rights theories, see R. Tuck, *Natural Rights Theories* (Cambridge University Press, 1979).

[5] On the importance of the eighteenth century as a 'Sattelzeit', see R. Kosselleck, 'Einleitung' in O. Brunner et al. (eds.), *Geschichtliche Grundbegriffe: Historisches Lexikon zut politisch-sozialen Sprache in Deutschland*, 9 vols. (Klett-Cotta, 2004), I, xv.

[6] H. Steiger, 'Völkerrecht und Naturrecht zwischen Christian Wolff und Adolf Lasson' in H. Steiger (ed.), *Von der Staatengesellschaft zur Weltrepublik?* (Nomos, 2009), 143: 'Seit dem Ende des 18. Jahrhunderts verlagerte sich das Gewicht immer mehr auf die Darstellung des positiven "Europäischen Völkerrechts"; am Ende unsere Epoche werden Lehrbücher des positiven "Völkerrechts" das Bild beherrschen.'

[7] For a revival of Kantian thought, see especially J. Rawls, *A Theory of Justice* (Harvard University Press, 2005); as well as J. Habermas, *The Divided West* (Polity Press, 2006).

republic, Kant subsequently settled on a federation of states as the foundation of international law. The reasons behind this move will be explored
in section IV, which also discusses the 'antinomies' of international right
and the obstacles to the creation of a compulsory international law. Finally,
section V analyses the idea of a 'permissive law' as a mediating device
between the ideal and the real world of international society.

II   Foundations of International Law: Three Topoi

Having lost the metaphysical certainties of the past, all early modern
scholars of international law battle to establish normative foundations for
the new 'law of nations'. What is the relationship between natural law and
'positive' international law? While Grotius allows for a 'natural' and 'positive' ('voluntary') international law,[8] Hobbes famously denied the existence of any 'positive' (external) international law by seeing international
law as part of the (non-enforceable) natural law of the 'state of nature'.[9] By
the early eighteenth century, the legal validity of 'positive' international
law had indeed become a major philosophical problem. For if 'positive'
international law existed, what was its relation to 'national law' and what
was the 'reason' behind its (presumed) status as 'law'? Three very different answers to this quest for the normative foundations of international
law are offered in the eighteenth century. These three answers reverber-
ate throughout that century, and only in the following century would one
solution come to dominate over the others.[10]

A   'Civil' Foundations: Wolff and the World Republic

A famous eighteenth-century attempt to provide a normative foundation
for 'positive' international law is made in the work of Christian Wolff.[11]
Wolff defines international law as 'the science of that law which nations or

---

[8] For the ambivalent position of Grotius in particular, see P. Haggenmacher, *Grotius et la doctrine de la guerre juste* (Presses Universitaires de France, 1983).

[9] T. Hobbes, *Leviathan*, ed. R. Tuck (Cambridge University Press, 1996), 244: '[T]he Law of Nations, and the Law of Nature, is the same thing ... [a]nd the same Law, that dicta-teth to men that have no Civil Government, what they ought to do, and what to avoid in regard to one another, dictateth the same to Common-wealths, that is, to the Consciences of Sovereign Princes, and Sovereign Assemblies; there being no Court of Natural Justice, but in the Conscience onely; where not Man, but God raigneth.'

[10] M. Koskenniemi, *The Gentle Civilizer of Nations: The Rise and Fall of International Law 1870–1960* (Cambridge University Press, 2010).

[11] C. Wolff, *Jus Gentium Methodo Scientifica*, trans. J. H. Drake (Oxford University Press, 1934 [1749]).

peoples use in their relations with each other and of the obligations corresponding thereto'.[12] Nations are here regarded as individual persons living in a 'state of nature'; and, originally, they 'used none other than natural law; therefore the law of nations is originally nothing except the law of nature applied to nations'.[13] This natural law is seen to constitute the 'necessary law of nations' or 'internal law of nations' because it 'binds nations in conscience'.[14] This law is said to be immutable,[15] and it is complemented by a changing 'positive' international law that externally imposes obligations on the modern state.

What is the normative foundation of this positive law; and whence does its 'legal' nature come from? In the famous words of Wolff, it is this:

> Nature herself has established society among all nations and binds them to preserve society. For nature herself has established society among men and binds them to preserve it. Therefore, since this obligation, as coming from the law of nature, is necessary and immutable, it cannot be changed for the reason that nations have united into a state. Therefore society, which nature has established among individuals, still exists among nations and consequently, after states have been established in accordance with the law of nature and nations have arisen thereby, nature herself also must be said to have established society among all nations and bound them to preserve society. *If we should consider that great society, which nature herself has established among men, to be done away with by the particular societies, which men enter, when they unite into a state, states would be established contrary to the law of nature, in as much as the universal obligation of all toward all would be terminated; which assuredly is absurd.*[16]

Wolff thus presupposes the existence of a world state behind international law.[17] What is the purpose of this world state (*civitas maxima*)? The metaphysical fiction is introduced to explain changes in and impose obligations under international law. To 'concretise' and 'externalise' universal natural law,[18] a universal positive law is required; and this positive law can only be

---

[12] Ibid., §1.

[13] Ibid., §3.

[14] Ibid., §4.

[15] Ibid., §5.

[16] Ibid., §7 (emphasis added).

[17] In the words of N. Greenwood Onuf, 'Civitas Maxima: Wolff, Vattel and the Fate of Republicanism' (1994) 88 *AJIL* 280, 296: 'Only by locating the *civitas maxima* at the apex of an ascending series of associations prescribed by the theory of corporations can we make sense of this proposition. The contemporary idea of an impersonal world-state connecting directly with individuals is irrelevant and, for Wolff, inconceivable ... Wolff's model is the *respublica composita*.'

[18] For the complex relationship between the necessary (natural) law and the positive (voluntary) law, see Wolff, *Jus Gentium Methodo Scientifica* (above n. 11), §22: 'The voluntary

adopted by a world state that gives it a commanding 'will'. Only a (hyposta-sised) world state can adopt 'voluntary' world civil law.

Within this world state, '[a]ll nations are understood to have come together into a state, whose separate members are separate nations, or indi-vidual states'.[19] This 'supreme state' is 'a kind of democratic government';[20] and the world state is entitled to adopt (positive) 'civil laws'.[21] These civil laws are adopted by the (fictitious) majority of the states,[22] as represented by a (fictitious) ruler of the supreme state.[23] These voluntary laws of nature are legally binding and can be externally enforced:

> In the supreme state the nations as a whole have a right to coerce the indi-vidual nations, if they should be unwilling to perform their obligation, or should show themselves negligent in it. For in a state the right belongs to the whole of coercing the individuals to perform their obligation, if they should either be unwilling to perform it or should show themselves neg-ligent in it. Therefore since all nations are understood to have combined into a state, of which the individual nations are members, and inasmuch as they are understood to have combined in the supreme state, the individual members of this are understood to have bound themselves to the whole, because they wish to promote the common good, since moreover from the passive obligation of one party the right of the other arises; therefore the right belongs to the nations as a whole in the supreme state also of coercing the individual nations, if they are unwilling to perform their obligation or show themselves negligent in it.[24]

---

law of nations is, therefore equivalent to the civil law, consequently it is derived in the same manner from the necessary law of nations, as we have shown that the civil law must be derived from the natural law in the fifth chapter of the eighth part of "The Law of Nature".

[19] Ibid., §9.

[20] Ibid., §10 and §19. The latter paragraph continues: 'The supreme state is a kind of demo-cratic form of government. For the supreme state is made up of the nations as a whole, which as individual nations are free and equal to each other. Therefore, since no nation by nature is subject to another nation, and since it is evident of itself that nations by com-mon consent have not bestowed the sovereignty which belongs to the whole as against the individual nations, upon one or more particular nations, nay, that it cannot even be con-ceived under human conditions how this may happen, that sovereignty is understood to have been reserved for nations as a whole. Therefore, since the government is democratic, if the sovereignty rests with the whole, which in the present instance is the entire human race divided up into peoples or nations, the supreme state is a kind of democratic form of government.'

[21] Ibid., §11. Within the Wolffian system of divided sovereignty, it is thus possible to envisage an international criminal law because states are entitled to 'punish' others (ibid., §272): 'The right belongs to every nation to punish another nation which has injured it.'

[22] Ibid., §20.

[23] Ibid., §21.

[24] Ibid., §13.

But can states be forced to obey the world law? Wolff answers this question affirmatively by means of a revolutionary innovation: the idea of divided sovereignty: 'Some sovereignty over individual nations belongs to nations as a whole. For a certain sovereignty over individuals belongs to the whole in a state.'[25]

This 'public' and 'universal' part of international law is joined by two 'private' sources of (positive) international law. First: there is the 'stipulative' law founded on the express consent of the states, and which arises from international treaties;[26] and second, there is customary law based on the tacit consent of states.[27] Yet importantly: neither of these 'sources' constitute real sources of international law as law. Not only are the stipulations 'not universal but particular'; both international agreements and custom simply 'cannot be considered as the law of nations' 'just as the private law for citizens ... is considered as having no value at all as civil law for a certain particular state'.[28] The 'private' law sources of international law are therefore not producing 'real' law. For what is 'law' within the law of treaties are only the binding norms that force states to obey their promises, and these rules form part of the voluntary law of nations (Figure 1).

B   Consensual Foundations: Vattel and Positive Law

Superficially, Vattel stands to Wolff like an apprentice to his master; yet Vattel not only 'de-scholasticises' Wolff's work;[29] he famously derives, while taking over much of Wolff's work, a number of very different conclusions.[30]

The central plank within Vattel's philosophy of international law is the postulated sovereignty of each state: '[t]he law of nations is the law of sovereigns';[31] and a state that wishes to be part of international society must be a sovereign state.[32] From this idea stems the outright rejection of

---

[25] Ibid., §15.

[26] Ibid., §23.

[27] Ibid., §24.

[28] Ibid., §23.

[29] For an excellent analysis of the methodological shift between Wolff and Vattel, see E. Tourme-Jouannet, L'Emergence doctrinale du droit international classique: Emer de Vattel et l'Ecole de droit de la nature et des gens (Pedone, 1998), 105 et seq.

[30] E. de Vattel, The Law of Nations, trans: J. Chitty (Johnson & Co., 1883 [1758]).

[31] Ibid., Preface, xvi.

[32] Ibid., Book I, §4: 'To give a nation a right to make an immediate figure in this grand society, it is sufficient that it be really sovereign and independent, that is, that it governs itself by its own authority and laws.'

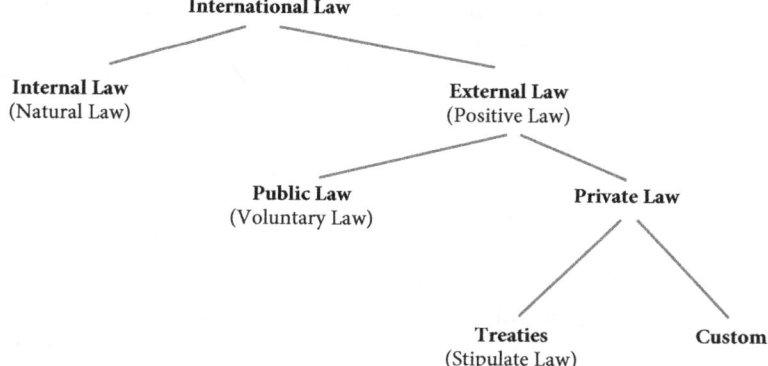

Figure 1.1 Wolff's Sources of International Law

a 'civil law' between states; and this famous rejection is announced at the very beginning in Vattel's 'Law of Nations' (1758):

> In the very outset of my work, it will be found that I differ entirely from Monsieur Wolf[f] in the manner of establishing the foundations of that species of law of nations which we call voluntary. Monsieur Wolf[f] deduces it from the idea of a great republic (*civitatis maximæ*) instituted by nature herself, and of which all nations of the world are members. According to him, the voluntary law of nations is, as it were, the civil law of that great republic. This idea does not satisfy me; nor do I think the fiction of such a republic either admissible in itself, or capable of affording sufficiently solid grounds on which to build the rules of the universal law of nations, which shall necessarily claim the obedient acquiescence of sovereign states. I acknowledge no other natural society between nations than that which nature has established between mankind in general. It is essential to every civil society (*civitati*) that each member have resigned a part of his right to the body of the society, and that there exist in it an authority capable of commanding all the members, of giving them laws, and of compelling those who should refuse to obey. Nothing of this kind can be conceived or supposed to subsist between nations. Each sovereign state claims, and actually possesses an absolute independence on all the others.[33]

Vattel here radically abandons the Wolffean foundation of positive international law: the (hypostasised) world state. While the establishment of civil society between men is seen as a necessary element to create binding law, 'civic association is very far from being equally necessary between

---

[33] Ibid., Preface, xiii.

nations, as it was between individuals': 'We cannot, therefore, say that nature equally recommends it, much less that she has prescribed it.'[34] And while there exists a mutual dependence between nations, nature 'has not imposed on them any particular obligation to unite in civil society'.[35] In other words: while there is a world *society*, there is no need for a world *state*; and while there thus exists a *natural* international law, there cannot be a *civil* international law.[36]

What, then, are the sources of international law? Apart from natural-law norms, which Vattel calls (following Wolff) the 'necessary law of nations',[37] he also acknowledges a 'voluntary law of nations'.[38] But in the absence of a – fictitious – world state adopting 'voluntary' laws binding on all states, how would Vattel define the relationship between the – unchanging – natural law and the – changing – positive international law? His answer, while not always clear, is revolutionary. The source of all *positive* international law lies in the consent of all states: 'I say, that all these alterations are deducible from the natural liberty of nations[.]'[39] For Vattel, all 'positive' international law – including voluntary law – is consensual law:

> These three kinds of law of nations, the Voluntary, the Conventional, and the Customary, together constitute the Positive Law of Nations. For they all proceed from the will of Nations; the Voluntary from their *presumed consent*, the Conventional from an *express consent*, and the Customary from *tacit consent*; and as there can be no other mode of deducing any law from the will of nations, there are only these three kinds of Positive Law of Nations.

[34] Ibid., Preface, xiv. Vattel continues (ibid.): 'We cannot, therefore, say, that nature equally recommends it, much less that she has prescribed it. Individuals are so constituted, and are capable of doing so little by themselves, that they can scarcely subsist without the aid and the laws of civil society. But, as soon as a considerable number of them have united under this same government, they become able to supply most of their wants; and the assistance of other political societies is not so necessary to them as that of individuals is to an individual ... States conduct themselves in a different manner from individuals. It is not usually the caprice or blind impetuosity of a single person that forms the resolutions and determines the measures of the public: they are carried on with more deliberation and circumspection; and, on difficult or important occasions, arrangements are made and regulations established by means of treaties.'

[35] Ibid., Preface, xiii.

[36] For an excellent discussion of the relation between Vattel and Wolff here, see P. Haggenmacher, 'Le Modèle de Vattel et la discipline du droit international' in P. Haggenmacher (ed.), *Vattel's International Law from a XXIst Century Perspective* (Nijhoff, 2012), 3 esp. 38–46.

[37] Vattel, *The Law of Nations* (above n. 30), Preliminaries, §7.

[38] Ibid., Preliminaries, §21.

[39] Ibid., Preface, xiv.

We shall be careful to distinguish them from the Natural or Necessary law of nations, without, however, treating of them separately. But after having, under each individual head of our subject, established what the Necessary law prescribes, we shall immediately add how and why the decisions of that law must be modified by the Voluntary law; or (which amounts to the same thing in other terms) we shall explain how, in consequence of the liberty of nations, and pursuant to the rules of their natural society, the external law which they are to observe towards each other differs in certain instances from the maxims of the internal law, *which nevertheless remains always obligatory in point of conscience.*[40]

All international law, including voluntary law,[41] is here effectively 'privatised'.[42] Not only do the sources of positive international law become (almost) equal in status, Vattel (almost) completely abandons the idea of an 'external' compulsory international law beyond the consent of each state.[43] The voluntary law is no longer a 'civil' law that allows states to be 'punished'.[44] It is that law of general state practice that (academic) commentators consider 'as the best available evidence of consent that might

---

[40] Ibid., Preliminaries, §27 (emphasis added).

[41] The concept of voluntary law is however extremely complex and multilayered. Koskenniemi describes it as Vattel's 'most central, yet most puzzling notion' in M. Koskenniemi, 'International Community: From Dante to Vattel' in P. Haggenmacher (ed.), *Vattel's International Law from a XXIst Century Perspective* (Nijhoff, 2012), 51, 73. For analysis of the concept, see also E. Reibstein, 'Die Dialektik der souveränen Gleichheit bei Vattel' (1958) 19 *ZaöRV* 607.

[42] In this sense also: Steiger, 'Völkerrecht und Naturrecht' (above n. 6), 148: 'Durch den Wegfall jeder Art von Staatengemeinschaft wird zudem das naturrechtliche Völkerrecht individualistisch.'

[43] In the words of F. S. Ruddy, *International Law in the Enlightenment* (Oceana Publications, 1975), 313: '[T]he voluntary Law of Nations reflected state practice, especially in reference to commerce and commercial treaties; precedence, self-defence and intervention; the prerogatives of territorial sovereignty; the rights of necessity and of innocent use; and in the importance, generally, of treaties to international relations.'

[44] Vattel, *The Law of Nations* (above n. 30), Book II, §7: 'It is strange to hear the learned and judicious Grotius assert that a sovereign may justly take up arms to chastise nations which are guilty of enormous transgressions of the law of nature, *which treat their parents with inhumanity like the Sogdians, which eat human flesh as the ancient Gauls, &c.* What led him into this error, was, his attributing to every independent man, and of course to every sovereign, an odd kind of right to punish faults which involve an enormous violation of the laws of nature, though they do not affect either his rights or his safety. But we have shown (Book I. § 169) that men derive the right of punishment solely from their right to provide for their own safety; and consequently they cannot claim it except against those by whom they have been injured. Could it escape Grotius, that, notwithstanding all the precautions added by him in the following paragraphs, his opinion opens a door to all the ravages of enthusiasm and fanaticism, and furnishes ambition with numberless pretexts? Mohammed and his successors have desolated and subdued Asia, to avenge the indignity done to the unity of the Godhead; all whom they termed associators or idolaters fell victims to their devout fury.'

reasonably be presumed'.[45] The distinction between a necessary international law and a voluntary international law is thus gradually reduced to
'an endorsement of current practice camouflaged by the supposedly self-
enforcing sanction of conscience'.[46] In this respect Vattel is much closer to
Hobbes than to Wolff.

C   Federal Foundations: Rousseau and the European Government

A third recurring theme within eighteenth-century discussions on international law and peace concerns (international) federalism. This third
strand acknowledges, like Vattel, the sovereign equality of states that
disallows – in the state of nature – a 'civil' law above the state; yet, unlike
Vattel, it urges states to 'found' such a civil law through a federal compact
between them.

The most elaborate project propagating a federation of states within the
eighteenth century is here offered by Saint Pierre;[47] yet his work would only
become famous in its Rousseauian 'restatement'.[48] And while Rousseau's
'A Lasting Peace' treats its predecessor with 'utmost freedom',[49] its central
problématique remains the same: how to combine internal welfare within
a state with the external warfare between states? If one admits 'that the
Powers of Europe stand to each other strictly in a state of war, and that all
the separate treaties between them are in the nature rather of a temporary
truce than a real peace', how can a 'public Law of Europe' be guaranteed?[50]

The answer Rousseau gives is this:

> If there is any way of reconciling these dangerous contradictions, it is to be
> found only in such a form of federal Government as shall unite nations by
> bonds similar to those which already unite their individual members, and
> place the one no less than the other under the authority of the Law. Even
> apart from this, such a form of Government seems to carry the day over
> all others; because it combines the advantages of the small and the large

---

[45] N. Greenwood Onuf, '*Civitas Maxima*: Wolff, Vattel and the Fate of Republicanism' (above n. 17), 300. And see now: Article 38(1)(d) Statute of the International Court of Justice.

[46] T. J. Hochstrasser, *Natural Law Theories in the Enlightenment* (Cambridge University Press, 2000), 181.

[47] C.-I. Castel de Saint-Pierre, *Projet pour rendre la paix pérpetuelle en Europe* (Utrecht, 1713).

[48] J.-J. Rousseau, *A Lasting Peace Through the Federation of Europe*, trans. C. E. Vaughan (Constable and Co., 1917).

[49] This was the opinion of C. E. Vaughan (ibid., 7): 'Rousseau has treated his original with the utmost freedom.'

[50] Ibid., 47.

State, because it is powerful enough to hold its neighbours in awe, because it upholds the supremacy of the Law, because it is the only force capable of holding the subject, the ruler, the foreigner equally in check.[51]

But how can this federal government be established? Contrasting it to the 'free and voluntary association' that already existed among the states of Europe, 'an authentic federation' is characterised as 'a genuine Body politic' that:

> must have a Legislative Body, with powers to pass laws and ordinances binding upon its members; it must have a coercive force capable of compelling every State to obey its common resolves whether in the ways of command or prohibition; finally, it must be strong and firm enough to make it impossible for any member to withdraw at his own pleasure the moment he conceives his private interest to clash with that of the whole body.[52]

The natural bond between the states of Europe consequently had to be transformed into a 'Constitution of the Federation of Europe'; and the latter would contain five articles:

> By the first, the contracting sovereigns shall enter into a perpetual and irrevocable alliance, and shall appoint plenipotentiaries to hold, in a specified place, a permanent Diet or Congress, at which all questions at issue between the contracting parties shall be settled and terminated by way of arbitration or judicial pronouncement. By the second shall be specified the number of the sovereigns whose plenipotentiaries shall have a vote in the Diet; those who shall be invited to accede to the Treaty; the order, date and method by which the presidency shall pass, at equal intervals, from one to another; finally the quota of their respective contributions and the method of raising them for the defrayal of the common expenses.
>
> By the third, the Federation shall guarantee to each of its members the possession and government of all the dominions which he holds at the moment of the Treaty, as well as the manner of succession to them, elective or hereditary, as established by the fundamental laws of each Province ... By the fourth shall be specified the conditions under which any Confederate who may break this Treaty shall be put to the ban of Europe and proscribed as a public enemy ... Finally, by the fifth Article, the plenipotentiaries of the Federation of Europe shall receive standing powers to frame – provisionally by a bare majority, definitively (after an interval of five years) by a majority of three-quarters – those measures which, on the instruction of their Courts, they shall consider expedient with a view to the greatest possible advantage of the Commonwealth of Europe and of its members, all and single.[53]

[51] Ibid., 38–9.
[52] Ibid., 59–60.
[53] Ibid., 61–4.

This constitutional scheme allows for 'civil' laws for the European federation that are adopted by a qualified majority of 'plenipotentiaries' on
behalf of their states. These laws could be enforced by executive and judicial means; and the advantages of such a federal government are clear and
numerous – both for each nation as well as the whole of Europe.[54]

Yet such a federal scheme has never been adopted. Why? For Rousseau,
the reason is not that it is not good but rather that 'it was too good to be
adopted'.[55] In light of the 'excessive self-love' of kings,[56] '[n]o Federation
could ever be established except by revolution'.[57] This conclusion leaves
Rousseau with the pessimism that undermines the very desirability of the
federal project. For if the only way to establish a federal Europe is revolution, the question arises 'whether the League of Europe is a thing more
to be desired or feared', because '[i]t would perhaps do more harm in a
moment than it would guard against for ages'.[58]

We shall see that the same idea would also cross the mind of the most
important legal philosopher of the eighteenth century: Immanuel Kant.

III   Kant and the 'Unsettled' Foundations of International Law

What is Kant's philosophical position towards the nature and foundation
of international law? In the early post-critical period, Kant lays out three
themes that are characteristic to his legal writings. First, he expressly links
the establishment of a perfect 'national' constitution 'to the problem of a
law-governed external relationship with other states'; indeed: the former
is 'subordinate' to the latter 'and cannot be solved unless the latter is also
solved'.[59] Second, as the solution for the lawful condition between states, he
suggests 'a federation of peoples';[60] and, third, since that federation is not
embedded in natural law, it must be positively 'founded'.[61]

---

[54] Ibid., 88–90.
[55] Ibid., 111.
[56] Ibid., 94–5.
[57] Ibid., 112.
[58] Ibid. In the famous footnote in Book III, Chapter 15 of his 'Social Contract', Rousseau had
      promised a deeper analysis of foreign relations and the political philosophy of 'confedera-
      tion' in a later work – yet he never did. For a summary of his international law writings, see
      however: S. Hoffmann and D. P. Fidler, *Rousseau on International Relations* (Clarendon
      Press, 1991).
[59] I. Kant, *Political Writings*, ed. H. Reiss (Cambridge University Press, 1991), 47.
[60] Kant here clearly follows Saint-Pierre and Rousseau, see G. Cavalar, *Pax Kantiana:
      Sytematisch-historische Untersuchung des Entwurfs 'Zum Ewigen Frieden' (1795) von
      Immanuel Kant* (Böhlau, 1992), 33.
[61] Like Hobbes, and unlike Wolff, the natural state is thus one of war, and peace therefore
      needs to be 'positively' founded. However, it is in my view, wrong to argue that Kant's

But what sort of federation he has in mind changes with the course of time. There are different and contradictory answers that the Königsberg philosopher gives. One answer applies, by analogy, the solution found for civil society to international society and thus argues in favour of a 'cosmopolitan constitution' establishing a federation above the individual states (A). But later on, this positive idea is replaced with a 'negative' substitute: an international federation of free states without the power to coerce (B). Both of these solutions are, while indebted to its immediate predecessors, original; yet they also show that Kant was himself a child of the 'unsettled' eighteenth century.

A The 'Cosmopolitan Constitution' and the World Republic

For Kant, international peace can only be established in a 'federation of peoples'. In his 'Idea of a Universal History with a Cosmopolitan Purpose' (1784), this is a federation 'in which every state, even the smallest, could expect to derive security and rights not from its own power or its own legal judgment, but solely from this great federation'.[62] The latter is 'a united power', whose united will adopts world laws.[63] Expressly referring to the plans by Abbé St Pierre and Rousseau, this *institutional* solution is justified by the suffering states can inflict on each other. It is this suffering that 'must force the states to make *exactly* the same decision (however difficult it may be for them) as that which man was forced to make, equally unwilling, in his savage state – the decision to renounce his brutish freedom and seek calm and security within a law-governed constitution'.[64] This solution is 'like a civil commonwealth' with a 'civil constitution', because 'nature aimed at a perfect civil union of mankind'.[65]

---

international law philosophy is 'an extremely Hobbesian account of the international state of nature' (Tuck, *The Rights of War and Peace* (above n. 3), 215). This seriously underestimates the intellectual debts to Wolff, Vattel and Rousseau, while it also downplays the originality of Kant's own solution in founding the normativity of international law. For the relationship between Kant and Rousseau in the context of international law, see in particular: O. Asbach, 'Internationaler Naturzustand und Ewiger Friede: Die Begründung einer rechtlichen Ordnung zwischen Staaten bei Rousseau und Kant' in D. Hüning and B. Tuschling (eds.), *Recht, Staat und Völkerrecht bei Immanuel Kant* (Duncker & Humblot, 1998), 203.

[62] I. Kant, 'Idea for a Universal History with a Cosmopolitan Purpose' in *Political Writings*, ed. H. Reiss (Cambridge University Press, 1991), 41, at 47.

[63] Ibid.

[64] Ibid., 48 (emphasis added).

[65] Ibid., 48–51.

Kant's answer to creating 'international' (better: cosmopolitan) law and peace thus lies in projecting the 'civic' solution into the international arena of states. States must exit the (international) state of nature and positively found a 'cosmopolitan system' in which a 'united power' legislates, executes and adjudicates over the individual 'citizens'.

This institutional solution is subsequently taken up and (minimally) developed in 'Theory and Practice' (1793):

> On the one hand, universal violence and the distress it produces must eventually make a people decide to submit to coercion which reason itself prescribes (i.e. the coercion of public law), and to enter into a *civil* constitution. And on the other hand, the distress produced by the constant wars in which the states try to subjugate or engulf each other must finally lead them, even against their will, to enter into a *cosmopolitan* constitution. Or if such a state of universal peace is in turn even more dangerous to freedom, for it may lead to the most fearful despotism (as has indeed occurred more than once with states which have grown to large), distress must force men to form a state which is not a *cosmopolitan* commonwealth under a single ruler, but a lawful federation under a commonly accepted international right.[66]

The passage contains a number of key confirmations. First, Kant advocates the adoption of a 'civil constitution' that is a 'cosmopolitan constitution'. Second, this cosmopolitan constitution will involve 'the coercion of public law'. Third, because the establishment of a world state is potentially dangerous for freedom if it is a state under a single ruler (universal monarchy), Kant prefers a 'federation', that is: a republican commonwealth. The latter is not the 'loose' federation of his late work, but 'a state of international right, based upon enforceable public laws to which each state must submit (by analogy) with a state of civil or political right among individual men'.[67] And to reinforce his plea for public laws, Kant not only ridicules the idea of the invisible hand in discourses on the international balance of powers,[68] he also holds – against Rousseau – that the theory of the federal world state is (still) possible in practice: 'For my own part, I put my trust in the theory of what the relationships between men and states *ought to be* according to the principle of right. It recommends to us earthly gods that maxim that we should proceed in our disputes in such a way that a universal federal

---

[66] I. Kant, 'On the Common Saying: "This May Be True in Theory, but It Does Not Apply in Practice"' in *Political Writings*, ed. H. Reiss (Cambridge University Press, 1991), 61, 90.

[67] Ibid., 92.

[68] Ibid: 'For a permanent universal peace by means of a so-called *European balance of power* is a pure illusion, like Swift's story of the house which the builder had constructed in such perfect harmony with all the laws of equilibrium that it collapsed as soon as a sparrow alighted on it.'

state may be inaugurated, so that we should therefore assume that it *is possible* (*in praxi*).'[69]

In conclusion: a first solution combines the idea of the world state – presumed by Wolff to be naturally existing – with the Rousseauian idea that such a state needs to be positively founded; and this founded cosmopolitan state would have to be a 'federation' – presumably along the lines that Rousseau had drafted, that is: a federation that acknowledges the continued political existence of individual states as moral persons; yet one that can enforce its laws through the right to be prosecuted through a 'punitive' war.

B   The Abandonment of the World Republic?

Only two years after 'Theory and Practice', Kant published his longest essay on the foundations of international law: 'Perpetual Peace: A Philosophical Sketch' (1795).[70] Written in the style of a peace *treaty* between states, the very form of the essay already signals a fundamental shift in his conception of the normative foundation of international law. No longer is international law founded on a cosmopolitan constitution, international law needs to be founded on the voluntary agreement between free states.

Kant's peace treaty has four components: the preliminary articles, the definite articles, the supplements and the appendices. The preliminary articles are designed to establish the preconditions for peace.[71] They are

---

[69] Ibid.

[70] I. Kant, 'Perpetual Peace: A Philosophical Sketch' in *Political Writings*, ed. H. Reiss (Cambridge University Press, 1991), 93. The essay is generally seen to be Kant's personal response to the Peace Treaty of Basel (1795), concluded by Prussia and revolutionary France. In the Treaty, Prussia ceded territory west of the Rhine so as to be permitted to swallow a part of Poland (to be shared with Austria and Russia). For an analysis of the third 'Polish Partition', see V. Kattan, 'To Consent or Revolt? European Public Law, the Three Partitions of Poland (1772, 1793, and 1795) and the Birth of National Self-Determination' (2015) 17 *Journal of the History of International Law* 247.

[71] What do they state? The first article clarifies that a temporary peace to prepare for war is not valid ('No conclusion of peace shall be considered valid as such if it was made with a secret reservation of the material for a future war.'). The second article states that a state cannot acquire another one ('No independently existing state, whether it be large or small, may be acquired by another state by inheritance, exchange, purchase of gift.'), because states are moral persons. The third article stipulates that standing armies are to be gradually abolished, while the fourth article criticises the credit system for financing wars ('No national debt shall be contracted in connection with the external affairs of the state.'). The fifth article prohibits violent interferences into the internal affairs of other states ('No state shall forcibly interfere in the constitution and government of another state.'), and the sixth preliminary article finally outlaws 'dishonourable stratagems' (poisoning and treason) that would undermine the trust of the enemy that a future peace might be possible.

'prohibitive laws'; yet, not all of them are said to be prohibitive in a strict sense.[72] By contrast, the 'definitive articles' positively 'institute' peace and end 'the state of nature, which is rather a state of war'.[73] In discussing these three articles, Kant returns to his first central theme: all law is connected; and here he distinguishes three constitutional levels:

> [T]he postulate on which all the following articles are based is that all men who can at all influence one another must adhere to some kind of civil constitution. But any legal constitution, as far as the persons who live under it are concerned, will conform to one of the three following types:
>
> (1) [A] constitution based on the *civil right* of individuals within a nation (*ius civitatis*).
> (2) [A] constitution based on the *international right* of states in their relationships with one another (*ius gentium*).
> (3) [A] constitution based on *cosmopolitan right*, in so far as individuals and states, co-existing in an external relationship of mutual influences, may be regarded as citizens of a universal state of mankind (*ius cosmopoliticum*).[74]

All public (positive) law is thus based on three 'constitutions';[75] and the constitutional categories are 'not arbitrary, but necessary': each of them on its own must be realised in order to create peace.[76] The three 'complementary

---

[72] This is, for example, the case for the second preliminary article. This is a prohibition to treat states as 'objects' capable of possession; and yet, in light of existing state practice, this prohibition is not directly effective. Kant explains: 'prohibitive' laws in a wider sense 'are not exceptions to the rule of justice', but 'allow for some *subjective* latitude according to the circumstances in which they are applied'. Put differently: they 'need not necessarily be executed at once, so long as their ultimate purpose (e.g. the *restoration* of freedom to certain states in accordance with the second article) is not lost sight of'. Delay in applying this prohibition is permitted 'as a means of avoiding a premature implementation which might frustrate the whole purpose of the article' (ibid., 97). Kant here introduces the idea of the 'permissive law', which will be discussed below.

[73] Ibid., 98.

[74] Ibid., 98, *footnote.

[75] On the concept of 'constitution' here, see O. Eberl and P. Niesen, *Immanuel Kant: Zum Ewigen Frieden* (Surkamp, 2011), 208–9: 'Wenn Kant sich am Ende des 18. Jahrhunderts in Friedensschrift und Rechtlehre für den Ausdruck "Verfassung" entscheidet, um den Rechtszustand nicht nur diesseits, sondern auch jenseits der Staaten zu bezeichnen, greift er ein in jüngster Zeit mehrdeutig gewordenes Konzept auf. Im hergebrachten und unspezifischen Sinne bezeichnet "Verfassung" einfach den Gesamtzustand des Gemeinwesens; im neuen, mit der Amerikanischen und der Französischen Revolution eingeführten terminologischen Sinn ist eine Verfassung dagegen ein positives Gesetz, dass die Rechtsbindung aller machthabenden Institutionen festlegt. Während das alte Verständnis ein empirisches ist, ist das neue ein normatives ... Sein Verfassungsbegriff für die globale Ordnung ist rechtlich-normativ, aber nicht demokratisch.'

[76] Kant, 'Perpetual Peace' (above n. 70), 99: 'This classification, with respect to the idea of a perpetual peace, is not arbitrary, but necessary.' See also I. Kant, 'Metaphysical First Principles

constitutions' are indeed mutually interlocking; and each of the three definitive articles consequently deals with one constitution:

Definite Article 1: 'The Civil Constitution of Every State shall be Republican.'

Definite Article 2: 'The Right of Nations shall be based on a Federation of Free States.'

Definite Article 3: 'Cosmopolitan right shall be limited to Conditions of Universal Hospitality.'

Unlike the preliminary articles (which are prohibitive laws), the definitive articles represent prescriptive laws. The first article thereby demands a link between the national and the international constitutions. For the requirement that state constitutions are 'republican' means, inter alia,[77] that the consent of the citizens is required to declare war; and this is seen to guarantee that states will only go to war when absolutely necessary.[78] The second article explains the need for an international constitution as follows:

> Each nation, for the sake of its own security, can and ought to demand of the others that they should enter along with it into a constitution, similar to the civil one, within which the rights of each could be secured. This would mean establishing a *federation of peoples*. But a federation of this sort would not be the same thing as an international state. For the idea of an international state is contradictory ... But peace can neither be inaugurated nor secured without a general agreement between the nations; thus a particular kind of league, which we might call a *pacific federation (foedus pacificum)*, is required ... This federation does not aim to acquire any power like that of a state, but merely to preserve and secure the *freedom* of each state in itself, along with that of the other confederated states, although this does not mean that they need to submit to public laws and to a coercive power which enforces them, as do men in a state of nature.[79]

---

of the Doctrine of Right' in Kant, *The Metaphysics of Morals*, ed. M. Gregor (Cambridge University Press, 1996), §43: 'So if the principle of outer freedom limited by law is lacking in any one of these three possible forms of rightful condition, the framework of all the others is unavoidably undetermined and must finally collapse.' It is therefore misleading to state that 'Kant argues that a peaceful global order can be created only by a cosmopolitan law [*Weltbürgerrecht*] that enshrines the rights of world citizens and replaces classical law among nations [*Völkerrecht*]' (J. Bohmann and M. Lutz-Bachmann, 'Introduction' in J. Bohmann and M. Lutz-Bachmann (eds.), *Perpetual Peace: Essays on Kant's Cosmopolitan Ideal* (MIT Press, 1997), 1, 2–3).

[77] On the very complex concept of 'republicanism', see Cavalar, *Pax Kantiana* (above n. 60), 142–56.

[78] On the famous empirical claim that democracies go less to war (with other democracies), see M. Doyle, 'Kant, Liberal Legacies and Foreign Affairs (Part I)' (1983) 12 *Philosophy and Public Affairs* 205–35 and Part II, 323–53.

[79] Kant, 'Perpetual Peace' (above n. 70), 102 and 104.

The passage seems to significantly depart from Kant's past position in three ways. First, he now denounces the very idea of an 'international state' as a contradiction in terms. *Inter*-national law conceptually means a law *between* nations; and if there were an international state, there would simply be no need for the second definitive article. This leads to a second point. The federation of states cannot have a civil constitution that allows for laws that can be enforced by a superior authority;[80] and there therefore cannot be any 'punitive war'.[81] Finally, the constitution must be based on the voluntary accession of states.[82]

The third definitive article finally deals with the cosmopolitan constitution. Substantially, it cannot – by subtraction – deal with relations within one state (Article 1), nor with relations between states (Article 2). Cosmopolitan law deals with the relationship between states and non-states. It is defined as 'the right of a stranger not to be treated with hostility when he arrives on someone else's territory'.[83] This right to hospitality is not the '*right of a guest* to be entertained' (asylum), but only the right to present oneself so as to enter into contact.[84] Importantly, this third article contains a prescriptive and a prohibitive element.[85] For while the prescriptive 'shall' positively indicates that there be a cosmopolitan right whose normative foundation appears to lie in the idea of a *civitas maxima*,[86]

---

[80] This is further spelled out in the 'Doctrine of Right' (above n. 76), §54: 'This alliance must, however, involve no sovereign authority (as in a civil constitution), but only an *association* (federation); it must be an alliance that can be renounced at any time and so must be renewed from time to time.'

[81] Kant, 'Perpetual Peace' (above n. 70), 96: 'A war of punishment (*bellum punitivum*) between states is inconceivable, since there can be no relationship of superior to inferior among them.'

[82] States should gradually crystallise around a federal 'focal point' – but no forceful or permanent adhesion is allowed (ibid., 104): 'For if by good fortune one powerful and enlightened nation can form a republic (which is by its nature inclined to seek perpetual peace), this will provide a focal point for federal association among the states. These will join up with the first one, thus securing the freedom of each state in accordance with the idea of international right, and the whole will gradually spread further and further by a series of alliances of this kind.'

[83] Ibid., 105.

[84] This right of physical *contact* is often identified with a right of economic *contract*. For an extensive discussion of Kant and international trade, see P. Kleingeld, *Kant and Cosmopolitanism: The Philosophical Ideal of World Citizenship* (Cambridge University Press, 2012), Chapter 5.

[85] This excellent point is made by Eberl and Niesen, *Immanuel Kant: Zum Ewigen Frieden* (above n. 75), 248.

[86] G. Cavallar, *Kant and the Theory and Practice of International Right* (University of Wales Press, 1999), 59; and see also K. Flikschuh, *Kant and Modern Political Philosophy* (Cambridge University Press, 2000), Chapter 5.

that right is limited to universal hospitality; and by means of this restriction, Kant indirectly prohibits all forms of imperialism and colonialism between states and non-state 'peoples'.[87]

IV The 'Antinomies' of International Right

There is a central antinomy at the heart of Kant's conception of international law, which he describes in 'Perpetual Peace' as follows:

> There is only one rational way in which states coexisting with other states can emerge from the lawless condition of pure warfare. Just like individual men, they must renounce their savage and lawless freedom, adapt themselves to public coercive laws, and thus form an international state (civitas gentium), which would necessarily continue to grow until it embraced all the peoples of the earth. But since this is not the will of the nations, according to their present conception of international right (so that they reject in *hypothesis* what is true in *thesi*), the positive idea of a world republic cannot be realised. If all is not to be lost, this can at best find a negative substitute in the shape of an enduring and gradually expanding federation likely to prevent war.[88]

And in the 'Doctrine of Right', we read:

> Since a state of nature among nations, like a state of nature among individual human beings, is a condition that one ought to leave in order to enter a lawful condition, before this happens any rights of nations, and anything external that is mine or yours which states can acquire or retain by war, are merely *provisional*. Only in a universal *association of states* (analogous to that by which a people becomes a state) can rights come to hold *conclusively* and a true *condition of peace* come about. But such a state made up of nations were to extend too far over vast regions, governing it and so too protecting each of its members would finally have to become impossible, while several such corporations would again bring a state of war. So *perpetual peace*, the ultimate goal of the whole right of nations, is indeed an unachievable idea. Still, the political principles directed toward perpetual peace, of entering into such alliances of states, which serve for continual approximation to it, are not unachievable ... Such an *association* of several *states* to preserve peace can be called a permanent congress of states, which each neighbouring state is at liberty to join.[89]

---

[87] Cavallar, *Pax Kantiana* (above n. 60), 227. On Kant and colonialism, see K. Flikschuh and L. Ypi (eds.), *Kant and Colonialism: Historical and Critical Perspectives* (Oxford University Press, 2014).

[88] Kant, 'Perpetual Peace' (above n. 70), 105.

[89] Kant, 'Doctrine of Right' (above n. 76), §61.

What arguments did Kant employ to explain this antinomy between reason and reality, between theory and practice? Two aspects must here be distinguished. First, Kant employs a series of empirical arguments to explain why nature obstructs the creation of an international state (A); and, second, there exist a number of 'conceptual' or normative reasons why Kant thinks there cannot be an 'international state' (B).

A   Empirical Obstacles to a Universal Civic State

For Kant, the *idea* of international law springs from the *empirical* existence of a plurality of states. For there simply would be no need for such a concept if all human beings had, from the beginnings of history, united into *one* general will under *one* constitution creating *one* state.[90] But this has not happened. There thus exists a multitude of peoples having constituted a multitude of states; and it is this *empirical* fact that gives rise to the law of nations, or better: the law *between* states.

But does nature not wish there to be only one state in the end? While 'Theory and Practice' postulated that nature unconditionally wants an international state governed by a civil constitution, the Kantian position has changed after 1795. Kant henceforth identifies the idea of an international state with a 'universal monarchy', whose 'soulless despotism' would 'finally lapse into anarchy' in light of the fact that 'laws progressively lose their impact as the government increases in range.'[91] Geography is here presented as an argument against the creation of (effective) law. But more importantly: nature itself has 'wisely separate[d] the nations' and uses 'two means to separate the nations and prevent them from intermingling – *linguistic* and *religious* differences'.[92] And since the social preconditions for a universal state are not fulfilled, 'unlike that universal despotism which

---

[90] If the physically possible (!) interaction between all human beings on earth is the reason for the assumption of an original community, why is the physically actual (!) interaction limited to states? The – perhaps – best explanation of this paradox comes from B. Ludwig, *Kants Rechtlehre* (Felix Meiner, Verlag, 2005), 131–2: 'Der *empirische* (mithin zufällige) Sachverhalt, daß der Erwerbende nicht zugleich mit *allen* Erdbewohnern "in ein Praktisches Verhältnis kommt", sondern zunächst nur mit denen, die sich mit ihm aktuel auf *dieselben* äußeren Sachen beziehen, führt dazu, daß, obgleich die *Idee* des allgemeinen Willens selbstverständlich alle praktischen Vernunftwesen einzubeziehen hat, der unmittelbar bewirkte Zustand der vereinigen Willkür nur einen Teil derselben umfaßt. Das – erst im öffentlichen Recht Thema werdende – Phänomen [!] des *Einzel*staates hat folglich seinen systematischen Ursprung in den empirischen Bedingungen der Erwerbung äußerer Sachen, speziell des Bodens.'

[91] Kant, 'Perpetual Peace' (above n. 70), 113.

[92] Ibid., 113–14.

saps all man's energies and ends in the graveyard of freedom, [perpetual] peace is created and guaranteed by an equilibrium of forces and a most vigorous rivalry'.[93] This rivalry is kept in check by nature, because 'nature also unites nations' under the concept of cosmopolitan right 'by means of their mutual self-interest' through 'the spirit of commerce'.[94]

In essence: the diversity within mankind demands only a degree of unity, and that unity-in-diversity is best preserved in a federation of states. Nature herself would see to this – mixed – result.[95]

B   Normative Obstacles against an International State

Why did Kant nevertheless not normatively advocate the idea of a (universal) state? In 'Perpetual Peace', Kant gives two reasons. Analytically, he considers the very idea of an 'international state' as contradictory: 'a number of nations forming one state would constitute a single nation'; '[a]nd this contradicts our initial assumption, as we are here considering the right of nations in relation to one another in so far as they are a group of separate states'.[96] The force behind this argument has often been misjudged.[97] For Kant's 'pure' theory of law, considers the idea of a people or 'nation' in exclusively legal terms. A state and its nation always coincide because a state 'constitutes' the nation (and not the other way around).[98] Because the

---

[93] Ibid., 114.

[94] Ibid.

[95] This is the essence of the 'First Supplement: On the Guarantee of a Perpetual Peace', where Kant famously writes (ibid., 108): 'Perpetual peace is *guaranteed* by no less an authority than the great artist Nature herself (*natura daedala rerum*).'

[96] Ibid., 102.

[97] For an extensive discussion of this point, Kleingeld, *Kant and Cosmopolitanism* (above n. 84), 59 et seq.

[98] According to this (Hobbesian) view, a multitude constitutes itself as a 'people' or 'nation' through the very act of creating a civil body, that is: a state. The notion of 'Staatsvolk' is here a pleonasm because 'Staat' and 'Volk' always coincide. This contrasts with the 'organic' (or in Kant's terminology: anthropological) view that considers the 'people' as an ethnic or cultural entity that pre-exists the state. The latter view can of course consider an international state of multiple national peoples, like the UK. J. Habermas therefore misreads the passage when he states (*The Divided West* (above n. 7), 127–8): 'In this context, Kant appears to treat "states" not only as associations of free and equal citizens in conformity with the individualism of modern constitutional law, but also in ethical-political terms, that is, as national communities. These collectivities consist of "peoples" or "nations" ... that are differentiated from one another by language, relation, and mode of life ... On this reading, the "contradiction" resides in the fact that the price the citizens of a world republic have to pay for the legal guarantee of peace and civil liberties would be the loss of the substantive ethical freedom they enjoy as members of a national community organized as an independent nation-state. In fact, this supported contradiction, over which generations of Kant interpreters have

latter is defined as a multitude of persons subject to a (sovereign) legislature, it analytically follows that there cannot be an 'inter-national' state but
only a cosmopolitan state.

But why does Kant not allow for such a *cosmopolitan* state – a state in
which all humanity is united into one nation? Why does he reject 'the positive idea of a *world republic*' in favour of 'the negative substitute in the
shape of an enduring and gradually expanding *federation*'? Kant admits
that states are under an obligation to leave the state of nature, which is 'a
non-rightful condition' that is 'in itself still wrong in the highest degree';[99]
yet he accepts that the obligation on states to leave the state of nature is not
the same as that imposed on individuals:

> [W]hile natural right allows us to say of men living in a lawless condition
> that they ought to abandon it, the right of nations does not allow us to say
> the same of states. For as states, they already have a lawful internal constitu-
> tion, and have thus outgrown the coercive right of others to subject them
> to a wider legal constitution in accordance with their conception of right.[100]

And again:

> [The] difference between the state of nature of individual men and of fami-
> lies (in relation to one another) and that of nations is that in the right of
> nations we have to take into consideration not only the relation of one state
> towards another as a whole, but also the relations of individual persons of
> one state towards the individuals of another, as well as toward another state
> as a whole. But this difference from the rights of individuals in a state of
> nature makes it necessary to consider only such features as can be readily
> inferred from the concept of a state of nature.[101]

Unlike the extreme normative pluralism that exists when each private person judges right and wrong in the state of nature, once civil societies have
been formed, normative progress through 'unification' has been made. In
order to protect the degree of 'public' order already reached, Kant thus

---

racked their brains, dissolves once we examine the premise underlying the argument. Kant
takes the French republic as his model and is forced into an unnecessary conceptual bind
by the dogma of the indivisibility of state sovereignty ... Had Kant read th[e] conception
of "divided" sovereignty from the US model, he would have realised that the "peoples" of
independent states who restrict their sovereignty for the sake of a federal government need
not scarify their distinct cultural identities.' Habermas is here, in my view, wrong about the
'cultural' conception of Kant's concept of 'people' but he is right in suggesting that Kant
cannot perceive a people as being subject to two legislatures.

99   Kant, 'Doctrine of Right' (above n. 76), §54.
100 Kant, 'Perpetual Peace' (above n. 70), 104.
101 Kant, 'Doctrine of Right' (above n. 76), §53.

considers that there exists a difference between the state of nature between individuals and the state of nature between states:

> The refusal by one State to enter into a civil condition with a particular State in its neighbourhood is not the same as refusing a civil condition between States as such. When, within the state of nature, a random number of persons decide to form a state, they create something ontologically different, namely an internally rightful constituted group of persons – which, as such, simply did not exist beforehand. By contrast, whenever a random number of previously distinct States join a Union of States that is itself similar to a State, nothing ontologically new has been created when compared to what had existed before. For there still exists a plurality of dis-united States – with the only difference that one State has changed its size and internal structure.[102]

In order to protect the 'internal' peace – and normative unification – that has already been achieved within a state, Kant not only prohibits any revolution from within, he also prohibits any other state from interfering into the internal affairs from without.[103] But more than that: while states are under an obligation, like individuals, to leave their state of nature, the means to achieve that end are different. While individuals are entitled to use force to positively 'found' a civil constitution, states are not allowed to establish the international constitution by means of war. (For a war against war is still war – and can never be a 'just war';[104] and even within the state of nature, wars of extermination or subjugation – that is: wars that forcefully merge one state with another – are prohibited.) Kant's legal philosophy here accepts states as distinct normative phenomena, and consequently rejects the violent creation of a world state.[105] Integration between states must thus be integration through law, not integration through war.

---

[102] J. Ebbinghaus, 'Kants Lehre vom Ewigen Frieden und die Kriegsschuldfrage' in *Gesammelte Aufsätze, Vorträge und Reden* (Olms, 1968), 24, 35 (my translation).

[103] The fifth 'preliminary article' states: 'No state shall forcibly interfere in the constitution and government of another state.'

[104] Kant's 'Doctrine of Right' distinguishes between three 'rights' with regard to war: the right to go to war (§56), the right during war (§57) and the right after war (§58). But importantly: these rights are rights within the state of nature and Kant emphatically denies a (conclusive) 'just war' as a contradiction in terms. It is thus wrong to claim that there is a Kantian theory of just war, and it is also unthinkable for Kant to justify a humanitarian intervention, contra: F. Téson, *A Philosophy of International Law* (Westview Press, 1998), 56: 'The Kantian thesis includes a theory of just war; it is the war waged in defense of human rights.'

[105] W. Kersting, *Kant über Recht* (mentis, 2004), 151: '[E]s kann kein Erlaubnisgesetz der Vernunft zur Gewaltnahme zum Zwecke der Errichtung eines Weltstaates geben, und daher kann sich die Befriedung durch Einzelstaatlichkeit nicht als Befriedung durch

What means of leaving the state of nature is suggested? The *exeundum* obligation expresses itself in the idea of a 'social contract' that creates a league of nations. Its single aim is the protection of peace under the territorial status quo.[106] The creation of a 'league' thus means no transfer of sovereign authority (as in a civil constitution); and the league cannot interfere in the states' internal affairs. The social contract between states is thus reduced to 'limit' states' external sovereignty. Kant identifies his idea of a league with a congress of states: 'Only by such a congress can the idea of a public right of nations be realized, one to be established for deciding their disputes *in a civil way, as if by a lawsuit*, rather than in a barbaric way (the way of savages), namely by war.'[107]

What does this 'as if' formula here mean? Negatively, it may mean that the (fictitious) Congress not only lacks legislative and executive powers but also lacks judicial powers.[108] Yet behind the 'as if' formula may equally stand a positive idea that finds a parallel in Kant's treatment of 'republicanism' under constitutional law. For Kant there famously accepts that, regardless of the constitutional arrangements within states,[109] the idea of republicanism can operate even outside a 'republic'. Wherever an (enlightened) monarch governs 'as if' s/he directly represented the people, republicanism is at play; and, in a similar vein, the 'as if' formula with regard to a 'civil law' above the state may thus refer to the idea that even in the absence of a single 'constitutional' moment that establishes a 'world state', the federation of states can act 'in a civil way'. The 'as if' formulation here refers not to a world *government* but to a form of world *governance* that needs to be

---

Weltstaatlichkeit vervollständigen. Es gibt im Kantischen Vernunftrecht Raum für Staatsgründungsgewalt, aber nicht für Weltstaatsgründungsgewalt.'

[106] Kant, 'Perpetual Peace' (above n. 70), 97. With reference to the second preliminary article Kant writes (ibid.): 'For in the case of the second article, the prohibition only relates to the *mode of acquisition*, which is to be forbidden hereforth, but not to the present *state of political possessions*. For although the present state is not backed up by the requisite legal authority, it was considered lawful in the public opinion of every state at the time of the putative acquisition.'

[107] Kant, 'Doctrine of Right' (above n. 76), §61.

[108] For the opposite view, A. Ripstein, *Force and Freedom* (Harvard University Press, 2009), 229–30: 'Because each nation has neither private purposes nor external objects of choice, the analogue of a rightful condition among states has a court but neither legislature nor executive. Such a court can resolve disputes about boundaries peacefully, but its resolution of disputes is only "as if before a court", because states can resolve their disputes peacefully by accepting the decision of a court as binding.' This interpretation reduces the 'as if' by pointing to the lack of an executive force enforcing a judgment.

[109] With Aristotle, Kant distinguishes between three 'forms of sovereignty' (autocracy/monarchy, aristocracy and democracy); while there exist two forms of government: republican and despotic.

permanently striven for. In this ideational sense, Kant unconditionally supports the idea (!) of the world state as a regulatory ideal;[110] but doubts that this ideal can ever be realised.[111]

V Excursus: Permissive Law(s) and International Right

The idea of a third class of 'permissive laws' to complement 'prohibitive' and 'prescriptive' laws has a distinctive pre-Kantian lineage. Kant here reacts and acts within an eighteenth-century context;[112] yet his understanding of the concept undergoes a remarkable evolution.[113] We first encounter the idea of a 'permissive law' in 'Perpetual Peace'. In a lengthy footnote that is meant to explain the difference between prohibitive laws in a strict and a wide sense, Kant takes the second preliminary article as his example and states:

> It has hitherto been doubted, not without justification, whether there can be permissive laws (*leges permissivae*) in addition to perceptive laws (*leges praeceptivae*) and prohibitive laws (*leges prohibitivae*). For all laws embody an element of objective practical necessity as a reason for certain actions, whereas a permission depends only upon practical contingencies ... [I]n the permissive law contained in the second [preliminary] article above, the initial prohibition applies only to the mode of acquiring a right in the future (e.g. by inheritance), whereas the exception from this prohibition (i.e. the permissive part of the law) applies to the state of political possessions in the present. For in accordance with this permissive law of natural

---

[110] Kant, 'Perpetual Peace' (above n. 70), 105.

[111] Can the idea of the international state ever be realised? According to Cavallar, *Pax Kantiana* (above n. 60), 209 this is possible if states voluntarily consent to subjecting themselves to compulsory laws; and importantly (ibid., 211): 'Kant kritisiert schließlich nie die freiwillige Stiftung einer kosmopolitischen Republik. Staaten könnten zusätzliche Schritte unternehmen, um über eine Föderation hinauszugehen, die bloß versucht, Kriege zu verhindern.' Yet for Kant, the idea that states as states would be willing agents favouring a process that would undermine their moral existence is unlikely, cf. Kant, 'Perpetual Peace' (above n. 70), 105: 'But since this [the world state based on voluntary association] is not the will of the nations, according to their present conception of international right (so that they reject *in hypothesi* what is true *in thesi*), the positive idea of a *world republic* cannot be realised. If all is not to be lost, this can at best find a negative substitute in the shape of an enduring and gradually expanding *federation* likely to prevent law.'

[112] On the 'scholastic' tradition of the idea of 'permissive laws', see B. Tierney, 'Permissive Natural Law and Property: Gratian to Kant' (2001) 62 *Journal of the History of Ideas*, 381; as well as M. Kaufmann, 'Was Erlaubt das Erlaubnisgesetz – und wozu braucht es Kant?' (2005) 13 *Jahrbuch für Recht und Ethik* 195.

[113] For a brilliant discussion of the idea of 'permissive law', see R. Brandt, 'Das Erlaubnisgesetz, oder: Vernunft und Geschichte in Kants Rechtslehre' in R. Brandt (ed.), *Rechtsphilosophie der Aufklärung* (de Gruyter, 1982), 233.

right, this present state can be allowed to remain even although the state of
nature has been abandoned for that of civil society.[114]

This definition points to a link between 'law' and (moral) 'necessity', which
seems to be broken for permissive laws. For certain types of actions, the
moral law thus stands at the crossroads: what it prohibits in the future, it
may nonetheless allow in the present. Later on, in another lengthy footnote, in the First Appendix to 'Perpetual Peace',[115] we find an explanation
of this first definition:

> These are permissive laws of reason, which allow a state of public right to
> continue even if it is affected by injustice, until all is ripe for a complete
> revolution or has been prepared for it by peaceful means. For any legal con-
> stitution, even if it is only in small measure *lawful,* is better than none at
> all, and the fate of a premature reform would be anarchy. Thus political
> prudence, with things as they are at present, will make it a duty to carry
> out reforms appropriate to the idea of public right. But where revolutions
> are brought about by nature alone, it will not use them as a good excuse
> for even greater oppression, but will treat them as a call of nature to create
> a lawful constitution based on the principles of freedom, for a thorough
> reform of this kind is the only one which will last.

This second definition reinforces the first one: once we enter civil or international society and the latter (unjustly) 'legalises' a tainted status quo, this
is still better than not moving towards some normative uniformisation.
Kant thus unconditionally prefers national or international constitutions –
even those that only are 'in small measure lawful' – to none at all.

But what is the normative function of permissive laws? An extensive
answer is given in the 'Metaphysics of Morals' where Kant associates
permissive laws with the 'Postulate of Practical Reason with Regard to
Rights'.[116] A permissive law is here characterised as a presumption of legality, which Kant ingeniously uses to explain the rational obligation of each
individual to exit the state of nature. And the best way to illustrate this
philosophical move is to refer to his complex philosophy of (property)
rights. Suffice to say here that Kant's fundamental idea behind (almost) all

[114] Kant, 'Perpetual Peace' (above n. 70), 97.
[115] Ibid., 118.
[116] Kant, 'Doctrine of Right' (above n. 76), §6: 'This postulate can be called a permissive law
(*lex permissive*) of practical reason, which gives us an authorization that could not be got
from mere concepts of right as such, namely to put all others under an obligation, which
they would not otherwise have, to refrain from using certain objects of our choice because
we have been the first to take them into our possession. Reason wills that this holds as a
principle, and it does this as practical reason, which extends itself *a priori* by this postulate
of reason.'

of his 'private' or 'natural' law philosophy is to explain how 'acquisitions' of external objects are possible.[117] His solution is that they must be possible because they are extensions of external liberty; and if they are to be possible permanently, there needs to be a 'public' or 'civil' law.[118] An individual that (unilaterally) claims property rights is thus justified in defending this right against everyone else, by means of a permissive law, because the claim to property is an invitation to enter into civil society.

But considering that he accepts that all (property) rights only become conclusive in 'a universal association of states (analogous to that by which a people becomes a state)',[119] why is there no permissive law to force states into entering into an international state? A partial answer to this question was already given above: once individuals have created a plurality of (sovereign) states, the existence of these states – as islands of public law – will itself be protected under a permissive law even if their creation is tainted by illegality. And because international law is defined as a relation *between* states, that is: a relation between moral *persons* and not physical objects, it is clear that 'the idea of the right of nations involves only the concept of an antagonism in accordance with principles of outer freedom by which each can preserve what belongs to it, but not a way of acquiring'.[120] And since states cannot 'acquire' property, the normative obligation on states to enter into a cosmopolitan state is here much lower.[121] The task of international law is thus exclusively to guarantee the coexistence of states in which property

---

[117] Brandt, 'Das Erlbaubnisgesetz' (above n. 113), 233: 'Die Lehre vom Privatrecht ist eine Theorie des erwerbbaren äußeren Mein und Dein[.]' Kant allows for the idea of 'innate' rights, that is: rights that are original and need not be aquired; yet for him these innate rights do not comprise property.

[118] Unlike Locke, property is not a 'natural right' that can be acquired by a person simply working the land. Such an idea of a 'unilateral' acquisition disregards that rights always impose obligations on others, and that in order to justify these obligations, these others must consent to the obligation imposed on them. For Kant, then, if an individual insists on the idea of 'rightful' property – as opposed to mere possession – it implicitly 'wills' civil society, for the idea of (non-provisional) property cannot be thought without the idea of public law. In claiming property rights, an individual thus insists on founding civil society; and because this idea of public law is a postulate of practical reason, the unilateral acquisition of property is provisionally justified – as long as it is followed by the creation of public law later on.

[119] Kant, 'Doctrine of Right' (above n. 76), §61.

[120] Ibid., §57.

[121] For the same conclusion, Ripstein, *Force and Freedom* (above n. 108), 228: '[A]s Kant understands states, they do not have external objects of choice. The state does not acquire its territory; its territory is just the spatial manifestation of the state. That is why Kant joins other eighteenth-century writers in supposing that the state's territory is more like its body than like its property.'

has become 'internally' conclusive, and the way to externally protect this solution is through a voluntary league of nations.

What normatively stabilises this voluntary league? The best answer here returns to the normative connection between internal (constitutional) law and external (international law):

> [A] state which claims immunity from international juridical coercion on the grounds of its juridical sovereignty domestically is for that reason juridically obliged to enter into rightful relations with other states: its very claim to sovereignty domestically obliges it internationally. The juridically sovereign state is a self-enforcer of its international obligations: given its juridical immunity it cannot be compelled by a higher authority but must compel itself. However, though not coercible, the obligation is not for that reason voluntarily incurred or even voluntarily discharged.[122]

A state that does not recognise the (external) sovereignty of other states thus undermines its own claim to (internal) sovereignty. This ingenious solution stands at the heart of Kant's international law: it is a solution that dialectically synthesises the central idea of all classic international law: the sovereign equality of all states.

VI   Conclusion

The normative foundations of international law remain debated and unsettled throughout the eighteenth century. Leaving aside the role of natural law, three possible foundations of *positive* international law here compete with each other. The first postulates the existence of a (united) general will within a fictitious world state. The latter can adopt 'voluntary' laws that will be binding on each of the states; and, in accepting binding international laws adopted by an authority above the states, this view must ultimately accept the idea of divided or shared sovereignty.[123] A second view rejects the metaphysical foundations of positive international law altogether and reconstructs the normative nature of international law around the sovereign equality of all states. All positive international law ultimately derives its 'normativity' from the consent of the states; and, while a lingering connection with natural-law theories is retained, this view ultimately leads to the complete 'positivisation' and 'privatisation' of international law.[124]

---

[122] K. Flikschuh, 'Kant's Sovereignty Dilemma: A Contemporary Analysis' (2010) 18 *Journal of Political Philosophy* 469 at 488.

[123] On this point, see section II(A) above.

[124] According to E. Tourme-Jouannet, *L'Emergence doctrinale du droit international classique* (above n. 29), 423 (my translation): 'Vattel is not one of the fathers of positivism or interstate voluntarism but simply the grand "engineer" of classic international law.'

A third view sits in the middle between these two positions. For while it rejects the 'natural' existence of a government above the states, it can envisage a positive (voluntary) law that can be enforced against a state's own will; yet this binding international law must be 'founded' through a federal compact.

All of these three views resurface in the work of Kant – this eighteenth-century prince of legal philosophy. Kant believes, with Wolff, in the *idea* of the world state as the ultimate normative fountain of all law, and this legal 'monism' strikingly contrasts with the legal dualism that would become a hallmark of modern international law;[125] yet, in light of the empirical and normative plurality of states, Kant comes to replace the (unrealisable) ideal of a world republic with the (realisable) idea of a voluntary federation of states. This federation is not 'naturally' given – but must be 'founded'; and without this federation there exists no 'public' international law. However, because states are 'sovereign', any federal union is confined to the 'negative' task of maintaining peace between states and it cannot 'positively' interfere into the 'internal' sphere that belongs to 'state' law. The free federation of states will thus not have a 'government', but the collectivity of the states is tasked to govern 'as if' subject to a civil constitution.

In retrospect, then, the eighteenth century is a battleground of – fascinating – old and new ideas. It is the century in which the 'old' international law dies and the modern international law is born.[126] That new – positive – international law will reach maturity in the next century; and, in many respects, the 'long' nineteenth century is, sadly, still with us – even if the owl of Minerva spread its wings in between two devastating World Wars. The second half of the twentieth century has however

---

[125] On this development, see only: Koskenniemi, *The Gentle Civilizer of Nations* (above n. 10), and J. von Bernstorff, Chapter 2 in this volume.

[126] The modern phrase 'Westphalian state order', so often found in international relations and (American) legal scholarship, is thus deeply misleading. No one has better said it than Haggenmacher, 'Le Modèle de Vattel et la discipline du droit international' (above n. 36), 48: 'Il ne s'agit nullement de nier l'immense importance politique de la paix de Westphalie qui (avec celle des Pyrénées) marque une césure dans l'histoire européenne en faisant échec aux visées hégémonique de la maison d'Autriche et en instaurant une manière de stabilité confessionnelle. Au demeurant l'objet du congés de paix n'était pas de créer de toutes pièces un nouvel ordre juridique internationale; tout au plus rééquilibrait-on la constitution du Saint-Empire, de manière à affaiblir la position de l'empereur ... S'il est vrai qu'avec eux s'ouvrit une nouvelle époque du système des Etats européens qui vit éclore les droit international comme discipline juridique propre, ce n'est pas pour autant à ces traités qu'on le doit. A vrai dire, ceux-ci forment bien le point de départ de ce qu'on appellera au temps de Vattel, à la suite de l'abbé de Mably, "le droit public de l'Europe fondé sue les traits"; mais ceci est toute autre chose que le prétendu "Westphalian Order"... Allant plus loin, il est même permis de se demander si l'on n'a pas indument projeté le modèle de Vattel un siècle en arrière.'

seen a remarkable revival of 'cosmopolitan' ideas, and especially, a return to the international law philosophy of Immanuel Kant. The rise of Kantian ideas and themes can thus today be found in discussions on the United Nations, as well as the European Union.[127]

---

[127] J. Habermas, *The Crisis of the European Union: A Response* (Polity Press, 2013); as well as R. Schütze, *From International to Federal Market: The Changing Structure of European Law* (Oxford University Press, 2017), Epilogue.

2

World Order through Law

The Politics of Kelsenian Positivism in International Law

JOCHEN VON BERNSTORFF

Positivism in international law means different things to different people. From a historical perspective famous early twentieth-century positivists, such as Hans Kelsen, Lassa Oppenheim or Dionisio Anzilotti, despite their common self-perception as representatives of a 'positivist' approach to international law, pursued quite diverse scientific and political projects through their writings. Apart from a common rhetorical denial of natural law, there are stark differences between the Kelsenian approach to international law and those of other 'positivists'. This chapter focuses on Hans Kelsen's approach to international law and attempts to situate it in the broader field of positivist authors. My general thesis on Kelsen and other contemporary positivists is twofold: twentieth-century international legal positivist approaches constituted further developments of – and critical reactions to – the late nineteenth-century tradition of German *Staatswillenspositivismus*. What is often portrayed as a common modern 'positivist' tradition was in fact a variety of different political and epistemological projects. While Oppenheim for instance adapted the basic premises of this tradition and turned it into a pragmatic approach in line with the British Empire's foreign policy prerogatives,[1] Kelsen in his critique of the voluntarist tradition radicalised methodological sensibilities of the late nineteenth-century German public law tradition and constructed a (utopian) cosmopolitan project for an effective world government.

In this chapter, I will first attempt to illustrate the deep structure of the Kelsenian approach to international law from an intellectual history perspective (section I). This will include the political, doctrinal and philosophical context in which Kelsen developed his fundamental critique of the then prevailing German 'positivist' international law theory. As a

---

[1] More on Oppenheim with references under section III.

second step, I attempt to illustrate the subversive and revolutionary force of Kelsen's critical methodology with a couple of examples (section II). By way of conclusion, I will add a few words on the differences between the Kelsenian approach and the pragmatic positivist tradition founded by Lassa Oppenheim. Oppenheim through his famous textbook, later edited by Hersch Lauterpacht, arguably became the most influential international legal 'positivist' of the first decades of the twentieth century (section III).

I   The Contextual Deep-Structure of the Kelsenian Approach to International Law

Hans Kelsen was a Viennese law professor in between the two World Wars, who is seen by many, in particular on the European continent, as one of the most outstanding, if not the most outstanding, jurist of the twenti-eth century.[2] He was an international lawyer, a legal theorist and eminent scholar of constitutional law. His extremely successful academic career, in the period before, between, and after the two World Wars, took him from Vienna, Cologne and Geneva to Harvard and Berkeley. Nearly all his moves and his emigration, however, were involuntary and came in response to life-threatening perils, persecution or political defamation which had an anti-Semitic background.

Kelsen was a radical modernist thinker, social democrat and liberal cosmopolitan. His vigorous defence of democracy and a cosmopolitan international legal order made him subject to harsh criticism from mainstream German scholars, most of whom were contemptuous of Weimar democracy and the League of Nations. His writings on international law include numerous articles: a monograph *On the Problem of Sovereignty*, a general textbook, Hague Lectures and a United Nations (UN) Charter Commentary.[3] Among Kelsen's students were outstanding international lawyers, namely Alfred Verdross, Josef L. Kunz, Hans Morgenthau and also Hersch Lauterpacht.

---

[2] See on the following section and Kelsen's international law theory more generally my partly identical contribution, 'Hans Kelsen and the Return of Universalism' in A. Orford et al. (eds.), *The Oxford Handbook of The Theory of International Law* (Oxford University Press, 2016).

[3] H. Kelsen, *Das Problem der Souveränität und die Theorie des Völkerrechts. Beitrag zu einer reinen Rechtslehre*, 2nd edn (J. C. B. Mohr, 1928), 87; H. Kelsen, *Principles of International Law* (Rinehart, 1952); H. Kelsen, *The Law of the United Nations* (Stevens, 1950).

To anticipate the findings of this particular interpretation of Kelsen's international legal theory, let me say at this point that the reconstructed doctrine of international law can be adequately grasped only if we place it within the tension-filled relationship between the two crucial goals of the international law theorist Hans Kelsen: (1) establishing a non-political method for the field of international law, and (2) promoting the political project – which originated in the interwar period – of a thoroughly legalised and institutionalised world order. Kelsen's approach to international law was characterised by the constant effort to advance these two prima facie conflicting goals through his writings on international law.[4]

Kelsen saw himself as the founder of a method of jurisprudence that was critical of ideology, the so-called 'pure theory of law'. This new jurisprudential methodology was to allow jurists to engage with law as a subject of study in a non-political, and thus purely 'scientific', way. In addition, as a political person, Kelsen developed during the interwar period – probably influenced by his experiences in World War I – into a committed internationalist, who saw the creation of an institutionalised legal community of states as the only path towards a more peaceful world order. Subsequently, Kelsen, as a legal scholar, found himself confronted with the problem of not being able to openly pursue his own political preferences for the 'cosmopolitan project' of an institutionalised rule of law in international relations, but was compelled to make the non-political method he postulated the yardstick also of his own legal-theoretical works when dealing with the legal material. Kelsen's solution was a methodologically guided critique of those theoretical and doctrinal constructs that stood in the way of his own political programme developed at the end of World War I. The explanatory approach laid out in this chapter thus reconstructs the inner connection between Kelsen's legal methodology and the cosmopolitan project underlying his fundamental critique of the *fin de siècle* mainstream German international legal scholarship. Kelsen's way of working, which seems largely 'destructive' towards the traditional doctrine of international law, can therefore be understood and explained as a strategy for uniting two goals whose impetus seems at first glance contradictory.

---

[4] I have developed this thesis more extensively in J. von Bernstorff, *The Public International Law Theory of Hans Kelsen*, trans. T. Dunlap (Cambridge University Press, 2010).

A   The Quest for Objectivity

The central project of the Pure Theory of Law was the creation of an 'objective' legal scholarship. In 1928, Kelsen described the state of German public law scholarship this way:

> The discipline becomes a mere ideology of politics ... In a society convulsed by world war and world revolution, it is more important than ever to the contending groups and classes to produce usable ideologies that allow those still in power to effectively defend their interests. That which accords with their subjective interest seeks to be presented as what is objectively right. And so the science of the state and the law must serve that purpose. It provides the 'objectivity' that no politics is able to generate on its own.[5]

The 'liberation' from political 'bondage' postulated in the Pure Theory of Law with such Enlightenment pathos is a struggle for the inherent autonomy of legal scholarship by a new scientific foundation. Already from the time of his habilitation in 1911, Hans Kelsen had been searching for a more 'scientific' method of jurisprudence. At the beginning of the twentieth century, Georg Jellinek's doctrine on state law was the measure of all things in German-language public law. Jellinek, the first dean of the Heidelberg law faculty, who was of Jewish background, had retained the Hegel-inspired assumption of the will of the sovereign state as the law's ground of validity, but enriched his theory of public law with sociological and psychological elements. His work symbolised the transition to a modern broadening of perspectives in German legal scholarship towards the integration of insights from the new neighbouring disciplines, as for example the emerging field of sociology. In Heidelberg, Kelsen, as a visiting researcher, attended Jellinek's seminar and felt repelled by the devoted band of disciples he felt Jellinek had gathered around himself. By now obsessed with the idea of putting legal positivism on a more objective scientific basis, he worked out a theoretical approach that turned against Jellinek's theoretical approach in two ways.[6] First, it completely displaced the Hegelian notion of will and the personification of the state as a subject capable of an exercise of will. Second, it radically rejected Jellinek's broadening to include sociological and psychological questions, which Kelsen wanted to purge entirely from the subject matter of jurisprudence.

---

[5] H. Kelsen, 'Juristischer Formalismus und Reine Rechtslehre' (1929) 58 *Juristische Wochenschrift* 1723–6.

[6] This is what Kelsen had to say in his autobiographical sketch: 'I was completely intoxicated by the feeling of embarking on a new path in my discipline.' 'Autobiography' in *Hans Kelsen Werke*, 6 vols., ed. M. Jestaedt (Mohr Siebeck, 2007), I, 41.

By applying contemporary neo-Kantian epistemological insights to juris-prudence, Kelsen became, with his project of the 'Pure Theory of Law' (1934) the *'Alleszermalmer'* ['universal destroyer'][7] of the traditional methodology in German-language jurisprudence.[8]

This modern revolt arose before and during World War I, in the collapse of the old Viennese world, which was marked by the rise of the 'masses', nationalism and anti-Semitism.[9] Moreover, the 'kakanian'[10] multi-ethnic state, whose unity had been secured, not least through an efficient, thor-oughly juridical administrative structure, was beginning to break apart. During the increasingly ideological usurpation of the societal discourse, Kelsen called for a scientific – that is, non-political – approach to the law. The project of the Pure Theory of Law, which was initially directed against the premises of the preceding German voluntaristic positivism (*Staatswillenspositivismus*), can thus be understood as a scholarly reaction to the centrifugal forces of the ideologised *Zeitgeist*.

The foundation of Kelsen's theory of international law was the 1920 mon-ograph *Das Problem der Souveränität und die Theorie des Völkerrechts* [*The Problem of Sovereignty and the Theory of International Law*]. This book, which, according to Kelsen himself, was largely already completed during World War I, was the second important monographic publication after Kelsen's habilitation thesis of 1911, *Hauptprobleme der Staatsrechtslehre* [*Chief Problems in the Theory of Public Law*].[11] The critical thrust of the 1920 monograph was directed against the main traditional approaches to international law theory by German-speaking theorists, from Adolf Lasson to Georg Jellinek, from Heinrich Triepel to Erich Kaufmann. In its constructive aspect, this monograph, with its emphasis on the primacy of international law, connected with the theory of international law devel-oped by C. Kaltenborn in the mid-nineteenth century. As an important

---

[7] As Theodor W. Adorno and Max Horkheimer said of Kant in *Dialektik der Aufklärung: Philosophische Fragmente* (Suhrkamp, 1998 [1947]), 100.

[8] The most compact and lucid recent account of the methodological orientation of the Vienna School from the perspective of the history of public law, along with extensive references, can be found in M. Stolleis, *A History of Public Law in Germany 1914–1945*, trans. T. Dunlap (Oxford University Press, 2004), 151–60. For a comprehensive analysis and interpretation of Kelsen's doctrine of international law, see H. Dreier, *Rechtslehre, Staatssoziologie und Demokratietherie bei Hans Kelsen* (Nomos, 1986).

[9] On this, see C. E. Schorske, *Fin-de-Siècle Vienna: Politics and Culture* (Knopf, 1979), 116–80.

[10] As Robert Musil famously depicted the dual Austrian monarchy being of both imperial and royal nature (in German *kaiserlich* and *königlich*, abbreviated 'k & k').

[11] H. Kelsen, *Hauptprobleme der Staatsrechtslehre entwickelt aus der Lehre vom Rechtssatze* (Mohr, 1911).

contribution to the development of the Pure Theory of Law, Kelsen's monograph had a lasting impact on the conception of international law by the three Viennese students and companions, Alfred Verdross, Joseph L. Kunz and Hersch Lauterpacht.

B   The Cosmopolitan Project

The first two decades of the twentieth century were a historical phase in which the pacifist-liberal currents in Europe and the United States regarded the inadequate development of the international legal system as the chief reason behind the outbreak of the war. If we shift our view to the broader environment of international law theory, it is apparent that Kelsen and his pupils, like a number of other authors of the interwar period, saw themselves as part of a modernisation movement in international law. This international movement for a new law of nations arose during World War I and reached its climax in the 1920s. The shared enthusiasm for a changed, more peaceful world order prompted legal scholars in various countries, coming from different methodological backgrounds, to try and prepare, in scholarly manner, the road to what they called 'a new international law'. As part of this movement, one could mention, in addition to the authors of the Vienna School, Lammasch, Nippold, Krabbe and Duguit from the pre-war generation, and for the younger generation, Scelle, Politis, Alvarez, Brierly and Lauterpacht.[12] During World War I, Kelsen had been an active office-holder of the declining Habsburg monarchy and – unlike the Austrian pacifist, politician and legal scholar Lammasch – he had refrained from publishing pacifist works or works promoting international understanding during the war.[13] But the publication of his monograph *The Problem of Sovereignty* in 1920 quickly made him into a pace-setter in international law theory within the renewal movement during the interwar period.

Driven by a spirit of enlightenment and cosmopolitan pacifism, these thinkers set out to destroy what they felt were the detrimental tenets of classic international law theory. At the centre of the critical analyses stood

---

[12] James W. Garner, in The Hague lectures in 1931, sought to provide an overview of the reform movement in the 1920s: 'Le Développement et les tendances récentes du droit international' in *Collected Courses of The Hague Academy of International Law* (Brill/Nijhoff, 1931), XXXV/I, 605–720.

[13] This probably had something to do with his involvement at the ministerial level of the Austrian war department during World War I, a position that was beneficial to his career; on this, see G. Oberkofler and E. Rabofsky, *Hans Kelsen im Kriegseinsatz der k.u.k. Wehrmacht. Eine kritische Würdigung seiner militärtheoretischen Angebote* (P. Lang, 1988), 13.

the concept of state sovereignty and its place within the international legal order. Although methods and results diverged strongly, what character-ised the representatives of this movement was a shared claim to moderni-sation, understood as a project of demystification of international legal theory. The dynamic of this movement sprang from the reaction against classical international law, which was regarded as the product of European pre-war nationalism.

For example, Brierly, in his inaugural lecture in 1924, emphasised that 'the world regards international law today as in need of rehabilitation'.[14] In light of this criticism, the theoretical landscape of international law in the nineteenth century seemed dominated by mystically transfigured notions of sovereignty. From this perspective, the traditional doctrines of inter-national law, with their 'subjective' orientation focused on the 'will' of the individual state, had contributed to the rupture of civilisation represented by World War I.[15] For the reformers, it was not only international politics, but also international legal scholarship infected by the dogma of sover-eignty that bore responsibility for the inadequate elaboration of the Hague order.[16] It was the League of Nations that initially served as a screen onto which the hopes for a more peaceful world order through new forms of collective security, arbitration and adjudication were projected.

Kelsen also saw in a reform of the international legal system – including a strong world organisation and compulsory adjudication – the key to a more peaceful world. His self-conception as it related to international law was thus fed by two central, basic beliefs that were not hard to find within the liberal, German-speaking bourgeoisie in Central Europe, which – not necessarily but often – had a Jewish background. First, the unrestrained faith in the specific validity and pacifying force of the legal form, also applicable in international relations; second, the belief in social progress

---

[14] J. L. Brierly, *The Basis of Obligation and Other Papers* (Clarendon, 1958), 68; on Brierly, see C. Landauer, 'J. L. Brierly and the Modernization of Transnational Law' (1993) 25 *Vanderbilt Journal of Transnational Law* 881–918; on the cultural-historical rupture of 1914, see M. Stolleis, *Der lange Abschied vom 19. Jahrhundert. Vortrag gehalten vor der Juristischen Gesellschaft zu Berlin am 22. Januar 1997* (de Gruyter, 1997).

[15] The criticism has focused above all on Jellinek's doctrine of self-obligation: J. L. Brierly, 'Le Fondement du caractère obligatoire du droit international public' in *Collected Courses of the Hague Academy of International Law* (Brill/Nijhoff, 1928), XXIII/III, 482–4; H. Lauterpacht, *The Function of Law in the International Community* (Garland, 1973 [1933]), 409–12.

[16] N. Politis, 'Le Problème des limitations de la souveraineté et la théorie de l'abus des droits dans les rapports internationaux', *Collected Courses of The Hague Academy of International Law* (Brill/Nijhoff, 1925), VI, 5–27.

through scientific – that is, 'objective' – understanding. The Pure Theory of Law regarded the supposedly ideologised jurisprudence of international law as an obstacle to the further development of the international legal system.[17] Kelsen shared this mindset with his closest student of international law, Joseph L. Kunz, and with Hersch Lauterpacht, who had studied with Kelsen in Vienna before emigrating to the UK.[18]

The belief in progress through 'objective' scientific understanding, on the one hand, and in the power of the pacifying medium of the law, on the other, is a cultural phenomenon of a vanished epoch of European jurisprudence in the late nineteenth and early twentieth centuries. Emerging out of the gradual demise of the Habsburg Empire, it found its most radical champion in Kelsen. In his short autobiography, Kelsen himself had depicted the Pure Theory of Law as a being decisively coined by the pre-World War I Austrian context.[19] After all, it had been the force of the law that had been perceived as holding together the multi-ethnic empire, bound to replace the missing 'homogeneous' society in the absence of common cultural foundations.

C The Methodological Toolkit

According to Kelsen, the quest for the epistemological Archimedean point outside of politicisation and subjectivity could succeed only through the formalisation of jurisprudential concepts. The legal form had to be purified – it had to be empty. Expelling the political could succeed only in a conceptual world that is subject to its own distinct, objectifiable laws. The latter entailed the basic principles of the unity and specificity of scientific cognition, logical coherence and a systematic internal structure free of contradictions.

These basic structures or postulates of Kelsenian thinking, already evident in his doctoral dissertation on Dante Alighieri in 1905,[20] had only

---

[17] According to Michael Hardt and Antonio Negri, this cosmopolitan impetus of the 'Pure Theory', Kelsen's quest for world government through law, made him the chief theorist of an 'imperial' global legal order: M. Hardt and A. Negri, *Empire* (Harvard University Press, 2001), Chapter 1.1.

[18] On the relationship between Lauterpacht and Kelsen, see M. Koskenniemi, 'Lauterpacht: The Victorian Tradition in International Law' (1997) 2 *EJIL* 218–25; A. Carty, 'The Continuing Influence of Kelsen on the General Perception of the Discipline of International Law' (1998) 9 *EJIL* 352–4. On Kelsen's relationship to J. L. Kunz, see Bernstorff, The Public International Law Theory of Hans Kelsen (above n. 4), 4 et seq. and 283–5.

[19] H. Kelsen, *Werke*, ed. M. Jestaedt (Mohr-Siebeck, 2007).

[20] On this, see Bernstorff, *The Public International Law Theory of Hans Kelsen* (above n. 4), Chapter 3A.

later been methodologically secured by the Neo-Kantian transcendental argument.

In the late nineteenth century, during Kelsen's studies, Hegel was unfashionable – and neo-Kantianism or, to be more precise, various versions of neo-Kantianism, were en vogue. Inspired by neo-Kantian epistemology, the first general point of attack for Kelsen was what he regarded as the lack of a stringent methodological distinction between *Sein* [Is] and *Sollen* [Ought], which made a scientific construction of public law impossible.[21] The concept of a strict and constitutive separation of scientific methodologies, the beginnings of which were already evident in Jellinek,[22] was radicalised by Kelsen, drawing on Georg Simmel, Wilhelm Windelband and Heinrich Rickert.[23] Kelsen regarded the multi-dimensional analysis of law, which was characteristic of Jellinek, as epistemologically inadmissible. Kelsen particularly found the use of insights from sociology and psychology in interpreting legal norms an unacceptable jumble of different methods. According to Kelsen's strict separation thesis, one could not derive from the 'Is-statements' of sociology any conclusions that were relevant for jurisprudence as a doctrine of normative 'Ought'. The principle difference in the explanatory *Denkform* (form of thinking) of the 'Is' and the normative *Denkform* of the 'Ought' revealed, in Kelsen's words, two 'separate worlds' that were irreconcilable.[24]

And yet, while insisting on the separation between these divergent methodologies, there was no question for Kelsen that there could be a mutual enrichment of 'Is-sciences' (*Seinswissenschaften*) like sociology, and legal scholarship:[25]

> Nor let it be said that the jurist may not also undertake sociological, psychological, or historical studies. On the contrary! These are necessary; except that the jurist must always remain aware that as a sociologists, psychologist,

---

[21] On the methodological dualism in his early work, see S. L. Paulson, 'Kelsen's Earliest Legal Theory: Critical Constructivism' in S. L. Paulson and B. L. Paulson (eds.), *Normativity and Norms: Critical Perspectives on Kelsenian Themes* (Oxford University Press, 1998), 23 et seq.; C. Heidemann, *Die Norm als Tatsache. Zur Normentheorie Hans Kelsens* (Nomos 1997), 24–8.

[22] On Jellinek's rejection of methodological syncretism, see G. Jellinek, *System der subjektiven öffentlichen Rechte* (Mohr, 1919), 17.

[23] Paulson, 'Kelsen's Earliest Legal Theory' (above n. 21), 29 et seq.

[24] H. Kelsen, *Hauptprobleme der Staatsrechtslehre, entwickelt aus der Lehre vom Rechtssatz*, 2nd edn with an added preface (J. B. Mohr, 1923), 8; on this, see G. H. von Wright, 'Is and Ought' in S. L. Paulson and B. L. Paulson (eds.), *Normativity and Norms: Critical Perspectives on Kelsenian Themes* (Oxford University Press, 1998), 365–7.

[25] H. Kelsen, 'Zur Soziologie des Rechts. Kritische Betrachtungen' (1912) 34 *Archiv für Sozialwissenschaft und Sozialpolitik* 602.

or historian he is pursuing a very different path from the one that leads
him to his specifically juridical insights. He must never incorporate the
results of his explanatory examination into his construction of normative
concepts.[26]

Legal 'science' was to be established as an autonomous, purely normative
discipline.[27] For Kelsen, the Pure Theory of Law was a 'theory of positive
law' in that its aim was to eliminate from the subject matter theories of substantive justice, morality and ethical considerations.[28] By distancing itself
from natural-law thinking, as well as from the methodologically 'syncre-
tistic' blending of 'Is' and 'Ought', the Pure Theory of Law attempted to
create the cognitive preconditions for the autonomous existence of a fully
contingent legal medium. Traditional legal doctrine constantly endangered this autonomy by creating ideological distortions and unreflected
discursive representations of the law and its institutions.[29] According to
Kelsen, legal positivism in this sense had to secure the autonomy of the
law, since 'only the positivistic understanding of the law creates the prerequisite for the existence of an autonomous legal order and legal "science",
while the natural law perspective allows the law, finally and ultimately, to
be absorbed into reason, morality, and nature, and legal scholarship into
ethics, politics, or even natural sciences'.[30]

   In international law, this process of autonomisation proved especially
difficult in that, contrary to the modern constitutional state, most of its
norms were of a customary-law nature. In addition, compared to state law,
its link to philosophical natural law continued to be very close. As a reaction to the renewed, fundamental challenge to legal character of international law during World War I, the 1920s had witnessed a renaissance of
natural-law theories in international legal scholarship.[31] Following World
War I, which contemporaries experienced as a civilisational rupture on a

---

[26] Kelsen, *Hauptprobleme* (above n. 24), 42; H. Kelsen, 'Law, State, and Justice in the Pure
Theory of Law' (1958) 57 *YLJ* 383; for a more comprehensive discussion of this problem, see
Dreier, *Rechtslehre* (above n. 8), 136–40.

[27] On the doctrine of the *Rechtssatz*: H. Kelsen, *Allgemeine Staatslehre* (J. Springer, 1925), 51.

[28] H. Kelsen, *Reine Rechtslehre* (Deuticke, 1934), 1; H. Kelsen, *Introduction to the Problems
of Legal Theory*, trans. B. L. Paulson and S. L. Paulson (Oxford University Press, 1992), 7.

[29] On the 'idea of the autonomy of jurisprudence', see A. Baratta, 'Rechtspositivismus
und Gesetzespositivismus: Gedanken zu einer "naturrechtlichen" Apologie des
Rechtspositivismus' (1968) 54 *Archiv für Rechts- und Staatsphilosophie* 337.

[30] Kelsen, *Das Problem der Souveränität* (above n. 3), 87.

[31] Josef Kohler, for example, saw the reason for the incompleteness of international law in the
fact that it still lacked the shared basis of a natural law, from which every law had to proceed:
J. Kohler, *Grundlagen des Völkerrechts* (Enke, 1918).

world-historical scale,[32] a growing longing for eternal values, metaphysics and a substantive foundation of the law had made itself felt. The old positivist law of nations had been unable to prevent neither the outbreak of the war nor the large-scale violations of the laws of war. Once again, the objective principle was sought out in the Christian doctrine of natural law, which in German *fin de siècle* jurisprudence was believed to have been overcome by the 'juristic method'. Under the impact of the gas-poisoned trenches, catholic natural law had been rediscovered in Germany, first by Cathrein, Mausbach and Schilling, and later by Kelsen's own pupil, Alfred Verdross[33] and in France by Louis le Fur.[34] Kelsen and Kunz also rejected these newer natural-law approaches with the goal of ensuring the 'purity of the science of international law'.[35]

The dichotomy of Is/Ought, and the specifically jurisprudential Ought-category they worked out allowed Kelsen and his students henceforth to castigate both sociological and ethical, as well as moral ascriptions and deductions, in the *legal* analysis of the law as methodologically inappropriate. As they saw it, this was the only way for the law to become a medium of contingent norm-creation on the international level, and, in general, the only way to enable a sober and, if necessary, critical assessment of the state of development of the law and its repercussions on society.

D   *The Critique of German* Staatswillenspositivismus *and the* Grundnorm *of International Law*

Starting from his strict separation of 'Is' and 'Ought', Kelsen had – already in his 'constructivist' phase – criticised the 'dogma of the will' in

---

[32] On this, see Stolleis: 'The world "after", after the "storms of steel", was hardly recognisable as an offshoot of the world "before". In that sense, 1914 remains an enormous rupture. It marked the first great explosion of aggression in the era of nationalism.' Stolleis, *Der lange Abschied* (above n. 14), 22.

[33] In 1918, immediately following the end of the war, the Jesuit Viktor Cathrein tried to revive the Christian roots of international law. The theologians Josef Mausbach and Otto Schilling, in their own monographs, drawing on the Spanish late scholastics, endorsed this view. See V. Cathrein, *Die Grundlage des Völkerrechts* (Herder, 1918); J. Mausbach, *Naturrecht und Völkerrecht* (Herder, 1918); O. Schilling, *Das Völkerrecht nach Thomas von Aquin* (Herder, 1918); A. Verdross, *Die Verfassung der Völkerrechtsgemeinschaft* (Springer, 1926).

[34] In France, Louis le Fur established a natural law theory of international law; see L. le Fur, 'La Théorie du droit naturel depuis le XVIIème siècle et la doctrine moderne' in *Collected Courses of The Hague Academy of International Law* (Brill/Nijhoff, 1927), 18/III, 259 et seq.

[35] On natural law in the doctrine of international law, see J. L. Kunz, *Völkerrechtswissenschaft und Reine Rechtslehre* (F. Deuticke, 1923), 72–4.

jurisprudence as the result of a blending of psychological and sociological Is-considerations and normative Ought-considerations.[36] In fact, from a strict normative perspective, the 'will' of the (assumed) personified state (*willensfähige Staatspersönlichkeit*) was nothing other than the central point of imputation for all acts of the organs of the particular state.[37] In this way, Kelsen had tried, already in his habilitation thesis, to replace the 'state as a legal person capable of will' with the concept of formal imputation.[38] Kelsen developed this approach further in *The Problem of Sovereignty* and the *Theory of International Law* and arrived at the assumption of the complete identity of state and law. The 'identity thesis' became the pivotal point in the sought-after revision of the conceptual apparatus of international law.

The provocative assumption that the state and the law were congruent terms for the legal scholar was based on two different strands of justification, though Kelsen often intertwined them in *The Problem of Sovereignty and the Theory of International Law*. The first strand is the demand for a strict separation between 'Is' and 'Ought' and the various 'Ought' categories described above, according to which the state can be represented in jurisprudence not as an Is/Ought causal construct, but exclusively as a normative legal order.[39] The second strand is Kelsen's theory or critique of 'juristic fictions' (*Juristische Fiktionen*), which was already part of Kelsen's critical methodology in his previous works. According to this theory, the notion of the state as a 'person' and 'bearer' of the law was a 'personifying fiction' (*personifikative Fiktion*) used by the prevailing doctrine.[40] With reference to Vaihinger's *Die Philosophie des Als-Ob*,[41] Kelsen recognised in the jurisprudential use of the concept of the '*willensfähige Staatsperson*' a doubling or 'hypostatisation'.[42] The real function of the legal person as a unifying point of imputation of norms became in traditional legal

---

[36] Kelsen, *Hauptprobleme* (above n. 24), 162 et seq.; see Heidemann, *Die Norm als Tatsache* (above n. 21), 35.

[37] Kelsen, *Hauptprobleme* (above n. 24), 189; on the notion of imputation and its origins in nineteenth-century German legal thought, see Paulson, 'Kelsen's Earliest Legal Theory' (above n. 21), 33 et seq.

[38] Paulson, 'Kelsen's Earliest Legal Theory' (above n. 21), 33; Paulson calls this early phase of Kelsen's legal theory the constructivist phase; on this phase, see also Heidemann, *Die Norm als Tatsache* (above n. 21), 23–33.

[39] Kelsen, *Hauptprobleme* (above n. 24), xvi.

[40] Kelsen, *Das Problem der Souveränität* (above n. 3), 18; Kelsen, 'Theorie der Juristischen Fiktionen' in H. R. Klecatsky (ed.), *Die Wiener Rechtstheoretische Schule*, 2 vols. (Europa Verlag, 1968), I, 1215 et seq.

[41] H. Vaihinger, *Die Philosophie des Als-Ob*, 2nd edn (Reuther & Reichard, 1913).

[42] Kelsen, *Das Problem der Souveränität* (above n. 3), 18.

scholarship a living, human-like figure, a state organism. The latter was mythically transfigured and endowed with primal omnipotence:

> Legal thinking is a thoroughly personifying one and – to the extent that it hypostatizes the persons it creates – can be compared to mythological thinking, which, anthropomorphically, suspects a dryad behind every tree, a spring god behind every spring, Apollo behind the sun, thus doubling nature as an object of cognition.[43]

The construction of the legal person, an achievement of nineteenth-century legal thought, was reduced by Kelsen down to its normative core. In Kelsen's eyes, this was merely a metaphor for the unity of a system of legal norms.[44] The notion of a dualism of state and law, according to which the 'unbounded Leviathan' had to be tamed by the law, was to be abolished by the identity thesis.[45] Kelsen saw the identity thesis as a fundamental break with the existing voluntaristic foundations of the science of the state and international law, as represented above all by Jellinek's *Allgemeine Staatslehre*.[46] He was the first author who attempted to break with this tradition of German *Staatswillenspositivismus* in international law on explicit 'positivist' premises. For him, in the debate over the 'source' or the 'validity ground' of international law, neither an argumentative strategy based solely on natural law or socio-biological or psychological assumptions, nor one based solely on positivism and consensus were sustainable by themselves. The doctrine of the a priori '*droit objectif*' (Scelle) or of Christian natural law (Verdross) were too vague; to become concrete, they had to resort after all to 'declaratory' positive law through a kind of metaphysical doubling. The doctrine of the consensus of the sovereign will of the states, for its part, required extra-positivistic standards to establish an objectivised, binding nature of international law vis-à-vis the will of individual states.[47] To that end, it had developed the constructs of an 'objective international law' derived from the nature of the community of states (Jellinek), the doctrine of the 'common will' (Triepel), and the 'tacit' or 'common consent' arising from silence (Oppenheim). Kelsen had thus attacked both the natural

---

[43] Ibid., 18 (translation by the author).

[44] M. Baldus, *Die Einheit der Rechtsordnung* (Duncker & Humblot, 1995), 158.

[45] Horst Dreier speaks of a 'profanisation' of the state in Kelsen: *Rechtslehre, Staatssoziologie und Demokratietheorie* (above n. 8), 208–13.

[46] On this see the discussion in Berstorff, *The Public International Law Theory of Hans Kelsen* (above n. 4), Chapter 2.

[47] For a fundamental language-analytical study of the various argumentative strategies concerning the 'basis of obligation', see M. Koskenniemi, *From Apology to Utopia* (Cambridge University Press, 2005), 268.

law and the consensus foundations of international law at their respective Achilles' heels: the lack of concreteness for natural law, and the absence of a binding normative nature in the voluntaristic-consensual theories. He developed the first in-depth structural critique of the semantic cage which this tradition had erected:

> The theory of international law, in particular, vacillates back and forth uncertainly between the antipodes of a state-individualistic and a human-universalistic perspective, between the subjectivism of the primacy of the legal order of the state and the objectivism of the primacy of international law ...[48]

Instead, in a radicalised neo-Kantian version of positivism, international law for Kelsen was valid because international lawyers assumed it to be valid. This hypothesis underlying international legal discourse is embodied in Kelsen's notion of the hypothetical *Grundnorm*, replacing the circular move between the sovereign will and the objective and binding law above the state. Through the hypothetical formulation of the Basic Norm, he sought to capture this paradox in the abstract idea of an – intellectually presupposed – binding nature of the law. Through the hypothetical articulation of the Basic Norm, international legal scholarship was to be freed from the need for an ultimate extra-legal foundation of the law. In his eyes, the hypothetical Basic Norm, as a placeholder[49] for the idea of a specifically legal validity, secured the 'objectivity' of the scholarly understanding of the law.[50]

Very much in the spirit of the interwar movement to modernise international law, the monumental 'dogma' of the sovereign will of the individual state was thus emphatically knocked off its pedestal by Kelsen and his students, its foundational role was being rejected. Kelsen's transcendental system of formal concepts, together with the assumption of the primacy

---

[48] Kelsen, *Das Problem der Souveränität* (above n. 3), 319–20.

[49] Here is the precise explanation of this by J. Raz, 'Kelsen's Theory of the Basic Norm' in S. L. Paulson and B. L. Paulson (eds.), *Normativity and Norms: Critical Perspectives on Kelsenian Themes* (Oxford University Press, 1998), 67: 'He [Kelsen] is able to maintain that the science of law is value-free by claiming for it a special point of view, that of the legal man, and contending that legal science adopts this point of view; that it presupposes its basic norm in a special, professional, and uncommitted sense of presupposing. There is, after all, no legal sense of normativity, but there is a specifically legal way in which normativity can be considered.'

[50] Alf Ross speaks in this context of Kelsen as a 'quasi-positivist': A. Ross, 'Validity and the Conflict between Legal Positivism and Natural Law' in S. L. Paulson and B. L. Paulson (eds.), *Normativity and Norms: Critical Perspectives on Kelsenian Themes* (Oxford University Press, 1998), 159–61.

of international law, created an international law without substantive state sovereignty; its place was taken by a legal cosmos which, hierarchical and structured through delegation, elevated international law philosophically above the state. Kelsen, in his construction of this monist legal universe, interestingly relied on Christian Wolff's concept of *civitas maxima* (through Kaltenborn) and not on Kant's essay on eternal peace.[51] I assume this was because Kant still retained a strong notion of substantial state sovereignty, which Kelsen did not want to endorse – sovereignty instead is relegated in the Pure Theory to nothing more than the formal attribute of the highest level of norms in a given legal system.

From the perspective of legal scholarship, universal law encompassed all legal norms as parts of a unified legal system. The norms of international law and national law were grounded in a unified theoretical conception of the law. Moreover, this conception reduced law to its 'pure' form, which, from the perspective of legal science, could take on any possible content. Freed from their *a priori* ethical and political limitations, international law and national law could be employed as a medium of potentially unlimited social change. The horizon was opened up – everything was possible. This included the realisation of world state structures as a possible goal of international politics. International law can look and operate like national law – it can, for instance, directly empower or obligate individuals. Thus, it can also take the form of national penal or administrative law. There is no categorical distinction between national and international law. The dualism of national and international law is being replaced by a continuum of various systemically connected emanations of the law, be they what we today call international, regional, transnational, national or local. Kelsen's use of the word 'universal' can thus be understood in a twofold sense: 'universal' stands for both the unity of international law and national law, and the contingent content of the medium of law as a 'form' that could be used in any conceivable way.

II The Limits of Objectivity

Kelsen's neo-Kantian formalisation of jurisprudence does not contain its own interpretive doctrine. For Kelsen, the process of the interpretation of a norm by the legal practitioner and the legal theorist defied complete

---

[51] On ideas of universal cooperation between or above the states in Kant and Wolff and on Kant's reluctance to wholeheartedly endorse the world state concept see Robert Schütze, Chapter 1 in this volume.

objectification. When it came to the realm of the application of the law, the Pure Theory of Law dispensed entirely with its own substantive theory of interpretation. Instead, such a theory was completely absorbed into the doctrine of the hierarchical structure of the legal system (*Stufenbaulehre*). According to the 'dynamic' variant of this theory, norm-application was considered a dynamic intellectual process moving from a higher to a lower norm in the hierarchical structure of the legal system. Applying a norm to a specific case creates an individualised lower norm through the reference to the text of a 'higher' norm. Kelsen describes this 'intellectual activity' of legally authorised courts and public officials as the act of 'authentic' interpretation.[52] In this process, the higher norm only to a limited extent predetermined the content of the new lower norm. Norm-application by authorised organs, such as courts or public officials thus involved an act of interpretation. The input by the higher level of norm-production created merely the semantic 'framework' that had to be respected by the lower norm. This act of interpretation by law-applying organs, which chose one of the possible readings within the outer semantic limits, was conceptualised as a creative act, as individualised legislation. As a theoretical consequence of this assumption, Kelsen erased the conceptual difference between adjudication and legislation.[53] Moreover, for Kelsen there was no 'scientific' method by which only one of the several readings of a norm could be identified as the 'correct' one. There was no 'objectively correct' interpretation of norms.[54] With interpretation came an unavoidable intrusion of subjectivity, politics, values and idiosyncratic preferences. While exposing the dilemma of interpretation, Kelsen stopped short of contributing to its methodological containment. Instead, he completely removed methodological questions regarding the act of interpretation from the Pure Theory's realm of cognition.[55]

---

[52] Kelsen, *Reine Rechtslehre* (above n. 28), 90; Kelsen, *Problems of Legal Theory* (above n. 28), 77.

[53] Through his realistic doctrine of the dynamic application of the law as interpretation, Kelsen comes closer to the communicative paradigm of later legal theories, like those of Jürgen Habermas, Pierre Bourdieu and Niklas Luhmann, than all other contemporary legal theories.

[54] Kelsen, *Reine Rechtslehre* (above n. 28), 96; Kelsen, *Problems of Legal Theory* (above n. 28), 81; this has important repercussions for the notion of democratic legitimacy, see for international adjudication: A. von Bogdandy and I. Venzke, 'Zur Herrschaft internationaler Gerichte: Eine Untersuchung internationaler öffentlicher Gewalt und ihrer demokratischen Rechtfertigung' (2010) 70 *Heidelberg Law Journal* 1–49.

[55] On this and the critique, see Bernstorff, *The Public International Law Theory of Hans Kelsen* (above n. 4), Chapter 6.

The lack of compulsory jurisdiction in most areas of international law, however, renders this problem particularly acute in international law. The pure theory of international law has no real answers to the question of the interpretation of norms by those who apply the law. The reappearance of the 'political' in the application of the law that Kelsen accepted as unavoidable is another way of describing the central conundrum of the law, which Jacques Derrida described as the '*Heimsuchung durch das Unentscheidbare*' and Niklas Luhmann as the '*Entscheidung des Unentscheidbaren*'.[56] Despite Kelsen's illuminating theoretical equation of adjudication and legislation, it remains problematic within this context that the Pure Theory of Law, as a theory of law, promotes the civilisational function of a specific judicial rationality without being able to explain it.

The issue of interpretation arises, however, not only in the area of the application of the law, but also on the level of international legal scholarship. To the question of the angle from which the legal scholar should interpret the monist legal system created by Kelsen, the latter has a particular answer, one that grants an unexpected amount of room to the 'political' with regard to the structure of the legal system. According to Kelsen, the makeup of the hierarchically structured legal system depends fundamentally on a basic interpretational decision that is prior to legal 'science', meaning it is 'political' in Kelsen's understanding. The question here is whether the monistic legal cosmos is constructed on the foundation of the primacy of national law or the primacy of international law. If state law is given primacy, it forms the highest level of norms, and international law is conceived as a subordinated system of norms derived from the respective national constitution. By contrast, if international law is given primacy, the state legal systems are subordinated subsystems of international law and are coordinated by it. For Kelsen, the primacy question is based on a fundamental political decision that cannot be answered by legal 'science'.[57] Looking at international law, the structure of the created transcendental world of scientific legal cognition itself depends, according to Kelsen, on a fundamental 'political' value-decision by the jurist.

Kelsen was thus trying to describe the political dimension of every form of international legal scholarship – that is, the question inherent in any discourse on international law, namely whether a norm is interpreted from the standpoint of a supraordinated system of international law, or

---

[56] J. Derrida, *Gesetzeskraft. Der mystische Grund der Autorität* (Suhrkamp, 1991), 49; N. Luhmann, *Das Recht der Gesellschaft* (Suhrkamp, 1993), 317.

[57] H. Kelsen, *Rechtsgeschichte gegen Rechtsphilosophie? Eine Erwiderung* (Springer, 1928), 317.

from the perspective of the sovereign individual state to which any binding norm must be traced back – by way of the so-called 'choice hypothesis'. Traditional doctrine according to Kelsen made the mistake of constant and unreflected changes between state-centred and universalising perspectives on international law ('*Wechsel des Erkenntnisstandpunktes*'). On the primacy question, he called for a single and coherent decision by the respective international lawyer on the chosen vantage point. If one considers that the doctrine of the primacy of state law entails, according to Kelsen, a denial of international law as an autonomous legal system, it becomes clear that Kelsen's construct of international law is subject to the provision of a fundamental political decision. One reason why Kunz and Verdross openly dissented from the 'choice hypothesis' was that central aspects of their shared cosmopolitan project – such as direct rights and obligations of the individual under international law and the post-sovereign empowerment of international organisations – depended on how this choice was made.[58]

However, Kelsen's formalised and deductive conceptual apparatus described above – that is, the claim to unity of cognition and hierarchical system-building – forced him to acknowledge that both primacy assumptions were inherently consistent. In a paradoxical way, Kelsen's formal understanding of legal scholarship, which sought to expel the political from the realm of legal cognition, generated in the choice hypothesis the far-reaching theoretical concession that legal cognition in international law, at its core, was also subjective and political in character.[59] In order to rescue his claim to objectivity, Kelsen demanded the jurist's transparent decision on whether the norms of international law should be interpreted on the basis of the primacy of state law or that of international law. To him, a 'science' of international law was still possible, in spite of a fundamental political decision on the part of the jurist about the posited total construct.

---

[58] On the quarrel over the Wahlhypothese, see Bernstorff, *The Public International Law Theory of Hans Kelsen* (above n. 4), 104–7.

[59] It would take until 1989 before Martti Koskenniemi, following David Kennedy, was able to reformulate Kelsens's critique of the continuous and unreflected change between the two epistemological standpoints (*Wechsel des Erkenntnisstandpunktes*) in international law with the help of the linguistic distinction between 'ascending' (primacy of national law-apology) and 'descending' (primacy of international law-utopia) arguments in international legal discourse. M. Koskenniemi, *From Apology to Utopia* (Cambridge University Press, 2005); D. Kennedy, 'Theses about International Law Discourse' (1980) 23 *German YBIL* 353–91; on Koskenniemi and Kelsen, see J. von Bernstorff, 'Sisyphus Was an International Lawyer: On Martti Koskenniemi's *From Apology to Utopia* and the Place of Law in International Politics' (2006) 12 *GLJ* 1015–35.

Scientific objectivity thus – in a more abstract sense – lay in making political preferences transparent and pursuing a strict deductive construction of the system on this basis.

III   Kelsen and Oppenheim: Two Radically Opposed 'Positivist' Projects

The 'objective' science postulated by Kelsen, which was to be achieved through the constructive uncoupling of the abstract concepts from the current content of the norms, already offered contemporary critics a two-fold point of attack under the slogan of a 'radical-logicistic metaphysics'.[60] Because of their distance from current law, the concepts generated by Kelsen's approach seemed to have little usefulness not only for those who applied the law, but also from the perspective of many mainstream legal scholars.[61] Moreover, the cosmopolitan project behind the central critical assumptions of the Pure Theory, which had resonated politically with the international reform movement, was not well received in the increasingly nationalist atmosphere in German international legal scholarship in the late interwar period.

What can be observed instead during this time is a turn to pragmatic consent-based approaches to international law. The father of this pragmatic approach is Lassa Oppenheim, who became highly influential in the UK, the United States and beyond through his famous textbook *International Law*. As Matthias Schmoeckel has shown, Oppenheim's academic roots must be situated in the German public law tradition of the German Empire. Like Triepel he was a pupil of the criminal law professor and legal philosopher Rudolf Binding. After his emigration to the UK he started his career as an international lawyer and based his approach on the fundamental theoretical assumptions of Jellinek and Triepel.[62] The validity of international law is based on 'common consent'

---

[60] A contemporary example of this critique is E. Kaufmann, *Gesammelte Schriften, III: Rechtsidee und Recht* (Schwarz, 1960), 198.

[61] Moreover, as Erich Kaufmann and Wilhelm Jöckel noted early on, they were not truly 'pure' in the sense of the Kantian categories. Both authors had pointed out that Kelsen's *Rechtsformbegriffe* were not transcendental legal concepts in the sense of pure legal categories, but merely highly abstracted 'general empirical concepts' of jurisprudence, which were by no means situated before any kind of experience. Ibid., 193; W. Jöckel, *Hans Kelsens rechtstheoretische Methode. Darstellung und Kritik ihrer rundlagen und hauptsächlichsten Ergebnisse* (Scientia, 1977 [1930]), 162.

[62] Matthias Schmoeckel, 'The Internationalist as a Scientist and Herald: Lassa Oppenheim' (2000) 11 *EJIL* 699.

of 'civilised' nations.[63] International law is a horizontal law between equal sovereign states. It therefore needs to be conceptualised as a separate legal system from (hierarchical) municipal law in line with Triepel's dualist theory. The lack of explicit consent by individual or newly recognised states is theoretically bridged by the assumption of implicit 'recognition' (Jellinek) or 'tacit consent' creating and reaffirming international customary law rules. 'Common interests', 'public opinion' and the 'balance of power' as well as decentralised enforcement theoretically step in as a cohesive force in order to make up for the lack of centralised (state-like) enforcement measures. Malleable concepts like 'common interests' and 'balance of power' used by Oppenheim are not accidently regularly synonymous with contemporary great-power (UK and United States) interests in international commerce through free navigation, transport and communication as well as in common scientific standards and selected humanitarian purposes.[64] While rhetorically focusing on empirical emanations of international law and denying the relevance of all extra-legal sources, Oppenheim's approach to international law, like the one taken by Jellinek, is ripe with psychological, sociological and political assumptions about a 'community of civilised states'. By merging fundamental voluntarist theories about the nature of the international legal order with a pragmatic and case-based style of presenting international legal doctrine, Oppenheim's 'international law' became the most successful textbook of the first decades of the twentieth century.

It is this particular blend of nineteenth-century voluntarist assumptions and a pragmatic and ideologically malleable usage of cases and legal materials through loaded background concepts such as 'common interests', 'international community' or 'family of nations' that has proven to be particularly successful in twentieth-century international law. It can be used for different political purposes, Walter Schücking's liberal-pacifist project works on the basis of this methodological basis, as do Karl Strupp's works on international law. Despite the at times strong rhetorical critique of Jellinek's theory of auto-limitation in the modernisation movement of the interwar period, the construct of sovereigns being bound by concrete

---

[63] On the following theoretical assumptions L. Oppenheim, *International Law: A Treatise*, 2 vols. (Longmans, 1905), I, §§ 3, 5–14.

[64] B. Kingsbury, 'Legal Positivism as Normative Politics: International Society, Balance of Power and Lassa Oppenheim's Positive International Law' (2002) 13 *EJIL* 401; and more recently M. G.-S. Rovira, *The Project of Positivism in International Law* (Oxford University Press, 2013).

expressions of their consent and overriding 'community interests', survived in the tradition of pragmatic positivism inaugurated by Oppenheim.

Monica Garcia-Salmones Rovira, in her book on Oppenheim, has labelled his approach as 'economic positivism' referring to the Anglo-American economic agenda promoted by Oppenheim's work. His works indeed are often apologetic of – and in line with – imperial British foreign policy and economic objectives, which can indeed justify using the label of 'economic positivism'. What is problematic about Rovira's thesis, however, is her attempt to subsume Kelsen's approach under the same label. As I have attempted to show, Kelsen's approach is an open break with the voluntarist tradition, on which Oppenheim relies. It is not only decisively un-pragmatic, but opposes all basic assumptions of Oppenheim's approach to international law ('tacit consent', 'common interests', 'family of nations' etc.). From both a methodological and a political perspective, Kelsen's theory of international law is an anti-Oppenheim project attempting to deconstruct all basic tenets of the tradition, on which Oppenheim's works on international law are built. And to portray Kelsen, who in his autobiography expressed that since World War I he supported socialist redistribution of wealth to the great masses, and who had not published a single line defending any general or concrete international economic project during his entire academic career, as a precursor of early European 'neoliberal' thought and as a towering figure of what is called 'economic positivism' seems unconvincing.[65]

IV Conclusion

But, by way of conclusion, what is the politics of Kelsen's universalist concept of international law in the twenty-first century? Michael Hardt and Antonio Negri have advanced a critical depiction of the current politics of Kelsenian cosmopolitanism. In their view, his sovereignty critique and his defence of the primacy of international law thesis as one possible option to construct the hierarchical monist legal universe make him a chief theorist of a twenty-first century 'imperial' global legal order.[66] In a somewhat similar vein, Carl Schmitt had criticised the Vienna School in the interwar period for justifying Allied interwar dominance over Germany through

---

[65] This is the assumption made by Rovira, ibid., 120 et seq. This interpretation seems to result from a misguided equation of Oppenheim's and Kelsen's approaches to international law and from contemporary (interwar German) stereotypes of 'liberal' legal scholarship.

[66] M. Hardt and A. Negri, *Empire* (Harvard University Press, 2001), Chapter 1.1.

the theory of monism. Are these critical depictions of the current politics of Kelsen's international law theory justified?

Yes and No. Yes, if these claims are meant to express that Kelsen and his school were among the first scholars to detect and explain how international law could be used to implement political projects through novel institutions and laws connecting the international and the national level, inter alia by directly empowering and holding to account private actors through international law in a monist legal system. And no, if 'chief theorist of an imperial global order' is meant to say that the Pure Theory *qua* theory promoted a specific political or even imperialist or economic project. Kelsen himself always maintained that both the primacy of international law perspective and the primacy of domestic law perspective were scholarly, valid and defendable perspectives. Moreover, the anti-ideological metaphor of the 'empty universal legal form' is not particularly well suited to defend from a scholarly perspective a particular economic or political project. The affirmative dimensions of Kelsen's Pure Theory, which can only be indirectly deduced from Kelsen's deconstruction of sovereignty, thus find a strong theoretical counterbalance in the Pure Theory itself. Not only that, according to Kelsen, the legal scholar is supposed to lay open his or her own political (cosmopolitan or national) preferences when analysing international law, but also, and more importantly, the fact that the Pure Theory creates a reflexive distance vis-à-vis the current contents of the international legal order. There is no inevitability, essentialism or romanticism as to the content of international legal structures. Rules and principles could be entirely different.[67] Without naïvely ignoring entrenched economic and political structures,[68] the metaphor of the empty universal form helps to throw the affirmative dimensions of current international legal discourse into relief. Imagining international law's 'foundation' or its 'constitution' as being empty, rather than one reflecting conventional 'family' or 'community' interests, thus creates a transformative potential. Vacating the constitutional space in order to fill it with new anti-hegemonic substance becomes an intelligible project.

---

[67] On 'false necessity' or the contingency of existing institutions, see R. Unger, *False Necessity*, 2nd edn (Verso, 2004).

[68] On 'false contingency' see S. Marks, 'False Contingency' (2009) 62(1) *Current Legal Problems* 1–21.

3

Tyranny and Constitutionalism beyond the State

AOIFE O'DONOGHUE*

I Introduction

Of late, a constitutional ethic has gained momentum amongst international legal academics.[1] This movement seeks to go beyond traditional international law tropes such as Westphalian sovereignty and subsidiarity to an understanding of the global legal order as incorporating public law components. With increasing frequency, a potential role, both normative and organisational, for a constitutional ethic beyond what is traditionally associated with the internal workings of a state is either recognised as pre-existing or declared emergent and is furthermost established amongst European Union (EU) scholars.[2] This chapter asks what has compelled international scholarship towards constitutionalism and what can be deduced about the nature of this scholarship from an analysis of its genesis.

Unquestionably public international law always contained a quality of 'publicness'. International law possesses foundational myths and legitimating language not contingent upon tropes from other systems. This is not to suggest an isolated legal system immune from cross-pollination but rather that the international legal order always possessed a separate publicness in its discourse and governance. These public elements comprise, amongst many others, the formation of international law, the structures of

*Thanks to Ruth Houghton, Máiréad Enright, Robert Schütze and Colin Murray for their comments on earlier drafts.

[1] This includes global constitutionalism/constitutionalisation, global administrative law, global legal pluralism, global public goods and EU constitutional law amongst several others.

[2] N. Walker, 'The Idea of Constitutional Pluralism' (2002) 65 *MLR* 317–59; P. S. Berman, 'A Pluralist Approach to International Law' (2007) 32 *YJIL* 301; G. Teubner, *Constitutional Fragments: Societal Constitutionalism and Globalization* (Oxford University Press, 2012); N. Krisch and B. Kingsbury, 'Introduction: Global Governance and Global Administrative Law in the International Legal Order' (2006) 17 *EJIL* 1.

international organisations and the operation of international courts and tribunals. Nonetheless, most obviously displayed in the constitutionalisation debate but clearly demonstrable elsewhere, is a move to adopt domestic constitutional tropes. This chapter seeks to ask why this has occurred, why lawyers whose concerns were not bound to questions of the rule of law, division of power, checks and balances, the incorporation of human rights or democratic legitimacy have become engrossed in such debates.

The underlying rationales for choosing what traditionally were and are domestic public law tools may range from a number of anxieties. These anxieties include: a perceived need to divest constituted power from a narrow set of global or regional actors, a role in underpinning both individual and collective rights, a provision to check both the legitimacy and legalism of power, the possibility of recognising diverse points of governance within the global or regional order, a perceived move beyond the state-consent-based order to something new but as yet unarticulated and, critically, to locate a global rule of law. While legal theory has been concerned with questions of legitimacy and power, whether this is a concern with regard to public international law was often dismissed as unnecessary in a contractual consent based legal order.[3] Yet, clearly an inner anxiety exists that has pushed scholars into considering whether public international law may gain in legitimacy from either recognising pre-existing constitutional accounts of existing formations, both institutional and legal, or from pushing the global order to adopt these structures onto itself. One potential explanation for the move towards public law is an underlying dread amongst international lawyers that law beyond the state underpins a system of tyrannical power;[4] that international law currently forms an a-constitutional order; that the accumulation of power beyond the state has yet to be entrenched with forms of legitimacy that would be expected when constituted power is exercised across a number of governance points. Global constitutionalism, in this scenario, provides a basis to make claims as to what is to be expected of a constitutional order.[5] Conversely,

---

[3] H. L. A. Hart, *The Concept of Law* (Clarendon Press, 1961), 227.

[4] For a discussion of international law and tyranny see M. Koskenniemi, 'Police in the Temple Order, Justice and the UN: A Dialectical View' (1995) 6 *EJIL* 325.

[5] E. De Wet, 'The International Constitutional Order' (2006) 55 *ICLQ*, 51; J. Klabbers et al., *The Constitutionalisation of International Law* (Oxford University Press, 2009); M. Kumm, 'The Legitimacy of International Law: A Constitutionalist Framework of Analysis' (2004) 15 *EJIL* 907; A. Peters, 'Compensatory Constitutionalism: The Function and Potential of Fundamental International Norms and Structures' (2006) 19 *Leiden JIL* 579; C. J. Schwöbel, *Global Constitutionalism in International Legal Perspective* (Martinus Nijhoff Publishers, 2011); E. U. Petersmann, 'The WTO Constitution and Human Rights' (2000) 3 *JIEL* 19, 20.

if a-constitutionality is the correct description of the current state of international law than tyranny may be the more appropriate term by which to describe its operation.

Describing the order as tyrannical neither proposes that there is no global legal order nor makes a claim towards anarchy. Rather, this chapter will develop a taxonomy of tyranny based in classical Greek philosophy, Machiavelli and the work of Hannah Arendt. These three models of tyranny focus on it as a form of governance order.[6] There are also several theories of tyranny that are omitted here including Erasmus, Kant, Schmitt and Montesquieu and, of course, tyranny is not unknown to scholarship beyond the state, for example, as a riposte to Kant's global government. However this chapter will maintain a narrow focus on establishing a taxonomy and placing this alongside international law.[7] Before beginning the discussion on tyranny, hegemony, anarchy and imperialism will also be discussed to contextualise the establishment of the taxonomy. This chapter, in looking to tyranny, asks what concerns ought global and EU scholars have when considering the structure of their proposed constitutional order.

II   Hegemony, Anarchy and Imperialism

Of course, tyranny sits amongst a plethora of other potential descriptors of international law. Anarchy, while not often a key part of international law (with the exception of 'failed states' and international relations scholarship), is often set as the ultimate failure in governance that strong legal structures forestall. Hegemony and imperialism both offer valuable insights into the choices that have gone into framing the global legal order. Both hegemony and imperialism may operate as part of a tyrannical order while anarchy is often placed at the opposite end of the governance spectrum from tyranny or as the only purported alternative to a tyrannical order.

A   Hegemony

Global, political, social, cultural and legal hegemony or the predominance, control or undue influence of one entity or group of entities over others is

---

[6] There are also several theories of tyranny that are omitted here including D. Erasmus and W. W. Barker (eds.), *The Adages of Erasmus* (University of Toronto Press, 2001); N. Machiavelli *The Prince* (Oxford University Press, 2005); C. Schmitt, *The Tyranny of Values* (Plutarch Press, 1996); Montesquieu: *The Spirit of the Laws* (Cambridge University Press, 1989).

[7] See R. Schütze, Chapter 1 in this volume.

now a central concern of many critical voices within international law.[8] As Wilhelm Grewe argues, successive hegemons shaped the foundations of international law.[9] From the fifteenth century to the first half of the twentieth century, attempts to establish European hegemony over America, Asia and Africa was dominant while in the post-World War II era the hegemony of the USSR and United States and, more recently, the United States alone are apparent (albeit the EU has also gained some critique on this basis). Hegemony has become a trope to explain the inequality behind the apparent sovereign equality of states.[10] As an idea, hegemony's heritage is at least as old as tyranny's and, as with tyranny, it has moved beyond the narrow confines of cities or states to global spheres of operation and also into the cultural, social, economic and political spheres.[11] Hegemonic influence may not always be consciously exerted or planned and indeed it is often much more complex in its operation.

Definitions of global or international hegemony vary, Michael Doyle describes it as 'controlling leadership of the international system as a whole' while Ilkenberry and Kupchan describe it as the ability to 'establish a set of norms that others willingly embrace.'[12] Within this idea of hegemony there are also issues of counter-hegemony, hegemonic stability and instability and questions of consent, coercion and socialisation in the adoption of norms. Like tyranny, for some, hegemony can be positive if it creates stability. For others, even in these circumstances, the tools necessary to establish and maintain that hegemony always create such inequality and harm

[8] M. Byers and G. Nolte (eds.), *United States Hegemony and the Foundations of International Law* (Cambridge University Press, 2003); D. Vagts, 'Hegemonic International Law' (2001) 95 *AJIL* 843; M. Koskenniemi, *The Politics of International Law* (Bloomsbury Publishing, 2011), 219. Koskenniemi, in focusing on Gramsci and Laclau, departs from other accounts that focus on international relations scholarship.

[9] W. Grewe, *The Epochs of International Law*, trans. M. Byers (de Gruyter, 2000); see also R. Keohane, *After Hegemony* (Princeton University Press, 1984); J. E. Alvarez, 'Hegemonic International Law Revisited' (2003) 97 *AJIL* 873; R. O. Keohane, *After Hegemony: Cooperation and Discord in the World Political Economy*, rev. edn (Princeton University Press, 2005).

[10] As early as 1908 Oppenheim argues that hegemony was antithetical to sovereign equality, L. Oppenheim, 'The Science of International Law: Its Task and Method' (1908) 2 *AJIL* 213. In contrast to regional or city state hegemons of earlier eras, including the Roman or the Five Hegemons in China, from the fifteenth-century attempts to create global hegemons became a possibility. Thucydides, *The Peloponnesian War* (Penguin, 1951).

[11] A. Gramsci, *Selections from the Prison Notebooks of Antonio Gramsci* (International Publishers, 1971); E. Laclau and C. Mouffe, *Hegemony and Socialist Strategy: Towards a Radical Democratic Politics* (Verso, 2001); J. Butler et al., *Contingency, Hegemony, Universality: Contemporary Dialogues on the Left* (Verso, 2000).

[12] M. W. Doyle, *Empires* (Cornell University Press, 1986), 40; G. J. Ikenberry and C. A. Kupchan, 'Socialisation and Hegemonic Power' (1990) 44 *IO* 283.

as to be a gratuitous use of power. Often drawing on the work of Gramsci, this critique suggests that hegemonic influence establishes what for some may be positive norms but for most others is an unjustified imposition of Euro-American exceptionalism.[13] Gramsci emphasised the role of cultural hegemony to demonstrate how capitalism is established, maintained and legitimised as well as the role of ideology in establishing what becomes represented as normal or common sense.[14]

The tools of technocratic, social and political elites in establishing hegemony is evident throughout international law where often the particular is presented as universal and hegemonic contestation reveals the political use of legality to establish a regime of benefit to a particular actor or set of actors.[15] Contemporary scholarship also understands there may be a move away from the state as the sole source of hegemonic power and the influence of a broader set of actors in the establishment of economic, political, social and cultural norms.[16] While this is often linked to globalisation this is not necessarily the case as the form and role of a hegemon can be in flux. Krisch in his study of international law and hegemony argues that hegemons typically instrumentalise law, reshape it in a hierarchical manner and supplant it with domestic legal tools that better suit their purposes.[17] But Krisch also points to a paradox within the international legal order, that to operate it requires power to enforce its norms.[18] This suggests a very close relationship between international law and hegemony where they appear locked together in substance, procedure and structure. The hegemon will establish and buttress the form of global order that will best suit its requirements both through coercion and acquiescence and this narrative reoccurs as differing hegemons assert themselves within international law.[19]

---

[13] A. Orakhelashvili, 'Hegemony, Multipolarity and the System of International Law' in M. Happold (ed.), *International Law in a Multipolar World* (Routledge, 2013), 114.

[14] Gramsci, *Selections from the Prison Notebooks of Antonio Gramsci* (above n. 11).

[15] S. Scott, 'The Impact on International Law of US Noncompliance' in M. Byers, G. Nolte (eds.), *United States Hegemony and the Foundations of International Law* (Cambridge University Press, 2003), 451; Keohane, *After Hegemony* (above n. 9); Koskenniemi, *The Politics of International Law* (above n. 8), 219–22.

[16] G. Z. Capaldo, *The Pillars of Global Law* (Ashgate, 2008), 22.

[17] N. Krisch, 'International Law in Times of Hegemony: Unequal Power and the Shaping of the International Legal Order' (2005) 16 *EJIL* 369.

[18] Ibid., 367.

[19] K. Williams et al., *Beyond Great Powers and Hegemons: Why Secondary States Support, Follow, or Challenge* (Stanford University Press, 2012); C. Schoenhardt-Bailey, *From the Corn Laws to Free Trade: Interests, Ideas, and Institutions in Historical Perspective* (MIT, 2006).

B   Anarchy

Anarchy, or the absence or rejection of authority, much like tyranny, is often the boogieman in debates regarding the global legal order. When anarchy arises in debates on international law it most often starts from two points: first, with Hadley Bull's highly influential *The Anarchical Society*[20] or, second, rather similarly to tyranny, as a catch-all phrase to mean chaos, lawlessness or disorder or 'total' anarchy. Rarely, if ever, is a third option, anarchy as a form of political philosophy, considered.[21] Much as hegemony, imperialism and tyranny are present from the classical period, so too anarchy but its modern form took shape during the Enlightenment. Kant placed anarchy alongside despotism, barbarism and republicanism as four forms of government, describing anarchy as law and freedom without force.[22] For Kant, anarchies fell short of the full sovereign state as law was merely recommendation not backed by force. A fuller theoretical version of anarchy emerged in the nineteenth century articulated by Pierre Joseph Proudhon.[23] Here, anarchy embraced stateless societies where activities and organisation are undertaken by voluntary associations.[24] After this period various strands of the political philosophy emerged that embrace both collectivism and individualism. In its latter form, it is often aligned with libertarianism while in its former it is regarded as closer to radical left politics.

Bull's work is critical in underpinning the absence of government or, in Waltz's terms, an absence of a higher common sovereign, as central to understanding international relations as an anarchy. This realist perspective is not negated by the presence of international law since, as with Kant, law is recommendation without the force to compel compliance.[25] Within this realist tradition, the influence of Hobbes and the anarchic state of nature is particularly influential, albeit Hobbes did not see international relations as being absent law but rather that law was consent-based.[26] For

---

[20] H. Bull, *The Anarchical Society: A Study of Order in World Politics* (Columbia University Press, 1977), 9.

[21] R. Amster et al. (eds.), *Contemporary Anarchist Studies: An Introductory Anthology of Anarchy in the Academy* (Routledge, 2009).

[22] I. Kant, *Anthropology from a Pragmatic Point of View* (Cambridge University Press, 2006).

[23] P. J. Proudhon, *What Is Property* (Cosimo, 2007).

[24] G. Chartier, *Anarchy and Legal Order: Law and Politics for a Stateless Society* (Cambridge University Press, 2013).

[25] K. Waltz, *Theory of International Politics* (McGraw-Hill, 1979); see also A. Wendt, 'Anarchy Is What States Make of It: The Social Construction of Power Politics' (1987) 46 *IO* 391.

[26] T. Hobbes, *Leviathan* (Penguin, 2014).

Bull, the presence of an international society with common rules and institutions is possible but is in a constant state of competition.[27] International law is partly socially constructed and is a product of habit.[28] Waltz argues that the presence of anarchy within international relations allows states the freedom to act as they so wish thus enabling autonomy to flourish, albeit this needs to be balanced against the claims of hegemony and imperialism[29] – in particular, whether a hegemon is necessary as a bulwark against anarchy.[30]

World government debates offer an intriguing description of the relationship between tyranny and anarchy. Tyranny and anarchy are set at opposite ends of a spectrum,[31] where tyranny is required to maintain world government as anything less would result in anarchy[32] – albeit whether this is better or worse than tyranny is rarely articulated, though clearly for Bull and Waltz some anarchy is always present within the international order. Pushing against this idea of anarchy is a constructivist approach which places international law at the heart of a global order based upon socially constructed rules.[33] International law and particularly the international rule of law becomes significant in fighting against politics 'understood as a matter of furthering subjective desires and leading to an international anarchy'.[34]

Alongside these debates lies a deeper understanding of anarchy as a form of governance albeit there is much contestation within this scholarship. While the popular depiction of anarchy is one of chaos and violence, the political theory rests in voluntary cooperation without the state.[35] Anarchy is critical of the relationship between capitalism, society, technology and

---

[27] Bull, *The Anarchical Society* (above n. 20), 49.

[28] Ibid., 133–7.

[29] Waltz, *Theory of International Politics* (above n. 25).

[30] S. Yee and J. Morin (eds.), *Multiculturalism and International Law: Essays in Honour of Edward McWhinney* (Brill, 2009), 117; F. D. Reism and O. Kessler, 'Constructivism and the Politics of International Law' in A. Orford et al. (eds.), *The Oxford Handbook of the Theory of International Law* (Oxford University Press, 2016), 347.

[31] M. Koskenniemi, 'The Politics of International Law' (1990) 1 *EJIL* 4, 28.

[32] S. Krasner, *Sovereignty: Organized Hypocrisy* (Princeton University Press, 1999), 42; J. Rousseau, *A Lasting Peace through the Federation of Europe and The State of War* (Constable and Co., 1917 [1756]); I. Kant, *Perpetual Peace* (1795); R. Müllerson, *Ordering Anarchy: International Law in International Society* (Brill, 2000), 134–47.

[33] Dos Reism and Kessler, 'Constructivism and the Politics of International Law' (above n. 30).

[34] Koskenniemi, 'The Politics of International Law' (above n. 31), 5.

[35] Chartier, *Anarchy and Legal Order* (above n. 24).

culture and includes strands of anarchfeminism and self-liberalisation.[36] Traditional legal orders, as systems that foster hierarchy and authority, alongside theories of crime, punishment and institutionalised structures such as marriage, are rejected. A focus on direct action, at odds with international law where the intermediaries (mostly in hierarchical structures) between the institutions creating law and its operationalisation, requires an anarchist rejection of the entire international legal order.[37] While anarchy is a much-used term within international legal debate, as a governance theory it has principled and considered proposals as to the cost of international law to individual lives and the need for resistance and is far from a call for chaos or Hadley Bull's state-dominated international society.

C   *Imperialism*

Imperialism or the control and authority, either direct or indirect, over another has historic ties with international law.[38] Colonialism and imperialism are often used as synonyms; however colonialism is a specific act of population transfer while the focus here is on imperialism as a broader process.[39] In their influential work Hardt and Negri, with a particular emphasis on globalisation, describe Empire as the political subject that regulates the sovereign power which governs the world.[40] For them, 'sovereignty has taken a new form, composed of a series of national and supranational organisms united under a single logic of rule'[41] and this is modern Empire. While the sovereignty of the nation state was the cornerstone of European Empire, as it was the extension of that sovereignty beyond state boundaries, for Hardt and Negri what constitutes contemporary Empire is its statelessness. This territorially linked definition of imperialism is quite a narrow construction – closer perhaps to colonialism – albeit

---

[36] H. J. Ehrlich, *Reinventing Anarchy, Again*, rev. edn (AK, 1996).

[37] U. Gordon, 'Dark Tidings: Anarchist Politics in the Age of Collapse' in R. Amster et al. (eds.), *Contemporary Anarchist Studies: An Introductory Anthology of Anarchy in the Academy* (Routledge, 2009), 253–356.

[38] A. Orford, 'The Past as Law or History? The Relevance of Imperialism for Modern International Law' (9 September 2011), IILJ Working Paper 2012/2 (History and Theory of International Law Series), University of Melbourne Legal Studies Research Paper No. 600, 14; A. Anghie, *Imperialism, Sovereignty and the Making of International Law* (Cambridge University Press, 2005); L. Benton and L. Ford, *Rage for Order: The British Empire and the Origins of International Law, 1800–1850* (Harvard University Press, 2016).

[39] J. A. Hobson, *Imperialism, A Study* (Cambridge University Press, 2011 [1902]), 4.

[40] M. Hardt and A. Negri, *Empire* (Harvard University Press, 2000), xi.

[41] Ibid., xii.

Hardt and Negri also recognise that juridical transformations provide an index of 'imperial constitution'.[42] In this chapter, imperialism incorporates both Hardt and Negri's Empire as well as imperialism as a broader contemporary construct, as such, recognising the theoretical break between sixteenth to twentieth century imperialism and that which has taken hold in the United Nations (UN) Charter era.[43] As Anghie points out the techniques and methods of imperialism are never consecutive; they coexist so the 'new form of Empire of Hardt and Negri ... coexists with very old forms of empire'.[44]

Legal, cultural, economic and social imperialism in combination all form part of the contemporary landscape that first was described in the nineteenth century.[45] Marxist literature made explicit the connections between capitalism and imperialism and that combination's link to the modern state form.[46] Hobson traces imperialism's association with hegemony and forms of what he calls internationalism going back to antiquity.[47] Hobson regards nineteenth-century imperialism as stimulating rivalry, creating false nationalism and as firmly anti-internationalist.[48] For Hobson, imperialism 'produces for popular consumption doctrines of national destiny and imperial missions of civilisation, contradictory in their true import, but subsidiary to one another as supports of popular Imperialism, it has evolved a calculating, greedy type of Machiavellianism, entitled "real-politik"'.[49] The critique of imperialism as it began to emerge in the early twentieth century was grounded in understanding it as a negative force for both those subject to imperialism but also the imperialists themselves.

Temporally, understandings of imperialism have moved both forward and backward from the nineteenth century to account for its influence across all governance eras. As such, contemporary methods of control and management operate in tandem with nineteenth-century ideas

---

[42] Negri and Hardt also perhaps overestimate the coming end of the state. Ibid., 9.

[43] Ibid., 4.

[44] Anghie, *Imperialism, Sovereignty and the Making of International Law* (above n. 38), 314.

[45] Hobson, *Imperialism, A Study* (above n. 39); E. W. Said, *Culture and Imperialism* (Vintage Publishers, 1994); J. A. Schumpeter, *Imperialism and Social Classes* (Ludwig von Mises Institute, 1955).

[46] V. I. Lenin, *Imperialism, the Highest Stage of Capitalism* (Penguin, 2019 [1916]); R. Luxemburg, *The Accumulation of Capital: A Contribution to an Economic Explanation of Imperialism* (Routledge, 2003 [1913]).

[47] Hobson, *Imperialism, A Study* (above n. 39), 6–9.

[48] Ibid.

[49] Ibid.,11.

of sovereignty and sixteenth-century notions of self-defence.[50] As von Bernstorff notes in this volume, Oppenheim's approach to economic positivism has been described as assisting British imperial policy and then permeating into international law.[51] Within this meshing of techniques, law continues the significant role it always had,[52] while in some instances this may be in maintaining and evolving administrative structures to maintain Empire,[53] exporting legal models across jurisdictions, inculcating racist stereotypes into law,[54] supporting political or economic structures that are instrumental to imperialism such as sovereignty or capitalism,[55] furthering gendered oppression, or in establishing a world order under which the rules of interaction establish a core and periphery that maintains control and authority within the minority's hands.[56] Law is an essential component of imperialism and, as Third World Approaches to International Law (TWAIL) scholarship demonstrates, this continues into the twenty-first century.[57]

III   Tyranny

A   Classical Greek Tyranny

As with the contribution of Allott in this volume, this discussion will begin in Greek antiquity. Whilst the classical Greek tradition often contains contradictory or, at the very least, unhelpfully vague definitions of the term, typically tyranny is associated with the coming to power of a force, either a single actor or group, other than by constitutional means.[58] Tyranny is an

---

[50] Anghie, *Imperialism, Sovereignty and the Making of International Law* (above n. 38), 314.

[51] Von Bernstorff, Chapter 2 in this volume.

[52] B. S. Chimni, *International Law and World Order: A Critique of Contemporary Approaches* (Sage Publications, 1993), 236–37; R. Knox, 'Valuing Race? Stretched Marxism and the Logic of Imperialism' (2016) 4 *London Review of International Law* 81.

[53] Benton and Ford, *Rage for Order* (above n. 38).

[54] M. W. Mutua, 'Savages, Victims, and Saviours: The Metaphor of Human Rights' (2001) 42 *HILJ* 201; Knox, 'Valuing Race?' (above n. 52).

[55] M. G.-S. Rovira, *The Project of Positivism in International Law* (Oxford University Press, 2013); S. Marks, *The Riddle of All Constitutions: International Law, Democracy, and the Critique of Ideology* (Oxford University Press, 2003), 10.

[56] C. Miéville, 'Multilateralism as Terror: International Law, Haiti and Imperialism' (2008) 19 *Finnish YBIL* 18; C. Miéville, *Between Equal Rights: A Marxist Theory of International Law* (Brill, 2005), 292–3.

[57] E. B. Pashukanis, 'International Law' in P. Beirne and R. Sharlet (eds.), *Pashukanis, Selected Writings on Marxism and Law* (Academic Press, 1980), 168–81.

[58] See variously, in K. A. Morgan (ed.), *Popular Tyranny: Sovereignty and its Discontents in Ancient Greece* (University of Texas Press, 2013); R. Boesche, 'Aristotle's Science of

exceptional form of governance rather than a permanent order and thus it is separate to monarchy, oligarchy or democracy, though for some it may be extrinsically linked to the weaknesses in each of these forms of governance. Critically, for the classical tradition it is not necessarily always a negative state of affairs.[59] Indeed, Lane argues that it may be viewed as benevolent.[60] This section will not present a unified idea of tyranny from the classical tradition but rather will attempt to bring together several strands of thought to suggest some common attributes.

Tyranny forms the starting point of Plato's Republic.[61] Here, tyranny is antithetical to the constitutional structures that possess the attributes of justice that resolve conflicting interests.[62] For Plato, tyranny forms the end point of collapsed governance; for example, tyranny springs from failed democracy but unlike democracy, the tyrant gains obedience by threat of violence. This link to democracy was contested by Aristotle who argued that Plato was unable to provide any historic examples for his claim.[63] For Plato, tyranny was connected to humanity's tyrannical form. Those who are tyrannical are ruled by lawless appetitive attitudes. Within tyranny there is little differentiation between the tyrant(s) and their subjects as both reflect and create the political order in which they live a life without reason.[64] Preferring rule through the educated class Plato acknowledges the ongoing tensions in choosing elitist governance.[65] However, it is from reason that perfect governance emerges and, as such, it must be limited to the few. Indeed, whilst rejecting tyranny Popper argues that Plato is adopting a form of totalitarianism.[66] Certainly Plato regarded hierarchy, even amongst citizens, as important in creating a common good and a

---

Tyranny' (1993) 14 *History of Political Thought* 1–25, 23; G. Anderson, 'Before Turannoi Were Tyrants: Rethinking a Chapter of Early Greek History' (2005) 24 *Classical Antiquity* 173.

[59] Anderson, 'Before Turannoi Were Tyrants' (above n. 58); V. Parker, 'The Semantics of a Political Concept from Archilochus to Aristotle' (1998) 126 *Hermes* 145.

[60] M. Lane, *Greek and Roman Political Ideas* (Penguin, 2014), 75. Also within Greek tragedy tyrant is most often simply a synonym for King: see Parker, 'The Semantics of a Political Concept from Archilochus to Aristotle' (above n. 59), 158.

[61] Plato, *The Republic* (trans. T. Griffith) (Oxford University Press, 2000).

[62] D. Roochnik, 'The Political Drama of Plato's Republic' in S. Salkever (ed.), *The Cambridge Companion to Ancient Greek Political Thought* (Cambridge University Press, 2009), 156–77.

[63] Ibid.: a critique of Plato that argues it is the basis of authoritarianism.

[64] Plato, *The Republic* (above n. 61), 254; R. Boesche, *Theories of Tyranny: From Plato to Arendt* (Penn State Press, 2010), 28–9.

[65] Roochnik, 'The Political Drama of Plato's Republic' (above n. 62).

[66] K. Popper, *The Open Society and its Enemies* (Princeton University Press, 1963), 533–7.

constitutional governance structure.[67] But even where good governance orders were established there is no guarantee of tyranny's absence. For instance, states which domestically would be considered democratic and constitutional can operate tyrannically in their imperial conquests. This was particularly significant in considering Athens's imperial governance of conquered territories.[68]

Boesche argues that Aristotle's view of tyranny, above other Greek iterations, is the most enduring in its effect.[69] For Aristotle, tyranny came in three forms, within barbarian countries in accordance with established law and practice, within Greece on an elective basis and, third, an entirely self-serving form that stands alongside oligarchy as an unjust or harmful system.[70] It is the third form which was the basis of his critique:

> For there is by nature both a justice and an advantage appropriate to the rule of a master, another to kingly rule, another to constitutional rule; but there is none naturally appropriate to tyranny, or to any other perverted form of government; for these come into being contrary to nature.[71]

Aristotle regarded the wish for power, pleasure and wealth which forms tyranny's driving force as potentially being held by groups or individuals. The impact of the 'Thirty Tyrants' in Athens, together with Aristotle's uneasiness regarding democracy's potential to descend into tyranny, extended it beyond the lone figure.[72] Aristotle acknowledged that tyranny may come about by choice as a group decide that their present governance is unsatisfactory but that ultimately tyranny will be for the tyrant's own ends.[73] As such, there are examples of elected tyrants or kings who became tyrannical by overreaching.[74] In its Aristotelian form tyrannies create 'economic incentives to depoliticise their subjects' and create a form of

---

[67] Boesche, 'Aristotle's Science of Tyranny' (above n. 58), 6.

[68] Lane, *Greek and Roman Political Ideas* (above n. 60), 112. See e.g. J. Barnes (ed.), *The Complete Works of Aristotle* (Princeton University Press, 1984).

[69] Boesche, 'Aristotle's Science of Tyranny' (above n. 58), 2.

[70] Aristotle, *Politics* (Penguin, 2000), 1285a39–1285b1; Boesche, 'Aristotle's Science of Tyranny' (above n. 58), 3.

[71] Aristotle, *Politics* (above n. 70), Part XVII.

[72] D. Teegarden, *Death to Tyrants!: Ancient Greek Democracy and the Struggle against Tyranny* (Princeton University Press, 2013), 15–56. Arendt argues that this fear of the masses or mob rule was also a consistent fear of the nineteenth century. H. Arendt, *The Origins of Totalitarianism* (Harcourt, 1951), 316.

[73] K. von Fritz, ïAristotleïs Contribution to the Practice and Theory of Historiographyï (University of California Publications in Philosophy, 1958), 137.

[74] Aristotle, *Politics* (above n. 70), 1310b18–20, 26–8.

governance that resembles the relationship between craftsman and tool.[75] It creates a system which establishes an unnatural political order which prohibits the development of humanity.[76] Tyrannies return governance to a pre-political state of dispersal which keeps individuals away from collective discussion or engagement that even a limited democracy allows.

Aristotle gives guidance to tyrants wishing to maintain power that Boesche categorises into five strands. First de-politicise the population; second, divide citizens to prevent them from organising politically against the tyranny; third, tyrants must know how to use and be effective with violence as well as maintaining a monopoly over it; fourth, they must be adept at deception including inventing terrors and bringing distant dangers near; and, finally, they must appear to rule constitutionally even if in reality their rule is arbitrary.[77] This advice provides an intriguing insight into the maintenance of tyranny albeit arguably it is of utility to anyone who wishes to maintain governance control no matter what their system.[78] Most important, however, as Boesche suggests, is that 'tyrants must make bows towards legality';[79] that while it remains an a-constitutional structure, it is important to retain the pretence of legality and critically constitutional legality. Donning the cloak of constitutional law is thus an essential characteristic for an Aristotelian tyranny.

Five core elements may be gleaned from this brief overview of Greek tyranny; the single or collective figure, tyranny's emergence outside of a constitutional structure, its relationship with imperialism, the benefit accrued to the tyrant(s) and, finally, the need to de-politicise governance. First, whilst the single tyrant is by far the most common form, this is by no means definitive. The firm link to democracy as mob rule or the Thirty Tyrants in Athens suggests that the form tyranny can take is myriad, thus enabling a much broader idea of a plurality of tyrants to coexist with single iterations and, as such, allows for the integration of more modern ideas of tyranny which will be discussed later, such as bureaucracies, technocracies or class.[80]

---

[75] Ibid., 1311a9ñ11; 1311a3ñ6; Boesche, 'Aristotle's Science of Tyranny' (above n. 58), 10; Aristotle, Nicomachean Ethics, 1161a30ñ1161b4.

[76] Aristotle, *Politics* (above n. 70), 1279a22ñ1279b10.

[77] Boesche, 'Aristotle's Science of Tyranny' (above n. 58), 18–20.

[78] T. Hale et al., *Gridlock: Why Global Cooperation Is Failing when We Need It Most* (Polity Press, 2013), 94.

[79] Boesche, 'Aristotle's Science of Tyranny' (above n. 58), 1–20. Boesche also discusses the tyrant's need to appear religious and to appear to rule like a king.

[80] K. A. Morgan, 'The Tyranny of the Audience in Plato and Isocrates' in K. A. Morgan (ed.), *Popular Tyranny: Sovereignty and its Discontents in Ancient Greece* (University of Texas

Second, gaining power outside of a constitutional structure is a common thread in classical discourse on tyranny; indeed tyrants are not regarded as constitutional bodies, albeit the lack of constitutionality appears to be a matter of gradation rather than a specific historical attribution to any particular tyrant. As such, whether a particular governance structure is a tyranny can appear to be in the eye of the beholder. Nonetheless, its a-constitutional structure establishes an idea of law and power being intertwined where tyranny creates an unjust system that merely has the attributes of a constitution rather than embodying constitutionalism.[81]

Third, we have tyranny's relationship with the exercise of imperial power. States can be considered tyrannical in their exercise of power beyond the state whilst maintaining a constitutional order at home. This is of particular consequence when considering whether democratic states acting beyond their state boundaries can claim to be less tyrannical in their actions because of their domestic structure.

Fourth, tyranny is generally to the advantage of a tyrant. As Aristotle argued:

> tyranny is just that arbitrary power of an individual which is responsible to no one, and governs all alike, whether equals or better, with a view to its own advantage, not to that of its subjects, and therefore against their will. No freeman willingly endures such a government.

Yet, as Lane also suggests, tyrants can be regarded as benevolent and, for Plato, were an inevitable reaction to the failures of governance that emerge from democracy. The advantage gained by being a tyrant may be material or political but is never regarded as purely altruistic on the part of the instigator(s) of tyrannical governance.

Fifth, tyranny seeks to de-politicise governance. In creating an order that denies humanity and natural democratic discussion it must operate in a space where deliberation and debate are denied.

What can be gleaned about the nature of tyrannies from this summation? Tyranny does not mean the absence of legality. Whilst it is a-constitutional it operates within a surround of law and indeed may lean towards couching decisions that ought to be political in their character as purely legal and technocratic in its attempts to de-politicise. Systems

---

Press, 2013), 182–3; K. A. Raaflaub, 'Stick and Glue: The Function of tyranny in fifth-century Athenian democracy' in K. A. Morgan (ed.), *Popular Tyranny: Sovereignty and its Discontents in Ancient Greece* (University of Texas Press, 2013), 182–3; B. M. Lavelle, *Fame, Money and Power: The Rise of Peisistratos and 'Democratic' Tyranny at Athens* (Michigan University Press, 2005).

[81] Aristotle, *Politics* (above n. 70), Book VII.

of governance which may be regarded as legitimate may be tyrannical or have traits in that direction; for Plato that included democracy; for others it is not democracy but it may be democracies acting beyond the state. The tyrannical system is to the benefit of the tyrant. What this advantage may be varies but there is a significant advantage to being a tyrant. When this advantage aligns with the interests of the population the benefits shared by the tyranny may be regarded as benevolent. Tyranny can emerge from other systems operating inefficiently and the intent can be benign or positive and have more generalised support, but tyranny remains the tool of the power-holders. Indeed, in looking towards pre-constitutional systems as tyrannical or alternatively as occasional moments where constitutional structures lapsed due to bad governance, thus including elected tyrants, there is a wider understanding of how tyranny operates. Whilst for Plato the focus was on the extra-legal character and Aristotle upon the pursuit of a particular interest, what is evident is that for both tyranny was a-constitutional.

B   Machiavelli

Whilst *The Prince* is Machiavelli's most famous work, *Discourses* offers a more nuanced account of his political philosophy, albeit neither book ought to be read in isolation.[82] As Strauss points out, tyrant (or other terms such as the common good) does not appear in *The Prince*, suggesting the word may have been too harsh to use in the context of the addressee.[83] Conversely, *Discourses* is replete with references to tyrant and tyranny. The fame of *The Prince* as well as Machiavelli's misgivings regarding the role of the Catholic Church and his 'template' for rule in *The Prince*, that read alone appears to be a validation of tyranny, has tainted both the invocation of his work and its actual content.[84] Contemporary accounts ranging from Skinner and McCormack to Strauss take a more deft approach which emphasises his preference for strong contestation, the role of the people

---

[82] N. Machiavelli, *The Prince* (Cambridge University Press, 1988 [1513]); N. Machiavelli, *Discourses on Livy* (Penguin, 2013 [1531]); L. Strauss, *Thoughts on Machiavelli* (The Free Press, 1958), 29, 133; his other major work *The Art of War* is not discussed here: N. Machiavelli, *The Art of War* (University of Chicago Press, 2003 [1521]).

[83] Strauss, *Thoughts on Machiavelli* (above n. 82), 26; W. R. Newell *Tyranny: A New Interpretation* (Cambridge University Press, 2013), 246.

[84] Machiavelli, *Discourses on Livy* (above n. 82); Newell, *Tyranny: A New Interpretation* (above n. 83), 246.

and his understanding of the power within governance, while still recognising some of the ambivalent elements of his work.[85]

Machiavelli is indebted to the classical period in his understanding of tyranny, many of the examples come from Antiquity and his discussions of Caesar, Tacitus and Athens, amongst references to Italian city states, form the core of his conclusions.[86] He argued that there were six intertwined forms of government. Monarchy that readily becomes Tyranny, Aristocracy that can become Oligarchy and Democracy which can tend towards Anarchy.[87] For him, all six were pernicious and the best form was a mixed government of monarchy, aristocracy and democracy as these three in tandem would prevent the descent towards their darker variants and prevent each sector of society from taking too much power into its own hands.[88]

Law was a clear instrument of governance for Machiavelli. For a state to succeed law must be strong from the outset and this may require a tyrannical figure to assemble those laws before passing the reigns on to a new form of government.[89] So Romulus was a tyrant, but one where the end was good. But to ensure this end the tyrant must safeguard that the authority they acquired is not passed to another. For Machiavelli one had to be a Scipio rather than a Caesar, for while both men held tyrannical power Scipio created the basis for Rome's Republic to continue strengthened and ultimately stepped aside while Caesar did the opposite. The pre-constitutional order may be tyrannical but the Commonwealth ought to follow a good law-giver to ensure longevity of non-tyrannical power. In such an instance a tyranny can be beneficial but only when it dissolves into (what would now be recognised as) constitutional government. While the creation of a legal order may be a positive side effect of time-limited tyranny – few other benefits followed. Tyrannies do not allow for progress within the state, which is why, for Machiavelli, tyranny is of most benefit to tyrants and not the people who, generally, hated them[90] – though Machiavelli also argues that where a tyrant has the support of the people or is a consensual

---

[85] J. P. McCormick, 'Machiavelli against Republicanism on the Cambridge School's "Guicciardinian Moments"' (2003) 31 *Political Theory* 615; Strauss, *Thoughts on Machiavelli* (above n. 82); Q. Skinner, *Machiavelli* (Oxford University Press, 1981).

[86] Newell, *Tyranny: A New Interpretation* (above n. 83).

[87] Machiavelli, *Discourses on Livy* (above n. 82), 10.

[88] Ibid., 12.

[89] Ibid., 117, 32–4.

[90] Ibid., 154.

creation it is the strongest argument in its favour, but again this is a time-limited variation.[91]

Tyranny may emerge at differing sites – for instance, the period prior to the formation of a new constitutional order or from the overthrow of a prince by a group who initially follow law but then give way to ambition and lust ultimately resembling the tyranny they rejected.[92] Further, those who benefited from the system may also attempt to restore a tyrannical order.[93] Personal ambition always establishes a fulcrum for tyranny that those who take power must guard against, as all are capable of evil inclinations.[94] For Machiavelli, crass ambition can be found in all groups in society though most notably amongst the nobles who will always turn a state to their entire benefit if left unchecked.[95] Similarly with the people or the monarch, the ambition of each requires they keep the other groups in check, and contestation and public debate is central to ensuring this happens.

Tyranny curtails the space available for political contestation and it is from here we have a nascent understanding of the process of constitution creation. Guardianship of liberty is an essential element of Machiavelli's Commonwealth due to both his distrust of humanity's natural inclinations towards tyranny but also his faith in the commons and the nobles to rail against a tyrannical agent working against their interests. No portion of society wishes to give way to the ambition of another and enshrining this form of check into the governance structure stands as a bulwark against tyranny. Machiavelli uses examples from Sparta, Venice and Rome to demonstrate what can happen if a constitutional structure does not ensure that interests within the state are unable to use the constitution as a means to both fulfil their own ambitions and to stifle the ambitions of others.[96] For Rome, it was contestation between the Senate and the People that ultimately lead to the Republic in its most perfect form; tyranny on its own was insufficient and ultimately tyranny lead to its downfall.[97] Indeed, once harm is done to such a governance order it can be impossible to restore. As Machiavelli describes after the deaths of Caligula and Nero, the Roman Senate was unable to take back power as an entirely new order was

---

[91] Strauss, *Thoughts on Machiavelli* (above n. 82), 271.

[92] Machiavelli, *Discourses on Livy* (above n. 82), 11.

[93] Ibid., 11.

[94] Ibid., 14.

[95] Ibid., 57; McCormick, 'Machiavelli against Republicanism on the Cambridge School's "Guicciardinian Moments"' (above n. 85), 634.

[96] Machiavelli, *Discourses on Livy* (above n. 82), 18–25.

[97] Ibid., 12, 18.

required.[98] In Republican Rome the constitutional nature of the office of Dictator was not a cause of tyranny.[99] Dictators could not eliminate other offices of state and their temporal limitations ensured that they did not give way to their baser qualities. Caesar cloaked himself in law and the office of Dictator in order to create a tyranny. Tyranny hid behind seeming lawfulness to the extent that the latter could not be resurrected once Octavian took over.[100] Law was present and operational; for Machiavelli tyranny is not the absence of law but when that law is corrupted or morphs into rule by law as it did under Caesar:

> That it is of evil example, especially in the Maker of a Law, not to observe the Law when made: and that daily to renew acts of injustice in a City is most hurtful to the Governor.[101]

Imperialism is also a key feature of both *The Prince* and *Discourses*, albeit in the former it is a balance between the expense of colonialism and the necessity of a reputation for meanness that is central to the argument.[102] In the latter there is a more nuanced take on both the need for Empire but also its pitfalls. Unlike Greek empires, according to Machiavelli, Rome succeeded in increasing its scale due to the nature of its Empire. For instance, part of the reason for Rome's success as an empire-builder was its extension of citizenship ensuring that the liberty of Rome spread out from the city but also vastly increasing the numbers available for its army, thus enabling further extensions of Empire.[103] But there is also a need to work within Roman law in imperialist expansion, again Caesar being the prime exemplar, as Machiavelli argues Roman emperors who stayed within the law earned 'far great praise'.[104] Yet Machiavelli also recognises that Rome laid great waste to the cities that surrounded it and, in doing so, the only reconciliation to those under its yolk was the offer of citizenship. For Machiavelli, this is the best form of expansionism.[105] Machiavelli was

---

[98] Ibid., 36.

[99] Albeit this differentiation has been challenged and whether dictatorship was in fact legalised tyranny is up for debate: A. Kalyvas, 'The Tyranny of Dictatorship: When the Greek Tyrant Met the Roman Dictator' (2007) 35 *Political Theory* 412, at 416–17, 426–8.

[100] Machiavelli, *Discourses on Livy* (above n. 82), 86.

[101] Ibid., 108.

[102] Machiavelli, *The Prince* (above n. 82), 9.

[103] Sparta, for instance, could not allow the individuals in the territory it conquered to become citizens. Machiavelli, *Discourses on Livy* (above n. 82), 151.

[104] Ibid., 36.

[105] Leagues being of the second order, albeit still workable: ibid., 162; see also R. Schütze, Chapter 1 in this volume, on discussions of Leagues in eighteenth-century international law.

not as clear that imperialism itself would have a negative impact on the imperialists (only when Empire was done badly); he is less concerned with imperial tyranny, though this is largely because of his preference for the Roman model and the extension of citizenship.[106]

Machiavelli also sets out a blueprint for the removal of the tyrant.[107] In such circumstances as to free a country from a usurper and a tyrant, the conspirers are entitled to act and to assassinate, although bloodshed is not inevitable. In this section of *The Discourses* Machiavelli sets out clear advice as to how to remove a tyrant, including how to run a conspiracy that will not reveal itself, and the need for clear planning after the removal of the tyrant.[108] Pointing to failures of Brutus and his co-conspirators he discusses how the removal of one tyrant can lead to another if the conspirators do not have a clear plan to establish liberty. Indeed, as within the Greek city states Machiavelli seems clear that the tyrant can be assassinated and that all tyrants must live with the knowledge that their removal is always a possibility.[109]

Machiavelli's view of tyranny is complicated by what can be somewhat contradictory messages. Much of *The Prince* is directed towards someone who, if they had read *Discourses*, would clearly recognise the attributes of a tyrant in their own operation. From *Discourses,* it is clear which form of government Machiavelli preferred, and it certainly was not tyranny. While everyone has the capacity for tyranny and will indeed choose that course of action if circumstances allow, the commons and nobles can also be the surest guard against tyranny. A tyrant may be necessary to create a state but only if they first ensure their power cannot be transferred to another. Imperialism can be beneficial but only under a single model. Tyrannicide is very much permitted and indeed encouraged. But here again only when there is a clear non-tyrannical strategy for the system to follow. Certainly, for Machiavelli tyranny was a-constitutional and while it may be critical in creating a constitutional order it cannot operate alongside one. Indeed, a functioning constitutional order will check tyrannies that emerge from any quarter, be that individual or group. A tyrant can be a law-giver. However, such lawfulness often masks a tyrannical intent to ultimately

---

[106] Doyle argues that Machiavelli was in favour of liberal imperialism; however, I would disagree with this interpretation in its modern form. M. W. Doyle, 'Liberalism and World Politics' (1986) 80 *American Political Science Review* 1151–69.

[107] Machiavelli, *Discourses on Livy* (above n. 82), 361.

[108] Strauss describes this section as a guide to tyrannicide: Strauss, *Thoughts on Machiavelli* (above n. 82), 26.

[109] Kalyvas, 'The Tyranny of Dictatorship' (above n. 99), 431.

usurp the governance order. Tyranny can be of benefit in creating a governance order but, in most cases, it causes a state to stand still or regress
and ultimately is of most benefit to the tyrant. Machiavelli stands at an
interesting crossroads for debate on tyranny. In both looking back towards
antiquity and in understanding his own contemporary governance order,
he would set a template for discussions of tyranny that would follow.

C   Arendt and Tyranny

Arendt's view of tyranny is very much tied to her consideration of totalitarianism and in particular the latter's emergence in the twentieth century
as a form of governance. Although not adhering to all of its precepts her
conception is also situated within the historical development of tyranny
since the classical period. According to Canovan, Arendt is attempting
to move away from imposed notions of governance dating from Plato
by accounting for human plurality in her work.[110] In doing so, Arendt
develops a particular view of tyranny which is both classical in its origins
but very much contemporary in its understanding of governance in the
modern era.

The role of law and its relationship with power and violence is particularly significant in Arendt's break from classical conceptions of tyranny.
Power, violence and law are three distinct elements and tyranny must be
understood in that frame. Arendt argues that the relationship between
law and power has been overshadowed by classical clichés suggesting that
eighteenth-century philosophy and more modern conceptions of government have erroneously relied upon classical categorisations of law, power
and interest and variations therein.[111] Arendt contends that there are two
sides to law; law as a limitation on power and contemporaneously power's
enforcement of law.[112] Arendt argues that what the Enlightenment incor-
rectly took from antiquity's creation of republics was the supremacy of the
rule of law. In doing so obedience to law simply replaced obedience to
men and the dichotomy between law and power, and, in particular, how
to bring about lawfulness became largely absent from consideration.[113]
As a result of this error Arendt argues tyranny mistakenly became a term

---

[110] M. Canovan, *Hannah Arendt: A Reinterpretation of Her Political Thought* (Cambridge
University Press, 1994), 207.
[111] H. Arendt, *On Violence* (Harcourt, 1969), 40; H. Arendt, 'The Great Tradition: I. Law and
Power' (2007) 74 *Social Science* 713–26.
[112] Arendt, 'The Great Tradition: I. Law and Power' (above n. 111).
[113] Arendt, *On Violence* (above n. 111), 40.

of art used to describe any lawless government or more particularly the difference between a lawful or constitutional government and a lawless or tyrannical government, or perhaps, to put it in constitutional terms, the absence or presence of the rule of law.[114] For Arendt this entirely misses how power and law interact. Arendt argues that tyranny raises the boundaries of law leaving behind a system which is not based on liberty, though, unlike totalitarianism, it still leaves room for action and, in doing so, it remains egalitarian in that it is the tyrant(s) against all others.[115]

Benhabib argues that Arendt regards constitutional government as a system where law acts as a hedge allowing people to orientate themselves whereas tyranny is more akin to a desert.[116] For Arendt, the work of Montesquieu is of particular import in breaking from the Platonic view of law and power. In recognising that power could be divided between the making of law, the executing of decisions and judging, Montesquieu – by recognising action and change – was able to depart from Plato's view of the inevitability of failure in all forms of governance and their ultimate dissent into tyranny.[117] Critically it was this introduction of what was to become a constitutional norm, the division of power, which was essential. For Montesquieu, danger lies where the only protection from tyranny is custom. Law, and what would become modern liberal constitutionalism, is required to prevent the emergence of tyranny. For Montesquieu, the separation of powers stood as a safeguard against tyranny as it prevented power from settling into one set of constituted power-holders and gave each point of governance the ability to curtail the action of the others if such activity was deemed *ultra vires*. Montesquieu brought about a break in democracy as potentially tyrannical with the introduction of a new form of constitution. A 'legally unrestricted majority rule, that is, a democracy without a constitution' suffocates dissent but new constitutionalism which renovates the classical form prevents this occurrence.[118]

Arendt divides power from violence and this is critical in her understanding of tyranny, in that it can (occasionally) exist without violence.[119] Power is all against one whereas violence is one against all; power doesn't

---

[114] Arendt, 'The Great Tradition: I. Law and Power (above n. 111), 714.
[115] Arendt, *The Origins of Totalitarianism* (above n. 72), 466; H. Arendt, *Between Past and Future* (Penguin Classics, 2006), 98.
[116] S. Benhabib, *The Reluctant Modernism of Hannah Arendt* (Rowman & Littlefield, 2003).
[117] Arendt, 'The Great Tradition: I. Law and Power' (above n. 111), 722; Montesquieu, *The Spirit of the Laws* (above n. 6), 72.
[118] Montesquieu, *The Spirit of the Laws* (above n. 6), 72.
[119] Arendt, *On Violence* (above n. 111), 37–42.

need to be justifiable as it is inherent within political action, but it needs to be legitimate whereas violence may be justifiable but not legitimate.[120] For Arendt, violence can destroy power but cannot substitute for it; the combination of force and powerlessness creates 'impotent forces' which leave very little behind.[121] She argues that this combination in classical theory is understood as tyranny. But, the fear of tyranny comes not from cruelty, which she argues can be countered by benevolent tyrants and enlightened despots. More exactly it is the impotence and futility which condemns both rulers and ruled that establishes our discontent with it as a form of governance.[122]

Powerlessness is key to understanding tyranny because it isolates the ruler from the ruled. The drive towards the establishment of a political community is absent in tyranny, no matter its benevolence, and the absence of the public realm removes power.[123] Yet, for Arendt, tyranny's short-term advantages – stability, security and productivity – in themselves pave the way towards its own end as these gains lead to participation and, from this, political action which in turn creates power beyond the tyrannical form bringing about its demise.

As was discussed in the previous sections, tyranny need not necessarily be a negative attribute of governance and indeed as Arendt suggests some have advocated it as a form of good governance.[124] For example, according to Arendt, Hobbes is proud to admit that the Leviathan amounted to a permanent government of tyranny, 'the name of Tyranny signifieth nothing more nor lesse than the name of Soveraignty'.[125] Arendt suggests that Hobbes was in actuality attempting to justify tyranny which she argues had not, up to that point, been honoured with a philosophical foundation.[126] By taking account of the rise of the bourgeois class, a property-owning elite where the acquisition of wealth can only be guaranteed by the seizure of power, Hobbes was advocating the creation of a form of tyranny.[127] Arendt regards Hobbes's commonwealth as leaving each individual powerless as

[120] Ibid., 50–2.
[121] Montesquieu, *The Spirit of the Laws* (above n. 6), 72202–3.
[122] H. Arendt, *The Human Condition* (University of Chicago Press, 1958), 202–3.
[123] Ibid., 221.
[124] Arendt, *The Origins of Totalitarianism* (above n. 72), 144–6.
[125] T. Hobbes, *Leviathan* (Cambridge University Press, 1996), 486.
[126] Arendt, *The Origins of Totalitarianism* (above n. 72), 144–6.
[127] Hobbes, *Leviathan* (above n. 125), 486; H. Arendt, *The Origins of Totalitarianism* (Harcourt, 1951), 144–6.

they are without the right to rise against tyranny leaving space only for the submission of power to the tyrannical body politic.[128]

Arendt's historic view of tyranny typically stands alongside three modern forms of domination: imperialism, bureaucracy and totalitarianism. Totalitarianism is a system of rule which is in nobody's interest, not even the rulers, and has no concern for individuals. Arendt clearly distinguishes between tyranny and totalitarianism; the latter insists on establishing each individual in a lonely state whilst the former leads to mere impotence. This makes totalitarianism far more dangerous and destructive. Unlike tyranny which is lawless, totalitarianism operates in accordance with what it presupposes to be the law of nature or history.[129] Tyrants never identify themselves with subordinates whereas the totalitarian leader must be all encompassing and be responsible for all, thus no criticism of any element of governance can be countenanced as it would be a censure of the leader and the system in its entirety.[130] For Arendt the fundamental difference between modern dictatorships and tyrannies is that terror is no longer aimed at opponents but, in ruling the masses, it has turned inward.[131] As such a rights discourse can remain in tyranny, particularly the right to resist the tyrannical power as it tends away from consistent arbitrariness. As such, one has to oppose it to be punished by it.[132] The tyrant takes away the right to possess rights whereas the totalitarian regime operates on the basis that none exist.[133] Arendt views totalitarianism as the absolute and most destructive form of governance that moves beyond all previous forms of negative regime.

Echoed in antiquity is Arendt's consideration of imperialism and its relationship with tyranny. For Arendt 'tyranny, because it needs no consent, may successfully rule over foreign peoples, it can stay in power only if it destroys first of all the national institutions of its own people'.[134] Using both the French and British imperial structures, with the former attempting to spread its values and cultures and the latter staying aloof from this enterprise, Arendt builds a picture of imperial tyranny in operation. Arendt argues that imperialism can only result in the destruction of

---

[128] Arendt, *The Origins of Totalitarianism* (above n. 72), 146; Arendt, *Between Past and Future* (above n. 115), 96.

[129] Canovan, *Hannah Arendt* (above n. 110), 88; Arendt, *The Origins of Totalitarianism* (above n. 72), 484.

[130] Arendt, *The Origins of Totalitarianism* (above n. 72), 374.

[131] Ibid., 6.

[132] Ibid., 433.

[133] Ibid., 297.

[134] Ibid., 128–9.

the nation state when the flag becomes a commercial asset and patriotism loses its value in its use for money-making purposes and centres this critique in a historical analysis of imperialism in the nineteenth century.[135] The British imperial structure is the exemplar, in that it attempted to keep national institutions separate with administrators consistently resisting any attempts to export justice or liberty from home.[136] In Roman imperialism, all became bound by a common law. In contrast, in modern imperialism this is absent. Consent is enforced and tyranny prevails no matter the domestic arrangement of the home nation state.[137] Thus, constitutional states acting outside their state boundaries may, much as in antiquity, be tyrannical.

Arendt suggests that rule by nobody – bureaucracy – may be one of the cruellest and most tyrannical forms of governance:[138]

> We ought to add the latest and perhaps most formidable form of such domination: bureaucracy or the rule of an intricate system of bureaus in which no men, neither one nor the best, neither the few nor the many, can be held responsible, and which could be properly called rule by Nobody. (If, in accord with traditional political thought, we identify tyranny as government that is not held to give account of itself, rule by Nobody is clearly the most tyrannical of all, since there is no one left who could even be asked to answer for what is being done.)

Bureaucracy establishes haphazard universal settlements and procedures from which there is no appeal. There is nobody behind the will out of which decisions emerge and, because of this, bureaucracy is more dangerous than mere arbitrary tyranny.[139] The creation of vast systems of faceless decisions from which no answers emerge creates a new form of tyranny that has become ever more present in the contemporary era.

For Arendt, tyranny is not of the kings and despots of history but has contemporary character. It lies not in totalitarian regimes but in other authoritarian forms, including bureaucracy and imperialism. Law is central to Arendtian tyranny as it is situated within lawlessness. Constitutional tyranny is not a possibility, not only due tyranny's existence only in the absence of law but also because constitutional norms such as division of

---

[135] Ibid., 125.
[136] Ibid., 131; see further, T. Frost and C. R. G. Murray, 'The Chagos Islands Cases: The Empire Strikes Back' (2015) 66 *Northern Ireland Legal Quarterly* 263–88.
[137] Arendt, *The Origins of Totalitarianism* (above n. 72), 125.
[138] Arendt, *The Human Condition* (above n.122), 40; H. Arendt, *The Promise of Politics* (Schocken, 2009), 78.
[139] Arendt, *The Promise of Politics* (above n. 138), 78.

power and the rule of law provide bulwarks against the descent of some forms of governance, such as democracy, into tyranny. It is the limitations to what tyranny can achieve that underlies the wish to have alternate forms of governance. Arendt points to the fear of tyranny coming from impotence and futility of action rather than a terror of cruelty. This limitation emerges from the absence of a public realm within tyranny and the push towards a plurality or political community that often signals the end of tyrannical governance. Constitutionalism is an agent against tyranny in that the division of power, its limits on majoritarian democracy, and the rule of law provide the lawful space in which plurality can occur, an anathema to tyrannical governance. As with antiquity, tyranny can be benevolent but this benevolence is caged by the need to keep the public realm from emerging, as such, it is inadequate. Arendt suggests that constitutional democracies can, particularly through imperialism but not just in that instance, be tyrannical in their dealings beyond the state. In combination, this understanding of tyranny means that it has a modern form and may be identifiable in contemporary governance.

IV   Understanding Tyranny?

Whilst this was not a comprehensive overview of Greek, Machiavellian or Arendtian tyranny, the purpose was to draw together some of the essential themes which underlie our understanding of tyranny and to suggest why there may be an underlying fear of being engaged in a system which has all or some of its traits. Each of the notions of tyranny clearly have contemporary resonances but perhaps more critically overlap in some of their articulations of its governance form. This chapter suggests that it is within this intersection between the two forms that we may find a common understanding of tyranny from which a taxonomy of tyranny may be adduced.

First, tyranny remains relevant. Some of its characteristics may evolve, as they did, for instance, during the Greek classical period, but there remains a common core to how it is understood. Second, tyranny is consistently a-constitutional. For Arendt, this includes a lawlessness that goes beyond the Greek construction, but, critically, such lawlessness does not suggest chaos or anarchy. Rather, it is the manner and form in how law emerges which is of import. For the Greeks law exists but as a form to de-politicise the public realm and with technocracy taking its place and while Machiavelli thought tyrants could be law-givers, they themselves had to depart office for the law to take effect. So too for Arendt, where the emergence of bureaucracy as a new form of tyranny demonstrates the de-politicisation and the creation of rule by Nobody, not in the complete absence of law but in a lawless realm where the public realm removes the legitimate creation of law and the politics to which it ought to adhere. Contestation of interests as central to the proper functioning of a constitutional order requires political engagement where de-politicisation is an anathema.

Third, constitutionalism plays a key role in understanding what tyranny is not. Good constitutional systems, for Arendt and Machiavelli, stand as bulwarks against tyranny. The rule of law, the division of power and the limits upon majoritarian politics are critical constitutional norms that prevent democracies in particular from descent into tyranny and ensure contestation. For the Greek tyrannical form this is not as straightforward, in that democracy was for Plato itself tyrannical or would ultimately descend towards it and so too for Aristotle when democracy moved beyond a limited class. But, critically, tyranny lacks the legitimacy that is associated with the other forms of constitutionalism identified in the Greek period. Thus, constitutionalism stands to defeat tyranny either by its creation out of a tyrannical system or its restoration after an interregnum.

Fourth, in both its emergence and its practice, tyranny may be benevolent. Nonetheless, there are limits to what its benevolence can achieve. For the Greeks, tyranny can emerge from bad or malfunctioning systems but its limitations are based on it being the tool of the power-holders. For Machiavelli, the tyrant can be a law-giver but that reputation depends on the tyrant passing power to a constitutional order. For both Machiavelli and Arendt, tyranny's limitations emerge from the absence of a public realm and contestation. Indeed, the more benevolent the tyranny the more likely it is to sow the seeds of its own ends as the push towards a public community and politics will become ever more pressing. The benevolence of a tyranny thus limits what can be achieved by that governance order.

Tyranny, whilst it may be benevolent, is generally to the benefit of the tyrant(s). As such, its fifth characteristic is that those holding power benefit most from the system. This does not necessarily mean avarice or cruelty but it does imply a governance order which inculcates a system of benefits to the holders of power within that system, ensuring that the monopoly over power will always accrue a profit.

Sixth, and finally, a domestically constitutional state may be tyrannical in actions beyond its borders. Imperialism is the key example for both the Greeks and Arendt, but the underlying thesis for both is important. Domestic constitutionalism is no bulwark against tyrannical action beyond the state and indeed both were able to point to clear examples where this was the case. Both considerations of tyranny regard such external tyranny as ultimately having a detrimental impact on those towards whom such action is pointed but also upon the tyrannical actors themselves.[140] For Machiavelli this is less clear, albeit it is only the Roman form of imperialism, which extends citizenship to conquered territories, that is beneficial – the only other form of 'good' expansionism being the creation of City-Leagues.

These six characteristics establish a taxonomy of tyranny under which a core understanding of its form may be uncovered. The resonances with some elements of contemporary governance is evident and in the next section this taxonomy will be utilised to grasp whether the current global legal order could be said to be in part or in sum tyrannical in nature and, if this is the case, whether this is the anxiety that pushes academic discourse towards constitutionalism beyond the state.

V Global Constitutionalism

The global constitutionalism debate is diffused in both its intent and form. The discussion that follows focuses on a normative understanding of constitutionalism. However, there are many more variants that are less concerned with such issues and instead focus on either institutionalism or a value-based understanding of a global constitutional order. By virtue of both its fast evolution and attention within scholarship, the EU constitutional debate is, by far, the furthest advanced. While there is increased discussion across the scholarship, there is a significant difference in the focus on normative discussions around checks and balances, division of power and democratic legitimacy that has evolved in EU law in comparison to the global variant. While the rule of law and constituent power are increasingly discussed in the global debate, concentration on the minutiae of constitutionalism remains relatively light.[141] The discussion of the rule of law that follows is intended to both engage with global constitutionalism and also wider debates on international law so as to understand if the absence or presence of the rule of law stands as perhaps an unacknowledged harbinger of tyranny's presence in the global realm.

---

[140] See R. Schütze, Chapter 1 in this volume, and his discussion of theoretical debates on combining internal state welfare and that of the broader state order.

[141] A. O'Donoghue, *Constitutionalism in Global Constitutionalisation* (2014, Cambridge University Press), 200–36; see Symposium (2016) 14 *International Journal of Constitutional Law* 608–711.

Generally considered to be a desirable element of any governance system the rule of law forms a core element of any order pertaining towards constitutionalism albeit its presence does not of itself establish the existence or a trajectory towards a constitutional order.[142] Focusing on instances where it is questionable whether it is rule of law or rule by law that subsists within international law this section asks whether there are resonances between attempts to identify the presence of the rule of law and the possibility of international law being regarded as possessing some elements of a tyrannical order. At times, what is tantamount to complacency regarding the presence of the rule of law within international law permeates debates on constitutionalism and beyond this to wider discussions on global governance. This tendency relies on an almost unquestioning belief in the rule of law's presence that arguably suggests that its absence may hint at something unpalatable about the legal order. Raz is correct in cautioning against using the rule of law to describe all the positive elements of a legal order, while Waldron's warning against regarding it as nothing more than the assertion that 'our side is great' is critical in considering international law.[143] At its core the rule of law requires law to be applied equally, created openly and administered fairly and it is from this basis that it is understood here.[144] The taxonomy of tyranny put forward, whilst not directly concerned with the rule of law as such, requires that aspects of these three elements of the rule of law be absent for tyranny to flourish.

The extension of governance alongside the creation, administration and adjudication of law beyond the state raises questions regarding why power is wielded at certain points, who the constituted power-holders are and from where they gain their legitimacy. From a more traditional perspective, some proffer that states make the law and thus, whilst it is imperfect, governance anxieties with its operation are not as seriously compromising as may be imagined.[145] Alternatively, states are the constituted power-holders, they are internally legitimate and thus they legitimately create law beyond the state.[146] Yet, there is a disjuncture between the constituent power-holders who choose the constituted power-holders within their state and their interests and the global interests in response to which

---

[142] O'Donoghue, *Constitutionalism in Global Constitutionalisation* (above n. 141), 14.

[143] J. Raz, *The Authority of Law* (Oxford University Press, 1979), 210; J. Waldron, 'Is the Rule of Law an Essentially Contested Concept' in J. Bellamy (ed.), *The Rule of Law and the Separation of Powers* (Ashgate, 2005), 119.

[144] O'Donoghue, *Constitutionalism in Global Constitutionalisation* (above n. 141), 31.

[145] J. Crawford, 'International Law and the Rule of Law' (2003) 3 *Adelaide Law Review* 24.

[146] Peters, 'Compensatory Constitutionalism' (above n. 5).

public international law and global public law respond.[147] Within a domestic constitutionalised system constituted power-holders act in the interests of constituent actors not, as in this instance, for global or other interests. Of course, this raises other questions regarding division of constituted power that are also necessary when considering tyranny.

Dyzenhaus argues for a distinction between rule of law and rule by law – the latter meaning compliance with whatever laws have been positively enacted no matter their content, whereas rule of law also requires adherence to the principles of legality. This legality is in line with Fuller's list of generality, publicity, non-retroactivity, clarity, non-contradiction, possibility of compliance, constancy and congruence, the majority of which must be complied with most of the time for a system to be in conformity with the rule of law.[148] Both also argue that rule by law is to some degree legitimate as it implies some degree of rule of law. However, what the tipping point from one to the other is remains obscure. Dyzenhaus goes on to argue that 'not only is the choice to abide by the rule of law a matter of political incentives, the same is true of the choice to use rule by law to achieve one's own ends ... [o]ne who is in a very powerful position will submit to ruling at various points away from the rule by law end of that continuum only when it is expedient to do so.'[149] As such, it is possible to have pockets of rule of law.[150] Nonetheless, having pockets or elements of legality may be on a continuum towards rule of law; they do not necessarily comport with a public law ethic that could be described as constitutional. Yet, can it be described as tyrannical, and is this what is pushing scholars towards proclaiming global governance as constitutional law?

Identification of the rule of law beyond the state comes in several forms. For instance, there is Henkin's oft-quoted statement that 'almost all nations observe almost all principles of international law and almost all of their obligations almost all the time', with some considering such

---

[147] J. L. Goldsmith and E. A. Posner, *The Limits of International Law* (Oxford University Press, 2005), 200; T. Macdonald and K. Macdonald, 'Non-Electoral Accountability in Global Politics: Strengthening Democratic Control within the Global Garment Industry' (2006) 17 *EJIL* 89.

[148] L. L. Fuller, *The Morality of Law* (Yale University Press, 1969), Chapter 2; and Raz, *The Authority of Law* (above n. 143), 223.

[149] D. Dyzenhaus, 'The Compulsion of Legality' in V. Ramraj (ed.), *Emergencies and the Limits of Legality* (Cambridge University Press, 2008), 37; see also D. Dyzenhaus, 'The Legitimacy of the Rule of Law' in D. Dyzenhaus et al. (eds.), *A Simple Common Lawyer: Essays in Honour of Michael Taggart* (Oxford University Press, 2009), 33–54.

[150] D. Dyzenhaus, *Hard Cases in Wicked Legal Systems: Pathologies of Legality* (Oxford University Press, 2010).

compliance as a satisfactory demonstration of a rule-of-law ethic.[151] There is also much reliance on the UN Charter as a core constitutional document in an international rule of law based on the UN as an organisation whose status emerges from its common place amongst members. For Fassbender this means that the 'United Nations is an organisation based on the concept of the rule of law. The organs of the UN are bound to comply with the rules of the UN Charter, which is the constitution of the United Nations.'[152] For Brownlie the 'moral purpose of the United Nations was the promotion of the rule of law'.[153] Although not arguing that the Charter established an international rule of law, he suggests that the concept is not unfamiliar to law beyond the state. A political willingness to employ the term certainly appears to exist, with UN Member States in 2005 affirming that 'an international order based on the rule of law and international law' was the ideal. But what is telling about this last statement is the notion that this was the ideal, perhaps acknowledging that it is not as firmly established as some commentators such as Fassbender might suggest.[154] The premise of an institution focused on the rule of law extends beyond the UN to other organisations such as the World Trade Organization (WTO). There the focus tends to be on its Dispute Settlement arm but it has a similar ethos that, without really defining its content, there is a rule of law beyond the state. We just have to identify it.[155]

Yet, contemporaneously, disquiet regarding increased governance beyond the state has become more consistent with questions of whether a rule of law or, perhaps in reality, rule by law endures. There are several examples of this angst. Some are based on the historical role law played in creating a global governance order that continues to favour the Global

---

[151] L. Henkin, *How Nations Behave: Law and Foreign Policy*, 2nd edn (Columbia University Press, 1979), 47.

[152] B. Fassbender, 'Targeted Sanctions and Due Process: The Responsibility of the UN Security Council to Ensure that Fair and Clear Procedures Are Made Available to Individuals and Entities Targeted with Sanctions under Chapter VII of the UN Charter', 20 March 2006, www.un.org/law/counsel/Fassbender_study.pdf, 19, 25, 28; B. Fassbender, 'The United Nations Charter as Constitution of The International Community' (1998) 36 *Columbia Journal of Transnational Law* 529; J. Wouters and M. Burnay, 'Introduction: The International Rule of Law: European and Asian Perspectives' (2013) 46 *Revue Belge de Droit International* 299–306.

[153] I. Brownlie, *The Rule of Law in International Affairs: International Law at the Fiftieth Anniversary of the United Nations* (Martinus Nijhoff, 1998), 1.

[154] Koskenniemi, 'Police in the Temple Order, Justice and the UN' (above n. 4).

[155] E. U. Petersmann, 'How to Promote the International Rule of Law-Contributions by the World Trade Organization Appellate Review System' (1998) *JIEL* 25; D. Cass, *The Constitutionalization of the World Trade Organization* (Oxford University Press, 2005).

North.[156] Others focus on the actual operation of the legal order. Bianchi questions whether the ad hoc nature of international law suggests an absence of the rule of law arguing that the exceptionalism in the period running up to the 2003 invasion of Iraq demonstrates a reliance on hard cases rather than rule of law in decision-making. This, he argues, undermines any constitutionalisation process.[157]

The multitude of international bodies, non-governmental organisations (NGOs) and corporations engaged in the administration of post-conflict territories poses questions as to what oversight and regulation they are subject to in their exercise of constituted power.[158] Critically such transitional governance raises issues around the open creation, equal implementation and fair administration of law with regard to the individuals living within their power.[159] Whilst bodies established beyond the state are often engaged with the implantation of human rights, criminal law, constitutionalism and economic transformation of the transitional states, this is only rarely reflected back on their own operation to hold them more fully accountable for their exercise of constituted power.[160] This raises questions regarding the rule of law but also checks and balances within the system.

Emerging first as a legislative body and second as a body with direct engagement with individual lives, the actions of the United Nations Security Council (UNSC) have caused much debate.[161] The UNSC's role as a legislative body has taken hold since the beginning of this century.[162] The creation of the International Tribunal for the Former Yugoslavia and

[156] Anghie, *Imperialism, Sovereignty and the Making of International Law* (above n. 38); Chimni, *International Law and World Order* (above n. 52).

[157] A. Bianchi, 'Ad-hocism and the Rule of Law' (2002) 13 *EJIL* 263, 270.

[158] M. Saul, *Popular Governance of Post-Conflict Reconstruction: The Role of International Law* (Cambridge University Press, 2014).

[159] E. de Brabandere, *Post-Conflict Administrations in International Law: International Territorial Administration, Transitional Authority and Foreign Occupation in Theory and Practice* (Martinus Nijhoff Publishers, 2009); S. Chesterman, *You, the People: The United Nations, Transitional Administration, and State-Building* (Oxford University Press, 2005); A. O'Donoghue, 'The Exercise of Governance Authority by International Organisations: The Role of Due Diligence Obligations after Conflict' in M. Saul and J. Sweeney (eds.), *International Law and Post-Conflict Reconstruction Policy* (Routledge, 2015), 45–66.

[160] R. Freedman, 'UN Immunity or Impunity?: A Human Rights Based Challenge' (2014) 25 *EJIL* 239.

[161] S. Talmon, 'The Security Council as World Legislature' (2005) 99 *AJIL* 175; I. Johnstone, 'Legislation and Adjudication in the UN Security Council: Bringing Down the Deliberative Deficit' (2008) 102 *AJIL* 275–308; Koskenniemi, 'Police in the Temple Order, Justice and the UN' (above n. 4).

[162] Alvarez, 'Hegemonic International Law Revisited' (above n. 9), 874; S. Talmon, 'The Security Council as World Legislature' (above n. 161).

the questioning of the UNSC's ability to create an adjudicative body was one of the first such actions and remains hotly debated.[163] The decision to pass Chapter VII resolutions requiring states to undertake legislative actions regarding – but not confined to – terrorism, coupled with the creation of Terror Lists (which include over 200 individuals) and a Committee designed to oversee this list, have added to these discussions. This has brought the UN body into a new governance position where the manner in which law is created and implemented is brought to the fore and is central in questioning whether the UNSC is acting *intra vires*.[164] Fassbender's Report on the UNSC and due process found that it did comply with all its obligations under the Charter, including several references to the rule of law, but this conclusion has been much contested.[165] Whilst this report led to the creation of an ombudsperson to review the terror listing process, this was a very limited step in a situation where the listing process itself and the system of appeal remains opaque.[166] In particular, the ombudsperson's remit still leaves many questions best exemplified by the cases taken by those fortunate to live within the jurisdiction of the ECJ and thus possessing an avenue to question their inclusion on the list.[167]

These examples may be added to by many others – for instance, the role of principally non-public actors in judicial activities within international economic law where hearings are most often heard in private and where the appeal processes are limited.[168] Or, the role of economic institutions such as the World Bank Group, the International Monetary Fund (IMF) or a supranational body such as the EU in setting both micro- and

---

[163] *Prosecutor v. Dusko Tadic* (Appeal Judgment), IT-94–1-A, International Criminal Tribunal for the former Yugoslavia (ICTY), 15 July 1999; D. Akande, 'The Legal Nature of Security Council Referrals to the ICC and its Impact on Al Bashir's Immunities' (2009) 7 *JICJ* 333.

[164] Security Council Resolutions 1373 (2001) and 1624 (2005), Security Council Committee pursuant to Resolutions 1267 (1999) and 1989 (2011) concerning Al-Qaida and associated individuals and entities, www.un.org/sc/committees/1267/aq_sanctions_list.shtml.

[165] Fassbender, 'Targeted Sanctions and Due Process (above n. 152); E. Cannizzaro, 'A Machiavellian Moment? The UN Security Council and the Rule of Law' (2006) 3 *International Organizations Law Review* 189–224.

[166] www.un.org/sc/suborg/en/ombudsperson; G. L. Willis, 'Security Council Targeted Sanctions, Due Process and the 1267 Ombudsperson' (2010) 42 *Georgetown JIL* 673.

[167] P. *Kadi and Al Barakaat International Foundation* v. *Council and Commission* [2008] ECR I-6351. See e.g. Cannizzaro, 'A Machiavellian Moment?' (above n. 165); O. Schachter, 'Self-Defence and the Rule of Law' (1989) 83 *AJIL* 259.

[168] M. Darrow, *Between Light and Shadow: The World Bank, the International Monetary Fund and International Human Rights Law* (Hart, 2003). There is a move within the WTO to open some of its hearings to the public which are advertised on its website www.wto.org/english/tratop_e/dispu_e/dispu_e.htm.

macro-economic policies within states, and the potential lack of owner-ship of global constitutionalism by constituent actors who may be subject to a preordained hegemonic constitutionalism.[169] Each of these suggest that international law has moved well beyond its sovereign equality base, if that ever existed, to a scenario where individual lives are now directly affected by decisions and actors which operate beyond the state. In such a scenario, the presence of the rule of law becomes a significant factor and allows us to question whether law is made openly, administered fairly and applied equally. If the conclusion is in the negative is it more honest to describe the system as rule by law and to question what the constitu-tionalisation process says about an order which, on this brief summation, appears to be entirely absent an ensconced rule of law.

These instances are not intended to create an apocalyptic or overly neg-ative image of international law. Rather, they are to be set against the very positive outlook of an operational rule of law that is presented in the con-stitutionalisation debate. It also demonstrates the types of anxieties that exist as constituted governance extends beyond the state. 'Finding' the rule of law at the international level is not about complying with Hart or Hobbes and coming to the conclusion that by their measure it is not a legal order and, following this, that constitutional questions as such are unnec-essary. Rather, it considers whether the public law ethic and the adoption of the rule of law *in situ* is a response to an entirely different issue, not the absence of law but the global governance order's creation of law, its adjudication and administration, and whether this could be considered presently to be a form of tyrannical governance. This is not to be confused with foundational discussions of how we perceive law within the global order when the traditional tropes of command and force have such lit-tle purchase. In particular, a traditional form of executive, legislature and judiciary cannot be relied upon to necessarily fill the roles that a domestic system requires and indeed where qualms regarding the form that global democracy may take have led some to argue that it will, as Plato feared, descend into tyranny.[170]

The underlying rationales for choosing what traditionally are domes-tic governance tools could have emerged from a number of anxieties,

---

[169] G. W. Anderson, 'Beyond "Constitutionalism Beyond the State"' (2012) 39 *Journal of Law and Society* 359, 378.

[170] M. Koenig-Archibugi, 'Is Global Democracy Possible?' (2011) 17 *European Journal of International Relations* 519, 520; D. Otto, 'Subalternity and International Law: The Problems of Global Community and the Incommensurability of Difference' (1996) 5 *Social & Legal Studies* 337, 357.

including: the divesting of power from a narrow set of global actors; a role in underpinning both individual and collective rights; a provision to check both the legitimacy and legalism of power; and the possibility of recognising diverse points of governance within the global order and, critically, to locate a global rule of law. These brief examples demonstrate that these anxieties are real. The question is what has global constitutionalism done in response to them. This is not a discussion of the existence of law beyond the state but rather whether there is a concern that there is a rule-by-law system rather than a rule-of-law system and whether this anxiety has its roots in a tyrannical view and to consider whether, in a legal order that has few, if any, democratic underpinnings or a division of power infused with checks or balances, the requirement of a strong rule of law becomes greater. In a differentiated system with a weak judicial arm it would be inadvisable to simply rely upon those with the law-making authority or constituted power to both establish and maintain the rule of law.

Raz argues that the rule of law ought not to be used to merely describe all the positive attributes of a particular legal system, yet this appears to be the form in which the rule of law has been accepted by some international scholars.[171] In such instances legalisation, institutionalisation and rule by law are confused with the rule of law and questions regarding international law's evolution. Koskenniemi contends that 'the rule of law hopes to fix the universal in a particular, positive space (a law, a moral or procedural principal or institution).[172] Too often its employment within global constitutionalism instead hides insufficiencies in global governance where perhaps more positively it could be used to critique the system. Critically, is it possible to call the anxieties and the push towards identifying a rule of law a wish to leave behind what could be described as a tyrannical order?

An assurance of democratic legitimacy within the global legal structure would militate towards simply accepting Fuller's procedural rule of law as satisfactory; however, the global order operates with very weak constraints thus requiring a more substantive approach.[173] Even if Fuller's formation were accepted, the basic substantive structure would have to set the parameters of both legal and political action to prevent the development of a 'wicked system'.[174] This problem may be remedied by a substantive rule of law capable of acting as a safety valve albeit presently this appears absent

---

[171] See, for a further discussion, Kumm, 'The Legitimacy of International Law' (above n. 5).

[172] M. Koskenniemi, *The Gentle Civilizer of Nations: The Rise and Fall of International Law 1870–1960* (Cambridge University Press, 2001), 507.

[173] Fuller, *The Morality of Law* (above n. 148), Chapter 2.

[174] Dyzenhaus, *Hard Cases in Wicked Legal Systems* (above n. 150).

from law beyond the state. While Fuller's arguments against a substantive rule of law are not without import, within the global order the lack of judicial positioning, strong democratic systems or other forms of restraint suggests rule of law in its substantive form would be necessary. If the argument is that the rule of law, either substantive or procedural, is absent or at the very least is weak within the global legal order, does this automatically imply that the governance order is tyrannical? This chapter has certainly not argued for an absence of law – there is plenty of law – but potentially this could be better described as rule by law.

A   Tyranny, International Rule of Law

Coming back to tyranny and its six characteristics: (i) its continued relevance; (ii) its a-constitutional content and lawlessness; (iii) constitutionalism as a bulwark against it; (iv) its potential benevolence; (v) the benefit accrued to tyrant(s); and finally (vi) that domestic constitutionalism does not necessarily prevent states from acting tyrannically beyond the state. From the foregoing discussion, it is certainly not obvious that international law contributes to a purely tyrannical governance order yet some of the issues raised in the previous discussion certainly suggest some of tyranny's attributes may be present.

Leaving its first element, its continued relevance, to the end, tyranny's a-constitutional character and Arendt's argument for lawlessness proffer some interesting insights. If we follow Fuller and Dyzenhaus, then rule by law requires rule of law and as such there is lawfulness. Thus, if international law remains, on the whole, a rule-by-law system, it does not quite meet the threshold of tyrannical power that Arendt would recognise. Yet, Greek tyranny remains relevant, particularly the notion that tyranny de-politicises and tends towards the technocratic. Certainly, the law may be instrumentalised and Bianchi's warning against ad hocism may suggest that replacing political with legal arguments can result in the political context being replaced. This is also linked to Arendt's view of bureaucracy, or the rule of Nobody, as the modern era's worst form of tyranny. The UNSC's Terror List or the creation of micro- and macro-economic policies beyond the state could be interpreted as falling into this category. This bureaucratic or technocratic turn towards expertise is not specific to law beyond the state but perhaps adds to the unease felt with regard to these actions and indeed the rise of global administrative law suggests that, at the very least, administration and, as such, bureaucracy, is a live issue.

Constitutionalism's role as a bulwark against tyranny is very close to this last argument and could be considered to be the biggest trigger for the turn to constitutionalism. If there is an acceptance that constitutionalism and tyranny cannot coexist then a push towards constitutionalism ought to resolve the issues identified in the last section. Indeed, it suggests that the real benefit of a constitutional ethic beyond the state is that it gives tools to scholars to offer critique when the continuum between rule by law and rule of law tends towards the former. Of course, beyond the rule of law constitutionalism also requires division of power combined with checks and balances, democracy and limits upon majoritarian politics, but the potential to both push for reforms – and be critical of areas that they do not reach what would be considered legitimate minimum standards of governance within states – provides the global constitutional ethic with a platform to push against any tyrannical tendencies within international law.

The potential for benevolence is also critical in understanding law beyond the state; examples such as the UN Sanctions Committee or the administration of states in transition demonstrate the positive tasks towards which international law contributes. It forms part and parcel of the governance system that creates the processes by which these are set up, administered and are held to account. Yet, the very lack of fulfilment of very basic levels of accountability and oversight taints this benevolence with tyrannical forms and, as previously discussed, limits what it can achieve. Both Arendt and the classical tradition agreed that tyranny included the seeds of its own end as benevolence created the groundwork and drive towards a public realm, while for Machiavelli contestation of interests drives others to bring tyranny to an end. This may also be part of the trigger towards the constitutional ethic, in that the existing benevolence is in itself fuelling a wish for the system to more fully engage and go further perhaps towards constitutionalism but also other governance possibilities.

In many ways, within the global governance order, the fifth characteristic is directly related to the sixth, that domestic constitutional structures do not necessarily mean that states acting beyond the state will not behave as tyrants. The rise of imperialism was concomitant with the rise of modern international law and both remain deeply intertwined.[175] Albeit authors such as Tully argue that constitutional language can accommodate anti-imperial undertakings through its flexibility, this has not prevented

---

[175] Anghie, *Imperialism, Sovereignty and the Making of International Law* (above n. 38); Chimni, *International Law and World Order* (above n. 52).

states from taking on the role of imperial actors.[176] This imperialism was largely led by states that had full domestic constitutional orders. In the contemporary era, TWAIL clearly demonstrates ongoing acts of imperialism suggesting that the spread of constitutionalism at the domestic level has not impeded this tendency.[177] Other authors also question whether it is possible to consider democracy at the domestic level as offering compensation for its absence beyond the state.[178]

To return to the first characteristic, the continued relevance of tyranny, whilst it is arguable whether the global governance order is fully or partially tyrannical and this chapter certainly cannot claim to sufficiently cover the constitutional ethic beyond the state to make such a claim, probing this possibility is critical. The relevance of tyranny is that it both questions the motivations for the push towards constitutionalisation and other public law forms but also adds an additional purpose to these debates in suggesting that, even if they are incorrect in their claims, they can usefully point to insufficiencies in global governance beyond the state. Perhaps this last element is the most important, that constitutionalism offers a basis to shine a spotlight on international law's tyrannical tendencies. It is thus essential that scholars in this field take the opportunity to offer critique rather than an ever-purposeful utopian view of the future of law beyond the state.

VI   Conclusion

This chapter is not intended to question the utility of the move towards a constitutional ethic within international, regional and supranational law, nor is it envisioned as an assault on the existence of law beyond the state. Rather, it is intended to add to the debate on constitutionalisation

---

[176] J. Tully, *Strange Multiplicity: Constitutionalism in an Age of Diversity* (Cambridge University Press, 1995), 31.

[177] N. White, *Democracy Goes to War: British Military Deployments in International Law* (Oxford University Press, 2009); P. Clark and Z. D. Kaufman, *After Genocide: Transitional Justice, Post-Conflict Reconstruction and Reconciliation in Rwanda and Beyond* (Columbia University Press, 2009); A. Anghie, 'Decolonising the idea of "Good Governance"' in B. Gruffydd Jones (ed.), *Decolonizing International Relations* (Rowman & Littlefield, 2006), 109.

[178] A. Duxbury, *The Participation of States in International Organisations* (Cambridge University Press, 2011), 299; and R. Bellamy, 'The Democratic Legitimacy of International Human Rights Conventions: Political Constitutionalism and the Hirst Case' in A. Føllesdal et al. (eds.), *The Legitimacy of International Human Rights Regimes: Legal, Political and Philosophical Perspectives* (Cambridge University Press, 2014), 243.

at the supranational and global levels by considering whether, in making the claims towards an already realised or in-train constitutional process, ought we ask what the impetus for identifying these processes is, why has it resulted in a turn to constitutionalism and what it means for law's place within global governance. Further if we find that a fear of tyrannical power is a partial explanation for the turn to constitutionalism (and this chapter is certainly suggesting this is the case), we can usefully engage the tools provided by it, and a public law ethic more broadly, to expose where gaps in global governance exist and advise where this tends towards the tyrannical. What is evident from this overview of tyranny is that ultimately it is always a-constitutional and it is this characteristic which this chapter suggests is the core rationale for the turn to constitutionalism. Tyranny and constitutionalism are not concomitant; thus, if there is an existent constitution, international law and governance cannot be tyrannical.

Thus, rather than relying on positive examples of where the rule of law is *in situ* to ignore where rule by law prevails, this new constitutional ethic could be utilised as a critique of existing fissures within law beyond the state. Instead of relying on an ever-positive account of the process of constitutionalisation to make a case for its existence by adding a tyranny-based understanding to the debate, an account of the failure to fully engage with the entire panoply of rule of law or other public law elements such a democratic legitimacy, checks and balances or a rights-based discourse would be required. Further it would make it necessary to consider what form constitutionalism must take if it is to leave behind all elements of tyranny.

The discussion of Antiquity, Machiavelli and Arendt – besides establishing the taxonomy – also suggests the constant threat of tyranny. This tyranny is not a straw man set up in opposition to anarchy to create false choices in governance but rather a fully articulated governance order which no system, constitutional or otherwise, can completely guard against. Whether this presence stems from, as Machiavelli suggests, humanity's avarice or the subtler manipulations that Arendt proposes, complacency about the nature of any governance order must be avoided. There is nothing inherent within the global order that makes it immune to tyranny. As such, when we consider constitutionalism as a potential fit for the global order, we ought to consider what those who have considered that choice before were concerned about preventing.

Global public law will need to take up the challenge of moving from tyrannical to constituted power. The incidences within global public law where tyranny's rudimentary elements may be found are far too frequent.

Yet the political and legal question is whether we wish to undertake fundamental reform based within constitutionalism or are we content with tyranny beyond the state and satisfied that the constitutional narrative may be used to cover the fissures that exist in the system rather than highlighting them. The existing ambiguities should not be used to enable an otherwise questionable constitutionalisation, or other public law process, to pass muster simply because it assuages our concerns that international law contributes to tyranny in law beyond the state.

4

New Order for Yet Another New World

Philosophy in a Time of Global Existential Crisis

PHILIP ALLOTT

I   Introduction

History-writing has been so obsessed with the intermittence of periods of pre-war and war and post-war, nationally and internationally, that we may be tempted to think that war is the default state of human coexistence. Since the end of the American Civil War in 1865 there have been so many new world orders and new world disorders that we may be inclined to conclude that the effort to govern the human world at the global level is now intrinsically hopeless. The world disorder that we are now experiencing, in the early twenty-first century, seems to present a radically new kind of challenge. It seems to be an existential crisis of society and government at all levels, which may be an existential crisis in the very ideas of society and government. As such, it is a devastating challenge for philosophy, as the means which the human mind has used to construct the order of society and government. It is a particular challenge for law, as the essential foundation of society and government.

The present author's *Eunomia: New Order for a New World* was first published in 1990. It proposes a new general philosophy of international law, as the universal law of a true international society comprising all subordinate human societies and all human beings. It was designed to change the world. It has not changed the world. The same author's *Eutopia: New Philosophy and New Law for a Troubled World* was published in 2016. It marks the five-hundredth anniversary of the publication of Thomas More's *Utopia* in 1516. It shares More's underlying authorial purpose of reviving the ancient tradition of philosophy to reveal the possibility of a better human future contained within the human world as it is. Idealist philosophy is made from ideas and ideals. Ideas can change the world. Ideals can make a better world. Philosophy is a form of human power with a world-transforming potentiality. The challenge to universal philosophy has never been greater than it is now. We must make an effort to restore the crucial world-making role of philosophy, before it is too late.

II The Mind in Search of Itself

That phrase echoes one of the dark sayings attributed to Heraclitus (*c.*550–*c.*480 BCE), the pre-Socratic Greek philosopher whose sayings haunted Greek and Roman philosophy. *I went in search of myself.*[1] That saying was a spark at the origin of a new mental universe, the universe of *philosophy*, seen not as the love of wisdom, but as the love of the human mind's self-searching. Human societies, always and everywhere, have had their own forms of self-knowing, expressed in social phenomena that we refer to generically as *mythology* and *religion*. Their wisdom may make a claim to universality, with potential power over all human societies and all human beings. But it is the function of *philosophy* to be not-mythology and not-religion. Its universality derives from the fact that all human beings have a human mind. Philosophy is a potential power of the human mind over all human societies and all human beings. And, in its derived forms, as natural science and engineering, it makes good on that claim in an amazing way – with a power to transform humanity's participation in the *natural world*, the primary habitat of the human species.

To understand the philosophical significance of the sayings of Heraclitus, it is necessary to understand the significance of his near-contemporary, the mathematician and mystic Pythagoras (*c.*570–*c.*480 BCE). The Greeks noticed that *mathematics* is the perfect model for transcendental thinking, that is to say, thinking about thinking. Mathematics does not picture or describe anything in the 'real' world. But everything in the physical world can be represented in mathematics. And, still more surprisingly, mathematics can be used to have an effect in the real world, especially by way of science and engineering. The 'square on the hypotenuse' exists only in the human mind, but, like all mathematical theorems, it forms part of a mathematical universe, a parallel universe located between the human mind and the natural world. Newton's equations are merely abstract/mathematical/

---

[1] C. H. Kahn, *The Art and Thought of Heraclitus: An Edition of the Fragments with Translation and Commentary* (Cambridge University Press, 1979), fragment XXVIII, 41. It is taken from H. Diels, *Die Fragmente der Vorsokratiker*, ed. W. Kranz, 6th edn (1951), and is customarily referred to as 'Diels-Kranz fragment 101'.

transcendental 'laws of motion', but they are applied by science and engineering at every moment of every day.[2]

The pre-Socratic philosophers saw that this is true not only of mathematics. It is true also of *language*. It is possible to use language abstractly, universally and transcendentally, to speak about everything without picturing or describing any particular thing in the 'real' world. And yet everything in the 'real' world can be represented within this 'universal' form. And, still more surprisingly, things said in the universal form – *tree, mind, body, God, truth, love, nation, society, law, humanity* – can also have creative and transformational effects in the real world. The discovery of universal abstract language changed fundamentally the human condition, giving to the human mind a new unlimited purposive power, exercised in thought, and through the communication of thought – a power over the mind-made human world, over humanity's participation in the natural world, over every aspect of human life, individual and collective.

Philosophy uses universal abstract language to explore the human mind itself, and the many mind-worlds that the mind has created, including human society. Its efforts are cumulative, with each philosopher responding dialectically to the ideas of other philosophers. The natural sciences produce ever more sophisticated accounts of humanity's physical participation in the natural world, including through the study of the human brain and nervous system. Mythology and religion continue to dispense their special form of wisdom, offering a particular understanding of the human condition, influencing the living of everyday life. Philosophy helps to form an ever-evolving self-consciousness within individual and collective human consciousness. Echoing the German philosopher Hegel, we may say that philosophy as a form of knowledge is the collected consciousness of past ages and the self-consciousness of the age in which it is produced.[3]

---

[2] 'I ... use the words Attraction, Impulse or Propensity of any sort towards a centre, promiscuously, and indifferently, one for another; considering those forces not Physically but Mathematically ... ': I. Newton, *The Mathematical Principles of Natural Philosophy* (1687), 2 vols., trans. A. Motte (1729), I, Definition VIII, 8–9.

[3] 'Thus that which each generation has produced in science and in intellectual activity, is an heirloom to which all past generations have added their savings, a temple in which all races of men thankfully and cheerfully deposit that which rendered aid to them through life, and which they had won from the depths of Nature and of Mind ... This is the function of our own and every age: to grasp the knowledge that is already existing, to make it our own, and in so doing to develop it still further and to raise it to a higher level ... The history which we have before us is the history of Thought finding itself, and it is the case with Thought that it only finds itself in producing itself ... These productions are the philosophical systems; and

The power of philosophy is capable of making any kind of world, from the very good to the very bad.[4] In principle, it is even capable of promoting the self-evolving and self-perfecting of the human species.[5] In the twenty-first century, we have inherited a philosophy of the whole human world that sustains a disastrous worldwide system of political, social, economic and cultural power. Philosophy teaches us that we are capable of making a better philosophy of a better human world.

Parmenides (c.515–c.440 BCE) began with the ultimate question. What is it for anything to 'be'? What is it for a human being to 'be'? We evoke

---

the series of discoveries on which Thought sets out in order to discover itself, forms a work which has lasted twenty-five centuries.' 'Every philosophy is the philosophy of its own day, a link in the whole chain of spiritual development, and thus it can only find satisfaction for the interests belonging to its own particular time.' G. W. F. Hegel, 'Introduction' in *Lectures on the History of Philosophy* (1805–30; published 1840), trans. E. S. Haldane (University of Nebraska Press, 1995 [1892]), I, 3, 5, 45.

'Whatever happens, every individual is a child of his time; so philosophy is its own time apprehended in thought'. G. W. F. Hegel, 'Preface' in *The Philosophy of Right* (1820), trans. T. M. Knox (Clarendon Press, 1952), 9. Hegel's dictum is vividly confirmed by dominant philosophies of the twentieth century. See below Part II.B.

'In this sense, therefore, history is to be regarded as ... the reflected consciousness of the human race; and it takes the place of a self-consciousness directly common to the whole [human] race; so that only by virtue of history does this [the human race] actually become a whole, a humanity.' A. Schopenhauer, *The World as Will and Representation* (1819/1844), 2 vols., trans. E. F. J. Payne (1958/1966), II, Chapter XXXVIII, 445. 'The motto of history in general should run: *Eadem, sed aliter* [the same, but different]', at 444.

4 Solon (c.640–c. 558 BCE), Athenian statesman and reformer, in his polemical hymn known as *Eunomia*, wrote on the stylistic cusp between the mythologising of abstraction and the concretising of abstraction. Eunomia is presented as the sister of Dike and Eirene, the three goddesses of order. Solon uses the abstract adjective *artia* (harmonious and orderly) to describe the essential virtue of Eunomia. Hesiod (middle of the eighth century BCE), in his *Work and Days*, had written of the three goddesses as embodying the order of the universe present in the natural world to whom the peasant prays for prosperity. After Solon, Order, Justice and Peace soon became the powerful concretised abstractions that they remain to this day. We may also note that Solon was struggling to bring what we would call constitutionalism to a society riven by chaos, vice and corruption – not the first or the last public-spirited person seeking to do the same thing.

5 [God speaking] 'We have given to you, Adam, no fixed seat, no form of your very own, no gift peculiarly yours, [in order that] you may feel as your own, have as your own, possess as your own the seat, the form, the gifts which you yourself shall desire. A limited nature in other creatures is confined within the laws written down by me. In conformity with your free judgment, in whose hands I have placed you, you are confined by no bounds; and you will fix limits of nature for yourself. I have placed you at the centre of the world, that from there you may more conveniently look around and see whatsoever is in the world ... You ... are the *molder and the maker of yourself*; you may sculpt yourself into whatever shape you prefer. You can grow downward into the lower natures which are brutes. Or you can grow upward from your soul's reason towards the higher natures that are divine.' G. P. della Mirandola, *On the Dignity of Man* (1486), trans. R. J. W. Miller (Hackett Publishing, 1965), 4–5.

a universal idea of 'being' in every 'is' sentence that we utter. We live every moment of our lives in an Istopia of our own making.[6] We create an Istopian human world that is our third habitat, alongside the natural world that sustains our living and the private world of our own minds.

Socrates and Plato, brothers-in-mind, saw that it thus matters a very great deal what universal ideas we have, what we do with them in making our mind-worlds and how we live in our mind-worlds in our everyday lives, as individuals and as societies. Hence Plato's most influential dialogue known to us as *Republic*, and the writings of Aristotle, his not entirely faithful pupil, especially in the books known to us as *Ethics* and *Politics*. They explore and propose universal ideas designed to enable us to live the best possible lives as individuals and as societies. That remains the ambition of those of us who think and write in their shadow.

The idea of the *ideal* – central to the philosophy of Socrates-Plato – is an exceptionally powerful universal idea. It acts in our mind as a destination that we cannot reach, a magnetic attraction that makes us do better things on the journey: *the just, the true, the good, the beautiful, the perfect* ...

> A pattern, then, said I [Socrates], was what we wanted when we were inquiring into the nature of ideal justice and asking what would be the character of the perfectly just man, supposing him to exist ... We wished to fix our eyes upon them as types and models ... Our purpose was not to demonstrate the possibility of the realization of these ideals ... Then were not we, as we say, trying to create in words the pattern of a good state?[7]

A dialectical interaction with the minds of the ancient Greek philosophers powerfully influenced philosophy in the Roman Republic and Empire, especially by way of Hellenistic Stoicism. And it influenced the theology of the Christian Church. The 'metaphysics' of Aristotle, deconstructing the idea of *being*, seemed helpful in imagining the 'being' of God. And 'natural law', reflecting the natural order of the universe, seemed capable of bringing order to an empire of great ethnic and cultural diversity. It also seemed capable of giving practical effect to the 'Will of God' within the great diversity of human societies in general.

---

[6] P. Allott, *The Health of Nations: Society and Law beyond the State* (2002), Chapter 1, on the land of Istopia. See P. Allott, *Eutopia: New Philosophy and New Law for a Troubled World* (Edward Elgar, 2016) for information on the lands known as Knowtopia and Eutopia.

[7] Plato, Republic, tr. P. Shorey, Book V, 472c–d, in *The Collected Dialogues of Plato*, ed. E. Hamilton and H. Cairns, Bollingen Series (Princeton University Press, 1961), 711. The idea of the *ideal* for Socrates-Plato is distinct from, but related to, the *Ideas* or *Forms* that are the universal content of an ultimate supernatural reality. See infra n. 19.

In the fourteenth century, William of Ockham (*c*.1285–*c*.1349) noticed that, in the meantime, something strange had happened. A twelfth-century Renaissance, and the universities that embodied it, had revived the study of the Greek and Roman philosophers. Some forms of philosophy, and one form of the theology of the Roman Christian Church, had managed to construct a virtual physics of a metaphysical mind-world, containing universal ideas as quasi-things, with a God whose attributes were a hyper-universalised version of universal human attributes. Some supernatural ideas had even been 'reified', made into ideas about virtual 'things' (*res*, in Latin).

Ockham's *nominalism* says: no; our universal ideas are just words – *nomina* ('nouns' or 'names' in Latin). To give a universalising name to something ('unicorn'; 'God') does not mean that there must be some really existing thing corresponding to that name. However, Ockam's own ideas developed over the course of his lifetime in an interesting, and often overlooked, way, reminiscent of the development in Ludwig Wittgenstein's thinking in the twentieth century. A closer reading of Ockham suggests that he eventually recognised that universal ideas *do* have some sort of existence, in that they are the way in which we are able to grasp reality and re-create it within our minds, leading us to act in conformity with them in the worlds that we inhabit. 'To be is to be known' (*eorum esse est eorum cognosci*, in Latin).[8] In that tentative development in Ockham's thinking is contained in embryo the whole drama of subsequent philosophy to the present day.

In the early seventeenth century, a new dialectical opposition was the catalyst in an intense new development of the philosophy of the mind. A new contrast emerged relating to our understanding of the nature of the mind, and its relation to our living of the human condition. René Descartes

---

[8] Relying especially on M. H. Carré, *Realists and Nominalists* (Oxford University Press, 1946). See further in P. Allott, *Invisible Power 2: A Metaphysical Adventure Story* (Xlibris, 2008), Appendix 1. 'To be is to be perceived' (*esse est percipi*) was a central thesis in the epistemology of George Berkeley (1685–1753), an idea misunderstood as proposing a form of absolute idealism (all 'reality' seen as nothing more than ideas in the human mind), whereas Berkeley was a leader in the tradition of English idealist empiricism. On Berkeley, see *Invisible Power 2*, Appendix 4.

'This misapprehension of philosophic method has veiled the very considerable success of philosophy in providing generic notions which add lucidity to our apprehension of the facts of experience. The depositions of Plato, Aristotle, Thomas Aquinas, Descartes, Spinoza, Leibniz, Locke, Berkeley, Hume, Kant, Hegel, merely mean that ideas that were introduced into the philosophic tradition must be construed with limitations, adaptations, and inversions, either unknown to them or even repudiated by them.' A. N. Whitehead, *Process and Reality: an Essay in Cosmology* (Cambridge University Press, 1929), 14.

(1595–1650) suggested that our mind is all that we know directly, so that the mind is the source of our knowledge of ourselves and of the world. It is within the mind itself that we must find the source of epistemological 'truth' and moral 'right'.

> I thence concluded that I was a substance whose whole essence or nature consists only in thinking … so that 'I', that is to say, the mind by which I am what I am, is wholly distinct from the body, and is even more easily known that the latter … After this I inquired in general into what is essential to the truth and certainty of a proposition … And as I observed that in the words *I think hence I am*, there is nothing at all which gives me assurance of the truth beyond this … I concluded that I might take, as a general rule, the principle, that all things which we very clearly and distinctly conceive are true, only observing, however, that there is some difficulty in rightly determining the objects which we distinctly conceive.[9]

Francis Bacon (1561–1626) took a different view. The activity of the mind is an interaction between the mind and the physical world in which our body lives. This interaction has its most privileged form in the natural sciences. But it is present in all our thinking, especially in the socialising of ideas, where the mind-in-the-individual and the mind-in-society tell each other what to think, and enlighten, control, mislead and abuse each other through ideas. *Nam et ipsa scientia potestas est* ('for knowledge is also power').[10]

The subsequent history of the interaction of these opposing ideas is often presented superficially as a struggle between (Continental European) *idealism* and (British) *empiricism*. It is true that a powerful series of British philosophers worked on the question of the relationship between the mind and the 'real' world. Does the mind make the world? Does the world make the mind? See Thomas Hobbes (1588–1679), John Locke (1632–1704), George Berkeley (1685–1753) and David Hume (1711–76). It is also true that influential Continental philosophers wrote in the spirit of Descartes, including Baruch Spinoza (1632–77) and Gottfried Leibniz (1646–1715) among many others, giving primacy to the intrinsic activity of the mind, leading to later forms of *idealism*, culminating in the work of G. W. F. Hegel (1770–1831) and his successors. But so-called British empiricism is better

---

[9] R. Descartes, *A Discourse of Method* (1637), trans. J. Veitch (Everyman's Library, 1912), Part IV, 26.

[10] F. Bacon, *De Hæresibus* (1597), in *The Works of Francis Bacon*, 15 vols., ed. J. Spedding and R. L. Ellis (Longmans, 1858–9), VII, 241. See also, T. Hobbes, *Leviathan* (1651), Chapter 9.

seen as a special form of idealism which Kant was able to integrate with so-called Continental idealism in a single system of ideas.[11]

John Locke is often presented as if his most significant idea was of the mind as *tabula rasa* ('blank sheet', in Latin). We are not born with any substantive ideas (such as 'truth' or 'the good' or 'justice') already present in our minds. Experience writes on the blank sheet. And it is this which has led people to class him and his followers as empiricists. But Locke was faced with the obvious fact that the mind is highly active in organising our relationship with the non-mind world.[12] If the mind can 'build worlds' from within itself, how precisely does it achieve this feat?[13]

Aristotle had considered the ways in which the special structures and systems of *language* allow us to communicate efficiently with each other. His 'logic', as it came to be called, seemed to be a set of rules for speaking efficiently and, perhaps even, for finding 'the truth'. And it is, indeed, a peculiar fact that we are able to judge the truth or untruth of *linked propositions*, not empirically, but as if they were part of a self-contained rule-governed process. *Lazy people do not work. All unemployed people do not work. Therefore, all unemployed people are lazy.* A possible, if improbable, empirical truth, but not a necessary conclusion arising from the linking of the premises. A more probable opinion is that some unemployed people are lazy. Politics, in particular, and social life in general, are full of such conclusions masquerading as logical inferences.

Aristotle went further, finding certain apparently normative structures of language: *identity* (p = p); *contradiction* (p or not-p); *difference* (p and not-p). Acceptance of these basic principles by the speaker and the hearer makes possible efficient communication. However, ignoring or manipulating them also gives great richness to communicated language, when we accept that the same thing is also different from itself, where we use contradictory truths dialectically, where we say that non-identical things are identical; for example, when we speak in metaphors: 'truth is beauty and

---

[11] It is interesting that we may see in classical Chinese philosophy a corresponding tension between the relative realism of Confucius and his various followers and the relative idealism of Mo Tzu and his various followers. See F. Yu-lan, *A History of Chinese Philosophy* (1931), 2 vols., trans. D. Bodde (Princeton University Press, 1952), I, *passim*; E. R. Hughes (ed. and trans.), *Chinese Philosophy in Classical Times* (Everyman's Library, 1942), *passim*.

[12] See Allott, *Invisible Power 2* (above n. 8), Appendices 3 and 4, on the problems that Locke creates for himself.

[13] Hegel puts words in the mouth of Descartes: 'I will build worlds for you [from within the mind]' ('*Ich will euch Welten bauen*'). Hegel, *Lectures on The History of Philosophy* (above n. 3), vol. III, sec. II, 247. The mind does, indeed, build many mind-worlds – supernatural, natural, social, personal. See Allott, *Eutopia* (above n. 6), Part One.

beauty truth'; 'dreaming spires'; 'we are what we eat'. Works of the creative imagination celebrate the possibility of manipulating the Aristotelian normativity of language.

Locke rejects the idea that we find truth by making deductions from transcendental universal ideas present in the mind. The mind converts sense-based 'impressions' into 'ideas' by using built-in *archetypes* – abstracted patterns which we use to generalise the infinite particularity of our sensual experience. And the mind creates higher-order *relations of ideas* (some of which are remarkably close to Aristotle's 'categories') – for example: *existence, substance, cause and effect, time, space*. Through *intuition* or *reason*, we use these mechanisms more or less spontaneously, but normatively, to produce richer ideas. In this sense, we are rational beings. So much for Locke the empiricist![14]

David Hume, the supposed nominalist sceptic, was determined, in his youthful *Treatise of Human Nature* (1738), to show that the mind contains no mysterious processes. It produces the ideas that human life requires it to produce. It produces more complex and general ideas, including very general and very abstract ideas, by using ideas to produce other ideas through what he calls *association of ideas*. Like Locke, Hume says that we use such more general ideas as templates to judge and order less general ideas. But, in producing and using such ideas, we are not governed merely by some mysterious thing called 'reason'. All other aspects of the mind are involved in our thinking – emotion, self-interest, custom and habit. Hence the all-too-familiar confusion and uncertainty of our 'rational' thinking and our 'moral' judgements.

For Immanuel Kant (1724–1804), it was the British philosophers, especially Hume, who provided the spur that led him into a new way of philosophy.[15] For Kant, the sceptical Humean challenge is the challenge to find the set of ideas which are *necessary* if we are to explain how it is *possible* for the mind to have *knowledge* of the physical world, other than as a random generalising of the 'perceptions' that come to us through the senses. The word 'possible' is the secret of the Kantian 'critical' method.

---

[14] '*Knowledge* then seems to me to be nothing but *the perception of the connexion and agreement, or disagreement and repugnancy of any of our ideas.*' J. Locke, *An Essay Concerning Human Understanding* (1690), ed. R. Woolhouse (Penguin Classics, 1997), IV.1, §2, 467.

[15] 'I freely admit: it was David Hume's remark [on the nature of causation] that first, many years ago, interrupted my dogmatic slumber and gave a completely different direction to my enquiries in the field of speculative philosophy.' I. Kant, 'Preface' in *Prolegomena to Any Future Metaphysics* (1783), trans. P. G. Lucas (Manchester University Press, 1953), 9. Kant dedicated the second edition of the *Critique of Pure Reason* (1781/87) to Francis Bacon.

It requires the mind to transcend itself still further – to find the rationality that makes rationality possible, not least the amazing rationality of the natural sciences. Such ultimate ideas about the mind's functioning must be *a priori* ideas, that is to say, not merely based on the investigation of human behaviour and experience, or on our knowledge of the functioning of the *human brain* as the physical basis of the mind's activity. Such ideas about the functioning of the mind are normative because they express the necessary conditions of rational thought. They make rational thinking and communication possible.

Kant proposes a model of a mind that 'makes' a real world in a *cooperative creative process* of interaction between the mind and a putative real world that is otherwise only known to us through the phenomena that it presents to the human senses. This seems to separate him fundamentally from Descartes and the idea of the autonomy of the mind in its coexistence with the world-outside-the mind, the world inhabited by the human body – an autonomy in the finding of 'true' knowledge and 'right' action. Kant suggests that we have capacities of the mind which allow us to bring order to our experience of the natural world – 'understanding' (*Verstehung*), which unifies our sensory perceptions of the world, and 'reason' (*Vernunft*) which makes a 'judgement' that brings order to the products of our understanding. The problem of the relationship between these two Kantian ideas has led to much of subsequent philosophy in the Western tradition.

Kant echoes Aristotle's normative analysis of the functioning of language. Kant even gives a central role to the Aristotelian word 'categories'. Aristotle suggested that the 'categories' are basic structures of our presentation of the world, making possible effective thinking and communicating. Kant's categories go much further. They are pre-formed tools with which we give 'form' to the formlessness of the natural world. They are *a priori* transcendental concepts allowing us to create, in our minds, a coherent order of the natural world.[16] We use these templates, as it were, to order our understanding of the putative external world. *Knowledge* is the end-product of the judgments of reason that we make about our understandings of the putative external world.

---

[16] 'I apply the term transcendental to all knowledge which is not so much occupied with objects as with the mode of our cognition of these objects, so far as this mode of cognition is possible *a priori*.' I. Kant, *Critique of Pure Reason* (1781–7), ed. and trans. N. Kemp Smith (MacMillan & Co., 1929), 59.

It follows, on this view, that our knowledge of the world is not merely *inductive* – the generalising of observed phenomena. It is *deductive-inductive*, in the sense that we use pre-existing patterns in the mind to make sense of the world. The *natural sciences* progress through an interaction between *a priori* ideas, including the foundational *paradigms* discussed by Thomas Kuhn,[17] and other existing scientific *hypotheses*, and the systematic observation of the physical world. Scientific knowledge is a collaborative process between the human mind and the natural world. Francis Bacon already knew this – contrary to the popular belief that he saw natural science as essentially inductive.[18] There remained the challenge of applying the new philosophy of mind to another world, our second habitat, the human world.

The long philosophical tradition that culminated in the work of Immanuel Kant had led the human mind to find within itself a universalising system of ideas explaining its own functioning, the programme of its programmes. This system of the functioning of the human mind reflects the functioning of the human brain. Our understanding of the *human* world must, therefore, be formed in an analogous way. But the human world is not a putative external physical world. It exists only in the human mind. It is a world made from ideas. To understand it, the mind must apply itself to itself, inductively and deductively.

It follows that the philosophy of the human world has the interesting characteristic, distinguishing it from the philosophy of the natural world, that we change the human world merely by thinking about it. It is a special case of what, in quantum mechanics, is called the Observer Effect. The observing of the observer alters that which is being observed. The human mind's study of itself has never been regarded as 'objective' or 'innocent', in the way that the natural sciences are seen as being, in principle, objective and innocent. (Their real-world effects are, however, frequently un-innocent in the extreme.) Human self-study has not succeeded in detaching itself

---

[17] For revisionist views of scientific method, see T. Kuhn, *The Structure of Scientific Revolutions*, 3rd edn (University of Chicago Press, 1970). P. Feyerabend, *Against Method* (Humanities Press, 1975).

[18] 'From the two kinds of axioms which have been spoken of arises a just division of philosophy and the sciences ... Thus, let the investigation of forms, which are (in the eye of reason at least, and in their essential) eternal and immutable constitute *Metaphysics*; and let the investigation of the efficient cause, and of matter ... constitute *Physics* ... Now my directions for the interpretation of nature embrace two generic divisions: the one how to educe and form axioms from experience; the other how to deduce and derive new experiments from axioms.' F. Bacon, *The New Organon* (1620), ed. F. H. Anderson (1960), Book II, Aphorisms IX, X, 129–30.

from what it is studying. The worlds that we make make us what we are. We master the universe with the power of our minds, but we are weak in the business of mastering our own minds.

Such is the power and the problem of the philosophy of human existence, and the cause of the intensely ambiguous role that ideas have played in the dramas of human history. At any particular time, our understanding of what it is to be human can be a very bad understanding, judged by its real-world effects.

Kant pays tribute to Plato but says that it may be that we understand Plato better than he understood himself.[19] Every succeeding philosophical generation has added to our understanding of Plato and Aristotle. We might say the same of Kant himself. Philosophy over the last two hundred years has responded voluminously to Kant, affirmatively or negatively.

Our present understanding of Kant must also take into account the fact that the natural sciences have progressed dramatically in the intervening period. Developments in evolutionary biology and the physiology of the human brain and nervous system have had an important effect on our understanding of the functioning of the human mind. Living species survive by responding to the challenge of their environment. The human mind enables human beings to survive in creative interaction with the natural world. The mind's *ordering* of its world can be seen as an expression of fundamental *ordering* capacities built into the physical structure and functioning of the brain, capacities which are now being intensely investigated in various disciplines in the natural sciences.[20]

---

[19] 'Plato made use of the expression "idea" in such a way as quite evidently to have meant by it something which not only can never be borrowed from the senses but far surpasses even the concepts of understanding (with which Aristotle occupied himself), inasmuch as in experience nothing is ever to be met with that is coincident with it. For Plato ideas are archetypes of the things themselves, and not ... merely keys to possible experiences ... I shall not engage here in any literary inquiry into the meaning which this illustrious philosopher attached to the expression. I need only remark that it is by no means unusual, upon comparing the thoughts which an author has expressed in regard to his subject, to find that we understand him better than he has understood himself.' Kant, *Critique of Pure Reason* (above n. 16), Second Division, Book I, sec. I, 310.

[20] 'Every mechanism in the brain – whether it does something categorizable as "cold cognition" (such as reasoning, inducing a rule of grammar, or judging a probability) or as "hot cognition" (such as computing the intensity of parental fear, the imperative to strike an adversary, or an escalation in infatuation) – depends on an underlying computational organization to give its operation its patterned structure, as well as a set of neural circuits to implement it physically.' L. Cosmides and J. Tooby, 'Evolutionary Psychology and the Emotions' in M. Lewis and J. M. Haviland-Jones (eds.), *Handbook of Emotions*, 3rd edn (Guilford Press, 2008), 116.

We also have to take account of the fact that the intensive study of *language* over the last two centuries suggests that language is an expression of an evolutionary ordering capacity embedded in the brain which determines the way in which the brain, and hence the mind, communicates with itself, and with other brains and minds. And *computer science* suggests something that is more than an analogy with the functioning of the mind. *Programmes* are transcendental (universal and prior) in relation to the information that they represent and process and the outcomes that they cause. Philosophy must now integrate into its self-searching of the human mind the ever-accelerating flood of the products of the natural sciences concerning the human being as a thinking being.

Taking account of these new understandings of the human phenomenon, we must ask our own version of the quintessential Kantian question.[21] *How is the human world possible?*

Kant said that his idea that the things that we perceive in the *natural world* are made by our mind to conform to concepts, instead of vice versa, might be compared with the idea of Copernicus that it is the observer on Earth who moves, not the stars.[22] Newton's universal system of ideas was a revolutionary response to the challenge left by Copernicus and Kepler. The present author's *Eunomia* and *Eutopia*[23] are designed to respond to the challenge of explaining the work of the human mind in organising the collective existence in the human species. They propose a universal *system of ideas* about the making of society and law, a system that sees all human societies as constituent societies of international society, and not vice versa.[24]

---

[21] I. Kant, *Critique of Pure Reason* (above n. 16), Intro., VI: 'The General Problem of Pure Reason', 55–8. How is pure mathematics possible? How is pure science of nature possible? How is metaphysics, as science, possible? And, later: How is morality possible? (*Critique of Practical Reason*, 1788). How are value and purpose possible? (*Critique of Judgment*, 1797).

[22] Kant, *Critique of Pure Reason* (above n. 16), Preface to the 2nd edn (1783), 22.

[23] For the original Eutopian 'project', see P. Allott, *The Health of Nations* (above n. 6), §§5.63 et seq.

[24] 'A system [of ideas] is an imaginary machine invented to connect together in the fancy [the imagination] those different movements and effects which are already in reality performed.' A. Smith, 'The History of Astronomy' in *Essays on Philosophical Subjects* (1795), ed. W. P. D. Wightman and J. C. Bryce (Oxford University Press, 1980), 66.

'But we need by no means assume that this contract [the social contract]... actually exists as a *fact*, for it cannot possibly be so ... It is in fact merely an *idea* of reason, which nonetheless has undoubted practical reality; for it can oblige every legislator to frame his laws in such a way that they could have been produced by the united will of a whole nation.' I. Kant, 'On the Common Saying: "This may be true in theory, but it does not apply in practice"'

G. W. F. Hegel (1770–1831) and A. Schopenhauer (1788–1860) were the last of the major philosophers in the great Platonic-Aristotelian tradition. Both of them admired Kant. Both of them used his ideas in particular ways which may seem to be philosophy at its most obscure, but which, remarkably, have had profound real-world consequences from which we are still suffering.

For Hegel, humanity's self-consciousness is an aspect of a World Mind (*Weltgeist*) living under the rule of a World Spirit (also *Weltgeist*). The World Mind manifests itself as Reason. He treats *spirit, mind* and *reason* as if they were Aristotelian/Kantian *categories* but gives them a practical role in the forming of our idea of the actual and changing human world. But, in Kant, the word 'reason' (*Vernunft*) had served merely as a logically necessary concept, to explain how 'understanding' (*Verstand*) unifies and universalises our perceptions of the external world – an idea flowing from Locke's use of the English word 'understanding'– a seventeenth-century usage, now out-dated, but lexically still available. (Kant had commissioned a German translation of Locke's *Essay on Human Understanding*.)

It may be that all these aberrations are caused by the fact that the German and French languages hopelessly confuse what in English are a rather well organised set of foundational philosophical terms – 'mind', 'spirit', 'soul', 'consciousness', 'idea', 'reason', 'rationality' and 'self'. Even a sharp philosophical eye may find it difficult to bring into clear focus the meaning of *Vernuft, Vorstellung, Verstand, Verstehen, Gedanke, Idee, Bewusstsein, Begriff* and *das Ich*. But such words, and analogous words in French, have been the *casus* of many philosophical battles and much intellectual confusion.[25]

(1793), trans. H. B. Nisbet, in *Kant's Political Writings*, ed. H. Reiss (Cambridge University Press, 1970), 61–92, 77.

'If the organism carries a "small-scale model" of external reality and of its own possible actions within its head, it is able to try out various alternatives, conclude which is the best of them, react to future situations before they arise, utilise the knowledge of past events in dealing with the present and the future, and in every way to react in a much fuller, safer and more competent manner to the emergencies which face it. Most of the greatest advances of modern technology have been instruments which extended the scope of our sense-organs, our brains or our limbs ... Is it not possible, therefore, that our brains themselves utilise comparable mechanisms to achieve the same ends and these mechanisms can parallel phenomena in the external world as a calculating machine can parallel the development of strains in a bridge?' K. Craik, *The Nature of Explanation* (Cambridge University Press, 1967 [1943]), 61.

25 See B. Cassin (ed.), *Dictionary of Untranslatables: A Philosophical Lexicon*, trans. S. Rendall et al., ed. E. Apter, J. Lezra, M. Wood (Princeton University Press, 2014 [2004]). This consists of 1,274 pages painfully illustrating the interlingual problem.

Hegel then proceeded to suppose that History (another materialised substantive) is the story of the progress of Reason manifesting itself as *Geist* (?Spirit or ?Soul or ?Mind), producing, incidentally, *Zeitgeist* (the spirit of a given time) and *Volksgeist* (the spirit of a given nation). This led him to judge his own time as a high point in human progress and to predict a human future which, among many other things, contains the 'state' as the terminus of human social organisation, and the 'nation' as the expression of the spirit of a unique people, and the 'nation state' as the archetypal and final expression of the organised social Spirit of his Age.

This, in turn, led to an outbreak of chronic historicism (history seen as containing deterministic laws), some of it declinist in spirit, and some of it progressive in spirit, causing Marx and Engels to find laws of history based on an inversion of Hegelianism – history determines ideas, rather than the other way round. And Darwinian evolutionary biology (from 1859) encouraged belief in some sort of determinism at the root of all organic existence, including human social existence. And the idea of the rational 'state' lent spurious philosophical prestige to the idea of all-human coexistence as the coexistence of states. Emmerich de Vattel (1714–67) used 'natural law' as a philosophical support for his idea of 'states or nations' as quasi-persons, but he also used a consoling rationalisation of the existing state of relations among the nations of Europe, as the governments of those nations saw those relations.[26] For Hegel, states or nations are living together in a Hobbesian state of nature, albeit under the rule of the World Mind and History.[27]

---

[26] E. de Vattel, *Le Droit des gens; ou, Principes de la loi naturelle appliqués à la conduite et aux affaires des nations et des souverains* [*The Law of Nations; or, Principles of Natural Law Applied to the Conduct and Affairs of Nations and of Sovereigns*] (1758).

[27] 'The nation state is mind in its substantive rationality and immediate actuality and is therefore the absolute power on earth. It follows that every state is sovereign and autonomous against its neighbours ... The fundamental proposition of international law ... is that treaties, as the ground of obligations between states, ought to be kept. But since the sovereignty of a state is the principle of its relations to others, states are to that extent in a state of nature in relation to each other. Their rights are actualized only in their particular wills and not in a universal will with constitutional powers over them. This universal proviso of international law therefore does not go beyond an ought-to-be ... '. Hegel, *The Philosophy of Right* (above n. 3), §§330, 333, 212–13.

'Tis often asked as a mighty Objection, *Where are*, or ever were, there any *Men in such a State of Nature*? To which it may suffice as an answer at present; That since all *Princes* and Rulers of *Independent* Governments all through the World, are in a State of Nature, 'tis plain the World never was, nor ever will be, without Numbers of Men in that State.' J. Locke, *Two Treatises on Government* (1690), ed. P. Laslett (Cambridge University Press, 1960/63), Second Treatise, Chapter II, §14, 317 (italics in original).

Schopenhauer accepted Kant's idea that the human mind re-presents the putative external world to itself in accordance with its own form of functioning, but suggested that this is not the whole of the functioning of the mind, which contains also what he expressed as *will*. His *Die Welt als Wille und Vorstellung* (1818/44) has been translated into English both as *The World as Will and Representation* and *The World as Will and Idea*. For Schopenhauer, the 'will' is a human life-force that acts in the 'real' world. The mind does not merely *understand* the world. It wills the world. And, for some strange reason, possibly personal and psychological, Schopenhauer sees the human will in the most negative possible light, as a naturally ruthless, aggressive, destructive, irrational force.

Schopenhauer's ideas, and his profound pessimism, powerfully affected countless intellectuals, including Nietzsche, Freud, Proust and Wittgenstein – and also Hitler, or so he himself said. It became the dominant zeitgeist of a disillusioned European 'waste-land' in the twentieth century, at the heart of an existential crisis of the European mind.

In the light of the tragi-comedy of human history, pessimism is reasonable.[28] But optimism is a possible, if courageous, attitude to adopt towards the inherent world-changing and world-perfecting power of philosophy.

'Now that I have laid down the true principles of political right, and tried to give the State a basis of its own to rest on, I ought next to strengthen it by its external relations, which would include the law of nations, commerce, the right of war and conquest, public right, leagues, negotiations, treaties etc. But all this forms a new subject that is far too vast for my narrow scope.' J.-J. Rousseau, *The Social Contract or Principles of Political Thought* (1762), Book IV, Chapter IX, in *The Social Contract and Discourses*, trans. G. D. H. Cole (Dent & Sons, 1913), 278. Sadly, the always-inspiring Rousseau did not return to this vast subject.

[28] '[The Roman Emperor] Antoninus [reigned 138–61 CE] diffused order and tranquility over the greatest part of the earth. His reign is marked by the rare advantage of furnishing very few materials for history; which is, indeed, little more than the register of the crimes, follies, and misfortunes of mankind.' E. Gibbon, *The History of the Decline and Fall of the Roman Empire*, 12 vols. (1776–88), I, Chapter 3.

'And the result of all this is, that war is now such an accepted thing that people are astonished to find anyone who does not like it; and such a respectable thing that it is wicked (I nearly said heretical) to disapprove of the thing of all things which is most criminal and most lamentable. How much more reasonable it would be to turn one's astonishment to wondering what evil genius, what a plague, what madness, what Fury first put into the mind of man a thing which had been hitherto reserved for beasts – that a peaceful creature, whom nature made for peace and loving-kindness ... should rush with such savage insanity, with such mad commotion, to mutual slaughter.' 'What is war, indeed, but murder shared by many, and brigandage, all the more immoral for being wider spread? But this view is jeered at, and called scholastic ravings, by the thick-headed lords of our day.' *The 'Adages' of Erasmus* (1515), trans. M. Phillips (Cambridge University Press, 1964), 310, 320.

'[Optimism] seems to me to be not merely an absurd, but also a really *wicked*, way of thinking, a bitter mockery of the unspeakable suffering of mankind.' A. Schopenhauer,

As our own version of Pascal's wager on the existence of God, we might take a bet on the permanent possibility of a better human future made by the best capacities of the human mind.[29]

III   An Existential Crisis of the European Mind

The nineteenth century was the first of two centuries like no others in the recorded history of the human world. Every aspect of the human world was transformed in an accelerating headlong rush. By the end of the nineteenth century, the public intellectual aspect of the human mind was experiencing a nervous breakdown. However, there was one aspect of the human world that hardly changed – the so-called 'international' world, inhabited by 'states' and ruled by diplomacy and war. It was the combination of these two phenomena – intellectual breakdown and international atavism – that caused the major disasters of the twentieth century. It seemed now that it was possible for the collective human mind to go mad.[30]

The World as Will and Representation (1819/1844), 2 vols., trans. E. F. J. Payne (Dover Publications, 1958/1966), I, Book 4, §59, 326 (italics in original).

[29] B. Pascal, *Pensées [Thoughts]*, trans. A. J. Krailsheimer (Penguin Classics, 1966), §418, 150–1.

'We always picture Plato and Aristotle wearing long academic gowns, but they were ordinary decent people like anyone else, who enjoyed a laugh with their friends. And when they amused themselves by composing their *Laws* and *Politics* they did it for fun. It was the least philosophical and least serious part of their lives: the most philosophical part was living simply and without fuss. If they wrote about politics it was as if to lay down rules for a madhouse. And if they pretended to treat it as something really important it was because they knew that the madmen they were talking to believed themselves to be kings and emperors. They humoured these beliefs in order to calm down their madness with as little harm as possible.' Pascal, ibid., §533, 216–7.

'For it was a witty and truthful rejoinder which was given by a captured pirate to Alexander the Great. The king asked the fellow, "What is your idea, in infesting the sea?" And the pirate answered, with uninhibited insolence – "The same as yours, in infesting the earth! But because I do it with a tiny craft, I'm called a pirate; because you have a mighty navy, you are called an emperor".' Augustine of Hippo (354–430 CE), *City of God*, trans. H. Bettenson (Penguin Classics, 1972), IV.4, 139.

See P. Allott, 'Curing the Madness of the Intergovernmental World', Alec Roche Lecture 2004, New College Oxford, www.squire.law.cam.ac.uk/eminent-scholars-archiveprofessor-pj-allott/pj-allott-curing-madness-intergovernmental-world.

[30] 'If the development of civilization has such a far-reaching similarity to the development of the individual and if it employs the same methods, may we not be justified in reaching the diagnosis that, under the influence of cultural urges, some civilizations, or some epochs of civilization – possibly the whole of mankind – have become neurotic?' S. Freud, 'Civilization and its Discontents' (1930), in *Civilization, Society and Religion*, trans. J. Strachey (Pelican, 1985), 38. Freud's primary interest was neurosis rather than psychosis. We may see symptoms of psychopathic social behaviour far and wide in the modern world.

The nineteenth century had started with the benign idea that the human phenomenon might be capable of being investigated in a way analogous to the method of the natural sciences. It might even be possible to find hypotheses capable of being the basis of reliable predictions, thereby rationalising public policy, and even offering effective prescriptions for living the good life, individually and collectively. This idea was the fruit of the marriage of the seventeenth-century scientific revolution and the eighteenth-century Enlightenment. Saint-Simon had proposed (1813) *la science de l'homme* (human science). His disciple, Auguste Comte, called the new movement *positivism* (1840) and gave the name *sociology* (1847) to the first of the new human sciences. In his *System of Logic* (1843), John Stuart Mill discussed the prospects of what he called the *moral sciences.* 'All that [sociology] asks is that the principle of causality be applied to social phenomena ... not as a rational necessity but only as an empirical postulate produced by legitimate induction.'[31] To which we may feel bound to respond: but most of human behaviour is the product not of causes, but of reasons and motives, dictated by the disorderly, unpredictable and mostly mysterious human mind.

Later in the century, human scientists began to practise a discipline known as *anthropology* – trying to generalise social phenomena from the study of sub-societal or pre-societal human groups, and other modestly organised societies all over the world. Others began to practise a discipline which came to be called *economics*. In the eighteenth century, there had been *political economy*, which was treated rather as a cousin of philosophy. 'Economics' would now see itself as the rational and technical study of specifically economic phenomena at an abstract and universal level.[32]

Historiography, theology and jurisprudence made a bow in the direction of the prestige of the natural sciences, trying to establish transcendental and objective credentials for themselves. Hermeneutics treated religious texts as cultural artefacts. Legal positivism tried to establish the idea of law as a logical system, separated from its inseparable cultural and social context. Phenomenology considered the systematic structure of

---

[31] E. Durkheim, *The Rules of Sociological Method* (1895), trans. S. A. Solovay and J. H. Mueller, ed. G. E. G. Catlin (Free Press, 1938), 141.

[32] 'Among the delusions which at different periods have possessed themselves of the minds of large masses of the human race, perhaps the most curious – certainly the least creditable – is the modern *soi-disant* science of political economy, based on the idea that an advantageous code of social action may be determined irrespectively of the influence of social affection.' J. Ruskin, 'Unto This Last' (1860), in *Unto This Last and Other Essays* (Everyman's Library, 1907), 115.

human thinking, separated from the products of thinking. A discipline known as *psychology* seemed set to replace philosophy, exploring the overwhelming complexity of the human mind as a biological and behavioural phenomenon, with its own intangible metaphysiology, the mysterious source of its powerful, strange and uncontrollable activity.

At the turn of the century (nineteenth to twentieth), all the higher aspects of the human mind, intellectual and imaginative, had developed a peculiar form of neurosis. They had become pathologically narcissistic, obsessively expressing their *form* as an integral part of their substance. In the visual arts, in music, in poetry, in the novel, the spectator no longer had the primary function of seeing the substance of a work, and judging its interest, its truth and its beauty. Those things had become secondary. The insistent focus was now on the form of the presentation, its surface.

These troubling symptoms were given a name: 'modernism'. Much intelligent, beautiful and memorable work was produced by the new intellectual narcissism, but the age-old cultural heritage of the human imagination had been shaken to its roots, and soon succumbed to populism, commercialism and tourism.

Professional philosophy had also come to be dominated by an obsessive discussion of its own medium – namely, language. It had ceased to contain an exploration of the possibilities of the good life for individuals and societies. And popularly accessible philosophy had surrendered its independence to pragmatism (socially determined truth and values), cognitive science (a naturalising of consciousness sometimes presented as if it were a philosophy of consciousness) and ideology (ideas as political power).

With all these new ways of thinking about the human condition, it came to seem that philosophy in the ancient tradition was no longer necessary. The self-searching of the human mind would be along bright new tracks, driven by a new spirit of exploration and discovery, abandoning the old highways and byways of speculative human self-consciousness. Philosophy must give way to its negation.[33] There were professional

---

[33] ' ... pragmatism became America's original school of philosophy and the nation's peculiar philosophical outlook'. J. P. Diggins, *The Promise of Pragmatism. Modernism and the Crisis of Knowledge and Authority* (University of Chicago Press, 1994), 38.

'We do not solve them [philosophical questions]; we get over them. Old questions are solved by disappearing.' J. Dewey, 'The Influence of Darwinism on Philosophy,' in *The Philosophy of John Dewey*, 2 vols., ed. J. J. McDermott (1981), I, 41. ' ... knowledge, mind and meaning are part of the same world that they have to do with, and ... they are to be studied in the same empirical spirit as natural science. There is no place for a prior philosophy.' W. van O. Quine, 'Ontological Relativity' in *Ontological Relativity and Other Essays* (Columbia University Press, 1969), 26. ' ... we can continue the conversation Plato began

philosophers, who had helped to marginalise philosophy in the public mind, with the impenetrable obscurity of their multi-volume writings. The news of the end of philosophy[34] was gladly received by an educated general public who had always been afraid of it, and suspicious of its pretensions.[35]

The naturalistic study of the human condition and the human mind had produced overwhelming masses of information, indigestible, incoherent and of wildly different levels of intellectual rigour.[36] We could pick and choose our own personal enlightenments from so much new self-knowledge. But, strangely, the human being seemed to be very little *wiser*, despite knowing so much more about itself.[37] And it had become

---

without discussing the topics [that] Plato wanted discussed … '; ' … cultural anthropology (in a large sense which includes intellectual history) is all we need.' R. Rorty, *Philosophy and the Mirror of Nature* (Princeton University Press, 1979), 391, 381.

'Unphilosophical philosophy [will be] the last that West Europe will know.' O. Spengler, *The Decline of the West* (1918), trans. C. F. Atkinson (Knopf, 1926), 45–6.

[34] M. Heidegger, *Das Ende der Philosophie und die Aufgabe des Denkens* (Verlag Günther Neske, 1961) (published in English as *The End of Philosophy*, trans. J. Stambaugh (University of Chicago Press, 1973)) suggests that philosophy should begin again at the beginning, with the pre-Socratic philosophers and the problem of 'being', and then take some wholly new direction, in order to rescue humanity from the disaster of contemporary civilisation. In the meantime, new movements of thought – structuralism, postmodernism, deconstructionism – were picking at the bones of traditional philosophy, demonstrating the ultimate contingency of all ideas, so that even the judgement of ideas in relation to each other (let alone the determination of their 'truth') is seen as an impossible enterprise, since an idea exists only in a context, and a context has no outer limits and no possible coherence. The human mind was wilfully stupefying itself.

[35] 'For if men judge that learning should be referred to action, they judge well; but in this they fall into the error described in the ancient fable, in which the other parts of the body did suppose the stomach had been idle, because it neither performed the office of motion, as the limbs do, nor of sense, as the head does; but yet, notwithstanding, it is the stomach that digests and distributes to all the rest; so if any man think philosophy and universality to be idle studies, he does not consider that all professions are from thence served and supplied.' ' … they are ill discoverers that think there is no land, when they can see nothing but sea'. F. Bacon, *The Advancement of Learning* (1605–33) (Everyman's Library, 1915), 2nd Book, 63, 94 (spelling modernised). '[The Bellman] had bought a large map representing the sea / Without the least vestige of land: / And the crew were much pleased when they found it to be / A map they could all understand.' L. Carroll, *The Hunting of the Snark* (1876), Fit the Second.

Michel de Montaigne (1533-92), master of constructive scepticism, recognised its limits: '[extreme scepticism] is the final trick of fencing [le dernier tour d'escrime] … when you abandon your arms to make your adversary get rid of his'. M. de Montaigne, *Essais* (1580) (ed. P. Villey, 1922), II, 308 (present author's translation).

[36] Allott, *The Health of Nations* (above n. 6), §§4.8 et seq., on the naturalising of the human phenomenon.

[37] 'And what caused this disorder in the mind of Europe? The free coexistence in all cultivated minds of the most diverse ideas, of the most contradictory principles of life and knowledge. That is what characterises a *modern* epoch … Well: the Europe of 1914 had perhaps

clear that the human 'sciences' would not discover any 'laws' of the human condition. The human mind, deprived of traditional philosophy and disappointed by the achievements of the professional naturalising of the human phenomenon, found itself empty and anguished in a human waste-land.[38] Confronted by the horrors of World War I, philosophy had no voice. Confronted by the crimes of the totalitarianisms, philosophy had no voice. The European mind fell victim to despair and shame. Nihilism became a dogma for some, a fashion for others.[39] Civilisational declinism was declining into civilisational endism.[40]

arrived at the limit of this modernism ... Every brain of a certain level was a crossroads for all schools of opinion; every thinker a Universal Exhibition of thoughts. There were works of the mind whose richness in contrasts and conflicting impulses suggested the bright lights of the capital cities of those times; one's eyes were burned and tired ... How much material, how much labour, how much ingenuity, how many plundered centuries, how many disparate lives brought together, were needed to make this carnival possible and enthrone it as a form of the highest wisdom and the triumph of humanity?' P. Valéry, 'La Crise de l'esprit [The Crisis of the Mind]' (1919), in *Œuvres*, 2 vols. (Bibliothèque de la Pléiade, 1957), I, 988–1014, 992 (present author's translation).

[38] T. S. Eliot's *The Waste Land* was published in 1922, expressing with intense imaginative accuracy the spirit of the age. 'One feels inclined to say that the intention that man should be "happy" is not included in the plan of "Creation".' S. Freud, 'Civilization and its Discontents' (above n. 30), 263–4. '[Philosophy] must set limits to what can be thought; and, in doing so, what cannot be thought.' 'What we cannot speak about we must pass over in silence.' L. Wittgenstein, *Tractatus Logico-Philosophicus* (1921), trans. D. F. Pears and B. F. McGuinness (Routledge, 1961), §4.114, §§7, 25, 74. '[Legal norms] are not valid by virtue of their content. Any content whatsoever can be legal; there is no human behaviour which could not function as the content of a legal norm.' H. Kelsen, 'The Pure Theory of Law: Its Method and Fundamental Concepts', trans. C. H. Wilson, 51 *Law Quarterly Review* (1935) 517–35, 518. 'Everything tends to make us believe that there exists a certain point of the mind at which life and death, the real and the imagined, past and future, the communicable and the incommunicable, high and low, cease to be perceived as contradictions.' A. Breton, *Manifestoes of Surrealism 2* (1930), trans. R. Seaver and H. R. Lane (University of Michigan Press, 1972), 123.

Among many other troubled spirits of the interwar years: P. Valéry, F. Kafka, O. Spengler, K. Čapek, J. Benda, J. Ortega y Gasset, T. Mann, A. Hitler, C. Chaplin, F. Lang, H. G. Wells, A. Huxley.

[39] ' ... l'Espoir, / Vaincu, pleure, et l'Angoisse atroce, despotique, / Sur mon crâne incliné plante son drapeau noir [...Hope, defeated, weeps, and Anguish, terrible, despotic, places its black flag over my lowered head]'. C. Baudelaire, 'Spleen' in *Les Fleurs du Mal* (1857/1861) (present author's translation). *Fin de siècle* was giving way to *fin des siècles*. 'Roma quanta fuit ipsa ruina docet [See Rome's greatness in its ruins]'. A medieval saying used by S. Serlio (1475–1554) in the frontispiece to Book III of his treatise on architecture.

[40] 'We civilisations know now that we are mortal. We had heard of worlds that had disappeared entirely, empires sunk without trace with all their men and all their machinery; lost in the unexplorable depths of the centuries with their gods and laws, their academies and their pure and applied sciences, with their grammars, their dictionaries, their classics, their romantics, their symbolists, their critics and the critics of their critics. We knew that

In the twentieth and twenty-first centuries, new manifestations of religion and mythology have flowed into the spiritual vacuum. The new mythology, when it does not take the form of totalitarian ideologies, takes the form of a fantasy-world in which alienated human beings play the roles of workers and consumers, aspiring to lead a good life whose meaning is defined by political, cultural and economic power. Modernism's de-magicking of an old world (*Entzauberung*) led to the grim re-magicking of a new world. Since 1945, there has been a new wave of declinist, endist and dystopian writing.[41]

IV   The Duty of Philosophy in a Time of Global Existential Crisis

The mental health of human societies, like the mental health of human beings, is always fragile. The self-constituting of a human society, like the self-constituting of a human person, is a permanent struggle. In both cases, a human form of entropy threatens self-ordering. In both cases, survival and flourishing depend on the unceasing application of countervailing human energy. These elementary facts of human existence take on a terrifying aspect when the self-constituting is at the level of all human societies and all human beings, when the struggle is a struggle for the survival and flourishing of the whole human species. The existential crisis of the twentieth-century has become, in the early twenty-first century, a global existential crisis.

Democracy and capitalism are among the greatest achievements of the human mind. They have a pedigree of ideas extending back as far as any religion. Dominating all three modes of a given society's self-constituting – ideal, real and legal – they can cause a society to develop, apparently without limit, in organisational complexity and in the creation of communal wealth. They are the product of all three forms of a society's theories – transcendental, pure and practical – conditioning the public mind of the society and the private minds of its members, as necessary to

the whole visible world is made of ashes, and that ashes mean something ... An extraordinary shudder passed through the very marrow of Europe. She felt, in every fibre of her thinking, that she no longer recognised herself, that she no longer resembled herself, that she was going to lose her consciousness, a consciousness acquired through centuries of survivable misfortunes, through thousands of men of the highest quality, through countless geographical, ethnic, historical chances.' Valéry, 'La Crise de l'esprit' (above n. 37), 988 (present author's translation).

[41] Among the most influential: G. Orwell, *Animal Farm* (1945); G. Orwell, *Nineteen Eighty-Four* (1949).

allow the society to survive and flourish. Over the brief course of recent centuries, democracy and capitalism have produced a staggering development of the human world in general. In the early twenty-first century, the democratic-capitalist model as a system of ideas seems to be under strain at its very foundations.[42]

(1) Governments have invented forms of managed democracy and managed capitalism – managed, that is to say, by the government. Democracy-capitalism contains an inherent totalitarian potentiality, given that it involves the organisation of every aspect of society, including mental organisation.[43] It requires masses of law, government and administration. All democratic-societies, even those regarded as 'liberal', require a great surrender of personal freedom, in exchange for immense aggregate gains that can be re-distributed. Tyranny in the name of democracy-capitalism is a permanent temptation for governments.[44] Many governments are now unable to resist that temptation.

(2) Populist democracy is the obverse of government-managed democracy. Capitalism is intrinsically populist, in the sense that it is the decisions of consumers that determine the fate of the capitalists, even if it

---

[42] For further discussion of this analysis of a society's self-constituting, see Allott, *Eutopia* (above n. 6), Chapter 11. For 'systems of ideas' and 'models', see above n. 24.

[43] 'The enchained possibilities of advanced industrial societies are: development of the productive forces on an enlarged scale, extension of the conquest of nature, growing satisfaction of needs for a growing number of people, creation of new needs and faculties. But these possibilities are gradually being realized through means and institutions which cancel their liberating potential, and this process affects not only the means but also the ends. The instruments of productivity and progress, organized into a totalitarian system, determine not only the actual but also the possible utilizations.' H. Marcuse, *One-Dimensional Man: Studies in the Ideology of Advanced Industrial Society* (Beacon Press, 1964), 255.

[44] '[A] dangerous ambition more often lurks behind the specious mask of zeal for the rights of the people than under the forbidding appearance of zeal for the firmness and efficiency of government. History will teach us that the former has been found a much more certain road to the introduction of despotism than the latter, and that of those men who have overturned the liberties of republics, the greatest number have begun their career by paying an obsequious court to the people, commencing demagogues and ending tyrants.' A. Hamilton in A. Hamilton et al. (eds.), *The Federalist Papers* (1788), no. 1 (The New American Library of World Literature, 1961), 35.

'In my opinion, the main evil of the present democratic institutions of the United States does not arise, as is often asserted in Europe, from their weakness, but from their irresistible strength. I am not so much alarmed at the excessive liberty which reigns in the country as at the inadequate securities which one finds there against tyranny.' A. de Tocqueville, *Democracy in America* (1835) (Everyman's Library, 1941/94), I, Chapter XIV, section entitled 'Tyranny of the Majority' 260.

is law and government that make capitalism possible.[45] On the other hand, the pure and practical theories of democracy support a system in which the opinions of the people are mediated through complex structures and systems. The general will is not the will of all. In particular, it is the job of democratic politics to reconcile all the particular opinions and interests of a society into a form that can influence government and the making of the law.[46] A spirit of random populism is now affecting the operation of political institutions at all levels – local, national and global.

(3) If everything is a matter of opinion, and everyone is entitled to an opinion, then all social structures are liable to be unsettled. We are witnessing what might be seen as a revolution, if it had a clearer focus and a specific location. It is a mental revolution, as much as it is a social revolution.[47] Its effects go far beyond the unsettling of the

---

[45] 'When we call a capitalist society a consumers' democracy we mean that the power to dispose of the means of production, which belongs to the entrepreneurs and capitalists, can only be acquired by means of the consumers' ballot, held daily in the market-place ... Thus the wealth of successful business men is always the result of a consumers' plebiscite, and, once acquired, this wealth can be retained only if it is employed in the way regarded by consumers as most beneficial to them. The average man is both better informed and less corruptible in the decisions he makes as a consumer than as a voter at political elections.' L. von Mises, 'Preface to 2nd Edition' in *Socialism: An Economic and Sociological Analysis* (1922), trans. J. Kahane (J. Cape, 1936), 21.

[46] 'There is often a great deal of difference between the will of all and the general will; the latter considers only the common interest, while the former takes private interest into account, and is no more than a sum of particular wills: but take away from these same wills the pluses and minuses that cancel one another, and the general will remains as the sum of the differences.' J.-J. Rousseau, 'The Social Contract' in *The Social Contract and Discourses*, trans. G. D. H. Cole (Everyman's Library, 1973), Book I, Chapter 3, 185.

'Like other tyrannies, the tyranny of the majority was at first, and is still vulgarly, held in dread, chiefly as operating through the acts of the public authorities. But reflecting persons perceived that when society is itself the tyrant ... its means of tyrannizing are not restricted to the acts which it may do by the hands of its political functionaries. Society can and does execute its own mandates: and if it issues wrong mandates instead of right, or any mandates at all in things with which it ought not to meddle, it practises a social tyranny more formidable than many kinds of political oppression ...'. J. S. Mill, *On Liberty* (1859), ed. A. Ryan (Penguin Classics, 2006), 10–11.

[47] 'There have been many internal revolutions in the government of countries, both as to persons and forms, in which the neighbouring states have had little or no concern ... The present revolution in France seems to me to be quite of another character and description; ... *It is a revolution of doctrine and theoretic dogma.* It has a much greater resemblance to those changes which have been made on religious grounds ... The last revolution of doctrine and theory which has happened in Europe is the Reformation.' E. Burke, *Thoughts on French Affairs* (1790) (Everyman's Library, 1910), 287. (Italics in original.) For a proposal to restore

foundations in *practical* theory of particular social forms, such as democracy and capitalism. The mental rebellion, if it is not a revolution, is also affecting, and powerfully, the *pure* theory of social forms, and even their *transcendental* theory.[48] Pure theory provides universalising concepts which are shared by most, perhaps all, societies, each society using them in its own way. *Family, city, society, government, state, nation, class, personal identity, religious identity, human identity.* Allied to these are high social values which have hitherto had a claim to universality. *Justice, fairness, equality, right, duty.* Societies are permutations of such ideas. A high value in its own right may be our judgement that the more successfully a society *constitutes itself ideally* from such ideas, the more successful that society is liable to be in surviving and flourishing. But all of them are, in the end, only ideas, and they can be unsettled very easily.

More fundamentally still, we may be witnessing an unsettling of the *transcendental* basis of social forms. It is possible that philosophy in the ancient tradition is being replaced, at least in its social context, by a populist and absolutist un-philosophy. The idea that the highest human values are not timeless and universal is an enduring product of the scepticism, pragmatism and nihilism that were at the centre of the existential crisis of the European mind in the twentieth century. They leave the true, the good, the just and the beautiful to be determined subjectively and socially. They leave the ideal to be determined by the actual. They leave us in the grip of a dehumanising fatalism.

A surprising and hopeful paradox is that the new populism may be fired by an intense and deep-seated criticism of existing social forms, not least democracy and capitalism, as systems failing to respect the true interests and the true aspirations of human beings, sensing that, in the name of social efficiency and the survival of the most ruthless, we are not doing justice to our highest human values.[49] Perhaps we should under-

---

a transcendental dimension to global social philosophy, see P. Allott, 'Europe and the Idea of the Transcendental: Human Rights and Other Imagined Entities' (2017) 10 *Annali di Scienze Religiose* 51–71.

[48] For the three theoretical levels of a society's self-constituting, see *Eutopia* (above, n. 6), §4.39.

[49] 'The epithets *sociable, good-natured, humane, merciful, grateful, friendly, generous, beneficent*, or their equivalents, are known in all languages, and universally express the highest merit, which *human nature* is capable of attaining. Where these amiable qualities are attended with birth and power and eminent abilities, and display themselves in the good government or useful instruction of mankind, they seem even to raise the possessors of

stand it as yet another cry of the oppressed. Could it be that, after all, the attraction of the ideal is deep enough within the human mind to survive, in the consciousness of human beings in general, even if it has deserted the minds of privileged members of society? The actual *does not* determine the ideal. The ideal *judges* the actual. Most human beings surely still know this.

Such is the context in which we approach the problem of the self-constituting of human society at the global level. Globalisation is a socialising of all-humanity. The emerging international society is an organic and gradual self-constituting of a new kind of human society, without a written constitution, without the organs of a constitution in their familiar form, but reflecting the fact that we share our coexistence as troublesome inhabitants of a single natural world. All human beings are now utterly dependent on all other human beings. We share the daunting task of surviving and flourishing as a species. The emerging international society already has a complex legal system, with efficient means of law-making, in *treaties* as a form of statute law, and *customary international law* as an expression of an organic form of law-making found throughout recorded human history. There is a mass of global *executive-branch* activity, operated by a vast international civil service in uncountable intergovernmental organisations. There are great numbers of *courts and tribunals* applying international law and national law. There is global *public opinion*, through the work of non-governmental organisations and in an amorphous *public mind*, expressing itself in global media of communication and in social media. It is the task of *philosophy* to provide the emerging international society with the self-consciousness of a true society.

The present author's *Eunomia* and *Eutopia* simply ignore the End of Philosophy proclaimed in the twentieth century. They resume the great tradition of human self-searching that has given us so much of the best in the self-creating and self-perfecting of the human species. They propose a revolution in our minds, a new Enlightenment.[50] War and disorder

---

them above the rank of *human nature*, and make them approach in some measure to the divine.' D. Hume, *An Enquiry Concerning the Principles of Morals* (1752/77), sec. II, part I, ed. T. Beauchamp (Oxford University Press, 1998), 78.

[50] For the postulation of a Law of Enlightenments at three-century intervals from the third century to the eighteenth century, see Allott, *The Health of Nations* (above n. 6), §3.18, fn. 15; *Eutopia* (above n. 6), §12.57.

shame our species. There can be a better future for the universal human society.[51]

---

[51] '[The law of nations] has not only the force of a pact and agreement among men, but also the force of a law; for the world as a whole, being in a way one single state, has the power to create laws that are just and fitting for all persons, as are the rules of international law.' F. de Vitoria, *Concerning Civil Power* (1528), §21, trans. G. L. Williams, in J. B. Scott, *The Spanish Origin of International Law* (Clarendon Press, 1934), App. C, para. xc.

'If we should consider that great society, which nature has established among men, to be done away with by the particular societies, which men may enter into, when they unite into a state, states would be established contrary to the law of nature, in as much as the obligation of all toward all would be terminated; which assuredly is absurd. Just as in the human body individual organs do not cease to be organs of the whole body, because certain ones taken together constitute one organ; so likewise men do not cease to be members of the great society which is made up of the whole human race, because several have formed together a certain particular society.' C. von Wolff, *The Law of Nations Treated according to a Scientific Method* (1749), Prolegomena to the 1764 edition, §7, trans. J. H. Drake (Clarendon Press, 1934), 11.

PART I

International Perspectives

B.   *Substantive Challenges*

5

The Real Utopia

International Constitutionalism and the Use of Force

MARC WELLER

I   Introduction

War is an 'activity fit only for beasts'. This is the view of Thomas More's Utopians. 'Unlike almost every other people in the world, they [the Utopians] think nothing so inglorious as the glory won in battle', he continues.[1]

Of course, utopia literally means 'un-place' – a place that does not, and cannot, ever exist. Hence, utopia offers a laboratory where ideas about human nature and human interaction can be tried out and experimented with in a way unconstrained by the realities of our human experience. But, even in that space which we cannot ever hope to reach in reality, and where our imagination can offer us a glimpse of the ideal global society, war apparently remains a fact of life. Depressingly, even the Utopians go to war, although strictly for what are determined to be 'good reasons'. These are:[2]

- to protect their own land
- to drive invading armies from the territories of their friends
- to liberate an oppressed people, in the name of compassion and humanity, from tyranny and servitude
- to repay and avenge injuries done to their friends.

In short, the Utopians believe in Article 51 of the United Nations (UN) Charter on individual and collective self-defence – although, sadly, we are not told whether they follow the interpretation of Bowett or Brownlie.[3] They have read Michael Reisman – they support humanitarian and

---

[1] T. More, *Utopia* (Cambridge University Press, 1988), 85.
[2] Ibid.
[3] Cambridge vs Oxford, famously disagreeing on the precise meaning of that provision.

pro-democratic intervention. Moreover, like Kelsen, they see in war a means to enforce legal obligations, or a sanction.

Of course, subsequently, utopianism has been identified with somewhat more pure designs for perpetual peace. These are proposals for social systems where there is no space for 'just war' principles of this kind. There has been a constant flow of such proposals, ranging from Sully (1559–1641), to the Abbé St Pierre, writing in 1713 just after having contributed to the negotiations of the Treaty of Utrecht, and some of the most notable figures in philosophy, including Leibnitz, Rousseau and Kant.[4] This tendency has continued to the present era dominated by the United Nations Charter, the UN era.[5]

The label 'utopian' is often attached to such proposals to delegitimise them as unreal before they have been read and considered. As Sully recounts, Henry IV was most reluctant to discuss with him his grand design for a perpetual peace in Europe, fearing that he would be classed as a romantic dreamer. And plans for perpetual peace have generally been described or denigrated as being as desirable as they are impossible to implement.

The utopian vision of a warless world is often contrasted with competing, and apparently more realistic approaches to managing large-scale social violence. Students of international affairs generally juxtapose the concept of utopia with terms like anarchy, realism, etc. It will be useful to consider these alternative concepts briefly in relation to the present state of development of international law, and then turn to analyse more particularly the character of the present international constitutional system, in particular as it relates to the use of force.

II   Types of International System and the Role of International Law

Our understanding of human nature – whether we are angels aiming for peace, or devils driving towards eternal war – colours our characterisation of the international system. There are four fundamental approaches:

- Anarchy or Empire
- 'Realist' or Balance of Power

---

[4] E.g. Esref Aksu, *Early Notions of Global Governance* (University of Wales Press, 2008).

[5] In the twentieth century, most notably Grenville Clark and Louis B. Sohn, *World Peace through World Law* (Harvard University Press, 1965); and a new effort by James Taylor Ranney, *World Peace through Law* (Routledge, 2018).

- The Common Interest or Society Approach
- An International Constitutional Order.

A   Anarchy or Empire

While we occasionally hear of the 'anarchical international society', anarchy and society are of course terms that stand in opposition to one another. Anarchy is a state of constant competition on the basis of pure power, cunning and deceit. The aim of the actors within the system are self-preservation, advancement of self-interest and the domination of others, ultimately to the point of Empire. A society, on the other hand, is based on the common belief that the interests of each participant in the system are best served through measured cooperation. Such cooperation is supported by rules which aim to bring about a modicum of stability and predictability in relations among the key actors, allowing them to advance their development undisturbed by constant conflict and clashes.

In an anarchical system, there is no international societal consensus and war is a matter of course. International law exists to a very limited extent in the shape of rules of mutual interest or convenience. This may include process rules relating to the commencement of hostilities, and perhaps quite limited, substantive rules relating to the conduct of war that appear mutually convenient (ransoming of members of the elite, no poisoning of wells, etc.). There may also be arrangements to allow for communications even within a generally hostile environment, for instance concerning the protection of ambassadors. Treaties of alliance may be concluded, but they remain tactical undertakings in this world governed by the dictates of Machiavelli. Crucially, there is no drive to establish or preserve a system, or a legal regime, in the common interest.

B   'Realist' or Balance of Power

Second, we have the so-called realist approach. Realists know that man is man's wolf. Violence is in our genes, and the best that can be done is to constrain the violent impulse of others through defensive preparations – the invincible Maginot line that was meant to preserve France from German aggression when World War II was looming – through deterrence, through alliances with others, and even through preventative wars. *Si vis pacem, para bellum* – if you want peace, prepare for war. The aim is to preserve a relatively stable system at the centre through balance of power politics, at times supported by *ad hoc* conference diplomacy to prevent wars that might unsettle the overall system. This is supported by international legal rules concerning cooperation in peacetime and rules restraining the temperament of war where it does occur. At the same time, the balance of power is stabilised, for instance through arms control agreements, at the turn of the past century addressing the principal perceived currency of national power – battleships.

There is an underlying agreement that the system as a whole is worth preserving in the common interest, along with at least its key actors. The system, rather than individual power politics, guarantees the survival of all. Hence, the survival of the system is in the common interest.

The problem is that the very same steps and measures that can safeguard the balance of power and the stability of the overall system can also be seen as preparations for violently overturning the system: *si vis bellum, para bellum*, instead of *si vis pacem, para bellum*. Some think that such preparations for war catastrophically resulted in the very war they were supposed to avoid. World War I erupted, in their view, more or less by accident, in consequences of the very alliances and preparations for rapid mass mobilisation that were meant to avoid war by being able credibly to deter it.

World War I turned from what was expected to be a limited campaign, allowing the warriors a hero's return by Christmas of 1914, into the gruesome *War to end all Wars*. In view of the improved technology of mass slaughter of the Great War which had killed off the 'flower of European youth', and that of some other nations, by the millions, war could no more be understood to be a glorious thing.[6]

C   *The Common Interest of Society Approach*

This experience led to the third, the legal or managerial approach of a society united by certain key values. It is assumed that mankind has indeed learnt that war is no longer a glorious pursuit – just as the Utopians did. No reasonable being would opt for war if there was any other alternative. As war by design is implausible, the system is geared towards avoiding war by accident. The aim is now not just to allow the system to survive along with its key actors more or less intact, but to avoid war altogether, given the demonstration of its limitless destructive power. Balance-of-power politics and conference diplomacy are replaced, or at least augmented, by international law and international institutions as means of war prevention.

---

[6] There were 20 million war deaths in World War I, the majority still being military personnel.

Earlier legal rules and institutions were functional, addressing commerce, communication and other practical needs brought about by advancing means of production and transport. The Danube River Commission is the often cited, early example of a functional legal regime created in the common interest and supported by an international constitutional instrument. However, after World War II, this cooperation was extended towards 'sovereign' issues, including those touching upon the preservation and very survival of the state. This time, international law and international organisations would also address what previously lay far outside of their remit – the problem of war itself. The world would unite to make war impossible, or at least less likely.

True, conflicts of interest will always arise, but these are to be addressed through what is called 'peaceful change'. In the League of Nations system, mechanisms for peaceful change consisted of a cascade of measures, starting with negotiation and mediation, directed conciliation through the Council of the League of Nations or the Assembly and, potentially, dispute settlement through legal means. There was a mechanism of supposedly automatic sanctions, and the possibility of collective military action against any transgressor. But crucially, the object of protection of the League was the League itself – the embodiment of the attempted international social contract. Hence, forcible action in response to a use of force was not only seen as a kind of collective form of self-defence on behalf of the victim, but it was described, in Article 16 of the Covenant, as action 'to protect the Covenant of the League'.

Of course, there were manifest deficiencies. There was no comprehensive compulsory jurisdiction and no comprehensive prohibition of the use of force. In view of the revanchism and nationalism of the time, a race was on to 'plug the gaps in the Covenant', again emphasising the legal approach. With the renunciation of war as a means of national politics in the Kellogg-Briand Pact, and the dispute settlement obligations of the Geneva General Act, it seemed that a comprehensive system of collective security was in place. However, key members were missing. The United States never joined, Japan withdrew after its invasion of Manchuria, as did Italy and Germany. The USSR was expelled.

Even if the system had been fully functional, it is doubtful that it could have prevented World War II. Despite the brilliance of the promise of the Kellogg-Briand Pact, Germany and others were still committed to the ideology of war and to overturning the Versailles system and all it stood for, including the League. The key states, or sadly, rather, their populations, were not yet genuinely willing to take the utopian step of renouncing the glory of war after all.

D   Constitutionalism and Utopia

The next model is furnished by the UN system, or what is generally called the modern international system. Modernity was in some ways surprisingly conservative. The UN Charter does translate the Kellogg-Briand Pact into the comprehensive prohibition of the use of force we are now familiar with. There was also a powerful executive body with a strong mandate to enforce peace. But critically, comprehensive, compulsory jurisdiction in relation to dispute settlement was lacking once again. Chapter VII of the Charter, at the time mainly directed at preventing a resurgence of violence on the part of the defeated Axis powers, or enemy states, was radical in its design. Chapter VI, on the other hand, directed at the system as a whole, including the principal victorious allies, did not really advance upon the League of Nations period – indeed, it is lacking the element of directed conciliation that had characterised the legal approach.

It will not be necessary here to rehearse the key features of the United Nations system. Let me remind you instead of the utopian design of the Abbé St Pierre I mentioned at the outset, proposed in 1713.

The Abbé proposed a 'society' among the sovereigns of Europe, to make 'peace unalterable'. This would extend beyond Europe, through alliances with the 'Mahometan Sovereigns' as he put it, and states in Asia would be assisted in establishing their own permanent society for peace. In essence, the organisation aimed at universality to the extent possible at the time. Indeed, just like Article 2(5) of the Charter, the system provided for an objective regime. According to the design of the Abbé, it would become operative in relation to all other states outside of its membership as soon as it reached the threshold of fourteen. From that point onwards, non-members would be compelled to join – compelled by war, incidentally.

The system would be maintained by a perpetual congress. Perhaps in analogy to the modern immunities appertaining to the UN and other international bodies, the congress would be installed in a free city, ensuring that it would not be beholden to a particular sovereign controlling the territory on which it was based.

In terms of substance, there was a pledge of non-intervention in the internal affairs of states – Article 2(7). Members would renounce the possibility to acquire territory by conquest or force – Article 2(4) of the Charter backed by Resolution 2625 (XXV) and a number of other standards. Disputes would be settled by the congress through directed conciliation or arbitration. A state using force in violation of this settlement would be declared 'the Enemy to the European Society' and war would be made upon it by all. In cases calling for urgent action, provisional measures *à la* Article 40 could be adopted. There was even provision for an Article 43 arrangement concerning the pre-assignment of troops for this purpose, and there would be a jointly appointed generalissimo, representing the Military Staff Committee, as it were. The expenses of the organisation would be met according to a levy determined in proportion to the revenues and riches of the respective states, much like the UN system of apportionment of budgetary expenses.

What is the point of rehearsing the elements of the design for perpetual peace put forward 250 years ago in this way? The aim is to demonstrate that utopia is not an 'un-place'. We are living in one. The League Covenant and its successor, the UN Charter, reflect all the major elements that would ordinarily be characterised as utopian when put forward as a programmatic proposal.

There clearly are deficiencies in the system, which is unsurprising given the context of its creation – managing the outcome of World War II – and the advance of time. It is over seventy years since San Francisco. The system was blocked for many years, due to the Cold War. Its revival has not been free of problems. The trouble is, we have caught up with modernity, and the early modern design of the UN System, at a time when reality is already post-modern.

The question is, though, whether the changes and growth in the organised international system that have taken place on this basis have moved us from the modern to a post-modern international system. That is to say, have we moved beyond utopia, towards international constitutionalism?

III   International Constitutionalism and the Use of Force

The international constitutional approach is not to be confused with the attempt to find *the* international constitution, for instance in the shape of the UN Charter, as some do. Instead, it considers to what extent the public functions we would expect to see performed within a constitutional system are being addressed within the international system.

In the classical international system of the Hegelian age, the only – or principal – actor was the state; modernity added international organisations. Post-modernity offers more potential actors in the public realm, and requires a more refined international constitutional mechanism to assess the relative legal personality, powers and functions of potentially a whole host of actors in addition to the state and international organisations. Accordingly, the international constitutional approach removes the state as the mono-dimensional holder of public powers. Through a theory of delegation, it argues that international competence is assigned at various layers, from the level of local government all the way up to the United Nations Security Council (UNSC), although it is clear that the state remains the principal holder of public powers, also in relation to the international realm. Hence, the international constitutional function of recognising relative competence and its extent on the part of particular actors is becoming increasingly complex.

Seen from this perspective, international constitutionalism is a project that identifies elements of public governance and investigates how such functions and powers are assigned and managed within the international system. We draw on the analogy of a constitution and use some relevant terms, but we do not proclaim that an international constitution as such exists. Instead, we look for the administration of international constitutional functions which we find necessary for a functioning legal system complying with the elements of good governance expected in all enlightened systems of governance.

Seen from this perspective, the state is just one layer of public authority. The international constitutional approach asks how the administration of public functions by a plurality of actors can be legitimised and controlled through law. And while it recognises this plurality, it still insists on retaining a special, particular identity for law – law to which essential constitutional principles including the demands of legitimacy, separation of powers and public authority subject to the rule of law, may well be applied. In this sense, principles of rule-of-law governance are attached to the exercise of public functions at whatever level they may be exercised.

When conceiving of an international constitutional framework, a number of elements become apparent:

- First, there is the issue of embeddedness. All international constituents accept that their legal identity is embedded in the overall, global constitutional system. States are born into this system, as are individuals and other internationally privileged actors. That means that their legal identity is not inherent or absolute. It is derived from a grant of authority transferred by individuals or groups to the corporate body involved. At the same time, such authority is delimited, and at times augmented, by the rules of the international system.
- The second issue concerns the unity of legal systems. The constituents of the constitutional system accept that their rights and interest will be safeguarded by the legal system, but do not trump the application of

the system. Universal legal rules of fundamental standing prevail over countervailing considerations, such as so-called vital national interests or appeals to the defunct concept of inherent state sovereignty. There is not necessarily a Kelsenian pyramid of legal authority. International law does not in itself constitute the state and establish a superior legal order. Rather, international law, in its most refined, substantive sense, reflects the principles and rules that must pervade all legal systems within the global order. There is a unity of legal systems.

- While the international legal order may not necessarily claim to be superior to national ones, given the two-way interaction of the domestic and the international – there are some issues of hierarchy. These concern fundamental values which orient the constitutional system, and which are accorded a superior status when translated into fundamental legal rules throughout the system. The concept of *jus cogens* and related categories ensure that such principles prevail.

- As was already noted, the international constitutional law approach in its formal sense considers the assignment of authority to particular actors or classes of actors in relation to the exercise of public powers. Given the profusion of actors, mechanisms for the validation of claims to competence need to be considered, also in relation to claims to the use of force.

- Formal constitutionalism also adds the principles of good and accountable governance in relation to the public powers assigned to the differing layers of public powers within the system.

- If all public authority is to be exercised in accordance with the substantial fundamental values and formal principles established for the legal system, then the individual constituents of the system, whether states, other corporate actors, groups or individuals, must be able to validate the application of the rule of law when public power is exercised in relation to them. Hence, there would need to be a mechanism to test the application of public powers, and the subjective claims to rights and obligations by constituents of the legal system according to law. In short, there would need to be a system offering judicial review or other remedies. This need not be a single court (a World Court, as it were), but this function can be distributed across the international constitutional system and exercised through a variety of means.

These general considerations apply to all aspects of governance in the international system, including the use of force. It will be convenient to consider each in turn, however briefly.

A   Constitutional Functions and the Use of Force

1   Embeddedness

The first requirement is a problematic one. Classically, the international system was very clearly seen to serve one ultimate aim: to facilitate the preservation of its exclusive constituents, the states. International law would have a role in managing their relations, but ultimately, self-preservation and the preservation of what was called vital national interests remained the overriding reserve put by states on the system.

As we already noted, the League of Nations somewhat shifted this balance. Rather than only proclaiming the sanctity of state interests, an important additional object of protection of the League was its own Covenant. A use of force was thus understood as an attack by one on the fundamental interest of all in the preservation of a functional system to maintain peace. The transfer of primary responsibility in relation to peace and security, and hence self-preservation, from individual states to the organs of the UN is made express in Articles 24 and 25 of the UN Charter. Critically, Article 51 on self-defence is placed within Chapter VII on collective security. Self-defence or self-preservation is part of collective security, rather than its antithesis; it applies provisionally until the UNSC has taken the measures necessary to preserve or restore international peace and security.

It is true, there have been some challenges to this interpretation of Article 51, arguing that the inherent right of self-defence still reflects the *ultima ratio* of the system – the survival of the state. We have the narrowest majority of the International Court of Justice (ICJ) to thank for a devastatingly unhelpful *codicil* to the Nuclear Weapons advisory opinion, which seems to suggest that in an extreme case of self-defence, the need to secure the preservation of the state might after all prevail over the highest order rules of international law.[7] But ultimately, it is difficult to dispute seriously at this point that the state is now so deeply embedded in the emerging constitutional order, and constrained by it, that the principle of the supremacy of the collective interest reflected in highest order rules cannot be seriously questioned.

---

[7] Legality of the Threat or Use of Nuclear Weapons, Advisory Opinion, 1996 ICJ para 105 (2) (E), adopted by seven votes to seven with the President's casting vote: 'However, in view of the current state of international law, and of the elements of fact at its disposal, the Court cannot conclude definitively whether the threat or use of nuclear weapons would be lawful or unlawful in an extreme circumstance of self-defence, in which the very survival of a State would be at stake.'

2   Unity of the Legal System and Specificity of Rules

International law claims that the legal rules on the use of force are recognised and accepted by the international community as a whole (as part of *jus cogens*). This is uncontested in principle. However, legal rules, including *jus cogens* rules, must be sufficiently specific and clear to fulfil their international constitutional function. True, *jus cogens* rules can contain what sometimes seem to resemble programmatic values elevated to the status of a substantive constitutional principle. However, rules that are not only programmatic, but also operational must be sufficiently specific when applied to particular circumstances. This applies with particular force where there is no dedicated central mechanism that offers an authoritative interpretation of such rules in all cases.

Clearly, there are significant disputes about the definition of the prohibition of the use of force. The dispute between Oxford and Cambridge (Brownlie vs Bowett) about the right reading of Article 51 noted above is perhaps a famous example. Proposals for additional exceptions to the prohibition of the use of force divide government and scholars alike, especially where humanitarian and pro-democratic intervention are concerned. And, we hear of new security challenges, demanding new answers, such as cyber wars, threats emanating from weapons of mass destruction and terrorism. But again, this debate has calmed down somewhat. Indeed, the General Assembly, in the Millennium plus Five Declaration, has quite clearly confirmed that the traditional rules on the use of force, and their established reading, is entirely sufficient to engage with these so-called new security challenges.

In fact, perhaps with the exception of the doctrine of humanitarian intervention, the concept of the prohibition of the use of force and of the right to self-defence can be taken to be relatively settled. Uncertainties arise in relation to factual claims made by states in support of their legal claims, or the abusive invocation of justificatory doctrines in this or that instance. However, this is a matter of authoritatively identifying the wrongful factual or legal argument at hand; it is not so much an issue of the indeterminacy of the legal rule in question. The vote in the UNSC of thirteen members to one – the Russian Federation – with one abstention in the case of the use of force concerning Ukraine confirms the ability to interpret and apply the relevant rules on the use of force in contested circumstances. What is lacking is the ability to enforce that finding in some instances.

3   Hierarchies

This issue of legal hierarchy in relation to the use of force can be addressed relatively easily. Clearly, the international system as it has evolved over the past thirty or so years has accepted the notion of high-order values enshrined in rules of international constitutional standing. The concepts of objective regime obligations *erga omnes*, *jus cogens*, serious violations of peremptory norms and individual criminal responsibility each offer a distinct legal effect, one adding to the other, with a view to retrenching universal values of the highest order within the legal system.

It is virtually uncontested that this extends to the prohibition of the use of force. Still, we need to note that this system has not always performed as these international constitutional concepts would suggest. Iraq in 2003 comes to mind, or more recently, Russian action in relation to Crimea and Eastern Ukraine. And yet, even in cases of violations that appear difficult to address and reverse, the fact that a violation occurred was manifest. In consequence, the transaction costs triggered by such conduct increased significantly.

4   Assignment of Authority

The next issue concerns the assignment of authority in relation to the use of force. This issue breaks down into three aspects: first, who is entitled to assign the authority to use force to particular actors in specific instances; second, how is the extent of the use of force that may be used determined; and third, how is the execution of the mandate granted in this way controlled or supervised?

a   Who Can Grant authority?   Let us turn first to the issue of assignment of authority to use force to particular actors in individual circumstances. Of course, it is axiomatic from theories of political organisation and the state that the establishment of a monopoly of force is a basic ingredient of any advanced social order. In relation to international law, the issue of the use of force is often presented as a touchstone when considering whether we can talk about a legal system at all.

States have renounced the use of force as a means of national policy and accepted the blanket prohibition of the use of force. They have formally transferred primary responsibility for international peace and security to the UNSC, and some have made additional provision in relation to regional organisations or arrangements. As was noted above, given the *erga omnes* nature of the prohibition of the use of force, its object of protection is in the first place itself, the rule and its credibility, as a key ingredient of an emerging international constitutional order. This is also confirmed by the rejection of conditions for the exercise of the right of collective self-defence, proposed, for instance, by Robert Jennings, that would require a pre-existing treaty of alliance, or an element of economic or other self-interest of the co-defending state. Such requirements are not consistent with the notion that the state concerned and its co-defenders are not only defending the victim state, but that the defence of the international legal order is at stake in cases of significant violation.

On the other hand, self-defence is still considered an inherent right that is not derived from a grant of authority. Its application is triggered by facts, rather than by an external decision. It applies if an armed attack occurs. If it does, the right is immediately available, without any process requirement, other than reporting to the UNSC. The Council can then exercise its process-based authority and suspend the right.

Other legal justifications for the use of force are process-based. They derive from a decision reached by a competent international organ, mainly the UNSC. The expansion of circumstances under which a forcible mandate can be granted by the Council, including counterterrorism, protection of civilians, offensive peacekeeping, forcible humanitarian or pro-democratic action, in addition to classical peace enforcement, has been generally accepted precisely because this practice is conditioned by the relevant process requirement.

Changes in the provisions of the Charter in this respect are under discussion – say the proposal to preclude the use of the veto in cases of genocide, or the argument that process-based authority may devolve from the UNSC to the UN General Assembly, or to regional organisations or agencies, under some circumstances. Some changes may have been endorsed through practice, concerning, for instance, the possible authorisation of regional humanitarian or pro-democratic action after the fact.

With respect to forcible humanitarian action and pro-democratic action carried out without a formal mandate from the UNSC, the principal disagreement concerns precisely the lack of a collective process that could control such action. Those favouring humanitarian or pro-democratic action have attempted to devise their own process criteria outside of the UNSC where the Council cannot act.

While the debate about forcible humanitarian action and pro-democratic action continues, a number of other challenges relating to the assignment of authority to authorise the use of force in the collective interest have been rejected. This includes, in particular, the US view about its claimed right to enforce unilaterally the disarmament obligations imposed upon Iraq by virtue of Resolution 678 (1991).

There are a number of other complex issues about the assignment of legal authority to use force. This applies both actively and passively. During the 1970s, the doctrine of national liberation movements generated a near consensus on the lawfulness of the use of force of pre-state actors in cases of struggle against classical colonialism and analogous cases. The claims of other non-state actors relating to the use of force have generally not been accepted – the label of terrorism being routinely applied to a wide variety of circumstances where non-state actors, or sometimes pre-state actors, seek to employ force.

Some argue that the advent of private security actors has added a new category of cases for consideration. However, this issue is best considered as one that is subsidiary to the right of the commissioning state, and remains an issue for inter-state regulation within the traditional framework of the rules on the use of force.

In the passive sense, new actors do seem to be capable of exposing themselves to the lawful international use of force, including terrorist actors, and non-state actors exercising control over territory, as confirmed by the UNSC.

In short, this is becoming an increasingly complex area, where the international system will need to adjust and refine its approaches, without the need to contemplate a radical review of our understanding of the use of force.

b   Determining the Extent of Force that Can Be Used   The amount of force that is permissible is regulated by customary international law and by process-based decision. In the case of self-defence, force is limited to what is strictly necessary to terminate an armed attack. The further customary law limitations on the exercise of the right to self-defence – including the principle of proportionality, necessity, compliance with humanitarian law etc. – also apply to collectively mandated uses of force. However, where force is used under mandates granted by collective agencies, the amount of force used can be graduated according to the view of what is strictly necessary of the authorising agency. This can go beyond terminating or reversing an armed attack. UN Security Council practice has at times been considered rather loose in this respect (Resolution 1973), although there has been a tendency to the more careful designation of what force may be used under what circumstances in the context of complex peacekeeping and enforcement missions.

c   Control over the Application of Force   In addition to the substantive rule, and process requirements attaching to its implementation, there is the issue of executive control. Obviously, we have departed from the highly centralised model foreseen in Chapter VII of the UN Charter in relation to all instances other than self-defence. Delegation of authority has taken place to a variety of actors of UN operations under UN command and control. These include regional organisations and arrangements, as foreseen in Chapter VIII of the Charter, but also unusual actors. These range from the legally unestablished Organisation for Security and Cooperation in Europe (OSCE) which is counted as a regional organisation or arrangement, to the North Atlantic Treaty Organisation (NATO), which is not, despite the fact that it has arrogated to itself collective security functions. It also includes the informal, so-called coalitions of the willing – a term that is often code for operations led by a global or regionally dominant power. The control requirement has been replaced by a reporting obligation in many such instances.

5   Accountability

The rule of law must apply throughout all aspects of international action if we are to speak of an emerging international constitutional system.

We have already noted that issues concerning the survival of the state, or vital national interests, are not beyond the law, but regulated by international law. There is no doubt that states at least feel compelled to justify any international use of force in terms of international law. It is more difficult to assess whether this also applies to international executive bodies, in particular the UNSC. The issue of hierarchy was famously displayed in the Lockerbie cases, and in the Bosnian Genocide debate relating to the continued application of Resolution 713. The correct and emerging view must surely be that any action concerning the use of force must be compliant with international law. The UNSC, itself based in a treaty, cannot be seen by virtue of Article 103 to have contracted out of *jus cogens* rules, which supervene a conflicting treaty provision.

In relation to states, the ICJ has made it clear on numerous occasions that any issue, however political, and however much it touches upon security interests of states, can be addressed as a matter of law. Indeed, it has pronounced itself in a number of important decisions on key aspects of the use for force, commencing with the *Corfu Channel* case and the Nicaragua litigation. The problem relates to the issue of comprehensive compulsory jurisdiction, as Serbia found, for instance, when seeking to challenge NATO's use of force.

6   Rule of Law Review

The absence of comprehensive compulsory jurisdiction is being cured in other areas of international law through an ever-denser network of dispute

settlement obligations arising from bilateral, regional and universal treaties, in relation to particular issue areas. However, this helpful trend is not
likely to impact on the issue of the use of force in anything but a marginal
way. Those seeking to assist the Ukraine in identifying *fora* to bring a case
relating to Crimea, for instance, will appreciate the difficulty. Increasing
subscription to the optional cause will not immediately resolve this issue, as
no great number of additional declarations is to be expected in the immediate future. Moreover, given the faculty of attaching reservations concerning national security, this mechanism does not always extend to cases
concerning the use of force. Still, the increasing litigation of use-of-force
cases in the ICJ is an interesting sign of the advancing legalisation even in
this area.

Finally, there is the question of judicial review in relation to the decisions or actions of executive agencies concerning the use of force. If there
is a move to monopolisation of the right to authorise force, good constitutional practice would require that this is balanced with the availability
of judicial review. This issue is at yet unresolved, given that the Lockerbie
case was not fully heard by the Court.

IV   Conclusion

International law is frequently criticised for its inability to end war as a
feature of international politics. It is of course clear that international law
can only reflect in its rules what the law-giver, traditionally the states, has
been willing to accept. It is also true that it cannot really be expected that
the threat of organised violence can be brought to an end altogether. In
that sense, we will, sadly, need to remain somewhat modest, as was the
case with Thomas More's Utopians.

What is at issue is the agreement that organised violence can only be
used in the common interest. The balancing between opposing values
through high-order norms on the use of force and its exceptions, and the
assignment of authority to determine when violence can be used in this
sense, are therefore crucial.

But perhaps surprisingly, the legal system on the use of force states that
states have been willing to accept, and have imposed upon themselves, is
principally utopian in character, both in terms of its substantive rules and
its process requirements. Indeed, around this central area of legal regulation, the international legal system has developed beyond Utopia, in ways
Sir Thomas More and his successors would have found difficult to imagine, or perhaps even to endorse.

Nevertheless, evidently we do not feel as if we are living in a paradise of perpetual peace. This however is not really an issue of legal process or substance. Instead, it is a civilisational mission that remains to be fulfilled – to transmit fully the sense of social de-legitimisation of war as a means of national policy that was begun nearly a hundred years ago, and was made manifest in the Kellogg-Briand Pact. In addition, the debate about war as a means of international policy has only just begun – a debate that will gain further in relevance once the utopia of standards and process we already have becomes fully effective.

6

Variable Geometry in the WTO

BERNARD M. HOEKMAN AND PETROS C. MAVROIDIS

I   The Issue

The agreements signed by Korea with the European Union (EU) and the United States, the ongoing Trans-Pacific Partnership (TPP) negotiations, and the launch of talks on a Transatlantic Trade and Investment Partnership (TTIP) agreement between the United States and the EU are evidence that trade dominates international relations. Not in the World Trade Organization (WTO)-level though, where the Doha round remains moribund.

Preferential Trade Agreements (PTAs) are resulting in increasing fragmentation of the rules of the game for businesses engaged in international trade, since the content of PTAs is idiosyncratic and they generate substantial information costs for traders. They are not the only game in town when it comes to negotiating deals within 'clubs'. The WTO offers another mechanism for Members to form 'clubs' that allow them to move forward on an agenda of common interest: conclusion of a Plurilateral Agreement (PA) under Article II.3 of the Agreement Establishing the WTO (the WTO Agreement). This provision permits subsets of the WTO Membership to agree to certain disciplines applying to signatories only. In contrast to a PTA, which must cover substantially all trade in goods,[1] and/or have substantial sectoral coverage of services,[2] PAs can be issue-specific.

In fact, PAs are not a novelty in international trade relations. They were quite prevalent under the pre-WTO General Agreement on Tariffs and Trade (GATT) regime, although different terminology was used to denote essentially the same function. In the Kennedy (1964–7) and Tokyo (1973–9) Rounds, a number of PAs (at the time called 'codes of conduct', or simply

---

[1] Article XXIV, General Agreement on Tariffs and Trade (GATT), 1994.
[2] Article V, General Agreement on Trade in Services, 1995.

'codes') were negotiated and bound only their signatories.[3] Examples include agreements on antidumping, technical barriers to trade (product standards), subsidies and countervailing measures, import licensing and customs valuation. Most of these agreements only attracted limited membership. During the Uruguay Round, as part of the move to create the WTO, virtually all of the GATT Codes were transformed into multilateral agreements that apply to all WTO Members.

The decision for a single undertaking was taken during the Uruguay round because the prevailing feeling was that the system was becoming unmanageable because different GATT members had assumed different obligations. Harmonisation of obligations assumed, it was felt, was necessary. Only two PAs were concluded during the Uruguay round, not as concession to single undertaking, but simply because the overwhelming majority of trading nations was unwilling to adhere to their disciplines, namely, the Agreement on Government Procurement (GPA), and the Agreement on Civil Aircraft.[4]

Two PAs only, against the hundreds of extant PTAs, raises the question why there is so little use of PAs.[5] In this chapter we assess the arguments for and against a more concerted effort to use (and accept the use of) PAs. The extant literature on PAs largely ignores the PTA dimension and centres on PAs vs the Single Undertaking/Most Favoured Nation (MFN) agreements, including so-called critical-mass agreements, under which commitments are negotiated among a set of countries that have the greatest stake/interest in an issue, with the benefits of whatever is agreed extended to all WTO Members, whether they join or not. The latter are often colloquially referred to as 'plurilateral agreements' but we shall reserve this term for WTO Annex 4 agreements, which may be applied on a discriminatory basis to signatories only.[6] We compare the statutory provisions regarding

---

[3] R. Stern and B. M. Hoekman, 'The Codes Approach' in J. M. Finger and A. Olechowski (eds.), *The Uruguay Round: A Handbook for the Multilateral Trade Negotiations* (World Bank, 1987).

[4] There were initially four PAs: the GPA, agreements on dairy products and on beef and the Agreement on Civil Aircraft. The beef and dairy agreements were terminated in 1997.

[5] Accommodating diversity in interests through greater use of critical-mass agreements that apply on a MFN basis was one of the recommendations of the Warwick Commission, *The Multilateral Trade Regime: Which Way Forward?* (University of Warwick, 2007) and has been advocated by a number of analysts – e.g., R. Z. Lawrence, 'Rulemaking Amidst Growing Diversity: A "Club of Clubs" Approach to WTO Reform and New Issue Selection' 9(4) *JIEL* (2006) 823.

[6] Critical mass has been a feature of both GATT-era and WTO negotiations with the aim of reducing free-riding to a minimum acceptable level. An example of a critical-mass agreement that was negotiated after the Uruguay Round was concluded is the International

the quintessential elements of PTAs and PAs viewed from the perspective of a multilateralist: the manner in which the multilateral regime prejudges (if at all) their substantive content; the conditions for membership and accession by new members; and institutional aspects such as transparency and dispute settlement procedures.

II   The Law

Despite the strong push towards multilateralisation of the Codes, four Tokyo Round codes were excluded from the single undertaking: the Agreement on Civil Aircraft, the International Dairy Agreement, the International Bovine Meat Agreement and the GPA. Article II.3 of the WTO Agreement explains that PAs do not create rights and/or obligations for non-signatories. Article X.9 of the WTO Agreement states that the Ministerial Conference of the WTO may decide to add an agreement to the existing set of PAs listed in Annex 4 'exclusively by consensus'. Existing agreements may be terminated if signatory WTO Members deem this appropriate, provided that they respect the statutory conditions to this effect. Termination did occur with respect to the dairy and bovine meat agreements: both were terminated by decisions of the General Council on 31 December 1997 and 17 December 1997 respectively. The Agreement on Civil Aircraft is still in force, but its disciplines on subsidies have been superseded by the WTO Agreement on Subsidies and Countervailing Measures and the GPA, which includes rules on public purchases of civil aircraft.[7] As a result its added value is limited to tariff treatment of aircraft.

Technology Agreement (ITA). Other critical-mass agreements include the Agreement on Basic Telecommunications and the Agreement on Financial Services, both concluded in the years immediately following the Uruguay Round. There have also been numerous sector-specific 'zero-for-zero' tariff agreements that were conditioned on the existence of a critical mass of participants (G. Hufbauer and J. Schott, 'Will the World Trade Organization Enjoy a Bright Future?', Petersen Institute for International Economics, Policy Brief 12-11 (2012)). See Bernard M. Hoekman and Michel M. Kostecki, *The Political Economy of the World Trading System* (Oxford University Press, 2009) for further discussion.

[7] The genesis of this PA was an effort by the EU and the United States to agree on more specific rules of the game in this area than prevailed in the pre-WTO years. The primary added value of the Civil Aircraft Agreement is the commitment by the thirty-one signatories to eliminate import duties on a specific list of products, including all non-military aircraft, civil aircraft engines, parts and components, all components and sub-assemblies of civil aircraft, and flight simulators and their parts and components. This applies on a MFN basis because the products involved are subject to the GATT. With regard to its market access dimension this PA is therefore an example of a critical-mass agreement.

A   Assessing the Impact of PAs and PTAs on WTO

Four aspects of PTAs and PAs are particularly relevant in assessing their impact on the trading system:

(a) coverage
(b) accession
(c) transparency
(d) dispute settlement.

We will take each one of them in turn.

1   Coverage

We start with PTAs. Article XXIV GATT, which deals with trade in goods, allows for free trade areas and customs unions if trade barriers after formation of the PTA do not rise on average;[8] all tariffs and other regulations of commerce are removed on substantially all trade within a reasonable length of time;[9] and they have been notified to the WTO Council.[10] Article V GATS imposes three conditions on economic integration agreements in the area of services: they must have 'substantial sectoral coverage', in terms of the number of sectors, volume of trade affected, and modes of supply; they must provide for the absence or elimination of substantially all measures violating national treatment in sectors where specific commitments were made in the GATS; and they may not result in higher trade barriers against third countries. The substantial sectoral coverage requirement is arguably weaker than the 'substantially all trade' criterion of Article XXIV.[11]

The determination of whether PTAs satisfy Article XXIV and/or Article V can be done only by WTO Panels following the advent of the Transparency Mechanism (2006), which limits multilateral review of notified PTAs to a mere transparency-exercise.

---

[8] Article XXIV: 5, GATT.
[9] Article XXIV: 8, GATT.
[10] Developing countries are not bound by Article XXIV as a result of the 1979 Decision on Differential and More Favorable Treatment of Developing Countries (the so-called Enabling Clause). This essentially removes the 'substantially all trade' test and allows for preferences between developing country PTA members (that is, the full removal of internal barriers – free trade – is not required).
[11] We say 'arguably' since this term has never been interpreted by the Committee on Regional Trade Agreements (CRTA, in charge of overseeing consistency of free trade areas and customs unions with the WTO) or by dispute adjudication Panels.

Horn et al. review the subject matter signed by the two main hubs (European Union and the United States) between 1992 and 2008 and identify over fifty areas subject to provisions in one or more PTAs, ranging from anti-corruption policies and macro-economic cooperation to environmental protection and antitrust policies.[12] The situation is similar for PTAs covering trade and investment in services. Many of the more recent vintage PTAs cover substantially more services and services policies than does the GATS.[13] These studies demonstrate that the content of more recent PTAs concerns in large part the treatment of regulatory measures. One explanation is that disciplines on NTBs (nontariff barriers) that go beyond non-discrimination are easier to contract across like-minded partners. Indeed, siding with Costinot, non-discrimination is an insurance policy for countries with a high level of domestic regulation as it ensured that products that do not meet their regulatory standards will be denied market access.[14] When negotiating a PTA, trading nations can 'select' their partners, and thus move towards 'deeper' integration without needing to worry about an erosion of domestic standards.

The WTO does not prejudge the content of PAs. The beef and dairy agreements were examples of narrow, product-specific arrangements; the GPA is an example of a PA that addresses a policy area that has wider coverage (purchases of goods and services by governments, a market that can represent 5 to 10 per cent of GDP). In principle, nothing in the legal statutes prohibits WTO Members from negotiating a PA that would consist of tariff reductions in one tariff line.[15] But could such types of agreements be accepted as being in the spirit of the overall economy of the Agreement? Clearly, we should not introduce through the window what we wanted to avoid coming in through the door. One would therefore expect that PAs focus on disciplining domestic instruments (non-tariff measures), as has been the case in the GPA, to date the only meaningful PA.

While Article X.9 of the WTO Agreement allows for WTO Members to agree to add new PAs (by consensus), this provision leaves open the question whether the consensus concerns a negotiated document or

---

[12] H. Horn et al., 'Beyond the WTO: An Anatomy of the EU and US Preferential Trade Agreements' (2010) 33 *The World Economy* 1565–88.

[13] M. Roy et al., 'Services Liberalization in the New Generation of Preferential Trade Agreements: How Much Further than the GATS?' (2007) 6(2) *World Trade Review* 1455–93.

[14] A. Costinot, 'A Comparative Institutional Analysis of Agreements on Product Standards' (2008) 75(1) *Journal of International Economics* 197–213.

[15] Subject of course to the PA being accepted by the WTO membership as a new Annex 4 agreement.

acceptance by the membership of a subset of Members seeking to negotiate a PA on a given subject. A careful reading of Article X.9 suggests that approval or rejection will be on the basis of the text that the interested countries (participating in the PA) have negotiated. There is a difference in this regard between the treatment of existing PAs and new ones. Of the four PAs that were included in Annex 4 of the WTO Agreement only one was subsequently modified: the GPA. The new GPA[16] entered into force in April 2014. Nonetheless, the final text of the new amended agreement was not approved by the WTO Membership. It sufficed that the Membership had approved the procedures for amending the original agreement.

Because of the consensus rule, any WTO Member can say no when the final text of a proposed PA is presented to them. Thus, plurilateral agreements are Pareto-sanctioned, since non-participants take the view that the agreement does not hurt them, whereas participants obviously take the view that the new agreement helps them achieve their goals. No one is worse off, and some are better off.

2   Accession

Article XXIV.5 GATT suggests that PTAs can be signed only between WTO Members: to the extent that a WTO Member grants an advantage to a non-WTO Member by signing a PTA, it would have to, by virtue of Article I GATT, automatically and unconditionally extend it to all WTO Members. Yet, practice has developed in a different way.[17] WTO Members, irrespective whether they enjoy developed- or developing-country status, notify the CRTA and/or the Committee on Trade and Development (CTD) of their PTAs, including those involving non-WTO Members.[18]

The WTO is silent regarding the conditions of subsequent accessions to a PTA. There is no right to accede to a PTA even if aspiring members are willing to match (or exceed) the liberalisation effort of the incumbents:

---

[16] WTO Doc. GPA/W/297 of 11 December 2006.
[17] Practice has arguably evolved in a way that violates the letter of WTO law as WTO Members that sign PTAs with non-WTO Members do not have to automatically and unconditionally extend benefits to all other WTO Members (assuming of course that they satisfy the statutory conditions for establishing a PTA).
[18] If one of the members of the PTA is a developed country, the PTA will be notified to CRTA, whereas if they are both developing countries, it will go to the CTD. EC–CARIFORUM is an example of the former (Bahamas is part of the agreement, but not a WTO Member), and Ukraine–Uzbekistan is an example of the latter. The Common Market of South America (MERCOSUR) involves developing countries only and yet, probably because of the size of the Brazilian market it had to be notified to both committees.

accession depends solely on the incumbents. As a result, PTAs are, in principle, closed clubs.[19]

The WTO does not provide for a minimum number of WTO Members that must agree to participate for a PA to be launched. The same is true for accession – there are no general provisions in the WTO defining criteria for accession to a PA. The terms for accession to the Annex 4 Agreements included at the end of the Uruguay Round are spelled out in each PA separately.[20] The terms of accession to a plurilateral agreement are determined by the contractual arrangement between incumbents and the new kid on the block.[21] Practice does not shed any additional light on this. Armenia and Chinese Taipei acceded to the GPA in 2011 and 2009, respectively, but it is difficult to compare the terms and conditions under which they joined with those of the incumbents.

3   Transparency

Countries intending to form, join or modify a PTA must notify this to the WTO and make available relevant information requested by WTO Members. Notified PTAs are considered on the basis of a factual presentation by the WTO Secretariat, to be concluded within one year of notification. WTO Members may ask questions or make comments concerning factual presentations of PTAs. The transparency mechanism for PTAs may help move the balance of assessments of PTAs back towards what was intended by the drafters of the GATT – *ex ante* review and engagement by the collective Membership on the design of a PTA, as opposed to what gradually emerged over time: ineffectual *ex post* assessments. However, the track record to date suggests that multilateral scrutiny is not an effective source of discipline on PTAs. The transparency mechanism does not have any teeth, and it was clear from the deliberations that preceded the creation of the mechanism that many WTO Members do not intend to use it as a means of exerting greater pressure on countries to abide by the rules. The fact that the process involves a 'consideration' of a PTA as opposed to an 'examination' is revealing in this regard.

The problem of under-supply of information is, course, not PTA-specific. It has been formally acknowledged by the WTO, which is taking

[19] E.g. Bhagwati and Panagariya (1999). Many PTAs are closed shops in that they do not have accession provisions, or, if they do, membership is limited to countries from a given geographic area.

[20] Article XII.3 WTO.

[21] Note that only WTO Members can accede to a PA whereas, as noted, WTO Members have concluded PTAs with non-WTO Members.

the first, very shy steps to fix it.[22] We doubt the announced changes will be meaningful. The heart of the issue is that those retaining private information will be unwilling to disseminate it for fear of providing self-incriminating facts. Why do it then? This is precisely why the EU regime, when dealing with similar instances, has empowered the common agent (the Commission) to go out and dig information that its holders might have no incentive to share. This makes perfect sense of course but, as we have argued elsewhere,[23] moving to a centralised regime presupposes a number of prerequisites that are simply not present at the WTO. For starters, the political will to empower the common agent must be present, and in a repeat interaction game (like the EU) one could argue that the incentive to act opportunistically is reduced. Practice shows this is not the case at the WTO, alas. The recent modifications, to which we referred above, are proof that, if at all, one should realistically expect cosmetic-only changes at the WTO-level. In a classic Bayesian framework where past performance is an indicator for future behaviour, one would be well-advised to downgrade hopes for meaningful change in this respect, the intellectual appeal of the EU model notwithstanding.

For PAs, transparency is ensured through the process of notification to the General Council and the need for the Council to approve any PA that is brought forward. As decisions to accept a PA are taken on the basis of consensus, all WTO Members having the opportunity to scrutinise the terms of a PA. If approved, a PA will be associated with the establishment of the types of WTO body that assist Members in the implementation of agreements, such as a Committee, with regular (annual) reporting on activities to the Council, and documentation that is open to all WTO Members. As noted above, the approval process has important legal repercussions: whereas challenges against PTAs are possible, challenges against approved PAs are legally impossible.

4 Dispute Settlement

It is possible that the same dispute is raised both in the PTA forum and before the WTO. In one WTO dispute so far, Argentina – Poultry Antidumping Duties, Argentina argued that Brazil was precluded from submitting the dispute to a WTO Panel since the very same dispute had already been adjudicated by a Common Market of South America (MERCOSUR) Panel. The WTO Panel dismissed Argentina's argument

---

[22] www.wto.org/english/news_e/news16_e/tpr_21dec16_e.htm.
[23] P. C. Mavroidis, *The Regulation of International Trade*, 2 vols. (MIT Press, 2015), II, 673–8.

because, inter alia, in its view Article 3.2 of the Dispute Settlement Understanding (DSU) did not require Panels to rule in any particular way and thus need not conform to decisions by other adjudicating fora. Some PTAs require disputes to be addressed through PTA-specific mechanisms. Thus, the North American Free Trade Agreement (NAFTA) provides that, for certain kinds of dispute (e.g. environmental disputes) that in principle could be subject to both NAFTA and WTO proceedings, the complainant is required to use NAFTA facilities exclusively.

Koremenos shows that roughly half of all existing PTAs contain dispute settlement rules. While many are quite inactive in settling disputes, in the future countries may find it more useful/appropriate to submit disputes to a PTA forum.[24] As the coverage of PTAs extends further beyond the WTO, this becomes more likely, as the DSU will not be applicable. There is, therefore, a strong likelihood of fragmentation in case law and interpretation of provisions, as well as less transparency than would arise if all disputes were addressed through a common dispute settlement mechanism.

Disputes under the GPA must be submitted to WTO Panels (and eventually the Appellate Body). This is beneficial for the development of the legal regime of the world trading system as judges can ensure consistency with other WTO case law in interpreting the meaning of the agreed contractual arrangement. Assigning the competence to adjudicate disputes coming under the purview of a PA to bodies other than WTO Panels would result in less legal certainty and diverging case law.

B   Overlap and Differences

Our discussion of the legal regime above reveals that there are similarities but also differences between PTAs and PAs from a systemic perspective. One important commonality is that both can be non-MFN. Both PTAs and PAs will be negotiated because there might be concerns about free-riding, and it is feasible (legal) to exclude non-parties. If exclusion is not possible, a critical-mass approach will need to be pursued, with the outcome applied on an MFN basis (such as the ITA or sector-specific tariff elimination agreements). PTAs and PAs are likely to involve discrimination and can give rise to trade diversion.[25]

---

[24] B. Koremenos, 'If Only Half of International Agreements Have Dispute Resolution Provisions, Which Half Needs Explaining?' (2007) 36 *Journal of Legal Studies* 189–221.

[25] As has long been noted in the literature on PTAs, diversion effects often will be a political precondition (driver) for a PTA. See G. Grossman and E. Helpman, 'The Politics of Free Trade Agreements' (1995) 85(4) *American Economic Review* 667–90 for a formal analysis.

This is not where commonalities end. Both instruments involve binding commitments that are enforceable. Why bother reviewing a PA or PTA that contains only best-endeavours provisions?

PAs differ from PTAs in many respects and it is important to recognise that the two mechanisms are by no means perfect substitutes, although they could, assuming certain contingencies, be alternative instruments to achieve the same goal. PTAs will often have as a major objective the integration of the markets of the participating countries on an explicitly discriminatory basis – something that is recognised and accepted by all WTO Members. This is not something that PAs are an appropriate vehicle for, since the potential for subsequent accessions is explicitly acknowledged.[26] PAs ensure greater transparency, a much closer 'connection' with day-to-day WTO activities and processes, and greater coherence when it comes to case law/dispute settlement. PAs also differ from PTAs in that the former have been, and most likely will be, (much) narrower in scope. PAs may deal with issues that are already subject to WTO disciplines or which cover matters that are not covered by the WTO. The GPA stayed a PA after the Uruguay Round because procurement is explicitly excluded from the reach of Article III GATT (national treatment) and the GATS[27] – although in contrast to the GATT, the GATS calls for negotiations on procurement of services to be launched two years after the entry into force of the agreement (i.e. 1997).[28] The GPA precedent suggests that one rationale or function of PAs could be as an instrument to allow WTO Members to deal with issues that are not (yet) covered by the WTO – any disciplines that are agreed among a subset of countries will not undercut existing commitments as there are none. This is not the case for PAs dealing with subjects that are already covered by the WTO. An example is the recent suggestion by some countries to negotiate PAs on services or on trade facilitation. In such instances a PA may undercut the MFN rule insofar as signatories apply commitments on a discriminatory basis. While this is detrimental to non-signatories, the alternative to a PA may be a PTA. Recall that a PA

---

[26] As noted previously each PA defines the applicable accession modalities and procedures; there is no explicit requirement in the WTO that states that that PAs be open to any WTO Member. Article XII.3 WTO simply states that 'Accession to a Plurilateral Trade Agreement shall be governed by the provisions of that Agreement.'

[27] Article XIII.1 GATS.

[28] Such talks have been taking place in the Working Party on GATS Rules since 1995 but no progress has been made on the subject – leaving the GPA as the only mechanism in the WTO dealing with procurement of services (as well as goods).

will have systemic benefits that a PTA does not – including greater transparency and inclusiveness (the prospect of eventual accession if countries decide to join at a future date).

III   The Pros and Cons of PAs

So far, we have painted a rather rosy picture for PAs, and one might wonder whether there are no disadvantages at all when this option is being pursued. Institutional players have made some waves, and literature has identified additional risks.[29] We take each argument in turn.

A   Opening Up to Controversial Issues

India in WTO discussions, and Sutherland et al., have argued that PAs might open the door to agreements among subsets of countries on controversial issues such as labour or environmental standards.[30] Existing WTO disciplines, as explained above, provide assurances that efforts to incorporate new PAs on controversial issues or that result in erosion of MFN can be blocked. The high threshold for approval of any new PA guarantees that WTO Members have the ability to block PAs that are deemed to be against the interests of non-signatories.

B   Erosion of MFN

Greater use of PAs will result in a multi-tier system with differentiated commitments and thus some erosion of the MFN principle – as club members would have the right to restrict benefits to other members. If PAs address areas not covered by the current WTO mandate, erosion of MFN is not an issue, although there will be a 'precedent-setting effect'. If PAs deal with matters covered by the WTO and entail preferential improvements in market access commitments, then the MFN principle will unavoidably be eroded. MFN will become conditional; that is, only those making the commitments will profit from it.

---

[29] See e.g. R. Wolfe, 'The WTO Single Undertaking as Negotiating Technique and Constitutive Metaphor' (2009) 12(4) *JIEL* 835–58 for discussion of the objections that can be raised against PAs.

[30] P. Sutherland et al., *The Future of the WTO: Addressing Institutional Challenges in the New Millennium (Consultative Board to the Director-General)* (WTO, 2004).

C A Two-Tier WTO

Wolfe notes that any PA will invariably include Organisation of Economic Cooperation and Development (OECD) member countries that may already have achieved much of whatever level of cooperation-cum-discipline that is agreed for an issue, and that many non-OECD countries are not going to have the capacity to participate in negotiations that will set a precedent.[31] Clubs will define the rules of the game in an area that will be difficult to change subsequently if and when initial non-signatories decide to participate. Experience illustrates that it is very difficult to amend (renegotiate) disciplines, so that a plurilateral approach may well become analogous to the *acquis communautaire* for prospective members of the EU; that is, non-negotiable. There may be a first mover's advantage that should not be under-estimated.[32]

This may be true, but the presumption that OECD countries will dominate PAs may not necessarily be correct. PAs also offer a mechanism that a broad set of WTO Members could use to move forward in an area where one of the large WTO members is not willing or able to participate. A PA that centres on operationalising 100 per cent duty-free, quota-free access for Least Developed Countries (LDCs) is a potential example – something that is currently not feasible for the United States to agree, but that has already been implemented by many other countries and where greater cooperation on issues like rules of origin among these countries could enhance the benefits for LDCs.

A PA approach may still result in a long-term bifurcation in the WTO Membership, splitting 'insiders' from 'outsiders'. This was the pattern that emerged in the GATT years, with very few countries subsequently joining the Tokyo Round codes after their initial negotiation. Many developing countries have argued that this is contrary to the basic character of the WTO and conflicts with the consensus-based approach that has historically been the norm.[33]

Much will depend on the substantive content of a PA and the intent of those countries that agree to negotiate a PA. Given the great heterogeneity in levels of development, social preferences, endowments and so forth that

[31] Wolfe, 'The WTO Single Undertaking as Negotiating Technique and Constitutive Metaphor' (above n. 29).
[32] This has been emphasised by the NGO community.
[33] 'Singapore Issues: The Way Forward', Joint Communication from Bangladesh, Botswana, China, Cuba, Egypt, India, Indonesia, Kenya, Malaysia, Nigeria, Philippines, Tanzania, Uganda, Venezuela, Zambia and Zimbabwe,' WTO document WT/GC/W/522, 12 December 2003.

prevails in the WTO, it is inevitable that a PA might address issues that are not seen to be priorities for some (many) WTO Members. This is arguably a good reason to have the PA option in the first place, as it allows countries to cooperate on a given policy area. But there is also the possibility that a group of countries may seek to negotiate a PA with the strategic objective of excluding others. Reports suggest that in the case of the TISA talks on services some of the participants do not want to include countries that they deem to be opposed to pursuing further liberalisation of services markets. If the club members end up agreeing to disciplines that are unacceptable to countries that are not part of the negotiations/agreement (e.g. by including provisions that greatly circumscribe the scope for state-owned enterprises to operate in specific sectors) the question then is whether a PA would be worse from a global-welfare/multilateral-system perspective than if these countries concluded a PTA. A world in which there are many PTAs that deal differently with a specific subject area could well be worse for global welfare (efficiency) than one in which the issue is addressed through a PA.[34] Of course, much depends here on the counterfactual – whether an issue is addressed in PTAs, and the weight that is accorded by the WTO Membership to maintaining a WTO that does not allow for additional distinctions across its Membership even if this generates less in the way of overall welfare gains (irrespective of their distribution).

D   Many Pay, Few Profit

PAs will impose additional costs on the rest of the WTO Membership by utilising the WTO 'infrastructure' – including operation of a Committee, making use of the WTO facilities, potential invocation of the DSU, calling on the Secretariat for support etc. The fact that the operation of a PA is centred in the WTO as opposed to occurring outside it is a positive feature but this does come with additional direct costs, as well as potential opportunity costs given limited Secretariat resources. There is a straightforward solution to this problem: signatories can be required to provide additional contributions to the WTO in order to cover the cost of implementing and administering PAs. They would need to incur these costs in any event if the PTA route is chosen instead, assuming that is feasible, or through another form of cooperation if it is not (e.g. if the issue involves regulatory

---

[34] This need not be the case as differences in preferences and circumstances may imply that it is more efficient for sets of countries to adopt different rules of the game (i.e. 'one size fits all' is not the first best solution).

cooperation). This might be particularly important since PAs could extend to areas on which there is no embedded expertise in the WTO Secretariat. Assuming unwillingness to outsource the servicing of the PAs, the WTO will need to be provided with additional expertise in the areas covered.

E   Reducing Issue Linkage

Moving down the PA track may imply that countries give up negotiating chips that could be used to obtain concessions in other areas in a multilateral negotiation. The fundamental premise underlying the Single Undertaking is that it permits issue linkage: country A can get something it wants by giving up something that country B wants and the trade may involve subjects that have nothing to do with each other. If PAs are negotiated for specific issues, the scope for such linkage may decline. Much depends here on the subject matter of a potential PA, and the ensuing contracting costs.[35] If it does not offer much in the way of negotiating leverage for the countries that are involved (i.e. nobody is inclined to 'pay' much if anything for a deal) the 'linkage downside' will be small. The absence of linkage potential might, under some circumstances, act as an incentive to join the PA in the first place if it reduces the opportunity cost of participation. There is of course no presumption that this will be the case, but the countries concerned will always have the option of not participating in the PA.

On the other hand, absence of linkage might prove a blessing in disguise. In Hoekman and Mavroidis (1994),[36] we criticised arguments for linking disciplines on competition law to tariff or other market access concessions. We feared that issues of paramount importance for the functioning of internal markets could be treated in a haphazard manner in the name of satisfaction of exporters' requests. Negotiators, by narrowing down the scope of their exercise to one negotiating objective, will strive, other things equal, towards addressing the substantive issues that arise in that area.

---

[35] Given uncertainty regarding the overall size of the 'cake' that is defined by an agreement that spans many issue areas, and the costs associated with negotiations, including the opportunity costs of delay, there may be good reasons for governments to pursue separate agreements as opposed to big-bang package deals where everything is conditional on everything else.

[36] B. M. Hoekman and P. C. Mavroidis, 'Competition, Competition Policy and the GATT' (1994) 17(2) *The World Economy* 121–50.

IV   Go for It: PAs, Variable Geometry and the WTO

A   Europeans Show the Way

Even the EU, a regime with arguably substantially greater homogeneity, allows for the establishment of PAs across a subset of its membership, the most notorious being the European Monetary Union (EMU). Besides the EMU, enhanced cooperation agreements (ECA) are possible for a subset of the EU Membership (Article 20 of the Treaty on European Union (TEU)). Although so far practice is scarce, many believe that in the future this could be an instrument that could propel further European integration.[37] As Bordignon and Brusco observe, 'heterogeneity among EU members has become so large that it is difficult to find common policies beneficial to all countries'.[38] They show that, when centralisation is not politically feasible, sub-union formation could be optimal if it takes into account the utility of excluded countries. If this is true for the EU, it is it even more so for the WTO. There are some features of the EU ECA-regime that, if adopted in the WTO, would strengthen the case for PAs:[39]

- Article 20 TEU makes clear that ECA should aim to 'further the objectives of the Union, protect its interests and reinforce the integration process'.
- Article 326.1 of the Treaty on the Functioning of the European Union (TFEU) underscores that ECAs shall not 'constitute a barrier to or discrimination in trade between Member States, nor shall it distort competition between them'.
- Article 329 TFEU suggests that at least nine out of twenty-seven EU Member States must propose an ECA.
- Article 328 TFEU explicitly states that ECAs should be open to all Member States that can demonstrate that they have met the requirements embedded in the authorising (ECA) decision.[40]

---

[37] R. Baldwin et al., 'Nice Try: Should the Treaty of Nice be Ratified?' (CEPR, 2001); B. Harstad, 'Flexible Integration? Mandatory and Minimum Participation Rules' (2006) 108(4) Scandinavian Journal of Economics 683–702.

[38] M. Bordignon and S. Brusco, 'On Enhanced Cooperation' (2006) 90 Journal of Public Economics 2063–90.

[39] Carlo M. Cantore, 'We're One but We're Not the Same' (2011) 3(3) Perspectives on Federalism 1–21 provides an excellent overview of the EU regime.

[40] Cantore, ibid., notes there are features of the ECAs that cannot find application in the WTO regime. For example, the 'no veto – no exclusion' regime is administered centrally by the European Commission. This is not – and will not be – the case in the current WTO regime.

Providing for a quorum, ensuring that PAs will be in line with the objectives of the WTO and agreeing *ex ante* to submit to arbitration/dispute adjudication disagreements as to whether accession requirements have been met could usefully be implemented in the current WTO legislative framework. What is needed are clear *ex ante* rules on PAs that ensure that such agreements are not vehicles for some countries to escape their general or specific WTO obligations and that the interests of small/poor countries are protected.

B   A Vehicle to Integrate those Left Behind

Lawrence discusses a number of criteria that would help ensure that what he calls the club-of-clubs option is facilitated while safeguarding the interests of those that are not interested in participating.[41] He suggests that PAs be restricted to subjects that are clearly trade-related; that any new PA be open to all WTO Members in the negotiation stage (i.e. participation in the development of rules should not be limited to likely signatories); and that PA members be required to use the DSU to settle disputes, with eventual retaliation being restricted to the area covered by the agreement (as is the case under the GPA).

It would be desirable to agree explicitly that 'open access' be a precondition for approval of any PA. Criteria to ensure that this is the case might be considered as well, such as prohibiting incumbents from ratcheting up the entry price for latecomers and making this enforceable through binding arbitration if contested.

LDCs are likely to be among the least able to engage in PA talks that focus on regulatory issues or matters that are not covered by the WTO. Whatever the subject of a PA, consideration could be given to extending whatever is negotiated amongst a club of WTO Members to all LDCs on a non-reciprocal basis. This would help reduce the extent of any discrimination, be one way to give meaning to the LDC waiver and ensure that PAs have a development dimension. Of course, the value of such action will depend on the capacity of the LDCs to benefit from (make use of) whatever is agreed among the PA members. In practice, even if a PA opens up market access opportunities for signatories, LDCs may not have the capacity to benefit, especially if a precondition is satisfying specific minimum standards. This suggests that to be effective any PA should include an aid-for-trade component – mechanisms to assist the LDCs improve

---

[41] Lawrence, 'Rulemaking Amidst Growing Diversity' (above n. 5).

their standards, regulation etc. to the level that is required to benefit from the PA. Such mechanisms will need to be tailored to address whatever the associated capacity-building needs are. One possibility would be to develop PA-specific 'platforms' that help LDCs, as well as other developing countries with an interest in acceding to the PA, to undertake diagnostic analysis, identify action plans and implement needed reforms with funding and assistance from high-income PA signatories. Including an operational aid-for-trade dimension in PAs could enhance the relevance of PAs for LDCs and other low-income countries and give them a development dimension.[42]

C   Hothouse for Regulatory Cooperation

Should a distinction should be drawn between matters that are already subject to WTO disciplines (i.e. the PA would be WTO+) as opposed to matters that are not (yet) subject to multilateral rules (i.e. it is WTO-X)?[43] If an issue area is already subject to the WTO, any PA will by definition result in greater fragmentation of applicable rules, whether the focus of the PA is on disciplines for certain policies and/or involves signatories granting discriminatory access to each other. If the PA is WTO-X, it may be precedent-setting but there is no issue of fragmentation or undercutting MFN as this rule does not apply. Given that an agreement on a WTO-X subject will need to be accepted by the WTO Membership there is no compelling reason why there would need to be restrictions on the types of WTO-X issues that might be addressed in a PA, beyond that they are 'trade-related'.

What about WTO+ PAs? Here a distinction can be made between WTO+ agreements that involve discriminatory market-access concessions and PAs that involve regulatory commitments and cooperation. The former are more likely to be problematical from a trading system perspective for reasons discussed previously (they imply targeted, narrow discrimination of the type that the rules on PTAs were intended to prevent).

---

[42] Given that PTAs may be used by countries as a substitute for non-reciprocal GSP-type programmes, PAs could also be conceived to be designed to advance specific development goals. For example, a PA might aim to promote technical expertise at the micro-level in dealing with conformity assessment; customs cooperation etc.

[43] Horn et al. in 'Beyond the WTO' (above n. 12) distinguish between WTO+ and WTO-X obligations in PTAs: the former cover matters that fall under the current mandate of the WTO but where commitments in the PTA-context are more comprehensive (e.g. deeper than MFN tariff cuts); the latter refer to policy areas currently not addressed by the WTO (e.g. cooperation on macro-economic policies).

The latter may also be discriminatory but any discrimination is more likely to be a side effect of whatever is jointly implemented (e.g. harmonisation of regulatory standards and practices). In such situations there may be little scope for free-riding by other countries. An example would be a PA on trade facilitation that involves signatories committing to specific actions (such as risk-assessment practices, collection and sharing of data on consignments) that ensures reciprocal 'green channel' treatment for goods. This implies better market-access conditions for signatories, but this is conditional on having previously put in place an agreed set of procedures, having made the necessary policy reforms and investments etc.

We claim that if a PA involves regulatory cooperation/convergence for a policy area that is covered by the WTO (i.e. is WTO+) or addresses a WTO-X issue, it is unlikely to have detrimental consequences for the trading system. However, if the PA involves discriminatory market access in an area that is covered by the WTO, it will matter whether the PA is a narrow/product-specific agreement or is broad-based. The former is likely to violate MFN and thus is likely to be precluded on that basis. The latter will also violate MFN. However, a broad-based agreement might also be pursued through a PTA. If this is a credible alternative to a PA, WTO Members need to consider the benefits that will come with a PA approach relative to a PTA – including greater transparency, potential for accession and gradual multilateralisation,[44] common dispute settlement etc. The clearest example of such a trade-off is the current discussion on a TISA (the Trade in Services Agreement currently under negotiation among various WTO members). If signatories to a TISA make specific commitments in areas that they have excluded from the reach of the GATS there may be no violation of MFN.[45]

D   Relax (Re-Think) Consensus

A constraint in pursuing the plurilateral route is that the incorporation of a PA into the WTO requires unanimity ('exclusively by consensus'). Greater use of PAs arguably will require a relaxation of this rule.[46] Some are of the

---

[44] One potential advantage of a PA is that the design of market access and national treatment commitments in the agreement is more likely to be consistent with (i.e. allow) 'docking' with the GATS at a later time.

[45] Of course, the issue becomes moot insofar as specific commitments are applied on a MFN basis.

[46] J. Tijmes-Lhl, 'Consensus and majority voting in the WTO' (2009) 8 *World Trade Review* 417–37.

view that no such change is needed and that non-members should be comfortable with the terms of any PA that is tabled.[47] What is the counterfactual to PAs? Is it a critical-mass MFN deal, the Single Undertaking with associated issue linkages, or continued deadlock – that is, no action? More likely is that those prevented from moving forwards in a PA will pursue more PTAs/deeper PTAs (if feasible), or issue-specific agreements *outside* the WTO that address regulatory policies that are not covered by existing WTO disciplines.[48] In both scenarios the WTO increasingly will become a set of 'minimum standards' – a global trade institution that establishes only certain baseline conditions.

Maintaining the strong consensus rule is arguably a recipe for inefficient outcomes. While presumably intended to ensure that any PA is consistent with multilateralism, it is arguably too strong a constraint. A rationale for the consensus rule may have been concern about countries putting forward subject areas simply because of the DSU or for 'strategic' reasons – such as controversial issues like labour standards. However, consensus is not needed to provide assurances that efforts to introduce PAs on controversial matters that are only weakly trade-related can be blocked. Relaxing the consensus requirement could be beneficial. Some have argued that if a 'substantial coverage' of world trade or world production of a particular commodity agrees, then this percentage (of world trade or production) should suffice for the PA to go ahead.[49] Others have argued that a two-thirds majority should suffice. Recall that the Enhanced Cooperation Agreements that are foreseen in the EU context only require participation by nine out of twenty-seven Member States in instances where consensus cannot be obtained on an issue.

We do like the idea of having Pareto-sanctioned PAs. One way to preserve it, inspired by practice in the International Standardisation Organisation, is that WTO Members that cast a negative vote should be required to justify opposition. It should not be that 'anything goes', thus allowing WTO Members to block deals that are beneficial to others which present no detriment to the opposing Members. Procedural obligations to this effect would reduce the potential for 'tactical' opposition that aims to extract promises (side-payments) in other areas, which could include all sorts of negative external effects. We support the arguments developed and

---

[47] Lawrence, 'Rulemaking Amidst Growing Diversity' (above n. 5).
[48] Or for that matter that build on WTO disciplines. The Anti-Counterfeiting Trade Agreement is an example.
[49] Hufbauer and Schott, 'Will the World Trade Organization Enjoy a Bright Future?' (above n. 6).

advanced by Lawrence,[50] WEF[51] and Draper and Dube,[52] who have suggested that a necessary condition for moving towards greater use of PAs is to address the concerns that have been expressed by WTO Members. One way of doing this is to focus on negotiating, upfront, a 'code of conduct' for PAs to be negotiated under the umbrella of the WTO. Qualified majorities – as suggested above – could be incorporated as one modality and buttressed by other principles that any PA should embody for it to be acceptable – such as aid for trade. A code of conduct could include, among other things, the underlying principles that: (a) membership is voluntary; (b) the subject of the plurilateral is a core trade-related issue; (c) those participating in plurilateral negotiations should have the means, or be provided with the means as part of the agreement, to implement the outcomes; (d) the issue under negotiation should enjoy substantial support from the WTO's membership; and (e) the 'subsidiarity' principle should apply in order to minimise the intrusion of 'club rules' on national autonomy.

V   Concluding Remarks

As tariffs gradually become a non-issue for international trade relations, negotiators shift their attention to the negotiation of NTBs. We explained above why non-discrimination is ill-suited to guarantee market access with respect to NTBs. Recognition and/or harmonisation on the other hand (e.g. the instruments that can effectively guarantee market access when NTBs are standing in the way) are for good reasons contracted across like-minded countries; that is, between club members.[53] Deeper integration will inevitably occur within clubs, and if the WTO cannot build bridges with them, its relevance can only decline. Deep integration is contracted now in PTAs, but it can also be contracted under the roof of

---

[50] Lawrence, 'Rulemaking Amidst Growing Diversity' (above n. 5).

[51] World Economic Forum, 'A Plurilateral "Club-of-Clubs" Approach to World Trade Organization Reform and New Issues' in *Global Agenda Council on the Global Trade System and FDI* (WEF, 2010).

[52] P. Draper and M. Dube, *'Plurilaterals and the Multilateral Trading System'*, E15 background paper (ICTSD, 2013).

[53] The theoretical case for this position is presented in Costinot, 'A Comparative Institutional Analysis of Agreements on Product Standards' (above n. 14); evidence has been supplied by many: see, inter alia, Juan A. Marchetti and Petros C. Mavroidis, 'I Now Recognize You (and Only You) as Equal: An Anatomy of (Mutual) Recognition Agreements in the GATS' in Ioannis Lianos and Okeoghene Odudu (eds.), *Regulating Trade in Services in the EU and the WTO, Trust, Distrust, and Economic Integration* (Cambridge University Press, 2012), 415–43.

PAs. The WTO should build its bridges with both, and privilege PAs for all the reasons mentioned above.

PAs offer a mechanism for subsets of WTO Members to move forward on issues of common concern, especially those that involve rule-making in areas that do not have a major market-access dimension. They could be the 'regulatory hothouse' for the WTO, the forum where originally plurilateral agreements become multilateralised at a later stage.

Absent the PA option, WTO Members may be induced to pursue PTAs more intensively, which will be less inclusive (open) than PAs, or to engage in cooperation outside the WTO (if the issue is a WTO-X subject), in the process replicating some of the WTO machinery (e.g. transparency related; dispute settlement). The continued relevance of the WTO also depends on its capacity to adapt to variable geometry. A WTO 2.0 should allow for clubs to be formed that would keep the umbilical cord to multilateralism intact.

The appetite for trade deals has been threatened by the recent election of Donald Trump, a trade sceptic, who won the election in the United States, one of the main hubs for trade deals, on a promise to abandon the TPP, and renegotiate NAFTA. Does his election affect our analysis so far? We think this is not the case. For starters he is not the first US President who runs on a trade sceptic-ticket. Obama, when a Congressman, voted against a series of trade deals, and then famously went on to negotiate and conclude not only TPP, but also the TTIP with the EU. Furthermore, his point has been that the United States loses out on its trade deals since it accumulates trade deficits. For the reasons explained in many publications, and most eloquently by Irwin,[54] this is simply wrong. Trade liberalisation is not a zero-sum game; it is a win-win, and gains from trade are not measured exhaustively in terms of trade surplus/deficit. At the moment of writing, Trump has not even hinted at acting upon his electoral bravado. In similar vein, the UK voted for Brexit in June 2016, and immediately initiated a reflection on the proper integration model to substitute for EU membership. If anything, the UK government has made it clear that the one thorny issue is migration, which, one should recall, does not even come under the current WTO mandate.

The key issue is to ensure that variable geometry, which is unavoidable, will not undo inclusiveness in the world trade regime. Those entrusted with guiding the WTO to its next decades should reflect on mechanisms that guarantee an osmosis between whatever the 'hothouses' of regulatory

---

[54] D. A. Irwin, 'The Truth About Trade' (2016) 95 *Foreign Affairs* 84–95.

cooperation will achieve, and the rest of the WTO. We have explored some of these avenues already, and the OECD issued a wonderful survey to this effect.[55] The question is how to minimise negative external effects of variable geometry for those that initially do not participate. PAs is the best fit at the moment of writing. The ways and means exist to ensure that the WTO will continue to provide the momentum for multilateral cooperation without reducing the appetite for those who want to go further, faster. The question is whether the stakeholders at the WTO will privilege the forest over a few individual trees.

During the recent Ministerial Conference in Buenos Aires (December 2017), the WTO membership agreed to embark on an examination that could eventually lead to an agreement on e-commerce. This issue has been on the table in one form or another since 1995. It now seems that there is finally some light at the end of the tunnel. What changed was that, without explicitly so stating, the WTO Membership gave this endeavour its blessing, even though it was clear from Day One that only a few of the WTO members would be on board. Something similar could happen with the other initiative that was launched during the Buenos Aires Ministerial Conference, namely, Investment Facilitation.

It could be that we are finally getting to the phase where envisaging a PA is no longer anathema in the WTO lexicon.

---

[55] T. Bollyky and P. C. Mavroidis, 'Trade, Social Preferences, and Regulatory Cooperation, the New WTO-Think' (2017) 20 *JIEL* 1–30.

7

New Challenges for Global
Environmental Governance

MARKUS W. GEHRING

I Introduction

Global environmental governance still occurs in silos in which different Conferences of the Parties (CoPs) are aware of the existence of a neighbouring regime but still fail to approach the questions in an integrated fashion. Twenty-five years ago, Cordonier Segger and Khalfan suggested that a coordination at the United Nations (UN) level would be the best governance reflection of the concept of sustainable development and its principle of integration at its core. This chapter argues that the only real unresolved challenge in international environmental governance is the lack of integration between the different regimes. Politically, this is a complex challenge because different ministries and units, at the national level, are in charge of different environmental conventions. Several CoPs have now also identified climate change as the main challenge in areas such as biodiversity loss, oceans and fisheries and sustainable natural resources governance more broadly but no legal integration is currently forthcoming. This chapter thus proposes that the interlinked concepts of sustainable development and the green economy could provide for such legal integration and that, in many fields, states are already adopting such laws.

A   Sustainable Development

Sustainable development, defined as 'development that meets the needs of the present without compromising the ability of future generations to meet their own needs', is a widely accepted goal of the global community.[1] Its underlying ideas have governed the practices of many cultures for

---

[1] World Commission on Environment and Development, *Our Common Future: Brundtland Report* (Oxford University Press, 1987). See also the explanation by M.-C. Cordonier Segger

thousands of years.[2] Significantly, from its inclusion in the Brundtland Report, those promoting more sustainable development did not focus on limiting economic activity but rather on redirecting it, in order to ensure the potential for long-term, sustained yields from the development process.[3] Sustainable development is closely related to, and may ideally become a core objective of, national and international law and policy. In governance terms, sustainable development calls for joined-up thinking and integrated decision-making.

Sustainable development according to Agenda 21 rests on three inter-linked pillars which are environmental protection, social inclusion and economic development.[4] Although these three pillars or dimensions have been criticised, they can serve an important purpose, particularly in conjunction with legal analysis. Indeed, in balancing these three priorities in an analogous manner to a proportionality analysis, neither priority should be completely ignored.[5]

The 2012 United Nations Conference on Sustainable Development in Rio (Rio+20), building on the 2002 World Summit on Sustainable Development (WSSD) in Johannesburg, refocused global awareness on the need for more environmentally sound and socially equitable economic development. Sustainable development has, in one formulation or another, been enshrined as an explicit objective in more than fifty binding international treaties.[6] It is central to the mandates of many international organisations,[7] and the subject of numerous 'soft law' declarations and standards.[8] Sustainable development and its principles guide domestic

---

and A. Khalfan (eds.), *Sustainable Development Law: Principles, Practises and Prospects* (Oxford University Press, 2004).

[2] C. G. Weeramantry, 'Achieving Sustainable Justice through International Law' in C. G. Weeramantry and M.-C. Cordonier Segger (eds.), *Sustainable Justice: Reconciling Economic, Social and Environmental Law* (Martinus Nijhoff, 2005), 15.

[3] M. Stillwell, 'Sustainable Development and Trade Law: Overview of Key Issues' in C. G. Weeramantry and M.-C. Cordonier Segger (eds.), *Sustainable Justice: Reconciling Economic, Social and Environmental Law* (Martinus Nijhoff, 2005), 87.

[4] UNCED, Agenda 21: Programme of Action for Sustainable Development, Report of the UNCED, vol. UN GAOR, 46th Sess., Agenda Item 21, UN Doc. A/Conf.151/6/Rev.1 (1992), 31 I.L.M. 874 (1992).

[5] Segger and Khalfan, *Sustainable Development Law* (above n. 1).

[6] Ibid., 32.

[7] Such as the World Trade Organization, UN Global Compact, the International Renewable Energy Agency (IRENA) or UN-REDD.

[8] M.-C. Cordonier Segger, 'Sustainable Development' in D. Armstrong (ed.), *Routledge Handbook of International Law* (Routledge, 2008), 355.

and international law in many areas of economic, social and environmental policy, particularly where these fields intersect.[9]

B   Green Economy and Sustainable Development

Broadly, green economy can be regarded as an approach that addresses aspects of all three pillars of sustainable development by connecting 'environment' and 'economics' to deliver human well-being and social equity through poverty reduction in accordance with Principle One of the 1992 Rio Declaration.[10] While not using the term in the 2012 Declaration on 'The Future We Want', the broader notion of green economy is reflected in that declaration. Green economy is designed to contribute to the eradication of poverty, sustain economic growth, enhance social inclusion, improve human welfare, create opportunities for employment and decent work for all, while maintaining the healthy functioning of the Earth's ecosystems. In this sense, many sustainable-development policies, such as fisheries or forestry policies could be seen as complying with the green economy objective because they enable states to become less dependent on liquidating environmental assets and sacrificing environmental quality while still allowing for economic growth. For global environmental governance that means that an integrated approach to the different environmental conventions and their interaction with related areas of law such as economic and human rights law is also in the interest of transitioning to the global green economy.

Prior to proceeding to a review and analysis of legal innovations, it is necessary to recognise that the green economy approach is not without its critics.[11] Some fear a renewed emphasis on an economic bottom line, to the detriment of environmental or social objectives.[12] Shawkat and Razzaque have aptly summarised the situation as follows: '[T]o many, the green economy is an instrument for the advancement of corporate

---

[9] M. W. Gehring, 'Sustainable International Trade, Investment and Competition Law' in M.-C. Cordonier Segger and A. Khalfan (eds.), *Sustainable Development Law: Principles, Practises and Prospects* (Oxford University Press, 2004); M. W. Gehring et al. (eds.), *Sustainable Development in World Investment Law* (Kluwer, 2010); M. W. Gehring and M.-C. Cordonier Segger (eds.), *Sustainable Development in World Trade Law* (Kluwer, 2005).

[10] United Nations Environment Management Group, *Working towards a Balanced and Inclusive Green Economy: A United Nations System-Wide Perspective* (UN, 2011), 33.

[11] J. Borel-Saladin and I. N. Turok, 'The Green Economy: Incremental Change or Transformation?' (2013) 23 *Environmental Policy and Governance* 209; C. L. Spash, 'Green Economy, Red Herring' (2012) 21(2) *Environmental Values* 95.

[12] Ibid.

interests, as it emphasises markets and businesses as a solution to environmental and economic problems. According to Simons, corporate human rights impunity is deeply embedded within the structures of the international legal system, allowing powerful states to create a globalised legal environment that fosters further corporate impunity. Therefore, enhancing economic interests of Transnational Corporations (TNCs) based in the North at the expense of human rights and environmental sustainability in the global South is a systemic issue, not simply the result of globalisation creating governance gaps, as Ruggie argues. Hence, the green economy is not a panacea for global economic, social, and environmental inequity.[13] In other words, the criticism here is that the green economy emphasises economic progress and perhaps environmental progress but might omit the social dimension that is such an integral part to sustainable development.

However, Rio+20 reaffirmed and underlined that sustainable development remains the overall context in which to view the transition to the global green economy. When viewed from a sustainable development perspective, the laws that can support the green economy provide a necessary coherence among economic, environmental and social objectives. This is also why, in the context of sustainable natural resources management, governments, especially, highlighted equity and employment, encouraging 'each country to consider the implementation of green economy policies in the context of sustainable development and poverty eradication, in a manner that endeavours to drive sustained, inclusive and equitable economic growth and job creation, particularly for women, youth and the poor'.[14]

II   Recent Legal Innovations

In a recent investigation, legal researchers in Africa, Latin America and the Caribbean, North America, Europe and the Asia Pacific regions tracked trends across a series of constitutional provisions and their judicial interpretations, as well as innovative national laws and their related regulations, institutions and standards.[15] The study identified a series of general

---

[13] A. Shawkat and J. Razzaque, 'Sustainable Development versus Green Economy: The Way Forward?' in S. Alam et al. (eds.), *International Environmental Law and the Global South* (Cambridge University Press, 2015), 603, 611.

[14] A/RES/66/288, 'The Future We Want', para. 62.

[15] This section is based on a recent research study with the UN Environment Programme that surveyed and analysed over 2,000 innovative legal instruments and provisions to facilitate the transition to a greener economy at the national, regional and international levels.

trends across the fourteen key sectors,[16] underlining the importance of 'increasing human wellbeing and social equity, and reducing environmental risks and ecological scarcities'. It concluded that '[a]cross many of these sectors, greening the economy can generate consistent and positive outcomes for increased wealth, growth in economic output, decent employment and reduced poverty'.[17]

The objective of the Compendium was to compile important national and subnational laws and regulatory instruments from around the world, documenting and highlighting innovative provisions which promote resource efficiency and sustainable consumption and production towards a transition to green economy on the pathway to sustainable development and poverty eradication.

A   Integrated Approaches at the International Level

At the international level, a multitude of new instruments are not just balancing social, economic and environmental concerns for sustainable development, but are actually increasingly adopting market-based instruments (MBIs) to provide green economy incentives for low-carbon development, for the stewardship of forest ecosystems enshrined within the goal of sustainable use of biodiversity. There are three trends that are particularly discernible: more MBIs, facilitating treaty provisions and courts and tribunals facilitating the transition to a green economy.[18]

First, international treaty regimes on environment and sustainable development are increasingly adopting international MBIs to achieve their ends. One example of an international market-based mechanism lies at the intersection of climate change and forest management. The new UN Reducing Emissions from Deforestation and Forest Degradation (REDD)

M. W. Gehring and A. Harrington (lead authors), *UNEP's Compendium of Innovative Laws Promoting Green Economy & Sustainable Development* (UNEP, 2016), http://wedocs.unep .org/bitstream/handle/20.500.11822/9947/compendium-innovative-laws-promoting-green-economy.pdf?sequence=1&isAllowed=y. See also for regional studies: M. Gehring and A. Kent, *Innovative Regulatory Frameworks Promoting Green Economy for Sustainable Development and Poverty Eradication in Europe* (UNEP, June 2013), http://ssrn.com/ abstract=2603713.

[16] The fourteen key sectors are: agriculture, forests, biodiversity, fisheries, marine/coastal, water regulation, sustainable tourism, energy, climate change, transportation, buildings and construction, manufacturing, mining and waste management/waste minimisation.

[17] Gehring and Harrington, *UNEP's Compendium* (above n. 15), 24.

[18] Early arguments by C. E. di Leva, 'The Conservation of Nature and Natural Resources through Legal and Market-Based Instruments' (2002) 11 *Review of European Community & International Environmental Law* 84.

system is an effort to create a financial value for the carbon stored in forests, offering incentives for developing countries to reduce emissions from forested lands and for investing in low-carbon paths to sustainable development.[19] As was seen in the Cancun CoP16 agreements on human rights, environmental and other safeguards,[20] and in the Warsaw CoP19 decision on REDD+,[21] which goes beyond deforestation and forest degradation, and includes the role of conservation, sustainable management of forests and enhancement of forest carbon stocks,[22] the mechanism is not without its challenges, especially because attracting private funding still remains difficult. But if it can be activated effectively, particularly now that the mechanism has been endorsed by the Paris Agreement, it also offers significant opportunities for the green economy.[23] It would provide a global market-based mechanism which would allow enhancement of the protection and sustainable management of forests while providing income for local communities without relying solely on government funds or official development assistance.

Concerning the energy sector, the Statute of the International Renewable Energy Agency (IRENA) has the potential to facilitate the use of market-based mechanisms for the transition to the green economy. The objective of IRENA is to:

> promote the widespread and increased adoption and the sustainable use of all forms of renewable energy, taking into account: (a) national and domestic priorities and benefits derived from a combined approach of renewable energy and energy efficiency measures; and (b) the contribution of renewable energy to environmental preservation, through limiting pressure on natural resources and reducing deforestation, particularly tropical deforestation, desertification and biodiversity loss; to climate protection;

[19] I. Fry, 'Reducing Emissions from Deforestation and Forest Degradation: Opportunities and Pitfalls in Developing a New Legal Regime' (2008) 17 *Review of European Community & International Environmental Law* 166.

[20] Report of the Conference of the Parties on its sixteenth session, held in Cancun from 29 November to 10 December 2010, Addendum Part Two: Action taken by the Conference of the Parties at its sixteenth session, Decisions adopted by the Conference of the Parties, UN Doc. FCCC/CP/2010/7/Add.1, 15 March 2011.

[21] Report of the Conference of the Parties on its nineteenth session, held in Warsaw from 11 to 23 November 2013, Addendum, Part Two: Action taken by the Conference of the Parties at its nineteenth session, UN Doc. FCCC/CP/2013/10/Add.1, Decisions adopted by the Conference of the Parties, 31 January 2014.

[22] See UN REDD Programme, www.un-redd.org/aboutredd.

[23] M. Gehring, M.-C. Cordonier Segger and J. Hepburn, 'Climate Change and International Trade and Investment Law' in R. Rayfuse and S. Scott (eds.), *International Law in the Era of Climate Change* (Edward Elgar, 2012), 84, 87.

to economic growth and social cohesion including poverty alleviation and sustainable development; to access to and security of energy supply; to regional development and to inter-generational responsibility.[24]

IRENA has already analysed most of its parties' potential for renewable energy and provides model laws to facilitate the transition to that form of energy production, offering feed-in tariffs which is another form of a market-based mechanism.

Second, international economic law, including trade and investment law can help rather than hinder the transition to a greener economy.[25] Several pathways for international economic law to support the green economy in the context of sustainable development can be identified.[26]

These provisions include:

(1) preambular recognition of sustainable development, the environment, and labour or human rights in trade and investment treaties, to inform interpretation of the accords

(2) use of exceptions to permit flexibility for green economy regulations, where appropriate, including general and specific exceptions, and recognition of permissible trade-related environmental measures from multilateral environmental agreements (The use of exceptions can be difficult because liberalisation commitments apply strictly if they fall outside the exception provisions which in turn can lead to stricter application in areas not covered.)

(3) commitments to cooperate, as part of trade and investment agreements, on shared parallel environmental and social work programmes, including control of harmful practices or substances which might increase due to increased trade, and also implementation of other treaties

(4) the activation of trade and investment law to directly achieve greener economic outcomes, such as through prohibitions on subsidies, especially fisheries where they encourage over-fishing; or liberalisation provisions in regional trade agreements to facilitate trade in environmental goods and services, or to develop markets and trade in renewable energy, organic agriculture, sustainable forest products; or

---

[24] See analysis by F. Zelli et al., *Global Climate Governance and Energy Choices - The Handbook of Global Energy Policy 340* (2013).

[25] See M. Gehring, 'Trade and Investment Measures for the Low-Carbon Economy' in I. L. Backer et al. (eds.), *Liber Amicorum Hans Christian Bugge* (Universitstforlaget, 2012).

[26] M. Gehring and M. Cordonier Segger (eds.), *Sustainable Developments in World Trade Law* (Kluwer Law International, 2005).

the use of investment law to ensure stability which can support, for instance, establishment of renewable energy (*PV Investors* v. *Spain*[27]).

Third, new decisions handed down by international courts and tribunals emphasise the role of the law in facilitating the transition to the green economy. One of the most important rulings guiding the global green economy was delivered by the Seabed Disputes Chamber of the International Tribunal for the Law of the Sea (ITLOS).[28] It had received a request for an advisory opinion on the question of liability of sponsoring states in the area (i.e. the seabed under the high seas) and how developing countries in particular could fulfil those obligations. This decision is important for the green economy because questions of liability and assigning liability are elements of a transition to a greener economy.[29]

Some scholars, such as Freestone, defined the case as a historic ruling.[30] The Opinion argued for 'highest standards of protection of the marine environment, the safe development of activities in the Area and protection of the common heritage of mankind'.[31] The Chamber recognised a 'responsibility to ensure'/'obligation of due diligence' with regards to liability[32] of the host state of the operator. This obligation applies equally to developing and developed countries[33] and as such could become important for the global transition to a green economy. The Court noted that '"due diligence" is a variable concept [which] may change over time as measures considered sufficiently diligent at a certain moment may become not diligent enough in light, for instance, of new scientific or technological knowledge'.[34] It highlighted that riskier activities will require higher

---

[27] *The PV Investors* v. *Spain*, UNCITRAL Arbitration Rules (November 2011).

[28] Responsibilities and Obligations of States Sponsoring Persons and Entities with Respect to Activities in the Area, Case No. 17, Advisory Opinion (ITLOS Seabed Disputes Chamber, 1 February 2011), 50 ILM 458 (2011), www.itlos.org/fileadmin/itlos/documents/cases/case_no_17/17_adv_op_010211_en.pdf.

[29] D. French, 'Supporting the Principle of Integration in the Furtherance of Sustainable Development: A Sideways Glance' (2006) 18 *Environmental Law and Management* 103.

[30] D. Freestone, 'Advisory Opinion of the Seabed Disputes Chamber of International Tribunal for the Law of the Sea on "Responsibilities and Obligations of States Sponsoring Persons and Entities with Respect to Activities in the Area"' (2011) 15 *ASIL*, Insights, www.asil.org/insights/volume/15/issue/7/advisory-opinion-seabed-disputes-chamber-international-tribunal-law-sea-.

[31] Responsibilities and Obligations of States (above n. 28), para. 159.

[32] See for the relationship between liability and due diligence, P.-M. Dupuy and J. E. Viñuales, *International Environmental Law* (Cambridge University Press, 2015), 253.

[33] Responsibilities and Obligations of States (above note 28), para. 163.

[34] Ibid., para. 117.

levels of due diligence.[35] The Seabed Chamber Advisory Opinion managed to strike a balance between economic activities and environmental and social concerns. In the transition to a green economy, liability provisions are important as more economic activity impacts directly on the environment.

While green economy cases are still rare in other areas of international law, they are becoming quite common in international trade law and World Trade Organization (WTO) law more specifically. While trade and environment cases have a long history,[36] recently mechanisms that countries claim were adopted to transition to a greener economy have come under scrutiny by the WTO dispute settlement mechanism, such as in the *China – Rare Earths* dispute.[37] This case offers important guidance for the sustainable use of natural resources, a key dimension of the global green economy and different approaches to ensure sustainable resource management have been chosen. In the dispute, China argued that the export restrictions that it imposed on these products are related to the conservation of its exhaustible natural resources, and necessary to reduce pollution caused by mining.[38] The plaintiffs disagreed, arguing that the restrictions are not designed to conserve the resources because they were lacking corresponding domestic conservation measures.[39] Essentially, the WTO Panel concluded that, by reference to Article XX of the General Agreement on Tariffs and Trade (GATT) 1994,[40] export duties and export quotas could not be justified.[41] They objected to the way China had designed the measure,

---

[35] 'Measures necessary to ensure': adoption of appropriate laws, regulations and administrative measures (*Pulp Mills* and 2001 ILC Harm Articles) 'to be kept under review so as to ensure that they meet current standards' (para. 222); 'may include the establishment of enforcement mechanisms for active supervision' (para. 218); contractual arrangements are alone insufficient. '[T]he liability of the sponsoring State depends upon the damage resulting from the activities or omissions of the sponsored contractor. But ... this is merely a trigger mechanism. Such damage is not, however, automatically attributable to the sponsoring State' (para. 201); 'precautionary approach is also an integral part of the general obligation of due diligence of sponsoring States' (para. 131); 'in light of the advancement in scientific knowledge, member States of the Authority have become convinced of the need for ... "best environmental practices" in general terms so that they may be seen to have become enshrined in the sponsoring States' obligation of due diligence' (para. 136).

[36] Gehring and Cordonier, Segger, *Sustainable Developments in World Trade Law* (above n. 26).

[37] China – Measures Related to the Exportation of Rare Earths, Tungsten and Molybdenum, WTO Doc. DS431, Panel Report, 26 March 2014.

[38] Ibid., 92.

[39] Ibid., 102.

[40] General Agreement on Tariffs and Trade, 30 October 1947, 55 UNTS 194.

[41] China – Measures Related to the Exportation of Rare Earths (above n. 37), 243.

finding that it did not fulfil the requirement of being necessary to protect human health (essentially because these Rare Earth minerals are mined at the same rate but for domestic production) and it was not a measure related to conservation of exhaustible natural resources.[42] The Panel agreed with China that the term 'conservation' in Article XX(g) GATT 1994 means more than simply 'preservation' of natural resources, and that every WTO Member can take its own sustainable development needs and objectives into account when designing a conservation policy,[43] in accordance with the general international law principle of sovereignty over natural resources reflected in various UN and other international instruments. The Panel then concluded that the export quota was not designed to conserve natural resources because no restrictions on the domestic level were adopted.[44] This dispute is important because it demonstrated that a state's policy commitment to transition to a greener economy should not override other international obligations such as general non-discrimination obligations (i.e. national treatment or most-favourite nation obligations). This is an important insight for the global green economy because to a certain extent, as in the International Court of Justice (ICJ) *Australia* v. *Japan* whaling case,[45] the WTO Panel recommends an international approach to conservation rather than a unilateral one.

In another recent case, the Ontario Feed-in Tariff (FIT) programme came under review due to a complaint by Japan and the European Union (EU). This is a particularly relevant WTO case for the green economy measures because it concerns the legality of a market-based instrument, here a FIT. In its ruling in December 2012, the Panel in Canada FIT provided important guidance as to the design of a FIT.[46] The dispute arose in September 2010, when Japan[47] and later the EU[48] complained about measures that impose domestic content requirements on Ontario's renewable

---

[42] Ibid., 105.

[43] Ibid., 98.

[44] Ibid., 105.

[45] *Whaling in the Antarctic* (*Australia* v. *Japan*: New Zealand intervening), Judgment, 31 March 2014, still unreported, available at www.icj-cij.org.

[46] Canada – Certain Measures Affecting the Renewable Energy Sector (Complaint by Japan); Canada – Measures Relating to the Feed-in Tariff Program (Complaint by the EU) [2013] WTO Doc. WT/DS412/AB/R, WT/DS426/AB/R (AB Report) ('Canada FIT').

[47] Canada – Certain Measures Affecting the Renewable Energy Sector (Complaint by Japan), DS412, www.wto.org/english/tratop_e/dispu_e/cases_e/ds412_e.htm.

[48] Canada – Measures Relating to the Feed-in Tariff Program (Complaint by the EU), DS426, www.wto.org/english/tratop_e/dispu_e/cases_e/ds426_e.htm.

energy industries.[49] In a nutshell, the plaintiffs raised two main arguments: first, it was argued that the scheme violates the 'national treatment' rule, which requires equal treatment for domestic and imported products, as stipulated in Article III(4) of the GATT 1994 and in Articles 2.1 of the Agreement on Trade-Related Investment Measures (TRIMs Agreement).[50] Second, it was contended that the Ontario FIT program is in violation of Article 3.1(b) of the Agreement on Subsidies and Countervailing Measures (SCM Agreement),[51] according to which subsidies that are contingent on the use of local content are prohibited.

The second question examined by the Panel was whether the local content requirement of the Ontario FIT program is a prohibited subsidy, according to the SCM Agreement. This is important for the global green economy because many feed-in tariff laws could be captured by this ruling. In order to answer this question, the Panel had first to determine whether the Ontario FIT program should be considered as a 'subsidy', according to the definition provided in Article 1.1 of the SCM Agreement. The Panel rejected the finding as a subsidy because the FIT price could not serve as the appropriate benchmark in the case,[52] otherwise public policy objectives such as the diversification of energy sources and the reduction of greenhouse gas emissions (mentioned in the report only as 'environmental impacts') could not be achieved. As an alternative approach, the Panel suggested the following benchmark for the determination of the 'prevailing market conditions'.[53] According to the Panel, the factors that must be considered in this respect included Ontario's aspiration to eliminate coal-fired plants, the Province's need to replace its energy production facilities and its commitment to encourage the production of energy from renewable sources.[54] The Panel further added that the correct comparison in this case would have been to compare the rate of return obtained by the FIT generators under the terms and conditions of the FIT and microFIT contracts with the average cost of capital in Canada for projects having a comparable risk profile in the same period.[55]

---

[49] Canada – Certain Measures Affecting the Renewable Energy Sector (Complaint by Japan); Canada – Measures Relating to the Feed-in Tariff Program (Complaint by the EU) [2012] WTO Doc. WT/DS412/R, WT/DS426/R (Panel Report) ('Canada FIT').

[50] Agreement on Trade-Related Investment Measures, 15 April 1994, 1868 UNTS 186.

[51] Agreement on Subsidies and Countervailing Measures, 15 April 1994, 1867 UNTS 14.

[52] Canada FIT (above n. 46), para. 7.320.

[53] Ibid., para. 7.322 (emphasis added).

[54] Ibid.

[55] Ibid., para. 7.323.

It is this last ruling (which was opposed by one Panel member in a separate opinion) that is of particular interest for the global green economy. In its decision, the Panel de facto recognised the special circumstances that are unique to investments in renewable energy. The Panel acknowledged that such projects cannot currently compete in the general energy market, that they include higher risk, that there are additional 'un-priced' social benefits for such projects[56] and that in the already distorted energy markets it could be that governmental support for this sector is in fact necessary. Accordingly, the Panel decided to interpret the term 'prevailing market conditions' in this case in a very expansive manner: by comparing the FIT rates only with projects that have a comparable risk profile, and by considering broader public considerations (such as environmental policies) as relevant for this legal test. The Panel's ruling thus appears to indicate that climate measures, if well designed, do not violate subsidy or other trade rules.

Unfortunately, in Japan's appeal relating to Article 1.1(b) of the SCM Agreement, the Appellate Body reversed the Panel's finding that Japan failed to establish that the FIT Programme and related FIT and micro-FIT Contracts confer a benefit within the meaning of Article 1.1(b) of the SCM Agreement, because the Panel erred in defining the relevant market and in its benefit analysis. In the light of these findings, the Appellate Body did not find it necessary to address Japan's alternative claim that the Panel acted inconsistently with Article 11 of the Dispute Settlement Understanding (DSU). The Appellate Body (AB) was unable to complete the analysis as to whether the challenged measures confer a benefit within the meaning of Article 1.1(b) of the SCM Agreement and whether Canada acted inconsistently with Articles 3.1(b) and 3.2 of the SCM Agreement. The AB did not take issue with the analysis of the public policy analysis of the Panel but rather criticised the way the Panel did not start with an analysis of the relevant market. So, in effect, while it might be slightly more onerous to make a green economy argument in subsidies cases, it is not impossible as the Panel's reasoning shows. While it would have been useful for the future 'trade-proof' design of green economy measures to have the complete analysis of the AB, both decisions provide a comprehensive framework for the design of FIT laws. This, in turn, is useful for future application of this MBI globally as we can now design feed-in tariffs which respect trade obligations while fulfilling their environmental and social purposes.

[56] Ibid., 135.

B   Integrated Approaches at the National Level

1   Climate Change

Mexico enacted the General Law on Climate Change, a ground-breaking law for Mexico and the region overall.[57] This law created an administrative mechanism that was charged with establishing and overseeing a carbon market within Mexico. Additionally, the law allows for the establishment of measures through which Mexico and Mexican entities could enter the existing global carbon mechanisms. Mitigation and adaptation strategies, their creation and their promotion, are also allowed and encouraged within Mexico under the new law.

The Canadian province of Alberta enacted the Climate Change and Emissions Management Act.[58] From the outset, the Act asserts the place of the province as the steward of the natural resources and environment in the province for current and future generations while also establishing the need to use these resources responsibly in order to promote the provincial economy. The Act establishes greenhouse gas emissions targets to be achieved by 2020 and vests the Lieutenant Governor with the necessary administrative and regulatory powers to achieve these goals. In order to further these goals, the Act provides for emissions credits, sinks and offsets for economic use and establishes the Climate Change and Emissions Management Fund, which is geared towards assisting in the development and implementation of adaptive measures to counter climate change. The Canadian province of Manitoba enacted the Climate Change and Emissions Reduction Act in order to protect the environment as well as to 'promote sustainable economic development and energy security'.[59] The Act notes that the majority of Manitoba's electricity sources are already clean and renewable and explains that the Act itself is geared towards creating even more progressive measures for the provincial environment and economy. These measures include setting emissions reduction targets starting in 2012 and extending to 2020 and establishing methods for calculating emissions offsets. Further, the Act implements green building requirements and vehicle emissions standards for the public and private sectors and requires that Manitoba Hydro implement a phase-out procedure for using coal.

---

[57] General Law on Climate Change (2012).
[58] Climate Change and Emissions Management Act, S.A. 2003, c. C-16.7.
[59] The Climate Change and Emissions Reductions Act, S.M. 2008, c. 17.

The Philippines' Climate Change Act[60] establishes the Climate Change Commission and requires the Commission to formulate a Framework Strategy on Climate Change that is renewable every three years. The Framework serves as the basis of a programme for climate change planning, research and development, and the monitoring of activities to protect vulnerable communities from the adverse effects of climate change.[61] Components of the Framework Strategy and Program on Climate Change are to include: (a) national priorities; (b) impact, vulnerability and adaptation assessments; (c) policy formulation; (d) compliance with international commitments; (e) research and development; (f) database development and management; (g) academic programmes, capability-building and mainstreaming; (h) advocacy and information dissemination; (i) monitoring and evaluation; and (j) gender mainstreaming.[62] Based on the Framework Strategy and Program on Climate Change, the Commission is to formulate a National Climate Change Action Plan. The Plan must include: (a) the assessment of the national impact of climate change; (b) the identification of the most vulnerable communities/areas; (c) the identification of the differential impacts of climate change on men, women and children; (d) the assessment and management of risk and vulnerability; (e) the identification of greenhouse gas mitigation potentials; (f) the identification of options; (g) prioritisation of appropriate adaptation measures for joint projects of national and local governments.[63] Consistent with the provisions of the Framework and National Climate Change Action Plan, the Local Climate Change Action Plan is set up to implement climate change action plans in their respective areas.[64] Due to the complexity and the widespread effects of climate change, when developing and implementing the National Climate Change Action Plan, and the local plans, the Commission must coordinate with non-governmental organisations (NGOs) and other concerned stakeholder groups.[65]

The contribution made by the General Law on Ecological Balance and Environment of Mexico is very valuable. Article 15 of this law provides that:

> In order to prepare and manage the environmental policy and issue the Official Mexican Standards and other instruments provided in this Law

---

[60] Philippines 2009 Climate Change and Emissions Reduction Act, An Act Mainstreaming Climate Change into Government Policy Formulations, Establishing the Framework Strategy and Program on Climate Change, Creating for this Purpose the Climate Change Commission, and for Other Purposes.

[61] Climate Change Act of 2009, s. 11.

[62] Ibid., s. 12.

[63] Ibid., s. 13.

[64] Ibid., s. 14.

[65] Ibid., s. 16.

related to the preservation and restoration of the ecological balance and environmental protection, the Federal Executive Power shall observe the following principles:

...

IV. Whoever carries out works or activities affecting or that may affect the environment, is obligated to prevent, minimise or repair the damage caused, as well as to assume the costs for such damage. In the same way, whoever protects the environment and exploits the natural resources in a sustainable manner must be provided with incentives.

In turn, Article 23 reads:

In order to contribute to the achievement of the environmental policy, the planning for urban development and housing, in addition to complying with the provisions of article 27 of the Constitution in the matter of human settlements, shall consider the following criteria:

...

VI. The authorities of the Federation, the States, the Federal Districts and Municipalities, within their jurisdiction, shall encourage the use of economic, fiscal, financial and financial instruments of urban and environmental policy, to induce behaviors consistent with the protection and restoration of the environment together with a sustainable urban development.

2 Biodiversity

Biodiversity plays an important role in laws throughout the globe, which make the clear connection between the need to develop the economy and to protect biodiversity. In order to achieve this, many states have set up administrative entities with specific charges to oversee the protection of biodiversity within a state or region.

The Canadian government has adopted the Species at Risk Act.[66] This Act specifically noted the interrelationship between Canadian natural heritage and economic status, taking into account Canada's international obligations regarding issues such as biodiversity as well as national commitments to conservation at all levels of government and on behalf of all peoples in Canada. Within this context, the Act establishes a number of specialised councils and administrative entities, and requires the creation of stewardship plans that involve environmental protection measures and information sharing requirements at many different levels of public and private involvement in wilderness activities. Japan's Basic Act

---

[66] Species at Risk Act, S.C. 2002, c. 29.

on Biodiversity sets fundamental principles for the conservation and sustainable use of biodiversity, and allocates the responsibilities among the state government, local governments, business entities, citizens and other private parties to ensure the performance of the conservation and sustainable use of biodiversity.[67] When implementing policies for conservation and sustainable use of biodiversity, the Act requires all governmental agencies to give necessary considerations to ensure the mutual organic coordination of prevention of global warming,[68] the creation of a sound material-cycle society and the creation of other policies for conservation of the environment.[69] The state should set a basic and comprehensive plan for conservation and sustainable use of biodiversity on a national level and the prefectural and municipal governments are responsible for implementing basic plans on conservation and sustainable use of biodiversity within their areas.[70] There is an Environmental Impact Assessment requirement at an early stage if a project has a potential impact on biodiversity.[71]

Chile recognised these themes in Law No. 19300, which provides in Article 34 that the state will administer a National System for Wildlife Protection Areas, including parks and marine reserves, with the aim of ensuring biological diversity, guaranteeing the preservation and conservation of the environmental heritage. Article 35 further provides that the State will promote and encourage the creation of protected wild areas on private property. Similarly, Costa Rica incorporates 'the sovereignty on the biological diversity as part of its natural heritage. The activities geared towards conservation, improvement, and if possible to the recovery of biological diversity in the national territory are of public interest; also focused on ensuring their sustainable use.'

Colombia also places importance on traditional knowledge, stating that it will promote the development and dissemination of knowledge, values, and technologies on environmental management and natural resources, and of indigenous cultures and other ethnic groups. Guatemala states that the Executive Branch will issue guidelines in relation to the following: (a) the protection of species or animal or vegetation specimens in danger of extinction; (b) the promotion of the development and use of conservation methods and enhancement of the flora and fauna of the country; (c) the establishment of a system of conservation areas with the aim of

---

[67] Basic Act on Biodiversity, Article 1.
[68] Ibid., Article 3 s. 5, Article 9.
[69] Ibid., Article 9.
[70] Ibid., Articles 4 and 5.
[71] Ibid., Article 25.

safeguarding the national genetic heritage, protecting and conserving special geomorphological phenomena, landscape, flora and fauna; (d) the importation of animal and plant species that damage the ecological balance of the country, and the exportation of unique species in danger of extinction; (e) the trade of illicit species considered in danger of extinction; and (f) the compliance with international conventions relating to the conservation of the natural heritage.

Honduras defines protected flora and fauna as those plant and animal species that should be subject to special protection due to their scarcity, condition in the ecosystem or in danger of extinction. Their exploitation, hunting, capture, commercialisation or destruction is prohibited under Honduran law. Additionally, the law provides that forest resources should be used and managed under the principle of biodiversity protection, sustainable yield and multiple-use concept of the resource, meeting their economic, ecological and social functions. The native ethnic groups shall receive special state support in relation to their traditional systems for the integral use of natural renewable resources, which should be studied with the aim of establishing their viability as a sustainable development model. The future development of these groups should be incorporated in the existing sustainable development norms and criteria. Nicaragua, in its General Environmental Law, states that in the case of indigenous peoples and ethnic communities contributing genetic resources, the state shall ensure that the use of these resources shall be granted under certain conditions determined in consultation with them.

Peru, an extremely diverse country in the region, has established laws relating to the sustainable exploitation of the natural resources, including conservation of biological diversity, through the recovery and protection of ecosystems, species and their genetic heritage. Under these laws, no circumstance or consideration can justify or excuse actions that could threaten or create a risk of extinction of any species, subspecies or the variety of flora or fauna. Venezuelan law also states that certain areas of the national territory will be declared ecosystems of strategic importance, namely: (i) when communities of plants and animals that represent highly relevant components in terms of food security are located within these areas; (ii) for the protection of human health and other living things; (iii) for medical pharmaceutical development; (iv) for the conservation of species; (v) for scientific research relating to the sustainable use of components of biological diversity; (vi) for the prevention of risks; and (vii) for national security and other types of interests of collective well-being.

Cuba's laws state that 'the endemic species, which are endangered, on the verge of extinction, which have special connotation and representative examples of the different types of ecosystems, as well as their genetic resources, are subject to special protection from the State, which includes the establishment of rigorous regulation mechanisms, control, management, and protection that guarantee their conservation and rational use'.

The Canadian province of Nova Scotia enacted a key law with regard to the protection of wildlife and the wilderness. In the 1989 Wildlife Act,[72] Nova Scotia committed itself to supporting biological diversity within the province in order to foster both environmental and economic benefits. This Act included the creation of a specific fund to assist in compliance, establishing wildlife management areas within the province in order to protect vulnerable species and providing assistance for wildlife research and education that benefits the province.

3 Sustainable Natural Resources

Many constitutions require state protection of national natural resources – particularly those associated with minerals and mining – and also establish public information requirements prior to the granting of licenses by the government.

The Constitution of Bhutan requires that '[the parliament] may enact environmental legislation to ensure sustainable use of natural resources and maintain intergenerational equity and reaffirm the sovereign rights of the State over its own biological resources'.[73] Bolivia's Constitution establishes that the state's actions must include the objective of 'promoting and guaranteeing the responsible and planned use of natural resources, and promoting industrialisation, by developing and strengthening the productive base in its different dimensions and at its different levels, as well as conserving the environment for the well-being of current and future generations'.[74] The Ecuadoran Constitution identifies sectors of strategic value, notably energy, communications, natural resources, transportation, biodiversity and water and establishes requirements for state action to ensure environmental protection in these areas. Further, the Ecuadorian Constitution establishes specific requirements regarding intellectual property, prohibiting any type of appropriation of collective knowledge in

---

[72] Chapter 504 of the Revised Statutes, 1989 as amended by 1990, c. 50; 1993, c. 9, s. 8; 1995–96, c. 8, s. 22; 1995–6, c. 25; 1998, c. 11, s. 29; 2001, c. 46; 2010, c. 2, s. 156; 2010, c. 4, ss. 41–43.

[73] Constitution of the Kingdom of Bhutan (2008), Article 5(4).

[74] Constitution of Bolivia (2009) Article 9, para. 6.

the fields of the sciences, technology and ancestral knowledge along with genetic resources that contain biodiversity and agrobiodiversity.

Article 120 of the Panamanian Constitution provides that natural resources should be used rationally – avoiding their depredation and ensuring their conservation, replenishment and permanence – while Article 121 states that natural resources should be used in a manner that avoids harming society, the economy and the environment. Constitutional relevance is also granted to the use of agricultural land for which, on the one hand, it is the owner's duty to appropriately use according to its eco-logical classification so as to avoid underuse and reduction of the produc-tive potential and, on the other hand, the suggestion in Article 126 that the state organise 'credit assistance to satisfy the financing needs of the agri-cultural activity and, especially, of the low-income sector and its organized groups and give special attention to the small and medium scale producer'. The Constitution of the Republic of El Salvador[75] in its Article 117 features an environmental clause that provides that it is the duty of the state to pro-tect the natural resources, as well as the diversity and integrity of the envi-ronment, in order to guarantee sustainable development. Furthermore, the protection, conservation, rational use, restoration or substitution of the natural resources is declared to be of social interest. The Honduran Constitution in Article 340 provides that 'the technical and rational exploi-tation of the nation's natural resources is useful and necessary for the public ... The country's reforestation and forest conservation are declared a national convenience and of collective interest.'

Additionally, some constitutions provide for specific rights to water, food, an adequate standard of living, a dignified life and/or the promotion of agriculture. A demonstrable trend in Latin American States is the incor-poration of the Earth, or 'Pacha Mama' as it is referred to in some consti-tutions, as an entity holding constitutional rights and protections. One of the distinctive and differentiating themes of the Ecuadorian Constitution is its declaration that 'nature will have those rights recognised for it in the Constitution'. This is complemented by the chapter on the 'Rights of Nature', which states that 'nature, or Pacha Mama, where it reproduces and makes life, is entitled to have its existence fully respected and to the maintenance and regeneration of its life cycles, structure, functions and

---

[75] Marco A. Gonzalez Pastora and Peter Lallas (eds.), *Introduction to Environmental Law in Central America: Building Regional Integration* (Fundación Doctor Manual Gallardoiro, 2007).

evolutionary processes'.[76] It then states that the primary obligations of the state are: 'to plan national development, eradicate poverty, promote sustainable development and the equitable redistribution of resources and wealth, in order to attain good living' and 'to protect the natural and cultural heritage of the country'.

In Latin America, several countries have classified property as having a constitutionally recognised social – as well as economic – function, thus requiring a different standard for evaluation by entities seeking to develop it. Social justice protections have been woven into these constitutional considerations as well. For example, the Brazilian Constitution has incorporated a strong socio-environmental component into its development policy, giving property a social function to be fulfilled with regard to environmental protection, while at the same time stressing, above all, that one of the guiding principles of the economic order resides in the definition of the environment. Similarly, Colombia shares Brazil's understanding of the social function of property and of its intrinsic relationship with its ecological function as part of its Constitution. The 1991 Colombian Constitution establishes that private 'property has a social function that entails obligations. As such, an ecological function is inherent to it'.[77] Article 47 of the Constitution of Uruguay rules that '[t]he protection of the environment is of general interest. People should refrain from any act that causes degradation, destruction or serious environmental pollution. The law shall regulate this provision and may provide penalties for offenders. Water is a natural resource essential for life. Access to safe drinking water and access to sanitation are fundamental human rights'.

In terms of specific forestry rights, the Constitution of Bhutan establishes the government's duty to ensure a minimum percentage of forest in its territory.[78] Additionally, the Guatemalan Constitution places special importance on protecting forests and declares that reforesting the country and conserving forests is an urgent national matter and in the interest of society and that forests as well as vegetation on the banks of rivers and lakes and within the vicinity of drinking-water sources will enjoy special protection.

The link between environmental concerns and economic practices within the forestry industry has been accepted throughout the world. The concept of sustainable forestry has been incorporated in the laws of states

---

[76] Constitution of Ecuador Ch. 7 (2008).
[77] 1991 Colombian Constitution (amended), Article 58.
[78] Constitution of the Kingdom of Bhutan (2008), Article 5.3.

across the globe and is an underpinning of recent forestry laws and practices. In addition to ensuring that forests are kept intact and safe from pollution as a general matter, many domestic legal regimes have come to focus on forestry practices as vital areas for regulation and protection of forests and the biodiversity within them. This includes measures to protect certain designated native forests, including the use of state funds to protect these areas.

Chilean Law 20283, relating to Native Forest Recovery and Forestry Development, promotes the objectives of protection, recovery and improvement of native forests with the aim of ensuring forest sustainability and environmental policy. The law creates a Competitive Fund for the conservation, restoration and sustainable management of the native forest, through which bonuses are awarded to help settle the costs of the mentioned activities. Further, the Chilean Budget Act annually reassesses a research fund for native forests, with the objective of promoting and increasing knowledge in matters related to native forest ecosystems, their management, preservation, protection, recovery and increase, notwithstanding the private contributions to complement it. The resources allocated for this procedure will be publicly competitive. Recent environmental valuation work in Kenya highlights the impact of forest ecosystem change to the national economy. A United Nations Environmental Programme (UNEP) supported Kenya Forest Service Report links the value of maintaining forests to the economy and has also stimulated the establishment of a steering committee on forest resource accounting, with efforts to include this accounting in official forest statistics.[79]

In order to oversee forestry practices, many states have turned to creating specialised administrative entities. These entities are often in control of the process required to obtain a permit for legal forestry and logging practices within a designated area as well as overseeing the industrial practices of those entities granted permits. Key concerns tend to focus on pollution of the areas being harvested as a result of harvesting practices as well as ensuring the use of sustainable forestry practices as required through laws and regulations.

This provides a legal framework for a national policy on payment for forest environmental services. The Decision stipulates the responsibilities

[79] Ministry of Environment of Kenya, *Technical Report on The National Assessment of Forest and Landscape Restoration Opportunities in Kenya 2016* (2016), http://afr100.org/sites/default/files/Kenya_Technical%20Report_Assessment%20of%20National%20Forest%20and%20Landscape%20Resto..._0.pdf.

and benefits of the payer and payees of forest environmental services (FES), the types of forest environmental service allowed, the norms of payments for use of service, the management of the money collected from FES and the responsibilities of the government agencies to the implementation of the policy on payment for FES. Further, Decree No. 99/2010/ND-CP on the Policy for Payment for Forest Environmental Services addresses the policy for payment for FES – including the types of environmental service that users pay to the suppliers[80] – the allowed suppliers and users of FES,[81] the management and use of the payment from FES, the rights and obligations of suppliers and users of FES and the responsibilities of state management agencies at various levels and of different sectors in implementing payment for FES.

Act 2780 of the province of Neuquén (Argentina) aims to establish guiding principles for the territorial management of native forests of the province as provided in Article 6 of the National Law 26331 on the Minimum Budgets for Environmental Protection of Native Forests. The aim of the National Law is to promote the conservation and sustainable use of native forests and promote activities for the conservation, recovery, enrichment, restoration, rehabilitation, research, sustainable management and use of native forests. However, the determination of compensation for environmental services is carried out through the Provincial Fund for Sustainable Use and Conservation of Native Forests which will be administered by the Ministry of Territorial Development or any administrative entity that replaces it in the future. Its destination will be indicated by the enforcement authority and will have the sole purpose of compensation for environmental or ecosystem services, conservation of native forests of the province and their environmental services and the promotion of sustainable use of native forests. To comply with the provisions established in the preceding article, the approval of conservation and sustainable management plans is required.

Costa Rican Law No. 36935 establishes the State Forestry Administration under the Ministry of Environment, Energy and Telecommunications (MINAET), through the National Forestry Financing Fund (FONAFIFO) and the National System for Conservation Areas (SINAC). Through negotiation for international and national cooperation projects, MINAET

[80] Decree No. 99/2010/ND-CP on the Policy for Payment for Forest Environmental Services, Article 4.
[81] Ibid. Articles 7 and 8.

requested financial support to strengthen and give continuity to the Payment for Environmental Services Programme, as well as to allow for the development and institutionalisation of other financing mechanisms, such as the sale of environmental services for the mitigation of greenhouse gases and the payment mechanism for the conservation of environmental services such as the water resources in Costa Rica.

Additionally, many states, particularly those in Africa, have enacted measures including the development of REDD and REDD+ programmes and their legal and societal incorporation. These measures include cooperation between state actors and international entities, such as the World Bank and UNEP, to further REDD goals such as law creation and programme generation. As an example of such measures, Ethiopia has situated its 'REDD Readiness Wheel' within the Climate Resilient Green Economy initiative developed by the Ethiopian government, explicitly incorporating REDD+ within the initiative that seeks to coordinate the main sectors of the economy to develop an environmentally sustainable growth path in Ethiopia. Forestry activities are part of Ethiopia's poverty reduction strategy and there are plans to extend participatory forest management across the country, which has the potential to contribute towards emission reductions as well as to greater empowerment and social equity. Ethiopia has recently secured funding from the World Bank's Forest Carbon Partnership Facility to continue to develop its national REDD+ strategy.

Forests are also explicitly included in Ethiopia's Climate Resilient Green Economy (CRGE) strategy, as 37 per cent of national greenhouse gas emissions come from the forestry and land-use sector. One of the four pillars of CRGE is the protection and re-establishment of forests for providing economic benefits and ecosystem services. CRGE seeks the protection and expansion of forest carbon stocks through reduced demand for fuelwood via fuel-efficient stoves, increased afforestation, reforestation and forest management. REDD+ was also integral in Ethiopia's Plan for Accelerated and Sustainable Development to End Poverty that promoted forest rehabilitation with the goal of increasing national forest cover. As a participant country in the World Bank's Forest Carbon Partnership Facility and a partner country of the UN-REDD Programme, Ethiopia now has the endorsement and finance to further develop a national REDD+ strategy and readiness.

There is a noticeable trend in state use of strategic action plans to evaluate economic policies and how they relate to the environment and forestry. This is of particular importance in the African region, where states are seeking to include REDD and REDD+ into their overall economic policies and practices. The African practices in this area demonstrate the importance of including all aspects of the market – regulatory, producer and consumer – into these plans. The African practices also highlight the importance of including sustainable development within these plans and focusing on the importance of poverty eradication as part of the state's economic development goals since poverty eradication is also an essential aspect of sustainable development, the green economy and green growth.

The Democratic Republic of the Congo has developed a 'REDD+ to a green economy' scenario as part of its analysis of policy reforms required for REDD+ with stakeholders and the Ministry of Planning, providing an example of what such transformation based on REDD+ investments. The REDD+ Framework Strategy, finalised in 2012, also includes direct reference to the importance of a green economy in REDD+ planning and processes. The Democratic Republic of the Congo's REDD+ framework includes direct reference to the green economy. Scenario analyses have been employed in the Democratic Republic of the Congo to establish REDD+ policy reform options and a pathway to 2035, and as part of this exercise, a 'REDD+ to a green economy' scenario was generated. The exercise raised awareness of the linkages between REDD+ and a green economy, including a variety of stakeholders, among them the Ministry of Planning. Also underway in the Democratic Republic of the Congo is sensitisation to and customisation of the Threshold-21 model. Threshold-21 is a simulation tool that can analyse different policy options to reach a desired goal. Developed by the Millennium Institute, the model integrates social, economic and environmental factors and can be customised to a country's context to support integrated planning as well as the monitoring and evaluation of results.

Illegal logging practices now serve as a threat to not only forests themselves but also the biodiversity within them and the lives of those who live near and work in them. The EU and its Member States have been at the forefront of this issue, as evidenced by the EU's laws on illegality in the timber industry. Additionally, France has enacted a similar piece of domestic legislation and has also adopted voluntary measures regarding the designation of products as legal timber. The use of voluntary measures is not just limited to the EU and has become important for producers in many states in order to certify to potential consumers that their products are legal. With an increasingly savvy market, particularly in the timber industry, these measures are important even if they are voluntary at this point.

III   Conclusions

This chapter has illustrated the role of law at international, regional and national levels to enable and incentivise an integrated approach to environmental governance as required by the concept of sustainable development and the green economy. It demonstrated that integration at the international level is possible and routinely occurs at the national level in legislation and decisions. Governance innovations at the national level highlight what could be discussed and eventually changed globally. As Cordonier Segger wrote in 2002: 'Without a comprehensive legal superstructure, nations find themselves bound to an increasingly complex web of unrealistic and at times contradictory legal obligations. The current situation is particularly unmanageable for developing countries.'[82] Only enhanced integration in global environmental governance as tested at the national level will address all new challenges in global environmental governance.

---

[82] M.-C. Cordonier Segger and A. Khalfan, 'Towards the World Summit on Sustainable Development: Crafting Legal Rules for Integrating Economic, Social and Environment Concerns' (Montreal, 8 April 2002), http://cisdl.org/public/docs/news/ArticleOp-Ed.pdf.

8

Tackling Mass Atrocity in a Globalised World

The International Criminal Court

OLYMPIA BEKOU

I Introduction

Crimes that 'shock the conscience of humanity' are as old as humanity itself. However, global responses to mass atrocity are a relatively recent phenomenon. In the absence of an international court to deal with crimes committed by individuals, the investigation and prosecution of genocide, crimes against humanity and aggression – the so-called core international crimes[1] – had been traditionally left to national criminal justice systems. Historically, however, trials before national courts have been the exception, not the norm.[2] As the exercise of criminal jurisdiction is a matter inextricably linked with state sovereignty, the possibility that an international institution could be seized with jurisdiction regarding such crimes took many years to materialise.

Whilst the idea of creating an international criminal court has a long history,[3] it was the Nuremberg trials that kick-started the efforts in earnest at the international level for a paradigm shift, from impunity to

---

[1] International crimes include both treaty crimes and core international crimes. Treaty crimes are crimes established by treaties and place obligations on states to either investigate and prosecute or extradite suspected perpetrators (the principle of *aut dedere, aut judicare*). Core international crimes are those which constitute the most serious crimes of concern to the international community. These crimes are criminalised and prosecuted both nationally and internationally, before international criminal courts and tribunals. See B. Broomhall, *International Justice and the International Criminal Court: Between Sovereignty and the Rule of Law* (Oxford University Press, 2005), 9–10.

[2] See e.g. the trial of Adolf Eichmann, one of the major organisers of the Holocaust. For a critical reflection on the Eichmann Trial, and international criminal justice generally, see H. Arendt, *Eichmann in Jerusalem: A Report on the Banality of Evil* (Penguin Books, 1994).

[3] J. Brierly, 'Do We Need an International Criminal Court?' (1927) 8 *British YBIL* 79.

accountability.[4] The recognition of individual criminal responsibility for core international crimes in the Nuremberg judgment[5] heralded the creation of a new field of law, that of international criminal law.

The Cold War led to a nearly fifty-year intermission regarding developing the discipline further, as efforts to create a permanent international criminal court in charge of dealing with core international crimes were stifled. Despite being called for in the immediate aftermath of the Nuremberg process, the International Criminal Court (ICC) did not materialise until after the atrocities in the former Yugoslavia and Rwanda in the early 1990s gripped public conscience, which led to the creation of the International Criminal Tribunal for the former Yugoslavia (ICTY), and the International Criminal Tribunal for Rwanda (ICTR),[6] respectively.

The ICC, a permanent treaty-based international institution, was established with the adoption of the Rome Statute ('ICC Statute') on 17 July 1998 with the conclusion of the negotiations at a multilateral conference in Rome,[7] and became operational on 1 July 2002.

The establishment of the ICC marks the creation of a permanent system of international criminal justice; a system with a universal sentiment, intended to make impunity the exception and ensure individual criminal accountability for 'the most serious crimes of international concern' through international investigations and prosecutions.[8] With the ICC firmly at its centre, the international criminal justice system relies on states, intergovernmental and non-governmental organisations to play their role in ending impunity. Indeed, as will be seen in the sections that follow, the very existence of this global institution is contingent on the interaction with other actors, not least because the Court does not have unfettered jurisdiction, unlimited resources or its own police force. Such synergies are therefore essential for the system to function and offer good insights

---

[4] B. V. A. Röling, 'The Nuremberg and Tokyo Trials in Retrospect' in M. C. Bassiouni and V. P. Nanda (eds.), *A Treatise on International Criminal Law* (Thomas, 1973), 590.

[5] Judgment of the Nuremberg IMT, reprinted in (1947) 41 *AJIL* 172, 221: 'That international law imposes duties and liabilities upon individuals as well as upon States has long been recognised ... Crimes against international law are *committed by men, not by abstract entities* and only by punishing individuals who commit such crimes can the provisions of international law be enforced.'

[6] Statute of the International Criminal Tribunal for the Former Yugoslavia, UNSC Resolution 827 (1993) (25 May 1993), UN Doc. S/RES/827 (1993), Annex, Article 8; Statute of the International Criminal Tribunal for Rwanda, UNSC Res. 955 (8 November 1944), UN Doc. S/RES/955, Annex, Article 7.

[7] Rome Statute of the ICC (signed 17 July 1998, entered into force 1 July 2002) 2187 UNTS 3 ('ICC Statute').

[8] Ibid., Article 1.

into the likely challenges other institutions operating on the global sphere might also face.

This permanent international criminal justice system does not operate to the exclusion of other (non-judicial) solutions. In the fight against impunity, other approaches have also been put forward, with varying degrees of success: from amnesties to truth and reconciliation commissions, to lustration and civil claims.[9] Whilst different transitional justice efforts have been used in different situations, judicial responses, which focus on the creation of international or internationalised courts, have remained a prominent option.[10]

Internationalised criminal courts, which combine international and domestic elements in terms of personnel and/or substantive law, offer an alternative forum for the pursuit of international criminal justice.[11] Examples include the Special Court for Sierra Leone,[12] the Extraordinary Chambers of the Courts of Cambodia[13], the Special Tribunal for Lebanon[14] and, more recently, the Central African Republic Special Criminal Court[15] and the Kosovo Specialist Chambers.[16] The establishment of the ICC did not halt the creation of other international(ised) Tribunals, whose jurisdiction covers specific situations and timeframes. Acknowledging their role in developing international criminal justice jurisprudence, such Tribunals will not be examined further in this chapter as, despite having been created with the support of the international community, they lack

---

[9] S. Cohen, 'State Crimes of Previous Regimes: Knowledge, Accountability and the Policing of the Past' (1995) 20 *Law and Social Inquiry* 7; K. Asmal, 'Truth, Reconciliation and Justice: The South African Experience in Perspective' (2000) 63 *MLR* 1; J. Dugard, 'Dealing with the Crimes of a Past Regime: Is Amnesty Still an Option?' (1999) 12 *Leiden JIL* 1001.

[10] M. J. Osiel, 'Why Prosecute? Critics of Punishment for Mass Atrocity' (2000) 22 *Human Rights Quarterly* 118.

[11] See, generally, C. P. R. Romano et al. (eds.), *Internationalized Criminal Courts: Sierra Leone, East Timor, Kosovo and Cambodia* (Oxford University Press, 2004).

[12] See www.rscsl.org/ and UNSC Resolution 1315(2000) S/RES/1315 (2000) 14 August 2000, www.rscsl.org/Documents/Establishment/S-Res-1315-2000.pdf.

[13] See www.eccc.gov.kh/en and www.eccc.gov.kh/sites/default/files/legal-documents/KR_Law_as_amended_27_Oct_2004_Eng.pdf.

[14] See UNSC Resolution 1757, S/RES/1757, 30 May 2007, www.stl-tsl.org/en/documents/un-documents/un-security-council-resolutions/225-security-council-resolution-1757 and https://www.stl-tsl.org/en/.

[15] See www.cps-rca.cf/fr and Loi organique no. 15.003 du 3 juin 2015 portant création, organisation et fonctionnement de la Cour Pénale Spéciale ('Loi organique portant création de la Cour Pénale Spéciale').

[16] See www.scp-ks.org/en and Law on Specialist Chambers and Specialist Prosecutor's Office, 3 August 2015, 05/L-053, www.kuvendikosoves.org/common/docs/ligjet/05-L-053%20a.pdf.

a truly global outlook. However, it is important to underline that where global institutions are created, it does not mean that other courts, with regional or local focus ought to cease to exist. Although proliferation of courts and tribunals may become an issue as far as providing a coherent response to mass atrocity is concerned, finding ways to collaborate, may ultimately achieve better results. However, this coexistence may be uneasy, as it will be seen in the sections that follow.

Returning to global institutions, with the ICC having marked its first fifteen years of operation, it is pertinent to consider some of its main achievements and challenges to assess its performance in the global environment. To do this, this chapter first revisits the context in which the ICC was established including some of its main aims and objectives. Mindful that putting an end to impunity continues to be elusive in many situations where mass atrocity occurs, the chapter reviews some key issues of the Court's first fifteen years in operation in order to explore its relevance as well as its limitations in a globalised world.

II The International Criminal Court: Establishment, Jurisdiction, Trigger Mechanisms

The rekindling of the international community's efforts to establish the ICC has its roots in 1989, and the question of a response to illicit trafficking in narcotic drugs and transnational crime. Unable to fight such transnational crimes alone, Trinidad and Tobago requested the creation of an international institution.[17] The debate crystallised in the United Nations General Assembly (UNGA), which asked the International Law Commission (ILC) to 'address the question of establishing an international criminal court or other international criminal trial mechanism'.[18] This was followed in the early 1990s, by the UNGA's request that the ILC 'continue its work on this question by undertaking the project for the elaboration of a draft statute for an international criminal court as a matter of priority'.[19] In 1992,

---

[17] United Nations, 'Overview of the International Criminal Court' in W. Driscoll et al. (eds.), *The International Criminal Court: Global Politics and the Quest for Justice* (The International Debate Education Association, 2004), 24.

[18] International criminal responsibility of individuals and entities engaged in illicit trafficking in narcotic drugs across national frontiers and other transnational criminal activities: establishment of an international criminal court with jurisdiction over such crimes, see UNGA Resolution 44/39, A/RES/44/39, 4 December 1989, www.un.org/documents/ga/res/44/a44r039.htm[1].

[19] Report of the International Law Commission on the Work of its Forty-Fourth Session, UNGA Resolution 47/33, A/RES/47/33, 25 November 1992 [6].

the ILC set up a working group which provided the 'the basic parameters' for a draft Statute.[20] Accordingly, the ILC produced a draft Statute in 1994,[21] and the UNGA established an Ad Hoc Committee to review arising issues.[22] A Preparatory Committee was subsequently formed in 1995, which met from 1996 to 1998 to discuss specific aspects of the text.

Following these early beginnings, the Preparatory Committee on the Establishment of an International Criminal Court focused on the text of the possible Statute for a proposed court, completing its work in April of 1998.[23] The report of the Preparatory Committee was debated at the Rome Conference, as the text of what became the ICC Statute contained many sets of square brackets, and issues such as jurisdiction or included crimes were yet to be finalised.[24] As the proposed Statute included areas which were sensitive both politically and in relation to the concept of sovereignty, such as the competence of the United Nations Security Council (UNSC), extradition, human rights, and international humanitarian law the negotiating process proved challenging.[25] In light of continuing perpetration of international crimes, the impetus for the creation of a global institution able to respond to such situations was clear.

Negotiation of the ICC Statute, namely, the United Nations Diplomatic Conference of Plenipotentiaries on the Establishment of an International Criminal Court ('the Rome Conference'), took place in Rome at the Food and Agriculture Organisation's headquarters between 15 June and 17 July 1998.[26] The participants in the negotiations included 160 States,

---

[20] J. Crawford, 'The ILC's Draft Statute for an International Criminal Tribunal' (1994) 88 *AJIL* 140.

[21] See, generally, Report of the International Law Commission on the Work of its Forty-Sixth Session, A/49/10, 2 May–22 July 1994, http://legal.un.org/ilc/documentation/6nglish/reports/a_49_10.pdf.

[22] UNGA, 'Establishment of an International Criminal Court' (9 December 1994), UN Doc. A/RES/49/53 [2].

[23] See Report of the Preparatory Committee on the Establishment of an International Criminal Court, Official Records of the United Nations Diplomatic Conference of Plenipotentiaries on the Establishment of an International Criminal Court (Reports and other documents), vol. III (Rome, Italy 15 June–17 July 1998), UN Doc. A/CONF.183/2; M. H. Arsanjani, 'The Rome Statute of the International Criminal Court' (1999) 93 *AJIL* 22.

[24] Report of the Preparatory Committee on the Establishment of an International Criminal Court (above n. 23), 15; Arsanjani, 'The Rome Statute of the International Criminal Court' (above n. 23), 22.

[25] Report of the Preparatory Committee on the Establishment of an International Criminal Court (above n. 23), 13; Arsanjani, 'The Rome Statute of the International Criminal Court' (above n. 23), 23.

[26] P. Kirsch and J. T. Holmes, 'The Rome Conference on the International Criminal Court: The Negotiating Process' (1999) 93 *AJIL* 2.

thirty-three intergovernmental organisations and a coalition of 236 non-governmental organisations (NGOs) under an umbrella organisation, the Coalition for the International Criminal Court (CICC).[27] Participants' numbers were high, particularly given the subject matter of this treaty. This was also the first international conference where NGOs had such a strong voice and were able to influence aspects of the Statute, such as the inclusion of provisions concerning victims and fair trial standards.[28]

Amidst considerable disagreement amongst the delegates and after six weeks of intense negotiations, the ICC Statute was adopted by an overwhelming majority on the 17 July 1998, with 120 votes in favour, 7 against and 21 abstentions.[29] The Statute came into force on the 1 July 2002: sixty days after the sixtieth ratification of the Rome Statute.[30] The elation that was felt in international law circles at the time, was matched only by surprise as many thought it impossible that the ICC Statute would attract the necessary ratifications only four years after being adopted.[31] This was a major achievement, not least because sovereignty was thought to be a major factor in states' reticence over what traditionally is a reserved domain.[32]

Whilst the intention for a global move towards international justice is evident, it must be noted that the ICC Statute, being an international treaty, only binds states which have accepted its jurisdiction through ratification or accession to it. By choosing to be bound by the ICC Statute, states demonstrate shared commitment to the aims and values embodied within it, such as international justice and respect for human rights.[33]

The ICC is able to exercise jurisdiction over crimes committed by natural persons,[34] in both the territory of a State Party and by nationals of a State Party.[35] In this sense, the Statute adopts a traditional approach regarding

---

[27] Arsanjani, 'The Rome Statute of the International Criminal Court' (above n. 23), 22.

[28] K. Anderson, 'The Ottawa Convention Banning Landmines, the Role of International Non-Governmental Organizations and the Idea of International Civil Society' (2000) 11 *EJIL* 91.

[29] States which voted against the ICC Statute: Iraq, Israel, Libya, China, Qatar, Yemen and the United States.

[30] ICC Statute (above n. 7); for information on the ratification of the ICC Statute see www.un.org/apps/news/story.asp?NewsID=3360&Cr=icc&Cr1#.WK7GHjuLTD4.

[31] Ibid.

[32] R. Cryer, 'International Criminal Law vs State Sovereignty: Another Round?' (2005) 16 *EJIL* 979, 981–3.

[33] ICC Statute (above n. 7), preamble.

[34] Ibid., Article 25.

[35] Ibid., Article 12.

the principles of jurisdiction.[36] The ICC possesses neither passive personality jurisdiction,[37] nor universal jurisdiction.[38] However, territorial jurisdiction implies that, when a crime falling under the Court's jurisdiction
has occurred on the territory of a State Party, the ICC could investigate
situations involving nationals of non-State Parties.[39] Additionally, the
ICC can investigate situations that occurred on the territory of non-State
Parties but which involved nationals of State Parties.[40]

Although the ICC exists independently from the UN Charter regime, it
can accept referrals of situations by the UNSC acting under its Chapter VII
powers, including those involving States not party to the ICC Statute, thus
considerably expanding the Court's potential reach.[41] Indeed, the situations in Sudan[42] and Libya,[43] both non-State Parties, have been referred to
the ICC by the Security Council by Chapter VII Resolutions.

Other ways to trigger the Court's jurisdiction involve a referral of a situation by a State Party[44] or the Prosecutor of the ICC, acting on his or her
own volition in accordance with Article 15 of the Rome Statute.[45] Self-
referrals, albeit not prohibited, had not been explicitly envisaged at the
time of drafting,[46] but have been a popular way of triggering the Court's
jurisdiction. Of the eleven situations under investigation at the time of
writing, five are self-referrals by States Parties, and three have been opened
using the Prosecutor's *proprio motu* powers.[47]

---

[36] See Part VII State Jurisdiction in J. Crawford, *Brownlie's Principles of Public International
Law*, 8th edn (Oxford University Press, 2012).
[37] I.e. jurisdiction over the nationality of the victims.
[38] O. Bekou and R. Cryer, 'The International Criminal Court and Universal Jurisdiction: A
Close Encounter?' (2007) 56 *ICLQ* 49–68.
[39] ICC Statute (above n. 7), Article 12.
[40] One such situation currently under preliminary examination before the Court involves
alleged crimes committed by UK soldiers (i.e. nationals of a state party) in Iraq (a non-
state party) in the context of the Iraq conflict and occupation from 2003 to 2008. See www
.icc-cpi.int/iraq.
[41] Ibid., Article 13(b).
[42] See UNSC Resolution 1593 (2005), S/RES/1593, 31 March 2005, www.icc-cpi.int/NR/
rdonlyres/85FEBD1A-29F8-4EC4-9566-48EDF55CC587/283244/N0529273.pdf.
[43] See UNSC Resolution 1970 (2011), S/RES/1970, 26 February 2011, www.icc-cpi.int/NR/
rdonlyres/081A9013-B03D-4859-9D61-5D0B0F2F5EFA/0/1970Eng.pdf.
[44] ICC Statute (above n. 7), Article 13(a).
[45] Ibid., Article 13(c).
[46] C. Kress '"Self-Referrals" and "Waivers of Complementarity"': Some Considerations in Law
and Policy' (2004) 2 *JICJ* 944.
[47] For situations under investigation see www.icc-cpi.int/pages/situations.aspx.

III   The ICC at 15: Globalisation of International Criminal Justice in Action

The field of international criminal justice is laden with grand aims, many enshrined in the ICC Statute's Preambular paragraphs, including reinforcing accountability; ending impunity; bringing justice to victims and affected communities; reconciliation; assisting peace and justice; and restoring the rule of law.[48] With the ICC in operation, expectations as to what this global institution could, or should do, have grown disproportionately to its ability to fulfil them.

It would be unrealistic to expect that the ICC could tackle all of the above within the first fifteen years of its operation. The ICC must also work within its own limitations; it is restricted in its function by the context in which it operates and the modalities of its constituting treaty (i.e. the ICC Statute). Issues of jurisdiction, budget, organisational efficiency and political will have all played a role in how the Court has performed, to date. Given the global context in which, by design, the ICC operates, there are clearly some areas where it has done well, and others where it needs to do better in order to fulfil its mandate. It is not possible to empirically measure the numbers of deaths and the instances of suffering that have been avoided, or, conversely, inflicted, as a result of the ICC's very existence.[49] However, measuring peoples' perceptions of the Court and employing performance indicators can assist in quantifying the ICC's success, or lack thereof, more generally.[50] For this chapter, whilst acknowledging the broader context, the focus is on selected key issues facing the ICC that better reflect, in the author's view, the global challenges faced by the Court.

After fifteen years of operation, the ICC is a fully fledged institution with the crimes under its jurisdiction and rules and procedures agreed to, some of which have also already been amended.[51] The definition of the crime of aggression, which owing to lack of agreement had been left out

---

[48] ICC Statute (above n. 7), preamble.

[49] G. Dancy and F. Montal, 'From Law versus Politics to Law in Politics: A Pragmatist Assessment of the ICC's Impact' (2017) 32 *AUILR* 645, 671–3.

[50] J. Clark, 'International War Crimes Tribunals and the Challenge of Outreach' (2009) 9 *International Criminal Law Review* 99, 113–15.

[51] For provisional amendment of the Rules of Procedure and Evidence (RPE) see www.icc-cpi .int/Pages/item.aspx?name=pr1194. Unlike the ad hoc Tribunals for the former Yugoslavia and Rwanda where RPE amendments were judge-led, it is important to highlight the role played by the Assembly of States Parties, the Court's governing body, in amending the ICC's RPE. Whilst the involvement of the Assembly of States Parties makes the process arguably more transparent, amendments can be slow, detached from the everyday practice of the Court and subject to political horse-trading.

of the ICC Statute at the end of the Rome Conference, was agreed upon during the first review conference in Kampala in 2010.[52] As the requisite number of ratifications of the amendment had been reached, in December 2017, the Sixteenth Assembly of States Parties adopted a Resolution activating the ICC's jurisdiction over the crime of aggression.[53] All four of the ICC's organs – Presidency, Chambers, Office of the Prosecutor (OTP) and Registry – are in operation. Improvements and developments are continually being made regarding the Court's day-to-day operation, including, for example, the former Registrar's *ReVision* project which aimed to reform the operation of the Registry.[54]

The ICC has had many firsts within its jurisprudence, which are too numerous to mention in this piece. Highlights include: the significance of the *Lubanga* case,[55] as the first case before the Court; the award of victims' reparations;[56] the ongoing *Ongwen* Trial,[57] the first Lord's Resistance Army commander to come before the Court, himself a former child soldier; the *Al Mahdi* case involving cultural property;[58] and the *Bemba* case, to name just a few.[59] As the ICC develops its own jurisprudence, it begins to leave its mark on international criminal justice. On the other hand, there are also a number of issues that have arisen including: procedural setbacks; the slow pace of justice;[60] the collapse of cases; the quality of some of the investigations;[61] witness tampering; and the overall cost and length (also

---

[52] The Crime of Aggression, ICC ASP RC/Res. 6, 11 June 2010, Annex I: Amendments to the Rome Statute of the International Criminal Court on the crime of aggression.

[53] For an up-to-date report of the ratification progress see http://crimeofaggression.info/documents//1/Status_Report-ENG.pdf. For the text of the activation resolution see https://asp.icc-cpi.int/iccdocs/asp_docs/Resolutions/ASP16/ICC-ASP-16-Res5-ENG.pdf.

[54] See, generally, The Registry, *Comprehensive Report on the Reorganisation of the Registry of the International Criminal Court* (ICC, 2016), www.icc-cpi.int/itemsDocuments/ICC-Registry-CR.pdf.

[55] *The Prosecutor* v. *Thomas Lubanga Dyilo*, Judgment Pursuant to Article 74 of the Statute, ICC-01/04–01/06, 14 March 2012.

[56] For information on individual and collective reparations awarded to victims of crimes committed by Germain Katanga see www.icc-cpi.int/Pages/item.aspx?name=pr1288.

[57] *The Prosecutor* v. *Dominic Ongwen*, Decision on Legal Representatives' Request Regarding Opening Statements ICC-02/04–01/15, 29 November 2016.

[58] *The Prosecutor* v. *Ahmad Al Faqi Al Mahdi*, Judgment and Sentence ICC-01/12–01/15, 27 September 2016.

[59] *The Prosecutor* v. *Jean-Pierre Bemba Gombo*, Judgment Pursuant to Article 74 of the Statute, ICC-01/05–01/08, 21 March 2016.

[60] G. Higgins, 'Fair and Expeditious Pre-Trial Proceedings: The Future of International Criminal Trials' (2007) 5 *JICJ* 394–5.

[61] See, generally, D. Groome, 'No Witness, No Case: An Assessment of the Conduct and Quality of ICC Investigations' (2014) 3 *Journal of Law and International Affairs* 1–112.

in terms of page numbers) of the decisions.[62] Instead of going through the details of the jurisprudence and the minutiae of particular findings, this chapter focuses on wider institutional challenges faced by a global justice Court, and how they may affect its success and future prospects. The four challenges identified, involve the Court's universality, independence, effectiveness and efficiency, cooperation with states and relationship with national jurisdictions. In selecting to focus upon these challenges, which are common also to other courts, the chapter aims to shed some light on how the ICC has responded to them and hopefully highlight some transferrable insights that may be proven useful to other courts.

A   Universality

The ICC was created on the promise of universality. Unlike the ad hoc or other internationalised Tribunals, with limited geographical, temporal or jurisdictional focus, the ICC, being a permanent institution with prospective jurisdiction, has been designed to be universal.

Universality therefore represents the first challenge the Court faces in fulfilling its global mission, including reconciling the ICC with all regions of the world. In recent years, the Court's relationship with Africa has been the focus of intense diplomatic and scholarly attention and certain actions by some African members have threatened the global justice system the Court represents.[63] As such, recent developments in relation to membership of this continent, will be examined below as well. From a global perspective, it is interesting to explore how a global institution may be perceived by one of the regions it is meant to serve, alongside others, and try to understand the tensions that may arise.

Few would have thought that fifteen years after its coming into force, the Statute would count 123 State Parties amongst its members.[64] High membership of the Court is particularly encouraging, given that criminal jurisdiction is traditionally regarded as a 'reserved domain', a sign of national sovereignty. As already noted, the entry into force of the ICC Statute in

---

[62] G. Sluiter and S. Vasiliev, 'International Criminal Court' (2007) 25 *Netherlands Quarterly of Human Rights* 329, 340.

[63] G. Werle et al. (eds.), *Africa and the International Criminal Court* (T. M. C. Asser Press, 2014); K. Diakité, *La Justice pénale internationale en Afrique. Aspects juridiques, défis et perspectives* (L'Harmattan, 2014); Société Africaine pour le Droit International (SADI), *L'Afrique et le droit international pénal* (Pedone, 2015).

[64] For a list of ratifications see https://asp.icc-cpi.int/en_menus/asp/states%20parties/Pages/the%20states%20parties%20to%20the%20rome%20statute.aspx.

July 2002 marked the beginning of a new system of international criminal justice; a universal system designed to ensure accountability for crimes under international criminal law. High membership is a desirable attribute of an institution purporting to be global, so achieving universality has been an issue high on the ICC's agenda.

While the objective of universality is not explicitly mentioned in the ICC Statute, the universal sentiment is evident; the Statute's preamble acknowledges the universality of the human experience and states that international crimes within the jurisdiction of the Court 'threaten the peace, security and well-being of *the world*' (emphasis added).[65]

The drafters of the ICC Statute realised that the Court is not, nor can it be, the only actor. In 2006, the ICC Assembly of States Parties adopted a Plan of Action aimed at achieving universality of the ICC Statute.[66] The Plan of Action recognises that such universality is imperative to ending impunity for the most serious international crimes, contributing to the prevention of such crimes, and guaranteeing lasting respect for and enforcement of international justice.[67] Additionally, it acknowledges that '[f]ull and effective implementation of the ICC Statute by all States Parties is equally vital to the achievement of these objectives'.[68] This illustrates wider objectives of universality than endowing the ICC with jurisdiction over all territories and people. The values and principles enshrined within the ICC Statute are also intended to become universally recognised and respected.

With every new ratification of the Rome Statute – including the most recent ones: Palestine and El Salvador – comes welcome progress towards achieving universality.[69] However, it is a disturbing truth that an overwhelming majority of the world's population is excluded from the jurisdiction of the ICC. Four of the five most populated states in the world – China, India, the United States of America and Indonesia – are not yet ICC State Parties.[70] Whilst such populations can come under ICC jurisdiction when a situation is referred to the Court by the UNSC, the repeated failure to

---

[65] ICC Statute (above n. 7), preamble, paras. 1 and 3.
[66] Strengthening the International Criminal Court and the Assembly of States Parties, ICC-ASP/5/Res. 3, 1 December 2006; Plan of Action of the Assembly of States Parties for Achieving Universality and Full Implementation of the Rome Statute of the International Criminal Court, ICC-ASP/5/Res. 3, Annex I (hereafter 'ASP Universality Plan of Action').
[67] ASP Universality Plan of Action (above n. 66), paras. 1 and 2.
[68] Ibid.
[69] For a list of ratifications see https://asp.icc-cpi.int/en_menus/asp/states%20parties/pages/the%20states%20parties%20to%20the%20rome%20statute.aspx.
[70] For a list of ratifications see ibid.

refer the situation in Syria[71] to the Court illustrates that the UNSC can often be deeply divided when dealing with matters of international criminal justice. Accordingly, though remarkable that 123 states are party to the ICC Statute, supporters of the international criminal justice system must continue to strive for universal ratification, so as to achieve justice at a global level. This requires government institutions to work together with global civil society, to continue to call upon states, which have not yet done so, to ratify the ICC Statute, including (permanent) members of the UNSC. However, given the international political climate at the time of writing, which sees an increase in nationalism and populism, the future currently appears uncertain regarding success with certain states.

With pessimism vis-à-vis ratification by states at the present time, the ICC also faces challenges in its relationship with existing members, particularly those located in Africa. Africa is the continent with the highest number of State Parties to the ICC Statute, with a total of thirty-three.[72] Moreover, four of the sixteen serving judges at the ICC are from African State Parties, not to mention the fact that the position of Prosecutor is also occupied by an African, Ms Fatou Bensouda from Gambia. It is also notable that much of the early support for the Court came from African States: to date, four ICC State Parties – Uganda, the Democratic Republic of the Congo, the Central African Republic and Mali – have referred situations occurring on their territories to the ICC.[73] Indeed, all but one of the eleven situations currently before the ICC originate from the African continent. When the Georgian investigation was opened, many thought: 'Finally, the ICC is out of Africa!' With the intended or actual African withdrawals however, some cynics may well have thought: 'Africa, is finally out of the ICC!' It is worth mentioning that a number of non-African situations are currently under preliminary examination.[74] As these situations progress and investigations are being opened, the ICC moves a step closer in fulfilling its global reach.

Before returning to the issue of withdrawals, the relationship between Africa and the ICC more broadly must be considered; it is no secret that

---

[71] For recent failures dating from 2014 see www.un.org/press/en/2014/sc11407.doc.htm and www.un.org/apps/news/story.asp?NewsID=55408#.WRIuDOUrLD4.

[72] For a list of ratifications see https://asp.icc-cpi.int/en_menus/asp/states%20parties/pages/the%20states%20parties%20to%20the%20rome%20statute.aspx.

[73] For situations under investigation see www.icc-cpi.int/pages/situations.aspx.

[74] For situations under preliminary examination see www.icc-cpi.int/pages/pe.aspx.

the relationship has not been straightforward.[75] Concerns have been expressed by certain African states that the ICC's perceived almost exclusive focus on investigations and prosecutions in Africa to date suggests that the Court is unfairly targeting Africa.[76] The ICC is often ironically described as 'the European Court for Africa', a reference to Western states' providing most of the Court's funding. However, the perceived bias against Africa can be easily dispelled, as most of the African situations currently before the ICC have been self-referred.[77] The fact that the two UNSC referrals, Sudan and Libya,[78] are also geographically located in Africa may be seen as an issue, but this is down to the balance of power at the UNSC, rather than an attempt to target Africa *per se*. Ultimately, the ICC, like any global court, must continue to be seen to investigate and prosecute, without distinction, all persons accused of committing the crimes under its jurisdiction, regardless of their location and nationality.

Returning to the issue of withdrawals and threats thereof, in late 2016, three states – Burundi,[79] South Africa[80] and Gambia[81] – announced their intention to withdraw from the ICC Statute.[82] Although saddening, legally, states are entitled to withdraw from a treaty in accordance with the provisions enshrined in that treaty; the procedure in the ICC Statute can be found in its Article 127.[83] Speculating on the motivation behind the inten-

---

[75] See, generally, O. Bekou and S. Shah, 'Realising the Potential of the International Criminal Court: The African Experience' (2006) 6 *Human Rights Law Review* 499–544.

[76] E. Keppler, 'Managing Setbacks for the International Criminal Court in Africa' (2012) 56 *Journal of African Law* 1, 6–7; see, generally, M. du Plessis et al., 'Africa and the International Criminal Court' (2013) 11 *Criminal Justice* 563–70.

[77] For situations under investigation see www.icc-cpi.int/pages/situations.aspx.

[78] See above nn. 42 and 43.

[79] Rome Statute of the International Criminal Court, Burundi: Withdrawal, C.N.805.2016. TREATIES-XVIII.10 (Depositary Notification), 27 October 2016, https://treaties.un.org/doc/Publication/CN/2016/CN.805.2016-Eng.pdf.

[80] Declaratory statement by the Republic of South Africa on the decision to withdraw from the Rome Statute of the International Criminal Court, C.N.786.2016.TREATIES-XVIII.10 (Depositary Notification), 19 October 2016, https://treaties.un.org/doc/Publication/CN/2016/CN.786.2016-Eng.pdf.

[81] Letter outlining Gambia's decision to withdraw from the Statute: PA 383/01/Part VI (117-NMG), 8 November 2016.

[82] Joe Bavier, 'Gambia Announces Withdrawal from International Criminal Court (26 October 2016)', *Reuters*, www.reuters.com/article/us-gambia-icc-idUSKCN12P335?il=0; Africa News 'Nkurunziza Signs Law Withdrawing Burundi's ICC Membership (18 October 2016)' *AN*, www.africanews.com/2016/10/18/nkurunziza-signs-law-withdra wing-burundi-s-icc-membership/; South Africa: SA Formally withdrawing form ICC, http://allafrica.com/stories/201610210877.html.

[83] ICC Statute (above n. 7), Article 127, para. 1. A State Party may, by written notification addressed to the Secretary-General of the United Nations, withdraw from this Statute. The

tion of these states to withdraw is beyond the scope of this chapter; however, a desire to protect their leaders has been evident in at least two of the above examples.

In the case of South Africa, it seemed to be a matter of internal politics around the Sudanese President Al Bashir's visit in 2015, and his departure from the country despite an order from the High Court of South Africa (Gauteng Division, Pretoria) ordering his arrest pursuant to an ICC arrest warrant.[84] The High Court of South Africa found in its decision on the matter that the notice of withdrawal from the ICC Statute without prior parliamentary approval, is unconstitutional and invalid.[85] As a result, on 7 March 2017, South Africa decided to revoke, with immediate effect, the instrument of withdrawal from the Rome Statute deposited by the government of South Africa with the Secretary-General of the United Nations on 19 October 2016, by notifying the UN Secretary-General.[86]

It is worth noting that pursuant to a decision issued by Pre-Trial Chamber II on 8 December 2016, the Chamber convened a public hearing to determine whether to make a finding of non-compliance by South Africa with the ICC's request for the arrest and surrender of Omar Al Bashir. The matter was also referred to the Assembly of States Parties and the UNSC, under Article 87(7) ICC Statute.[87] On 6 July 2017 the Pre-Trial Chamber in its decision on the matter found that 'South Africa failed to comply with its obligations under the Statute by not executing the Court's request for the arrest of Omar Al-Bashir and his surrender to the Court while he was on South African territory.'[88] However, it decided against a referral to the Assembly of States Parties or the Security Council for non-compliance.

---

withdrawal shall take effect one year after the date of receipt of the notification, unless the notification specifies a later date.

[84] See, generally, *Southern African Litigation Centre* v. *Minister of Justice and Constitutional Development and Others*, High Court of South Africa (Gauteng Division, Pretoria) 27740/2015 (24 June 2015); for information on the Al Bashir Case at the ICC see www.icc-cpi.int/darfur/albashir.

[85] See, generally, *Democratic Alliance* v. *Minister of International Relations and Cooperation and Others*, High Court of South Africa (Gauteng Division, Pretoria) 83145/2016 (22 February 2017).

[86] Rome Statute of the International Criminal Court, South Africa: Withdrawal of Notification of Withdrawal, C.N.121.2017.TREATIES-XVIII.10 (Depositary Notification), 7 March 2017, https://treaties.un.org/doc/publication/CN/2017/CN.121.2017-Eng.pdf.

[87] *The Prosecutor* v. *Omar Hassan Ahmad Al Bashir*, Decision convening a public hearing for the purposes of a determination under Article 87(7) of the Statute with respect to the Republic of South Africa, ICC-02/05–01/09, 8 December 2016.

[88] See *Situation in Darfur, Sudan in the Case of the Prosecutor v Omar Hassan Ahmad Al-Bashir, Decision under article 87(7) of the Rome Statute on the non-compliance by South*

Gambia's withdrawal from the ICC was reversed following the newly elected President Adama Barrow's taking of office who confirmed that Gambia will not be withdrawing from the ICC after all.[89] On 10 February 2017, Gambia's Permanent Mission to the UN delivered to the UN Secretary-General notification of the country's rescission of its withdrawal from the ICC Statute.[90]

At the time of writing, the only country that has followed through with their withdrawal from the ICC is Burundi. Its withdrawal took effect on 27 October 2017. On 25 October 2017, the ICC Prosecutor was authorised by Pre-trial Chamber III to open a *proprio motu* investigation in a decision first issued under seal.[91]

Moreover, the African Union (AU) has scaled up its anti-ICC approach; during the twenty-eighth Ordinary Summit of the AU, the regional body adopted an 'ICC Withdrawal Strategy'.[92] Despite its name, the strategy does not actually call for mass withdrawal. Instead, it adopts a two-pronged approach calling on more research to be done on the so-called 'collective withdrawals' and outlines a timeline for proposed Rome Statute amendments (i.e. reform) that AU members would like to see being agreed upon. These include, among others, Head of State or Government immunity, whilst in office.[93] Furthermore, in its Thirtieth Summit, the AU decided to seek an advisory opinion from the International Court of Justice on the

---

Africa with the request by the Court for the arrest and surrender of Omar Al-Bashir, Pre-Trial Chamber II, ICC-02/05-01/09, 6 July 2017, www.icc-cpi.int/CourtRecords/CR2017_04402 .PDF.

[89] See Adama Barrow, President of the Republic of Gambia, 'First Press Conference in Banjul' (questions and answers at The President's first press conference, 28 January 2017), www .youtube.com/watch?v=I9O_t514Gzc.

[90] See Rome Statute of the International Criminal Court, Gambia: Withdrawal of notification withdrawal C.N.62.2017.TREATIES-XVIII.10 (Depositary Notification), 10 February 2017, https://treaties.un.org/doc/Publication/CN/2017/CN.62.2017-Eng.pdf.

[91] See www.icc-cpi.int/burundi. A public version of the said decision was published on 9 November 2017. See *Situation in the Republic of Burundi, Pubic Redacted Version of 'Decision Pursuant to Article 15 of the Rome Statute on the Authorization of an Investigation into the Situation in the Republic of Burundi'*, ICC-01/17-X-9-US-Exp, Pre-Trial Chamber III, 25 October 2017 ICC-01/17-X, 25 October 2017, www.icc-cpi.int/CourtRecords/ CR2017_06720.PDF.

[92] www.hrw.org/sites/default/files/supporting_resources/icc_withdrawal_strategy_ jan._2017.pdf.

[93] See Elise Keppler, 'AU's "ICC Withdrawal Strategy" Less than Meets the Eye', 1 February 2017, www.hrw.org/news/2017/02/01/aus-icc-withdrawal-strategy-less-meets-eye; Allan Ngari, 'The AU's ICC Strategy Presents a New Avenue for Dialogue as Much as it Urges Withdrawal' Institute for Security Studies, 14 February 2017, https://issafrica.org/iss-today/ the-aus-other-icc-strategy.

question of immunities of heads of state and government and other senior officials.[94]

The above developments challenge the ICC's global outlook. ICC membership in Africa is under attack. Leaving the ICC is not the answer to the African States' problems, as there is no other body that could replace the Court's functions. Moreover, the tumultuous relationship between Africa and ICC seems to have had a spill-over effect in other situations. On 17 March 2018 the Republic of the Philippines deposited a written notification of withdrawal from the Rome Statute.[95] If a State Party has concerns over its relationship with the Court, then leaving the ICC family is not the answer; instead, trying to find solutions from within, through constructive dialogue and exchanges is a safer way to ensure that impunity does not take the place of justice. For other global courts, what this experience shows is that international institutions ought to cater for the differing needs their diverse membership entails. This calls for navigating regional challenges when interacting with certain regions, particularly where there is a widely held perception of bias.

The experience with Africa has also brought up another issue, that of regionalisation. The only instance of regional international criminal justice prosecution in practice is that of former Chad President Hissène Habré before the Extraordinary African Chambers. A hybrid court, established within the Senegalese justice system to deal with the atrocities in Chad between 1982 and 1990,[96] there was no scope for it to compete with the ICC. However, the question as to whether a regional court would be incompatible with the ICC remains and is likely to arise again in the future, also in Africa. The Malabo protocol,[97] aimed at expanding the jurisdiction of the African Court of Justice and Human Rights to include a criminal chamber with jurisdiction over core international crimes, may in

[94] See Decisions, Declarations and Resolution Assembly of the Union, Thirtieth Ordinary Session, 28–29 January 2018, Addis Ababa, Ethiopia, https://au.int/sites/default/files/decisions/33908-assembly_decisions_665_-_689_e.pdf.

[95] See www.icc-cpi.int/Pages/item.aspx?name=pr1371. A preliminary examination into the situation of the Philippines was opened by the ICC prosecutor on 8 February 2018. See www.icc-cpi.int/Pages/item.aspx?name=180208-otp-stat.

[96] Ministère Public c. Hissein Habrè, Judgment CAE, 30 mai 2016, www.chambresafricaines.org/pdf/Jugement_complet.pdf.

[97] For the Malabo Protocol see www.au.int/web/sites/default/files/treaties/7804-treaty-0045_-_protocol_on_amendments_to_the_protocol_on_the_statute_of_the_african_court_of_justice_and_human_rights_e.pdf.

the future lead to jurisdictional conflicts.[98] Whilst regional efforts should not be *a priori* incompatible with the global court, more work needs to be done to clarify the effect of such developments in practice.

In recent years, a number of initiatives have been employed in an effort to diffuse the tensions and solve the ICC's 'Africa problem', ranging from a dialogue with the AU, to debates before the Assembly of States Parties meetings.[99] The relationship between Africa and the ICC has become a standing item in such meetings, where, besides the anticipated attacks towards the Court (see e.g. Burundi's statement in the general debate),[100] there are efforts on behalf of most other states, including many from Africa, to support the Court in the delivery of its mandate, reaffirming their commitment towards the ICC.[101]

With a view to the future, if the ICC were to undertake all activities in a transparent and accountable manner, it would contribute to the restoration of trust in the Court and to the strengthening of its legitimacy across the world, including also across Africa.

B   Independence, Efficiency and Effectiveness

Achieving universality regarding the Court's membership is not sufficient, on its own, for the ICC to succeed in performing its global function. As with any court, be it national or international, ensuring that the ICC is independent, efficient and effective is key to its success. Consequently, preserving the Court's integrity ought to be an important aim, if the ICC were to become truly universal. A court's independence is one – if not *the* – defining and distinguishing feature of a justice system operating in accordance with the rule of law.

Ensuring that the ICC is independent as an institution but also that each of its organs enjoys such independence, played a central part in the

---

[98] G. Werle and M. Vormbaum (eds.), *The African Criminal Court: A Commentary on the Malabo Protocol* (T. M. C. Asser Press, 2017); M. Sirleaf, 'The African Justice Cascade and the Malabo Protocol' (2017) 11 *International Journal of Transitional Justice* 71–91; C. B. Murungu, 'Towards a Criminal Chamber in the African Court of Justice and Human Rights' (2011) 9 *JICJ* 1067–88.

[99] K. M. Clarke et al., *Africa and the ICC: Perceptions of Justice* (Cambridge University Press, 2016), 2.

[100] https://asp.icc-cpi.int/iccdocs/asp_docs/ASP15/GenDeba/ICC-ASP15-GenDeba-Burundi-ENG.pdf.

[101] At the time of writing, on the occasion of change in the Court's presidency, a number of states wrote to the Court to express their strong support. See www.icc-cpi.int/Pages/item.aspx?name=pr1378.

negotiations during the Rome Conference. As a result, independence per-meates the entire ICC Statute, from the preamble through to the obliga-tions imposed upon judges to ensure their independence.[102] In addition, the OTP is not only independent from outside actors, but, importantly, it is also independent from the other organs of the Court.[103]

However, this independence is not absolute, and certain concessions are envisaged in the way the system has been set up to function: for instance, the power of the UNSC to refer situations involving non-State Parties under Article 13(b) of the ICC Statute, and its power to defer or suspend proceedings for up to a year pursuant to Article 16, are two areas in which the independence of the Court has been qualified. While Article 13(b) of the ICC Statute opens up the possibility that the Court may exercise jurisdiction over non-State Parties, as we have seen in the case of Sudan or Libya,[104] thus expanding the Court's jurisdictional ambit and further-ing the Court's global reach, the question of when that jurisdiction may be triggered is subject to the high politics of UNSC decision-making. Similarly, enabling the UNSC to prevent the Court from acting, in line with Article 16, interferes in the Court's independence, as the judicial function of the Court is submitted to the politics of the UNSC. Needless to say, both scenarios are subject to the veto power enjoyed by the five per-manent members of the UNSC.[105] Whereas in the case of referrals a veto would block the ICC from exercising jurisdiction, in the case of Article 16 deferrals, a veto would allow the Court to continue with its investigations and prosecutions and as such, it has been described as the 'only positive function of the veto power'.[106]

Equally important as actual independence is the *perceived* independ-ence; the ICC and its organs must not only be independent, but also be seen to be independent. The legitimacy of the ICC (i.e. the degree to which its investigations, trials and decisions) are accepted by those subject to its jurisdiction, depends to a large extent upon the degree to which the Court is perceived to be independent. Challenges to the Court's legitimacy in recent years demonstrate the role that independence plays in the course

---

[102] ICC Statute (above n. 7), Article 40.
[103] Ibid., Article 42.
[104] Above n. 78.
[105] As an example, consider the complexities around acting on the situation in Syria; see, gen-erally, S. Adams, *Failure to Protect: Syria and the UN Security Council* (Global Centre for the Responsibility to Protect, Occasional Paper Series, 2015), www.globalr2p.org/media/files/syriapaper_final.pdf.
[106] F. Lattanzi, 'Compétence de la Cour pénale internationale et consentement des états' (1999) 103 *Revue Générale de Droit International Public* 425, at 443.

of promoting the universality and integrity of the Statute and cooperation with the Court. Critics of the Court frequently raise the perception of bias to justify their action in respect to the Court.[107]

The reason why any actor – be it a State Party, international institution or non-governmental organisation – lends support to the ICC is so as to enable it to be effective in the fulfilment of its mandate.[108] By pursuing the universality of the Statute and preserving its integrity, and by encouraging cooperation with the Court and implementing the principle of complementarity,[109] these actors are contributing not only to the effectiveness and efficiency of the ICC specifically, but the effectiveness and efficiency of the Rome Statute system as a whole. Effectiveness can be measured in any number of possible ways, but in general terms, each seeks to measure the extent to which the Rome Statute system fulfils its objectives. Effectiveness and efficiency are inextricably linked. The more efficient that the Court is, the more effective it is, and the more credible it will be as a deterrent to the commission of core international crimes in the future. However, this translates at a more practical level in the ICC being increasingly expected to achieve more with less resources.[110]

Encouraging and supporting the Court to improve its efficiency is obviously desirable. However, at the same time, the Court's budget needs to remain appropriate and it ought to be ensured that efficiency is not used as an excuse for resource shortages, which, in turn, may give rise to inefficiencies caused by capacity shortfalls. Insufficient resources ultimately impact upon the ability of the Court to effectively carry out the activities necessary in order to deliver upon its global mandate envisaged in the Statute. While it is important that the Court continues to make efficiency savings in its operation, it is necessary to consider whether the savings made are sufficient to absorb the cost of the increase in workload and whether such savings are, in fact, sustainable.

The experience from the ICC highlights the important role that independence and efficiency play with regard to fulfilling its mandate. When

---

[107] A prime example of this is the perceived anti-African bias. See discussion of Africa and the ICC above.

[108] See ICC Statute (above n. 7), Article 88; it should be noted that there is a clear obligation under the ICC Statute for states to make national procedures available for all forms of cooperation; see O. Bekou, 'A Case for Review of Article 88, ICC Statute: Strengthening a Forgotten Provision' (2009) 12 *New Criminal Law Review* 468–83.

[109] ICC Statute (above n. 7), Tenth preambular paragraph, Article 1 and Article 17. See below.

[110] Resolutions adopted by the Assembly of States Parties (Resolution ICC-ASP/14/Res.1) ICC-ASP/14/20 (26 November 2015).

building global institutions, it is important to ensure that independence and efficiency are guaranteed, both in law, but also in the actual practice.

C   Cooperation

The third major challenge that impacts on the ICC's successful contribution to global justice is that of an effective enforcement system. As the Court has neither its own army, nor a police force, cooperation between the Court, states and international organisations is required in order for the ICC to be able to conduct its investigations and prosecutions. The ICC Statute does not permit trials *in absentia*.[111] Securing the accused's presence and having the evidence required to convict, is dependent upon such cooperation.[112] The late Judge Antonio Cassese poignantly observed with regard to the ICTY:

> The Tribunal remains very much like a giant without arms and legs – it needs artificial limbs to walk and work. And these artificial limbs are state authorities. If the cooperation of states is not forthcoming, the [Court] cannot fulfil its functions.[113]

The above applies also to the ICC. Cooperation constitutes a key pillar of the proper functioning of the international criminal justice system as a whole. It also represents a major challenge that can threaten the smooth functioning of the global justice system established by the Statute. It is, therefore, essential for the operation of the ICC that states combine their efforts to assist the Court with its investigations and prosecutions, by executing requests for arrest and surrender, detention and transfer of suspects to the custody of the Court[114] and by providing assistance in collecting evidence, or providing other types of assistance outlined in the Statute.[115]

Three categories of cooperation may be identified, which will be considered in turn. The first category is bilateral cooperation. Fostering a constructive dialogue between the ICC and the national authorities responsible for cooperation is necessary, not least to ensure the timely execution of cooperation requests. In addition, encouraging more states

---

[111] ICC Statute (above n. 7), Article 63.

[112] Ibid., Part IX, International cooperation and judicial assistance.

[113] A. Cassese, 'On the Current Trends towards Criminal Prosecution and Punishment of Breaches of International Humanitarian' (1998) 9 *EJIL* 2, 13.

[114] ICC Statute (above n. 7), Article 59.

[115] Ibid., Article 93(1).

to sign the Agreement on Privileges and Immunities (APIC),[116] as well as to accept the relocation of witnesses, ensure the protection of victims and agree to receive convicted detainees for the enforcement of their sentences[117] or regulating interim release,[118] would further enhance good cooperation.

The presence and participation of victims in proceedings before the ICC is essential to help rebuild their lives in the aftermath of mass crimes. Victim participation is one of the key attributes of the ICC.[119] According to the Rome Statute system of justice, they must, without fear or apprehension, participate in trials at the ICC with their legal representatives to seek justice for the atrocities and suffering that they have endured.[120]

Facilitating their appearance, protection and reparations is therefore key to the Court's success. Relocation agreements contribute towards ensuring that victims and witnesses are better protected in a suitable geographical and cultural environment that serves to guarantee both their security and confidence.[121]

Another key issue in strengthening the ICC regime is the importance of states enacting national implementing legislation. Signing and ratifying the ICC Statute can constitute a powerful demonstration of political commitment to its values and objectives. However, in order to establish the envisaged system of international criminal justice, it is necessary for states to also implement ICC Statute provisions in their domestic legal systems. Such implementation requires states to review their existing domestic legislation, assess its compatibility with the ICC Statute and make appropriate amendments or adopt specific legislation. Accordingly, states who have ratified the ICC Statute must be encouraged to integrate into their national

---

[116] See Agreement on the Privileges and Immunities of the International Criminal Court (ICC-ASP/1/3); the APIC was adopted 9 September 2002, and entered into force 22 July 2004.

[117] Agreements on the enforcement of sentences are currently in force between the ICC and the governments of Argentina, Austria, Belgium, Denmark, Finland, Mali, Norway, Serbia, Sweden and the United Kingdom of Great Britain and Northern Ireland. See also a Court-developed booklet to promote the signature of such agreements, www.icc-cpi.int/news/seminarBooks/Cooperation_Agreements_Eng.pdf.

[118] See e.g. Cooperation Agreement on interim release and release of ICC detained person on the Argentine territory, pursuant to decisions of the Chambers of the Court, www.icc-cpi.int/Pages/item.aspx?name=pr1360.

[119] ICC Statute (above n. 7), Article 68.

[120] T. M. Funk, *Victims' Rights and Advocacy at the International Criminal Court*, 2nd edn (Oxford University Press, 2015).

[121] See Report of the Court on Cooperation, ICC-ASP/15/9, 11 October 2016, https://asp.icc-cpi.int/iccdocs/asp_docs/ASP15/ICC-ASP-15-9-ENG.pdf

legislation core international crimes, as well as provisions allowing for effective and efficient cooperation with the ICC, an obligation under the Statute.[122]

The implications of such implementations within domestic legal systems include increased ability of states to investigate and prosecute the core international crimes: genocide, war crimes and crimes against humanity. In turn this would allow states to maintain control over cases, rather than the ICC. Additionally, such implementation facilitates cooperation between states and the Court which enables the ICC to operate effectively. As discussed, the ICC's lack of enforcement mechanism makes the willingness and ability of states to cooperate, such as to surrender of alleged perpetrators, serve documents, collect evidence and facilitate the appearance of witnesses etc., essential to the Court's ability to fulfil its mandate. To this end, to allow the ICC to discharge its functions requires further measures.

For State Parties to be able to fulfil their cooperation obligations with the ICC, they must also sign, ratify and implement the Agreement on Privileges and Immunities of the ICC.[123] The APIC provides the ICC, officials, staff, as well as victims and witnesses, with the privileges and immunities necessary to perform their duties in an independent, unconditional and efficient manner.[124] However, to date, more than half of the State Parties do not have cooperation legislation; there are only seventy-seven Parties to the APIC and just fourteen relocation agreements.[125]

The future of international criminal justice is reliant upon building capacity at the national level.[126] Capacity-building is an area which will be returned to when discussing the final challenge facing the Court, in the section that follows. As regards the cooperation challenges, it is also vital to strengthen cooperation between the ICC and non-State Parties to ensure the universality of the Court's enforcement action. It is pleasing to note in this regard that it was the United States, a non-State Party to the Rome Statute, that handed over the Lord's Resistance Army commander Dominic

---

[122] ICC Statute (n. 7), Part IX, International cooperation and judicial assistance.

[123] Above n. 116.

[124] APIC (above n. 116), Articles 13–18, and Articles 19–20.

[125] See information obtained through the Cooperation and Judicial Assistance Database, https://cjad.nottingham.ac.uk.

[126] See, generally, O. Bekou, 'Building National Capacity for the ICC: Prospects and Challenges' in T. Mariniello (ed.), *The International Criminal Court in Search of its Purpose and Identity* (Routledge, 2015); M. Bergsmo et al., 'Complementarity after Kampala: Capacity Building and the ICC's Legal Tools' (2010) 2 *Georgetown JIL* 791–811.

Ongwen to the authorities in the Central African Republic, who then took the decision to surrender him to the ICC for trial in The Hague.[127]

Finally, it is pivotal for the ICC to build upon its pre-existing multi-faceted cooperation with international civil society, including intergovernmental organisations such as the Commonwealth, human rights and humanitarian organisations, victims' associations and regional organisations. There is a lot still to be done in terms of cooperation. Tackling non-cooperation, for example, is also a key issue and severely affects the Court's efficiency.[128] The treaty basis of the ICC restricts the available options. This is an inevitable fault in the institutional design of this court, which as a treaty regime is limited to making judicial findings of non-cooperation and referrals to the Assembly of States Parties, or the UNSC, in cases of UNSC referrals.[129]

Like any global institution, the ICC does not operate in a vacuum and is reliant on other actors and actions to be able to perform its functions. If cooperation is not forthcoming, the ability of the Court to operate would be seriously curtailed. Strengthening such cooperation is more likely to lead to a strong institution. Ensuring that a strong enforcement system is in place should be part of the institutional design of any court aimed at delivering justice at the global level.

D   Relationship with National Courts: Complementarity

The fourth and final challenge faced by the ICC relates to its relationship with national criminal justice systems. The ICC Statute is premised on the principle of complementarity, which gives priority of action to national courts, and limits the jurisdiction of the ICC to cases where there is clear unwillingness or inability to act.[130] It is important to recall that the ICC is, and should only be, a court of last resort.[131] As stipulated by Article 17 of the ICC Statute, situations and cases are only admissible when states with concurrent jurisdiction are unwilling or unable genuinely to conduct

---

[127] Report of the Registry on the voluntary surrender of Dominic Ongwen and his transfer to the Court, 22 January 2015, ICC-02/04–01/05. See www.icc-cpi.int/CourtRecords/CR2015_01648.PDF.

[128] A. Jones, 'Non-Cooperation and the Efficiency of the International Criminal Court' in O. Bekou and D. Birkett (eds.), *Cooperation and the International Criminal Court: Perspectives from Theory and Practice* (Brill Nijhoff, 2016), 185–209.

[129] ICC Statute (above n. 7), Article 87(5) and (7).

[130] Ibid., Article 17.

[131] See e.g. P. Kirsch, 'The Role of the International Criminal Court in Enforcing International Criminal Law' (2007) 22 *AUILR* 539, 543.

investigations into, and prosecution of, suspected international crimes within the Court's jurisdiction.[132] The ICC does not replace the work of national jurisdictions; each state must be able to try crimes committed on its territory, including those under the jurisdiction of the ICC. Indeed, states, by ratifying the Rome Statute, have neither abandoned nor restricted their sovereignty; the ICC is activated only when national proceedings are not forthcoming. The competence of the Court is not meant to displace national authorities.[133] On the contrary, it is the primary responsibility of all ICC State Parties to investigate and prosecute the authors of the most serious crimes.

It is evident then that the success of the ICC should not be assessed through the volume of cases pending before it, but rather by the exponential growth of matters within its jurisdiction in national courts.[134] Addressing mass atrocity before national courts offers multiple advantages, as internalising the responsibility to investigate and prosecute crimes under national law slowly builds a domestic culture of justice and the rule of law.[135] Additionally, to avoid being subject to an ICC investigation, and potentially arising political and diplomatic disputes, states may initiate their own investigations and prosecutions into impugned situations. National and even local trials are more visible and comprehensible by the affected population and they usually seem more legitimate to the local communities.[136] This is supported by experiences of the ad hoc tribunals,[137] the work of the ICC until now, and proceedings of hybrid tribunals such as the Special Court for Sierra Leone and the Special Tribunal

---

[132] ICC Statute (above n. 7), Article 17.

[133] J. T. Holmes, 'The Principle of Complementarity' in R. Lee (ed.), *The International Criminal Court: The Making of the ICC Statute* (Kluwer Law International, 1999), 41.

[134] See Statement by Luis Moreno-Ocampo, Prosecutor of the International Criminal Court, Ceremony for the solemn undertaking of the Chief Prosecutor of the International Criminal Court (16 June 2004); the absence of cases before the Court was hailed as a measure of the ICC's success by the Court's first prosecutor.

[135] The OTP, 'Report on Prosecutorial Strategy' (The Hague, 14 September 2006) 4; see e.g. J. Stromseth, 'Justice on the Ground: Can International Criminal Courts Strengthen Domestic Rule of Law in Post-Conflict Societies?' (2009) 1 *Hague Journal on the Rule of Law* 87–97; see e.g. C. Sriram, 'Globalising Justice: From Universal Jurisdiction to Mixed Tribunals' (2004) 4 *Netherlands Quarterly of Human Rights* 7–32.

[136] See C. Sriram, 'Revolutions in Accountability: New Approaches to Past Abuses' (2003) 19 *AUILR* 301, 383; C. Stahn, 'The Geometry of Transitional Justice: Choices of Institutional Design' (2005) 18 *Leiden JIL* 425, 449; J. Stromseth, 'Pursuing Accountability for Atrocities After Conflict: What Impact on Binding the Rule of Law' (2007) 38 *Georgetown JIL* 251, 260.

[137] Namely, ICTY and ICTR.

for Lebanon.[138] All have demonstrated limitations of a justice process that is both geographically and temporally remote from the societies that have experienced mass atrocity.[139] In contrast, national procedures can have a great societal impact, especially for the victims of core international crimes.[140]

While state willingness is essentially a matter of politics,[141] the ability to investigate and prosecute core international crimes depends largely on institutional capacity and preparedness. It is not uncommon, following mass atrocity, that national jurisdictions lack the necessary operational capacity to address the complex and numerous crimes committed within a specific context. However, it must be noted that the ICC cannot deal with each and every situation.[142] The Court has finite resources and is usually detached from the territories on which atrocity takes place. This poses a number of problems in gathering and accessing evidence, approaching witnesses and ensuring their safety, as well as achieving the visibility that is often needed to bring closure to the victims.[143] As the domestic capacity of states dealing with the aftermath of mass atrocity is often significantly reduced, there are a number of common challenges.

Building on the issue of lack of national legislation implementing the ICC Statute, this absence of specific legislation addressing core international crimes as such, might lead to their investigation and prosecution

---

[138] See e.g. ICTR and the ICTY Case Law Database, United Nations Mechanism for International Criminal Tribunals 'Cases', www.unmict.org/en/cases/ictr-icty-case-law-database.

[139] The ad hoc tribunals were created under the UNSC's Chapter VII powers and could therefore fall back on the UNSC's powers of enforcement, though they have not done so in practice. See Statute of the International Criminal Tribunal for the Former Yugoslavia (above n. 6), Article 8; see Statute of the International Criminal Tribunal for Rwanda (above n. 6), Article 7; see Agreement between the United Nations and the Lebanese Republic on the Establishment of a Special Tribunal for Lebanon, UNSC Res. 1757 (30 May 2007) UN Doc. S/RES/1757, Annex; see e.g. Sriram, 'Globalising Justice' (above n. 135).

[140] Other reasons that suggest that local proceedings are more favourable to the remoteness of international proceedings are discussed in M. Bergsmo et al., 'Complementarity and the Construction of National Ability' in C. Stahn and M. M. El Zeidy (eds.), *The International Criminal Court and Complementarity From Theory to Practice* (Cambridge University Press, 2011), 800.

[141] See also, Y. Lijun, 'On the Principle of Complementarity in the ICC Statute of the International Criminal Court' (2005) 4 *CJIL* 121, 123.

[142] C. Stahn, 'The Geometry of Transitional Justice (above n. 136), 449.

[143] J. Turner, 'Nationalizing International Criminal Law' (2005) 41 *Stanford JIL* 1, 24; M. Drumbl, *Atrocity, Punishment and International Law* (Cambridge University Press, 2007), 148; see The OTP, 'Paper on Some Policy Issues before the Office of the Prosecutor' (The Hague, September 2003), 4; other reasons that suggest that local proceedings are more favourable to the remoteness of international proceedings are discussed in Bergsmo et al., 'Complementarity and the Construction of National Ability' (above n. 140), 800.

as 'ordinary crimes'. While not legally problematic, 'ordinary crimes' lack the stigma of the core international crimes and may not carry the same significance in the eyes of the victims, perpetrators and the wider international community.[144] Moreover, the elements of international crimes are often more complex than those of ordinary domestic law crimes. They, therefore, require legislation that is highly precise and adapted to the grave nature and complexity of international crimes.[145] In the aftermath of mass atrocity the situation is further exacerbated by lack of necessary infrastructure, potential lack of confidence in judicial structure, disputed authority, and weak economy which is common in post-conflict and transitional societies.[146] A criminal justice system does not require only laws, but infrastructure including courtrooms, detention and imprisonment centres, as well as properly trained and experienced personnel such as judges and police investigators.[147] Building national capacity to deal with mass atrocity, is therefore key to the success of the system put forward by the Rome Statute.[148]

The emergence of the concept of 'positive complementarity' has been seen by many as the solution to the absence of a legal basis in the Statute to ensure comprehensive assistance with capacity-building.[149] The initial

---

[144] See W. Ferdinandusse, 'The Prosecution of Grave Breaches in National Courts' (2009) 7 *JICJ* 723, 729–34.

[145] M. Bergsmo and P. Webb, 'Innovations at the International Criminal Court: Bringing New Technologies into the Investigation and Prosecution of Core International Crimes' in H. Radtke et al. (eds.), *Historische Dimensionen von Kriegsverbrecherprozessen nach dem Zweiten Weltkrieg* (Nomos, 2007), 205.

[146] As such they had been highlighted at a special panel on complementarity hosted by South Africa and Denmark, the focal points for complementarity on 2 June 2010, in the course of the Review Conference; International Criminal Court Assembly of States Parties, Review Conference, Resolution ICC-ASP/8/Res. 9 (25 March 2010), adopted by consensus at the 10th Plenary Meeting.

[147] See e.g. E. Baylis, 'Reassessing the Role of International Criminal Law: Rebuilding National Courts through Transnational Networks' (2009) 50 *Boston College Law Review* 1, 49; S. Straus, 'How Many Perpetrators Were There in the Rwandan Genocide? An Estimate' (2004) 6 *Journal of Genocide Research* 85; see also M. Bergsmo et al., *The Backlog of Core International Crimes Case Files in Bosnia and Herzegovina*, 2nd edn (Torkel Opsahl Academic EPublisher, 2010), www.fichl.org/fileadmin/fichl/documents/FICHL_3_Second_Edition_web.pdf.

[148] M. Ellis, 'The International Criminal Court and its Implication for Domestic Law and National Capacity Building' (2002) 15 *Florida JIL* 215, 239.

[149] ICC Statute (above n. 7), Article 93(10). Notably the ICC Statute provides very limited scope for such assistance; see e.g. C. Stahn, 'Complementarity: A Tale of Two Notions' (2008) 19 *Criminal Law Forum* 87–113; W. Burke-White, 'Proactive Complementarity: The International Criminal Court and National Courts in the Rome System of International Justice' (2008) 49 *HILJ* 53–108; P. Akhavan, 'The Lord's Resistance Army Case: Uganda's

concept, first appeared in the OTP's 2006 Report on Prosecutorial Strategy, to describe the active encouragement of states to conduct national proceedings and, where appropriate, to provide the necessary assistance to enable them to do so.[150] Until 2010, the notion of positive complementarity was perceived only as a prosecutorial strategy. In the view of the OTP, positive complementarity 'encourages genuine national proceedings where possible; relies on national and international networks; and participates in a system of international cooperation'.[151]

Positive complementarity received much attention ahead of and during the first Review Conference in Kampala, in 2010, which gave further prominence to positive complementarity in the stocktaking exercise that formed part of the Conference.[152] A Resolution adopted at the Conference transformed what was the common understanding of positive complementarity until then, and changed its character from a purely prosecutorial strategy to the basis for engaging in capacity-building.[153] Recognising that the ICC is not a development agency, the onus on developing such capacity-building was shifted at the Review conference from the Court to:

> all activities/actions whereby national jurisdictions are strengthened and enabled to conduct genuine national investigations and trials of crimes included in the Rome Statute, without involving the Court in capacity building, financial support and technical assistance, but instead leaving these actions and activities for States, to assist each other on a voluntary basis.[154]

Positive complementarity therefore focuses on the technical and financial assistance provided to states in order to build their capacity to oversee investigations and prosecutions of core international crimes.[155] This means strengthening both the expertise and capacity of domestic legal

---

Submission of the First State Referral to the International Criminal Court' (2005) 99 *AJIL* 403–21; see e.g. F. Gioia, 'Reverse Cooperation' and the Architecture of the ICC Statute: A Vital Part of the Relationship between States and the ICC?' in M. Malaguti (ed.), *ICC and International Cooperation in Light of the Rome Statute* (Argo, 2011), 75–101.

[150] The OTP, 'Report on Prosecutorial Strategy' (above n. 135).

[151] Ibid., 5.

[152] See Strengthening the International Criminal Court and the Assembly of States Parties, ICC-ASP/8/Res. 3, Annex IV 'Topics for Stocktaking', Eighth Plenary Meeting of the ASP (26 November 2009); see also, generally, Bergsmo et al., 'Complementarity and the Construction of National Ability' (above n. 140).

[153] Complementarity, ICC ASP RC/Res. 1, Ninth Plenary Meeting of the ASP (8 June 2010).

[154] Report of the Bureau on Stocktaking: Complementarity, ICC-ASP/8/Res. 9, Appendix, Tenth Plenary Meeting of the ASP (25 March 2010) 16.

[155] Ibid., 17.

actors including judges, prosecutors, lawyers, clerks and security forces.[156] The principle of complementarity operates to reduce the 'impunity gap' between individuals who are prosecuted by the ICC and those who are not, and between situations that are subject to investigation by the ICC and those that are not.[157]

It is only when national legal actors are familiar with international norms that the guarantees of a fair and equitable trial can be ensured. Arguably, national jurisdictions are very important to ensuring the success of the ICC regime.

In the fifteen or more years that the ICC has been operational, there has been a realisation of the continued importance of national jurisdictions in the success of the global institution. Although this interrelationship had been envisaged in the Statute, the position of each of the two levels – national and international – in the international criminal justice system is beginning to crystallise. With the institution-building phase complete and the Court being fully operational, the shift towards ensuring that national courts discharge their role under the Statute is clear. For this and other courts, strengthening the interface between the domestic and the international remains a global challenge.

IV   Conclusions

In assessing the role international criminal justice plays in a globalised world, the operation of the ICC as the main focus of this effort was scrutinised. In this journey through the Court's life to date, four major challenges were chosen. They are by no means the only ones. Universality, independence, efficiency and effectiveness, cooperation and complementarity, have left a hallmark on the Court's record. It is beyond doubt that the first fifteen years of the ICC have been remarkable in the world of international criminal justice. As the enthusiasm of the early years subsides, one thing is clear: the ICC is entering the era of pragmatism. The first fifteen years saw some fascinating developments, quite a few achievements and many challenges. The time has come to reflect upon them and consider how to support and improve the ICC and the Rome system of justice as a whole.

Whilst the ICC occupies the central position in the international criminal justice system, other courts and tribunals also play their distinct roles. As the ad hoc Tribunals for Rwanda, and the Former Yugoslavia have

---

[156] Ibid., 8.
[157] Ibid., 3.

completed their mandates, new Tribunals, such as the Kosovo and Central African Republic special criminal courts and an International, Impartial and Independent Mechanism to Assist in the Investigation and Prosecution of Persons Responsible for the Most Serious Crimes under International Law Committed in the Syrian Arab Republic[158] have been set up. At the same time, national courts both look towards the ICC for direction and begin to play their own role in investigating and prosecuting core international crimes.

The road to global justice is not however problem-free. International criminal justice and the ICC continue to dominate headlines. For some, the ICC may seem to be in crisis. However, it is also a stable institution, which despite the challenges, continues to grow and will, no doubt, be present in the years to come. In terms of globalisation, the Court, with its trials and tribulations, its victories and setbacks, is a vivid example of the multifaceted areas involved in administering international criminal justice at the international level. The experiences and lessons learnt from this process may be useful in other areas where global solutions for global problems are sought.

---

[158] On 19 December 2016, the IIIM was established following the adoption of Resolution A/71/L/48. See www.un.org/ga/search/view_doc.asp?symbol=A/71/L.48. A similar independent mechanism to investigate violations in South Sudan has been called for. See www.ohchr.org/EN/NewsEvents/Pages/DisplayNews.aspx?NewsID=21386&LangID=E   and https://unmiss.unmissions.org/human-rights-experts-call-independent-body-investigate-conflict-related-crimes-south-sudan.

PART II

European Perspectives

A. *Formal Foundations*

9

European International Law

BRUNO DE WITTE

I Introduction

The two parts in which this volume is divided reflect the view that one can meaningfully distinguish between 'international' and 'European' perspectives on global governance. This chapter somewhat qualifies that distinction by noting that the *European perspective* is also an *international* perspective. Indeed, first the European Communities and later the European Union (EU) came into being as creatures of international law, as they were established by means of international treaties concluded by states. Today still, two international treaties, the Treaty on European Union (TEU) and the Treaty on the Functioning of the European Union (TFEU), form the legal foundations of the European integration process, as they together act as the hierarchically superior source of the EU legal order. It logically follows from this fact that EU law could still be considered to be part and parcel of international law, so that the European perspective on governance and globalisation can then be qualified as a subform of the international perspective. Hence also the choice of this chapter's hybrid title.

The way in which the EU is, on the one hand, deeply nested in international law, but has also, on the other hand, developed an arm-length's relationship with the 'rest' of international law, will be described in this chapter. The first part of the chapter will highlight the international legal features of EU law, whereas the second part will, as a counterpart, describe the way in which both the EU Member States and the Court of Justice of the EU (CJEU) have sought to develop the identity and autonomy of the EU legal order within the wider world of international law.

II   The International Legal Features of EU Law

Many of the features of EU law make it look like a quasi-federal system, with the TEU and TFEU fulfilling the function of a constitution for that quasi-federal system.[1] Indeed, a large part of EU law scholarship has taken the view, for many years already, that the EU, whilst certainly not yet a federal state, is also no longer an international organisation, but rather a legal construct that is somewhere in between those two poles in a category all of its own; this is often expressed by saying that the EU is a *sui generis* entity, although sometimes more focused concepts are proposed such as that of a 'constitutional order of states',[2] a 'federation of States'[3] or a 'plurinational federation'.[4] If, however, one reads textbooks on international law or the law of international organisations, their authors unanimously consider that the EU is still an international organisation and is still situated *within* international law. These authors have a strong formal argument to support their view, namely the fact that the EU, apart from having been created through international treaties, continues until today to rely heavily on that international law pedigree.

Indeed, beyond the fact (already noted in the introduction to this chapter) that the European integration process was effectively launched and carried forward by means of international treaties, the current rule of recognition of EU law (i.e. the rule that allows us to decide whether a norm is part of EU law or not[5]) is whether a particular norm can be traced back, directly or indirectly, to the text of the TEU and the TFEU.[6] For example, the fact that the EU Charter of Fundamental Rights is a binding element of EU law is justified by the attribution of binding legal force to that document in Article 6 TEU. Or, to use a more mundane example, the decision by the European Commission to allocate funding for student mobility between European universities is part of EU law because that decision is based on an EU Regulation establishing the Erasmus programme which, in turn, finds its legal basis in Article 165 TFEU that allows the EU to enact incentive measures for the promotion of student mobility.

---

[1] See, for this constitutional perspective on EU law, C. Möllers, Chapter 10 in this volume.

[2] A. Dashwood, 'States in the European Union' (1998) 23 *EL Rev* 201.

[3] R. Schütze, *European Constitutional Law* (Cambridge University Press, 2012), 79.

[4] A. Bailleux and H. Dumont, *Le Pacte constitutionnel européen* (Bruylant, 2015), 200–63.

[5] The notion of the 'rule of recognition' is used here in the sense famously developed by H. L. A. Hart, *The Concept of Law* (Oxford University Press, 1997).

[6] For the sake of convenience, we neglect the fact that there is actually a third 'founding' Treaty of the EU, namely the European Atomic Energy Treaty, which is legally independent from, and equivalent to, the TEU and TFEU, but whose policy scope is very limited.

The EU's original pedigree in international law has, thus, not been cancelled in the course of time, and is forcefully revived on a number of occasions, most clearly perhaps when the Treaties on which the EU is based are being reformed, as they repeatedly have been in the past forty years: these major political events invariably take the legal form of treaty amendments; that is, acts of international law. Often, in the past decades, ideas were floated, and even concrete plans developed, that aimed at transforming the European Communities (or later the EU) into 'something altogether different' (legally speaking), but none of those attempts resulted in a rejection of the EU's international legal pedigree. On the contrary, each Treaty amendment project provides the Member States with a new opportunity to reaffirm their 'mastership' over their legal creature. Take for instance the latest major revision treaty, the Treaty of Lisbon. In concluding that instrument, the Member States inscribed the following text in Article 1 TEU: 'By this Treaty, the HIGH CONTRACTING PARTIES establish among themselves a EUROPEAN UNION ... on which the Member States confer competences to attain objectives they have in common.' The subtle shift from 'High Contracting Parties' to 'Member States' (both terms designating the same entities), the description of the EU as the passive recipient of competences, and even the quaint use of capital letters, are all traditional features of the international legal tradition which the EU Member States apparently liked to rehearse on this occasion. One may add to this that the Member States also frequently describe the EU as an international organisation when they conclude other international treaties. Indeed, there are many multilateral treaty provisions that use the terms 'international organisation' or 'regional economic international organisation' (REIO) where it is clear from the context that the (only) organisation that is intended by that term is the EU.[7] Furthermore, we may also note that the EU continues to be considered as 'just' an international organisation under the constitutional law of many of its Member States. Today, it is true, some national constitutions contain clauses dealing specifically with the transfer of powers to the EU, but many countries continue to adopt a generic approach of allowing transfers of powers, or limitations of sovereignty, for the benefit of 'international organisations' or 'international institutions' without making special reference to the EU,[8] and it is clear

---

[7] See, among many other examples, the UNESCO Convention on the Protection and Promotion of the Diversity of Cultural Expressions (2005), Article 27.

[8] See M. Claes, 'Constitutionalising Europe at its Source: The "European Clauses" in the National Constitutions: Evolution and Typology' (2005) 24 *YEL* 81.

from the context that those generic references to international organisations include the EU.

It is also interesting to note that the CJEU never stated in so many words that the EU's legal order was situated *outside* the scope of international law. In its famous early judgments *van Gend en Loos* and *Costa*, the Court sought to differentiate the European Economic Community (EEC) Treaty from 'other' or 'ordinary' international treaties, but that otherness was not pushed to the conclusion that the EEC Treaty had created something other than an international organisation.[9] Much has been made of the fact that the Court held, in its *van Gend en Loos* judgment of 1963, that the EEC Treaty had created 'a new legal order of international law', whereas it dropped the last three words one year later in *Costa* when it simply spoke of 'a new legal order'. This has been interpreted, by a number of commentators, as a deliberate tearing away of Community law from its international legal moorings. Yet, the way in which the Court described the peculiar characteristics of the EEC Treaty was very similar in both those early judgments, so it would be very odd if that description had led, in 1963, to the conclusion that this was a special legal order *still of international law*, and only one year later to the opposite conclusion that it was a special legal order *no longer of international law*. In the many years that have passed since its *Costa* judgment, the Court of Justice never sought to develop a doctrine affirming the non-international nature of the EU. In fact, there was no need for the Court to adopt the premise that the Union was 'something other' than an international organisation in order to affirm and protect the advanced features of European law since international law is extraordinarily flexible as to the content of the cooperation between states. On the few occasions on which the Court gives an indication of the kind of legal entity the EU might be, it tends to use tautological categories, as in a recent judgment in which it described the EU as a 'union based on the rule of law'.[10]

---

[9] See, however, the Opinion of AG Poiares Maduro in the *Kadi* case, who stated that the ECJ, in *van Gend en Loos*, had considered the EEC Treaty to form a new legal order which was 'beholden to, but distinct from the existing legal order of public international law' (Opinion in Joined Cases C-402/05 P and C-415/05 P, *Kadi and Al Barakaat* v. *Council and Commission*, ECLI:EU:C:2008:11, para. 21). The ECJ, in fact, did not quite use those words in its 1963 judgment *van Gend en Loos*, nor at any later time.

[10] Case C-583/11 P *Inuit Tapiriit Kanatami* v. *Parliament and Council*, ECLI:EU:C:2013:625, para. 91 (emphasis added). Note the shift from 'Union' (the species) to 'union' (the genus). The small-u term is left undefined, and should not be read as denying that EU law belongs to international law. Curiously, the concept of 'international union' was of common usage

The view that EU law is international law also appears reasonable when one looks at the broader picture of international cooperation. Advanced international organisations are being created year after year, and display one or several of the characteristic supranational features of the EU.[11] For example, many international organisations have organs possessing the power to adopt operational decisions that are binding on states, and occasionally such decisions can even be adopted by a majority vote; that is, against the wishes of single Member States of the organisation.[12]

III   The European Union as an Autonomous Legal Order of International Law

Like other treaties establishing an international organisation, the TEU and TFEU are somewhat hybrid instruments. Such treaties may lay down mutual rights and obligations between the parties but they also, unlike other treaties, create a new 'internal legal order' for the organisation.[13] In the case of the EU, that internal legal order is particularly rich and complex, and displays many features that, taken in combination, can hardly be found anywhere else in the world of international law, such as: the broad and flexible nature of the competences conferred on the EU, extending into almost all areas of law-making; the existence of a (partially) common currency and a common (though derivative) citizenship; the decision-making regime, marked by the involvement of institutions not controlled by the Member State governments and by recourse to majority voting in the state-controlled Council of Ministers; the relatively effective mechanism of state compliance; and the habit of obedience by national courts to their duty to apply EU law. It is evident, therefore, that the EU possesses,

---

in the nineteenth and early part of the twentieth centuries to describe the early international regimes for technical cooperation.

[11] See W. Schroeder and A. Müller, 'Elements of Supranationality in the Law of International Organizations' in U. Fastenrath et al. (eds.), *From Bilateralism to Community Interest: Essays in Honour of Bruno Simma* (Oxford University Press, 2011), 358.

[12] For a general view, see J. von Bernstorff, 'Procedures of Decision-Making and the Role of Law in International Organizations' (2008) 9 *GLJ* 1939; N. D. White, 'Decision-Making' and J. Wouters and P. De Man, 'International Organizations as Law-Makers' both in J. Klabbers and A. Wallendahl (eds.), *Research Handbook on the Law of International Organizations* (Edward Elgar, 2011), 225 and 190 respectively.

[13] On this hybrid nature of treaties establishing international organizations, see A. Peters, 'Das Gründungsdokument internationaler Organisationen als Verfassungsvertrag' (2013) 68 *Zeitschrift für öffentliches Recht* 1.

more than any other international organisation in the world, its own autonomous legal order within the broader world of international law.[14]

The most obvious way in which that autonomous legal order manifests itself within international governance is by creating, or helping to create, new norms of international law. The EU contributes to the development of international law, and hence also to the development of global governance, in the same three main ways as states do:[15] through its unilateral practice (which may contribute to the emergence of rules of customary international law);[16] through concluding treaties with non-EU states or international organisations; and through its activity as a member of some multilateral organizations, such as the World Trade Organization (WTO). But the EU is not just a new subject of international law alongside the states; its existence affects international governance in quite distinct and novel ways. Two such distinct features will be highlighted in the following pages: on the one hand, the EU has partially substituted its Member States as actors of international governance, and even where it does not substitute them, it constrains the choice of governance venues which those Member States possess (section A below); on the other hand, the EU legal order has developed a very particular position on the incorporation of the norms of international governance in which the EU and its Member States participate; that position is welcoming in principle, but reluctant in many particular cases (section B below).

A   The EU's Partial Replacement of its Member States on the International Governance Scene

The development of the EU's treaty-making power reflects directly on the international legal actorness of its Member States. Indeed, the EU has almost entirely *replaced* its Member States as an international actor in a number of policy fields, such as international trade or international fisheries regulation. The Member States have had to accept abandoning their

---

[14] See, generally, on the extent to which international organizations possess their own autonomous legal order: R. Collins and N. White (eds.), *International Organizations and the Idea of Autonomy* (Routledge, 2011).

[15] Recent collections of contributions on this theme include: B. Van Vooren et al. (eds.), *The EU's Role in Global Governance: The Legal Dimension* (Oxford University Press, 2013); and D. Kochenov and F. Amtenbrink (eds.), *The European Union's Shaping of the International Legal Order* (Cambridge University Press, 2013).

[16] See, on this aspect of the interaction between EU law and general international law, F. Hoffmeister, 'The Contribution of EU Practice to International Law' in M. Cremona (ed.), *Developments in EU External Relations Law* (Oxford University Press, 2008), 54 et seq.

power to conclude treaties in those areas that are within the EU's exclusive competence.[17] In many other areas, such as environmental protection or immigration, the EU and the Member States share their treaty-making competence. In the practice of the EU's external relations, the dividing line between exclusive and shared competences is, however, often rather blurred, which leads to constant disputes between the Member States and the supranational EU institutions (the Commission and the Parliament) as to whether an envisaged international agreement should be considered to fall within the EU's exclusive competence or whether, on the contrary, some elements of the agreement fall within shared competences so as to justify the additional participation of all the Member States as parties to the agreement.[18] The recent Opinion 2/15 relating to the EU–Singapore Agreement was expected to bring some judicial clarification in this matter, but did so only to a limited extent.[19]

In the areas of shared competence, the Member States remain actors of international legal relations. Their governments preserve a choice between either addressing a given transnational policy problem within the context of the EU, or acting within the context of another (regional or global) international organisation, or even acting by means of a series of bilateral negotiations with individual countries or by means of informal transgovernmental networks. In such cases, the EU site of governance can be seen as competing with institutionalised sites of *global law-making*, some of which pre-dated the European organisations, such as the International Labour Organisation (ILO) and the Hague Conference on Private International Law, whereas others were developed in the post-war period as part of the broad United Nations (UN) family, such as the General Agreement on Tariffs and Trade (GATT) and WTO, the World Intellectual Property Organisation, the UN Economic Commission for Europe, the Codex Alimentarius Commission etc. This *choice of law-making venue* is denied to them when the EU has acquired exclusive competence on a given subject matter; but even when a choice exists, it can be influenced by the activity of EU institutions, in particular by the Commission, that can propose a new piece of EU legislation in order to prevent the Member States from

[17] See discussion of this point in B. de Witte, 'The Emergence of a European System of Public International Law: The EU and its Member States as Strange Subjects' in J. Wouters et al. (eds.), *The Europeanisation of International Law* (T. M. C. Asser Press, 2008), 39.

[18] For a recent survey of the evolution of that controversy, see F. Erlbacher, 'Recent Case Law on External Competences of the European Union: How Member States Can Embrace their Own Treaty', *CLEER Papers* 2017/2.

[19] Opinion 2/15, *Free Trade Agreement between the EU and Singapore*, ECLI:EU:C:2017:376.

moving to another forum, or may, on the contrary, admit that another international venue is more appropriate and encourage the Member States to act within that other venue.

Looking at this question from the perspective of the EU Member States, we can see that their choice of venue is affected both by the dynamics of the EU's domestic legislative process and by the participatory structure of the competing international law-making venue. As long as the pertinent international setting does not allow for the EU itself to participate,[20] it is for the Member States to participate individually or jointly as subjects of the international legal order, and/or to allow for the EU to legislate on the same matter. However, that choice of the Member States is not only constrained by the *political* pressure that the Commission and the European Parliament may bring to bear in favour of the 'EU route', but also by the legal implications of the EU's internal competence allocation, which affects states' individual room for manoeuvre at the international level. Where the EU is not itself represented in the international forum but holds exclusive competence under EU law with regard to (part of) the subject matter in question, Member States need to act as 'trustees' of the EU.[21] In Opinion 2/91 (International Labour Organisation (ILO) Convention), the Court of Justice of the EU held that where constitutional rules of the international organisation presented an obstacle to the EU's exercise of competence, such competence would need to 'be exercised through the medium of the Member States acting jointly in the Community's interest'.[22] Following the choice of an international venue, this can oblige Member States to establish a joint negotiating position which is binding on them.

---

[20] See e.g. Article 1 of the International Labour Organisation (ILO) Constitution, according to which ILO membership is only open to states; Article 19(5)(d) requires ILO Members to ratify Conventions, even where other authorities' consent is needed internally. Interestingly, although the EU is not a member of the Council of Europe, it does participate in most Council of Europe conventions by means of ad hoc participation clauses in those conventions. See, generally, F. Hoffmeister, 'Outsider or Frontrunner? Recent Developments under International and European Law on the Status of the European Union in International Organizations and Treaty Bodies' (2007) 44 *CML Rev* 1.

[21] M. Cremona, 'Member States as Trustees of the Union Interest: Participating in International Agreements on Behalf of the European Union' in A. Arnull et al. (eds.), *A Constitutional Order of States? Essays in EU Law in Honour of Alan Dashwood* (Hart, 2011), 435.

[22] Opinion 2/91, *ILO Convention No. 170*, ECLI:EU:C:1993:106, paras. 5 and 37; confirmed in C-45/07, *Commission* v. *Greece (IMO)*, ECLI:EU:C:2009:81, para. 31.

B *The EU's Cautious Incorporation of International Governance Norms*

As soon as an international agreement is concluded by the EU, international law starts acting as a constraint on it. In this respect, the EU is facing the same choices as a state on how to organise the implementation, application and judicial enforcement of those international norms within its domestic legal system. The TFEU contains the very international law-friendly rule stating that EU agreements are binding on the institutions of the EU and also, as the case may be, on its Member States,[23] which has been interpreted by the Court of Justice in a monist fashion as making those international law norms part of the EU legal order upon their entry into force.[24] However, the legal force of this reception rule is, in fact, very variable. Increasingly, the Union seeks to insert clauses into international agreements that guarantee the prevalence of existing or future EU law over the obligations contained in the agreement. The most blatant form of this 'reverse primacy' is the so-called disconnection clauses that the EU manages to insert into many Council of Europe conventions. According to these clauses, EU law dealing with subject matter covered in the relevant convention shall continue to apply between EU Member States, so that, on those matters, the convention provisions will only apply to non-EU Member States.[25] Even in the absence of such conflict rules that preserve the integrity of the Union's own law, the prevalence of the international agreements may be limited by the fact that their self-executing nature is denied by the Court of Justice (as is notoriously the case with WTO law).[26] Finally, as highlighted in the *Kadi* judgment of 2008, the primacy

[23] Article 216, second para., TFEU.

[24] The founding case in this respect is Case 181/73, *Haegeman v. Belgium*, ECLI:EU:C:1974:41, para. 5. See discussion of this question by E. Cannizzaro, 'Neo-Monism of the European Legal Order' in E. Cannizzaro et al. (eds.), *International Law as Law of the European Union* (Martinus Nijhoff, 2011), 57.

[25] For a discussion of these disconnection clauses and similar devices aiming at preserving the integrity of pre-existing or future EU law against conflicting international obligations, see M. Cremona, 'Disconnection Clauses in EC Law and Practice' in C. Hillion and P. Koutrakos (eds.), *Mixed Agreements Revisited: The EU and its Member States in the World* (Hart, 2010), 160.

[26] See, for a detailed discussion, M. Mendez, *The Legal Effects of EU Agreements: Maximalist Treaty Enforcement and Judicial Avoidance Techniques* (Oxford University Press, 2013). See also, among many other writings on this question: P. Eeckhout, 'The Integration of Public International Law in EU Law: Analytical and Normative Questions' in P. Eeckhout and M. López Escudero (eds.), *The European Union's External Action in Times of Crisis* (Hart, 2016), 223; K. S. Ziegler, 'Beyond Pluralism and Autonomy: Systemic Harmonization as a Paradigm for the Interaction of EU Law and International Law' (2016) 35 *YEL* 667.

of international agreements recognized by Article 216(2) TFEU concerns *secondary* EU law, but the application of international agreements within the EU legal order may be denied if they conflict with the Treaties themselves or with the unwritten principles of primary EU law.[27]

The relationship between EU law and other forms of international law is, in fact, seen by the Court of Justice as a relationship between distinct legal orders. For example, in a judgment of 2012, the CJEU characteristically held that:

> Security Council resolutions, on the one hand, and Council common positions and regulations, on the other hand, originate from distinct legal orders. Measures within the framework of the United Nations and the European Union are adopted by organs with autonomous powers, granted to them by their basic charters, that is to say, the treaties that created them.[28]

The emphasis on the *autonomy of the EU institutions* (as in the citation above) or on the *autonomy of the EU legal order* as a whole (as in the *Kadi* judgment) has become a frequent feature of the CJEU's case law. Yet, the concept of autonomy is rather fuzzy. It has been developed initially to describe the special relationship between the EU legal order and the laws of its Member States,[29] and only at a later stage to describe the relations of the EU legal order with its broader international legal environment.[30] Also, in its external dimension, autonomy may mean two quite different things: either that EU law, as a specialised international legal order, *deviates* from the general rules of international law on one or other point; or that the EU *fails to comply* with specific international obligations and gives priority instead to its own internal rules.

The *first meaning of autonomy*, namely the capacity to adopt special legal rules that deviate from the general rules of international law, is unproblematic. The general rules of international law are default rules which states can set aside and replace by more suitable rules in their mutual relations.

---

[27] Joined Cases C-402/05 P and C-415/05 P, *Kadi and Al Barakaat* v. *Council and Commission*, ECLI:EU:C:2008:461. Among the many scholarly contributions dealing with the implications of that judgment for the relation between EU law and the rest of international law, see the collection of essays in (2009) 28 *YEL* 533–697.

[28] Case C-380/09 P, *Melli Bank* v. *Council*, ECLI:EU:C:2012:137, para. 54.

[29] On this dimension, see in particular the study by R. Barents, *The Autonomy of Community Law* (Kluwer Law International, 2004).

[30] For contributions that seek to connect the internal and external dimension of EU law autonomy, see B. de Witte, 'European Union Law: How Autonomous Is its Legal Order?' (2010) 65 *Zeitschrift für öffentliches Recht* 141; and J. W. van Rossem, 'The Autonomy of EU Law: More Is Less?' in R. A. Wessel and S. Blockmans (eds.), *Between Autonomy and Dependence* (T. M. C. Asser Press, 2013), 13.

This is particularly true for treaties establishing international organisations, in which the founding States are free to equip 'their' organisation with institutional mechanisms and operational rules of their own liking with hardly any limits to their creativity. In an Advisory Opinion of 1996, the International Court of Justice affirmed that 'constituent instruments of international organizations are ... treaties of a particular type; their object is to create new subjects of law endowed with a certain *autonomy*, to which the parties entrust the task of realizing common goals'.[31]

A *second* and stronger *meaning of autonomy* is the capacity for a particular system to give priority to its own internal rules over and above external international obligations. This is a form of autonomy that is typical for those international organisations that are subjects of international law, and have used their capacity to conclude international agreements with states or other international organisations. When acting as subjects of international law, they may be led – just like states – to incur obligations under international law which may appear, at some point in time, to conflict with their own internal rules. In view of the multiplication of such external legal commitments of the EU, it is possible that they may occasionally enter into conflict with the EU's own domestic law.

In *Kadi*, the European Court of Justice (ECJ) thus refused the application of 'external' international obligations in order to preserve fundamental norms of the 'internal' legal order of the EU, namely the right of defence and the right to property. The wisdom of the Court's attitude has been very widely discussed in the literature, but from the point of view that concerns us here, namely that of the relation between the EU legal order and the surrounding international legal environment, the judgment did not imply a major change. In particular, the Court did not call into question its well-established view that international agreements of the EU form part of the EU legal order upon their ratification and entry into force. The Court did, however, repeat the unsurprising view that international obligations concluded by the EU cannot prevail over the highest norms of the internal EU legal order. In defending that position, which is very similar to that adopted by national courts when confronted with a conflict between international and national constitutional law, the ECJ highlighted the autonomy of the special legal order which the EU Member States have decided to create.

---

[31] ICJ, *Legality of the Use by a State of Nuclear Weapons in Armed Conflict*, Advisory Opinion of 8 July 1996, para. 19 (emphasis added).

The doctrinal concept of the autonomy of EU law had appeared in the Court of Justice on a number of occasions in the past, when it was used by the Court in a preventive way, namely in several of its Opinions dealing with the legality of projected external agreements of the EC: Opinion 1/91 (about the European Economic Area (EEA) Agreement, first version), Opinion 1/92 (about the EEA Agreement, second version) and Opinion 1/00 (about the European Common Aviation Area). In each of those three Opinions, the theme of the autonomy of the Community legal order is mentioned recurrently, and relates essentially to the preservation of the Court's own exclusive power to interpret Community law.[32] The creation, in the external agreements submitted to the Court's assessment, of mechanisms of dispute settlement between the parties raised the possible danger that the Court's own interpretation of provisions of Community law would be constrained by rival interpretations of the same provisions by another court or court-like structure. On this ground, the CJEU declared in Opinion 1/91 the first version of the EEA Agreement to be contrary to the EC Treaty, whereas in Opinion 1/92 and Opinion 1/00 it found that the autonomy of the EC legal order was not endangered, and therefore the envisaged agreements could be concluded by the Community as they stood.[33]

In Opinion 2/13, dealing with the accession of the EU to the European Convention on Human Rights (ECHR), the autonomy of the EU legal order was again used by the CJEU in this preventive way; that is, in order to stop the Union from acceding to an international treaty (the ECHR), thereby preventing that treaty from becoming a fully fledged part of the EU legal order and, more to the point, preventing the compulsory jurisdiction of the European Court of Human Rights (ECtHR) from constraining the CJEU's own position as the supreme authority for the interpretation and validity of EU law.

When assessing, in Opinion 2/13, the compatibility of accession to the ECHR with the primary law of the EU, the CJEU relied heavily on the twin concepts of the autonomy and specific characteristics of the EU

---

[32] The autonomy theme is also prominent in Opinion 1/09 on the European and Community Patents Courts, although there it is used (ostensibly at least) to protect the role of national courts as 'ordinary courts' of EU law – as against an Agreement that entrusted the application of EU patent law to an international court.

[33] For precise references to, and further discussion of, these cases, see B. de Witte, 'A Selfish Court? The Court of Justice and the Design of International Dispute Settlement beyond the European Union' in M. Cremona and A. Thies (eds.), *The European Court of Justice and External Relations Law: Constitutional Challenges* (Hart, 2014), 33.

legal order. Whereas the 'specific characteristics' had been indicated by the EU Member States themselves as a legal benchmark for the accession agreement (they did so by means of Protocol No. 8 attached to the Lisbon Treaty), the Court seamlessly shifted its benchmark from these 'specific characteristics' to the broader and encompassing notion of 'autonomy'. It thereby managed to inflate the 'specific characteristics' criterion to such vast proportions that the Draft Accession Agreement failed to meet it on a number of points. In this manner, the doctrine of the autonomy of the EU legal order was effectively used by the Court to Justice to thwart the will of the EU Member States to see accession to the ECHR coming about. Thus, the concept of specific characteristics acquired a much wider meaning in Opinion 2/13 than the Member States had intended: it became the modestly sounding entrance gate through which the CJEU was able to smuggle in the 'Trojan horse' of autonomy that enabled it to destroy the draft accession agreement.[34]

On previous occasions, the Court had used the notion of the autonomy of the EU legal order as a barrier to the conclusion or application of external agreements and, in particular, to the creation of new international jurisdictions, but on those earlier occasions these external agreements were not *required* by primary EU law but simply *contemplated* by the EU institutions (this is also the case with the investment dispute settlement mechanisms which the EU seeks to include in its current 'deep trade' agreements[35]). In the case of the ECHR Accession Agreement of 2013, however, the EU negotiators had sought to implement a TEU obligation: primary EU law *requires*, in Article 6(2) TEU, accession to the ECHR and thereby also, and necessarily, requires acceptance of the Strasbourg

---

[34] CJEU, Opinion 2/13, *Accession to the ECHR*, ECLI:EU:C:2014:2454. Among the very many scholarly comments on this Opinion, those that focus on the role played by the concept of autonomy include: D. Halberstam, '"It's the Autonomy, Stupid!" A Modest Defense of Opinion 2/13 on EU Accession to the ECHR, and the Way Forward' (2015) 16 *GLJ* 105; P. Eeckhout, 'Opinion 2/13 on EU Accession to the ECHR and Judicial Dialogue: Autonomy or Autarky' (2015) 38 *Fordham International Law Journal* 1; J. Odermatt, 'When a Fence Becomes a Cage: The Principle of Autonomy in EU External Relations Law', EUI Working Paper MWP 2016/07. Some authors had anticipated the role that this notion of autonomy would play in the Court's attitude towards ECHR accession: C. Eckes, 'EU Accession to the ECHR: Between Autonomy and Adaptation' (2013) 76 *MLR* 254; and T. Lock, 'Walking on a Tightrope: The Draft ECHR Accession Agreement and the Autonomy of the EU Legal Order' (2011) 48 *CML Rev* 1025.

[35] The compatibility of those dispute settlement mechanisms with the autonomy of the EU legal order is disputed but not yet settled by the Court of Justice; see discussion of this question by S. Hindelang, 'Repellent Forces: The CJEU and Investor–State Dispute Settlement' (2015) 53 *Archiv des Völkerrechts* 68.

Court's adjudicative role in respect of EU law. By adding Protocol No. 8 to the Lisbon Treaty, the Member States had indeed formulated some conditions to be respected in negotiating the accession, but they certainly cannot be suspected of having added Protocol No. 8 in order to nullify the clear accession mandate of Article 6(2) TEU. And yet, this is what the CJEU did in its Opinion 2/13: it took the wording of Protocol No. 8, developed this into a fully fledged autonomy doctrine echoing its earlier case law, and used that doctrine to effectively neutralise the mandate of Article 6(2) TEU – since some of the objections made by the Court in Opinion 2/13 could not possibly have been met by the negotiators of the Accession Agreement. One can explain this in two ways: either the CJEU thinks that the autonomy of EU law (and the protection of its own role, in particular) is a supra-constitutional principle prevailing even over the text of the Treaties (but nothing in the language used in Opinion 2/13 points in this direction), or else it has effectively adopted a *contra legem* interpretation of primary EU law. Either way, the doctrine of autonomy of EU law was used in a quite problematic way here. In the earlier cases, the doctrine was used to protect the integrity of the Court's role in interpreting and applying EU law. But accession to the ECHR, on the terms of the draft accession Agreement, would not actually have undermined that role. The ECtHR, admittedly, interprets the domestic law of the ECHR's contracting parties on some occasions. It has to make up its own mind when faced with conflicting interpretations of domestic law offered by the parties to a case; otherwise, it could not decide whether the Contracting State has committed a violation of the ECHR. For example, in order to decide whether an interference with the Convention is 'prescribed by law', the ECtHR has to assess whether the relevant national measures are laid down in a clear and accessible legal text or court doctrine.[36] Similarly, if the EU were to accede to the Convention, the ECtHR would necessarily be led to endorse the interpretations of EU law provided either by the applicant or the defendant. It is true that the Court of Justice would not be present in the Strasbourg courtroom to correct the interpretation of EU law given by the applicant, or by the Commission representing the EU as defendant, but this situation has always existed in relation to the domestic law of the Convention states: their supreme court is not present during the proceedings to give its own

---

[36] On the extent to which the ECtHR is necessarily led to interpret domestic law of the state involved in the dispute, see D. Spielmann, 'Le Fait, le juge et la connaissance. Aux confins de la compétence interprétative de la Cour européenne des droits de l'homme' in *Les Limites du droit international – Essais en l'honneur de Joe Verhoeven* (Bruylant, 2015), 319.

authoritative interpretations of national law. There is really no way out from this situation: if the EU is ever to become a party to the Convention, the ECtHR will have to be able to interpret, at least minimally, EU law, in order to be able to assess whether the ECHR has been infringed. The Strasbourg Court simply cannot 'keep its hands off' from EU law entirely. In this connection, one may also note that the Court of Justice itself does not hesitate to interpret other international agreements whose interpretation is primarily entrusted to an international body. Take for example the WTO Agreements. The fact that that those Agreements are enforced by the WTO's Dispute Settlement Body, whose interpretation of WTO law is authoritative, has not prevented the CJEU from proposing its own interpretation of WTO rules when necessary for its own purposes.[37] So, why should the mirror situation be any different: why should the CJEU jealously deny to other international adjudication bodies any kind of interpretative activity relating to EU law? The invocation of the autonomy of the EU legal order in Opinion 2/13 is, at bottom, a blunt refusal to admit the logical consequences of accession to the ECHR system, and by displaying the autonomy doctrine in this way, the Court of Justice has overruled the choice made by the EU Member States governments when they agreed the new text of Article 6 TEU. It was rightly noted that:

> by designating the EU as an exceptional entity, the Court keeps other institutional actors involved in European integration – including the member states – guessing as to what may or may not be compatible with its basic structure, while reserving for itself the authority to pronounce on the necessary contours of this new legal order.[38]

IV Conclusion

This volume's conceptual separation between an international and a European dimension of global governance makes complete sense to the extent that 'European' refers to the legal order of the EU. Indeed, that legal order forms a separate whole, and relatively clear rules of recognition allow us to decide whether a legal action or a legal norm belongs to that legal order or not. Yet, at the same time, and as this chapter has sought to point out, that distinction is somewhat blurred by two factors. The *first factor* is

---

[37] One example among many is the Court's Opinion 1/08 of 30 November 2009, *GATS Schedules of Specific Commitments*, EU:C:2009:739.

[38] T. Isiksel, 'European Exceptionalism and the EU's Accession to the ECHR' (2016) 27 *EJIL* 565, 577.

that EU law is also, in a meaningful way, a sub-area of international law rather than 'something else'. The same European states who conclude international treaties with other countries have also created the EU by means of a series of treaties, and they continue to consider themselves as masters of the overall political and legal destiny of the EU. These same Member States have, however, allowed their 'creature' to develop, in the course of time, a sophisticated legal order that is equipped with autonomous institutions, including some (such as the Commission, the Parliament and, above all, the Court of Justice) that have shown a constant tendency to develop the autonomous nature of that legal order when faced with international norms or mechanisms that are external to it. This autonomy of the EU legal order has had an impact on the evolution of international law generally, which is the *second factor* blurring the international/European distinction. Thus, the autonomous development of EU law has led to changes in the international status and role of the EU Member States (most obviously by excluding them altogether from some policy domains); it has contributed to containing the domestic effect of international treaties (by effectively shielding the EU's regulatory autonomy against international treaty obligations); and it has limited the degree to which the EU could engage with other international cooperation venues (by the Court's denial of EU participation in international treaties with effective dispute settlement mechanisms).

10

Constitutional State of the European Union

CHRISTOPH MÖLLERS

I Introduction

For the sixty years of its existence, defining the European Union (EU) or its predecessors as an institution *sui generis* has been a useful cloak of conceptual laziness.[1] Still, it remains difficult to find an adequate place for the EU within the landscape of international law and international governance. On the one hand, it may serve as a sign either of encouragement (or warning) how far the institutional integration of modern states can go. On the other hand, it is far from clear which lessons are to be learnt from this part of the world for other regions or even for the entire world. On the one hand, it seems to be increasingly clear that the most fruitful conceptual approaches to the EU treat it as one form of federal polities among others.[2] On the other hand, it is hard to ignore the fact that European integration takes place in a legal world of sovereign states, a fact that confers upon this integration a particular meaning and maybe, at least for the time being, brings about certain limitations. Finally, the legal discourse on European integration is more and more determined by actual political events. For years, it has been an indication of an academic introvert not to address the euro crisis in the context of European integration, in 2015 thousands of refugees arrived at the borders of the EU every day, many of them washed

---

[1] R. Schütze, *European Union Law* (Cambridge University Press, 2015), 63–5. Cohen and Vauchez notice that the assumption of a legal order *sui generis* empowered the early functionaries of the community vis-à-vis international and constitutional lawyers. A. Cohen and A. Vauchez, 'The Social Construction of Law: The European Court of Justice and its Legal Revolution Revisited' (2011) 7 *Annual Review of Law and Social Science* 417 at 424.

[2] O. Beaud, *Théorie de la Fédération* (Presses Universitaires de Frances, 2009); C. Schönberger, 'Die Europäische Union als Bund' (2004) 129 *Archiv des öffentlichen Rechts* 81; R. Schütze, *From Dual to Cooperative Federalism: The Changing Structure of European Law* (Oxford University Press, 2009).

up dead at the coasts, and as I write this the UK tries to make sense (or not) of the Brexit decision. A conceptual analysis has to keep its distance from the news, but only to a certain degree, and less so the more the events shake the concepts themselves.

This chapter is an effort in descriptive constitutionalism. My argument here is less about how the EU should be designed, but rather about what the state of the Union expresses about its constitution.[3] After a very short introduction into questions that are classically part of the debate on the topic of European constitutionalism, questions that seem however more and more fruitless today, I will organise the text around the distinction between legislative, executive and judicial functions. This structure implies that a working balance of political and legal constitutionalism is best organised around a system of legitimate branches.[4]

II Beyond: Traditional Conceptual Distinctions and their Limits for the Actual State of the EU

The debate on European constitutionalism should free itself from some conceptual questions that have defined it for decades, and take its ambiguities for granted instead of trying to resolve them in theory.

Yes, it makes sense to talk about European constitutional law.[5] But, yes, there are considerable institutional differences between the EU and its member states. Yes, there is considerable friction between a legal and a political concept of constitutionalism.[6] But it is no news that the EU as well as the Member States have to combine politicisation and juridification in order to set up a system that is perceived as legitimate. Yes, the Member States remain sovereign in the, quite contested,[7] legal sense of public international law.[8] But the way they make use of this sovereignty is

---

[3] For the kind of normative argument, I would embrace in this context: C. Möllers, 'Pouvoir Constituant – Constitution – Constitutionalisation' in J. Bast and A. von Bogdandy (eds.), *Principles of European Constitutional Law* (Hart, 2011), 169; C. Möllers, *The Three Branches: A Comparative Model of Separation of Powers* (Oxford University Press, 2015), 51–80.

[4] Möllers, *The Three Branches* (above n. 3), 80–101.

[5] Schütze, *European Union Law* (above n. 1), 43–76.

[6] For the attempt to integrate instead of juxtaposing them, see Möllers, 'Pouvoir Constituant – Constitution – Constitutionalisation' (above n. 3), 169.

[7] For a general account D. Grimm, *Sovereignty* (Columbia University Press, 2015); cf. J. H. H. Weiler and U. Haltern, 'Autonomy of the Community Legal Order: Through the Looking Glass' (1996) 37 *HILJ* 411.

[8] For an intelligent attempt to rethink that: H. M. Heinig, 'Verfassung im Nationalstaat: Von der Gesamtordnung zur europäischen Teilordnung?' (2016) 75 *Veröffentlichungen der Vereinigung der Deutschen Staatsrechtslehrer* 65.

widely defined by the law of the EU factually and normatively – even if they leave the EU. Normatively, it is perfectly possible to legally leave the EU, which is an important difference to more integrated federations. Factually, European law has created an intertwinement amongst the Member States as well as between them and EU institutions that seems to be rather difficult, if not impossible, to disentangle.[9] Whatever it means legally to 'leave' the EU, practically, many political and even legal bonds will remain or be substituted by formally different, but substantially comparable rules.

Yes, Europe is the site of a plurality of legal orders and it defies any strong assumption of normative unity.[10] Yet, it is not clear if this is new or specific to the European legal space or better understood as the normal state of heterogeneous federalism. Neither can we deny that the law of the EU serves as a resounding instrument of de-fragmentation and unification of legal relations between its Member States as well as between them and its citizenry.[11] Again, the state of the Union seems to be too complex for a purely conceptual effort along the traditional lines of constitutional theory.

III   Legislation: The Stasis of European Political Constitutionalism

A   Unstable Political Fault Lines and the Problem of Hegemony

Historically, the emergence of political constitutionalism has a variety of sources: independence from a colonial regime, liberation from authoritarianism or apartheid or the realisation of a political identity that has been prepared in non-political contexts. In any case, such constitutive processes do not have to create a homogeneous people. If there is any emerging consensus in a fuzzy debate, it is that the 'no demos thesis'[12] is built on wrong

---

[9] For the complex discussion on the 'Brexit', see the contributions on www.verfassungsblog .de/tag/brexit/.

[10] Cf. the contributions in M. Avbelj and J. Komárek, *Constitutional Pluralism in the European Union and Beyond* (Hart, 2012).

[11] C. Möllers, 'Fragmentierung als Demokratieproblem?' in C. Franzius et al. (eds.), *Strukturfragen der Europäischen Union* (Nomos, 2010), 150–72.

[12] D. Grimm, 'Does Europe Need a Constitution?' (1995) 1 *ELJ* 282. See also J. H. H. Weiler, 'Does Europe Need a Constitution? Demos, Telos and the German Maastricht Decision' (1995) 1 *ELJ* 219.

assumptions concerning the democratic subject.[13] We will not have to wait for a homogeneous European people to emerge, it never will.

This does not mean that the challenges are not demanding: what seems to be necessary for a democratic polity are relatively stable fault lines of political conflict between parties or political preferences. The early American republic in which parties appeared quite unexpectedly on the scene is an important example of the integrating effect of such conflicts. Substantial questions of foreign or economic policy,[14] not the least about the Federal Bank, could fuse with the institutional question of the status of the federation into a stable bipartisanism.[15] For a while, the EU seemed to develop into this direction along a classical left/right divide of two party blocks within the European Parliament.[16] This development is now interrupted and probably stalled by a set of recent developments, although the debate on austerity and budgetary restraint illustrated that there may still be a meaningful distinction between the political right and left on the European level. The existence of the same divide in other political conflicts confirms this point.[17] But for institutional as well as political reasons, even this debate – although concerning fundamental questions of the EU – rarely took place in the European Parliament (EP), but mostly within and among Member States and their party systems: the EP simply did not have a relevant say in the solution of the euro crisis that could have served to spark a debate. For the same reason the conflict was, to a certain degree, overwhelmed by Member State identities and their political (over-)identification with their respective domestic banking systems. The main issue – after all – being money that was raised and spent by Member States. The disparate interests of borrowers and lenders could, therefore, create new political conflict lines within and without the Eurozone. Even countries that do not typically endorse austerity may have an interest in controlling other countries that received guarantees (Italy). Even countries that received guarantees may have an interest in a formally equal treatment of other receiving countries (Ireland/Portugal versus Greece). Even countries that did not receive support may not play along the same

---

[13] There are several reasons for that, comparative: B. Anderson, *Imagined Communities: Reflections on the Origin and Spread of Nationalism* (Verso, 1983); theoretical: C. Möllers, 'Multi-Level Democracy' (2011) 24 *Ratio Juris* 247.

[14] So coherent that the parties could switch sides in the Federal conflict.

[15] S. Elkins and E. McKitrick, *The Age of Federalism: The Early American Republic 1788–1800* (Oxford University Press, 1995), Ch. VII.

[16] Cf. S. Hix, *What's Wrong with the Europe Union and How to Fix It* (Polity, 2008).

[17] Migration and social policy would be other examples.

political lines, independently from their governments' political ideology (France, Italy versus Germany).[18] Moreover, all these differing views may be judged as legitimate from a domestic democratic point of view. Let us take the case of Germany. Its stance on austerity may be politically, morally and economically flawed. It resembled a short-sighted and selfish plea for the kind of 'ordo-liberalism' in which nobody else believes.[19] But it was surely representative of a majority of voters whose taxes were in question. That democratically legitimate decisions may be wrong is a truism often neglected in political and constitutional theory especially of the left-liberal kind. In addition, the migration crisis of 2015 created a strange frontline, at the end between Germany and the rest. Finally, Brexit has so far created an unexpected procedural unity between the now twenty-seven Member States towards the UK.

Furthermore, the political process within the EP has changed. For the EP, the right/left divide has become less important than the distinction between the grand coalition of Europeanists and the opposition of Eurosceptics from the right and the left.[20] The classical political conflict between left and right has been cornered by the institutional question of more or less Europeanisation, and, different from the early American republic, both conflicts seem incapable of being integrated into one. This constellation is not necessarily undemocratic. The Swiss system in which the government has been backed by an all-party coalition for decades may serve as a role model.[21] But this kind of political consensus may not only have reached its limits even in Switzerland, it also needs compensatory mechanisms like a robust federalism and a lively system of direct democracy.

It is not entirely clear how meaningful democratic contestation along these overlapping and blurred lines can be possible.

The fragmentation of political fault-lines then leads to a stasis in political constitution-building, in which the central political conflict between parties that one may label as European 'federalists' and 'sovereigntists' cannot serve as bundlers of political contestation. Instead, the coexistence of conflicts between pro-European centrists and right and left sceptics with a plethora

[18] For the debate between France and Germany about the Banking Union, see D. Howarth and L. Quaglia, 'Die Bankenunion als Krönung der Wirtschafts- und Währungsunion?' (2015) *Integration* 44, 50–1.
[19] 'Of Rules and Order', *The Economist*, 9 May 2015.
[20] Euro-scepticism is better represented in the EP than in the average national parliament: P. Manow and O. Döring, 'Electoral and Mechanical Causes of Divided Government in the European Union' (2008) 41 *Comparative Political Studies* 1349.
[21] See e.g. the recommendations in *The EEAG Report on the European Economy* (CESifo, 2014), 55–73.

of overlapping but differing political conflicts between Member States does not give any support for a genuine Europeanisation of democratic politics. It is not clear whether there is any institutional solution to that problem.

This is all the more problematic because it is accompanied by a crisis of coalition-building between the Member States.[22] Hegemony has become a topic in the EU. Traditionally, hegemony has been an anti-liberal concept.[23] It appeals to the quest for true political power behind mere legal form. But there is neither such a thing as formless political power, nor a necessity for federal systems to be under the spell of a hegemon. While German state-building was unthinkable without Prussian hegemony, there is no comparable story to tell about a federal hegemon in India or the United States. Do we have to think about hegemony in constitutional terms for the EU? In fact, the voting mechanism within the Council has always been designed for the prospect of possible positive or negative state coalitions. If we talk about hegemony of one state today, this is the result of the crisis of coalition-building within the Member States. It was part of the European project that some Member States would be more powerful than others. But especially the role Germany plays at the moment seems to depart from this scheme, and this departure may become even more dramatic after the UK has finally left the Union. This is dangerous because action by Member State coalitions cannot lead to positive or negative nationalisms the same way the action of a hegemon can. In a more consolidated federal polity such a crisis of one decision-maker would shift powers to other branches or organs. If the states do not find common ground in the (European) Council, the EP has to take over. That this is not happening and that we are, instead, talking about hegemony, shows that the 'sovereigntist party', whatever its normative point is, still provides us with a fairly accurate account of the locus of legitimacy and power within the EU.

B   Conflicting Member State Preferences

The EU is a system of executive federalism in which European legislation is still mostly carried out by the Member States.[24] This creates the difficult

---

[22] F. Fabbrini, 'States' Equality v States' Power: The Euro-Crisis, Inter-State Relations and the Paradox of Domination' 17 *CYELS* (2015) 3.

[23] For Gramsci see T. R. Bates, 'Gramsci and the Theory of Hegemony' (1975) 36 *Journal of the History of Ideas* 351; H. Triepel, *Die Hegemonie. Ein Buch von führenden Staaten* (W. Kohlhammer, 1938).

[24] R. Schütze, 'From Rome to Lisbon: "Executive Federalism" in the (New) European Union' (2010) 47 *CML Rev* 1385.

question of how to adequately attribute political and administrative action to a particular political subject. This is highly relevant to an analysis of the state of political constitutionalism. Who is addressed when 'the EU' is criticized? The institutional setting has become so complex that both narratives, the story about bureaucratic Brussels as well as the story about Member States hiding behind international obligations, have created respective truth-value for themselves.[25] But this does not mean that both levels of political action are equally rational in their competing claim. While there is a stringent justification for a consolidation of European competences, Member States' policies, even if representing their electorates, seem to suffer from self-contradicting preferences. The necessity of European cooperation and coordination is accepted for many policy fields, while the externalities of this cooperation are often interpreted as an act of usurpation by 'the EU'. Many Member States and their democratic constituencies want a monetary union without substantial economic coordination, or an equal application of European law without control by central supranational organs. In short, in many contested cases, the Member States cultivate self-contradictory preferences and use them against the process of integration.

The border protection regime is another case in point. Before the dramatic outbreak of the crisis in the summer of 2015, most Member States could live with a deeply inhumane policy scheme because it was not perceived as a part of their own domestic political action. While state borders have been virtually substituted through European borders, the fact that thousands and thousands died at these borders only resounded in those Member States in which state and European borders were identical, namely in Italy and Malta. It is clear that the German public would not have tolerated the dying of thousands of people in the North Sea without feeling compelled to press for a policy change. But as long as the border was far away, it could be perceived as a foreign one.

This mechanism seems characteristic for the state of democratic constitutionalism at the European level. It is less a democratic deficit, but rather a democratic akrasia, a weakness of the will, at the level of the Member States who articulate and realise policy preferences but reject the immediate implications of these very preferences. From the point of view of democratic theory, this is a dramatic problem that leads to an institutional Catch-22. By attributing negative implications of EU policies that

[25] R. Putnam, 'Diplomacy and Domestic Politics: The Logic of Two-Level Games' (1988) 42 *IO* 427.

are sanctioned by the Member States to the EU level, political preferences shift against the EU and prevent the process from finding satisfying institutional answers. All institutions seem to distrust each other. The making of the Banking Union is a case in point.[26] Neither an intergovernmental solution nor the Commission were considered feasible. In the end, the supervision ended up with the European Central Bank.

C   Lack of Governmental Institutions

Taking democratic nation states as a role model, the division of labour between Commission, European Parliament and the Council seems particular, but not completely unheard of. The Member States remain powerful and so are the intergovernmental organs. The real problem in this setting is less the distribution of competences as such, but its lack of generality within the system, in the words of a Resolution of the EP: 'the lack of a credible single executive authority enjoying full democratic legitimacy and competence to take effective action across a wide spectrum of policies'.[27] As long as the institutional tasks within the EU are differentiated along different policies there is an immense degree of horizontal fragmentation.[28] This kind of fragmentation seems specific to the EU because it differs from the vertical differentiation which is a normal feature of asymmetric federalism that is organised around diverse forms of differentiated integration. One example is EU foreign relations: for classical federal systems foreign politics always provided a crucial point of political self-definition. It guaranteed institutional unity and had an immense potential for internal integration. 'If we are to be one nation in any respect, it clearly ought to be in respect to other nations.'[29] The organisation of external relations is, therefore, especially telling about the state of integration. In the EU, the difference between external trade policy, where the Commission has a strong role and classical international politics, which is still run by important Member States, tells a dramatic story about these differences.[30]

---

[26] C. Möllers, 'Some Reflections on the State of European Democracy with Regard to BU and ECB' in S. Grundmann and H. W. Micklitz (eds.), *The European Banking Union and Constitution* (Hart, 2018).

[27] European Parliament Resolution of 16 February 2017 on possible evolutions of and adjustments to the current institutional set-up of the European Union (2014/2248(INI)), lit. D.

[28] A. Rosas and L. Armati, *EU Constitutional Law: An Introduction* (Hart, 2012), 20; Schütze, *European Union Law* (above n. 1), 153.

[29] Federalist Papers No. 42 (1788) [James Madison].

[30] Rosas and Armati, *EU Constitutional Law* (above n. 28), 244–50; Schütze, *European Union Law* (above n. 1), 189, 204–12.

The most important effect of this is the lack of a truly governmental power that is responsible for political leadership, for the agenda-setting, within the EU. The debate on the 'Economic Government' has illustrated this void. Either an economic government is a real government, or it remains an agent of other political actors that define its agenda. There is no way to sectoralise the 'economical' from the political. The shifting role of the Commission that seemed for a while to develop into a governmental organ shows the problem. With the institutionalisation of the President of the European Council, the fragmentation of European para-governmental powers started, a linear development towards a government by the Commission was interrupted. And with the election of 2014 the idea of a politicized Commission was immediately kept within tight political and institutional constraints: the Grand Coalition centrism within the EP that raises the question as to what 'politicisation' of the European Commission can mean and the delicate role of the Commission as a mediator between Member States that is not allowed to look partisan.[31] Traditionally, the political role of the Commission was to defend European institutions and programmes against the Member States. Another understanding would define the Commission as the executor of a political majority in the EP. But today's Commission seems to do neither. It is flexible towards powerful Member States and it refuses to give determined vision of its own towards the future of European institutions.[32] Politicisation has become asymmetrically dependent on certain Member States.

Today, the role of the EU head of government is opaquely distributed between the President of the European Council, the President of the Commission, the High Representative for Foreign Affairs and Security Policy and the heads of important Member State governments. This makes it increasingly more difficult to address the EU, with support or critique, as a responsible – more or less identifiable – political actor.

D   The Decline of Formal Legislation and the Myth of 'Negative Integration'

The output of formal legislative acts according to the co-decision procedure has been steadily declining[33] while the role of the European Council

---

[31] M. Hartlapp and Y. Lorenz, 'Die Europäische Kommission – ein (partei)politischer Akteur?' (2015) 43 *Leviathan* 64.

[32] Just look at the European Commission's *White Paper on the Future of Europe*, 2017, IP/17/385.

[33] D. Chalmers and M. Chaves, 'Union Democratic Overload and the Unloading of European Democracy' in O. von Cramme and S. B. Hobolt (eds.), *Democratic Politics in a European*

as an informal agenda-setter has been gaining traction, probably since the Treaty of Maastricht. So, there is a political output of the EU, but the way this output is created displays a considerable distrust of the traditional institutional setting. The Member States are striking back. This seems, at first glance, to feed into a current critique of the EU as a negative regulator that enables market forces to act within a common space. The economic constitution of the common market, so the story goes, favours negative integration[34] and a decline of social regulation at the level of the Member States. The governance of the EU may look like a neoliberal project, a neo-liberalism that is engrained in its form of constitutionalism.[35]

It is far from clear if this assumption corresponds to the institutional reality.[36] There is no doubt that the erosion of market barriers between Member States has considerable impact on their ability to regulate. Certain European rules, for example concerning public procurement[37] and priva-tisation of public services, significantly change the relation between pri-vate and public power. However, there is little doubt that the EU itself is a very active regulator. Many of its regulatory efforts cannot be understood as simply adhering to a free-market ideology. This is the case, for example, in the fields of environmental law, consumer protection, chemicals and even data protection.[38] It is also necessary to clarify the baseline of regula-tory normality implied by such critique. A European rule that, for some Member States, constitutes a scaling down of intervention may be an intro-duction of a new form of regulation for others. The same is true for some of the criticisms of the jurisprudence of the Court of Justice of the European Union (CJEU). Again, the basic freedoms have a market-liberalising effect that is non-trivial. But it is not always self-evident to what degree much-debated decisions actually influence the balance of social and economic power. Take the example of *Viking* and *Laval*,[39] two of the most widely criticised decisions of the CJEU, for legal as well as for political reasons. All

---

Union under Stress (Oxford University Press, 2014), 155–79, 162–4.

[34] F. Scharpf, *Governing in Europe: Effective and Democratic?* (Oxford University Press, 1999); A. Somek, *Individualism. An Essay on the Authority of the European Union* (Oxford University Press, 2008).

[35] C. Crouch, *Post-Democracy* (Polity, 2004); or *The Strange Non-Death of Neo-Liberalism* (Polity, 2013).

[36] C. Möllers, 'Krisenzurechnung und Legitimationsproblematik in der Europäischen Union' (2015) 43 *Leviathan* 339.

[37] C. McCrudden, *Buying Social Justice: Equality, Government Procurement, & Legal Change* (Oxford University Press, 2007).

[38] See also V. Kosta, *Fundamental Rights in EU Internal Market Legislation* (Hart, 2015).

[39] Case C-438/05, *Viking Line* [2007] ECR I-10779; Case C-341/05, *Laval* [2007] ECR I-11767.

we know indicates that the political implications of this jurisprudence are ambiguous, even with regard to the power of trade unions.[40] In any case and despite all problems, there is still a considerable regulatory output that should raise serious doubts about too-sweeping attempts to portray the EU as an instrument of neoliberalism.

The point here is that the decline of formal legislation and the inaccurate assumption of negative integration stem from the same assumption, namely the fundamental lack of political legitimacy in the standard legislative process. Even if it is fundamentally unclear why this process should be more deficient than many processes of European domestic legislation, the fact of this distrust is in itself undeniable. It may be the expression of a democratic preference for a national governmental level that deserves respect.[41]

E   Crippled Member States?

With the European Council becoming the main agenda-setter of European politics, domestic political legitimacy of the Member States becomes a more urgent problem for European constitutionalism. In its international origins, the European project was both dependent on the political legitimacy of the states as well as an instrument to insulate policy from them. This also meant that the European level itself could be read as the equivalent of a functional independent agency.[42] This rendered early integration in a different manner, dependent on the state of domestic democracy. States could obstruct, like France under Charles de Gaulle's 'empty chair' policy, but there was no direct spill-over of democratic deficiencies to the European level. Today, we can see such effects in both directions. For many young democracies, European structures should and do operate as a supporting framework. But when state democracies like Hungary become authoritarian under the condition of a Union that is both more integrated than in the 1960s and more intergovernmental than in the 1980s, this may endanger the legitimacy of the whole project. And are there also reversed effects? Did the European approach to the euro crisis erode Member State democracies like Greece or Portugal? It seems difficult to make a clear case. There is little doubt that the Eurozone created wrong incentives and that

---

[40] Cf. the studies in M. Freeland and J. Prassl (eds.), *Viking, Laval and Beyond* (Hart, 2015), esp. Chapter 19 by M. Bobek, 323.

[41] Möllers, 'Multi-Level Democracy' (above n. 13).

[42] This is still Peter Lindseth's reading of the EU; cf. P. Lindseth, *Power and Legitimacy: Reconciling Europe and the Nation-State* (Oxford University Press, 2010).

governments were misled by investment banks. There is also little doubt that austerity politics have failed and were anyhow mostly aiming at the rescue of banks. On the other hand, states being blackmailed by globalised players is not a phenomenon limited to the EU; nor were the states innocent in the matter. They, after all, were either dysfunctional and corrupt or extraordinarily dependent on financial markets in the first place. Even the fact that states of the Eurozone have lost one important macro-economic instrument – devaluation – is ambivalent. Even before the euro, monetary policy, in most states, was in the hands of independent national central banks. And some states explicitly wanted to avoid the risks of devaluation through their membership of the euro.[43]

The pattern of mutual destabilisation between the EU and Member State levels makes it even harder to find an institutional solution to the question of how to preserve the political integrity of the Member States. The cases of Austria,[44] Hungary and Poland have displayed helplessness.[45] The core problem is that neither can a court[46] claim sufficient legitimacy to evaluate the political system of a member state as a whole,[47] nor do the European organs seem to be politically weighty enough to fulfil this task. Finally, the Member States have a strong incentive to ignore democratic deficiencies of other Member States.[48]

F   Conclusion: The Missing Architecture of Political Constitutionalism

The institutional design of the standard EU of (soon to be) 27 within the legislative co-decision procedure presents by all accounts a fairly good model for the democratic legitimacy of such a vast federal polity. But this institutional set-up has lost more and more of its relevance for different

---

[43] P. de Grauwe, *Economics of Monetary Union*, 10th edn (Oxford University Press, 2014), 34–6.

[44] On this failed action, see F. Schorkopf, *Die Maßnahmen derXIV EU-Mitgliedstaaten gegen Österreich* (Springer, 2002).

[45] C. Möllers and L. Schneider, *Demokratieschutz in der EU* (Mohr, 2018).

[46] On this idea, see D. Halberstam, 'Constitutional Heterarchy: The Centrality of Conflict in the European Union and the United States' in J. L. Dunoff and J. P. Trachtman (eds.), *Ruling the World? Constitutionalism, International Law and Global Governance* (Cambridge University Press, 2009), 326–55, 350–5.

[47] For systemic criteria A. von Bogdandy and M. Ioannidis, 'Systemic Deficiency in the Rule of Law: What It Is, What Has Been Done, What Can Be Done' (2014) 51 *CML Rev* 59–96.

[48] European Commission Communication, 'A New Framework to Strengthen the Rule of Law', COM (2014) 158 final.

reasons:[49] the Eurozone has become more and more the space of relevant political action,[50] and the Member States have discovered more and more intergovernmental means to bypass the institutions. The lack of a coherent architecture of political constitutionalism is less the result of a democratic deficit than of a lack of coherent preferences and of trust in the other actors.

IV The Executive: Emergency Constitution and Democratic Technocracy

A The Ambivalent Development of Parliamentarism

The rise of the executive and the fall of parliaments have been announced since the beginnings of parliamentary rule. But serious comparative and empirical corroboration of this narrative remain rare. At first glance European integration shows a different picture. The EP has been steadily gaining in power and is today the only politically relevant parliament beyond the state worldwide. It is important to keep this in mind, even if it is not the whole story. For, at a second glance, we observe at least three different, equally disturbing phenomena.[51] First, there is a serious trade-off on the level of Member States. European integration claimed powers in fields that are normally governed by constitutional rules for foreign politics. Under these regimes, national parliaments suffer from a loss of decision-making and control powers. Second, the EP is inhibited by the general external and internal problems of the legislative process that we discussed above. Third, emergency situations seem to create an executive and/or technocratic regime that leaves less room for formal legislative input. These developments must be taken seriously; this also means giving them a more thorough analysis.

B Technocratic Regimes 1: Agencies

Is the 'rise of the unelected' part of the constitutional development in the European Union?[52] A first indicator is the much-described flourishing of

---

[49] For a more optimistic reading that takes the euro crisis as a mere exception: B. de Witte, 'Euro Crisis Responses and the EU Legal Order: Increased Institutional Variation or Constitutional Mutation?' (2015) 11 *ECLR* 434.

[50] J. Bast, 'Article 26 AEUV (TFEU)' in E. Grabitz et al. (eds.), *Kommentar EUV/AEUV*, 58th edn (Beck, 2016), para. 7A. But did it fundamentally change the structure? M. Dawson and B. de Witte, 'Constitutional Balance in the EU after the EU-crisis' (2013) 76 *MLR* 817.

[51] D. Curtin 'The Challenge of Executive Dominance in Europe' (2014) 77 *MLR* 1.

[52] F. Vilbert, *The Rise of the Unelected* (Cambridge University Press, 2007).

the European system of independent agencies.[53] This development is probably less due to the problem of coping with factual complexity in certain regulatory contexts, and more to do with an institutional conflict between Member States and the European Commission. As long as the Member States connect the execution of European law with their sovereignty, the setting up of European agencies serves as a compromise between the two classical options of European administration: either leaving action to the states or giving it to the Commission. The debate about independent agencies has become less dramatic the more we have learned about the level of control that is yielded by Commission and Member States.[54] Therefore, it does not seem plausible to interpret the system of independent agencies as a technocratic counter-government that is compromising a political concept of legitimacy of the EU. To be sure, the constitutional means to avoid such silent erosions of legitimacy are still sketchy. While ten years ago scholars could see the first signs of a developing non-delegation doctrine on the horizon,[55] the more recent jurisprudence of the CJEU has taken another path.[56] This may be for good reasons. Comparative law offers very few examples of efficient non-delegation standards.[57] There may also be better ways to achieve the aim of upholding democratic legitimacy.[58] It remains, however, a worrisome sign that the Court of Justice appears to have given up on the classical constitutional project of taming administrative discretion through the means of law. But this is a critique of the CJEU that does not imply the system of independent agencies in its current state to be running wild. The tasks that are carried out by these agencies are too technical and too fragmented to justify such an assumption.

C   Technocratic Regimes 2: The EURO Crisis

The management of the euro crisis has been – to many observers – the epitome of the use of executive emergency powers. Comparisons ranged from the French Directoire before Napoleon to Schmittian concepts.[59] But

---

[53] E. Chiti, 'The Emergence of a Community Administration: The Case of European Agencies' (2000) CML Rev 309; and E. Chiti, 'European Agencies' Rulemaking: Powers, Procedures and Assessment' (2013) 19 ELJ 93.

[54] D. Curtin, Executive Power in the European Union (Oxford University Press, 2009), 146–65.

[55] R. Schütze, '"Delegated" Legislation in the (new) European Union: A Constitutional Analysis' (2011) 74 MLR 661. Case 9/56, Meroni v. High Authority [1958] ECR 133.

[56] Case C-270/12, United Kingdom v. Parliament & Council (ESMA), EU:C:2014:18.

[57] Möllers, The Three Branches (above n. 3), 114–18.

[58] C. R. Sunstein, 'Nondelegation Canons' (2000) 67 University of Chicago Law Review 315.

[59] E.g. J. White, 'Emergency Europe' (2015) 63 Political Studies 300.

it is dubitable if this is an accurate description. While there is no space for detailed institutional analysis here,[60] it is clear that the strong intergovernmental side of the rescue is different from a technocratic regime.[61] There is no doubt that the raw and unformalised intergovernmentality of the euro-rescue does not live up to any demanding ideal of democratic self-determination. But it is, on the other hand, hard to deny that the ongoing crisis was a conflict between Member States in which the opposing parties each could claim considerable democratic legitimacy, for example with regard to Greece and Germany. It is also hard to see what political room for manoeuvre was given to the notorious Troika, consisting of the Commission, the European Central Bank (ECB) and the International Monetary Fund (IMF). These three are, more or less, technocratic institutions, but they were carrying out a politically determined agenda that was defined by the Council of Ministers for Economics and Finance (ECOFIN). Again, the idea that specific measures of a given state are essentially dictated by a group of other states has no democratic flavour whatsoever, but it is also misunderstood as the action of a technocratic regime. If one does not want to reconstruct the whole story as the result of a capitalist conspiracy, it seems again more appropriate to talk about a political conflict between Member States for which genuine European rules were either missing or bypassed, and that was, therefore, deeply underformalised.

Still, this assumption needs at least two qualifications. The form of the European Stabilisation Mechanism (ESM) obviously resembles international financial institutions like the IMF. But due to its being built on money that comes from the Member States, it can only be legitimately controlled by Member State parliaments. The state of its legitimacy is, therefore, defined by Member State constitutional law. Liberating it from the impression of an arcane technocracy is a task that cannot be solved on the European level as long as there is no European source for its finances.[62] There will be no representation without taxation.[63]

Second, crucial for an adequate understanding of the crisis mechanisms is the interpretation of the role of the Commission in the control of austerity measures within the Member States. This is an issue that is both very

[60] K. Tuori and K. Tuori, *The Eurozone Crisis: A Constitutional Analysis* (Cambridge University Press, 2014).

[61] For a different reading that stresses the relevance of independent technocratic institutions, see A. Vauchez, *Démocratiser l'Europe* (Seuil, 2014).

[62] Curtin, 'The Challenge of Executive Dominance in Europe' (above n. 51).

[63] For a general point, see L. Martin, 'Taxation, Loss Aversion, Accountability', Working Paper, Department of Political Science, Yale University, 2014.

contested and quickly developing. In any case, it is telling about the state of European constitutionalism that the analysis of the law that empowers the Commission is not sufficient (in some contexts maybe not even necessary) to get an impression of its political relevance. If we suppose that we cannot attribute the same democratic legitimacy to the Commission as to a functioning Member State government, it seems problematic to confer upon the Commission such control powers as was done in the much criticised Six-Pack and Two-Pack regulations.[64] According to one interpretation, these powers could enable the Commission to wield wide control over the budgets of the Member States and that means to substitute one core element of the domestic democratic process with a technocratic decision. But there are at least two caveats to this interpretation, one legal, one political. The legal argument reminds us of the fact that these powers are not mandatory, but that they refer to a political process in the Council in which only sanctions against Member States can be included. The political observation tells us that we cannot, so far, see that the Commission has the political will and the political power to execute these budgetary rules. The cautionary treatment of France since the euro crisis is a point in case. Generally, the violation of the budget rules has more and more become the rule rather than an exception. This may be good news for political critics of austerity measures. But the Commission does look less like an independent institutional actor than like a moderator between Member States as it is missing a political agenda of its own. If this observation is correct, the problem of EU integration seems to lie less in too much technocracy than in too much diplomacy.

D   In Particular: The European Central Bank

From a legal point of view, the ECB can claim a maximum amount of institutional legitimacy within the European legal order. It enjoys an explicit constitutional status,[65] though it is not as completely insulated from external control as it claimed to be.[66] One might even argue that its constitutional status as an independent organ has deeper roots than the rule of Article 130 of the Treaty on the Functioning of the European Union (TFEU). Pierre Rosanvallon has argued for the German Bundesbank that

---

[64] See C. Antpöhler, 'Emergenz der europäischen Wirtschaftsregierung' (2012) 72 *ZaöRV* 353.

[65] Article 13 TEU; Article 282 TFEU.

[66] Case C-11/00, *Commission* v. *ECB* [2003] ECR I-7417; CFI Case T-496/11, *United Kingdom* v. *ECB*, EU:T:2015:133.

its independence had a constitutive mandate stemming from the German experience with inflation in the early 1920s.[67] This argument still seems to be valid with regard to the German public. It nevertheless is somewhat ironic, given that a highly expertocratic institution is built on a narrative that is at least factually contestable. While the Weimar Republic was successful in dealing with inflation by democratic and politically responsible means, it finally collapsed under the consequences of deflationary politics.

From the perspective of constitutionalism, the status of the ECB is a vice rather than a virtue. One might even doubt if we can attribute second-order legitimacy to it. While the independent US Federal Reserve is a creature of Congress, of an egalitarian and reversible political process, the ECB is basically set in stone. Even if there was a political process on the European level, this process would not be able to amend its fundamental structure.[68] But democratic legitimacy is maintained only under the condition of amenability. Put differently, political constitutionalism is built on the fundamental trust of all members of a community that majority decisions will be acceptable for all possible minorities; that is, for everybody. This trust did not exist between the Member States that created the ECB. It did especially not exist between France and Germany.[69] Moreover, the constitutional status of the ECB is part of an institutional environment in which the meaning of the highest political offices is unclear and contested. We saw that there is no responsible head of government in the EU.[70] Consequently, the President of the ECB assumes a role and authority that is remarkably weightier than that of any other head of a central bank. Would it be possible to imagine an American Republic in which the office of the Chairman of the Federal Reserve is older, more deeply constitutionally entrenched and less contested than the office of the President of the United States? Functionalism has created an institutional monstrosity.[71]

In a traditional transmission-belt model of democratic administration, the lack of political legitimacy is compensated by a clear statutory mandate. This was the German argument for a normative focus on price stability for the ECB, different from the Federal Reserve that is also obliged

---

[67] P. Rosanvallon, *Democratic Legitimacy: Impartiality, Reflexivity, Proximity* (Princeton University Press, 2011), 115–19.

[68] A. Blinder, *The Quiet Revolution* (Yale University Press, 2004), 8–9.

[69] H. James, *Making the European Monetary Union* (Belknap Press, 2012).

[70] Above, section C 'Technocratic Regimes 2: The EURO Crisis'.

[71] Pufendorf's comment on the Holy German Empire as 'monstro simile' was meant as a description rather than as an evaluation: S. von Pufendorf, *Die Verfassung des deutschen Reiches* (1667), ed. H. Denzer (Insel, 1994), 198–9.

to take employment into consideration. Despite many challenges from governance theory there is still a good case to be made for well-defined mandates.[72] But the definition of a mandate only functions in specific contexts. Even if one accepted the restrictive economic approach of the ECB mandate as a matter of policy, one would wonder if it makes sense as an institutional solution, given the factual dependence between monetary and economic policies. Can this mandate really prevent the ECB from becoming a democratically illegitimate economic government? Or, rather, does it work like the mandate of an environmental agency that, because of its clear mandate, must put all its resources in the protection of clean water while ignoring air pollution? As a matter of fact, there is a political process going on within the ECB concerning its own mandate. This process is less an indicator of usurpation of competences[73] than of an ill-designed legal framework. Setting up a Central Bank as the guardian of a currency without other political actors in the field of economic policy at hand implies that this institution does not only apply rules, but also sees itself as responsible for the survival of the currency. This kind of protection will always work beyond a given mandate.

Within the political framework we developed, the ECB is more problematic for left-wing politics than for conservatives and more problematic for sovereigntists than for Europeanists. The combination of liberal monetary politics as executed in the SMT, OMT, and QE programmes on the one hand and its tough stance towards the Greek government has allowed the ECB to escape being defined in clear political terms. But this achievement can also be seen as a problem. Maybe the ECB did not feel at liberty to be more flexible towards the Greek government because it had already used up its political credit with regard to fiscally conservative Member States. This is mere speculation, but it illustrates that the independence of the ECB, contrary to what is often assumed, may not be increased through the European construction: as the argument often goes, the ECB is an institution without a clear political counter-process. Hence, its independence may be even bigger and more problematic than in the case of national central banks.[74] But the fragmentation of European politics could make the Bank more dependent. It might be much more difficult for an agency to please fighting factions than to cope with a political process from which

[72] D. Epstein and S. O'Halloran, *Delegating Powers* (Cambridge University Press, 1999).

[73] This is, of course, the view of the German Federal Constitutional Court's preliminary ruling: 14th of January 2014 – 2 BvR 2728/13 et al.

[74] G. Majone, 'Rethinking European Integration after the Debt Crisis', UCL Working Paper 3/2012.

it is supposed to deviate once in a while. The bad news is that this kind of dependence does not produce any convincing form of legitimacy because it is hidden within a structure that claims expertise and autonomy from politics. The specific problem of the ECB might not be too much independence, but a complex network of informal dependencies.

This problem becomes more dramatic because we know that this political conflict is not only part of the environment of the ECB, but of its internal discourse. The federal structure of the Governing Council led to an internalisation of the conflict between the Member States, albeit with different decision-making rules. One does not have to take sides in this conflict to see that this threatens the core of the ECB's claim to legitimacy. If decisions are taken according to political criteria in the first place, then it should be done in the open and left to elected officials.

A final problem for the ECB lies in the dramatic loss of credibility with regard to expertocratic arguments in the field of economic politics. The decline of expertise at the European level began perhaps with the now infamous paper of the European Commission for European Monetary Union (EMU),[75] and it went on with the policy recommendations of the IMF, especially for Cyprus and Greece that were endorsed and executed by the 'institutions'. To be sure, there is no governing without expertise, and no expertise without flaws. But the misrepresentation of these institutions were not simple mistakes, they were not accidental. They were the result of an institutional political agenda that was clothed in the language of the economically factual. Neither independent expertise nor democratic politics explain them, but the agenda of institutions that pursue their self-preservation.

E   Conclusion

Technocracy and executive action have always played a pivotal role in EU law. But it would be wrong to describe the state of European constitutionalism as being captured by these two phenomena. At least two points have to be made to complete the picture. First, in parliamentary systems Member States' governments are backed by parliamentary majorities as well as by public sentiment. This is true for the German approach to the euro crisis and the French critique of the Service Directive. To be sure, this is not

---

[75] European Commission, 'One Money, One Market: An Evaluation of the Potential Benefits and Costs of Forming an Economic and Monetary Union' (1990) 44 *European Economy*, http://ec.europa.eu/economy_finance/publications/publication_summary7520_en.htm.

true for the Greek fight against austerity, whose outcome still seems to be the result of unequal Member State power, because, second, technocratic regimes are still firmly embedded in, albeit unjustly distributed, political power of Member States. A fatalist narrative about the rise of technocracy in neoliberalism does not seem specific enough for the description of the EU. What we see are states looking for means to secure their political preferences, and a deep distrust between them that favours static, highly entrenched and formally de-politicised institutions.

V   Law: The Limits of Judicial Governance

The idea of a *Rechtsgemeinschaft* that has played a pivotal rule at least in the German debate on the European integration consists of two almost untranslatable connotations. A *Gemeinschaft* is a thick community kept together by traditional bonds. *Recht* is 'law', but it is also alluding to rightness and justice in a way that undermines any purely formal concept of legalism. Other Member States have different legal cultures and divergent ideas of the meaning and the normative status of law and of 'integration' as a synonym for a formalised way of de-differentiating a multinational community. The formality of law can be read as an instrument to abstract from differing understandings of the meaning of law and differing expectations of what can be achieved through law. But the more integrated the community gets, the easier do these differing understandings come to the fore. If law is accepted to be just a technocratic means to an end, then there might be a good case to bend the rules for a benign and politically accepted intention. But if legality is seen as an end in itself and if breaking one rule is just an indication for the dissolution of the whole legal order, then there is no room for a political or economic discretion in addressing European law. The idea of an autonomous value of law that might trump a sound political process is probably also deeply German,[76] and not shared by the legal cultures of all other Member States. But more interesting than the origins of diversity is the fact of diversity in itself. It significantly changes the role of the CJEU, which becomes, paradoxically, through the different meanings of law, more of a political actor because these different

---

[76] www.infratest-dimap.de/umfragen-analysen/bundesweit/umfragen/aktuell/mehrheit-hat-kein-vertrauen-in-medien-berichterstattung-zum-ukraine-konflikt/. The German Federal Constitutional Court is constantly polled as the most trustworthy institution in Germany. Walter Hallstein's strong belief in the integrating force of law for the European integration is also well known: see W. Hallstein, *Die Europäische Gemeinschaft* (Econ, 1973), 53.

understandings are very much part of national political identities. Therefore, the way the CJEU treats EU law, especially its readiness to establish a hierarchy of norms that binds European organs as well as the Member States, is also part of the political identity of the EU. The critical German reception of the *Pringle*[77] and *OMT*[78] decisions is only the most visible point in case. The opt-out of Poland and the UK with regard to the Charter of Fundamental Rights is another example. And these questions of a juridico-political identity do not only concern the state of legal principles but also the internal organisation of the European courts. All of these are constitutional issues for the EU.

A   The Institutional Crises of Human Rights in Europe

While human rights have become something like the least common denominator in international law despite much critical literature, they are more and more growing into a source of contestation within the EU. The triangle of national constitutional courts, CJEU and European Court of Human Rights (ECtHR) has not necessarily produced an increase in human rights protection. There is a difference between human rights and human rights regimes that human rights lawyers sometimes ignore. It must be considered not only by political scientists, but also by lawyers for two reasons. First, as long as the interpretation of human rights depends on differing concepts of liberty, there is no such thing as an optimal protection of human rights. One might even wonder if it is really easier to create a union of common rights protection than to create a political union. Second, courts cannot avoid being political actors at least with regard to their own institutional interests. In the best case, there is a convincing convergence between their internal institutional preferences and their formal function as defined by law. But in the normal case these two overlap without being identical. This is nothing unusual, but it becomes problematic when the gap between the jurisprudence of a court and its institutional interests is connected with a competition with other courts. It becomes more precarious when this conflict relates to virtually open-ended and highly politicised norms like human rights. All this gets even more dramatic when the conflict between the courts represents a conflict

---

[77] M. Ruffert, 'Case Note Pringle' (2013) *JuristenZeitung* 257; P. Kirchhof, 'Stabilität von Recht und Geldwert in der Europäischen Union' (2013) *Neue Juristische Wochenschrift* 1.

[78] Cf. the reactions reported on www.faz.net/-gqu-84kbk and U. di Fabio, 'Nur Mut, Bundesverfassungsgericht!', *Frankfurter Allgemeine Sonntagszeitung*, 21 June 2015, 22.

between different levels of public authority, which creates another layer of politicisation. An example for this is the first Data Retention decision of the CJEU.[79] Leaving open the merits of the case, it is interesting that the Court of Justice complained about the lack of determinacy in the Directive with regard to different issues: the kind of crimes that could trigger the use of saved information as well as the procedures to get access to them. But this omission was not an accidental failure of the European legislator with regard to a minimum rule-of-law standard. It was a deliberate decision in order to protect the powers of the Member States in the fields of criminal law and criminal procedure. In a concededly extreme reading, this decision could lead to a considerable politically unwanted degree of harmonisation in these two fields.

It is part of the irritating features of the academic debate that the question of how to organise the overlapping layers of human rights regimes is often answered by extremely weak and non- or at best para-juridical notions like 'cooperation', 'dialogue' or, with a hint at international law, 'comity'.[80]

Such formulas are fair enough as self-descriptions of courts vis-à-vis the institutional conflicts in which they are entangled. But nobody would mistake a will to cooperation expressed by different governments with a rule of international law. It is mysterious why the academic observer should do just that with regard to courts. This holds at least as long as one does not assume that everything courts utter is law. To the contrary, the only justification for the independent (i.e. non-responsible) power of courts is their obligation towards the law.[81] Without being naïve about the determinacy of rules, it seems critical to lead a discussion about the inter-level conflicts that is not satisfied with political formulas. To be sure, there is also a highly technical discussion, especially on Art. 51 of the Fundamental Rights Charter.[82] But it remains remarkable that the basic question if a given case should be reviewed by separate standards or by concurrent standards is not

---

[79] Case C-293/12, *Digital Rights Ireland*, EU:C:2014:238.

[80] A.-M. Slaughter, 'A Global Community of Courts' (2003) 44 *HILJ* 191; D. Thym, 'Vereinigt die Grundrechte!' (2015) *JuristenZeitung* 53; K.-H. Ladeur and L. Viellechner, 'Die transnationale Expansion staatlicher Grundrechte' (2008) 46 *Archiv des Völkerrechts* 42; A. Voßkuhle, 'Multilevel Cooperation of the European Constitutional Courts' (2010) 6 *ECLR* 175.

[81] Möllers, *The Three Branches* (above n. 3), 84–96.

[82] F. Fontanelli, 'The Implementation of European Union Law by Member States under Article 51 (1) of the Charter of Fundamental Rights' (2014) 20 *CJEL* 193; E. Hancox, 'The Meaning of "Implementing" EU Law under Article 51(1) of the Charter: Åkerberg Fransson' (2013) 50 *CML Rev* 1411.

answered by any concerted political decision. We see dramatic differences even between the constitutional courts of relatively similar legal orders like the Austrian[83] and the German[84]. But we see no basis for these paths in decisions by a political decision-maker, be it a national or a European one.

B   Two Examples of Misplaced Legal Constitutionalism: Autonomy and Mutual Recognition

For the reasons developed above, it seems too simplistic to criticise the already infamous Opinion 2/13[85] of the CJEU from a perspective that is limited to human rights protection. It is neither clear if more courts generally provide more rights protection nor does such a limitation seem appropriate with regard to the genuinely federal problems that are created by the accession.[86] This neither means that the opinion was correct nor that the level of rights protection against the actions of EU organs is currently satisfying. But it seems, at least for our purposes, more interesting to look at the structure and value of two central organising principles of the argument: the autonomy of European legal order and the principle of mutual recognition.

The principle of autonomy has already served in other opinions as a tool to achieve two goals: to identify the integrity of the EU legal order with the institutional fact of its exclusive reviewability by the CJEU and to immunize the EU law from the interference of other international legal orders.[87] Whatever the merits of these two doctrines may be, it is quite obvious that the CJEU does not only apply such a principle to EU law, but also works against the use of comparable principles by other legal orders. For the CJEU, there is neither a level of autonomy of international[88] nor one of Member State law[89] that is comparable to the standards it applies to its own legal order. This kind of European constitutional exceptionalism seems

---

[83] Cf. M. Pöschl, 'Verfassungsgerichtsbarkeit nach Lissabon' (2012) *Zeitschrift für öffentliches Recht* 587.

[84] BVerfGE 126, 286 (2010) *Honeywell*; C. Möllers, 'Case Note Honeywell' (2011) 7 *ECLR* 161.

[85] Opinion 2/13, *ECHR II*, EU:C:2014:2454.

[86] For an insightful analysis, see D. Halberstam, '"It's the Autonomy, Stupid!" A Modest Defense of Opinion 2/13 on EU Accession to the ECHR, and the Way Forward' (2015) 16 *GLJ* 105.

[87] Opinion 2/94, *ECHR I* [1996] ECR I-1759; Case C-459/03, *Commission v. Ireland (MOX Plant)* [2006] ECR I-4635.

[88] Case C-402/05P, *Kadi and Al Barakaat International Foundation v. Council and Commission* [2008] ECR I-6351.

[89] Case C-399/11, *Melloni*, EU:C:2013:107.

contestable because it is far from clear how it can be justified beyond the self-reference of the court to its own jurisprudence.[90] From a theoretical point of view, 'autonomy' sounds like a version of a Kelsenian Grundnorm model with the irritating implication that all other legal orders, Member State as well as international, have to be understood as derivatives of EU law. This is neither a convincing theory nor does it render any justice to what Kelsen tried to explain with his theory.[91] From a theoretical point of view the claim to autonomy of one legal order towards any other is non-sensical. As long as levels of public authority are as intertwined as they are today it is hard to imagine how the autonomy of EU law that deserves this name could be imagined. It is a dream, but not necessarily a nice one.

From a constitutionalist point of view, one would have to look for a substantial backing of such a kind of principle. Of course, there is no consensus of which principles or rights are necessary and sufficient to build a legitimate constitutional order, but there are some obvious candidates: individual and collective self-determination; the protection of personal dignity and equality; and objective goods like social security or the protection of natural resources. The point here is that the principle of autonomy seems to be lacking any constitutional substance. To put it into the distinction developed above: by applying autonomy, the court protects its institutional interests without being able to explain how these interests could converge with any normative framework that deserves protection under the idea of a European constitutionalism. This is even more problematic because since the amendment of Article 6(2) TFEU the argument against accession has to dwell on the highest and seemingly unalterable place within the hierarchy of norms. Therefore, there is no legitimate political or individual claim that would be able to get rid of this reading of autonomy.

Similar observations apply to the principle of mutual recognition that plays an important role in Opinion 2/13[92] and which has made a somewhat unlikely career from a regulatory model in the aftermath of *Cassis de Dijon*[93] to a constitutional principle that is now another central argument to exclude the European Convention from the EU legal order.[94] Again

---

[90] G. de Búrca, 'The EU, the European Court of Justice and the International Legal Order after *Kadi*' (2010) 51 *HILJ* 1.

[91] J. von Bernstorff, *The Public International Law Theory of Hans Kelsen* (Cambridge University Press, 2010).

[92] Paras. 168, 191–4.

[93] Case 120/78, *Cassis de Dijon* [1979] ECR 649.

[94] K. Lenaerts, 'The Principle of Mutual Recognition in the EU's Area of Freedom, Security and Justice' (2015), Lecture in Honour of Sir Jeremy Lever, www.law.ox.ac.uk/sites/files/

the question remains on which legitimate grounds this principle could be founded. Here, we have at least some candidates. Mutual recognition seems like a typically federal principle that formalises a general trust into the institutional legitimacy of different jurisdictions within a plural polity.[95] This trust is a reference to political and legal procedures, above all, within the Member States. But there is a rub. Historically, it is exposed by the fact that the constitutionalisation of mutual recognition, as distinguished from the introduction of the regulatory principle by the Commission, came at the very moment when the basis for this trust became more dubious, especially after the accession of Middle and Eastern European states after 1989.[96] The law reacted to growing heterogeneity with a principle that created the normative fiction of homogeneity. Systematically, the normative gist of the principle is not entirely clear.[97] Respect for the procedures of the members of a polity is a common feature in federal systems. But the concrete instantiation the principle of mutual recognition takes within the EU legal order creates suspicion that goes beyond this historical context. The principle has been used in order to shield individual rights complaints from further judicial review.[98] It thus works as a substitute for sovereign immunity from external judicial review, now empowered by European law. The rationale behind that principle is, therefore, not the autonomy of Member State action, but the effectiveness of European rules that should not be reviewed twice. This applies especially in asylum cases and it is the source of the well-known conflict between the CJEU and the ECtHR concerning the individual or systemic review of cases.[99] So even if there were a good argument for the position of the CJEU, it remains remarkable to constitutionalise a principle that prioritises effectiveness over individual rights. The, often misplaced, complaint about the technocratic nature of the European integration seems finally to find an adequate location.

oxlaw/the_principle_of_mutual_recognition_in_the_area_of_freedom_judge_lenaerts.pdf.

[95] P. Lerche, 'Föderalismus als nationales und internationales Ordnungsprinzip' (1962) 21 *Veröffentlichungen der Vereinigung der deutschen Staatsrechtelehrer* 66, 85.

[96] Just after the fall of the Iron Curtain, the Dublin Convention of 15 June 1990, OJ 1997 C 254/1 introduced the Dublin system of 'mutual trust' dealing with asylum applications. And shortly before the Eastern Enlargement in 2004, Council Regulation (EC) No. 343/2003 (*Dublin II*) of 18 February 2003, OJ 2003 L 50/1 integrated the mutual trust system in the EU.

[97] D. Chalmers et al., *European Union Law* (Cambridge University Press, 2014), 640; M. Möstl, 'Preconditions and Limits of Mutual Recognition' (2010) 47 *CML Rev* 405.

[98] See e.g. concerning the European Arrest Warrant Case, C-399/11, *Melloni*, EU:C:2013:107.

[99] *M.S.S. v. Belgium and Greece*, App. No. 30696/09, ECtHR, 21 January 2011; *Tarakhel v. Switzerland*, App. No. 29217/12, ECtHR, 4 November 2014.

It is perhaps more than a metaphorical connection that both principles – autonomy and mutual recognition – primarily serve the goal of exclusion of different legal orders and of asylum seekers whose rights protection is treated in a summary way. This is nothing new. Here, the old European Court of Justice (ECJ) shows up again, which was always especially careful when external affairs had to be reviewed.[100] This may invite us to be less enthusiastic about generally acclaimed judgments like *Schrems*.[101] The problem with that is perhaps less that the apex court of federal polity has a certain propensity for uniformity and harmonisation, but rather the way this is covered under principles which are not treated as the result of a European political constitutionalism as applied by a court, but as, in the case of autonomy, a purely conceptual principle, and, in the case of mutual recognition, as respect for the Member States where they do not deserve it. Both principles could be read as part of a semantic constitution behind which the court's version of legal authoritarianism appears.

C Double Dependency: The Internal Constitution of the CJEU

The legitimacy of the CJEU is an old topic of European law, but the way it is addressed is changing. This change is welcome from a theoretical point of view. While the traditional critique centred around the output of the Court, its dramatic foundational decisions and its lenient treatment of the EU competences, more recent literature is more interested in its organisation and procedures. This is a wise move as it is methodically problematic to conflate the question of institutional legitimacy with the question of the 'right' answer to substantial legal problems. While the external constitutional perspective has to treat the question of whether there is a judicial review of European acts that gives legality an adequate role in the European polity, an internal question has to wonder how plausible the claim of the Court of Justice is to be a truly judicial institution.

Looking at the European apex court, at least three problems can be identified. For all we know, the appointment procedure has considerably improved through the integration of the Article 255 committee.[102] To be sure, there is no settled background model for critique, because it is far

---

[100] M. Kottmann, *Introvertierte Rechtsgemeinschaft* (Springer, 2014), Chapter 3.

[101] Case C-362/14, *Schrems*, ECLI:EU:C:2015:650.

[102] J.-M. Sauvé, 'Selecting the European Union's Judges: The Practice of the Article 255 Panel' in M. Bobek (ed.), *Selecting Europe's Judges* (Oxford University Press, 2015), 78; T. Dumbrovský et al., 'Judicial Appointments: The Article 255 TFEU Advisory Panel and Selection Procedures in the Member States' (2014) 51 *CML Rev* 455.

from clear which is in general the ideal procedure for the appointment of judges. While it is basically uncontested that members of governments must be elected or appointed in a political procedure, there are at least three models for the appointment of judges: political election, bureaucratic appointment or some kind of cooptation.[103] Still, one can point to possible improvements. The introduction of the committee is able to guarantee a minimum standard of professional qualification and to prevent political favours. But considerable problems remain. The fact that every Member State sends one judge combined with the possibility to reappoint judges creates a considerable degree of institutional dependence. This is hardly compatible with the normative idea of an independent judiciary.[104] The principle of independence excludes all formal legal reactions to actions of a judge. Any form of reappointment is in clear violation of this demand. That each Member State can claim one member of the Court expresses not only a representational concept hardly compatible with the role of a court of the Union legal order. It also produces an uneasy combination with the reappointment problem as the rules build a clear axis of dependence between the judge and his or her national government.

Even more questionable seem certain elements of the internal organisation of the court. This concerns the strong role of the President in assigning cases[105] – causing internal hierarchies to develop within the court – and the fact that the presidency of the Court is elected by the judges. What at first glance looks like a feature of judicial self-organisation is, at closer inspection, an internal political process of its own that may undermine the legitimacy of the Court. The incentive to trade votes to an office for votes in cases is too obvious. We only have anecdotal evidence for this claim. However, as with judicial independence, this is less about empirical facts than about normative structures that cast doubts about the motivation for judicial action. This is all the more problematic when the elected office of the presidency yields powers that may undermine the formal equality of the judges.[106] If the assignment of cases is neither rule-bound nor the result

---

[103] This model is still favoured by some international organisations though it has created politicised casts in many countries. For the political fights about the Spanish 'Consejo General del Poder Judicial', see M. M. Guerrero, 'Grundlagen und Grundzüge staatlichen Verfassungsrechts: Spanien' in A. von Bogdandy et al. (eds.), *Handbuch Ius Publicum Europaeum, Band I* (C. F. Müller, 2007), 625, 672–3.

[104] Möllers, *The Three Branches* (above n. 3), 101–2.

[105] Article 15(1) of the Rules of Procedure of the Court of Justice of 25 September 2012 (OJ 2012 L 265), as amended on 18 June 2013 (OJ 2013 L 173).

[106] Besides Article 15, see also Articles 9, 20, 27, 53(3), 56, 75(1), 78, 105(1) and 133 of the Rules of Procedure.

of an egalitarian process and if the role of the assignor is defined internally, we get internal politicisation. This process may be different from the political process that we observe at the ECB. Nonetheless it seems misplaced and dysfunctional. We cannot even exclude the possibility that such a process works along comparable lines, trading votes for offices in decisions that concern politically contested lines between the supranational organs of EU and its Member States or between clubs of Member States.

From the perspective of constitutionalism, one has to draw a careful line between naïve expectations of rationality in the judicial system and justified critique. Every court has internal political processes. The higher and the more powerful the court gets, the more politicised is its internal life. The specific problem with the CJEU lies on a different level. The combination of reappointment and internal inequality creates a set of interdependencies for normal judges that make it difficult to accept them as agents of legality. As a matter of speculation, one might wonder if the two strands of dependency pull in different directions and could neutralise each other. While the reappointment option pulls the court towards the interests of Member States, the presidentialisation of the CJEU looks, as with the case of the Commission, like an immune reaction that creates institutional autonomy through a tighter internal control. But for one, the Commission is a political-administrative organ which, indeed, needs legitimacy as an institution while the court needs legitimacy for single decisions done by different groups of judges. And second, even the fact that dependencies may pull in different directions does not belie the wish for an institutional set-up with less dependency.

VI   General Conclusions

A   *The Stability of the Transitory, or Finality Revisited*

For a long time, the EU-friendly narrative had a strong institutional story to tell. By means of deeper integration, the EU would become a bi-cameral Federation with the Commission as coalition government and the Member States as remaining, but contained, political players. The result of such a development would have fewer similarities with the constitutional systems of vast unions like the United States or India, but rather would resemble Switzerland: a multi-linguistic state with a fragmented public sphere, with strong, even 'sovereign', cantons and a centrist grand coalition government that, by means of an informal compromise, de facto cannot be voted out of office. The strength of this, or any comparable narrative, lies less in its (rapidly declining) probability of becoming true than in its normative function as a yardstick for the real state of the Union. This becomes clear when we look for a counter-narrative, which seems to be utterly missing amongst Euro-sceptics of all sorts. To be sure, that does not mean that they are normatively wrong, but it will help us to reconsider the old question of finality of European integration.

The urge to look for a finality to European integration is inspired by the powerful European (!) state tradition that led to a segmentation of the global territory into sovereign states. This story has never been entirely true,[107] but it is especially strange with regard to an entity like the EU that is supposedly meant to overcome the state just in order to build a new and bigger one. The statement, usually accredited to Walter Hallstein – that European integration functions like a bicycle that either goes forward or falls – should be put under closer scrutiny. It was probably only plausible in itself as long as the idea of a European state was too far away to become a real political prospect. In addition, the multiple crises in Europe, that all seem to be following a centrifugal institutional trajectory, are a vivid reminder of the value of the acquired state of integration. Even if there are many reasons for more integration it is no longer perceived as a quasi-natural process that is basically implied by the politics which Member States pursue and the character of the problems that they are aiming to solve. The British plea before Brexit to erase the formula of 'ever closer union' from the Treaty is, despite its pettiness, telling in two regards. First, there is indeed a normative case to take the political process of integration out of the status of evolutionary growth. This also means that the question of finality is the wrong question. We find ourselves in a political union that deserves to be improved like any other political community. Maybe the internal contradictions of this union are more striking than those of others. But this is only an argument for reform, not the definition of the final destination of the integration process. On the other hand, the British demand gives hope even for advocates of a deeper integration. It documents an utter lack of imagination on the side of the critics of the European project. For, on a fundamental level, it presents a purely negative demand. There seems to be no genuine political project attached to Euro-scepticism.

---

[107] B. Badie, *L'État importé* (Fayard, 1992).

B   Limits of Institutional Engineering and the Byzantinism of the European Institutions

The European institutions have undergone dramatic changes in the past thirty years. Compared to the design of the European construction before the Single European Act of 1987 the EU of today looks completely different in depth and width. The construction has also become much more complicated, it is a byzantine political structure whose formal procedures are only understood by experts, an underappreciated deficit of its political constitutional quality. Both developments, the dramatic changes and the complexity of their results, document the fundamental ambivalence in which the European political project is caught. Insight into the necessity to cooperate is connected with a fundamental distrust that is expressed in the refusal to act without formalised veto-positions and sectoralised procedures. We observe an institutional failure that cannot be cured by institutional means. Either the Member States get ready to let political power go or the European construction will remain flawed. This readiness for institutional change can only be the result of a deeper exchange of European societies, of an inner Europeanisation that so far seems to have lost track of institutional development.

11

Subsidiarity as a Principle of EU Governance

KATARZYNA GRANAT

I Introduction

Today's European Union (EU) has a complex structure of cooperative federalism that raises substantial challenges of governance. The subsidiarity principle has emerged as the pre-eminent organising principle for the allocation of powers among the EU's different levels of government; that is, among the European institutions such as the Commission, the Council and the Parliament, and the Member States and their regional or local government structures.

Following its introduction in the Maastricht Treaty, the subsidiarity principle has been elevated in status by the Lisbon Treaty through the introduction of a specific, formal protocol for the assessment and enforcement of subsidiarity in all EU legislation. Commensurate with its increased legal status, the subsidiarity principle and the issues it raises have kept both scholars and practitioners in institutions, parliaments and governments engaged in recent years.

Against this background, this chapter describes the key aspects of the subsidiarity principle, including its roots and substantive content and shows subsidiarity at work in specific cases of governance. The chapter highlights the contribution of subsidiarity to the European project but also underlines its shortcomings and presents proposals for reform.

At its core, the principle of subsidiarity raises questions about the appropriate place for political and legal power.[1] It is applicable to the exercise of competences in areas shared between Member States and the EU.[2] Subsidiarity is 'called upon to arbitrate the tension between integration and

---

[1] G. de Búrca, 'Re-Appraising Subsidiarity's Significance after Amsterdam', Harvard Jean Monnet Working Paper 7/99, 43.
[2] A. G. Toth, 'Is Subsidiarity Justiciable?' (1994) 19 *EL Rev* 268, 269.

proximity in all matters dealt with by the Union and its Member States'.[3] Being a 'constitutional safeguard of federalism', subsidiarity attempts to restrain the EU's exercise of shared powers.[4] In other words, subsidiarity 'only determines whether in a particular case, which is already within Community competence, action should be taken at the Community or at the national level'.[5]

II   Background of the Subsidiarity Principle

The principle of subsidiarity expressed in Article 5(3) of the Treaty on European Union (TEU) organises the system of EU governance by declaring that 'in areas which do not fall within its exclusive competence, the Union shall act only if and in so far as the objectives of the proposed action cannot be sufficiently achieved by the Member States, either at central level or at regional and local level, but can rather, by reason of the scale or effects of the proposed action, be better achieved at Union level'. As further detailed in that provision, the EU institutions apply subsidiarity in the legislative process and the national parliaments ensure its compliance in accordance with Protocol No. 2 on the application of the principles of subsidiarity and proportionality included in the Lisbon Treaty.

III   Origins of the Idea of Subsidiarity

The roots of the modern notion of subsidiarity can be traced to Pope Pius XI's Encyclical *Quadragesimo Anno* (1931).[6] In the Encyclical the Pope discusses a principle of social order that reflects the principle of subsidiarity:

> Just as it is gravely wrong to take from individuals what they can accomplish by their own initiative and industry and give it to the community, so also it is an injustice and at the same time a grave evil and disturbance of right order to assign to a greater and higher association what lesser and subordinate organizations can do. For every social activity ought of its very

---

[3]   K. Lenaerts, 'The Principle of Subsidiarity and the Environment in the European Union: Keeping the Balance of Federalism' (1993) 17 *Fordham International Law Journal* 846, 848.

[4]   R. Schütze, *From Dual to Cooperative Federalism: The Changing Structure of European Law* (Oxford University Press, 2009), 247.

[5]   A. G. Toth, 'The Principle of Subsidiarity in the Maastricht Treaty' (1992) 29 *CML Rev* 1079, 1082.

[6]   See e.g. J. Isensee, *Subsidiaritätsprinzip und Verfassungsrecht* (Duncker & Humblot, 2001), 18 et seq.; D. Z. Cass, 'The Word that Saves Maastricht? The Principle of Subsidiarity and the Division of Powers within the European Community' (1992) 29 *CML Rev* 1107, 1110.

nature to furnish help to the members of the body social, and never destroy and absorb them.[7]

The quote expresses a preference for allocating responsibilities to the lower levels of organisation, as long as they are capable to exercise them effectively, mirroring the two key elements of subsidiarity as known in the EU.

Still, important differences between the European and the Catholic versions of subsidiarity remain. The EU subsidiarity is narrowly focused on democratic public bodies; the Catholic version considers society as a whole.[8] Moreover, the EU subsidiarity principle is not a derivative of its Catholic understanding, but might have developed independently from *Quadragesimo Anno*.[9]

Federalism and liberalism, especially in the German tradition, provide alternative intellectual roots of subsidiarity.[10] The German federalist notion of the state focuses on the different components of the state, their functions and relationships amongst each other. For example, the work of Althusius, von Humboldt and Hegel offers clues of the subsidiarity principle.[11] Liberalist theory, in turn, contains elements of subsidiarity as an organising principle: in the liberalist tradition the state is legitimate only to the extent it is organised from the bottom up and thus in accordance with the principle of subsidiarity.[12] However, there are limits to this parallel as the liberalist perspective focuses on the relation of the individual and the state, and arguably has less to say on intermediary levels of organisation, while the subsidiarity principle can be applied to each layer of government.[13]

IV   Development of Subsidiarity in German and EU Law

A   Germany

From the German scholastic tradition, the subsidiarity principle found its way into the German Basic Law and from there into the EU. Although the subsidiarity principle is not explicitly included in the Basic Law the argument can be made that it is part of the German constitution.

---

[7] *Quadragesimo Anno*, point 79, English translation available at http://w2.vatican.va/content/
    pius-xi/en/encyclicals/documents/hf_p-xi_enc_19310515_quadragesimo-anno.html.
[8] N. W. Barber, 'The Limited Modesty of Subsidiarity' (2005) 11 *ELJ* 308, 310.
[9] Ibid. See also Isensee, *Subsidiaritätsprinzip und Verfassungsrecht* (above n. 6), 71.
[10] Isensee, *Subsidiaritätsprinzip und Verfassungsrecht* (above n. 6), 35.
[11] Ibid., 37.
[12] Ibid., 45.
[13] Ibid., 46.

The historical background to the creation of the Basic Law of 1949 suggests an environment receptive to the subsidiarity principle even though it did not enter the constitutional text itself. The draft prepared by the Constitutional Convention at Herrenchiemsee in 1948 tried to introduce formally the subsidiarity principle, an attempt that ultimately failed for several reasons.[14] The drafters at Herrenchiemsee shied away from using the term subsidiarity because of its potential religious connotations.[15] Furthermore, it was felt that there was no need to explicitly introduce subsidiarity because Article 1 of the proposed draft already included a firm commitment against an overreaching state.[16]

Following the convention at Herrenchiemsee the final text of the Basic Law was prepared and approved by the Parliamentary Council of 1949. Again no explicit reference to subsidiarity was made but arguably this should not be interpreted as a rejection of the principle.[17] Instead, the Council expected the Basic Law to be of a provisional nature and thus refrained from entering areas that were not yet fully developed such as the developing economic and cultural elements of nascent post-war Germany.[18] However, overall, the drafters of the Basic Law were driven by the general idea of moving away from the collectivist state of the recent past to an order based on ethical individualism.[19]

Finally, the Basic Law created a state structure that was inherently federal and this federalist outlook carried with it the idea of subsidiarity.[20] The *Länder* that were part of the process of creating and approving of the constitution had an interest in limiting the powers of the federal level to the necessary minimum.[21]

Beyond these indications for the presence of the subsidiarity principle in the minds of the drafters of the Basic Law at the time we can also consider the text itself and look for provisions reflecting that principle.[22] For example, and most fundamentally, the federal structure of the German state is built up from below. Article 30 of the Basic Law on the sovereign powers of the *Länder* states that the *Länder* exercise the state powers unless specifically provided otherwise by the Basic Law. Certain areas are explicitly

[14] Ibid., 143.
[15] Ibid.
[16] Ibid.
[17] Ibid., 145.
[18] Ibid.
[19] Ibid., 146.
[20] Ibid., 147.
[21] Ibid., 147.
[22] Ibid., 223 et seq.

allocated to the federal level (Article 73), whilst in other cases the Basic Law establishes certain conditions that determine whether the *Länder* or the state should act (Article 72).

Article 72 of the Basic Law in its original form simply required that a law met certain conditions specifically relating to 'the uniformity of living conditions beyond the territory of any Land' for the federal level to be able to act in that matter. This original wording was found to be non-justiciable as any law could easily be drafted such as to fulfil this requirement.[23]

Since 1994 Article 72(2) of the Basic Law provides that in the field of concurrent legislative competences the Federation should act 'if and to the extent that the establishment of equivalent living conditions throughout the federal territory or the maintenance of legal or economic unity renders federal regulation necessary in the national interest'. In particular, the newly added necessity clause has proved to carry a restrictive force for federal legislation requiring in each case the state to demonstrate a specific need to act. This amended provision can thus be seen as a prototypical expression of the subsidiarity principle in constitutional law.[24] It grants primacy to the federal level in the exercise of competence shared with the *Länder*, in the sense that when the conditions of Article 72(2) of the Basic Law are fulfilled and the federal level decides to act then this matter is closed to the *Länder*.[25] However, the federal government is required to justify its actions with reference to the conditions enumerated in Article 72(2) of the Basic Law.[26] Note that the federal government is not obligated to act in all matters that concern equivalent living conditions and legal or economic unity: if the *Länder* can achieve the relevant objectives themselves, for example by adjusting their respective laws or jointly coordinating new legislation, then this is a valid alternative to the action at the federal level.[27] Both these aspects are arguably also present in the EU subsidiarity principle: first, once the EU decides to act and the conditions are met then the Member States can no longer regulate on their own and, second, there is no compulsion on the EU to act in all cases where the national level cannot achieve the objective sufficiently and where it would be better achieved at the EU level.

Article 72(2) of the Basic Law prescribes certain limits to the applicability of the subsidiarity principle. First, it speaks to the exercise of

---

[23] Ibid., 230.
[24] Ibid., 358.
[25] Ibid., 359.
[26] Ibid.
[27] Ibid., 360.

competence by two levels only – the federal and the *Länder* level – thereby excluding other units of government such as municipalities, and civic organisations.[28] In comparison, the Lisbon Treaty included for the first time as the locus of the exercise of competence the 'central level or at regional and local level' of the Member States, establishing a distinction that was missing in the Maastricht Treaty which simultaneously highlights that the national level itself is multilayered.[29] Second, Article 72(4) of the Basic Law leaves discretion to the federal level about returning competences to the lower level if and when the conditions of Article 72(2) of the Basic Law are no longer fulfilled, instead of automatically returning such matters to the *Länder*.[30] In contrast, the TEU does not provide for a similar provision on when the competence should be returned to be exercised by the Member States.

Hence Article 72(2) of the Basic Law requires a dual test examining whether there is a case for legislation at the federal level in addition to reviewing whether the legislation goes beyond what is necessary to achieve the objectives set in that provision.[31] The Basic Law granted the Federal Constitutional Court a possibility to review the compatibility of federal legislation with the subsidiarity principle, on the application of the *Bundesrat* or of the government or legislature of a *Land*.[32] In contrast to the judicial review, a political safeguard of subsidiarity, which would have included granting the *Bundesrat* a role as a parliamentary watchdog of subsidiarity principle, did not gain the necessary support.[33]

The Federal Constitutional Court has actively fulfilled its role, building case law on the enforcement of the subsidiarity principle. However, the Court's interpretation of the tests involved in Article 72(2) of the Basic Law remains unclear, in the sense that the Court has not given precise criteria as to what the 'equal living conditions' or 'national interest' are.[34]

---

[28] Ibid.

[29] De Búrca, 'Re-Appraising Subsidiarity's Significance after Amsterdam' (above n. 1), 16.

[30] Isensee, *Subsidiaritätsprinzip und Verfassungsrecht* (above n. 6), 360.

[31] G. Taylor, 'Germany: The Subsidiarity Principle' (2006) 4 *International Journal of Constitutional Law* 115, 120.

[32] Article 93(2a) of the Basic Law. This judicial safeguard did not exist before 1994 since both the German scholarship and the Federal Constitutional Court perceived Article 72(2) of the Basic Law as expressing a political decision of the federal legislator to legislate. See M. Rau, 'Subsidiarity and Judicial Review in German Federalism: The Decision of the Federal Constitutional Court in the Geriatric Nursing Act Case' (2003) 4 *GLJ* 223, 227.

[33] Deutscher Bundestag, Bericht der Gemeinsamen Verfassungskommission, Drucksache 12/6000, 5.11.93, 33.

[34] Rau, 'Subsidiarity and Judicial Review in German Federalism' (n. 32), 233.

This state of affairs resembles the European discussion on the subsidiarity jurisprudence of the Court of Justice of the European Union (CJEU) discussed below. Despite such limitations, a series of cases where the Court has found the federal legislation incompatible with the subsidiarity principle (e.g. the 'Junior Professors' case[35]) have led to a further amendment of Article 72(2) of the Basic Law in 2006, restricting its applicability to a limited number of subject areas of concurrent competence.[36] Specifically, the subsidiarity test now only applies to subjects such as, for example, residence of foreign nationals, public welfare, law relating to economic matters (mining, industry, trade, commerce etc.), regulation of educational training or state liability.

B   EU

The idea of subsidiarity in the EU can be traced back to the Treaty of Rome of 1957.[37] Some of the provisions of the European Economic Community (EEC) Treaty deal with questions concerning the distribution and exercise of competences between the Community and the Member States and explore possible approaches and criteria that are reminiscent of the later subsidiarity principle. For example, Article 100 EEC Treaty concerning the approximation of laws granted the Council a competence regarding laws that 'have a direct incidence on the establishment or functioning of the Common Market'. In addition, Article 235 EEC Treaty allowed the Council to legislate in areas where the Treaty does not explicitly give it a competence when it 'appears necessary to achieve, in the functioning of the Common Market, one of the aims of the Community'.

Scholars have found in these provisions reflections of the idea of subsidiarity as well as aspects of its later implementation such as conditions setting out necessity for the EU to act.[38] Similarly, the concept of directives established in Article 189 EEC Treaty incorporates aspects of subsidiarity: the EU level sets out the overall objective and leaves it to the Member States to implement laws to achieve the objective.[39] However, overall these

---

[35] G. Taylor, 'Germany: A Slow Death of Subsidiarity?' (2009) 7 *International Journal of Comparative Law* 139, 143.

[36] Ibid., 146.

[37] Lenaerts, 'The Principle of Subsidiarity and the Environment in the European Union' (above n. 3), 852.

[38] C. Calliess, *Subsidiaritäts-und Solidaritätsprinzip in der Europäischen Union* (Nomos, 1996), 31–5.

[39] Ibid.

connections appear peripheral and do not present tangible direct evidence of the presence of the subsidiarity principle as early as the Rome Treaty.[40]

This changed later on in the run-up to the reforming treaties and later the Maastricht Treaty. An early draft proposal for an EU Treaty by the European Parliament (EP) in 1984 both emphasized the multilayered nature of the EU as well as explicitly called upon the subsidiarity principle in circumscribing its competences.[41] Subsidiarity as such was first included in the Treaty text in the Single European Act of 1987, where it concerned Community action in the area of environmental policy and limited Community action in that field to cases where the objectives of the policy can be better achieved at the Community level than by Member States individually.[42]

The Maastricht Treaty subsequently took the notion further and first defined the 'clear legal core of subsidiarity', that forms the basis of subsidiarity today.[43] During the negotiations of the Maastricht Treaty the Member States adopted different stances towards subsidiarity reflecting their idiosyncratic interests and political conditions, which can be illustrated with reference to the positions of the UK and Germany. In the UK, subsidiarity was primarily seen as a restraint on what was perceived as an excessive tendency towards political integration, which clashed with the strong established notion of primacy of the UK Parliament in all matters.[44] In contrast, the debate in Germany was driven by the *Länder* and their fear of losing powers relative to the federal state and the EU. As such, subsidiarity was viewed mostly as a tool for implementing the German federalist model in the EU.[45] Furthermore, the *Länder* together with the European organisations of the regions pushed for recognition of the three levels of organisation (Union, national state and region) that appeared only in the subsequent Lisbon version of the subsidiarity principle.[46]

At its introduction with the Maastricht Treaty, subsidiarity was welcomed as 'an important, if undervalued' part of the relation between Community and Member States and a form of division of power between them,[47] yet it was simultaneously criticised as a step back, weakening the

[40] Ibid.
[41] Ibid., 36.
[42] Article 130r(4) EEC Treaty.
[43] De Búrca, 'Re-Appraising Subsidiarity's Significance after Amsterdam' (above n. 1), 14.
[44] Calliess, *Subsidiaritäts-und Solidaritätsprinzip in der Europäischen Union* (above n. 38), 51 et seq.
[45] Ibid., 53.
[46] Ibid., 54.
[47] Cass, 'The Word that Saves Maastricht?' (above n. 6), 1134.

Community and slowing down European integration.[48] Although some indicated that even without subsidiarity 'one could [also] have lived quite happily and in peace in the European home', the principle was here to stay.[49]

C Reimport of EU Subsidiarity to the German Basic Law

Article 23 of the German Basic Law, which was introduced in 1992 before the ratification of the Maastricht Treaty by Germany, establishes the principles of participation of Germany in the EU and is a reimport of the subsidiarity principle to the German constitutional system.[50] According to this provision, Germany participates in the development of an EU 'that is committed to democratic, social and federal principles, to the rule of law, and to the principle of subsidiarity, and that guarantees a level of protection of basic rights essentially comparable to that afforded by this Basic Law'.

The article establishes the subsidiarity principle as an important tie between German law and EU law, working in both directions at the same time. It provides a policy framework for Germany's participation in the EU. For instance, the representatives of Germany at the EU level have to adhere to the subsidiarity principle in both the division and the exercise of competences.[51] Furthermore, by committing Germany to a Europe based on subsidiarity, it reflects and re-emphasises the prominence of the principle for German constitutional law.[52] Embedding subsidiarity in the EU Treaties, Germany's own commitment to the principle for the organisation of the federal state received renewed attention.[53]

V Components of the Subsidiarity Principle

The EU principle of subsidiarity has two dimensions: a material and a procedural one.[54] There are two prongs to the verification of material subsidiarity, labelled the *national insufficiency test* and the *comparative efficiency test*.[55] The first test – the Union shall act 'only if and in so far as the

---

[48] Toth, 'The Principle of Subsidiarity in the Maastricht Treaty' (above n. 5), 1105.
[49] P. Pescatore, 'Mit der Subsidiarität leben' in Ole Due et al. (eds.), *Festschrift für Ulrich Everling* (Nomos, 1995), 1094.
[50] Isensee, *Subsidiaritätsprinzip und Verfassungsrecht* (above n. 6), 334.
[51] Ibid., 371.
[52] Ibid., 371.
[53] Ibid., 334.
[54] A. E. de Noriega, *The EU Principle of Subsidiarity and its Critique* (Oxford University Press, 2002), 105.
[55] Schütze, *From Dual to Cooperative Federalism* (above n. 4).

objectives of the proposed action cannot be sufficiently achieved by the Member States' – means that a Member State has 'inadequate means at its disposal for achieving the objectives of the proposed action.'[56] The second test requires that the Union shall act if the objectives of the proposed action can rather 'by reason of the scale or effects of the proposed action, be better achieved at Union level'. Hence, the EU should not act 'unless it could *better* achieve the objectives of the proposed action'.[57]

The principle of subsidiarity in the EU is based on a test that is different from that in German law. In comparison to the German Basic Law, which recognises the 'necessity' of federal action for the achievement of equivalent living conditions and legal and economic unity, the TEU looks at the insufficient achievement of the objective of the action at the national level and their comparatively more efficient achievement at the EU level. This can be contrasted with Article 72(2) of the Basic Law which in principle allows the federal level to act even if the *Länder* could achieve the relevant objective as long as the action concerns the establishment of equivalent living conditions or the maintenance of legal or economic unity.

In addition, the EU version of subsidiarity does not refer to the notion of 'necessary in the national interest' indicated in Article 72(2) of the Basic Law. Instead it assesses which level of government is better placed to achieve the objective of the legislation, thereby allocating powers by comparison rather than exclusion. In this sense, the EU subsidiarity principle can be seen to embody federal proportionality, asking whether EU action 'unnecessarily restricts national autonomy';[58] that is, without providing sufficient benefits.

Finally, within the criteria justifying federal action, the EU notion of subsidiarity does not require legislation to necessarily be in the interest of the nation, like in Germany, or rather the Union; however, it has to aim at achieving one of the objectives of the Treaties. Nonetheless, the objective of the legislation is not questioned per se by subsidiarity, only at what level of government a given objective can be best achieved.

Since the EU subsidiarity principle was first introduced by the Maastricht Treaty, the tests have been elaborated on. First, the 'Overall Approach' annexed to the Conclusions of the European Council meeting in Edinburgh established guidelines providing for more clarity in answering

---

[56] K. Lenaerts, 'Subsidiarity and Community Competence in the Field of Education' (1994) 1 *Columbia Journal of European Law* 1, 22.
[57] Schütze, *From Dual to Cooperative Federalism* (above n. 4), 250.
[58] Ibid., 263.

the question of whether the Community should act.[59] These include, first, testing whether the issue at stake has transnational aspects that cannot be satisfactorily regulated by Member States.[60] Second, the guidelines suggest that a Community action satisfies the subsidiarity principle when 'actions by Member States alone or lack of Community action would conflict with the requirements of the Treaty ... or would otherwise significantly damage Member States' interests'. Three examples are given in the text: the need to correct distortion of competition; avoidance of disguised restrictions on trade; and strengthening of economic and social cohesion. The final guidance principle makes the compliance with the subsidiarity principle conditional on the 'clear benefits [of Community action] by reason of its scale or effects compared with action at the level of Member States'. In addition, the 'Overall Approach' provides that subsidiarity reasoning has to be 'substantiated by qualitative or, wherever possible, quantitative indicators'.[61] The 'Overall Approach' also instructs the EU institutions to observe the subsidiarity principle when they examine Community proposals. Specifically, the Commission is obliged to include a subsidiarity assessment in its pre-legislative consultations, as well as a recital in the proposal that assesses the compatibility with the principle of subsidiarity and, where necessary, provide more detail in an explanatory memorandum.[62]

Second, the Inter-Institutional Agreement established that the Commission, while exercising its right of initiative, and the EP and the Council, while exercising their respective powers, should 'take into account' the subsidiarity principle.[63] In addition, the agreement provides that the explanatory memorandum in any Commission proposal should include a subsidiarity assessment.

The development of these guidelines culminated in the protocol 'on the application of the principles of subsidiarity and proportionality' added to the Amsterdam Treaty, which borrows the idea of subsidiarity as a 'dynamic concept'[64] from the Edinburgh Conclusions and restates that compliance with subsidiarity must be demonstrated by 'qualitative or, wherever possible, quantitative indicators'.[65] The Amsterdam Protocol

---

[59] European Council in Edinburgh, 11–12 December 1992, Conclusions of the Presidency.

[60] Ibid., 20.

[61] Ibid.

[62] Ibid., 23.

[63] Inter-institutional declaration on democracy, transparency and subsidiarity, Bull. EC 10–1993, 119. The declaration is referred to rather by scholars than by the EU institutions themselves.

[64] Article 3, Protocol on the application of the principles of subsidiarity and proportionality.

[65] Ibid., Article 4.

echoes the requirement that both the 'national insufficiency test' and the 'comparative efficiency test' must be met for subsidiarity compliance.[66]

In addition, the Amsterdam Protocol repeats the provisions regarding the form of action, which should be 'as simple as possible', and more specifically fulfil the requirement of choosing directives over regulations.[67] This provision is placed in the Amsterdam Protocol alongside the guidelines for the assessment of subsidiarity. In fact, the choice of the type of legal act can be seen to be much closer to the idea of a proportionality principle, as it rather concerns a 'how' question.[68] The 'General Approach' of the Edinburgh Council is hence more accurate in this respect, as it placed the provision on the form of action under the third paragraph of Article 3b EC Treaty ('nature and extent of Community action'), wherein the proportionality principle is currently enshrined.[69]

At the time, the Edinburgh Guidelines and the Inter-Institutional Agreement were perceived as 'vague and only indicative'.[70] They did however represent an effort to make subsidiarity 'operational',[71] suggesting a procedural dimension to the subsidiarity principle and demanding that the Community conducts an inquiry before undertaking legislative steps.[72] Similarly, the Amsterdam Protocol was also often regarded as a mere extract of the central principles established in the Edinburgh 'Overall Approach', thereby not adding much value in itself.[73] Nonetheless, the Amsterdam criteria are today still referred to in the subsidiarity assessments of the Commission[74] and national parliaments alike.[75] Neither

---

[66] Ibid., Article 5.

[67] Ibid., Article 6.

[68] So also qualified in Calliess, *Subsidiaritäts-und Solidaritätsprinzip in der Europäischen Union* (above n. 38), 567. De Búrca sees these provisions as 'the linkage' between subsidiarity and proportionality. See also de Búrca, 'Re-Appraising Subsidiarity's Significance after Amsterdam' (above n. 1), 30.

[69] Conclusions of the Presidency (above n. 59), 212.

[70] I. Pernice, 'Framework Revisited: Constitutional, Federal and Subsidiarity Issues' (1995) 2 *CJEL* 403, 408.

[71] C. Timmermans, 'Subsidiarity and Transparency' (1999) 22 *Fordham International Law Journal* 106, 108.

[72] P. Lindseth, *Power and Legitimacy: Reconciling Europe and the Nation-State* (Oxford University Press, 2010), 195.

[73] Calliess, *Subsidiaritäts-und Solidaritätsprinzip in der Europäischen Union* (above n. 38), 66.

[74] Report from the Commission on Subsidiarity and Proportionality, 18th Report on Better Lawmaking covering the year 2010, COM (2011) 344, 2.

[75] See e.g. House of Commons, 'Reasoned Opinion on the Draft Directive of the European Parliament and of the Council on Improving the Gender Balance among Non-Executive Directors of Companies Listed on Stock Exchanges and Related Measures', COM (2012) 614.

the Lisbon Treaty nor the Inter-Institutional Agreement on Better Law-Making of 2016 have provided any new criteria in this respect.

VI   Enforcement within the EU

Whilst the Amsterdam Protocol established the conceptual criteria against which subsidiarity should be assessed in any given case, the role of subsidiarity in the EU's governance is also shaped by its enforcement, primarily through the CJEU and national parliaments. This section discusses the relevant mechanisms for both institutions and highlights their limitations.

A   Enforcement of Subsidiarity by the CJEU

The introduction of the subsidiarity principle in the Maastricht Treaty opened it to judicial enforcement by the CJEU. Initially it was expected that a flood of litigation might be triggered.[76] However, since the entry into force of the Maastricht Treaty subsidiarity challenges have played a role in fewer than twenty cases before the CJEU, with some of these repeating previous challenges.[77]

The CJEU's jurisprudence on the subsidiarity principle[78] has been widely criticised, in particular, the Court's alleged unwillingness to 'deal with subsidiarity frontally' and its 'misleading interpretation' of the principle, because of a focus on procedural aspects, instead of a more substantive cost/benefit test for the necessity of EU action.[79] Moreover, the Court's case law has been described as a 'drafting guide', which means that, as long as EU institutions use the Court's vague vocabulary and draft EU legislation accordingly, the Court has no ground to annul such an act on the basis

---

[76] Toth, 'The Principle of Subsidiarity in the Maastricht Treaty' (above n. 5), 1101.

[77] P. Craig, 'Subsidiarity: A Political and Legal Analysis' (2012) 50 *JCMS* 72, 80. Some argue that the CJEU conducted subsidiarity review under a different heading, see T. Horsley, 'Subsidiarity and the European Court of Justice: Missing Pieces in the Subsidiarity Jigsaw?' (2012) 50 *JCMS* 267, 270.

[78] See especially CJEU's cases: Case C-84/94, *United Kingdom* v. *Council* [1996] ECLI:EU:C:1996:431 (Working Time Directive); Case C-233/94, *Germany* v. *Parliament and Council* [1997] ECLI:EU:C:1997:231 (Deposit-Guarantee Schemes); and Case C-491/01, *British American Tobacco (Investments) and Imperial Tobacco* [2002] ECLI:EU:C:2002:741.

[79] G. Martinico, 'Dating Cinderella: On Subsidiarity as a Political Safeguard of Federalism in the European Union' (2011) 17 *European Public Law* 649, 655.

of a subsidiarity violation.[80] The Court was urged to develop a 'doctrinal framework' on subsidiarity to increase the transparency and justification of the legislative acts, instead of relying on the manifest-error doctrine.[81]

Partially the principle of subsidiarity itself is blamed for the low number of Court cases since it is seen as a 'catch-all formula of good government and common sense, rather than a well-defined political or philosophical principle,' and without 'clear legal content'.[82] Another given justification is the adherence of the Court to the separation of powers: the Court tried to avoid 'substituting its own judgment for that of the institutions, in assessing a choice which was ultimately perceived as political'.[83] Another explanation offered sees the 'idea of integration' as an important driver of CJEU jurisprudence, which may be endangered by the 'anti-integration' character of the subsidiarity principle, which is directed specifically against the growth of EU competences.[84] Finally, the low number of cases is explicated by the fact that adoption of legislative acts requires a qualified majority, implying that a sufficient number of Member States saw EU action in compliance with subsidiarity.[85]

The CJEU has been under greater scrutiny due to the broadening of EU competences and the extension of majoritarian decision-making by the Lisbon Treaty.[86] The Court is expected to enhance the control over the exercise of EU competences and advance a counter-majoritarian approach when reviewing EU legislation.[87] Lack of the Court's case law declaring a subsidiarity breach should not be preventing bringing such EU legislative acts before the Court.[88] In this respect, the impact assessments attached

---

[80] S. Weatherill, 'The Limits of Legislative Harmonization Ten Years after Tobacco Advertising: How the Court's Case Law Has Become a Drafting Guide' (2011) 12 *GLJ* 827.

[81] M. Kumm, 'Constitutionalising Subsidiarity in Integrated Markets: The Case of Tobacco Regulation in the European Union' (2006) 12 *ELJ* 503.

[82] De Noriega, *The EU Principle of Subsidiarity and its Critique* (above n. 54), 96 and 139.

[83] A. Biondi, 'Subsidiarity in the Courtroom' in Andrea Biondi et al. (eds.), *EU Law after Lisbon* (Oxford University Press, 2012), 213, and earlier Toth, 'The Principle of Subsidiarity in the Maastricht Treaty' (above n. 5), 1102.

[84] De Noriega, *The EU Principle of Subsidiarity and its Critique* (above n. 54), 7. This approach of the members of the Court de Noriega drew from their doctrinal writings.

[85] Craig, 'Subsidiarity: A Political and Legal Analysis' (above n. 77), 81.

[86] M. P. Maduro and L. Azoulai, 'Introduction' in M. P. Maduro and L. Azoulai (eds.), *The Past and the Future of EU Law: The Classics of EU Law Revisited on the 50th Anniversary of the Treaty of Rome* (Hart, 2010), xix.

[87] Ibid.

[88] J. Ziller, 'Le Principe de subsidiarité' in J.-B. Auby and J. Dutheil de la Rochèr (eds.), *Traité de droit administratif européen* (Bruylant, 2014), 533.

to draft legislative acts can possibly facilitate subsequent judicial review of subsidiarity.[89]

B   Enforcement of Subsidiarity by National Parliaments

In contrast to enforcement by the CJEU, which itself is an unelected EU body, the involvement of national parliaments in the subsidiarity scrutiny embodies an aspect of EU governance that may help address concerns over democratic legitimacy, the EU's so-called 'democracy issue'.[90] To analyse this issue it is useful to consider the notions of 'input' and 'output' legitimacy, two 'legitimising beliefs' for the exercise of governing authority.[91] Input-oriented legitimacy means that 'political choices are legitimate if and because they reflect the "will of the people", that is, if they can be derived from the authentic preferences of the members of a community'.[92] Under output-oriented legitimacy 'political choices are legitimate if and because they effectively promote the common welfare of the constituency in question'.[93] Viewed from this perspective, the transfer of competence from the national level to the EU brings with it concerns over legitimisation if the EU authorities and laws fall short in input and output legitimacy relative to their national counterparts.

Several attempts have been made to address these concerns. The first approach has been to increase the role of the directly elected EP in the legislative process. Indeed, the EP is the 'winner' in the Lisbon Treaty, due to the extension of the ordinary legislative procedure, whereby decisions are taken jointly by the EP and the Council, and the conferral of more control over the appointment of the President of the EU Commission.[94]

The second attempt to strengthen the EU's democratic legitimacy has been to reinforce the role of national parliaments within the European legislative process. The Lisbon Treaty introduced the so-called Early Warning System (EWS) as a new way to safeguard subsidiarity that involves the national parliaments. This permits the national legislatures to be involved

---

[89] Craig, 'Subsidiarity: A Political and Legal Analysis' (above n. 77), 78.
[90] J. H. H. Weiler, 'The Transformation of Europe' (1991) 100 *YLJ* 2403, 2472.
[91] F. W. Scharpf, *Governing in Europe: Effective and Democratic?* (Oxford University Press, 1999), 6.
[92] Ibid.
[93] Ibid.
[94] P. Craig, *The Lisbon Treaty: Law, Politics, and Treaty Reform* (Oxford University Press, 2010), 36.

in the enforcement of the main principle by which a limit is placed on the exercise of shared powers by EU institutions.

Under this new procedure, the Commission, the EP and the Council shall forward draft legislative acts to national parliaments, providing a justification regarding the principle of subsidiarity and proportionality for each proposal, including a detailed statement to enable the appraisal of compliance with these principles.[95] National parliaments are then granted eight weeks from the date of transmission of a draft legislative act to submit a reasoned opinion to the Presidents of the European Parliament, the Council and the Commission explaining why the draft is not in compliance with the principle of subsidiarity.[96] The institution from which the draft originates should 'take account' of the reasoned opinions received. Reasoned opinions count as votes: each national parliament has two votes; in a bicameral parliament, each of the two chambers has one vote. If the number of reasoned opinions exceeds certain thresholds, one of two procedures may be triggered.[97]

First, under the 'yellow card', if the reasoned opinions issued by national parliaments are equal to at least one-third of all the votes allocated to national parliaments, the draft must be reviewed. For proposals in the area of freedom, security and justice, the respective threshold is one-quarter of the votes of national parliaments. Subsequently, the initiating institution may decide to maintain, amend or withdraw the draft, and is require to give reasons for its decision.[98]

Second, in the procedure labelled as the 'orange card', if the reasoned opinions against a proposal within the ordinary legislative procedure represent at least the majority of votes assigned to national parliaments, the Commission must review the draft legislative act. The Commission may then decide to maintain, amend or withdraw the draft. If it decides to maintain the draft, the Commission should present its own reasoned opinion on the compliance of the draft with the subsidiarity principle.[99] This reasoned opinion of the Commission, together with the reasoned opinions of the national parliaments, is then forwarded to the EU legislator for consideration. If a majority of 55 per cent of the votes in the Council or a majority of the votes cast in the EP is of the opinion that the proposal is contrary to the principle of subsidiarity, the legislative procedure is halted.

[95] Protocol No. 2, Articles 4 and 5.
[96] Ibid., Article 6.
[97] Ibid., Article 7(1).
[98] Ibid., Article 7(2).
[99] Ibid., Article 7(3).

The experience thus far suggests that national parliaments have been actively participating in the EWS. By the end of 2016 they have issued 350 reasoned opinions.[100] So far the 'orange card' has never been invoked, but the 'yellow card' has been triggered three times: for the so-called Monti II proposal on the right to strike; for the proposal establishing the European Public Prosecutor's Office; and for the proposal amending the Posted Workers Directive.[101] In neither case did the reasoned opinions of the national parliaments convince the Commission of a subsidiarity breach. In the first case the Commission decided to withdraw the proposal follow-ing the 'yellow card' because of the possible future lack of support in the EP and in the Council.[102] In the second case it elected to continue to work on the proposal without any amendments but taking 'due account' of the reasoned opinions.[103] This was not surprising especially since the Lisbon Treaty expressly provides that in a case of lack of unanimity on the proposal in the Council, nine Member States can proceed with enhanced coopera-tion to establish the Office.[104] In fact, in October 2017 the regulation estab-lishing the EPPO was adopted by twenty Member States which were part of the EPPO enhanced cooperation at the time.[105] Finally, in the case con-cerning the amendment of the Posted Workers Directive the Commission decided to maintain the proposal.[106] However, as of March 2018, the pro-posed amendment has not yet been adopted by the EU legislator.

Overall, national parliaments see the EWS as in need of improvement. This concerns especially quality of the Commission replies to the reasoned

---

[100] Own calculation on the basis of Commission Annual Reports on Subsidiarity and Proportionality, COM (2011) 344; COM (2012) 373; COM (2013) 566; COM (2014) 506; COM (2015) 315; COM (2016) 469; and COM (2017) 600.

[101] COM (2012) 130; COM (2013) 534; and COM (2016) 128 respectively. See F. Fabbrini and K. Granat, '"Yellow Card, but No Foul": The Role of the National Parliaments under the Subsidiarity Protocol and the Commission Proposal for an EU Regulation on the Right to Strike' (2013) 50 *CML Rev* 115; D. Fromage, 'The Second Yellow Card on the EPPO Proposal: An Encouraging Development for Member State Parliaments' (2016) 36 *YEL* 5–27.

[102] See e.g. Commission reply to the Polish Sejm of 12 September 2012, Ares (2012)1058907.

[103] Communication from the Commission to the European Parliament, the Council and the National Parliaments, COM (2013) 851, 13.

[104] Article 86(1) TFEU.

[105] Council of the EU, Press Release 580/17, 12 October 2010.

[106] Communication from the Commission to the European Parliament, the Council and the National Parliaments on the proposal for a Directive amending the Posting of Workers Directive, with regard to the principle of subsidiarity, in accordance with Protocol No. 2, COM (2016) 505.

opinions, as well as adjustments in the eight-week deadline (e.g. by excluding the Christmas period and the parliamentary summer recess).[107]

Besides the EWS, Member States notify on behalf of a national parliament or its chamber an action on grounds of subsidiarity violation before the Court.[108] Accordingly, the rules of action of annulment (Article 263 of the Treaty on the Functioning of the European Union (TFEU)) apply before the Court, while at the Member State level it is for national law to specify the rights of the parliament in this procedure.[109] So far no such subsidiarity action has ever been brought by national parliaments.

Viewed through the lens of input and output legitimacy, the EWS has arguably helped partially to address the EU's democratic deficit. The formal involvement of national parliaments, as well as their active use of the new tools, suggests that the preferences of the voters have received a greater voice in the EU legislative procedure, thereby improving input legitimacy. Furthermore, consistency with the subsidiarity principle ensures that government takes place at the level that is best placed to regulate specific functions, thereby achieving better outcomes for the community. However, these potential improvements in legitimacy are limited by the apparent lack of consequences of the reasoned opinions issued by national parliaments in the EWS. Many proposals for reform thus tend to focus on making the input of national parliaments more consequential for the legislative outcome as discussed in greater detail in section VIII below.

VII   The Subsidiarity Principle in Practice

As indicated above, an assessment of the subsidiary principle needs to consider the concrete implications of any enforcement mechanism. The following section therefore discusses the application of the subsidiarity principle in practice, both by the Court and by national parliaments, and argues that this can be challenging. Subsidiarity as a principle of governance helps to decide when the EU is more apt to enforce a certain policy; that is, whether its objective cannot be sufficiently achieved at the national level and can be better attained at the EU level. The ease with which this test can be applied depends on the policy area and the objectives at hand. This section illustrates this aspect by considering two specific areas of interest,

---

[107] COSAC, 24th Bi-annual Report: Developments in European Union Procedures and Practices Relevant to Parliamentary Scrutiny, 4 November 2015, 17 et seq.

[108] Protocol No. 2, Article 8.

[109] K. Granat, 'Institutional Design of the Member States for the Ex Post Subsidiarity Scrutiny' in M. Cartabia et al. (eds.), *Democracy and Subsidiarity in the EU* (Il Mulino, 2013), 427.

namely, internal market legislation and fundamental rights legislation. With regard to the achievement of the internal market, the problem is that it appears too easy to conclude that the subsidiarity principle points in the direction of undertaking certain action at the EU level, simply because of the inherent cross-border nature of the objective. With regard to the governance of fundamental rights, issues arise if subsidiarity is simply applied mechanically, without due respect for the wider-ranging objectives of fundamental rights policy.

A   Internal Market

The review of EU legislation based on Article 114 TFEU, such as the Tobacco Products Directive, underlines the deficiencies of the subsidiarity test.[110] The national parliaments challenged the Commission proposal for the Tobacco Products Directive under the EWS, issuing nine reasoned opinions.[111] The reasoned opinions argued that the Commission did not prove disparities between tobacco products in the Member States and therefore did not establish the presence of a threat to the functioning of the internal market.[112] It was also underlined that the Member States have already contributed to increasing health protection by measures such as banning smoking in public spaces or selling in vending machines.[113] Moreover some parliaments underlined that the large number of foreseen delegated acts impeded subsidiarity assessment of the proposal.[114]

The threshold for the 'yellow card' was not reached and the EU legislator adopted the proposal with some changes in 2014. The Directive prohibits cigarettes with characterising flavours (e.g. menthol) and introduces health warnings on packages of tobacco and related products which consist of a picture and text health warnings covering 65 per cent of the front and back of the packages. Moreover, it provides safety and quality requirements for electronic cigarettes.

Subsequently, three cases concerning the new Directive were brought before the Court. Some of the challenges contested whether the prohibition

---

[110] COM (2012) 788.
[111] Two of those reasoned opinions (Bulgarian parliament and Italian Chamber of Deputies) were issued after the eight-week deadline.
[112] Reasoned opinion of the Greek parliament, 20 February 2013, 4.
[113] Reasoned opinion of the Bulgarian parliament, 28 February 2013, 2.
[114] Reasoned opinions of the Danish parliament, 4 March 2013, 1; the Italian Senate, 30 March 2013, 1; and the Romanian Chamber of Deputies, 26 February 2013, 1.

of menthol cigarettes[115] and the new rules on e-cigarettes complied with Article 5(3) TEU.[116] The cases show the Court's reasoning and appear to provide the most structured discussion of subsidiarity to date in the case law. The Court's Advocate General (AG) provided the most extensive opinion in the *Poland* v. *Parliament and Council* case, referring to that opinion in the other proceedings.[117] This is therefore the opinion that is reviewed in this chapter to show the challenges of subsidiarity analysis with regard to legislation based on Article 114 TFEU.

The AG included in the subsidiarity review an analysis of the substance of the EU measure and of the statement of reasons.[118] Within the substantive test, the AG outlined two different limbs of the test, one negative and one positive, which de facto represent simply different labels for the national insufficiency test and comparative efficiency test discussed earlier.[119] Under the negative limb the AG enumerated three components: (1) the technical and financial capabilities of the Member States to resolve the problem; (2) the national, regional and local features central to the issue at stake; and (3) the cross-border dimension of the problem that is impossible to address at national level.[120]

Of these, the last one appears to be the most important and the AG's opinion focused on it. As was shown earlier, the Amsterdam Protocol referred to this test as a guideline to justify action at the EU level.[121] The 'cross-border activity test' was also used in the earlier *Vodafone* case in the opinion of AG Maduro,[122] who argued that the EU should act whenever it had 'a special interest in protecting and promoting economic activities of a cross-border character', and that 'the national democratic process is likely to fail to protect cross-border activities'.[123] Generally speaking, the EU should take action in cases where the transnational dimension of an

---

[115] C-547/14, *Philip Morris Brands and Others* [2016] ECLI:EU:C:2016:325; and C-358/14, *Poland* v. *Parliament and Council* [2016] ECLI:EU:C:2016:323.

[116] C-477/14, *Pillbox 38* [2016] ECLI:EU:C:2016:324.

[117] Opinion of AG Kokott delivered on 23 December 2015, C-358/14, *Poland* v. *Parliament and Council* [2015] ECLI:EU:C:2015:848. According to the AG, the *Philip Morris Brands and Others* and *Pillbox 38* cases concern subsidiarity 'only briefly' (see [2015] ECLI:EU:C:2015:853, para. 273 and [2015] ECLI:EU:C:2015:854, para. 159 respectively).

[118] Opinion of AG Kokott, C-358/14, para. 140.

[119] Ibid., para. 142.

[120] Ibid., paras. 151–3.

[121] Article 5 of Protocol on the application of the principles of subsidiarity and proportionality annexed to the Treaty establishing the European Community.

[122] Case C-58/08, *Opinion of Advocate General Poiares Maduro in Vodafone and Others* [2009] ECLI:EU:C:2009:596.

[123] Ibid., para. 34.

issue means that national processes may fail, in turn increasing the added value of EU legislative intervention.[124]

The AG indicated that 'as a rule' Member States cannot sufficiently achieve the aim of Article 114 TFEU which is elimination of obstacles to cross-border trade.[125] In this context, Poland argued that marketing of menthol-flavoured tobacco does not have a cross-border dimension. This was due to diverse consumption patterns and economic structures among the Member States, and the possibility to provide 'health-related action' by the Member States with the biggest markets (Poland, Slovakia and Finland).[126] However, the AG disagreed and underlined that the objective of the Directive – removal of obstacles for the trade of tobacco products and a simultaneous guarantee of a high level of health protection – can be achieved only when all characterising flavours are prohibited.[127] The AG pointed out that differences in the Member States are irrelevant: the key question is whether there is or will be cross-border trade in this area and whether the Member States can 'efficiently' remove these obstacles on their own.[128] The AG concluded that there exists a 'lively' cross-border trade in the tobacco market, with different national rules on characterising flavours, leading to a problem that the Member States cannot tackle themselves. Thus, the EU legislator did not commit a manifest error in its subsidiarity assessment.[129] Already this part of the AG's reasoning shows that when cross-border trade is concerned, EU level regulation almost automatically wins.

With regard to the positive limb of the subsidiarity test, the AG framed this test as a question of 'added value' meaning that 'the general interests of the European Union can be better served by action at that level than by action at the national level'.[130] Although, as the AG pointed out, this might be an 'automatic' case with regard to Article 114 TFEU legislation, it still

---

[124] Establishing that an activity has a cross-border character and thus demands an EU action is not always a straightforward task. For example, AG Maduro in the *Vodafone* case distinguished between the harmonisation of the wholesale and retail roaming prices. While it was hard to dispute that wholesale roaming prices had a cross-border character, the Member States could have regulated retail prices after the harmonisation of the wholesale prices. Yet, AG Maduro explained that EU-level regulation of the retail prices was indispensable, as they represented only a small part of domestic communications and thus there was a risk that the national regulator will not protect this cross-border activity.

[125] Opinion of AG Kokott, C-358/14, para. 154.

[126] Ibid., para. 155.

[127] Ibid., para. 157.

[128] Ibid., para. 158.

[129] Ibid., paras. 159–60.

[130] Ibid., para. 162.

demands a quantitative and qualitative test.[131] The AG established that the market at stake has a 'substantial trade volume and affects the lives of millions of Union citizens every day' ('quantitative test') and that the issue at stake is 'beyond national boundaries' confirming a common European interest ('qualitative test').[132] Again, no manifest error of assessment was evident in the Commission's reasoning and hence the Directive passed also the positive aspect of the subsidiarity test.[133]

Finally, the AG assessed the procedural subsidiarity angle, since Poland argued that the Commission's Directive is insufficiently justified, as only one recital of the Directive's preamble concerns subsidiarity.[134] The AG agreed that the Directive only repeated the text of Article 5(3) TEU.[135] Despite this 'empty formula' used by the EU legislator, the AG found that other recitals in the preamble, even though they do not directly reference subsidiarity but rather justify the use of Article 114 TFEU, are nonetheless relevant to the issue at stake due to the overlap in the reasoning applicable to internal market and subsidiarity provisions.[136] Moreover, the AG underlined that the explanatory memorandum in the Commission proposal and the impact assessment discussed the insufficiency of national rules and the added value of EU action and were available to EU institutions and national parliaments in the legislative procedure.[137] Still, the AG advised the EU legislature to avoid 'empty formulas' and substantiate the preamble with regard to the subsidiarity principle in future legislative acts.[138] In sum, the AG found that the EU violated neither the substantial nor the procedural aspect of the subsidiarity principle.[139]

The Court in its judgments confirmed that the Directive's provisions prohibiting placing on the market mentholated tobacco products in the *Philip Morris Brands and Others* and in *Poland* v. *Parliament and Council* cases and the rules applicable to electronic cigarettes and to refill containers in the *Pillbox 38* case are compatible with the principle of subsidiarity.[140] The Court established that the initial, political review of subsidiarity is in the hands of national parliaments while the Court has to decide whether

---

[131] Ibid., paras. 164–5.
[132] Ibid., para. 167.
[133] Ibid., para. 168.
[134] Ibid., para. 175.
[135] Ibid., para. 177.
[136] Ibid., para. 180.
[137] Ibid., paras. 182–5.
[138] Ibid., para. 188.
[139] Ibid., para. 189.
[140] See C-547/14, paras. 213–28; and C-477/14, paras. 142–51.

the EU legislature 'was entitled to consider, on the basis of a detailed statement, that the objective of the proposed action cannot be better achieved at EU level'.[141]

The Court indicated that the objectives of the Directive were 'interdependent'.[142] Even if the objective of the Directive to ensure a high level of protection of human health could be better achieved at the national level, its other objective, improvement of the functioning of the internal market for tobacco, would be shattered if the menthol-flavoured tobacco would be permitted in some Member States and prohibited in others.[143] In this light, the EU was better placed to achieve the objectives of the Directive. In addition, the subsidiarity principle does not aim at setting limits on EU action based on the situation in a specific Member State assessed individually but instead demands that action can be better achieved at EU level because of the Treaty objectives.[144] The Court disagreed that the objective of human health protection could be better achieved at the national level, since menthol cigarettes are consumed only in three Member States. In fact, at least an additional eight Member States had a market share greater than the EU-wide share.[145] With regard to the procedural aspect of the claim, the Court argued that the wording of the Directive, as well as its context and the circumstances of the case have to be taken into account. The CJEU concluded that both the proposal and the impact assessment offered 'sufficient information' showing 'clearly and unequivocally' the benefits of EU action.[146] Because Poland participated in the legislative procedure it could not claim to be unaware of the grounds behind the Directive.[147] In turn, in the assessment of the proportionality principle, the Court considered a procedural requirement that any burden upon the economic operators should be minimised and commensurate with the sought objective as per Article 5 of Protocol No. 2. The jobs and revenue lost due to the prohibition were mitigated by the transitional period until 2020 and by the expected decrease in the number of smokers.[148]

---

[141] C-358/14, paras. 112 and 114.
[142] Ibid., para. 118.
[143] Ibid., para. 117.
[144] Ibid., para. 119.
[145] Ibid., para. 120.
[146] Ibid., paras. 122–3.
[147] Ibid., para. 125.
[148] Ibid., paras. 100–1.

Clearly, the reasoning of the Court is much more succinct in comparison to the AG Opinions, not breaking down the subsidiarity assessment into positive and negative limbs. Moreover, with regard to the procedural aspect the CJEU is much more generous towards the EU legislature, and does not criticise the use of wording in the preamble. In addition, the Court draws a clear distinction between the political and judicial review of subsidiarity in the Directive. This is even more visible in the *Pillbox 38* case where the Court did not give any thought to the reasoned opinions issued during the legislative procedure, stating that the reasoned opinions are part of the political monitoring of subsidiarity principle under Protocol No. 2.[149]

The case highlights the difficulties of enforcing subsidiarity in practice, in particular in instances concerning the internal market, where an almost automatic prejudice for EU action appears to apply. Nonetheless, one can argue that despite the evident cross-border implications of internal market issues, a meaningful subsidiarity review may still be applied, if a profound study of the issue at stake is offered by the impact assessment. Moreover, subsidiarity could be tied to the question of the harmonisation method chosen by the EU and whether the adopted approach minimises the disruption necessary to achieve the stated objectives.[150] Yet, this approach seems closer to the proportionality review since it concerns the applied means.

B   *Fundamental Rights*

The second area that exposes the difficulties in the application of the subsidiarity principle concerns EU legislative proposals or acts with a fundamental rights objective. It has been argued that '[t]here is mismatch between the function of the principle of subsidiarity as defined in EU law and the function of fundamental rights standard-setting in the EU'.[151] Legislative acts that express a fundamental right (or as is used in this chapter, those with a fundamental rights objective) often concern relations within Member States rather than among them.[152] Moreover, the nature of fundamental rights, their focus on values, stands in contrast to a

---

[149] C-477/14, para. 147. The referring national court invoked the reasoned opinions of national parliaments arguing subsidiarity violation by the Tobacco Products Directive and no proof of divergent national regulation for electronic cigarettes.

[150] R. Schütze, 'Deciding when the EU Should Act', Durham Law School Research Briefing no. 26 (2015).

[151] E. Muir, 'The Fundamental Rights Implications of EU Legislation: Some Constitutional Challenges' (2014) 51 *CML Rev* 219, 240.

[152] Ibid.

subsidiarity test that concentrates on the effectiveness of the government level at stake.[153] The example of the 'Women on Boards' proposal and the reasoned opinions issued in this respect highlight the problems at stake.

In 2012 the Commission put forward a proposal for a Directive to promote gender equality in economic decision-making, specifically on boards of companies listed on stock exchanges.[154] The proposal followed up on an earlier, rather unsuccessful, pledge of the Commission encouraging self-regulation of publicly listed companies to increase the number of women on boards.[155] The proposed Directive set a target of 40 per cent for women in director positions on non-executive boards by 2020, or by 2018 in case of listed companies that are public undertakings.[156] Crucially, in the selection procedure, the female candidate is chosen when she has equal qualification to a male candidate in terms of suitability, competence and professional performance, unless an objective assessment taking account of all criteria specific to the individual candidates tilts the balance in favour of the male candidate. The proposal put forward some examples of sanctions for infringements of national provisions implementing the Directive with regard to the selection process (e.g. administrative fines or annulment of the appointment).[157]

The proposal was anchored in the EU competence to adopt measures ensuring the application of the principle of equal opportunities and equal treatment of men and women.[158] In support of the consistency of the proposal with the principle of subsidiarity, the Commission underlined the legal diversity in the Member States which resulted in a range from 3 per cent to 27 per cent of women within the boards.[159] Relying on its Impact Assessment, the Commission emphasised that female representation on boards will not reach 40 per cent by 2020 without further measures. The legal diversity across Member States was apt to produce problems in the functioning of the internal market, such as exclusion from public procurement, because of the lack of compliance with national binding quotas in

---

[153] Ibid., 241.

[154] Proposal for a Directive of the European Parliament and of the Council on improving the gender balance among non-executive directors of companies listed on stock exchanges and related measures, COM (2012) 614.

[155] 'Women on the Board Pledge for Europe' MEMO/11/124, 1 March 2011, http://europa.eu/rapid/press-release_MEMO-11-124_en.htm. The pledge was signed only by twenty-four companies.

[156] Article 4 of the proposal.

[157] Article 7(2) of the proposal.

[158] Article 157(3) TFEU.

[159] Explanatory Memorandum, 9.

another Member State. In sum, as only an EU-level action could effectively achieve a 40 per cent quota allowing for equal opportunities and equal treatment of men and women in matters of employment and occupation and diminish the internal market related problems, the proposal was in conformity with the subsidiarity principle.

Eight parliamentary chambers issued reasoned opinions on this proposal, and the threshold for the 'yellow card' was not met. The Czech Chamber of Deputies and the Danish Folketing highlighted a subsidiarity violation, since affirmative measures should be taken by national initiatives.[160] The UK House of Commons stated that the Commission did not offer strong evidence on the cause of female underrepresentation and the problems encountered within the internal market that would justify the EU action.[161] Another chamber established a subsidiarity violation by the draft Directive on the basis that it focused only on non-executive boards requiring less specialist knowledge and hence confirming gender stereotypes.[162] Finally, some parliaments argued that reforms at the national level have recently begun.[163]

This study of the reasoned opinions indicates that they were predominantly issued by national parliaments of Member States that had no existing legal quota and relatively high shares of women on boards. In those Member States corporate governance codes often regulate gender equality matters. In contrast, national parliaments of Member States with relatively low shares of women on boards tended not to submit a reasoned opinion.

Arguably despite the Commission's protestations to the contrary, the 'Women on Boards' proposal only marginally concerned situations of a truly transnational context, with substantive cross-border effects. Such a case would exist in only a limited set of cases; for instance, if a female member of a non-executive board applied for a similar position in another Member State in accordance with the free movement rules.[164] The proposed Directive – an example of a genuine fundamental rights legislation – however forced national parliaments to assess whether gender equality should be offered better protection, although an explicit cross-border dimension was not present. In fact, there have been cases

---

[160] Reasoned opinions of the Czech Chamber of Deputies, 6 December 2012, point 5; and the Danish parliament, 14 December 2012, 1.
[161] Reasoned opinion of the UK House of Commons, 18 December 2012, point 22.
[162] Reasoned opinion of the Polish Chamber of Deputies, 4 January 2013, 4.
[163] Reasoned opinion of the Dutch Tweede and Eerste Kamer, 18 December 2012, 1.
[164] Recital 13 of the proposal's preamble.

where fundamental rights legislation concerned transnational situations, for example the Commission proposal on the right to strike.

In the area of fundamental rights, a more open-ended approach to subsidiarity based on the issues of 'process', 'outcome' (capacity of the levels of authority to deal with certain issues) and 'willingness' rather than simply treating it as an efficiency measure may be called for.[165] For example, on the one hand, in terms of process and willingness, fundamental rights issues may best be dealt with at the national level, because this has 'the information, the capacity and the political legitimacy to intervene'.[166] On the other hand, process and willingness also suggest that the EU or international level might be better placed to act as it is 'less mired in the immediacy of a local political situation [and] is the more appropriate actor in certain human rights matters, since it is more likely to have the will, the independence, the wider experience and the normative authority to act'.[167] As regards outcome, the national level may be better placed to protect fundamental rights through constitutional values and political institutions, while monitoring of existing national protections might be better dealt with at the international level.[168] As these examples show, the result of this multifaceted assessment is an 'inevitable interaction between those different levels and actors in adopting and carrying through a particular policy in a given sphere'.

In this light, the 'Women on Boards' proposal may improve the situation in those Member States lagging behind in gender equality. For instance, Malta, Hungary and Greece had very low shares of women on boards, ranging between 3 and 6 per cent. The EU Directive could assist these Member States in overcoming national problems, such as the entrenched positions of national parties on the issue of women in society. The 'Women on Boards' proposal thus presented a more suitable measure to move towards gender equality on companies' boards as compared to a national level regulation.

This discussion of the 'Women on Boards' proposal highlights the issues arising in the application of the subsidiarity principle to fundamental rights legislation. A purely efficiency-based assessment may fail to do justice to the more wide-ranging ambitions of fundamental rights and their importance for the EU. Like proposals concerning the internal market,

---

[165] De Búrca, 'Re-appraising Subsidiarity's Significance after Amsterdam' (above n. 1), 2–3.
[166] Ibid., 4.
[167] Ibid.
[168] Ibid.

proposals that have as their objective the protection of fundamental rights put a spotlight on certain limits and basic problems with the application of the subsidiarity principle in practice, thereby motivating the search for proposals to reform the current practice.

VIII   Reform Proposals

Over time, the EWS as introduced by the Lisbon Treaty has been perceived as insufficient for safeguarding against the EU's 'competence creep'. For example, both the Netherlands and the UK have conducted systematic and wide-ranging reviews of EU legislation to assess whether and how the EU should act.

The Dutch report has shown that EU proposals raise concerns with regard to their proportionality and substance.[169] With regard to the subsidiarity principle itself, some 'points of action' in the report clearly highlighted that the issue at stake 'can best take place at national level' or that they do not have a 'transnational character'. However, in this assessment the Dutch tested only the national insufficiency prong of the subsidiarity principle, without looking into the EU's comparative efficiency.[170]

The British 'Balance of Competences Review' produced a series of reports on the effects of EU law on the UK legal system. In a report dedicated to the subsidiarity and proportionality principles it stated that the evidence on how subsidiarity is applied in practice is 'mixed': on the one hand respect for subsidiarity is growing; on the other hand subsidiarity has not proven to be an effective brake on EU legislation.[171] Since the outcome of the 'Balance of Competences Review' generally did not confirm the UK government's position, especially with regard to free movement, the British delegations did not use it in the negotiations with in the EU.[172]

---

[169] Ministerie van Buitenlandse Zaken, Testing European legislation for subsidiarity and proportionality – Dutch list of points for action. See also Michael Emerson, 'The Dutch Wish-List for a Lighter Regulatory Touch from the EU', CEPS Commentary, 1 July 2013, http://ceps.eu/book/dutch-wish-list-lighter-regulatory-touch-eu.

[170] See A. Duff, 'Why the Dutch Version of the Balance of Competence Review Will Not Please the Brits' (2013), http://blogs.lse.ac.uk/europpblog/2013/08/27/why-the-dutch-version-of-the-balance-of-competence-review-will-not-please-the-brits/.

[171] Review of the Balance of Competences between the United Kingdom and the European Union, Subsidiarity and Proportionality, para. 2.32.

[172] C. O'Brien, 'Cameron's Renegotiation and the Burying of the Balance of Competencies Review', http://ukandeu.ac.uk/camerons-renegotiation-and-the-burying-of-the-balance-of-competencies-review/. Also, the House of Lords criticised lack of publicity of the review and lack of any overall summary of the findings of the reports. See House of Lords,

The Dutch and the British reports suggest that countering the competence creep of the EU cannot be the main reason why national parliaments should be involved in the EU legislative process. Instead, the main reason for enhancing of the role of national parliaments in the EU lies in the democratic legitimacy that their involvement brings to EU legislation. In line with this view, the UK in the renegotiation process of its EU membership called for 'a bigger and more significant role for national parliaments' to bring about democratic accountability.[173] The negotiations of UK membership in the EU have led to what is termed 'Tusk's proposal' putting forward a number of issues such as competitiveness, Eurozone relations and sovereignty, which included a section on proposed amendments to the EWS.[174]

In Tusk's proposal national parliaments may submit reasoned opinions stating that an EU draft legislative act violates the principle of subsidiarity submitted within twelve weeks from the transmission of that draft. If these reasoned opinions represent more than 55 per cent of votes allocated to national parliaments (i.e. at least thirty-one of the fifty-six available votes), the opinions will be 'comprehensively discussed' in the Council. If the EU draft legislative proposal is not changed in a way reflecting the concerns of national parliaments in their reasoned opinions, the Council will discontinue the consideration of that draft.

This proposal differs from the current 'yellow' and 'orange' card schemes of the Lisbon Treaty in a number of ways concerning in particular the timeframe, applicable thresholds and the effects of these procedures. First, Tusk's proposal gives national parliaments more time for the analysis of proposals and drafting reasoned opinions as compared to the current eight-week deadline. Second, although the mechanism of assignment of votes to national parliaments remains unchanged, Tusk's proposal offers a different threshold of votes to be met by national parliaments: whilst at least nineteen are necessary for a 'yellow card' and at least twenty-nine for an 'orange card', thirty-one are required to meet the threshold in Tusk's proposal. The new procedure thus requires only slightly more votes than the existing 'yellow' and 'orange card'. Third, the most substantial change

---

European Union Committee, 12th Report of Session 2014–15, 'The Review of the Balance of Competences between the UK and the EU', 18.

[173] David Cameron, EU speech at Bloomberg, delivered 23 January 2013, www.gov.uk/government/speeches/eu-speech-at-bloomberg.

[174] Draft Decision of the Heads of State or Government, meeting within the European Council, concerning a New Settlement for the United Kingdom within the European Union, EUCO 4/16, 2 February 2016.

concerns the consequences of activating the new procedure. Tusk's proposal insists on stopping the legislative procedure if the requests of national parliaments are not met, while the 'orange card' provided for discontinuation only if the Council finds a subsidiarity breach.

On the one hand Tusk's proposal seems to demand a more active response from EU institutions than the 'orange card'. On the other hand, and crucially in light of the perception of the initiative, Tusk's proposal does not grant national parliaments a veto power on any aspect of a Commission proposal. Tusk's proposal makes discontinuation of the legislative procedure conditional on the non-accommodation of the 'concerns' expressed in the reasoned opinions, with the ultimate decision taken by the Council, and thereby away from the national parliaments. In contrast, the rejected 'red card' initiative proposed in the Convention on the Future of Europe asked for a requirement of the Commission to withdraw its proposal in light of opposition from a two-thirds majority of national parliaments. Compared to this initiative, Tusk's proposal can hardly be seen as a 'red card'.[175] However, avoiding the introduction of a veto for national parliaments without further checks may be regarded as one of the benefits of the Tusk's proposal, as it prevents adding another veto player to the already often lengthy horse-trading over EU policy.

Finally, discussion in the Council could also mean that depending on the relationship between parliaments and their governments represented in the Council, ministers might show more or less flexibility with the 'concerns' of their own national parliaments and thus affect whether a consensus on stopping or continuing with the legislative procedure can be achieved.

As this final limit of Tusk's proposal suggests, a substantive strengthening of the role of national parliaments could take place by granting them more control over their governments in the Council. One of the ways that has been suggested to achieve this greater role for national parliaments would be to adopt a procedure similar to some existing national procedures with regard to the so-called flexibility clause expressed in Article 352 TFEU.[176] This clause allows the EU to act by unanimous decision of the Council where this is necessary to achieve one of the stated objectives of the Treaties even in cases where the EU does not yet have the requisite

---

[175] CONV 540/03, 6 February 2003, 3.
[176] See R. Schütze, 'Reply to Call for Evidence Questions on Subsidiarity, Proportionality, and Article 352 TFEU', www.gov.uk/government/consultations/subsidiarity-and-proportionality-review-of-the-balance-of-competences.

powers. In Germany and the UK a parliamentary approval in the form of an act of the national parliament is necessary before the representative of the government in the Council can support a draft legislative act based on Article 352 TFEU in the Council.[177] Of course, demanding an act of parliament for every EU legislative act might have a negative impact on the speed and efficiency of the decision-making. Even worse, the applicability of this mechanism to every EU legislative draft may diminish the value of such a procedure, making the parliament act *ex officio* or simply rubber-stamping approvals. This is why a requirement of prior agreement by parliament should be limited to the most important cases, specifically those where a national parliament has issued a reasoned opinion at an earlier stage of the EU legislative procedure. Such an approach would likely also make the approval process more deliberate. The number of reasoned opinions issued would then provide the EU institutions with a more accurate indication of possible opposition in the Council. For example, in the case of the Tobacco Products Directive, only the Polish representative voted against the proposal in the Council, even though its own parliament did not adopt a reasoned opinion.[178] A final advantage of strengthening national parliaments through the national Rules of Procedures of the parliamentary constitutions is that it would not demand an EU Treaty amendment and may thus be easier to achieve.

The proposals discussed here share a common focus on the outcome of parliamentary involvement. They seek to ensure that substantial disapproval by national parliaments has consequences for the EU legislative procedure, without giving the parliaments an outright veto on legislation. They can thus be usefully considered as targeting the output legitimacy of the EU.

IX   Conclusion

This chapter has studied the role of the subsidiarity principle in the governance of the EU. It has shown the development of subsidiarity from its conceptual roots in the papal Encyclical *Quadragesimo Anno* through its incubation period in the German Basic Law to its formal introduction to the EU in the Maastricht Treaty. With the Lisbon Treaty, the subsidiarity

---

[177] European Union Act 2011, s. 8; §8 Gesetz über die Wahrnehmung der Integrationsverantwortung des Bundestages und des Bundesrates in Angelegenheiten der Europäischen Union (IntVG).

[178] See Council of the EU, 7763/14, 14 March 2014.

principle gained a new enforcement mechanism, beyond the CJEU, in the form of the EWS.

The analysis of two areas of competence, the internal market and fundamental rights, and the enforcement of subsidiarity either by the CJEU or national parliaments, identified conceptual and practical limitations inherent in the current use of subsidiarity as a principle of governance. These problems suggest that in its current practice subsidiarity may be unable to deliver fully on its promised benefits for limiting the EU competence creep and addressing the democratic deficit of the EU institutions.

Reforms currently under discussion focus predominantly on improving the output legitimacy through procedural tweaks, such as the red card 'light' of Tusk's proposal, although with the result of the UK referendum on 23 June 2016 on so-called Brexit indicating a preference to leave the EU the future of these proposals remains highly uncertain. As the analysis of the application of subsidiarity in the areas of the internal market and fundamental rights policy has shown, more substantial rethinking of the conceptual core of subsidiarity, beyond the established national inefficiency and EU comparative efficiency tests, may be necessary to perfect the subsidiarity principle as a governance tool that achieves a desirable balance between the EU and its constituent components.

12

Citizenship's Role in the European Federation

DIMITRY KOCHENOV*

I Introduction

The significant impact that European Union (EU) citizenship has on the nationalities of the Member States and the day-to-day functioning of EU law, including both its substance and its scope, is now as clear as day.[1] EU citizenship – the first truly meaningful citizenship status in the world not directly associated with a state – clearly came to affect the nationalities of the Member States it is derived from – including at the level of the rules of their acquisition – and also the material scope of EU law, both in substance, de facto, and in theory, by offering an avenue for a novel approach to the 'activation' of EU law, making sure that a case at hand is not 'wholly internal',[2] through an appeal to the 'substance of [EU citizenship]

---

*For the full version of the argument presented in this chapter, please consult my 'On Tiles and Pillars', which appeared in D. Kochenov (ed.), *EU Citizenship and Federalism: The Role of Rights* (Cambridge University Press, 2017), 3. I am grateful to Robert Schütze for his comments and patience. The splendid assistance of Jacquelyn Veraldi is gratefully acknowledged.

[1] E. Spaventa, 'Earned Citizenship – Understanding Union Citizenship through its Scope' in D. Kochenov (ed.), *EU Citizenship and Federalism: The Role of Rights* (Cambridge University Press, 2017); D. Kochenov, 'Member State Nationalities and the Internal Market: Illusions and Reality' in L. W. Gormley and N. Nic Shuibhne (eds.), *From Single Market to Economic Union: Essays in Memory of John A. Usher* (Harvard University Press, 2012); E. Spaventa, 'Seeing the Wood Despite the Trees?' (2008) 45 *CML Rev* 13.

[2] A. Tryfonidou, 'Reverse Discrimination in Purely Internal Situations' (2008) 35 *LIEI* 43; P. Van Elsuwege and S. Adam, 'Situations purement internes, discriminations à rebours et collectivités autonomes après l'arrêt sur l'*Assurances soins flamande*' (2008) 44 *CDE* 655, 662–78; N. Nic Shuibhne, 'Free Movement of Persons and the Wholly Internal Rule' (2002) 39 *CML Rev* 731; R.-E. Papadopoulou, 'Situations purement internes et droit communautaire' (2002) 38 *CDE* 95; M. Poiares Maduro, 'The Scope of European Remedies' in C. Kilpatrick et al. (eds.), *The Future of Remedies in Europe* (Hart, 2000); H. Tagaras, 'Règles communautaires de libre circulation, discriminations à rebours et situations dites "purement internes"' in M. Dony (ed.), *Mélanges en hommage à Michel Waelbroeck*, 2 vols. (Bruylant, 1999), II.

rights'.[3] This being said, uncertainty persists about the formal role that EU citizenship ought to be endowed with in the context of the delimitation of powers between the EU and the Member States:[4] the issue going to the very core of European federalism.[5] This chapter, besides saying a couple of words about the current role of EU citizenship in impacting the nationalities of the Member States (section II), focuses on the arguments in favour of endowing EU citizenship with a formal structural role in determining the scope of EU law, engaging with the critics of such an approach to EU citizenship, especially European Court of Justice (ECJ) President Lenaerts,[6] and siding with the main proponents of this approach, especially Advocate General Sharpston.[7] It deploys three distinct arguments in

---

[3] S. Platon, 'Le Champ d'application des droits du citoyen européen après les arrêts [*Ruiz*] *Zambrano, McCarthy et Dereçi*' (2012) 48 *RTDEur* 21; M. J. van den Brink, 'EU Citizenship and EU Fundamental Rights' (2012) 39 *LIEI* 273; M. Hailbronner and S. Iglesias Sánchez, 'The European Court of Justice and Citizenship of the European Union' (2011) 5 *VJICL* 498.

[4] D. Kochenov, 'The Right to Have *What* Rights? EU Citizenship in Need of Clarification' (2013) 19 *ELJ* 502; van den Brink, 'EU Citizenship and EU Fundamental Rights' (above n. 3); Spaventa, 'Earned Citizenship' (above n. 1).

[5] See, most importantly, R. Schütze, *From Dual to Cooperative Federalism: The Changing Structure of European Law* (Oxford University Press, 2010). For the key analyses of the EU as a federation besides Schütze, see e.g. K. Lenaerts, 'Constitutionalism and the Many Faces of Federalism' (1990) 38 *AJCL* 205; S. Oeter, 'Federalism and Democracy' in A. von Bogdandy and J. Bast (eds.), *Principles of European Constitutional Law*, 1st edn (Hart, 2006), 53; E. Delaney, 'Managing in a Federal System without an "Ultimate Arbiter"' (2005) 15 *Regional and Federal Studies* 225; S. Fabbrini (ed.), *Democracy and Federalism in the European Union and the United States* (Routledge, 2005); J.-C. Piris, 'L'Union européenne: vers une nouvelle forme de fédéralisme?' (2005) 41 *RTDEur* 243; R. D. Kelemen, *The Rules of Federalism* (Harvard University Press, 2004); K. Lenaerts, 'Interlocking Legal Orders in the European Union and Comparative Law' (2003) 52 *ICLQ* 873; M. Burgess, *Federalism and the European Union* (Routledge, 2000); L. F. Goldstein, *Constituting Federal Sovereignty* (Johns Hopkins University Press, 2001); K. Nicolaïdis and R. Howse (eds.), *The Federal Vision* (Oxford University Press, 2001); K. Lenaerts, 'Federalism and the Rule of Law' (2010) 33 *Fordham International Law Journal* 1338; D. Sidjanski, 'Actualité et dynamique du fédéralisme européen' (1990) 341 *Revue du marché commun* 655; F. W. Scharpf, 'The Joint Decision Trap' (1988) 66 *Public Administration* 239; M. Cappelletti et al. (eds.), *Integration through Law*, 5 vols. (Walter de Gruyter, 1986), I(3). Judge Pierre Pescatore highlighted the 'caractère fédérale de la constitution européenne', as far back as in the beginning of the 1960s: P. Pescatore, 'La Cour en tant que juridiction fédérale et constitutionnelle' in *Dix ans de jurisprudence de la Cour des Communautés Européennes* (Université de Cologne, 1963), 522.

[6] K. Lenaerts and J. A. Gutiérrez-Fons, 'Epilogue on EU Citizenship: Hopes and Fears' in D. Kochenov (ed.), *EU Citizenship and Federalism: The Role of Rights* (Cambridge University Press, 2017); D. Düsterhaus, 'EU Citizenship and Fundamental Rights: Contradictory, Converging, or Complementary?' in D. Kochenov (ed.), *EU Citizenship and Federalism: The Role of Rights* (Cambridge University Press, 2017).

[7] E. Sharpston, 'Citizenship and Fundamental Rights – Pandora's Box or a Natural Step Towards Maturity' in P. Cardonnel et al. (eds.), *Constitutionalising the EU Judicial*

favour of broadening the Court's view of EU citizenship rights: theoretical, textual and historical. At the core of the discussion is the idea that EU citizenship rights cannot be construed as excluding human rights[8] and should thus take all the values the EU is building upon – as expressed in Article 2 of the Treaty on the European Union (TEU) – most vividly into account.[9] In the context of this analysis the EU is approached as an anthropocentric federation created for the benefit of the citizens (section III). The rights individuals enjoy under EU law (section IV) are then construed as EU citizenship rights (section V), by definition and in contrast with the entitlements of the third-country nationals (section VI). This perspective paves the way to endowing EU citizenship with a renewed structural function in the context of EU federalism (section VII).[10] This is done by associating the enjoyment of a broad spectrum of rights of EU citizenship with a potential to activate the scope of EU law, thereby protecting EU citizens via the supranational level of the law regardless of the connection of the particular situation at hand with the internal market, which is currently at the core of the federal bargain.[11]

II   EU Citizenship's Impact: Superseding the Derivation Logic

Although branded as derivative,[12] EU citizenship, besides supplying the holders with supranational rights beyond their states of origin, also alters

---

   System: Essays in Honour of Pernilla Lindh (Hart, 2012); D. Kochenov, 'A Real European Citizenship: A New Jurisdiction Test' (2011) 18 *CJEL* 55.

[8] Sharpston, 'Citizenship and Fundamental Rights' (above n. 7).

[9] D. Kochenov, 'The *Acquis* and its Principles: The Enforcement of "Law" vs. the Enforcement of "Values" in the European Union' in A. Jakab and D. Kochenov (eds.), *The Enforcement of EU Law and Values* (Oxford University Press, 2017).

[10] D. Kochenov and R. Plender, 'EU Citizenship: From an Incipient Form to an Incipient Substance?' (2012) 37 *EL Rev* 369; Sharpston, 'Citizenship and Fundamental Rights' (above n. 7).

[11] For the criticism of the current status quo, see e.g. G. Peebles, "'A Very Eden of the Innate Rights of Man"?' (1997) 22 *Law and Social Inquiry* 581, 605; P. Allott, 'European Governance and the Re-Branding of Democracy' (2002) 27 *EL Rev* 60; D. Kochenov, 'The Citizenship Paradigm' (2013) 15 *CYELS* 197; C. O'Brien, 'I Trade Therefore I Am' (2013) 50 *CML Rev* 1643; P. Caro de Sousa, 'Quest for the Holy Grail' (2014) 20 *ELJ* 499; D. Kochenov, 'Neo-Mediaeval Permutations of Personhood in Europe' in L. Azoulai et al. (eds.), *Ideas of the Person and Personhood in European Union Law* (Hart, 2016); C. O'Brien, '*Civis capitalist sum*: Class as the New Guiding Principle of EU Free Movement Rights' (2016) 52 *CML Rev* 937.

[12] D. Kochenov, '*Ius Tractum* of Many Faces' (2009) 15 *CJEL* 169.

the essence of the Member State nationalities it is derived from,[13] including the rules of loss and acquisition of such nationalities. Simply put, although the acquisition and the loss of nationality are not among the issues which the Union is empowered to regulate,[14] the very existence of the internal market[15] amplified by the notion of EU citizenship makes the retention of the pre-existing modes of regulation of such de jure extra-*acquis*[16] issues by the Member States clearly unsustainable. It goes without saying that the general duty of loyalty is at work in this field of law just as in any other:[17] the Member States cannot, when acting within their sphere of competence, imperil the achievement of the goals of integration by undermining the nature and functioning of the EU citizenship status. This basic point is particularly clear following the ECJ's decision in *Rottmann*.[18] The same

---

[13] Article 9 of the Treaty on the EU (TEU); Article 20 of the Treaty on the Functioning of the EU (TFEU), OJ C115/1, 2009.

[14] E.g. Opinion of Poiares Maduro, AG in Case C-135/08, *Janko Rottmann*, EU:C:2010:104, [2010] ECR I-1449, para. 17: 'la détermination des conditions d'acquisition et de perte de la nationalité, – et donc de la citoyenneté de l'Union –, relève de la compétence exclusive des États membres' (also see the references cited therein). This notwithstanding the famous *obiter dictum* in *Micheletti* that decisions on nationality should be taken by the Member States with 'due regard of Community law': Case C-369/90, *Mario Vicente Micheletti et al. v. Delegación del Gobierno en Cantabria*, EU:C:1992:295, [1992] ECR I-4239, para. 10. In practice, the Union took part in the framing of state nationality laws on several occasions, all during the pre-accession process, when dealing with the Member States-to-be. For analysis see D. Kochenov, 'Pre-Accession, Naturalization, and "Due Regard to Community Law": The European Union's "Steering" of Citizenship Policies in Candidate Countries during the Fifth Enlargement' (2004) 4 *Romanian Journal of Political Science* 71.

[15] Article 26(2) TFEU.

[16] On the concept of the *acquis* see C. Delcourt, 'The *Acquis Communautaire*: Has the Concept Had its Day?' (2001) 38 *CML Rev* 829.

[17] D. Kochenov, 'Case C-135/08, Janko Rottmann v. Freistaat Bayern, judgment of 2 March 2010 (Grand Chamber)' (2010) 47 *CML Rev* 1831.

[18] Case C-135/08, *Janko Rottmann*, EU:C:2010:104, [2010] ECR I-1449; see e.g. for a brief selection in this sea of reactions: S. Adam and P. Van Elsuwege, 'Citizenship Rights and the Federal Balance between the European Union and its Member States' (2012) 37 *EL Rev* 176; A. Tryfonidou, 'Redefining the Outer Boundaries of EU Law' (2012) 18 *European Public Law* 493; H. U. Jessurun d'Oliveira, 'Case C-135/08 *Janko Rottman v. Freistaat Bayern* Case Note 1' (2011) 7 *ECLR* 138; G.-R. de Groot and A. Seling, 'Case C-135/08 *Janko Rottman v. Freistaat Bayern* Case Note 2' (2011) 7 *ECLR* 150; A. Hinarejos, 'Extending Citizenship and the Scope of EU Law' (2011) 70 *CLJ* 309; R. Palladino, 'Il Diritto di soggiorno nel "proprio" Stato membro' (2011) 2 *Studi sull'integrazione europea* 311; L. J. Ankersmit and W. W. Geursen, '*Ruiz Zambrano*: De interne situatie voorbij' (2011) *Asiel & Migrantenrecht* 156; P. Van Elsuwege, 'Shifting Boundaries?' (2011) 38 *LIEI* 263; D. Kochenov, 'Annotation of Case C-135/08, *Rottmann*' (2010) 47 *CML Rev* 1831; G.-R. de Groot, 'Overwegingen over de *Janko Rottmann*-beslissing van het Europese Hof van Justitie' (2010) 1(5/6) *Asiel & Migrantenrecht* 293; H. U. Jessurun d'Oliveira, 'Ontkoppeling van nationaliteit en Unieburgerschap?' (2010) *Nederlandsch Juristenblad* 785; S. Iglesias Sánchez, '¿Hacia una

considerations apply both to the status as such and to the enjoyment of the rights associated with the supranational status.[19]

The internal market and EU citizenship work together to transform the nationality policies of the Member States not by empowering the Union to act in the field of the conferral of nationalities by the Member States, but simply by bringing a profound change to the whole meaning of the Member States' nationalities in contemporary Europe. This evolution is the key to the understanding of the dynamic development of the legal essence of EU citizenship of the near future, as it affects access to supranational status as well as the delimitation of the scope of EU law. EU citizenship has emerged as a federal citizenship[20] endowed with a structural significance in the edifice of EU law. As EU citizenship plays a fundamentally important role in the shaping of EU federalism, the line which could be drawn between the legal concepts of Member State nationality and EU citizenship is becoming ever more flexible and contested.

Already today several Member States differentiate at a formal level between EU citizens and third-country nationals in their naturalisation procedures. These differences are not minor at all. In Italy, for example, the length of minimal legal residence in order to qualify for naturalisation is drastically different for the two categories in question: while EU citizens naturalize in four years, third-country nationals have to wait six years longer.[21] In the near future, the number of Member States to introduce such differences as well as the reach of the differences themselves is likely to proliferate, reflecting the importance of EU law in providing EU citizens with virtually unlimited access to de facto unconditional residence and work in the territory of the Union, thus removing EU citizens who chose

---

nueva relación entre la nacionalidad estatal y la cuidadanía europea?' (2010) 37 *Revista de Derecho Comunitario Europeo* 933.

[19] Kochenov, 'A Real European Citizenship' (above n. 7).

[20] For the analyses of the European citizenship from a federal perspective, see Kochenov (ed.), *EU Citizenship and Federalism* (above n. 1); C. Schönberger, 'European Citizenship as Federal Citizenship' (2007) 19 *European Review of Public Law* 63. See also: G. L. Neuman, 'Fédéralisme et citoyenneté aux Etats Unis et dans l'Union européenne' (2003) 21 *Critique Internationale* 151; A. P. van der Mei, 'Freedom of Movement for Indigents' (2002) 19 *Arizona Journal of International & Comparative Law* 803; T. Fischer, 'European Citizenship' (2002) 5 *CYELS* 357; F. Strumia, 'Citizenship and Free Movement' (2006) 12 *CJEL* 714; C. Timmermans, 'Lifting the Veil of Union Citizens' Rights' in N. Colneric et al. (eds.), *Festschrift für Gil Carlos Rodríguez Iglesias* (Berliner Wissenschafts-Verlag, 2003). For a truly magisterial analysis, see C. Schönberger, *Unionsbürger. Europas föderales Bürgerrecht in vergleichender Sicht* (Mohr Siebeck, 2006).

[21] Legge N. 91/1992; G. Zincone and M. Basili, 'Country Report: Italy', EUDO Citizenship Observatory RSC Paper, EUI, 2009, 13.

to reside outside of their Member State of nationality from the category of simple 'foreigners'. Formal naturalisation simplifications thus come on top of the EU law guarantees, which infinitely simplify the meeting of *any* standard naturalisation requirements.[22] Ultimately, the establishment of diverging naturalisation requirements for EU citizens and third-country nationals means that a distinction is made between the acquisition of EU citizenship (necessarily coupled with a Member State's nationality) and the mere acquisition of another Member State nationality. This is a fundamental development, bound to have far-reaching consequences for the legal essence of both legal statuses in question.

Naturalisation in the Member State of residence is already less important by far for EU citizens than for the third-country nationals. This is so because a number of key rights formerly associated with state nationality are granted to EU citizens directly by the EU legal order. Among these are virtually unconditional rights of entry, residence, taking up employment and, crucially, non-discrimination on the basis of nationality.[23] An oft-cited phrase coined by Gareth Davies attributes to Article 18 of the Treaty on the Functioning of the EU (TFEU) – provocatively, but no doubt correctly – the abolition of the nationalities of the Member States.[24] Currently it is not Member State nationality, but EU citizenship, which provides Europeans with the most considerable array of rights, so long as, by virtue of this status, rights in (still[25]) twenty-eight states instead of only one are extended and any discrimination on the basis of nationality is prohibited. Unquestionably, thus, EU citizens not having the nationality of the Member State where they reside are not, any more, simple 'foreigners' in the EU.[26]

---

[22] Consequently, those Member States' nationals who naturalise in their new Member State of residence automatically fall within the scope of EU law even when they lost their previous Member State's nationality, since EU law permitted them to meet the necessary residence requirements: Opinion of Poiares Maduro, AG in Case C-135/08, *Janko Rottmann*, EU:C:2010:104, [2010] ECR I-1449, paras. 10–11.

[23] For a critical analysis see Kochenov, '*Ius Tractum* of Many Faces' (above n. 12), 206 (and the literature cited therein).

[24] G. Davies, '"Any Place I Hang My Hat?"' (2005) 11 *ELJ* 43; Evans put it slightly differently: 'possession of the nationality of one Member State rather than that of another loses all real significance': see A. Evans, 'Nationality Law and European Integration' (1991) 16 *EL Rev* 190, 195.

[25] D. Kochenov, 'EU Citizenship and Withdrawals from the Union: How Inevitable Is the Radical Downgrading of Rights?' in C. Closa (ed.), *Secessions and Withdrawals* (Cambridge University Press, 2017).

[26] But see C-524/06, *Huber* v. *Germany*, EU:C:2008:724, [2008] ECR I-9705 (on the legality of placing resident EU citizens who are not German nationals on the register of foreigners in Germany). Cf. K. Hailbronner, 'Are Union Citizens Still Foreigners?' in P. Minderhoud and N. Trimikliniotis (eds.), *Rethinking the Free Movement of Workers* (Wolf, 2009).

This shift from foreigners to European citizens coupled with the tensions it brought about did not affect the core understanding of the federal compact in Europe, however: the creation of EU citizenship notwithstanding, as Ulrich Everling rightly put it, the Member States 'hold responsibility for their peoples',[27] underscoring the crucial importance of their nationalities, to which they alone hold the key,[28] even if loyalty to EU law is required when such a key is used.[29] As a consequence, EU citizenship, though a legal status which is '*autonome*'[30] – autonomous of the nationalities of the Member States – does not exist without a nationality of a Member State, numerous academic[31] and institutional[32] calls for such a development notwithstanding.

This being said, the EU tends not to notice *ex lege* and thus not to protect any of its most vulnerable citizens: the poor,[33] the uneducated,[34] the

[27] U. Everling, 'The European Union as a Federal Association of States and Citizens' in A. von Bogdandy and J. Bast (eds.), *Principles of European Constitutional Law*, 1st edn (Hart, 2006).

[28] See Article 1 Convention Governing Certain Questions Relating to the Conflict of Nationalities, The Hague, 12 April 1930, entered into force 1 July 1937, 179 LNTS 89, 99. This position is also confirmed by the fact that the Court respects the Declarations made by the Member States in clarifying the meaning of their nationalities in the context of EU law. See C-192/99, *Kaur*, EU:C:2001:106. Cf. A. Sironi, 'Nationality of Individuals in Public International Law' in A. Annoni and S. Forlati (eds.), *The Changing Role of Nationality in International Law* (Routledge, 2014).

[29] See also Case C-135/08, *Janko Rottmann*, EU:C:2010:104, [2010] ECR I-1449, para. 56; Case C-369/90, *Mario Vicente Micheletti et al.* v. *Delegación del Gobierno en Cantabria*, EU:C:1992:295, [1992] ECR I-4239, para. 10. For analyses, see Iglesias Sánchez, '¿Hacia una nueva relación entre la nacionalidad estatal y la cuidadanía europea?' (above n. 18); Kochenov, 'A Real European Citizenship' (above n. 7), 77.

[30] C-135/08, *Janko Rottmann*, Opinion of AG Poiares Maduro, EU:C:2009:588, ECR I-1449, paras. 11, 23: 'Tel est le miracle de la citoyenneté de l'Union: elle renforce les liens qui nous unissent à nos États (dans la mesure où nous sommes à présent des citoyens européens précisément parce que nous sommes des nationaux de nos États) et, en même temps, elle nous en émancipe (dans la mesure où nous sommes à présent des citoyens au-delà de nos États).'

[31] E.g. D. Kostakopoulou, 'European Union Citizenship and Member State Nationality' in J. Shaw (ed.), 'Has the European Court of Justice Challenged Member State Sovereignty in Nationality Law?', EUI Working Paper RSCAS 2011/5; Jessurun d'Oliveira, 'Ontkoppeling van nationaliteit en Unieburgerschap?' (above n. 18).

[32] E.g. most recently, European Economic and Social Committee, 'Opinion on a More Inclusive Citizenship Open to Immigrants (own-initiative opinion)' (Rapporteur P. Castaños, SOC/479, 16 October, 2013): 'The Committee proposes that, in future, when the EU undertakes a new report of the Treaty (TFEU), it amends Article 20 so that third-country nationals who have stable, long-term resident status can also become EU citizens' (para. 1.11).

[33] Case C-86/12, *Alokpa and Others* v. *Ministre du Travail, de l'Emploi et de l'Immigration*, EU:C:2013:645, [2013].

[34] Case C-333/13, *Dano*, EU:C:2014:2358, [2014].

criminal,[35] the mothers of children with special needs.[36] The 'good' EU citizen, as the ECJ teaches us,[37] is thus the one – and only the one – who meets the expectations of the internal market: to exist in the eyes of EU law it is indispensable to earn, to be relatively healthy and be engaged across borders; that is, to be able to contribute to the internal market the EU is creating. The legal plight of all those not falling within this image of the 'good' is interpreted away as having no connection to EU law.[38] In this sense Union citizenship is definitely 'neo-mediaeval': it is the personal circumstances of the holder, not the formal legal status as such, which play the crucial role in determining whether EU law – the law that has extended the status – would actually apply to the situation of the concrete individual or not.[39]

Notwithstanding the slowed-down progress towards a formal legal status of equal citizens in the EU, it is clear that the successful development of the internal market is bound to diminish the legal effects of particular Member States' nationalities even further. There are three main consequences. The first is the widening of the gap between EU citizens and third-country nationals in the EU even further. The second is the obvious need to adapt the Member States' nationalities to the new reality, constructing legal statuses more aware of their limitations. The diminution in importance of the nationalities of the Member States as legally meaningful statuses naturally reaffirms the rise of EU citizenship to the most prominent position in regulating the rights of EU citizens. Third, and most crucially, the rules of determination of the scope of EU law need to prevent the Union from failing its most vulnerable citizens in a situation when the national-level protections are bound to weaken as indicated above.

This is the core preoccupation of this chapter: having seen the overwhelming impact of the supranational legal status on the nature and scope of the nationalities of the Member States in the European federal context, how can

---

[35] Case C-348/09, *P.I.* v. *Oberbürgermeisterin der Stadt Remscheid.*, EU:C:2012:300, [2012]; and Case C-378/12, *Onuekwere* v. *Secretary of State for the Home Department*, EU:C:2014:13 [2014]; U. Belavusau and D. Kochenov, 'Kirchberg Dispensing the Punishment' (2016) 41 *EL Rev* 557.

[36] Case C-434/09, *McCarthy* v. *Secretary of State for the Home Department*, EU:C:2011:277, [2011] ECR I-3375.

[37] L. Azoulai, 'Transfiguring European Citizenship: From Member State Territory to Union Territory' in D. Kochenov (ed.), *EU Citizenship and Federalism: The Role of Rights* (Cambridge University Press, 2017).

[38] O'Brien, 'I Trade Therefore I Am' (above n. 11); Caro de Sousa, 'Quest for the Holy Grail' (above n. 11); D. Kochenov, 'Citizenship of Personal Circumstances in Europe' in D. Thym (ed.), *Reinventing European Citizenship* (Hart, 2017).

[39] Kochenov, 'Neo-Mediaeval Permutations of Personhood in Europe' (above n. 11).

those nationals who do not qualify as 'good enough' for protection in the context of the internal market be protected? The justice-deficit-prone[40] Union should be prevented from appealing to the fundamental principles of the delimitation of competences between the EU and the Member States when a justification for denying rights and dignity to the most vulnerable citizens is sought thereby.[41] The Union thus has to turn to the citizen not at the level of *rights* per se, but by rethinking, instead, the scope of the limitations perceived as inherently built into its own law in order to ensure that a humane law[42] is created at the supranational level, protecting, rather than punishing the vulnerable in need of protection. Only by reconsidering the approach to the core principles of the vertical delimitation of powers in the EU can such a result be achieved, thereby ensuring that the EU is not anymore perceived by those it was created to help as an 'actor of injustice'.[43] It is crucial, in this context, to remember the EU's roots as an anthropocentric federation and all of its law has always been presented as focusing uniquely on creating additional opportunities for EU citizenship and improving their lives.

A hope has recently arisen in the academic doctrine[44] inspired by conceptually significant signs coming from the ECJ[45] and the rich history of critiquing the status quo,[46] that the core assumptions underlying EU law

---

[40] D. Kochenov et al. (eds.), *Europe's Justice Deficit?* (Hart, 2015). Cf. D. Kochenov, 'EU Law without the Rule of Law' (2015) 34 *YEL* 74; A. Williams, *The Ethos of Europe* (Cambridge University Press, 2009); F. de Witte, *Justice in the EU* (Oxford University Press, 2015).

[41] D. Kochenov, 'Citizenship without Respect', Jean Monnet Working Paper 08/2010; O'Brien, 'I Trade Therefore I Am' (above n. 11); N. Nic Shuibhne, 'The Resilience of EU Market Citizenship' (2010) 47 *CML Rev* 1597.

[42] C. O'Brien, *Unity in Adversity* (Hart, 2017); N. Ferreira and D. Kostakopoulou (eds.), *The Human Face of the European Union: Are EU Law and Policy Humane Enough?* (Cambridge University Press, 2016).

[43] G. de Búrca, 'Conclusion' in D. Kochenov et al. (eds.), *Europe's Justice Deficit?* (Hart, 2015).

[44] E.g. Caro de Sousa, 'Quest for the Holy Grail' (above n. 11); K. Lenaerts, '"Civis Europæus Sum"' in P. Cardonnel et al. (eds.), *Constitutionalising the EU Judicial System* (Hart, 2012); Kochenov, 'A Real European Citizenship' (above n. 7); Platon, 'Le Champ d'application des droits du citoyen européen' (above n. 3); van den Brink, 'EU Citizenship and EU Fundamental Rights' (above n. 3); Hailbronner and Iglesias Sánchez, 'The European Court of Justice and Citizenship of the European Union' (above n. 3); Spaventa, 'Seeing the Wood Despite the Trees?' (above n. 1). A whole new wave of EU citizenship scholarship literature was inspired by a spectacularly well-argued, detailed, and forward-looking Opinion of AG Eleanor Sharpston in *Ruiz Zambrano*.

[45] See the whole line of cases commenced with Case C-135/08, *Janko Rottmann*, EU:C:2010:104, [2010] ECR I-1449; Case C-34/09, *Ruiz Zambrano* v. *Office national de l'emploi (ONEm)*, EU:C:2010:560, [2010] ECR I-1177; Case C-434/09, *McCarthy* v. *Secretary of State for the Home Department*, EU:C:2011:277, [2011] ECR I-3375.

[46] Writing as early as 1986, David Pickup argued that 'The just and common sense principle must be that the nationals of *all* Member States are entitled to the same treatment by

and leading to the commodification of the individual could be giving way to a somewhat more mature – constitutional – approach to personhood in EU law.[47] The change could be driven by placing EU citizenship status and the essence of the rights this status is associated with at the core of EU constitutionalism, allowing the two to take a notable place among the main factors delimiting the material scope of EU law, thus putting the EU federal bargain on a more coherent, logical and just foundation.[48] The cases of Dr Rottmann and Mr Ruiz Zambrano – criticised for the lack of doctrinal clarity[49] and simultaneously praised for almost boring predictability, if not inevitability[50] – played a particularly important role here. *Rottmann* teaches us that EU law, at least potentially, restrains the national law of the Member States in all situations 'capable of causing [EU citizens] to lose the status conferred by Article 17 EC [now 9 TEU and 20 TFEU] and the rights attaching thereto',[51] since any such situation would fall, '*by reason of its nature and its consequences*, within the ambit of European Union law'.[52] *Ruiz Zambrano* built on this, clarifying that any measures, 'which have the effect of depriving citizens of the Union of the *genuine enjoyment of the substance of the rights* conferred by virtue of their status as citizens of the Union',[53] are equally within the ambit of EU law. EU citizenship, through the rights associated therewith, seemingly acquired the ability to affect the material scope of EU law directly.

The starting assumption behind the recent hopes has been that simple respect for rights cannot be enough: without giving EU citizenship at least

---

any given Member State. To say otherwise is to promote discrimination which is, in effect, based upon the difference in nationality of the victim': D. Pickup, 'Reverse Discrimination and Freedom of Movement of Workers' (1986) 23 *CML Rev* 135.

[47] For the legal significance of the persons/citizens divide, see e.g. L. Bosniak, 'Persons and Citizens in Constitutional Thought' (2010) 8 *ICON* 9; L. Azoulai, 'L'Autonomie de l'individu européen et la question du statut', EUI Working Paper, LAW 2013/14. Cf. D. Kostakopoulou, *The Future Governance of Citizenship* (Cambridge University Press, 2008); L. Azoulai et al. (eds.), *Ideas of the Person and Personhood in European Union Law* (Hart, 2016).

[48] Caro de Sousa, 'Quest for the Holy Grail' (above n. 11); Kochenov, 'A Real European Citizenship' (above n. 7).

[49] N. Nic Shuibhne, 'Seven Questions for Seven Paragraphs' (2011) 36 *EL Rev* 161; U. Šadl, 'Case – Case Law – Law' (2013) 9 *ECLR* 205.

[50] G. Davies, 'The Entirely Conventional Supremacy of Union Citizenship and Rights' in J. Shaw (ed.), 'Has the European Court of Justice Challenged Member State Sovereignty in Nationality Law?', EUI Working Paper, RSCAS 2011/5. Kochenov, 'Annotation of Case C-135/08, *Rottmann*' (above n. 18).

[51] Case C-135/08 *Janko Rottmann*, EU:C:2010:104, [2010] ECR I-1449, para. 42.

[52] Ibid., para. 42 (emphasis added).

[53] Case C-34/09, *Ruiz Zambrano* v. *Office national de l'emploi (ONEm)*, EU:C:2010:560, [2010] ECR I-1177, para. 42 (emphasis added).

a minimally significant structural role in the delimitation of competences between the Union and the Member States, a simple insistence on rights is bound to result in the exacerbation of the problems the EU faces, since the internal market logic would still play a key role in the distribution of the rights the EU is protecting – precisely what one would seek to avoid when attempting to turn market constitutionalism into full-fledged constitutionalism.[54] Citizenship should thus be approached as contestation territory,[55] playing a structural role in the organisation of power in the federal Union.[56]

III   An Anthropocentric Federation

Nothing less than a *fédération européenne* is the *finalité* of the EU's endeavour according to the Plan Schuman,[57] which started the project to transform Europe over the decades to follow.[58] Federalism, famously characterised by Wechsler as 'the means and the price of the formation of the Union',[59] is thus among the core aspects of the Union's DNA,[60] a fundamental tool for bringing about a tamed cooperation-oriented constitutionalism to the Member States,[61] by limiting their democratic,

[54] J. H. H. Weiler, 'Bread and Circus' (1998) 4 *CJEL* 223.

[55] For a coherent theory of citizenship-building uniquely on this idea, see the work of Engin Isin, e.g. E. Isin, 'Citizenship in Flux' (2009) 29 *Subjectivity* 367.

[56] On citizenship in the federal contexts, see e.g. V. Jackson, 'Citizenship and Federalism' in A. T. Aleinikoff and D. Klusmeyer (eds.), *Citizenship Today* (Carnegie Endowment for International Peace, 2001). For analyses of the European and comparative perspectives, see Schönberger, 'European Citizenship as Federal Citizenship' (above n. 20); Neuman, 'Fédéralisme et citoyenneté aux Etats Unis et dans l'Union européenne' (above n. 20); van der Mei, 'Freedom of Movement for Indigents' (above n. 20); Fischer, 'European Citizenship' (above n. 20); Strumia, 'Citizenship and Free Movement' (above n. 20); Timmermans, 'Lifting the Veil of Union Citizens' Rights' (above n. 20). For a truly magisterial analysis, see Schönberger, *Unionsbürger* (above n. 20).

[57] See the Schuman Declaration (1950), https://europa.eu/european-union/about-eu/symbols/europe-day/schuman-declaration_en. Cf. J. H. H. Weiler, 'The Schuman Declaration as a Manifesto of Political Messianism' in J. Dickson and P. Eleftheriadis (eds.), *Philosophical Foundations of European Union Law* (Oxford University Press, 2012).

[58] J. H. H. Weiler, 'Journey to an Unknown Destination' (1993) 31 *JCMS* 417.

[59] H. Wechsler, 'The Political Safeguards of Federalism' (1954) 54 *Columbia Law Review* 543 (he obviously had the United States, not the EU, in mind).

[60] Weiler, 'The Schuman Declaration as a Manifesto of Political Messianism' (above n. 57).

[61] W. Kymlicka, 'Liberal Nationalism and Cosmopolitan Justice' in S. Benhabib (ed.), *Another Cosmopolitanism* (Oxford University Press, 2006); G. Davies, 'Humiliation of the State as a Constitutional Tactic' in F. Amtenbrink and P. van den Bergh (eds.), *The Constitutional Integrity of the European Union* (T. M. C. Asser Press, 2010), 147. For critical engagements with the recent breakdown of this strategy, see Jan-Werner Müller's works: J.-W. Müller, 'The EU as a Militant Democracy' (2014) 165 *Revista de estudios políticos* 141; 'Should the

economic[62] and most recently also monetary and budgetary decisions.[63] As Schönberger rightly put it, federalism in 'the European Union is uniquely European in the same sense that other federalisms are uniquely American, German, or Swiss'.[64] The dialogue about the exact placement of the vertical border of competences is constantly ongoing.[65]

The federal Union does not exist in disconnect from its inhabitants. It has always profiled itself as a coming-together of states[66] for the greater well-being of the individual, or 'integrative federalism' in Lenaerts's words,[67] consciously putting an emphasis on the 'legal heritage'[68] of freedom, prosperity and unity generated thereby. EU citizenship – 'the fundamental status'[69] – is in fact traceable to the ideas of the first President of

---

European Union Protect Democracy and the Rule of Law in its Member States?' (2015) 21 *ELJ* 141; and the contributions in C. Closa and D. Kochenov (eds.), *Reinforcing Rule of Law Oversight in the European Union* (Cambridge University Press, 2016); A. von Bogdandy and P. Sonnevend (eds.), *Constitutional Crisis in the European Constitutional Area* (Hart, 2015); M. Bánkuti et al., 'Hungary's Illiberal Turn' (2012) 23 *Journal of Democracy* 138. See also, R. Uitz, 'Can You Tell When an Illiberal Democracy Is in the Making?' (2015) 13 *ICON* 279; T. Koncewicz, 'Of Institutions, Democracy, Constitutional Self-Defence, and the Rule of Law' (2016) 53 *CML Rev* 1753; L. Pech and K. L. Scheppele, 'Illiberalism Within' (2017) 19 *CYELS* 3.

[62] A. J. Menéndez, 'Whose Justice? Which Europe?' in D. Kochenov et al. (eds.), *Europe's Justice Deficit?* (Hart, 2015).

[63] For the EMU members, that is: M. Adams et al. (eds.), *The Constitutionalisation of European Budgetary Constraints* (Hart, 2014); F. Amtenbrink and R. Repasi, 'Compliance and Enforcement in Economic Policy Coordination in EMU' in A. Jakab and D. Kochenov (eds.), *The Enforcement of EU Law and Values* (Oxford University Press, 2017).

[64] Schönberger, *Unionsbürger* (above n. 20), 67. Cf. B. Dubey, *La Repartition des competences au sein de l'Union européenne à la lumière du fédéralisme Suisse* (Helbing & Lichtenhahn, 2002).

[65] Indeed, this is one of the main markers of a truly functioning federation. One could elevate it to the rank of a principle of ambivalence: O. Beaud, 'The Allocation of Competences in a Federation' in L. Azoulai (ed.), *The Question of Competence in the European Union* (Oxford University Press, 2014), 26.

[66] The typology of federations is much richer than just the 'coming-together' type: A. Stepan, 'Federalism and Democracy' (1999) 10(4) *Journal of Democracy* 19. For a call to be flexible when operating within particular theoretical frameworks of federalism, see H. K. Gerken, 'Our Federalism(s)' (2012) 52 *William and Mary Law Review* 1549. For good overviews of federalism literature see e.g. R. L. Watts, 'Federalism, Federal Political Systems, and Federations' (1998) 1 *Annual Review of Political Science* 117; D. J. Elazar, 'Contrasting Unitary and Federal Systems' (1997) 18 *International Political Science Review* 237.

[67] Lenaerts, 'Constitutionalism and the Many Faces of Federalism' (above n. 5), 263.

[68] Case 26/62, *van Gend en Loos*, EU:C:1963:1, [1963]; see also F. Jacobs (ed.), *EU Law and the Individual* (North Holland, 1976); O. Due, 'The Law-Making of the European Court of Justice' (1994) 63 *Nordic JIL*.

[69] Case C-184/99, *Grzelczyk* v. *Centre public d'aide sociale d'Ottignies-Louvain-la-Neuve*, EU:C:2001:458, [2001] ECR I-6193, para. 31. See also e.g. Case C-413/99, *Baumbast and*

the High Authority.[70] Indeed, it is the citizens who were supposed to be the core beneficiaries of integration: the internal market is for them to realise their potential[71] in whatever they chose to do; the area of freedom, security and justice is for them to enjoy across all the EU territory.[72] This is how the well-known story goes: the citizens endow the Union with legitimacy through their supposed democratic engagement and control,[73] and reap the benefits of integration – especially prosperity and peace – in return.[74]

The core principles of European law, in particular supremacy and direct effect, which we are now prone to take for granted, were created with the citizen in mind, both as an objective and as a means of distilling these principles.[75] The 'anthropocentric nature'[76] of the Union is thus at least as

---

R v. Secretary of State for the Home Department, EU:C:2002:493, [2002] ECR I-7091; Case C-34/09, Ruiz Zambrano v. Office national de l'emploi (ONEm), EU:C:2010:560, [2010] ECR I-1177, para. 41.

[70] W. Hallstein, Der Schuman Plan (Vittorio Klostermann, 1951), 18; see also H. P. Ipsen and G. Nicolaysen, 'Haager Konferenz für Europarecht und Bericht über die aktuelle Entwicklung des Gemeinschaftsrechts' (1965) 18 Neue Juristische Wochenschrift 339. For the analysis of the history of the concept, see A. Wiener, 'European' Citizenship Practice (Westview Press, 1998); W. Maas, 'The Genesis of European Rights' (2005) 43 JCMS 1009; W. Maas, Creating European Citizens (Rowman & Littlefield, 2007).

[71] Article 3(3) TEU.

[72] Article 3(2) TEU. Cf. H. van Eijken and T. Marguery, 'The Federal Entrenchment of Citizens in the European Union Member States' Criminal Laws' in D. Kochenov (ed.), EU Citizenship and Federalism: The Role of Rights (Cambridge University Press, 2017). On EU territory, see O. Golynker, 'European Union as a Single Working-Living Space' in A. Halpin and V. Roeben (eds.), Theorising the Global Legal Migration (Hart, 2009), 151. Cf. D. Kochenov, 'The EU and the Overseas' in D. Kochenov (ed.), EU Law of the Overseas (Kluwer Law International, 2011).

[73] A. von Bogdandy, 'The Prospect of a European Republic' (2005) 42 CML Rev 913; Lenaerts and Gutiérrez-Fons, 'Epilogue on EU Citizenship: Hopes and Fears' (above n. 6). The number of sceptical scholarly works refusing to take this story for granted is growing, however: Menéndez, 'Whose Justice? Which Europe?' (above n. 62); G. Davies, 'Social Legitimacy and Purposive Power' in D. Kochenov et al. (eds.), Europe's Justice Deficit? (Hart, 2015); Allott, 'European Governance and the Re-Branding of Democracy' (above n. 11); A. Somek, 'The Individualisation of Liberty' (2013) 4 Transnational Legal Theory 258; A. Somek, 'On Cosmopolitan Self-Determination' (2012) 1 Global Constitutionalism 405; J. Přibáň (ed.), Self-Constitution of European Society (Routledge, 2016).

[74] Alexander Somek retells this cliché story much better (and dismisses it brilliantly): Somek, 'The Individualisation of Liberty' (above n. 73), 258–60. The recent economic crisis introduces an important correction to this part of the story too: integration does not necessarily bring about prosperity.

[75] B. de Witte, 'Direct Effect, Primacy, and the Nature of the Legal Order' in P. Craig and G. de Búrca (eds.), The Evolution of EU Law, 2nd edn (Oxford University Press, 2011).

[76] Case C-378/97, Wijsenbeek, EU:C:1999:144, [1999] ECR I-6207, Opinion of AG Cosmas, para. 83.

prominent in the Union's core vision of itself as the federal idea of the vertical division of powers between the national and the supranational legal orders. Indeed, naming the citizen the direct beneficiary of supranational law and implying, quite esoterically probably, that such law is endowed by the citizens with democratic credentials[77] – two stories which date back to the early days of integration[78] – was a crucial step away from the classical visions of international law, potentially replacing 'diplomacy' logic with 'democracy' logic in Allott's terms.[79] These are then the stories lying behind the Union's constitutionalisation,[80] now the most accepted symbolic presentation of the Union's legal nature[81] and 'who cares what it "really" is?'[82]

That the Treaties speak of Europeans as citizens of the Union is an important Maastricht addition to the preceding era of a supranational citizenship hidden in the 'informal resources of the *acquis*' in Antje Wiener's poignant phrase.[83] Virtually every federation in the world is marked by

---

[77] Case 26/62, *van Gend en Loos*, EU:C:1963:1, [1963] (the case refers both to the role of the representative institutions at the supranational level and to the structural role of what is now Article 267 TFEU in empowering the individuals). Is it not ironic, as Alexander Somek has noted, that looking at the core of this argument, it is clear that the presumption of the lack of clarity of the law (which is at the core of the preliminary reference procedure) has been used to justify its supreme force in the national constitutional context?: Somek, 'Is Legality a Principle of EU Law?', available at: www.academia.edu/24524007/ Is_legality_a_principle_of_EU_law.

[78] For one of the early analyses, see e.g. P. Pescatore, 'Fundamental Rights and Freedoms in the System of European Communities' (1970) 18 *AJCL* 343; Jacobs (ed.), *EU Law and the Individual* (above n. 68).

[79] P. Allott, 'The European Community Is Not the True European Community' (1991) 100 *YLJ* 2485. Even if, as Joseph Weiler reminds us, *van Gend en Loos* could be decided uniquely on international law grounds too: J. H. H. Weiler, 'Rewriting *Van Gend en Loos*' in O.Wiklund (ed.), *Judicial Discretion in European Perspective* (Kluwer, 2003).

[80] J. H. H. Weiler, 'The Transformation of Europe' (1991) 100 *YLJ* 2401.

[81] J. H. H. Weiler, *The Constitution for Europe* (Cambridge University Press, 1999); G. de Búrca and J. H. H. Weiler (eds.), *The Worlds of European Constitutionalism* (Cambridge University Press, 2011). But see P. L. Lindseth, *Power and Legitimacy: Reconciling Europe and the Nation-State* (Oxford University Press, 2010).

[82] J. H. H. Weiler and U. Haltern, 'The Autonomy of the Community Legal Order' (1996) 37 *HILJ* 411, 422. For a brilliant account of the inherent limitations of the 'constitutional' and 'sovereign' narrative, see P. Eleftheriadis, 'Begging the Constitutional Question' (1998) 36 *JCMS* 255.

[83] A. Wiener, 'Assessing the Constructive Potential of Union Citizenship' (1997) 1 *European Integration Online Papers* 17. Abundant literature on EU citizenship predated the formal articulation of the status in the Treaties: Hallstein, *Der Schuman Plan* (above n. 70), 18; R. Plender, 'An Incipient Form of European Citizenship' in E. Jacobs (ed.), *EU Law and the Individual* (North Holland, 1976), 39; A. Evans, 'European Citizenship' (1984) 32 *AJCL* 679; A. Evans, 'European Citizenship' (1982) 45 *MLR* 497; G. van den Berghe and C. H. Huber, 'European Citizenship' in R. Bieber and D. Nickel (eds.), *Das Europa der zweiten*

an intricate layered citizenship arrangement[84] – either expressly articulated or not[85] – and the European Union is not an exception in this regard, boasting a meaningful supranational personal legal status from the very inception of the integration project.[86] The status is 'additional',[87] coexisting with the Member State nationalities and 'not replacing them'.[88] In fact, given the mutual interdependence between the two, from *van Gend en Loos*, where the supranational 'legal heritage' was conferred directly on the Member States nationals, to *Rottmann*, where the possession of the status of Member State national was potentially protected by the Union to ensure the continuous enjoyment of the supranational citizenship additional to it,[89] it would not be an exaggeration to claim that the EU's federal constitutional nature and its citizenship matured together, gradually gaining the acceptance of commentators and practitioners, becoming entrenched ever more firmly in the law and the quotidian practice of human lives, until the point when the inhabitants of several Member States came to think of discrimination on the basis of nationality of a particular Member State as a horrible aberration.[90] Thinking this way is most atypical, of course: let us not forget, after all, that the core task of citizenship in any system is

---

Generation, 2 vols. (Nomos, 1981), II; M. Sica, *Verso la cittadinanza europea* (LeMonnier, 1979); M. Stuart, 'Recent Trends in the Decisions of the European Court' (1976) 21 *Journal of the Law Society of Scotland* 40; A. Lhoest, 'Le Citoyen à la une de l'Europe' (1975) 18 *Revue du marché commune* 431; R. Plender, 'The Right of Free Movement in the European Communities' in J. W. Bridge et al. (eds.), *Fundamental Rights* (Sweet & Maxwell, 1973); E. Grabitz, *Europäisches Bürgerrecht zwischen Marktbürgerschaft und Staatsbürgerschaft* (Europa Union Verlag, 1970).

[84] Jackson, 'Citizenship and Federalism' (above n. 56); Schönberger, 'European Citizenship as Federal Citizenship' (above n. 20); E. Delaney and L. Barani, 'The Promotion of "Symmetrical" European Citizenship' (2003) 25 *Journal of European Integration* 93.

[85] Vicky Jackson demonstrated that not all the federations expressly recognize sub-national citizenships, using Canada and India as examples: Jackson, 'Citizenship and Federalism' (above n. 56), 134–7, 140.

[86] Wiener, *'European' Citizenship Practice* (above n. 70); Condinanzi et al., *Cittadinanza del'Unione e libera circolazione delle persone* (Giuffrè, 2003); cf. Kochenov and Plender, 'EU Citizenship' (above n. 10).

[87] Article 20(1) TFEU continues as follows: 'and [shall] not replace national citizenship'.

[88] Article 9 TEU. This is what can be referred as EU citizenship's *'Ius Tractum'* nature: Kochenov, *'Ius Tractum* of Many Faces' (above n. 12).

[89] Case C-135/08, *Janko Rottmann*, EU:C:2010:104, [2010] ECRI-1449, para. 42. Cf. Kochenov, 'Annotation of Case C-135/08, *Rottmann*' (above n. 18); de Groot, 'Overwegingen over de *Janko Rottmann*-beslissing van het Europese Hof van Justitie' (above n. 18); Iglesias Sánchez, '¿Hacia una nueva relación entre la nacionalidad estatal y la cuidadanía europea?' (above n. 18).

[90] J. Gerhards, 'Free to Move?' (2008) 10 *European Societies* 121.

to mark those who do and who do not 'belong', its core function being to serve as an instrument of exclusion.[91]

IV   Supranational Rights

It is true that a citizen can benefit from a legal system in a number of ways. Sometimes the very possession of the status can be perceived as gratifying: citizenship can trigger emotions. The most straightforward way to benefit from citizenship, however, is by availing oneself of the rights shaped, distributed and enforced by the legal system in question among its subjects. Modern citizenship, a formal, thin and equal status of legal attachment to a legal-political system *is* chiefly about rights. Even the Oxford English Dictionary defines 'citizenship' as 'the position or status of being a citizen with its rights and privileges'.[92]

In the EU context, as the internal market was gradually taking shape, it came to produce precisely this: an array of directly enforceable rights – the majority of them referred to as fundamental freedoms in contemporary eurospeak[93] – for the citizens to enjoy. Many more rights were gradually added later. The contemporary Part II TFEU, dealing with the citizenship of the Union, lists an array of rights, many of which have parallels in the

---

[91] E.g. M. J. Gibney, 'The Right of Non-Citizens to Membership' in C. Sawyer and B. K. Blitz (eds.), *Statelessness in the European Union* (Cambridge University Press, 2011) (and the literature cited therein).

[92] *Oxford English Dictionary* (Oxford University Press, 2012). Cf. C. Joppke, 'The Inevitable Lightening of Citizenship' (2010) 51 *European Journal of Sociology* 37; C. Joppke, *Citizenship and Immigration* (Polity, 2010), Chapter 3; D. Kochenov, 'EU Citizenship without Duties' (2014) 20 *ELJ* 482; D. Husak, 'Ignorance of Law and Duties of Citizenship' (1994) 14 *Legal Studies* 105; M. Perry, 'Taking Neither the Rights-Talk Nor the "Critique of Rights" Too Seriously' (1984) 62 *Texas Law Review* 1405. While modern democratic citizenship based on duties is inconceivable, legal systems based on duties are certainly as viable as legal systems based on rights: classical Canon Law was built on the ideology of duties and the papal *plenitudo potestatis*, leading the state theorists of the Papal States to deny 'the very principle of a constitutional government as an objectionable heresy': R. C. Van Caeneghem, 'Constitutional History: Chance or Grand Design?' (2009) 5 *ECLR* 447, 457. Obligation is key to Jewish law too: R. Cover, 'Obligation: A Jewish Jurisprudence of the Social Order' (1985) 5 *Journal of Law & Religion* 65.

[93] For a wonderful classical presentation of the EU internal market law built on the four freedoms, see C. Barnard, *The Substantive Law of the EU* (Oxford University Press, 2013). Cf. A. Tryfonidou, *The Impact of Union Citizenship on the EU Market Freedoms* (Hart, 2015) (and the literature cited therein). On the intricacies of the gradual transformation of 'freedoms' into 'rights', see A. Tryfonidou, 'The Federal Implications of the Transformation of the Market Freedoms into Sources of Fundamental Rights' in D. Kochenov (ed.), *EU Citizenship and Federalism: The Role of Rights* (Cambridge University Press, 2017).

free movement and freedom of establishment of workers elsewhere in the Treaties, introducing some tensions into the structure.[94]

Although unquestionably forming the most popular core, free movement and the other internal market and Part II TFEU rights, are not the only list of rights known to EU law. In parallel, and as a result of a cocktail of the whims of fashion and well-articulated (as well as fully justifiable) threats from the national courts,[95] basic human rights were added by the ECJ to this construct,[96] producing a two-tier rights system, now reinforced by a direct Treaty reference to the European Convention on Human Rights (ECHR) principles and the constitutional traditions of the Member States,[97] and a Charter of Fundamental Rights of the Union (CFR) at the supranational level to complement (and at times override and undermine) the national rights protection mechanisms.[98] The ECJ is not too rights-eager at times,[99] being officially reluctant to double the efforts of the Council of Europe in the same field.[100] Although EU law is by definition inspired by the ECHR, a clear message from the *Herren der Verträge* that

---

[94] Tryfonidou, 'The Federal Implications of the Transformation of the Market Freedoms into Sources of Fundamental Rights' (above n. 93); C. O'Brien, 'Social Blind Spots and Monocular Policy Making' (2009) 46 *CML Rev* 1107; S. O'Leary, 'Developing an Ever Closer Union between the Peoples of Europe?' Mitchell Working Paper 6/2008, 14–24.

[95] The *Bundesverfassungsgericht* is widely considered the most vocal and authoritative among these. See BVerfGE 37, 271, 2 BvL 52/71 (29 May 1974); BVerfGE 73, 339, 2 BvR 197/83 (22 October 1986); BVerfGE 89, 155, 2 BvR 2134/92, 2 BvR 2159/92 (12 October 1993). For an analysis of the whole story see E. C. Mayer, 'Multilevel Constitutional Jurisdiction' in A. von Bogdandy and J. Bast (eds.), *Principles of European Constitutional Law*, 1st edn (Hart, 2006), 410–20. See also BVerfGE 63, 2267 (2009). For analysis, see e.g. D. Thym, 'In the Name of Sovereign Statehood' (2009) 46 *CML Rev* 1795; C. Wohlfahrt, 'The Lisbon Case' (2009) 10 *GLJ* 1277; A. Steinbach, 'The Lisbon Judgment of the German Federal Constitutional Court' (2010) 11 *GLJ* 367.

[96] For the full story, see B. de Witte, 'The Past and Future of the European Court of Justice in the Protection of Human Rights' in P. Alston (ed.), *The EU and Human Rights* (Oxford University Press, 1999); J. H. H. Weiler and N. J. S. Lockhart, '"Taking Rights Seriously" Seriously' (I and II) (1995) 32 *CML Rev* 51 and 669, respectively.

[97] Article 6(3) TEU. The provision reads as follows: 'Fundamental rights, as guaranteed by the European Convention for the Protection of Human Rights and Fundamental Freedoms and as they result from the constitutional traditions common to the Member States, shall constitute general principles of the Union's law.'

[98] Joined Cases C-411/10 and C-493/10, *N.S. and M.E.*, EU:C:2011:865, [2011] ECR I-13905, paras. 78–80; Case C-399/11, *Melloni* v. *Ministerio Fiscal*, EU:C:2013:107, [2013], paras. 37 and 63. See also Opinion 2/13, EU:C:2014:2454, [2014], paras. 193 and 195.

[99] Spaventa, 'Earned Citizenship' (above n. 1); N. Nic Shuibhne, 'Limits Rising, Duties Ascending' (2015) 52 *CML Rev* 889; D. Kostakopoulou, 'When EU Citizens Become Foreigners' (2014) 20 *ELJ* 447.

[100] For a critical analysis of this aspect of the recent jurisprudential moves, see e.g. G. Davies, 'The Right to Stay at Home: A Basis for Expanding European Family Rights' in

ECHR law should be taken somewhat more seriously by the Court and other institutions[101] met with overwhelming resistance from the ECJ.[102] So the principled idea of substantively adhering to Council of Europe human rights standards is seemingly out of favour of late with the ECJ, for some hermeneutic procedural and quasi-structural – read essentially irrelevant, from the point of view of human rights protection – reasons.[103]

This does not ultimately alter the fact that the Court is obviously bound by the ECHR, even if not directly, in all that it does for two reasons in addition to the requirements of EU law itself.[104] The first are the expectations of the national constitutional courts – the *Solange* logic.[105] The

---

D. Kochenov (ed.), *EU Citizenship and Federalism: The Role of Rights* (Cambridge University Press, 2017); N. Nic Shuibhne, '(Some of) the Kids Are All Right' (2012) 49 *CML Rev* 349.

[101] Indeed, there can be no other explanation for the binding requirement on the EU to accede to the ECHR now contained in Article 6(2) ECHR. See also Protocol 8 relating to Article 6(2) TEU on the accession of the Union to the European Convention on the Protection of Human Rights and Fundamental Freedoms, OJ 2012 C326/273. Cf. V. Kosta et al. (eds.), *The EU Accession to the ECHR* (Hart, 2014); P. Gragl, *The Accession of the European Union to the European Convention on Human Rights* (Hart, 2013). The subject is not new, of course. For a classical early treatment, see F. Capotorti, 'A propos de l'adhésion éventuelle des Communautés à la Convention européenne des droits de l'homme' in R. Bieber and D. Nickel (eds.) *Das Europa der Zweite Generation*, 2 vols. (Nomos, 1981), II.

[102] Opinion 2/13, EU:C:2014:2454, [2014]. Cf. D. Halberstam, '"It's the Autonomy, Stupid!" A Modest Defense of Opinion 2/13 on EU Accession to the ECHR, and the Way Forward' (2015) 16 *GLJ* 105; and P. Eeckhout, 'Opinion 2/13 on EU Accession to the ECHR and Judicial Dialogue' (2015) 38 *Fordham International Law Journal* 955. See also Opinion 2/94, EU:C:1996:140, [2014].

[103] Opinion 2/13, EU:C:2014:2454, [2014], para. 192: '[W]hen implementing EU law, the Member States may, under EU law, be required *to presume* that fundamental rights have been observed by the other Member States, so that ... they *may not check* whether that other Member State has actually, in a specific case, observed the fundamental rights guaranteed by the EU.' Piet Eeckhout made a most persuasive argument that federalism and the issues of the division of competences between the EU and the Member States cannot, as such, possibly play any role here, since, no matter which level of government is responsible, the fundamental values, as expressed in the ECHR have to be respected, as rightly put by Eeckhout 'for the CJEU ... to assume that responsibility and division of competences are one and the same, is not an example of proper judicial reasoning, to say the least'. It is thus clear that the ECJ simply deploys 'autonomy' as a flimsy pretext to ensure that its own jurisdiction is unchecked: Eeckhout, 'Opinion 2/13 on EU Accession to the ECHR and Judicial Dialogue' (above n. 102).

[104] Let us not forget that Article 6(3) TEU, codifying famous case law, refers to the ECHR as a source of general principles of EU law.

[105] Mayer, 'Multilevel Constitutional Jurisdiction' (above n. 95), 410–20. On the scrutiny of the proposals aiming to extend *Solange* logic to make it police the essence of the national constitutional orders of the Member States using EU citizenship as a trigger, see J. Croon-Gestefeld, 'Reverse *Solange*: Union Citizenship as a Detour on the Route to European Rights Protection against National Infringements' in D. Kochenov (ed.), *EU Citizenship*

second are the expectations of the European Court of Human Rights (ECtHR), which are no less legitimate. Both the national courts – and not only *Bundesverfassungsgericht* or *Corte Costituzionale* – and the ECtHR can always check whether fundamental rights are indeed respected in the EU. The first functions by potentially limiting the reach of EU law within the national legal system, while the second is about the real and present danger of the ECtHR changing its mind on the courtesy of *Bosphorus*, thereby declining to presume an equal level of protection of the said rights in EU law.[106]

The CFR is an ambiguous latecomer to this feast.[107] The principal point of it seems to lie in the limitations of Article 51 CFI and the fears of the Union's domination over the Member States in the rights field, using rights as a pretext to expand jurisdiction.[108] Probably ironically, the added value

---

and *Federalism: The Role of Rights* (Cambridge University Press, 2017); D. Kochenov, 'On Policing Article 2 TEU Compliance' (2014) 33 *Polish YBIL* 145.

[106] *Bosphorus* v. *Ireland*, App. No. 45036/98 (30 June 2005). The number of far-reaching discrepancies between EU law and ECtHR law seems to be growing, especially after the ECJ hinted in the ill-advised Opinion 2/13 that the EU's own structural considerations prevail over the protection of human rights, see Opinion 2/13, EU:C:2014:2454, [2014], para. 192: '[W]hen implementing EU law, the Member States may, under EU law, be required *to presume* that fundamental rights have been observed by the other Member States, so that ... they *may not check* whether that other Member State has actually, in a specific case, observed the fundamental rights guaranteed by the EU.' Piet Eeckhout made a most persuasive argument that federalism and the issues of the division of competences between the EU and the Member States cannot, as such, possibly play any role here, since, no matter which level of government is responsible, the fundamental values, as expressed in the ECHR have to be respected, as rightly put by Eeckhout 'for the CJEU ... to assume that responsibility and division of competences are one and the same, is not an example of proper judicial reasoning, to say the least'. It is thus clear that the ECJ simply deploys 'autonomy' as a flimsy pretext to ensure that its own jurisdiction is unchecked: Eeckhout, 'Opinion 2/13 on EU Accession to the ECHR and Judicial Dialogue' (above n. 102). Cf. Case C-542/13, *M'Bodj* v. *Belgium*, EU:C:2014:2452, [2014]; *S.J.* v. *Belgium*, App. No. 70055/10 (19 March 2015), especially the dissenting opinion of Judge Pinto de Albuquerque, paras. 3–4. Cf. also the ECJ's Joined Cases C-411/10 and C-493/10, *N.S. and M.E.*, EU:C:2011:865, [2011] ECR I-13905; and Case C-394/12, *Abdullahi* v. *Bundesasylamt*, EU:C:2013:813, [2013] with the ECtHR's *M.S.S.* v. *Belgium and Greece*, App. No. 30696/09 (21 January 2011) and *Tarakhel*, App. No. 29217/12 (4 November 2014).

[107] G. de Búrca, 'The Drafting of the European Union Charter of Fundamental Rights' (2001) 26 *EL Rev* 126; P. Eeckhout, 'The EU Charter of Fundamental Rights and the Federal Question' (2002) 39 *CML Rev* 945; P. Pescatore, 'La Coopération entre la Cour communautaire, les juridictions nationales et la Cour européenne des droits de l'homme dans la protection des droits fondamentaux: enquête sur un problème virtuel' (2003) 466 *Revue du marché commun* 151.

[108] See also Article 6(1)(2) TEU. It is probably ironic that the former Vice-President of the Commission connected the proper functioning of EU law in the future with the necessity to abolish this provision (SPEECH/13/677, Centre for European Policy Studies, 2013) and

of this document, as Haltern so rightly underlined, is not absolutely clear, the long judicial and academic struggle with it notwithstanding: 'Does the ... Charter offer better protection of fundamental rights? The Charter itself says no.'[109] Member States have been steadily watering down the scope of the Charter, on the road to elevating it to the level of the primary law of the EU, the last round taking place at its incorporation into the structure of the Treaties in a binding form.[110] Combined with the preference for structure over substance in the area of human rights protection abundantly demonstrated by the ECJ, not the least in its Opinion 2/13, the picture that emerges is unsettling.[111] This puzzling reality cannot alter the basics described above, however: the essence of the Rule of Law consists precisely in making sure that the law is controlled by law,[112] necessarily implying being subjected to external checks, including those coming from international (i.e. the Council of Europe (CoE)) law.[113] The EU is lucky also to have the 'national' level in this respect: in the face of the serious arguments coming from the national courts, the ECJ is bound to oblige again. The picture of rights at stake is thus multifaceted and dynamic. What seems to be undoubtedly the case is that the rights protected by EU law cannot possibly be read as being limited by the Charter: approaching the Charter as a limit to fundamental rights protection – although theoretically possible[114] – would be an aberration of the law.

---

that some scholars share this perspective: e.g. A. Jakab, 'The EU Charter of Fundamental Rights as the Most Promising Way of Enforcing the Rule of Law against EU Member States' in C. Closa and D. Kochenov (eds.), *Reinforcing Rule of Law Oversight in the European Union* (Cambridge University Press, 2016).

[109] U. Haltern, 'On Finality' in A. von Bogdandy and J. Bast (eds.), *Principles of European Constitutional Law*, 1st edn (Hart, 2006). See also, J. H. H. Weiler, 'Editorial: Does the European Union Truly Need a Charter of Fundamental Rights?' (2000) 6 *ELJ* 95. For a magisterial analysis, see M. Dougan, 'Judicial Review of Member State Action under the General Principles and the Charter' (2016) 53 *CML Rev* 1201, 1226–9.

[110] For an analysis, see H. Kaila, 'The Scope of Application of the Charter of Fundamental Rights of the European Union in the Member States' in P. Cardonnel et al. (eds.), *Constitutionalising the EU Judicial System* (Hart, 2012) 299 (analysing the reframing of Article II-111 of the Treaty Establishing a Constitution for Europe, which never entered into force. This provision is now Article 51 CFR, however.

[111] Kochenov, 'EU Law without the Rule of Law' (above n. 40).

[112] Cf. G. Palombella, *È possibile la legalità globale?* (Il Mulino, 2012); G. Palombella, 'The Rule of Law and its Core' in G. Palombella and N. Walker (eds.), *Relocating the Rule of Law* (Hart, 2009).

[113] R. Dworkin, 'A New Philosophy of International Law' (2013) 41 *Philosophy and Public Affairs* 2.

[114] This could even be the reason behind drafting the CFR in the first place: A. Knook, 'The Court, the Charter, and the Vertical Division of Powers in the European Union' (2005) 42 *CML Rev* 367.

V   EU Citizenship Rights

There can be no doubt that the absolute majority of the supranational rights, whatever their precise terminological framing and specific source in the relevant case law, Treaties and legislation, has traditionally amounted in essence to supranational *citizenship* rights. The scope of the main bulk of these has traditionally been connected to a strictly delimited body of the 'nationals of the Member States for the purposes of Community law'[115] (later formally branded 'EU citizens') finding themselves within the ambit of EU law: the scope *ratione personae* of EU law is, however dynamic, a relatively simple construct.[116]

Which rights should be associated with the status of EU citizenship is not a purely theoretical matter. In addition to giving citizenship meaning, rights have serious potential to reshape the federal delimitation of powers in the EU in the world where being able to enjoy the 'substance of rights associated with the status' of EU citizenship is key to the delimitation of the boundaries of the material scope of EU law. The interest in the exact framing of EU citizenship rights is on the rise,[117] the fifty-year-old practice of framing the majority of core supranational rights as de facto citizenship rights notwithstanding.

An argument has been made, championed by President Lenaerts, that only the rights explicitly mentioned in Part II TFEU are 'true' citizenship rights.[118] This view seems, with respect, too narrow. The arguments against such a narrow view are threefold. They can be grounded in the structure of rights and the textual analysis of Part II TFEU in the Treaties; in the role played by the (pre-)citizenship status throughout the history of EU law in the context of the framing of rights; as well as, most importantly, in the arguments relating to the essential and indispensable connection between

---

[115] Case C-192/99, *The Queen v. Secretary of State for the Home Department, ex parte Manjit Kaur* [2001] ECR I-1237. For a detailed discussion of this issue, see e.g. Kochenov, '*Ius Tractum* of Many Faces' (above n. 12), 186–90.

[116] For the best scholarly account to date, see Spaventa, 'Seeing the Wood Despite the Trees?' (above n. 1). Cf. 'Earned Citizenship' (above n. 1).

[117] See e.g. Lenaerts and Gutiérrez-Fons, 'Epilogue on EU Citizenship: Hopes and Fears' (above n. 6); S. Iglesias Sánchez, 'Fundamental Rights and Citizenship of the Union at a Crossroads' (2014) 20 *ELJ* 464; Kochenov, 'The Right to Have *What* Rights?' (above n. 4); Sharpston, 'Citizenship and Fundamental Rights' (above n. 7); van den Brink 'EU Citizenship and EU Fundamental Rights' (above n. 3). See also S. O'Leary, 'The Relationship between Community Citizenship and the Protection of Fundamental Rights in Community Law' (1995) 32 *CML Rev* 519.

[118] See most recently Lenaerts and Gutiérrez-Fons, 'Epilogue on EU Citizenship: Hopes and Fears' (above n. 6).

citizenship and fundamental rights overwhelmingly accepted in the literature. To narrow the scope of EU citizenship rights to what we find mainly in Article 20 TFEU, which does not contain any core fundamental rights, would thus run counter to the historical functioning of the personal legal status in European supranational law, would be contrary to the Treaty text and structure and would also amount to implying that the EU has created what can essentially be referred to (given the list in Article 20 TFEU) as citizenship without rights – which is as implausible as it is unfortunate. Let us look at all the three groups of arguments against the narrow reading poisoning the recent case law on EU citizenship starting with the structural-textual and proceeding to legal-theoretical and, lastly, legal-historical.

A   Text

The textual and structural arguments are very simple. Part II TFEU does *not* contain an exhaustive list of rights for EU citizens to benefit from. The language of the Treaty is unequivocal: Article 20(2) TFEU states: 'Citizens of the Union shall enjoy the rights and be subject to the duties provided for in the Treaties. They shall have, inter alia ... ', then lists the rights. That the list of these '"inter alia" rights' can be extended by using the special procedure of Article 25 TFEU thus most logically emerges, first, as a possibility offered by the drafters to enlarge the EU citizenship rights' list *sensu stricto* – the specific list of Article 20 TFEU, each element of which has a corresponding article elsewhere in Part II TFEU – as opposed to the list of rights 'provided for in the Treaties', including the unwritten ones, which, as Article 20(2) TFEU indicates, can also be tapped into by EU citizenship.[119] Alternatively, second and probably more importantly, Article 25 TFEU can provide a way to coin new rights hitherto unknown to EU law. Both the possibility of coining *sensu stricto* rights and of using the rights not available in the Treaties provide sufficient explanation for the existence of Article 25 TFEU. To use the provision meant to *extend* the scope of rights following an open list of examples as a justification (as Lenaerts and

---

[119] One example of such a right among many others, which is unwritten and thus not expressly mentioned in Part II TFEU, is the ability to benefit from equality in a wholly internal situation also outside the territorial scope of EU law, which the Court relied on in Case C-300/04, *Eman and Sevinger*, EU:C:2006:545, [2006] ECR I-8055, para. 61. For analysis see D. Kochenov, 'EU Citizenship in the Overseas' in D. Kochenov (ed.), *EU Law of the Overseas* (Kluwer Law International, 2011) 199; L. F. M. Besselink, 'Annotation of *Spain* v. *UK, Eman en Sevinger*, and ECtHR Case *Sevinger and Eman* v. *The Netherlands*' (2008) 45 *CML Rev* 787.

Gurtiérrez-Fons do)[120] for limiting the scope of rights, thereby depriving EU citizenship of all the breadth of the rights in the Treaties – which Article 20 TFEU refers to but does not expressly cite – is thus a most problematic move of legal reasoning with which it is difficult to agree, as Martijn van den Brink also underlines.[121]

When approached from a strictly textual perspective, the question concerning the precise extent of European citizenship rights[122] thus cannot receive a clear-cut answer; EU citizenship rights seems to be a much roomier category than the list of Article 20 TFEU. Lastly, as clearly follows from *Rottmann*,[123] having citizenship *as such* – the supranational-level status – is clearly protected by the EU law and unequivocally connected to an undisclosed set of rights, which is a construct arguably not rooted in Article 20 TFEU, but in the general broader understanding of what citizenship entails.

B   Theory

Second, turning to the legal-theoretical framing of the essence of citizenship, the commonly accepted vision of citizenship rights in the academic doctrine is much broader than the contents of the list in Article 20 TFEU. The fact that such a position on the issue is articulated by respected scholars too numerous to mention,[124] as well as illustrious members of the Court, renders this broad view of citizenship rights in the context of EU law eminently defendable.[125] Eleanor Sharpston articulates this position with crystal clarity:

> Whilst a civilised society extends the protection afforded by fundamental rights guarantees to all those who are present on their territory, this does

---

[120] Lenaerts and Gutiérrez-Fons, 'Epilogue on EU Citizenship: Hopes and Fears' (above n. 6).

[121] M. J. van den Brink, 'The Origins and the Potential Federalising Effects of the Substance of Rights Test' in D. Kochenov (ed.), *EU Citizenship and Federalism: The Role of Rights* (Cambridge University Press, 2017).

[122] Kochenov, 'The Right to Have *What* Rights?' (above n. 4).

[123] Case C-135/08, *Janko Rottmann*, EU:C:2010:104, [2010] ECR I-1449, para. 42. Cf. Kochenov, 'Annotation of Case C-135/08, *Rottmann*' (above n. 18).

[124] E.g. Iglesias Sánchez, 'Fundamental Rights and Citizenship of the Union at a Crossroads' (above n. 117); van den Brink, 'EU Citizenship and EU Fundamental Rights' (above n. 3); Hailbronner and Iglesias Sánchez, 'The European Court of Justice and Citizenship of the European Union' (above n. 3); J. Shaw, 'Citizenship of the Union', Jean Monnet Working Paper 6/1997; O'Leary, 'The Relationship between Community Citizenship and the Protection of Fundamental Rights in Community Law' (above n. 117).

[125] Even the lawyers who see this position as largely undesirable agree on the soundness of the legal reasoning behind it, e.g. D. Düsterhaus, 'EU Citizenship and Fundamental Rights: Contradictory, Converging or Complimentary?' in D. Kochenov (ed.), *EU Citizenship and Federalism: The Role of Rights* (Cambridge University Press, 2017).

not alter the fact that the people who (*par excellence*) have rights – including, of course, fundamental rights – are citizens. Article 19(1) TEU ... states that '[t]he Court of Justice ... shall ensure that in the interpretation and application of the Treaties the law is observed.' Viewed in that light, it becomes clear that it would be unthinkable for the Court to interpret the scope and content of the citizenship provisions in the Treaty without recourse to fundamental rights.[126]

Advocate General Sharpston stated this very important point in her *Ruiz Zambrano* Opinion in similarly convincing fashion, advocating 'true citizenship, carrying with it a uniform set of rights and obligations in a Union under the rule of law in which respect for fundamental rights must necessarily play an integral part.'[127] This reasoning, which can only seem innovative in the through-the-looking-glass reality of the Union in Europe, gained traction. Advocate General Szpunar fully endorses Eleanor Sharpston's view in his Opinion in *Alfredo Rendón Marín* and *CS*, in the course of his discussion of the exact meaning of the 'substance of rights', refusing to treat 'fundamental rights' as separate from 'citizenship rights' and thus respecting the age-old tradition on which Eleanor Sharpston's approach equally rests:

> The term 'substance of the rights' employed by the Court inevitably calls to mind the concept of 'the essential content of the rights' or 'the essence of the rights', *particularly of fundamental rights* well known in the constitutional traditions of the Member States and in EU law as well.[128]

Indeed, we can safely agree that citizenship without fundamental rights would be too much of a departure from the basic tenets of constitutionalism[129] to allow even in the context of the constitutional market, which is the EU today.[130] For the Court to refuse fundamental rights to citizens could thus amount to failing to ensure that 'the law is observed' in the sense of Article 19(1) TEU – a move as shameful as a new *Stork* would have been.[131] In *Stork* the ECJ found almost sixty years ago that its obligation to ensure 'that the law is observed' prohibited it from taking into account the fundamental rights of the parties reflected *in casu* in the provisions of

---

[126] Sharpston, 'Citizenship and Fundamental Rights' (above n. 7), 267.

[127] Case C-34/09, *Ruiz Zambrano* v. *Office national de l'emploi (ONEm)*, ECLI:EU:C:2010:560, [2010] ECR I-1177, Opinion of AG Sharpston, para. 3.

[128] Case C-165/14, *Rendón Marín* v. *Administración del Estado*, EU:C:2016:675, [2016]; and Case C-304/14, *Secretary of State for the Home Department* v. *C.S.*, EU:C:2016:75, [2016], Opinion of AG Szpunar, para. 128 (footnotes omitted).

[129] Sharpston, 'Citizenship and Fundamental Rights' (above n. 7).

[130] Nic Shuibhne, 'The Resilience of EU Market Citizenship' (above n. 41).

[131] Case 1/58, *Stork* v. *High Authority*, EU:C:1959:4, [1959].

the German Basic law. In other words, it refused to take any fundamental rights arguments into account.

It is worrisome of course that *Stork* logic seems to be more and more *en vogue* in Kirchberg. If a constitutional system is alive and well, the fundamental rights of citizens cannot easily be ruled out due to a particularly narrow reading of the text of the Treaties in the name of a vague goal of protecting the delimitation of powers in a federation. A citizenship without fundamental rights is as problematic as a legal system which does not take fundamental rights into consideration as a matter of principle, while pretending to be constitutional. Indeed, this is precisely why *Stork* was overruled a lifetime ago. The protection of surrogate 'citizenship rights' devoid of 'fundamental rights' thus equals acting on a truly questionable assumption which could mean the denial of the very existence of citizenship in the EU. If taken seriously, such an assumption sits uneasy with the text of the Treaties and the principle of conferral, flying in the face of *Herren der Verträge* expressing an unequivocal wish 'to establish citizenship common to nationals of their countries'.[132] It is thus highly unlikely that the 'substance of rights' will merely remain a 'curious belly-rumble on the part of ECJ judges'[133] in Martijn van den Brink's no less curious turn of phrase. Protecting EU citizenship without protecting the fundamental rights of citizens is impossible and is bound to result in a legal aberration.

C History

The third argument is historical. Historically, individuals with an EU-recognised legal status as Member State nationals for the purposes of EU (then EEC) law enjoyed – just as EU citizens do now – a much broader spectrum of rights 'in the Treaties' and elsewhere in written and also unwritten EU law than what President Lenaerts claims to be the scope of citizenship rights. Whether this has been stated directly in the Treaties[134] or not[135] did not matter much in practice. In the numerous contexts where

---

[132] Recital 10 of the preamble to the TEU (first appeared as recital 8 of the preamble to the TEU, Maastricht, 7 February 1992, entered into force 1 November 1993, OJ 1992 C191/1, 31 ILM 253).

[133] Van den Brink, 'The Origins and the Potential Federalising Effects of the Substance of Rights Test' (above n. 121), 95.

[134] As is the case with the provision of services, for instance, as confirmed in Case C-147/91, *Ferrer Laderer*, EU:C:1992:278, [1992] ECR I-4097, para. 7.

[135] As is the case with the freedom of movement of workers, for instance: Case 75/63, *Hoekstra v. Administration of the Industrial Board for Retail Trades and Businesses*, EU:C:1964:19, [1964] ECR 347; Case 61/65, *Vaassen-Göbbels* v. *Management of the Beambtenfonds*

supranational rights could most legitimately be construed as applicable to all the persons falling within the scope of EU law, the Court limited its reach to those in possession of supranational-level (i.e. EU citizenship) status.[136]

The type of brand applied to describe the personal status is largely irrelevant in this context: internal market law – and the crucial connection to the persons it would empower – functioned quite well before the word 'citizenship' formally made it into the Treaties.[137] 'Member State nationals for the purposes of EU law' described the same group of people which is now called 'EU Citizens' well,[138] even if the personal scope of supranational law has been significantly upgraded as a result of the Maastricht terminological shift.[139] Supranational rights were (and still largely are) there to endow the nationals of the Member States – Europeans[140] – with extra opportunities, *not* so much the foreigners present in Europe.[141] Once the

---

voor het Mijnbedrijf, EU:C:1966:39, [1966] ECR 377; Case 44/65 *Hessische Knappschaft* v. *Maison Singer et fils*, EU:C:1965:122, [1965]; Case 66/85, *Lawrie-Blum* v. *Land Baden-Württemberg*, EU:C:1986:284, [1986] ECR 2121. For a drastic example of how far-reaching the implications of this are, showing that even the criminal liability of third-country nationals is potentially greater than that of EU nationals as a result for the same offence, cf. Case C-230/97, *Awoyemi*, EU:C:1998:521, [1998] ECR I-6781 (Mr Awoyemi, a third-country national having moved from one Member State to another, failed to exchange his Community-model driving licence and could not question the proportionality of the criminal penalty imposed on him by the Belgian state since provisions on free movement in the EC Treaty did not apply to him) with Case C-193/94, *Skanavi and Chryssanthakopoulos*, EU:C:1996:70, [1996] ECR I-929.

[136] Importantly, Article 18 TFEU case law is limited to EU citizens. For analysis, see P. Boeles, 'Europese burgers en derdelanders' (2005) 12 *Sociaal-economische wetgevin* 502. Cf. T. Hervey, 'Migrant Workers and Their Families in the European Union' in J. Shaw and G. More (eds.), *New Legal Dynamics of the European Union* (Clarendon Press, 1995); R. Plender, 'Competence, European Community Law and Nationals of Non-Member States' (1990) 39 *ICLQ* 599, 605.

[137] Kochenov and Plender 'EU Citizenship' (above n. 10).

[138] The obvious scholarly disappointment notwithstanding: Plender, 'An Incipient Form of European Citizenship' (above n. 83).

[139] Spaventa, 'Seeing the Wood Despite the Trees?' (above n. 1).

[140] The Member States are free to determine who 'their' EU citizens are, even if they make a narrow judgment, excluding some of their nationals from the scope of 'nationality for the purposes of EU law' (*Kaur*), which is the correct contemporary understanding of 'nationals of the Member States' in the context of Articles 9 TEU and 20 TFEU. This being said, the Member States are not free not to recognise each other's nationalities when legally conferred (*Micheletti*), discriminate between 'natural born' and naturalised citizens (Case 136/78, *Auer*, EU:C:1979:34, [1979] ECR 437, para. 28) or deviate from the core principles of EU law in ruling on their nationality (*Rottmann*).

[141] The lines between citizens and foreigners are often blurred: P. Järve, 'Sovetskoje nasledije i sovremennaja ètnopolitika stran Baltii' in V. Poleshchuk and V. Stepanov (eds.), *Ètnopolitika*

Treaty of Maastricht made the formal move of introducing supranational citizenship into the framework of EU law, all the classical EU citizenship case law – in Eleanor Sharpston's enlightening and thorough analysis[142] – becomes about securing of the enjoyment of *fundamental rights* by the citizens in question.

Ironically – and clearly reflecting the intention of the drafters[143] – the Charter has not affected this situation much: 'everybody' in the Charter is the 'everybody' the arcane Article 51 CFR can see: the 'everybody' within the (personal, for our purposes) scope of EU law. Let us not forget that the majority of those who are not in possession of EU citizenship are thus excluded – and this is in line with the Court's case law on the scope of non-discrimination on the basis of nationality: the core boundary between 'us' and 'them' in any citizenship law, including the supranational law in Europe.[144] This demonstrates with sufficient clarity EU citizenship's traditional, rather than innovative nature. EU citizenship thus fits surprisingly well within the ambit of Brubacker's proverbial definition as an ideal 'instrument and an object of social closure'.[145]

VI   Non-Citizens and EU law

The situation of EU citizens and third-country nationals in any Member State is categorically different,[146] allowing talk of an 'unfulfilled promise of

---

stran Baltii (Nauka, 2013); D. Kochenov and A. Dimitrovs, 'EU Citizenship for Latvian Non-Citizens' (2016) 38 *Houston JIL* 55.

[142] Sharpston, 'Citizenship and Fundamental Rights' (above n. 7).

[143] Knook, 'The Court, the Charter, and the Vertical Division of Powers in the European Union' (above n. 114); de Búrca, 'The Drafting of the European Union Charter of Fundamental Rights' (above n. 107).

[144] Kochenov, 'Neo-Mediaeval Permutations of Personhood in Europe' (above n. 11); F. Strumia, 'Remedying the Inequalities of Economic Citizenship in Europe' (2011) 17 *ELJ* 725.

[145] R. Brubaker, *Citizenship and Nationhood in France and Germany* (Harvard University Perss, 1992), 23.

[146] The EU and the Member States announced on a number of occasions that this difference is bound to be reduced, the third-country nationals gradually coming to be treated as EU citizens. However, as Directive 2003/109/EC overwhelmingly demonstrates the differences are there to stay. For the assessment of the legal position of the third-country nationals in the EU see e.g. Kochenov, '*Ius Tractum* of Many Faces' (above n. 12), 225–9; M. Hedemann-Robinson, 'An Overview of Recent Legal Developments at Community Level in Relation to Third country Nationals Resident within the European Union, with Particular Reference to the Case-law of the European Court of Justice' (2001) 38 *CML Rev* 525; H. Staples, *The Legal Status of Third-Country Nationals Resident in the European Union* (Kluwer Law International, 1999); I. Ward, 'Law and the Other Europeans' (1997)

European citizenship.[147] The outgrowth of the personal scope of some of the freedoms to encompass third-country nationals is fairly recent[148] and only compares with difficulty with the intensity and scope of the rights EU citizens are endowed with:[149] almost all the entitlements third-country nationals enjoy in the EU legal system are de facto and also de jure dependent on a number of conditions, not stemming directly and exclusively from the status of legal presence in the EU, which allows questioning some of the literature glorifying the treatment of non-citizens in the EU, misleadingly comparing third-country nationals with citizens.[150] Agreeing with Étienne Balibar, fortress Europe still is, in numerous vital respects, a system of *apartheid européen*:[151] the internal market remains a Morgana's castle and thus has nothing to offer those who 'do not belong',[152] showing these people an entirely different Europe and an entirely different law compared to the one which EU citizens know and enjoy.[153]

EU law guarantees the non-availability of the core achievements of the united Europe to the (permanent resident) foreigner, numerous solemn declarations notwithstanding.[154] At issue is not the mistreatment of those

---

35(1) *JCMS* 79; S. Peers, 'Towards Equality: Actual and Potential Rights of Third-Country Nationals in the European Union' (1996) 33 *CML Rev* 7.

[147] W. Maas, 'Migrants, States, and EU Citizenship's Unfulfilled Promise' (2008) 12 *Citizenship Studies* 583.

[148] D. Thym, 'EU Migration Policy and its Constitutional Rationale' (2013) 50 *CML Rev* 709. For a critical overview of the secondary legislation in force, see e.g. S. Carrera et al., 'Labour Immigration Policy in the EU' (2011) *CEPS Policy Brief* 240; D. Acosta Arcarazo, *The Long-Term Residence Status as a Subsidiary Form of EU Citizenship* (Brill-Nijhoff, 2011).

[149] For global overviews, see D. Thym and M. H. Zoetewij-Turhan (eds.), *Rights of Third-Country Nationals under EU Association Agreements* (Brill-Nijhoff, 2015); A. Wiesbrock, *Legal Migration in the European Union* (Brill-Nijhoff, 2010).

[150] E.g. D. Acosta Arcarazo, 'Civic Citizenship Reintroduced?' (2015) 21 *ELJ* 200; A. Wiesbrock, 'Granting Citizenship-Related Rights to Third-Country Nationals' (2012) 14 *European Journal of Migration and Law* 63; Acosta Arcarazo, *The Long-Term Residence Status as a Subsidiary Form of EU Citizenship* (above n. 148).

[151] É. Balibar, *Nous, citoyens d'Europe?* (La Découverte, 2001), 190–1.

[152] For an enlightening perspective on how this could be changed: Boeles, 'Europese burgers en derdelanders' (above n. 136).

[153] D. Kochenov and M. J. van den Brink, 'Pretending There Is No Union' in D. Thym and M. H. Zoetewij-Turhan (eds.), *Rights of Third-Country Nationals under EU Association Agreements* (Brill-Nijhoff, 2015) 63; S. Iglesias Sánchez, 'Fundamental Rights Protection for Third Country Nationals and Citizens of the Union' (2013) 15 *European Journal of Migration and Law* 137.

[154] See, most importantly, Presidency Conclusions, Tampere European Council (15–16 October 1999). Para. 21 of the Conclusions reads as follows:

> The legal status of third-country nationals should be approximated to that of Member States' nationals. A person, who has resided legally in a Member State

who are not EU citizens but rather, the failure to extend the same legal, political and social reality to these people – let us not even call this 'rights' – ensuring that all that Europe has been about over the last half a century simply does not exist for them: free movement and non-discrimination on the basis of nationality are the first which spring to mind. Where an EU citizen benefits from the Union with its territory and opportunities, a foreigner is by law confined to Slovenia, France, or Portugal, with the borders as transparent, as often absurdly impenetrable. This is a story of unity hidden from foreign eyes.[155] Indeed, this is precisely what *apartheid* stands for:[156] imagining some other legal planet and legally exiling to it all those you do not want to accept in full, while allowing them to work in your town and walk the same streets.[157]

The picture could not be more different for the nationals of the Member States of the Union. 'Europe', whatever we find in the tabloids, is profoundly entrenched both as a reality and as an opportunity. The European Union has thus gradually emerged, to agree with Ulrich Everling, as 'a Federal Association of States and Citizens'.[158]

VII   Structural Role for EU citizenship?

As we have seen, the scope of EU citizenship rights in the EU is clearly *not* limited to what Part II TFEU chose to list. Before and unless a broader array of rights of EU citizenship assumes the role of the federal

---

for a period of time to be determined and who holds a long-term residence permit, should be granted in that Member State a set of uniform rights which are as near as possible to those enjoyed by EU citizens; e.g. the right to reside, receive education, and work as an employee or self-employed person, as well as the principle of non-discrimination *vis-à-vis* the citizens of the state of residence. The European Council endorses the objective that long-term legally resident third-country nationals be offered the opportunity to obtain the nationality of the Member State in which they are resident.

[155] Kochenov and van den Brink, 'Pretending There Is No Union' (above n. 153).

[156] See e.g. South African Bantu Homelands Citizenship Act, 1970, which instituted the denaturalisation of the black majority during Apartheid. Cf. J. Dugard, 'South Africa's Independent Homelands' (1980) 10 *Denver Journal of International Law & Policy* 11.

[157] For an extreme example, see K. Rundle, 'The Impossibility of an Exterminatory Legality' (2009) 59 *University of Toronto Law Journal* 65, 69–76. For a contemporary EU example, see Kochenov and Dimitrovs, 'EU Citizenship for Latvian Non-Citizens' (above n. 141); D. Kochenov et al., 'Do Professional Linguistic Requirements Discriminate?' (2013) 10 *European Yearbook of Minority Issues* 137.

[158] Everling, 'The European Union as a Federal Association of States and Citizens' (above n. 27).

denominator in the EU, EU citizenship remains largely one of the tools within the context of the internal market, summoned to serve the Union at the price of closing our eyes to the simple fact that as far as the framing of any legal system is concerned, the relationship between citizenship and the market is necessarily not harmonious, but in acute conflict: issues of equality and vulnerability cannot possibly be decided on the basis of someone's employability or market worth. Proportionality and legality lose their appeal, seeing their functions paralysed and their effectiveness, as legal tools, undermined,[159] in a context where market considerations as opposed to core human rights and values provide the frame for every outstanding issue. Instead of correcting absurdity and prejudice, the Union is not infrequently their generator and enforcer.[160] The negative implications of this are amplified by the fact that the problematic status quo is so much part of the day-to-day that not enough scholarly and political attention is paid to the negative potential of the current deployment of citizenship in the context of the EU's constitutionalism – the royal garb without an emperor, affecting the lives of us all.[161]

The fundamental dissonance between the essence of the internal market and the essence of citizenship notwithstanding, the main interpretation of the scope of Part II TFEU has to this day mostly been inspired by what Sir Richard Plender around forty years ago called the 'incipient form of European citizenship'.[162] This 'incipient form' was rooted in what is now the Internal Market, Title IV TFEU, *not* the EU Citizenship, Part II TFEU. It thus largely assumes that EU citizenship is only deployable as an element of the internal market. This is the *decorative citizenship of the EU*. The core mantras of decorative EU citizenship are simple. EU citizenship has consistently been presented by the powers that be as, even if not the least relevant, then definitely somewhat of an auxiliary factor in determining the crucial *koiné* of Union law and the delimitation of its depth and scope as the law stands to date. In the half-hearted and oft-quoted words of the Court of Justice, it is one of those parts of the *acquis* which is,

---

[159] Somek, 'Is Legality a Principle of EU Law?' (above n. 77); Kochenov, 'EU Law without the Rule of Law' (above n. 40); S. Tsakyrakis, 'Disproportionate Individualism' in D. Kochenov et al. (eds.), *Europe's Justice Deficit?* (Hart, 2015).

[160] Gráinne de Búrca had a sense that this was the case long ago, writing that equality 'does not have a single coherent role in [EU] law': G. de Búrca, 'The Role of Equality in European Community Law' in A. Dashwood and S. O'Leary (eds.), *The Principle of Equal Treatment in EC Law* (Sweet & Maxwell, 1997), 14.

[161] Weiler, *The Constitution for Europe* (above n. 81).

[162] Plender, 'An Incipient Form of European Citizenship' (above n. 83), 39.

quite astonishingly, not supposed to affect the material scope of EU law.[163] Federalism and the respect of the Member States' perceived autonomy and authority is usually the only sweet pill to make this excessive modesty *vis-à-vis* citizenship tolerable.[164]

Once it is recognised that the logic of citizenship makes it indispensable to separate EU citizenship from the internal market in terms of its day-to-day operation and, probably more importantly, in terms of the mode of shaping the scope of EU law, it becomes possible to speak of the emergence of a *structural citizenship of the EU*. While the structural and decorative functions of EU citizenship could possibly overlap in some circumstances, such overlaps, although probably tolerable for purely practical reasons, are unlikely to shape clarity and foster crisp legal reasoning. The two are natural rivals, clarity necessarily being occluded when they operate hand in hand.

The guiding role of the Court in the federal context is indispensable[165] – the institutional structure cannot of itself, contrary to what Herbert Wechsler used to advocate on the example of US federalism for instance,[166] be enough to build and ensure the lasting operation of a robust federal legal system.[167] It is thus for the Court to make the fundamental choices and to convince both the citizens and their Member States that the choices made are correct and viable in the long term. As EU law stands today, issues with justice and the overwhelming internal market bias radiating from EU institutions could be taken as signs that the Court has so far not been as effective in shaping clarity about the law as one would have wished.

The Court can always rely on internally coherent attempts to interpret the grievances of European citizens away.[168] Law alone is not enough, however – the social fabric matters too – and here the Court's efforts along internal market lines can prove problematic: a good court convinces and

---

[163] E.g. Joined Cases, C-64–5/96, *Uecker and Jacquet*, EU:C:1997:285, [1997] ECR I-3182, para. 23; Case C-148/02, *Garcia Avello* v. *Belgium*, EU:C:2003:539, [2003] ECR I-11613, para. 26.

[164] N. Nic Shuibhne, 'Recasting EU Citizenship as Federal Citizenship: What Are the Implications for the Citizen when the Polity Bargain Is Privileged?' in D. Kochenov (ed.), *EU Citizenship and Federalism: The Role of Rights* (Cambridge University Press, 2017).

[165] Indeed, passive federal-level courts are dangerous: J. O. Newman, 'The "Old Federalism"' (1982–3) 15 *Connecticut Law Review* 21.

[166] Wechsler, 'The Political Safeguards of Federalism' (above n. 59).

[167] L. A. Baker, 'Putting the Safeguards Back into the Political Safeguards of Federalism' (2001) 46 *Villanova Law Review* 951.

[168] K. Lenaerts, 'The Court's Outer and Inner Selves' in M. Adams et al. (eds.), *Judging Europe's Judges* (Hart, 2013). See also J. H. H. Weiler, 'Epilogue: Judging Europe's Judges – Apology and Critique' in the same volume.

inspires. The first consideration for such a court to take into account is the constant necessity to remember that it is undesirable to interpret away the key notions' very core. Consistent attempts to move in this direction are bound to work against the legitimacy of the judiciary[169] and, by extrapolation, of the whole of the Union in the eyes of its citizens, thus emerging as utterly counterproductive.[170]

In the light of the above the answer to the question 'which role for European citizenship?' is abundantly clear: EU citizenship, associated with the broadest array of rights, is bound to assume a structural role, should the ideals of dignity, equality, democracy and the rule of law prevail, to say nothing of the mere structural coherence of the primary law at hand, which must obviously be respected too.

---

[169] The courts' only basis for strong claims to legitimacy is reason: the more people are not convinced, the less legitimacy the institution enjoys: M. Kumm, 'The Idea of Socratic Contestation and the Right to Justification' (2010) 4 *Law and Ethics of Human Rights* 142.

[170] O'Brien, 'Social Blind Spots and Monocular Policy Making' (above n. 94); O'Leary, 'Developing an Ever Closer Union between the Peoples of Europe?' (above n. 94). It is possible to speak about 'contamination' of economic free movement of persons law with some restrictive rules originating in the Court's inconclusive approach to EU citizenship. See Case C-94/07, *Raccanelli* v. *Max-Planck-Gesellschaft*, EU:C:2008:425, [2008] ECR I-5939, para. 37; Case C-213/05, *Geven* v. *Land Nordrhein-Westfalen*, EU:C:2007:438, [2007] ECR I-6347; Case C-158/07, *Förster* v. *Hoofddirectie van de Informatie Beheer Groep*, EU:C:2008:630, [2008] ECR I-8507.

PART II

European Perspectives

B. *Substantive Solutions*

13

Integration and Constitutionalisation in EU Foreign and Security Policy

RAMSES A. WESSEL

I Introduction

The European Union's (EU) presentation of its foreign and security policy has been ambivalent from the outset. In the context of the present book it is perhaps the best example of a combination of national, EU and international legal elements that is increasingly under pressure from not only globalisation, but also from the EU's own ambitions to partly shift its attention from its own Member States to the rest of the world. The ambiguity follows from the fact that Member States continue to see (or at least present[1]) the Common Foreign and Security Policy (CFSP) as a policy area that has not developed beyond the intergovernmental European Political Cooperation (EPC) of the 1970s and 1980s, while neglecting an integrationist and constitutional undercurrent that is boosted by both internal

---

[1] Although primarily made for domestic consumption, the following representation of CFSP by the UK Foreign Secretary while explaining the result of the 2007 Lisbon negotiations to Parliament is striking: 'Common foreign and security policy [CFSP] remains intergovernmental and in a separate treaty. Importantly ... the European Court of Justice's jurisdiction over substantive CFSP policy is clearly and expressly excluded. As agreed at Maastricht, the ECJ will continue to monitor the boundary between CFSP and other EU external action, such as development assistance. But the Lisbon treaty considerably improves the existing position by making it clear that CFSP cannot be affected by other EU policies. It ring-fences CFSP as a distinct, equal area of action.' Secretary of State for Foreign and Commonwealth Affairs (David Miliband), HC Debs. 20 February 2008, col. 378. Similar views were reported to have been shared by France's Prime Minister François Fillon and the Spanish Foreign Minister Miguel Moratinos; 'Debate on the European External Action Service, European Parliament', CRE 07/07/2010–12, European Parliament, Strasbourg, 7 July 2010, www.europarl.europa.eu/sides/getDoc.do?pubRef=-//EP//TEXT+CRE+20100707?+ITEM-012+DOC+XML+V0//EN.

See more extensively: P. J. Cardwell, 'On "Ring-Fencing" the Common Foreign and Security Policy in the Legal Order of the European Union' (2015) 64(4) *Northern Ireland Legal Quarterly* 443–63.

and external developments. While this view is certainly no longer supported (if ever[2]) by the current treaty provisions, the question is whether – ironically – the continued intergovernmental representation of CFSP did not serve as a vehicle for further integration in that field. Indeed, a less visible integration perhaps – as CFSP is much less used as a legal basis for policy making than other external relations provisions – but nevertheless one that has changed the position of CFSP in the EU and hence the commitments of the Member States, the role of the institutions and the way the EU is perceived by other states in relation to its role in global governance.[3]

Yet, it is difficult to change the image of CFSP. It has been argued that there is a 'tradition of otherness'[4] which continues to keep alive the notion that CFSP is a policy of the joint Member States rather than of the Union (admittedly, the term *Common* Foreign and Security Policy may support that notion, although the argument is never made in relation to the other *common* policies within the EU). This chapter aims to highlight the consolidation of EU foreign policy – as well its constitutionalisation as part of the Union's legal order – and will do so from both an internal and an external perspective.[5] Internally, subsequent treaty modifications as well as institutional adaptations have led to a further 'normalisation' of CFSP in the Brussels policy-making machinery. Externally, the need for a clearer EU foreign policy stance flowed from the increasingly undeniable external dimension of successful internal policies. Yet, both the internal and the external dimensions are sides of the same coin; they are intertwined and basically reveal the Union's coming of age as a polity with the ambition to validate the external potential of its internal development. As we will see

---

[2] R. A. Wessel, 'Lex Imperfecta: Law and Integration in European Foreign and Security Policy' (2016) 1 *European Papers: A Journal on Law and Integration* 439–68. This chapter is a further developed version of that shorter piece. See earlier already R. A. Wessel, 'The Dynamics of the European Union Legal Order: An Increasingly Coherent Framework of Action and Interpretation' (2009) 1 *ECLR* 117–42; M. E. Smith, *Europe's Foreign and Security Policy: The Institutionalization of Cooperation* (Cambridge University Press, 2004).

[3] See more extensively on the external perception of the EU: C. Eckes and R. A. Wessel, 'The European Union: An International Perspective' in T. Tridimas and R. Schütze (eds.), *The Oxford Principles of European Union Law*, I: *The European Union Legal Order* (Oxford University Press, 2018), 74–102.

[4] Cardwell, 'On "Ring-Fencing"' (above n. 1), 445.

[5] Parts of the argumentation used in this contribution were developed over the years in earlier publications. See the references throughout this chapter and more particularly: B. van Vooren and R. A. Wessel, *EU External Relations Law: Text, Cases and Materials* (Cambridge University Press, 2014).

this also complicates seeing the governance of CFSP as a template (or perhaps a laboratory[6]) for other forms of international cooperation.

From the outset (the 1992 Maastricht Treaty) much has been written on the position of CFSP in the Union and its legal nature.[7] This chapter has no intention of repeating these analyses. Rather, it purports to take a fresh look at the current treaty provisions. In fact, taking these provisions at face value (rather than dwelling on informal interpretations that may serve certain political goals) may allow for a clearer view of the result of the negotiations and the texts Member States agreed on. Too many analyses reveal a poor or selective reading of the treaty texts and seem to be affected by the 'tradition of otherness' which prevents seeing CFSP in a new light and in the context of an EU that is redefining its contribution to global governance.[8]

Looking at a policy area from an integrationist perspective is largely left to political scientists and international relations scholars.[9] Indeed, those disciplines have extensively analysed EU foreign policy from different theoretical perspectives, including European-Integration Theory (EIT).[10] While earlier studies followed the classic works on the internal aspects of integration, the development of the external dimension (through CFSP as well as other external relations policies) triggered new integration analyses.[11] In general, research in political science and European Studies concluded on a 'move beyond intergovernmentalism' in CFSP.[12] Yet – and that seems

---

[6] See the Introduction to this volume by R. Schütze.

[7] For an overview see e.g. Wessel, 'The Dynamics of the European Union Legal Order' (above n. 2). See recently also M. Cremona, 'The CFSP-CSDP in the Constitutional Architecture of the EU' in S. Blockmans and P. Koutrakos (eds.), *Research Handbook on EU Common Foreign and Security Policy* (Edward Elgar, 2018).

[8] Cf. D. Kochenov and F. Amtenbrink (eds.), *The European Union's Shaping of the International Legal Order* (Cambridge University Press, 2014); B. Van Vooren et al. (eds.), *The Legal Dimension of Global Governance, What Role for the EU?* (Oxford University Press, 2013).

[9] Yet, 'integration through law' has of course been part of the debates. Key publications include: M. Cappelletti et al. (eds.), *Integration Through Law: Europe and the American Federal Experience* (de Gruyter, 1985); S. Weatherill, *Law and Integration in the European Union* (Oxford University Press, 1995); D. Augenstein (ed.), *'Integration through Law' Revisited: The Making of the European Polity* (Ashgate, 2012).

[10] An overview can be found in J. Bergmann and A. Niemann, 'Theories of European Integration' in K. E. Jørgensen et al. (eds.), *The SAGE Handbook of European Foreign Policy*, 2 vols. (Sage, 2015), I, 166–82.

[11] See e.g. the analyses by R. Ginsberg, 'Conceptualizing the European as an International Actor: Narrowing the Theoretical Capability-Expectations Gap' (1999) *JCMS* 429–54, 432; B. Tonra and T. Christiansen, 'The Study of EU Foreign Policy: Between International Relations and European Studies' in B. Tonra and T. Christiansen (eds.), *Rethinking European Union Foreign Policy* (Manchester University Press, 2004), 1–9.

[12] P. M. Norheim-Martinsen, 'Beyond Intergovernmentalism: European Security and Defence Policy and the Governance Approach' (2010) 48(5) *JCMS* 1351–65; H. Sjursen,

to be a hallmark of international relations and political science studies – the application of different theories results in different outcomes (or: whatever the outcome, there is always a theory to explain it). Thus, while a neofunctionalist approach may be able to explain the development of CFSP and the further integration into the EU's legal-political framework, intergovernmentalism will be able to let us know why this is in fact not the case since in the end European integration is determined by states' interests.[13]

Nevertheless, it has been argued that:

> EIT is capable of providing the answer to the question why European foreign-policy cooperation has developed in a specific historic way and not in another ... Secondly ... EIT contributes to our understanding of which actors drive integration processes in the foreign policy domain and through which channels and mechanisms ... Third, EIT ... also has the potential to explain European foreign-policy non-decisions and inaction.[14]

For legal scholars the extensive debates in international relations, European studies and political science may be relevant in the sense that they show us where to look when we wish to study European integration. And, in a way, the same theoretical approaches are at the background of our choices to focus on the role of the Commission or the European Parliament, or on the voting procedures in the Council when defining the nature of, for instance, CFSP. Yet, also as the present chapter will testify, *legal* integration has a somewhat different focus. In particular in relation to EU foreign policy, our

---

'Not So Intergovernmental After All? On Democracy and Integration in European Foreign and Security Policy' (2011) 18(8) *JEPP* 1078–95; A. Juncos and K. Pomorska, 'Invisible and Unaccountable? National Representatives and Council Officials in EU Foreign Policy' (2011) 18(8) *JEPP* 1096. And, true to their character, these academic disciplines came up with new ways to describe the new modes of cooperation, using terms like 'transgovernmentalism' (S. Hoffmann, 'CSDP: Approaching Transgovernmentalism?' in X. Kurowska and F. Breuer (eds.) *Explaining the EU's Common Security and Defence Policy: Theory in Action* (Palgrave MacMillan, 2011)) or 'supranational intergovernmentalism' (J. Howorth, 'Decision-Making in Security and Defense Policy: Towards Supranational Inter-Governmentalism?' (2012) 47(4) *Cooperation and Conflict* 433–53). Yet, also note the term 'progressive supranationalism' coined by (then) Director of the Council's legal service, R. Gosalbo-Bono, 'Some Reflections of the CFSP Legal Order' (2006) 43 *CML Rev* 337–94.

[13] Bergmann and Niemann, 'Theories of European Integration' (above n. 10) point to the importance of quite a number of different theories in relation to European foreign policy: federalism, neofunctionalism, intergovernmentalism, the governance approach, policy-network analysis, new institutionalism and social constructivism. In addition, a special role is often devoted to the theory of 'Europeanisation', also in relation to European foreign policy. 'Europeanisation' focuses on the impact of the European integration process on Member States. See e.g. B. Tonra, 'Europeanization' in K. E. Jørgensen et al. (eds.), *The SAGE Handbook of European Foreign Policy*, 2 vols. (Sage, 2015), I, 184–96.

[14] Bergmann and Niemann, 'Theories of European Integration' (above n. 10), 176.

aim is to note shifts and developments on the basis of new legal provisions (or new interpretations of provisions). We compare competences and confront actors with the legal choices they made. We look for (in)consistencies and try to make sense of paradoxical provisions. In doing so, we indeed have an internal as well as an external perspective: internally, more integration would mean that CFSP has become more similar to other (more supranational) policies (section III below); externally, integration would be triggered by the simple need for the Union to act in a more unified and coherent fashion (section IV). First of all, however, we will reassess the position of CFSP within the EU on the basis of the current treaty provisions (section II).

II   The Current Position of CFSP in the EU Treaties

A   *The Purpose of CFSP*

So, let's see what we are dealing with. The first reference to CFSP can be found in the preamble to the Treaty on European Union (TEU), where the signatories state to be:

> RESOLVED to implement a common foreign and security policy including the progressive framing of a common defence policy, which might lead to a common defence in accordance with the provisions of Article 42, thereby reinforcing the European identity and its independence in order to promote peace, security and progress in Europe and in the world.

Three key elements are already evidenced by this statement: (i) the signatory states not only aim at implementing CFSP, they also intend to work on the further development of a common defence (policy); (ii) all of this is meant to promote peace, security and progress, both in Europe and in the rest of the world; (iii) the European identity and its independence will be reinforced through the implementation of CFSP and the further development of a common defence policy. The latter is particularly important for the narrative of the present contribution: CFSP is important to reinforce the European identity.

At the same time CFSP is a *foreign* policy and its main objectives relate not to the EU itself but to the rest of the world, while stimulated by the EU's own integration. Article 5(3) TEU phrases this as follows:

> In its relations with the wider world, the Union shall uphold and promote its values and interests and contribute to the protection of its citizens. It shall contribute to peace, security, the sustainable development of the Earth, solidarity and mutual respect among peoples, free and fair trade, eradication of poverty and the protection of human rights, in particular

the rights of the child, as well as to the strict observance and the development of international law, including respect for the principles of the United Nations Charter.

And, Article 21(1) TEU even more extensively provides:

> The Union's action on the international scene shall be guided by the principles which have inspired its own creation, development and enlargement, and which it seeks to advance in the wider world: democracy, the rule of law, the universality and indivisibility of human rights and fundamental freedoms, respect for human dignity, the principles of equality and solidarity, and respect for the principles of the United Nations Charter and international law.
>
> The Union shall seek to develop relations and build partnerships with third countries, and international, regional or global organisations which share the principles referred to in the first subparagraph. It shall promote multilateral solutions to common problems, in particular in the framework of the United Nations.

Specific references to CFSP are absent. Indeed, the 2009 Lisbon Treaty consolidated the Union's external relations objectives and CFSP is just one of the means to attain these objectives. The requirement of consistency in Article 21(3) TEU is meant to prevent a fragmentation of the Union's external action (see below).

Zooming in on the objectives (Article 21(2) TEU) reveals their extraordinarily broad scope. Aside from perhaps issuing a declaration of war, there is very little that does not fall within the purview of these objectives:

> The Union shall define and pursue common policies and actions, and shall work for a high degree of cooperation in all fields of international relations, in order to:
>
> (a) safeguard its values, fundamental interests, security, independence and integrity;
> (b) consolidate and support democracy, the rule of law, human rights and the principles of international law;
> (c) preserve peace, prevent conflicts and strengthen international security, in accordance with the purposes and principles of the United Nations Charter, with the principles of the Helsinki Final Act and with the aims of the Charter of Paris, including those relating to external borders;
> (d) foster the sustainable economic, social and environmental development of developing countries, with the primary aim of eradicating poverty;
> (e) encourage the integration of all countries into the world economy, including through the progressive abolition of restrictions on international trade;
> (f) help develop international measures to preserve and improve the quality of the environment and the sustainable management of global natural resources, in order to ensure sustainable development;

(g) assist populations, countries and regions confronting natural or man-made disasters; and

(h) promote an international system based on stronger multilateral coop-eration and good global governance.

Articles 3(5) and 21 TEU give a double response to the question as to what kind of international actor the EU is, and how it relates to the international order. On the one hand, there is the substantive answer. These provisions in the TEU impose substantive requirements on EU international relations by stating that there are certain fundamental objectives which shall guide its internal and external policies.[15] On the other hand, these provisions also impose a strong methodological imperative upon EU international action: it must pursue its action through a multilateral approach based on the rule of law. Yet, no clear link is made between these objectives and the means to attain them; but CFSP is clearly needed to make this work.

B Consistency Between CFSP and Other External Relations Policies

Article 21 TEU is the first provision in Title V that was invented to inte-grate (but also still partly separate) the EU's external relations. The title is named 'General provisions on the Union's external action and specific provisions on the Common Foreign and Security Policy'. One could argue that the first Chapter (called 'General Provisions of the Union's External Action') is indeed general in the sense that it aims to regulate EU external relations in general, whereas Chapter 2 entails 'Specific Provisions on the Common Foreign and Security Policy'. Yet, Article 21(3) TEU establishes a legal connection between the different parts. Indeed, it imposes a binding obligation of coherence in EU external relations, illustrating that coher-ence is not merely an academic notion but a tangible legal principle of EU primary law. It provides that:

> The Union shall ensure consistency between the different areas of its exter-nal action and between these and its other policies. The Council and the Commission, assisted by the High Representative of the Union for Foreign Affairs and Security Policy, shall ensure that consistency and shall cooper-ate to that effect.

---

[15] See also J. Larik, 'Entrenching Global Governance: The EU's Constitutional Objectives Caught between a Sanguine World View and a Daunting Reality' in B. Van Vooren et al. (eds.), *The Legal Dimension of Global Governance, What Role for the EU?* (Oxford University Press, 2013), 7–22.

Indeed, paragraph 3 of Article 21 TEU can be considered the *lex generalis* coherence obligation in EU external relations. Thus, what this paragraph does is connect the list of policy objectives in 21(2) to each other, and to the functioning of pertinent legal principles, by imposing a legally binding obligation of coherence between all EU internal and external policies which must pursue them. Specifically through the case law of the Court of Justice, the obligation of loyalty has become directly connected to the objective of 'ensur[ing] the coherence and consistency of the action and its [the Union's] international representation'.[16]

The TEU contains four other provisions which pertain to coherence in its material and institutional dimensions. All in their own way, these provisions strengthen the relationship (or in fact, the integration) between CFSP and other external relations policies.[17]

- Article 13(1) TEU imposes coherence as one of the overarching purposes for the activities of the EU institutions: 'The Union shall have an institutional framework which shall aim to promote its values, advance its objectives, serve its interests, those of its citizens and those of the Member States, and ensure the consistency, effectiveness and continuity of its policies and actions.' The explicit reference to the Member States can be read as meaning that it concerns not merely coherence between policies and action of the Union itself (horizontal), but also between that of the Union and its Member States (vertical).
- Article 16(6) TEU imposes on the General Affairs Council an obligation of substantive policy coherence between the work of the different Councils, and a specific obligation for the Foreign Affairs Council since it 'shall elaborate the Union's external action on the basis of strategic guidelines laid down by the European Council and ensure that the Union's action is consistent'.
- Article 18(4) TEU imposes a specific coherence obligation on the EU High Representative (HR) with a strong institutional dimension, as it relates to the connection between the work of the HR and that of the Commission: 'The High Representative shall be one of the Vice-Presidents of the Commission. He shall ensure the consistency of the

---

16 See e.g. Case C-266/03, *Commission* v. *Luxembourg* [2005] ECR I-4805, para. 60, and Case C-476/98, *Commission* v. *Germany* [2002] ECR I-9855, para. 66. See for a recent analysis of the principle of consistency, M. Estrada Cañamares, '"Building Coherent Responses": Coherence as a Structural Principle in EU External Relations' in M. Cremona (ed.), *Structural Principles in EU External Relations Law* (Hart, 2018), 244–62.

17 This analysis of the provisions on coherence and consistency is partly based on Chapter 1 of Van Vooren and Wessel, *EU External Relations Law* (above n. 5).

Union's external action. He shall be responsible within the Commission for responsibilities incumbent on it in external relations and for coordinating other aspects of the Union's external action.'

– Article 26(2) TEU contains an obligation of substantive policy coherence specifically for the EU's Common Foreign and Security Policy: 'The Council and the High Representative of the Union for Foreign Affairs and Security Policy shall ensure the unity, consistency and effectiveness of action by the Union.'

Furthermore, in the Treaty on the Functioning of the Union (TFEU), we find coherence obligations that do not relate to the institutions as such, but are predominantly substantive in the nature of their requirement.

– Article 7 TFEU is found in Title II of that treaty, under the heading 'Provisions Having General Application' and states that: 'The Union shall ensure consistency between its policies and activities, taking all of its objectives into account and in accordance with the principle of conferral of powers.' Because this article is of general application and not specific to EU external relations, it must be read as requiring substantive, positive coherence between EU internal policies and EU external policies.
– Part Five of the Treaty on the Functioning of the Union concerns 'external action by the Union'. Article 205 TFEU is the first and general provision of that Title and reads that 'the Union's action on the international scene, pursuant to this Part, shall be guided by the principles, pursue the objectives and be conducted in accordance with the general provisions laid down in Chapter 1 of Title V of the Treaty on European Union'. This article is a cross-reference to Articles 21 and 22 TEU and has a triple consequence. First, any of the external competences listed in Part Five of the TFEU (common commercial policy, development policy, and so on) must be conducted in line with the coherence obligation of Article 21(3) TEU. Second, any of these competences must all pursue the objectives listed in Article 21(2) TEU. Third, where Article 22(1) TEU states that 'the European Council shall identify the strategic interests and objectives of the Union', Article 205 TFEU is yet another confirmation that this EU institution is given the principal role in ensuring overarching coherence across all EU external policies.

In three competence-specific articles we also find obligations to maintain coherence. In Article 208(1) TFEU concerning development policy there is an obligation that it pursue 'the principles and objectives of the Union's external action' (e.g. an obligation of horizontal coherence with Articles

3(5) TEU and 21(2) TEU), and a vertical obligation of coherence stating that 'the Union's development cooperation policy and that of the Member States complement and reinforce each other'. In Article 212 TFEU concerning economic, financial and technical cooperation with third countries we find similar obligations: one of horizontal coherence but this time with EU development policy, and one of vertical coherence with Member States' respective policies. Finally, Article 214 TFEU concerning humanitarian aid, is formulated in similar terms: a general reference to the EU's principles and objectives in external relations, and the need for EU measures and those of Member States to 'complement and reinforce each other'. This is thus a reciprocal obligation of substantive, positive, policy coherence.

All in all, by simply reading the Treaties one can only conclude that everything is geared towards an integration of the overall external relations regime, of which CFSP forms an integral part.

C   Legal Basis and Competence

However, this conclusion brings us to the question of the attention that is also paid by treaty provisions to separating CFSP from all other Union policies. The fact that CFSP – including Common Security and Defence Policy (CSDP) – is the only policy area, with perhaps one exception,[18] that is not regulated by the TFEU but by the TEU may be interpreted differently. The TFEU is usually considered to be the operational treaty, whereas the TEU may be seen as the constitutional foundation, providing the legal-constitutional framework for the EU's actions. Perhaps ironically, this would allude to a 'higher' or 'more important' status of CFSP norms as they seem to form part of the constitutional set-up of the Union. At the same time, we know that it owes this special position to fears by certain Member States that aligning CFSP with some former Community policies could make an end to what they perceive as the 'intergovernmental' nature of CFSP.[19]

---

[18]   Although not formally framed as a 'policy area', Article 8 TEU forms the basis of the EU's 'neighbourhood policy'.

[19]   The intergovernmental nature is often related to Declarations 13 and 14 annexed to the Treaties, which indicate that CFSP does not affect 'the responsibilities of the Member States, as they currently exist for the formulation and conduct of their foreign policy nor of their national representation in third countries and international organizations' and that it 'will not affect the existing legal basis, responsibilities, and powers of each Member State in relation to the formulation and conduct of its foreign policy, its national diplomatic service, relations with third countries and participation in international organizations'. Yet, a close

Indeed, the textbook classification of CFSP as 'intergovernmental' often conceals the fact that CFSP decisions are taken by the Union – following strict rules and procedures – and not by the Member States. Article 2(4) TFEU clearly refers to CFSP as an EU competence:

> The Union shall have competence, in accordance with the provisions of the Treaty on European Union, to define and implement a common foreign and security policy, including the progressive framing of a common defence policy.

CFSP is not the sum of national foreign policy issues; CFSP is primarily an EU policy. And, in the words of Keukeleire and Delreux:

> it is questionable whether EU foreign policy must automatically – and on all levels – be seen as a substitute or as a transposition of individual Member States' foreign policies to the European level. The specificity and added value of an EU foreign policy can be precisely that it emphasizes different issues, tackling different sorts of problems, pursuing different objectives through alternative methods, and ultimately assuming a form and content that differs from the foreign policy of its individual members.[20]

Yet, the legal basis to be used by the Union to adopt CFSP Decisions is to be found in the 'Specific Provisions on the Common Foreign and Security Policy' (Chapter 2 of Title V TEU). The intention does not seem to be to set CFSP aside from other policies; the term 'specific provisions' is rather to be read in relation to the 'general provisions' on external relations (Chapter 1 of Title V TEU). In fact, also as far as external relations are concerned, the TEU and TFEU are clearly linked. Part V of the TFEU (bearing the very general title 'The Union's External Action') starts with a reference in Art. 205 to Title V of the TEU:

> The Union's action on the international scene, pursuant to this Part, shall be guided by the principles, pursue the objectives and be conducted in accordance with the general provisions laid down in Chapter 1 of Title V of the Treaty on European Union.

So, Union action *pursuant to this Part* of the TFEU (which includes the Common Commercial Policy, Development Cooperation, Economic, Financial and Technical Cooperation with Third States, Humanitarian Aid, Restrictive Measures, International Agreements, the Union's Relations with International Organisations and Third Countries and Union Delegations,

---

reading of these Declarations reveals that they mainly state the obvious and repeat rules that are also reflected in the general principle of conferral.

[20] S. Keukeleire and T. Delreux, *The Foreign Policy of the European Union* (Palgrave Macmillan, 2014), 18–19.

as well as the Solidarity Clause) *shall be conducted in accordance with* the general provisions on external action in the TEU. This seems to indicate a subordination of this TFEU Part to general TEU provisions on external action. At least it reveals the intention of the treaty legislator to consolidate the different provisions on external action, despite the positioning of CFSP in the TEU. At the same time, it underlines that CFSP may be placed in the TEU, but that the general provisions on EU external relations are also put there. Title V of the TEU is therefore presented as the basis for EU external relations, including CFSP.[21]

Another link is made by the general competence of the Union 'to define and implement' CFSP, which is laid down in the TFEU (Article 2(4)) and the more concrete legal bases that can indeed be found in the 'specific provisions' in the TEU. And despite their specificity, action of the Union on the basis of the CFSP provisions is also to be 'conducted in accordance with' the general principles (Article 23 TEU). Unfortunately, the distinction between CFSP and other external action is not made clear by the Treaties. 'The Union's competence in matters of common foreign and security policy shall cover all areas of foreign policy and all questions relating to the Union's security, including the progressive framing of a common defence policy that might lead to a common defence' (Article 24(1) TEU). Considering that the TFEU mentions many other areas where the EU has external competences, one will have to conclude that 'foreign policy' is everything that is not covered by other competences. That this is easier said than done will become clear in the next section.

It is well known that CFSP is formed on the basis of 'specific rules and procedures' (Article 24(1) TEU): the exclusion of the use of the 'legislative acts'[22] (Article 23(1) TEU; and thereby the use of the legislative procedure which is the regular decision-making procedure for other Union policies), unanimity rather than qualified majority voting (QMV) as the default voting rule,[23] the 'specific role of the European Parliament and of

---

[21] All of this is again confirmed by Article 24(2) TEU: '*Within the framework of the principles and objectives of its external action*, the Union shall conduct, define and implement a common foreign and security policy ... '. Emphasis added.

[22] Note that this does not imply that CFSP acts are not binding on Member States. See R. A. Wessel, 'Resisting Legal Facts: Are CFSP Norms as Soft as They Seem?' (2015) 20 *European Foreign Affairs Review* 123–45.

[23] Unanimity continues to form the basis for CFSP decisions, 'except where the Treaties provide otherwise' (Article 24(1) TEU). In that respect it is interesting to point to the fact that apart from the previously existing possibilities for QMV under CFSP, it is now possible for the Council to adopt measures on this basis following a proposal submitted by the High Representative (Article 31(2) TEU). Such proposals should, however, follow a specific

the Commission' and the fact that 'the Court of Justice of the European Union shall not have jurisdiction with respect to these provisions, with the exception of its jurisdiction to monitor compliance with Article 40 of this Treaty [decision on the legal basis] and to review the legality of certain decisions as provided for by the second paragraph of Article 275 [restrictive measures against natural or legal persons]'.

Yet, many policy areas have their own rules and exceptions. The fact that CFSP – to accommodate the strong political preferences of certain Member States – was placed in another treaty is clearly compensated by the many links and cross-references between the Treaties. And, despite their public presentation of CFSP as an intergovernmental form of cooperation, the Member States drafted the Treaties as to allow for a far-reaching integration of foreign policy into the Union's external relations regime; thereby allowing for a further integration dynamic on the basis of the Union's external action.

III   Internal Pressures Towards Integration

This integration dynamic is first of all set in motion by internal developments triggered by the treaty provisions. Thus, the consolidation of EU external policies was not only accompanied but also boosted by a revised role for the Institutions. At the same time the Court of Justice seems to push for a further alignment of CFSP and other policies.

A   A New Institutional Set-Up

Perhaps the most visible body representing the Union's ambitions to consolidate its external relations is the European External Action Service (EEAS). Much has been written on the status and position of this new body.[24] The

---

request by the European Council, in which, of course, Member States can foreclose the use of QMV. In addition, QMV may be used for setting up, financing and administering a start-up fund to ensure rapid access to appropriations in the Union budget for urgent financing of CFSP initiatives (Article 41(3) TEU). This start-up fund may be used for crisis management initiatives as well, which would potentially speed up the financing process of operations. In addition, QMV may be extended to new areas on the basis of a decision by the European Council (Article 31(3) TEU).

[24] See M. Gatti, *European External Action Service: Promoting Coherence through Autonomy and Coordination* (Brill|Nijhoff, 2016). And earlier e.g. B. Van Vooren, 'A Legal Institutional Perspective on the European External Action Service' (2011) 48 *CML Rev* 475–502, 500–1; as well as G. de Baere and R. A. Wessel, 'EU Law and the EEAS: Of Complex Competences and Constitutional Consequences' in J. Bátora and D. Spence (eds.), *The European External*

EEAS, mentioned only in Article 27(3) TEU, was formally established by a Council Decision in 2010, and was officially launched in January 2011.[25] Its set-up is ambiguous. In a way, the EEAS can be seen as a continuation of a process that defined the former EPC and the establishment of the early CFSP: a decades-old struggle of the Union seeking to project a strong, coherent voice on the international scene; counterbalanced by the Member States' wish to retain control over various aspects of international relations. At the same time the EEAS was created to overcome this fragmentation. The idea is to bring together policy preparation and implementation on external relations into one new body, under the auspices of the High Representative for CFSP. In terms of policy fields covered by the new EEAS, the current structure remains a typical EU-type compromise. It is *not* an EU institution, which significantly constrains its power to legally influence EU external decision-making. Furthermore, the EU external action service has no say whatsoever in the Common Commercial Policy, where the Commission remains very firmly in the driver's seat. Development policy is more opaque, where both the EEAS and the Commission have been given a role in the policy-making process. Similarly, in the domain of EU external energy policy, the EEAS has 'some kind' of role to play, but disagreement persists as to its exact relationship with the European Commission.

The preamble of the Council Decision reaffirms that coherence remains the final objective of setting up the EEAS, and does this by copying and pasting the text of Article 21(3) second paragraph TEU (see above). In all practical terms the EEAS may be seen as the EU's Foreign Ministry, which does not at all deny that other 'Ministries' (the Commission's Directorates General) may engage in their own external relations. Article 2 of the EEAS Decision indicates that CFSP may be its core business, but also hints at a more general role in EU external relations:

> (1) The EEAS shall support the High Representative in fulfilling his/her mandates as outlined, notably, in Articles 18 and 27 TEU:
> – in fulfilling his/her mandate to conduct the Common Foreign and Security Policy ('CFSP') of the European Union, including the

---

Action Service: European Diplomacy Post-Westphalia (Palgrave MacMillan, 2015), 175–93. A thorough legal analysis was done by S. Blockmans et al., *EEAS 2.0: A Legal Commentary on Council Decision 2010/427/EU Establishing the Organisation and Functioning of the European External Action Service*, ed. S. Blockmans and C. Hillion (CEPS/Sieps/EUI, 2013); and by the same authors *European External Action Service 2.0: Recommendations for the 2013 EEAS Review* (CEPS/Sieps/EUI, 2013).

25 Council Decision 2010/427/EU of 26 July 2010 establishing the organisation and functioning of the European External Action Service, OJ 2010 L 201/30.

Common Security and Defence Policy ('CSDP'), to contribute by his/her proposals to the development of that policy, which he/she shall carry out as mandated by the Council and to ensure the consistency of the Union's external action,

- in his/her capacity as President of the Foreign Affairs Council, without prejudice to the normal tasks of the General Secretariat of the Council,
- in his/her capacity as Vice-President of the Commission for fulfilling within the Commission the responsibilities incumbent on it in external relations, and in coordinating other aspects of the Union's external action, without prejudice to the normal tasks of the services of the Commission.

(2) The EEAS shall assist the President of the European Council, the President of the Commission, and the Commission in the exercise of their respective functions in the area of external relations.

Deep disagreement existed throughout the negotiation process on the EEAS's position in the EU institutional set-up. On the one hand, there was Member State agreement that 'the EEAS should be a service of a *sui generis* nature separate from the Commission and the Council Secretariat',[26] while Parliament's opinion was that it should be connected to the Commission. The final result laid down in Article 1(2) reveals that Parliament has lost out in the final compromise. Article 1 of the EEAS Decision provides that the EEAS is 'functionally autonomous' and 'separate' from the Council Secretariat and Commission. Given the negotiation history to the EEAS ('equidistance'), these notions should be interpreted as meaning that in supporting the High Representative, the EU diplomatic service does not take instructions from the Council or the Commission. Its instructions come from the *office of* the High Representative,[27] who is in her turn accountable to the EU institutions proper – notably also the Parliament. The EEAS is certainly part of a 'command structure' which runs vertically via the High Representative, then through to the Council and up to the European Council, with a strand of accountability connecting it to Parliament. However, the EEAS is horizontally not an institutional participant in the EU's institutional balance, or part of an Institution itself.[28]

---

[26] October 2009 Presidency Report, DOC 14930/09, 6.

[27] Heads of the EU delegations can also receive instructions from the Commission 'in areas where they exercise powers conferred upon it by the Treaties'. Otherwise the delegations only receive instructions from the High Representative (Article 5(3) EEAS Decision).

[28] See more extensively van Vooren, 'A Legal Institutional Perspective on the European External Action Service' (above n. 24); and De Baere and Wessel, 'EU Law and the EEAS' (above n. 24).

An interesting institutional integrationist development took place with the creation of the 'Union delegations'. On the basis of Article 221(1) TFEU (!) 'Union delegations in third countries and at international organisations shall represent the Union.' In the absence of any further description in the Treaties, their mandate is based on Article 5 of the EEAS Decision and turns them into an integral part of the EEAS,[29] with the Head of Delegation (clearly an EU official appointed by the High Representative, who receives instructions from the High Representative and the Commission) exercising 'authority over all staff in the Delegation, whatever their status, and for all its activities', including the staff members seconded by Member States. Yet, the EEAS is often presented as a CFSP body, whereas Article 221 TFEU indicates that delegations represent the Union as a whole.[30] At the same time the link with the High Representative for Foreign and Security Policy is clear. Article 221(2) TFEU states that 'Union delegations shall be placed under the authority of the High Representative of the Union for Foreign Affairs and Security Policy. They shall act in close cooperation with Member States' diplomatic and consular missions.' The 'HR/VP' in turn combines her function with the one of Vice-President of the Commission and Chairperson of the Foreign Affairs Council (Article 18 TEU). This is referred to as 'triple-hatting', and is again hoped to support attaining coherence in EU external relations (Article 21(3) TEU).

Significantly, a study commissioned by the European Parliament found that most stakeholders now agree that the *sui generis* positioning of the EEAS was a mistake: the Commission perceives the construction of the EEAS as a loss of power that ought to be regained or protected, while Member States believe the priorities set out by the EEAS often compete

---

[29] Yet, see the judgment of the General Court in the *Elti* v. *EU Delegation to Montenegro* case, where it argued that 'the legal status of the Union Delegations is characterised by a two-fold organic and functional dependence with respect to the EEAS and the Commission' (Case T-395/11, para. 46). In a similar case on the former Commission delegations, the Court came to the same conclusion (Case T-264/09, *Technoprocess* v. *Commission and EU Delegation to Morocco*, ECLI:EU:T:2011:319, para. 70). While different interpretations are possible, at least the Court underlined that in order for the delegations to represent the Union as a whole, they need to work both for the EEAS and the Commission.

[30] See also Article 5(7) EEAS Decision, indicating that the delegation 'shall have the capacity to respond to the needs of other institutions of the Union, in particular the European Parliament'.

with their own national priorities.[31] The hybrid position of the EEAS, and in particular the position of the HR/VP, was put on the agenda again at the start of the new Juncker Commission in November 2014. Juncker preferred to have the new High Representative, Federica Mogherini, as fully operational Vice-President. 'Mogherini's symbolic decision to install her office in the Berlaymont building, the appointment of Stefano Manservisi, an experienced hand at the Commission, as her Chef de Cabinet, and the recruitment of half of her cabinet from Commission staff, have served her well in striving to attain that goal.'[32] Yet, it is questionable whether this is the best solution. While it will still be possible for the High Representative to use her EEAS office for her HR functions, her closest staff will be in the Berlaymont Building and it will remain difficult to clearly separate the issues, possibly triggering member states that are particularly sensitive on the issue of Commission involvement in CFSP to open a new battle front. Thus, while a closer entanglement between EEAS and other external policies is to be welcomed from a consistency perspective, time will tell whether this somewhat bold move did not come too soon. In any case, recent studies reveal that the role of the Commission in relation to foreign policy is often underestimated.

This is nevertheless one of the best examples of the internal dynamics pushing towards a further 'normalisation' of CFSP. While the Commission undeniably retained control over (important) parts of the EU's external relations, the HR/VP does function as a bridge-builder as she is forced to align the different external policies.[33] At the same time, since the entry into force of the Treaty of Lisbon, a new interinstitutional agreement between the European Parliament and the Commission foresees the involvement of the former by the latter in the CFSP:[34] 'Within its competences, the Commission shall take measures to better involve Parliament in such a way as to take Parliament's views into account as far as possible in the area

---

[31] J. Wouters, et al., *The Organisation and Functioning of the European External Action Service: Achievements, Challenges and Opportunities* (European Parliament, Directorate-General for External Policies of the Union, Directorate B, Policy Department, 2013), 93.

[32] S. Blockmans and F. S. Montesano, 'Mogherini's First 100 Days: Not the Quiet Diplomat', CEPS Commentary, 12 February 2015.

[33] See for a recent evaluation of the function post-Lisbon N. Herwig, 'The High Representative of the Union: The Quest for Leadership in EU Foreign Policy' in J. Bátora and D. Spence (eds.), *The European External Action Service: European Diplomacy Post-Westphalia* (Palgrave MacMillan, 2015), 87–104.

[34] Cardwell, 'On "Ring-Fencing"' (above n. 1), 459.

of the Common Foreign and Security Policy.'[35] 'Within its competences':
yet, the traditional view is that these competences are extremely limited
in relation to CFSP. Again, however, this picture needs to be nuanced. The
limited formal competences of the Commission in the CFSP area have not
led to the Commission being completely passive in this field. From the outset, the Commission has been represented at all levels in the CFSP structures. Within the negotiating process in the Council, the Commission is
a full negotiating partner as in any working party or Committee (including the Political and Security Committee(PSC)). The President of the
Commission attends European Council and other ad hoc meetings. The
Commission is in fact the 'twenty-ninth Member State' at the table; it
safeguards the *acquis communautaire* and ensures the consistency of the
action of the Union other than CFSP. In the implementation of CFSP
Decisions the Commission's role is however formally non-existent as delegation of executive competences from the Council to the Commission
is prevented by the fact that CFSP acts are not legislative acts (Article 29
TFEU). Nevertheless, practice from the outset showed an involvement of
the Commission in the implementation of CFSP Decisions, not in the least
because other measures were in some cases essential for an effective implementation of CFSP policy decisions. Some studies even reveal a considerable influence of the Commission on one of the most sensitive dimensions
of CFSP, the security and defence policy and the military missions.[36]
Regardless of these competences and practices of the Commission under
CFSP, it is not difficult to conclude that this institution is nowhere near the
pivotal position it occupies in the other areas of the Union. Although it is
not formally excluded by Article 17 TEU, the Commission lacks its classic
function as a watchdog under CFSP. The absence of an exclusive right of
initiative also denies the Commission another indispensable role it has in
other areas.

B   Legal Bases

Perhaps the best example of a necessary combination of CFSP and other
EU rules is formed by the regulation of restrictive measures. In fact,

---

[35] Framework Agreement on Relations between the European Parliament and the European
Commission (2010) 20 November 2010, OJ 304/47, Article 10.
[36] M. Riddervold, '(Not) in the Hands of the Member States: How the European Commission
Influences EU Security and Defence Policies' (2015) 54(2) *JCMS* 353–69.

legislative decisions taken by the Union in this area depend on a prior CFSP decision. Article 251(1) TFEU provides:

> Where a decision, adopted in accordance with Chapter 2 of Title V of the Treaty on European Union [the provisions on CFSP], provides for the interruption or reduction, in part or completely, of economic and financial relations with one or more third countries, the Council, acting by a qualified majority on a joint proposal from the High Representative of the Union for Foreign Affairs and Security Policy and the Commission, shall adopt the necessary measures. It shall inform the European Parliament thereof.

Paragraph 2 adds that this procedure is also to be followed whenever a CFSP decision provides for restrictive measures against natural or legal persons and groups or non-state entities.

While other CFSP decisions do not automatically affect the creation of Union legislative acts, it remains clear that they form part of the Union's legal order and that all decisions related to a certain external policy are to be interpreted taking their content into account and irrespective of their place in the Treaties (see also the rules on consistency referred to above). Apart from the example of restrictive measures, which present a CFSP decision as the foundation for subsequent action, no automatic hierarchy exists. Article 40 TEU simply provides:

> The implementation of the common foreign and security policy shall not affect the application of the procedures and the extent of the powers of the institutions laid down by the Treaties for the exercise of the Union competences referred to in Articles 3 to 6 of the Treaty on the Functioning of the European Union.
>
> Similarly, the implementation of the policies listed in those Articles shall not affect the application of the procedures and the extent of the powers of the institutions laid down by the Treaties for the exercise of the Union competences under this Chapter.

In other words, in adopting CFSP decisions the Council should be aware of the external policies in the TFEU, and vice versa. Despite its 'balanced' approach, Article 40 implies that foreign policy measures are excluded once they would interfere with exclusive powers of the Union, for instance in the area of Common Commercial Policy (CCP). This may seriously limit the freedom of the Member States in the area of restrictive measures (above) or the export of 'dual goods' (commodities which can also have a military application).[37] The current text of Article 40 TEU forces

---

[37] Council Regulation 1334/2000/EC setting up a Community regime for the control of exports of dual-use items and technology, OJ 2000 L 159/1; in the meantime replaced by Council Regulation 428/2009/EC setting up a Community regime for the control of

the Court to take a different view on the relationship between CFSP and other areas of external action. No longer should an automatic preference be given to a non-CFSP legal basis whenever this is possible. One could argue that Article 40 is merely a confirmation of the principle of consistency, now that it no longer establishes a hierarchy between CFSP and other policies.[38] At the same time, the fact that Article 40 does not really add anything to the treaty regime may be interpreted as confirming a separate status of CFSP, which again underlines what has been termed the 'integration–delimitation paradox', which from the outset has characterised the position of CFSP in the treaties.[39]

Despite the fact that a combination of legal bases in CFSP and other external policies remains difficult because of the diverging decision-making procedures and instruments,[40] an integrationist pull can again come from the Union's unified external objectives. Indeed, as argued by Merket on the basis of a study of the relationship between development and security policy, 'Objectives of conflict prevention, crisis management, reconciliation and post-conflict reconstruction cannot be assigned to one or the other EU competence, forging an indissoluble link between development cooperation and the CFSP.'[41] Yet, obviously it would have been easier when CFSP and other policies could be combined in single legal instruments.

C   Integrationist Case Law?

Whereas the consistency requirement hints at a combination of legal bases, the different CFSP procedures and instruments preclude that. In fact,

---

exports, transfer, brokering and transit of dual-use items, OJ 2009 L 134/1. Exception was only made for certain services considered not to come under the CCP competence. For these services (again) a CFSP measure was adopted: Council Joint Action 2000/401/CFSP concerning the control of technical assistance related to certain military end-uses, OJ 2000 L 159/216.

[38] Pre-Lisbon, Article 47 TEU contained the clear rule that 'nothing in the TEU shall affect the EC Treaty'. See also Case C-91/05, *Commission* v. *Council (Small Arms/ECOWAS)* [2008] ECR I-3651. See further: C. Hillion and R. A. Wessel, 'Competence Distribution in EU External Relations after ECOWAS: Clarification or Continued Fuzziness?' (2009) 46 *CML Rev* 551–86.

[39] H. Merket, 'The European Union and the Security-Development Nexus: Bridging the Legal Divide', PhD thesis, defended at the University of Ghent, Belgium, 2015; see on this issue in particular Chapter 2.

[40] See e.g. Joined Cases C-164–5/97, *Parliament* v. *Council*, ECLI:EU:C:1999:99, para. 14, in which the Court held that no combination of legal bases is possible 'where the procedures laid down for each legal basis are incompatible with each other'.

[41] Merket, 'The European Union and the Security-Development Nexus' (above n. 39), Chapter 3.

the combination of the different CFSP procedures/instruments and the requirement of consistency seems to form a key challenge for the Court of Justice.[42] The role of the Court in relation to CFSP has been subject to legal analysis over the years,[43] yet new case law has more recently led to many more analyses.[44] A clear example is Hillion, who convincingly argued that the view that the Court is not competent at all in the area of CFSP can no longer be upheld. He summarised the areas in which the Lisbon Treaty has created a competence for the Court in relation to CFSP as follows:

> First, it has made it possible for the Court, albeit within limits, to *exercise judicial control* with regard to certain CFSP acts, thus abolishing the policy's conventional immunity from judicial supervision. Second, it has recalibrated the Court's role in *patrolling the borders* between EU (external) competences based on the TFEU and the CFSP, turning it into the guarantor of

---

[42] Arguments in this section are further developed in Wessel, 'Resisting Legal Facts' (above n. 22).

[43] S. Griller, 'The Court of Justice and the Common Foreign and Security Policy' in A. Rosas et al. (eds.), *Court of Justice of the European Union – Cour de Justice de l'Union Européenne, The Court of Justice and the Construction of Europe: Analyses and Perspectives on Sixty Years of Case-law – La Cour de Justice et la Construction de l'Europe: Analyses et Perspectives de Soixante Ans de Jurisprudence* (T. M. C. Asser Press, 2013), 675–92; G. de Baere and P. Koutrakos, 'The Interactions between the Legislature and the Judiciary in EU External Relations' in P. Syrpis (ed.), *The Judiciary, the Legislature and the EU Internal Market* (Cambridge University Press, 2012), 243–73; L. Saltinyté, 'Jurisdiction of the European Court of Justice over Issues Relating to the Common Foreign and Security Policy under the Lisbon Treaty' (2010) 119 *Jurisprudence* 261; A. Hinarejos, *Judicial Control in the European Union: Reforming Jurisdiction in the Intergovernmental Pillars* (Oxford University Press, 2009).

[44] See, most notably C. Hillion, 'A Powerless Court? The European Court of Justice and the Common Foreign and Security Policy' in M. Cremona and A. Thies (eds.), *The European Court of Justice and External Relations Law* (Hart, 2014), 44–70; C. Hillion, 'Decentralised Integration? Fundamental Rights Protection in the EU Common Foreign and Security Policy' (2016) *European Papers* 55; C. Eckes, 'Common Foreign and Security Policy: The Consequences of the Court's Extended Jurisdiction' (2016) 22 *ELJ* 492; G. Butler, 'The Coming of Age of the Court's Jurisdiction in the Common Foreign and Security Policy' (2017) 13 *ECLR* 673; M. Cremona, 'Effective Judicial Review is of the Essence of the Rule of Law: Challenging Common Foreign and Security Policy Measures before the Court of Justice' (2017) *European Papers* 671; P. Koutrakos, 'Judicial Review in the EU's Common Foreign And Security Policy' (2018) 67 *International and Comparative Law Quarterly* 1; C. Hillion and R. A. Wessel, 'The Good, the Bad and the Ugly: Three Levels of Judicial Control over the CFSP' in S. Blockmans and P. Koutrakos (eds.), *Research Handbook on EU Common Foreign and Security Policy* (Edward Elgar, 2018); and J. Heliskoski, 'Made in Luxembourg: the Fabrication of the Law on Jurisdiction of the Court of Justice of the European Union in the Field of the Common Foreign and Security Policy' (2018) *Europe and the World: A Law Review* (forthcoming).

the latter's integrity. Third, the Treaty has generalized the Court's capacity to *enforce the principles underpinning the Union's legal order.*[45]

This role of the Court should not be unexpected, given the intertwining of CFSP and other external Union policies – in particular through the principle of consistency referred to above. This would also explain the major change initiated by the Lisbon Treaty: no longer is the Court's role explicitly excluded in relation to CFSP; rather the general rule seems to be that the Court is competent unless its role is excluded in a specific situation.[46]

This leads to a role for the Court in relation to CFSP in different situations.[47] First of all, as we have seen, restrictive measures taken on the basis of CFSP acts against natural or legal persons fall under the scrutiny of the Court (Article 24(1) TEU in conjunction with Articles 275 and 263 TFEU). Second, there is the situation under Article 40 TEU, calling for a balanced choice for either a CFSP or another legal basis of decisions (e.g. trade or development cooperation). In the 2012 Case C-130/10, *European Parliament* v. *Council the Court,* the Court was given a first chance to develop an approach towards the function of Article 40.[48] Being confronted with the question of the appropriate legal basis for 'restrictive measures directed against certain persons and entities associated with Usama bin Laden, the Al-Qaeda network and the Taliban',[49] the Court held that Article 215 TFEU (following a previous CFSP decision) rather than Article 75 TFEU (in the Area of Freedom, Security and Justice (AFSJ)) was the correct choice, despite the limited role of the European Parliament in relation to the CFSP/Article 215 procedure. The context of peace and security proved to be decisive for the Court's conclusion. The Court did not shy away from referring to CFSP provisions as well and seemed to focus on the distinction between internal policies and external action.[50]

---

[45] C. Hillion, 'A Powerless Court?' (above n. 44).

[46] Hinarejos, *Judicial Control in the European Union* (above n. 43), 150.

[47] See more extensively and for many case law references Hillion, 'A Powerless Court?' (above n. 44).

[48] Case C-130/10, *Parliament* v. *Council,* ECLI:EU:C:2012:472.

[49] Council Regulation (EU) No. 1286/2009 of 22 December 2009 amending Regulation (EC) No. 881/2002 imposing certain specific restrictive measures directed against certain persons and entities associated with Usama bin Laden, the Al-Qaeda network and the Taliban, OJEU L 346/42 (2010).

[50] Cf. Hillion, 'A Powerless Court?' (above n. 44).

These legal basis questions are relevant for the point this chapter aims to make. As argued by Advocate General Kokott in a similar case:

> At first sight this might all seem a question of technical detail which certainly does not hold the same excitement as many literary treatments of the subject of piracy. Nevertheless, the problem at issue here has considerable political and even constitutional implications because it is necessary to define more sharply the limits of the common foreign and security policy and to delimit it from other European Union policies.[51]

This became clear also when the Court had a chance to revisit the issue in the so-called *Mauritius* case.[52] Here the Court chose context over content and argued that the EU–Mauritius Agreement, concluded in the framework of Operation Atalanta, was rightfully based within CFSP.[53] Yet, this does not limit the application of procedural EU rules and principles. In the words of Peers:

> the Court's ruling means that any CFSP measure can be litigated before it, as long as the legal arguments relate to a procedural rule falling outside the scope of the CFSP provisions of the Treaty (Title V of the TEU). For instance, it arguably means that the Court would have the power to rule on the compatibility of proposed CFSP treaties with EU law, since that jurisdiction is conferred by Article 218 TFEU and not expressly ruled out by Article 275. But such disputes might often include arguments about the substance of the measure concerned (for instance, whether it would breach the EU's human rights obligations), and it could be awkward to distinguish between procedural and substantive issues in practice.[54]

Third, international agreements in the area of CFSP are concluded on the basis of the general EU provisions in this regard (Article 218 TFEU), despite some specific procedural rules, and no exception is made in relation to legality control by the Court.[55] It has further been noted – and in a

---

[51] View of AG Kokott in Case C-263/14, *European Parliament* v. *Council*, ECLI:EU:C:2015: 729, 28 October 2015, para. 4.

[52] Case C-658/11, *European Parliament* v. *Council (Mauritius Agreement)*, ECLI:EU:C:2014:2025. See C. Matera and R. A. Wessel, 'Context or Content? A CFSP or AFSJ Legal Basis for EU International Agreements – Case C-658/11, European Parliament v. Council (Mauritius Agreement)' (2014) *Revista de Derecho Comunitario Europeo* 1047–64.

[53] A similar conclusion was drawn by AG Kokott in the more recent Tanzania case, Case C-263/14, *European Parliament* v. *Council*, ECLI:EU:C:2015:729, 28 October 2015.

[54] S. Peers, 'The CJEU Ensures Basic Democratic and Judicial Accountability of the EU's Foreign Policy', EU Law Analysis, 24 June 2014, http://eulawanalysis.blogspot.nl/2014/06/the-cjeu-ensures-basic-democratic-and.html.

[55] T. Tridimas, 'The European Court of Justice and the Draft Constitution: A Supreme Court for the Union?' in T. Tridimas and P. Nebbia (eds.), *European Union Law for the Twenty-First Century: Rethinking the New Legal Order*, I: *Constitutional and Public Law. External*

way confirmed by the *Mauritius* case – that Article 218(11) does not seem to exclude EU agreements that relate 'exclusively or principally' to the CFSP from the Court's scrutiny.[56] In the end, all international agreements (whether not, wholly or partly) CFSP agreements, are agreements for which the Union as such is internationally formally responsible. It would therefore be difficult to maintain the view that the Court could not scrutinise CFSP international agreements or CFSP parts in agreements. In any case, the Article 40 TEU situation could by itself already cause the Court to assess international agreements in their entirety. In Case C-658/11 on the EU–Mauritius Agreement (and more recently confirmed in Case C-263/14, *Tanzania*), the Court underlined its jurisdiction in relation to CFSP-related agreements where the right of the European Parliament (EP) to be informed is concerned. All cases can be seen as underlining that CFSP is part and parcel of the Union's constitutional set-up.

Fourth, whereas the Court in the *Mauritius* case argued that the simple fact that there is a CFSP relation does not deprive Parliament from its constitutional prerogatives, in another recent case it had already argued that a CFSP link could not form a reason to deny an individual the right to bring a case. And in *H. v. Council* – a case brought by a staff member of the EU Police Mission in Bosnia and Herzegovina (EUPM) – the Court set clear limits to the exclusion of CFSP-related matters from its jurisdiction :

> T]he scope of the limitation, by way of derogation, on the Court's jurisdiction ... cannot be considered to be so extensive as to exclude the jurisdiction of the EU judicature to review acts of staff management relating to staff members seconded by the Member States the purpose of which is to meet the needs of that mission at theatre level, when the EU judicature has, in any event, jurisdiction to review such acts where they concern staff members seconded by the EU institutions.[57]

Overall, the Lisbon Treaty thus seems to have strengthened the Court's role as a Constitutional Court, allowing it to enforce the fundamental EU principles across the board.[58] The Treaties do not provide reasons to

---

Relations (Hart, 2004), 128; G. de Baere, *Constitutional Principles of EU External Relations* (Oxford University Press, 2008), 190.

[56] Hillion, 'A Powerless Court?' (above n. 44); as well as P. Eeckhout, *EU External Relations Law* (Oxford University Press, 2011), 498.

[57] Case C-455/14P *H v. Council*, ECLI:EU:C:2016:569.

[58] Cf. C. Hillion, 'Conferral, Cooperation and Balance in the Institutional Framework of EU External Action' in M. Cremona (ed.), *Structural Principles in EU External Relations Law* (Hart, 2018), 117–74. And earlier: D. M. Curtin and I. F. Dekker, 'The European Union from Maastricht to Lisbon: Institutional and Legal Unity Out of the Shadows' in P. Craig and G. de Búrca (eds.), *The Evolution of EU Law*, 2nd edn (Oxford

exclude CFSP from this holistic approach, simply because it finds its basis in another treaty. On the contrary. What becomes clear is that many of these cases, irrespective of their clear CFSP context, might be about an application of more general rules and principles. Thus, one could say that the Court (merely) underlines a Union-wide application of, inter alia, rules on role of the European Parliament in the procedure to conclude international agreements,[59] legal protection by the different EU and/or national courts,[60] regulations for (seconded) staff to EU bodies and missions,[61] or of rules on public procurement.[62]

The obvious question is whether Article 24(1) TEU does not simply provide an exhaustive list of the powers of the Court in relation to CFSP. After all, the text of that provision is quite clear:

> The Court of Justice of the European Union shall not have jurisdiction with respect to these provisions, with the exception of its jurisdiction to monitor compliance with Article 40 of this Treaty and to review the legality of certain decisions as provided for by the second paragraph of Article 275 of the Treaty on the Functioning of the European Union.

Taking into account our analysis above, the answer seems to be that it remains difficult to see a role for the Court in pure CFSP situations, in which the context of other EU external relations is absent. The most obvious lack of judicial control is apparent when competences and decision-making procedures *within* the CFSP legal order are at stake. This means, for instance, that neither the Commission, nor the EP can commence a procedure before the Court in cases where the Council has ignored their rights and competences in CFSP decision-making procedures in a

---

University Press, 2011), 155–86, 170. This is not to say that the Court did not have this role prior to the Lisbon Treaty; see e.g. D. M. Curtin and R. A. Wessel, 'Rechtseenheid van de Europese Unie? De rol van het Hof van Justitie als constitutionele rechter' (2008) 10 *SEW Tijdschrift voor Europees en economisch recht* 371–8; as well as D. M. Curtin and R. H. van Ooik, 'Een Hof van Justitie van de Europese Unie?' (1999) *SEW Tijdschrift voor Europees en economisch Recht* 24–38.

[59] See also C-130/10, *Parliament* v. *Council*; Case C-658/11, *European Parliament* v. *Council* (*Mauritius Agreement*); and Case C-263/14, *Tanzania*.

[60] Case 72/15, *Rosneft*: 'Since the purpose of the procedure that enables the Court to give preliminary rulings is to ensure that in the interpretation and application of the Treaties the law is observed, in accordance with the duty assigned to the Court under Article 19(1) TEU, it would be contrary to the objectives of that provision and to the principle of effective judicial protection to adopt a strict interpretation of the jurisdiction conferred on the Court by the second paragraph of Article 275 TFEU, to which reference is made by Article 24(1) TEU ...'.

[61] Case C-455/14P, *H* v. *Council*, ECLI:EU:C:2016:569.

[62] Case C-439/13P, *Elitaliana*, ECLI:EU:C:2015:753.

situation where CFSP as a legal basis is not disputed. This brings about a situation in which the interpretation and implementation of the CFSP provisions (including the procedures to be followed) is left entirely to the Council (or perhaps worse: to individual Member States). Remembering their preference for 'intergovernmental' cooperation where CFSP is concerned, it may be understandable that Member States at the time of the negotiations had the strong desire to prevent a body of 'CFSP law' coming into being by way of judicial activism on the part of the European Court of Justice, but it is less understandable that they were also reluctant to allow for judicial control of the *procedural* arrangements they explicitly agreed upon (although it is acknowledged that it may be difficult to unlink procedures and content).

At the same time, given the dynamics of the Lisbon approach to consolidating the EU's external relations, it will be increasingly difficult to deny a link with other policies, allowing the Court to take CFSP-dimensions into account in its assessment of those policies. Arguments can be found why the current treaty regimes also allow for an extended role for domestic courts in relations to CFSP.[63]

Yet, what about the two notions that are often said to differentiate CFSP norms from other EU norms: primacy and direct effect?[64] The question of primacy and direct effect of CFSP norms is far from new. Earlier, it has been contended that these principles cannot be said to be completely alien to the CFSP legal order.[65] Furthermore, Declaration No. 17 on primacy explicitly refers to both the TFEU and the TEU: 'in accordance with well settled case law of the Court of Justice of the European Union, the Treaties and the law adopted by the Union on the basis of the Treaties have primacy over the law of Member States, under the conditions laid down by the said case law'. Obviously, one could argue that there is not so much case law in the area of CFSP; yet this could also be seen as a reference to the *Segi* case in which the Court had already claimed the Union-wide application of primacy.[66]

Indeed, both the legal nature and the normative content of CFSP decisions may form an obligation for Member States to allow for direct effect and primacy in their national legal order in specific cases. This would also

---

[63] See more extensively Hillion and Wessel, 'The Good, the Bad and the Ugly' (above n. 44).

[64] According to the first principle a Court would need to set aside a national rule in case of a conflict with an EU norm; on the basis of the second principle EU norms can in principle be invoked in domestic proceedings.

[65] Gosalbo-Bono, 'Some Reflections of the CFSP Legal Order' (above n. 12).

[66] In a similar vein: Case C-105/03, *Pupino* [2005] ECR I-05285.

be in line with the general demand laid down in Article 19(1) TEU that 'Member States shall provide remedies sufficient to ensure effective legal protection in the fields covered by Union law.' Once individuals are confronted with rights or obligations on the basis of CFSP decisions that are 'sufficiently clear and unconditional' it may become difficult for national courts to ignore an important EU decision simply because its status has not been regulated in as much detail as some other EU instruments. Effective legal protection includes the protection of fundamental rights,[67] which (as underlined by Article 6(3) TEU) 'shall constitute general principles of the Union's law'.

All in all, while enforcement of CFSP decisions as such remains difficult, the case law of the Court reveals that the 'special position' of CFSP should not affect general principles of EU law, that there may be good reasons to opt for CFSP rather than for any other external policy and that individuals have a right to effective protection. Admittedly, apart from perhaps the restrictive measures, not many CFSP decisions have a substantive impact on the EU's legal order or on the position of individuals.[68] Yet, the foreseen extended role of the Union in global governance may change this.

IV   External Pressures Towards Integration

Integration in European foreign policy is not only triggered by an internal institutional dynamic, but increasingly also by external reactions to the EU's global ambitions and its more visible posture in the international arena. The ambition of the Union to 'play along' calls for an adaptation of the Union to the rules and customs of international law. This is indeed a two-way street: while we have seen that the Union aims to contribute to global governance, it also has to find its place in a legal order that has states as its primary subjects.

At the same time, the internal debates (partly described above) have to a large extend resulted in navel-gazing. The outside world is less interested

---

[67] Including the right to access to justice. See also C. Eckes, *EU Counter-Terrorist Policies and Fundamental Rights: The Case of Individual Sanctions* (Oxford University Press, 2009). See also the *Rosneft* case (above n. 60).

[68] See also Cardwell, 'On "Ring-Fencing"' (above n. 1), 461: 'The reasoning set out above leads to a conclusion that the practice of the CFSP, beyond sanctions, remains declaratory in nature. "Declaratory" is a criticism that has been levelled at the CFSP since its creation, and whilst declarations may have some foreign policy impact, it is curious that these are the hallmark of the policy, instead of the instruments which have been specifically created for its use. The extent to which non-CFSP measures are used already suggests that actions and policies toward third countries or issues are there but not badged as such under the CFSP.'

in internal (horizontal as well as vertical) competence battles. This had led the Union to develop its so-called 'comprehensive approach', which as observed by Merket:

> indicates a tendency to move away from pre-determined off-the-shelf solutions or politically correct but vague calls for coherence. This is replaced by a gradual systematisation of mechanisms that stimulate continuous interaction between all relevant stakeholders in order to arrive at made-to-measure comprehensive approaches continuously adapted to the specific needs of any given situation.[69]

The question is to what extent outside pressures help the EU to integrate and consolidate its external relation regime.

A   External Representation

It is not to be expected that the international legal order will be adapted to allow the EU to fully play its role as a global actor. In fact, the Union's demands – often related to its complex internal division of competences – may increasingly annoy third states for whom it may remain unclear with whom they are actually dealing.[70] The current treaty regime therefore aims to streamline the Union's external representation. While this is also clearly driven by internal developments, the external pressure is obvious as well.[71]

Traditionally, diplomatic relations are established between states and the legal framework is strongly state-oriented. As an international organisation enjoying international legal personality, the EU is allowed to enter

---

[69] Merket, 'The European Union and the Security-Development Nexus' (above n. 39), Conclusions of Chapter 6.

[70] A recent example is the Draft Agreement on the Accession of the EU to the European Convention on Human Rights, which contains many complex innovations to allow the Union to participate in what was set-up as a system for states only. On the various aspects see e.g. the special issue of the *GLJ*: www.germanlawjournal.com/volume-16-no-01/.

[71] See recently on this topic: S. Duquet, 'The Contribution of the European Union to Diplomatic and Consular Law', PhD-thesis, KU Leuven (2018); and earlier J. Wouters and S. Duquet, 'Unus inter plures? The EEAS, the Vienna Convention and International Diplomatic Practice' in J. Bátora and D. Spence (eds.), *The European External Action Service: European Diplomacy Post-Westphalia* (Palgrave MacMillan, 2015). See earlier R. A. Wessel, 'Can the European Union Replace its Member States in International Affairs? An International Law Perspective' in I. Govaere et al. (eds.), *The European Union in the World: Essays in Honour of Marc Maresceau* (Martinus Nijhoff Publishers, 2013), 129–47; as well as R. A. Wessel and B. van Vooren, 'The EEAS's Diplomatic Dreams and the Reality of International and European Law' (2013) 20(9) *JEPP* 1350–67.

into legal relations with states and other international organisations.[72] At the same time, its external competences are limited by the principle of conferral (Article 5 TEU), and in many cases the EU is far from exclusively competent and shares its powers with the Member States. Indeed, the TEU mandates that 'essential state functions'[73] of the Member States are to be respected by the Union and it is in diplomatic relations in particular that one may come across these state functions.[74] Yet, the Treaties reveals the EU's new diplomatic ambitions, in particular through the establishment of the EEAS, which has been called 'the first structure of a common European diplomacy'.[75]

International representation is a core element of international (diplomatic) law. The first indent of Article 3(1) of the Vienna Convention on Diplomatic Relations lists as a task of embassies: 'Represent the sending state in the receiving state'.[76] Several EU Treaty articles provide a solid basis for the Union to establish a formal and substantive presence as a single, fully matured diplomatic actor represented in third countries and international organisations.[77] As regards the physical presence through its delegations, EU activities are based on Article 221(1) TFEU: 'Union Delegations in third countries and at international organisations shall represent the Union.' The ambition flowing from this new provision in the TFEU should be quite clear: the Union no longer wishes to have an international presence through delegations of only one of its institutions (e.g. Commission delegations), or through the diplomats of the Member State holding the rotating presidency.[78] The purpose of this new treaty provision

---

[72] R.A. Wessel and J. Odermatt (eds.), *Research Handbook on the EU's Engagement with International Organisations* (Edward Elgar, 2018).

[73] Cf. Article 4(2) TEU.

[74] The EEAS Decision acknowledges this in Article 5(9): 'The Union delegations shall work in close cooperation and share information with the diplomatic services of the Member States'. See also B. Van Vooren, 'A Legal-Institutional Perspective on the European External Actions Service', *CMLR*, 2011, 475–502, who points out that due to consistency obligations this should be read as a general obligation to cooperate between the EEAS and the national diplomatic services (at 497).

[75] *Consular and Diplomatic Protection: Legal Framework in the EU Member States*, Report of the EU CARE project, December 2010, 31; available at http://www.careproject.eu/images/stories/ConsularAndDiplomatic-Protection.pdf.

[76] Article 3(a) of the Vienna Convention on Diplomatic Relations.

[77] Articles 220 and 221 TFEU in conjunction with Articles 3(5) and 21(1) TEU.

[78] But see the EEAS document 'EU Diplomatic Representation in Third Countries – First half of 2012', Council of the European Union, Doc. 18975/1/11, REV 1, 11 January 2012, which reveals that in some countries the EU is still represented by a Member State.

was to have 'less Europeans and more EU';[79] that is, a single diplomatic presence for the Union speaking on behalf of a single legal entity active globally.

The transformation from Commission delegations into embassies proper was not purely formal, but was in some cases accompanied by added powers to at least some of those representations abroad. While all 139 Commission delegations[80] were transformed into EU delegations mere weeks after the entry into force of the Lisbon Treaty, 54 were immediately transformed into 'EU embassies' in all but name.[81] This meant that these 'super-missions' were not merely given the new name, but also new powers in the form of an authorisation to speak for the entire Union (subject to approval from Brussels); and the role to coordinate the work of the member states' bilateral missions. Prominent exclusions among those fifty-four delegations were those to international bodies, of which there are seven: New York (UN), Geneva (UN and WTO), Vienna (IAEA, UNODC, UNIDO, OSCE), Strasbourg (Council of Europe), Addis Ababa (AU), Paris (UNESCO and OECD) and Rome (FAO, WFP, IFAD, Holy Sea, and Order of Malta).[82] The Union still has to work out how to handle EU representation in multilateral fora under Lisbon.[83] However, it is certainly the EU's ambition to 'progressively' expand these powers to other EU delegations as well.[84]

---

[79] A. Missiroli, 'The New EU Foreign Policy System After Lisbon: A Work in Progress' (2010) 15(4) *European Foreign Affairs Review* 427–52.

[80] See www.eeas.europa.eu/delegations/index_en.htm.

[81] A. Rettman, 'EU Commission "Embassies" Granted New Powers', *EU Observer*, 21 January 2010. Yet, see the many differences between Union delegations and national embassies: P. Kerres and R. A. Wessel, 'Apples and Oranges? Comparing European Union Delegations to National Embassies', CLEER Paper, 2015/2.

[82] UN: United Nations; WTO: World Trade Organization; IAEA: International Atomic Energy Agency; UNODC: United Nations Office on Drugs and Crime; UNIDO: United Nations Industrial Development Organisation; OSCE: Organisation for Security and Cooperation in Europe; AU: African Union; UNESCO: United Nations Educational, Scientific and Cultural Organisation; OECD: Organisation for Economic Cooperation and Development; FAO: Food and Agriculture Organisation; WFP: World Food Programme; IFAD: International Fund for Agricultural Development.

[83] Rettman, 'EU Commission "Embassies"' (above n. 81). Similarly, A. Rettman, 'Ashton Designates Six New "Strategic Partners"', *EU Observer*, 16 September 2010, quoting an EU official on the importance of the EEAS for the role of Mrs Ashton in external representation: 'Lady Ashton has de facto 136 ambassadors at her disposal'.

[84] See e.g. EEAS, 'EU Diplomatic Representation in Third Countries – Second Half of 2011', 11808/2/11 REV 2 (Brussels, 25 November 2011), and EEAS, 'EU Diplomatic Representation in Third Countries – First Half of 2012', 18975/11 (Brussels, 22 December 2011). These documents always start with two paragraphs quoting Article 221 TFEU and an excerpt from the Swedish Presidency report on the EEAS of 23 October 2009, which set

So far, the representation by the Union delegations largely followed the pre-Lisbon practice which was developed on the basis of the experience with the Commission delegations. Representation by the Union did not replace representation by the Member States. Indeed, as Article 5(9) of the EEAS Decision provides: 'The Union delegations shall work in close cooperation and share information with the diplomatic services of the Member States.' Yet, ongoing budget cuts may trigger Member States to close some of their own representations and to rely more on the new 'EU embassies'. This may be unthinkable for most of the larger Member States at this moment, and the current EEAS legal regime does not yet include this option. Obviously, any transfer of powers will depend on the consent of the Member States, as they may have good reasons to continue a bilateral representation. After all, essential elements of a relationship between a Member State and a third state may not be covered by the EU's competences or a special relationship may exist between an EU state and a third country, either due to historical ties and/or geographic location.[85] Nevertheless, one medium-sized Member State openly discussed the possible benefits of a transfer of certain consular tasks and the collection of information to Union delegations.[86]

The development of the external representation through the High Representative, but above all by establishing 'Union delegations', was certainly also triggered by the demands and customs of the international diplomatic system. The arrangements concluded with third states reveal that the Union has adopted the rules of the game and has in fact 'contracted-in' to the rules of international diplomatic law.

B   An EU Contribution to International Law?

Another external trigger for further integration in the area of foreign policy is formed by the need for the Union to co-design the international

---

out the Member States' view on the scope of the EEAS in relation to the HR mandate. On that basis these reports continue by stating that the 'responsibility of representation and coordination on behalf of the EU has been performed by a number of Union delegations as of 1 January 2010, or later', and insofar as they have not taken over such functions, pre-Lisbon arrangements and the role of the Presidency continue to apply.

[85] C. Cusens, 'The EEAS vs. the National Embassies of EU Member States?' in P. Quinn (ed.), *Making European Diplomacy Work: Can the EEAS Deliver?*, EU Diplomacy Paper 08/2011 (College of Europe, 2011), 11–13, 12.

[86] See the report by the Netherlands Ministry for Foreign Affairs, 'Nota modernisering Nederlandse diplomatie' (8 April 2011), 10 and 18, www.rijksoverheid.nl/documenten-en-publicaties/notas/2011/04/08/nota-modernisering-nederlandse-diplomatie.html.

rules, now that it is becoming more affected by them. In other words: the coming of age of the EU as a global actor also slowly turns the EU from a passive recipient into an active contributor to the further development of international law. As we have seen, the EU Treaties contain the idea that the EU should – at least partly – shift its focus from its own Member States to third states. By now the EU has a legal relationship with almost all states in the world and it is an active participant in many international organisations (either directly or through its Member States). It has been held that the EU is a global normative actor,[87] in particular in the promotion of its own values and by influencing global policy-making. Yet, influencing policies is not the same as influencing legal norms. International law is known for its quite strict rules on what it considers to be a legitimate source. The question is to what extent EU practice may indeed contribute to international law-making.[88]

It remains important to underline that – irrespective of the clear link between many internal and external policies – the Union has a choice to participate in either international law-making or to legislate domestically. In the words of De Witte and Thies: 'the competence allocation under the Treaties does not distinguish, in principle, between internal and external competences of the EU and therefore does not establish any "venue preference". In other words, where the EU has competence to legislate, it can do so in any accessible venue.'[89] Yet, as also underlined by these authors, there may be legal constraints. While internal legal constraints flow for the rules and principles in the EU Treaties, external constraints are related to the fact that the Union, as a non-state actor, may have limited access to traditional international law-making procedures and venues. An interesting effect, however, is that law-making at the global level may trigger increased

---

[87] See e.g. I. Manners, 'Normative Power Europe: A Contradiction in Terms?' (2002) 40(2) *JCMS* 235–58; H. Sjursen, 'The EU as a Normative Power: How Can this Be?' (2006) 13(2) *JEPP* 235–51; R. Whitman (ed.), *Normative Power Europe: Empirical and Theoretical Perspectives* (Palgrave, 2011); and T. Forsberg, 'Normative Power Europe, Once Again: A Conceptual Analysis of an Ideal-Type' (2011) 49(6) *JCMS* 1183. See also some chapters in N. Witzleb et al. (eds.), *The European Union and Global Engagement: Institutions, Policies and Challenges* (Edward Elgar, 2015).

[88] See also F. Hoffmeister, 'The Contribution of EU Practice to International Law', M. Cremona (ed.), *Developments in EU External Relations Law* (Oxford University Press, 2008).

[89] B. de Witte and A. Thies, 'Why Choose Europe? The Place of the European Union in the Architecture of International Legal Cooperation' in B. Van Vooren et al. (eds.), *The EU's Role in Global Governance: The Legal Dimension* (Oxford University Press, 2013), 23–58, 34. For a more extensive development of some ideas presented here, see R.A. Wessel, 'Flipping the Question: The Reception of EU Law in the International Legal Order' (2016) *Oxford Yearbook of European Law*, 533–61.

activity of the Union in that area, and vice versa. De Witte and Thies described this in terms of upstream and downstream 'sequencing', pointing to an ever stronger interaction between internal and external policy-making.[90] Thus, international agreements may trigger new legislation at EU level (for instance in the area of food safety, private international law or the rights of disabled persons), which in turn strengthens the international role of the Union in these areas in discussions on implementation or revision of agreed rules, principles or standards.[91]

Taking a broader perspective than just CFSP, the EU can influence the international legal order in different ways. Obviously, the most common way for the EU to influence international law, or to contribute to it, is by concluding an international agreement. Treaties form a key source of international law. As a matter of EU law, the competence to conclude international agreements is undisputed.[92] The EU is a party to well over 1,000 treaties.[93] With the increasing internal competences the scope of the Union's legal dealings with third states was extended to almost all areas covered by the treaties. The EU's Treaties Database thus lists international agreements in the areas of Agriculture, Coal and Steel, Commercial Policy, Competition, Consumers, Culture, Customs, Development, Economic and Monetary Affairs, Education, Training, Youth, Energy, Enlargement, Enterprise, Environment, External Relations, Fisheries, Food Safety, Foreign and Security Policy, Fraud, Information Society, Internal Market, Justice, Freedom and Security, Public Health, Research and Innovation, Taxation, Trade, and Transport. Both bilateral and multilateral agreements form a source of international law and, as a major global player, the EU may substantially influence the text of an agreement. Yet, the question may be rightfully posed whether this can be seen as EU law forming a source of international law. After all, in many cases substantive EU law may not exist at the time of the negotiations and the EU is simply one of the parties. Thus, we have seen an active role played by the EU in such

---

[90] De Witte and Thies, 'Why Choose Europe?' (above n. 89), 36.

[91] More extensively on this interaction: R. A. Wessel and J. Wouters, 'The Phenomenon of Multilevel Regulation: Interaction between Global, EU and National Regulatory Spheres', *International Organizations Law Review*, 2007, 257–89.

[92] Cf. Opinion 1/2003 on the Lugano Convention: 'whenever Community law created for the [EU] institutions powers within its internal system for the purpose of attaining a specific objective, the Community has authority to undertake international commitments necessary for the attainment of that objective even in the absence of an express provision to that effect'.

[93] See the Treaties Office Database of the European External Action Service, http://ec.europa .eu/world/agreements/default.home.do.

diverging areas as security issues, environmental policies, financial governance or migration.[94]

Apart from international agreements, the EU may influence the international legal order through the issuing of unilateral acts, which on the basis of international law bind the Union vis-à-vis third states both in relation to internal market issues[95] as well as on foreign policy. Once the Union has succeeded in formulating a policy, this may result in the creation of expectations on the side of the third party. It is generally held that apart from the Member States and the institutions, the third states involved must be able to rely on the official decisions of an organisation.[96] Thus, the legal effects of EU Decisions would reach beyond the internal system of the EU legal order. This considerably extends the scope of the effect of EU external action. Potentially, it not only includes a wide range of decisions taken in the framework of the Union's foreign and security policy, but also the vast amount of declaration issues by the Union (or the High Representative for Foreign and Security Policy) on an almost daily basis. Obviously, the statements must have been phrased in a way to trigger legitimate expectations on the side of third states which are to be upheld by the Union.

Third, the EU may contribute to the development of international customary law. Traces, at least, of a 'European' influence of international norms are already to be found in the effects of the case law of the European Court of Human Rights. A case in point may be the tension between the international rules on the immunity of international organisations and the demands laid down in Article 6 of the European Convention on Human Rights in relation to the right to fair trial and the interpretation of the Court that this implies that international organisations are to cater for a system of 'equivalent protection' compared to that of states.[97] Fourth, the EU may

---

[94] See e.g. the contributions to B. Van Vooren et al. (eds.), *The EU's Role in Global Governance: The Legal Dimension* (Oxford University Press, 2013).

[95] An example being the EU's Generalised Scheme of Preferences' (GSP), which allows for developing country exporters to pay less or no duties on their exports to the EU. This gives them vital access to EU markets and contributes to their economic growth. See Regulation (EU) No. 978/2012 of the European Parliament and of the Council of 25 October 2012 applying a scheme of generalised tariff preferences and repealing Council Regulation (EC) No. 732/2008.

[96] Cf. J. Klabbers, *The Concept of Treaty in International Law* (Kluwer Law International, 1996), 94.

[97] See on the relevant case law e.g. A. Reinisch and U. A. Weber, 'In the Shadow of Waite and Kennedy: The Jurisdictional Immunity of International Organizations, The Individuals Right of Access to the Courts and Administrative Tribunals as Alternative Means of Dispute Settlement' (2004) 1 *International Organizations Law Review* 59–110. See on a recent view by a number of European lawyers: Brief of European Law Scholars and Practitioners as Amici Curiae in Support of Plaintiffs-Appellants, Case *Delama Georges et al. v. United*

influence international law-making through participation in international organisations.[98] Apart from its participation in a number of actual international organisations, the institutionalisation of the role of the EU in the world is reflected in its position in international regimes in various policy fields. The position of the EU in international institutions is part and parcel of its foreign policy and it is at these fora that a *structural* role of the EU in global governance becomes most visible. Moreover, it is this role that has become more interesting now that it becomes clear that many EU (and national) rules find their origin in decision-making processes in other international organisations. The question of how effective the EU has been in influencing the outcome of law and policy-making processes at international institutions is again one that has primarily been on the table of non-lawyers. Overall – and despite major internal turf-battles – the view is that the EU's influence is quite substantive,[99] and that it largely practices what it preaches in terms of the promotion of values.[100]

While the above-mentioned examples are the most clear expressions of the EU's contribution to international law-making, the Union's role in 'shaping the international legal order'[101] is much more extensive. Conceptions of 'normative power Europe' have in particular been developed in International Relations Theory and EU Studies and aim to draw attention to 'the EU's "promotion of norms in a normative way"– ie the promotion of multilateralism and of values such as respect for international law, human rights and democracy, through non-coercive means'.[102]

Nations et al., United States Court of Appeals, No. 15–455, 2015, www.ijdh.org/wp-content/uploads/2015/06/EuroLaw-Amicus-Brief.pdf.

[98] Cf. S. Blavoukos and D. Bourantonis (eds.), *The EU Presence in International Organizations* (Routledge, 2010); Wessel and Odermatt (above n. 72).

[99] See e.g. K. E. Jørgensen and K. Laatikainen (eds.) *Routledge Handbook on the European Union and International Institutions: Performance, Policy, Power* (Routledge, 2013). For a general overview of different opinions see C. Hill and M. Smith, 'Acting for Europe: Reassessing the European Union's Place in International Relations' in C. Hill and M. Smith (eds.), *International Relations and the European Union*, 2nd edn (Oxford University Press, 2011).

[100] Cf. S. Lucarelli, 'Values, Principles, Identity and European Union Foreign Policy' in S. Lucarelli and I. Manners (eds.), *Values and Principles in European Union Foreign Policy* (Routledge, 2006). See for legal analyses of this matter: M. Cremona, 'Value in EU Foreign Policy' in M. Evans and P. Koutrakos (eds.), *Beyond the Established Legal Orders: Policy Interconnectedness between the EU and the Rest of the World* (Hart, 2011).

[101] Cf. Kochenov and Amtenbrink (eds.), *The European Union's Shaping of the International Legal Order* (above n. 8).

[102] G. de Búrca, 'EU External Relations: The Governance Mode of Foreign Policy' in B. Van Vooren et al. (eds.), *The EU's Role in Global Governance: The Legal Dimension* (Oxford University Press, 2013), 39–58, 39–40.

The question then is to what extent the promotion of norms can lead to actual law-making. In that respect it is well-known that EU views may function as a reference point in many areas. On the basis of their cooperation with the EU, third states may even (be forced to) adopt elements of EU law in their domestic legal orders. The more close the relationship with the EU is (candidate countries, associated countries, countries participating in the European Neighbourhood Policy, countries that are dependent on the EU for parts of their development etc.) the more frequent this will be the case.

Generally, it is clear that to be successful as a 'normative power', the EU will have to adapt its strategies to the norms on international law-making. Again, this causes an external pressure on the external representation of the EU and the way in which it succeeds in aligning its internal policies and actors towards a unified force in foreign policy.

V   Conclusion

The EU's foreign and security policy represents a clear paradox. Set up as a largely intergovernmental network, the aim of most Member States was to limit integration in the area. Yet, both internal and external factors put the intergovernmental nature into perspective and the Union's legal order as well as the global system pulled CFSP closer to other policy areas. Ironically, this seems to have happened while the perception of 'otherness' was not affected; or perhaps *because* this perception was not affected. In a way it is surprising how limited the effects of treaty changes and internal and external developments have been on the perception of the nature of CFSP. Most probably, the same amount of integration could not have been reached if the issues had been laid out on the table.

Despite the fact that one stream in literature has always pointed to the clear links between CFSP and other Union policies, legal scholarship traditionally has been slow in picking up on real-life developments. The focus on legal texts sometimes blurs our view of what is going on in reality. As we have seen, other academic disciplines (such as political science and European studies) have been more clear on the integrationist tendencies in CFSP. Yet, these days many more lawyers would agree with Cardwell that 'the perspective of the CFSP as being intergovernmental is not only out-dated but misleading because it stresses that the Member States are the only significant actors in it and that anything which concerns the world beyond the borders of the EU must take place within CFSP'.[103]

---

[103] Cardwell, 'On "Ring-Fencing"' (above n. 1), 456.

At the same time, while political scientists may more easily take things as they come, lawyers struggle with inconsistencies and paradoxes. As indicated by Merket, for instance, 'one of the main post-Lisbon challenges for EU external action will therefore be to solve this integration-delimitation paradox. In other words, how to reconcile the remaining plea for delimitation of the CFSP, with the equally strong call for coherence, integration and comprehensiveness.'[104]

This chapter aimed to show that this is not a challenge we should fear. And that the development of CFSP is as much connected to internal integrationist tendencies as to external demands to the new kid on the (state-centred) block.

---

[104] Merket, 'The European Union and the Security-Development Nexus' (above n. 39), Chapter 1.

14

Intergovernmentalism in the Wake of the Euro-Area Crisis

ALICIA HINAREJOS

I Introduction

The euro-area crisis exposed long-standing flaws in the design of the European Union's (EU) Economic and Monetary Union and threatened the very existence of the euro. As the crisis deepened, Member States and EU institutions scrambled to address its causes and contain its effects. One of the features of this multifaceted and, at times, piecemeal response was the predominance of the executive, which led to what can be considered a resurgence of intergovernmentalism as a means of cooperation among Member States. This chapter will focus on this feature of EU and Member State action in the wake of the crisis, exploring its causes, manifestations and consequences.[1]

II Executive Dominance and Intergovernmentalism

The aftermath of the crisis saw an increase in the predominance of executive power at the EU level.[2] National executives took the lead in grappling with different solutions to the crisis, acquiring an even more central role in economic reform and governance. But it is not only national executives – and

---

[1] An earlier version of this chapter was first published as part of A. Hinarejos, *The Euro Area Crisis in Constitutional Perspective* (Oxford University Press, 2015). By permission of Oxford University Press.

[2] On executive dominance in general, see D. Curtin, 'Challenging Executive Dominance in European Democracy', Amsterdam Law School Legal Studies Research Paper No. 2013–77; on intergovernmentalism after the crisis, see, generally, C. Bickerton, D. Hodson and U. Puetter, et al., 'The New Intergovernmentalism: European Integration in the Post-Maastricht Era' (2014) 53 *JCMS* 703. See also K. Armstrong, 'Differentiated Economic Governance and the Reshaping of Dominion Law' in M. Adams et al. (eds.), *The Constitutionalization of European Budgetary Constraints* (Hart, 2014), 72 et seq.

by extension the European Council and the Council – that have gained in power as a result of the crisis; other EU executive institutions have also seen their role strengthened. This is the case for the Commission, which has been tasked with implementing duties in economic surveillance and enforcement, and which has acquired a central role in implementing and monitoring conditionality and adjustment programmes attached to financial assistance provided through the European Stability Mechanism (ESM).[3] It is also the case for the European Central Bank (ECB), whose role has similarly grown and will continue to do so with the establishment of the Single Supervisory Mechanism.[4] Some voices in the literature have referred to this phenomenon of growing dominance of the executive (both national and supranational) as 'executive federalism'.[5]

In sum, the crisis has resulted in the increased dominance of the executive at both national and supranational levels, including executive expert bodies such as the Commission and the ECB. In particular, national governments played a central role in the aftermath of the crisis. This dominance of the executive – and, especially, of national executives – has manifested itself in three main ways.

First, national executives, in general, have been the visible leaders of reform, whether this has taken place through the Community method, within the EU framework but outside the Community method or outside the EU framework altogether.

Second, within the EU framework, the predominance of national executives has resulted in the European Council and the Council adopting a more central role in economic governance – aided by the Commission in an implementing capacity – often acting by unanimity or consensus (or always in the case of the European Council) and without resorting to the adoption of legislation through the Community method.

---

[3] The ESM Treaty foresees that the Commission carry out assessment tasks following receipt of a request for assistance, and participate in negotiating and monitoring conditionality attached to ESM financial assistance.

[4] The ESM Treaty also allocates tasks to the ECB, which is to be involved in the negotiations regarding conditionality attached to ESM financial assistance. The ECB's Outright Monetary Transactions Scheme also links assistance to countries in financial difficulties – through bond-buying – to compliance with ESM conditionality.

[5] J. Habermas, 'Europe's Post-Democratic Era', The Guardian (10 November 2011). Crum defines it 'as a governance model where 'new powers are uploaded to the European level, but political control remains with the (creditor) states and surveillance takes place through depoliticized procedures and technocratic institutions'. B. Crum, 'Saving the Euro at the Cost of Democracy' (2013) 51 JCMS 614, 615.

And third, secretive intergovernmental negotiations have resulted, at times, in measures of international law adopted outside the EU legal framework altogether, albeit with some ties to it.

III The Resurgence of Intergovernmentalism and its Causes

A Resurgence

The second and third manifestations amount to the adoption of decisions and the conducting of policy by means other than by Community method, whether within or without the EU framework. Accordingly, they have been seen as a resurgence of intergovernmentalism as a method of cooperation between the Member States.

There is no single definition of intergovernmentalism in law,[6] but the label is commonly used to refer to a kind of decision-making where there is a predominance of the executive, and that lacks some or all of the features of supranationalism or the Community method:[7] in its purest form, decisions are adopted by the Member States by unanimity and without the involvement of supranational institutions, and the decision-making process results in decisions that lack the supranational features of EU law. Some authors have suggested a distinction between those situations where Member States act completely outside the EU legal framework, on the one hand, and those where Member States act within the EU legal framework, but without wanting to commit – fully or at all – to the Community method: these authors would reserve the label of intergovernmentalism for the first type of situation, and suggest the label of 'intensive transgovernmentalism' for the second.[8] While the distinction between the two types of situation (acting within the EU framework without relying on the Community method, and acting fully outside the EU framework) is useful and should be borne in mind, this chapter will nevertheless speak of 'intergovernmentalism' across the board.

---

[6] As regards the use of the term in law: D. Thym, 'The Intergovernmental Constitution of the EU's Foreign, Security and Defence Executive' (2011) 7 *ECLR* 453, 466. See also P. Craig, 'Integration, Democracy and Legitimacy' in P. Craig and G. de Búrca (eds.), *The Evolution of EU Law*, 2nd edn (Oxford University Press, 2011), 32–3. As regards the use of the term in political science: C. Bickerton et al., 'The New Intergovernmentalism' (above n. 2).

[7] Craig, 'Integration, Democracy and Legitimacy' (above n. 6), 32–3.

[8] H. Wallace, 'The Institutional Setting' in H. Wallace and W. Wallace (eds.), *Policy-Making in the European Union*, 4th edn (Oxford University Press, 2000), 33–4; G. Majone, *Dilemmas of European Integration: The Ambiguities and Pitfalls of Integration by Stealth* (Oxford University Press, 2005), 163 et seq.

Within the framework of EU law, the European Council has emerged as main decision-maker,[9] acting by unanimity and without significant parliamentary contribution. Although the coordination of economic policies was always supposed to take place through the adoption of Council guidelines (more specifically, a Council recommendation based on conclusions of the European Council),[10] there has been an unprecedented emphasis on more effective coordination since the crisis, with the European Council and the Council at its helm. While the Commission plays a very significant role within the new framework for economic governance and there are efforts to include the European Parliament (EP) to a limited degree (e.g. by holding debates at certain points during the European Semester)[11] there is no doubt that this model of economic governance and budgetary surveillance is no application of the Community method.[12]

Nevertheless, the most obvious expression of the resurgence of intergovernmentalism has been the adoption of international agreements that are outside the EU legal framework but have important ties

---

[9] See e.g. Curtin, 'Challenging Executive Dominance in European Democracy' (above n. 2); P. de Schoutheete and S. Micossi, 'On Political Union in Europe: The Changing Landscape of Decision-Making and Political Accountability', CEPS Essay No. 4 (February 2013); S. Fabbrini, 'After the Euro Crisis: The President of Europe. A New Paradigm for Increasing Legitimacy and Effectiveness in the EU', *EuropEos Commentary*, No. 12, June 2012.

[10] According to Article 121(2) of the Treaty on the Functioning of the EU (TFEU):

The Council shall, on a recommendation from the Commission, formulate a draft for the broad guidelines of the economic policies of the Member States and of the Union, and shall report its findings to the European Council.

The European Council shall, acting on the basis of the report from the Council, discuss a conclusion on the broad guidelines of the economic policies of the Member States and of the Union.

On the basis of this conclusion, the Council shall adopt a recommendation setting out these broad guidelines. The Council shall inform the European Parliament of its recommendation.

[11] In fact, the EP may make use of the 'Economic Dialogue' instrument (expressly provided in five measures of the Six-Pack) to engage in discussion with other institutions or with national representatives at any point of the European Semester. On the genesis and nature of the economic dialogue, see C. Fasone, 'The Struggle of the European Parliament to Participate in the New Economic Governance', EUI Working Paper RSCAS 2012/45.

[12] Although the Commission does suggest in its Blueprint that the Broad Economic Policy Guidelines and Employment Guidelines could perhaps be adopted as legislative instruments through the ordinary legislative procedure in the future. Further proposals include that the potential decision to require a revision of a national budget be adopted through the ordinary legislative procedure, and that the ESM Treaty be integrated into the EU framework, so that the EP can be involved in scrutinising the ESM: 'Blueprint for a Deep and Genuine Economic and Monetary Union: Launching a European Debate', COM (2012) 0777 final, 38. The Commission also proposed the strengthening of the EP's role by granting it normal budgetary control over the ECB's activity as banking supervisor: ibid., 39.

to it.[13] These include the Treaty establishing the European Stability Mechanism, initially signed by seventeen Member States in order to create the ESM as an international organisation (not an EU agency). A similar mechanism was used to create the European Financial Stability Facility (EFSF), the predecessor of the ESM, this time through the signature of an executive international agreement and the creation of a private company set up under Luxembourg law.[14] Additionally, the Treaty on Stability, Coordination and Governance (TSCG) was also adopted as an international agreement by a majority of EU members, but not all;[15] and an international agreement was adopted to regulate certain aspects of the Single Resolution Fund.[16] Finally, the Euro Plus Pact occupies a greyer area: while it is undeniably intergovernmental in nature, it is perhaps not outside the EU legal framework to the extent that the previous instruments are, since it is more or less integrated within the European Semester.[17]

It has already been mentioned that these international instruments have nevertheless significant links to the EU legal system; this is because of their allocation of tasks to EU institutions, which will be discussed in more detail below, and because of the general duty placed on Member States not to breach EU law, even when acting within the sphere of international law.[18] The TSCG itself acknowledges the primacy of EU

---

[13] See also the analysis in A. Dimopoulos, 'The Use of International Law as a Tool for Enhancing Governance in the Eurozone and its Impact on EU Institutional Integrity' in M. Adams et al. (eds.), *The Constitutionalization of European Budgetary Constraints* (Hart, 2014).

[14] B. de Witte, 'Using International Law in the Euro Crisis: Causes and Consequences' *Arena Working Paper* No. 4, www.sv.uio.no/arena/english/research/publications/arena-publications/workingpapers/working-papers2013/wp4-13.pdf, 4 et seq.

[15] Signed on 2 March 2012 by all EU Member States apart from the UK, the Czech Republic and Croatia (the last one joined the EU subsequently).

[16] The agreement establishes the conditions under which participating Member States will levy the financial contributions from banks and will transfer these resources to the Single Resolution Fund: Agreement on the transfer and mutualisation of contributions to the Single Resolution Fund, signed on 21 May 2014 by all Member States except Sweden and the UK. Final text: Document 8457/14, ECOFIN 342. The international agreement complements the SRM Regulation: Regulation (EU) No. 806/2014 of the European Parliament and of the Council of 15 July 2014 establishing uniform rules and a uniform procedure for the resolution of credit institutions and certain investment firms in the framework of a Single Resolution Mechanism and a Single Resolution Fund and amending Regulation (EU) No. 1093/2010. See further Hinarejos, *The Euro Area Crisis in Constitutional Perspective* (above n. 1), Chapter 3.

[17] Hinarejos, *The Euro Area Crisis in Constitutional Perspective* (above n. 1), Chapter 3.

[18] See de Witte, 'Using International Law in the Euro Crisis' (above n. 14), 15 et seq.; P. Eeckhout and M. Waibel, 'The United Kingdom' in U. Neergaard, C. Jacqueson and G. Skovgaard Ølykke (eds.), *Proceedings from the XXVI FIDE Congress, I: The Economic*

law,[19] and the same instrument – but not the ESM Treaty – foresees its eventual integration within the EU legal framework after five years.[20]

While the adoption of instruments of international law seems to have intensified as a result of the crisis, it should be borne in mind that groups of Member States have resorted to this type of action often in the past. Past *inter se* agreements (i.e. international agreements signed by some, but not all, EU Member States) include instruments such as the Schengen framework or the Prüm Convention, in the area of justice and home affairs, and the Social Policy Agreement.[21] In all these cases, a group of Member States decided to push integration further through an instrument of international law. The future integration of these instruments into the EU legal framework was expressly foreseen at the time of their adoption, and took place at a later stage. The use of instruments of this kind has declined in more recent years,[22] but their recent revival is not surprising in the wake of the crisis, especially in areas where the EU did not have the necessary powers or resources.[23]

B   Causes

The reasons for the dominance of the executive in the aftermath of the euro-area crisis are manifold. First, it is unsurprising that national

---

and Monetary Union: Constitutional and Institutional Aspects of the Economic Governance within the EU (2013), 617 et seq.

[19] Article 2(2) TSCG.

[20] Article 16 TSCG.

[21] De Witte, 'Using International Law in the Euro Crisis' (above n. 14), 2. The Schengen Agreement of 14 June 1985 on the Gradual Abolition of Checks at their Common Borders, and the Convention that implements it (19 June 1990); the Prüm Convention of 27 May 2005 on the stepping up of cross-border cooperation, particularly in combating terrorism, cross-border crime and illegal migration. The Social Policy Agreement was signed by 11 of the Member States in December 1991.

[22] De Witte argues that the decline in popularity of international instruments is illustrated by the creation of the enhanced cooperation mechanism at Amsterdam, and the deletion from the Treaties of the provisions inviting Member States to adopt *inter se* agreements in certain fields: de Witte, 'Using International Law in the Euro Crisis' (above n. 14), 2.

[23] The Euro Plus Pact, for example, concerns areas of national competence. Regarding the ESM Treaty, the Court of Justice of the EU (CJEU) stated, in *Pringle*, that the EU did not have the power to create a permanent mechanism such as the ESM, or at least that Member States were under no obligation to act within the EU legal framework for these purposes and were free to do so outside the EU legal framework: Case C-370/12, *Pringle v. Ireland*, ECLI:EU:C:2012:756, judgment of the Court of Justice of 27 November 2012, [64]–[67]. Additionally, the EU itself did not have enough resources to fund either the EFSF or the ESM, and non-euro countries were not willing to fund these mechanisms indirectly by increasing the EU budget. Finally, the case of the TSCG is different: operating through primary law was considered desirable for symbolic reasons, but an amendment of the TFEU was blocked by two countries (the UK and the Czech Republic).

executives would come to be seen as leaders or agenda-setters of reform. The problems and potential solutions to the crisis were of such political significance and sensitivity that it would have been unthinkable for the Heads of State or Government not to have taken a leading role in the quest for recovery; it was furthermore crucial to calm down markets and private investors, and this could only be done by showing the involvement of the national executives at the highest level. Moreover, voices in the political science literature have referred to the crisis of democracy at national level as a contributing factor to this new wave of intergovernmentalism.[24] Other explanatory factors for the predominance of the executive, in general, include the perceived need for speedy or decisive action in the aftermath of the crisis, for which the executive power is comparatively better suited. Executive power often grows and consolidates in times of crisis or emergency; an obvious example would be the effects of 9/11 on US governance and beyond.[25]

Second, it should be remembered that the EU has limited legislative competence in this area, and it was thus limited in what it could do to address the crisis. It is unsurprising that a limited legislative competence at the EU level has resulted in limited use of the Community method; instead, international law instruments have been used to a certain degree (such as in order to create the ESM, which could not have been done within the EU framework according to the Court of Justice's ex-post assessment in *Pringle*)[26] and economic governance within the EU framework has moved away from a purely rule-making model – premised on the Community method – and towards an executive decision-making model,[27] or at least a combination of the two.

Third, there were political and practical reasons for the creation of the EFSF and the ESM and the adoption of the TSCG outside the framework of the EU. In both cases, the distinction between euro and non-euro Member States and the desire or need to integrate at different speeds, or to different degrees, has played a role: the EFSF was created outside the EU

---

[24] Bickerton et al. 'The New Intergovernmentalism: European Integration in the Post-Maastricht Era' (above n. 2), 8 et seq.

[25] Curtin, 'Challenging Executive Dominance in European Democracy' (above n. 2), 4–5.

[26] The CJEU stated, in *Pringle*, that the EU did not have the power to create a permanent mechanism such as the ESM; or at least that Member States did not have an obligation to act within the EU framework and were free to do so outside the EU legal framework: *Pringle*, [64]–[67]. There were of course additional practical reasons for the creation of the ESM outside the EU framework; these will be discussed below.

[27] De Schoutheete and Micossi, 'On Political Union in Europe' (above n. 9), 5; Curtin, '*Challenging Executive Dominance in European Democracy*' (above n. 2), 10.

framework because far greater resources were needed than those available from the EU budget,[28] and non-euro countries were understandably reluctant to fund this mechanism – aimed at safeguarding the stability of the euro area – either directly or indirectly.[29] A similar reasoning applies to the creation of the ESM. The adoption of an international agreement on certain aspects of the Single Resolution Fund seems to have responded to German concerns over the existence of an appropriate legal basis in the Treaties.[30] As regards the TSCG, an amendment of the EU Treaties was blocked by the UK. While adoption of EU secondary legislation through the enhanced cooperation procedure may have been possible, action through primary law was considered preferable for symbolic reasons and in order to send a clear signal that would calm down the markets.[31] The resulting treaty was adopted outside the EU framework and signed by all Member States at the time, apart from two non-euro countries, the UK and the Czech Republic. Thus, the need for multi-speed or differentiated integration has been one of the factors leading Member States to resort to international law instruments.

Finally, intergovernmental decision-making (in the sense of avoiding use of the Community method, be it with or without the EU framework) offers a high degree of flexibility and control to Member States – due to the fact that they are free, in principle, from enforcement and control, whether

---

[28] The 'parallel' but much smaller mechanisms created within the EU framework, the EFSM, had much less firepower (upper limit of €60 billion). See Article 2(2) of Council Regulation 407/2010 and analysis and further references in de Witte, 'Using International Law in the Euro Crisis' (above n. 14), 4. In contrast, the EFSF had access to greater resources (those of the participant Member States).

[29] De Witte, 'Using International Law in the Euro Crisis' (above n. 14), 3–4.

[30] The agreement establishes the conditions under which participating Member States will levy the financial contributions from banks and will transfer these resources to the Single Resolution Fund: Agreement on the transfer and mutualisation of contributions to the Single Resolution Fund, signed on 21 May 2014 by all Member States except Sweden and the UK. Final text: Document 8457/14, ECOFIN 342. The international agreement complements the SRM Regulation: Regulation (EU) No. 806/2014 of the European Parliament and of the Council of 15 July 2014 establishing uniform rules and a uniform procedure for the resolution of credit institutions and certain investment firms in the framework of a Single Resolution Mechanism and a Single Resolution Fund and amending Regulation (EU) No. 1093/2010. The combination of an EU measure with an intergovernmental agreement seems to respond to concerns regarding the limits of Article 114 as a proper legal basis: see further Hinarejos, *The Euro Area Crisis in Constitutional Perspective* (above n. 1), Chapter 3.

[31] Some voices in the literature have argued that Member States should not be allowed to resort to intergovernmental treaties when EU action through enhanced cooperation is legally possible; but note the approach taken by the CJEU to enhanced cooperation in *Pringle*: K. Tuori and K. Tuori, *The Eurozone Crisis: A Constitutional Analysis* (Cambridge University Press, 2013), 173–5.

judicial or democratic. Yet this freedom from external pressure is a double-edged sword that raises two different kinds of concerns: on the one hand, the lack of effective enforcement may translate into a lack of effectiveness and credibility. On the other hand, if intergovernmental decision-making turns out to be effective as a mechanism of cooperation, issues such as the lack of transparency, judicial control, and democratic legitimacy become the more pressing. Both sets of concerns will be discussed in turn.

IV   Intergovernmentalism, Credibility and Use of EU Institutions

While Member States may seek to be free from external enforcement and control when cooperating in highly sensitive areas, this freedom may come at a high price, as it may result in a lack of credibility for their commitments.

Aware of the problems associated with the lack of enforcement, Member States have sought to temper the use of intergovernmentalism since the crisis with the use of EU institutions as enforcers. This has happened within the EU framework of fiscal and economic governance, where the Commission has been given implementing and enforcement duties, but the phenomenon can be most clearly seen in those instances where the Member States have acted outside the EU legal framework altogether. Of the three instruments of international law adopted so far, two allocate tasks to EU institutions: the TSCG tasks the Commission with monitoring whether signatories have implemented the 'golden rule' or debt brake into national law; the Court of Justice is given jurisdiction to review whether signatories have discharged the same duty properly.[32] The ESM Treaty relies on the Commission and the ECB as 'agents' in the implementation and monitoring of ESM conditionality and adjustment programmes; finally, the Court of Justice is given jurisdiction in disputes between ESM members over the interpretation of provisions of the ESM Treaty.

Although some aspects of this use of EU institutions still remain unclear or problematic – especially concerning judicial review[33] – the Court of Justice considered it to be in accordance with EU law in *Pringle*, as long

---

[32] Article 8 TSCG, pursuant to Article 273 TFEU.

[33] See further Hinarejos, *The Euro Area Crisis in Constitutional Perspective* (above n. 1), Chapter 8; some of the questions regarding the use of EU institutions outside the EU framework (specifically whether those institutions are still subject to the Charter of Fundamental Rights in these situations) have since been answered in Joined Cases C-8–10/15 P, *Ledra Advertising*, ECLI:EU:C:2016:701. See further Section V below.

as this use did not 'alter the essential character of the powers conferred on those institutions by the EU and FEU Treaties'.[34] The applicants had argued that the tasking of EU institutions by a group of Member States should not be allowed outside the context of enhanced cooperation; this argument was rejected by the Court in relation to situations like the one at stake in that case, where the Union had no specific power to act – which meant, at least, that Member States were under no obligation to cooperate within the EU legal framework and free to do so outside.[35] Additionally, in the case of the ESM Treaty – the subject matter of the *Pringle* decision – all Member States had given their consent to the use of EU institutions, albeit that the Court did not mention this as a requirement. On the contrary, neither the UK nor the Czech Republic gave their consent to the allocation of tasks to EU institutions in the TSCG; however, the legality of this allocation has not been challenged before the Court.[36]

The use of the EU institutions serves an additional purpose; by relying on the EU institutions to implement – unpopular – aspects of these agreements, the signatories avoid having certain countries enforce discipline directly on their peers.[37] The interposition of 'neutral' EU institutions seeks to avoid politically toxic dynamics, as well as to provide a veneer of legitimacy.

---

[34] Case C-370/12, *Pringle* v. *Ireland* (above n. 23), [158] et seq. See further P. Craig, 'Pringle and Use of EU Institutions outside the EU Legal Framework: Foundations, Procedure and Substance' (2013) 9 *ECLR* 263; S. Peers, 'Towards a New Form of EU Law?: The Use of EU Institutions outside the EU Legal Framework' (2013) 9 *ECLR* 37; de Witte, 'Using International Law in the Euro Crisis' (above n. 14), 20–3. In the case of the Court, Article 273 TFEU allows Member States to extend its jurisdiction 'under a special agreement between the parties', to 'any dispute between Member States which relates to the subject matter of the Treaties'. Regarding other institutions, a similar allocation of tasks outside the EU framework had already been considered acceptable in the *Bangladesh* and *Lome* cases. In these cases, however, all Member States had given their consent to the use of the institutions in this way. Joined Cases C-181/91 and C-248/91 *European Parliament* v. *Council and European Council* v. *Commission (Bangladesh)* [1993] ECR I-3685; Case C-316/91, *European Parliament* v. *Council (Lome)* [1994] ECR I-625.

[35] On a broader reading, it could also be taken to mean that enhanced cooperation was not even available. On *Pringle* and the scope of enhanced cooperation, see Hinarejos, *The Euro Area Crisis in Constitutional Perspective* (above n. 1), 106 et seq. On the resort to international law when enhanced cooperation is available: Tuori and Tuori, *The Eurozone Crisis* (above n. 31), 172 et seq. See also Craig, 'Pringle and Use of EU Institutions outside the EU Legal Framework' (above n. 34).

[36] Peers, 'Towards a New Form of EU Law?' (above n. 34), 53–5.

[37] De Schoutheete and Micossi, 'On Political Union in Europe' (above n. 9), 2.

V Executive Dominance and Democratic Control

The predominance of the executive at the EU level is generally linked to concerns regarding transparency and lack of effective democratic control, whether from the EP or from national parliaments.[38] A certain predominance of the executive power in the context of the EU is nothing new, given the technocratic pedigree of the European project.[39] But the resurgence of intergovernmentalism in the aftermath of the crisis has exacerbated these concerns,[40] as the shunning of the Community method resulted in considerable migration of economic executive powers from the national sphere,[41] without extending democratic oversight at the EU level substantially. The strengthened role of independent expert bodies – mainly the Commission and the ECB, although the growing 'agentification' of financial supervision has also raised concerns – compounds this problem.

Outside the EU legal framework (i.e. when Member States have signed international agreements such as the ESM Treaty and the TSCG) national parliaments have been involved in the ratification process.[42] Beyond that, the treaties themselves do not foresee a significant role for national parliaments, albeit that this has been tempered in certain cases by requirements imposed by national constitutional courts.[43] In general, the mechanisms of financial assistance created through international treaties, such as the ESM, operate in a non-transparent manner and are subject to strict confidentiality rules, which has prompted accountability concerns.[44] On its

---

[38] Curtin, 'Challenging Executive Dominance in European Democracy' (above n. 2).

[39] Ibid., 6–7 and, more broadly, P. Lindseth, *Power and Legitimacy: Reconciling Europe and the Nation-State* (Oxford University Press, 2010).

[40] See e.g. M. Ruffert, 'The European Debt Crisis and European Union Law' (2011) 48 *CML Rev* 1777; Fabbrini, 'After the Euro Crisis' (above n. 9); R. Lastra and J. Louis, 'European Economic and Monetary Union: History, Trends, and Prospects' (2013) 32 *YEL* 57, 195 et seq. Concerns have been voiced by the EP also; e.g. MEPs have called for the integration of the ESM within the EU framework (and the Community method): see e.g. 'MEPs Call for Dismantling of EU Bailout Troika', *EU Observer*, 16 Jan 2013, http://euobserver.com/economic/122738.

[41] On the effects on national parliaments: C. Hefftler and W. Wessels, 'The Democratic Legitimacy of the EU's Economic Governance and National Parliaments', IAI Working Papers No. 13, 2013.

[42] This is different when we consider measures such as the Euro Plus Pact, which is neither a measure of EU law nor an international agreement in need of domestic ratification.

[43] The German Constitutional Court required parliamentary control over the Greek Loan Facility and ESM expenditure: BVerfG, 2 BvR 987/10 et al., Decision of 7 September 2011, and BVerfG, 2 BvR 1390/12 et al., Decision of 12 September 2012. See further Hinarejos, *The Euro Area Crisis in Constitutional Perspective* (above n. 1), Chapter 8.

[44] The German Constitutional Court has imposed transparency requirements. See above n. 43. The Finnish Constitutional Law Committee has imposed accountability requirements

part, the EP was neither involved at adoption, nor is there much room for its involvement after that. Unsurprisingly, this institution has argued that greater parliamentary involvement at the EU level is desirable, and has expressed concerns over the intergovernmentalist trend that manifests itself both within and without the EU framework.[45] More specifically, it has voiced concerns over its lack of involvement in the operations of the ESM, calling for the integration of this mechanism within the EU legal framework and the Community method.[46]

Other institutional voices are slightly less critical of these post-crisis developments. In 2012, the Commission argued for further fiscal and economic integration within the EU framework, rather than without (and, in the same spirit, for the future integration of the ESM into the EU framework).[47] The Commission considered that the matters of democratic legitimacy and accountability would become problematic if 'intergovernmental action of the euro area were significantly expanded beyond the current state of play'.[48] Conversely, the Commission was of the opinion that, as long as EMU is developed on the basis of existing Treaty provisions, no 'insurmountable accountability problems exist'.[49] The Commission's view is that, at the national level, national democratic processes continue to

---

on the functioning of the ESM in PeVL 13/2012; see Tuori and Tuori, *The Eurozone Crisis* (above n. 31), 219 and 195–9; see also P. Leino and J. Salminen, 'The Euro Crisis and its Constitutional Consequences for Finland: Is there Room for National Politics in EU Decision-Making?' (2013) 9 *ECLR* 451.

[45] The EP has expressed its regret over 'the lack of parliamentary scrutiny of the Troika, the EFSF and the ESM', and has stressed 'that the Euro Summit and the Eurogroup are informal bodies for discussion and not institutions for decision-making in the governance of the Economic and Monetary Union': European Parliament Resolution of 12 December 2013 on constitutional problems of a multitier governance in the European Union (2012/2078(INI)), [28], [33].

[46] MEPs have called for the integration of the ESM within the EU framework (and the Community method): see e.g. 'MEPs Call for Dismantling of EU Bailout Troika' (above n. 40). See also the broader critique offered by Lastra and Louis, 'European Economic and Monetary Union' (above n. 40), 57, 195 et seq.

[47] 'Blueprint for a Deep and Genuine Economic and Monetary Union' (above n. 12), 33–4. For the Commission's take on the future of EMU, see also its Communications to the EP and Council, 'Towards a Deep and Genuine Economic and Monetary Union: Ex Ante Coordination of Plans for Major Economic Policy Reforms', COM (2013) 166 final, and 'Towards a Deep and Genuine Economic and Monetary Union: The Introduction of a Convergence and Competitiveness Instrument', COM (2013) 165 final.

[48] 'Blueprint for a Deep and Genuine Economic and Monetary Union' (above n. 12), 36.

[49] 'The Lisbon Treaty has perfected the EU's unique model of supranational democracy, and in principle set an appropriate level of democratic legitimacy in regard of today's EU competences. Hence, as EMU can be further developed on this Treaty basis, it would be inaccurate to suggest that insurmountable accountability problems exist': ibid., 35.

legitimise and determine economic and budgetary decisions, as national parliaments continue to have decision-making power; and that at the EU level, limited coordination and surveillance powers are sufficiently legitimised directly by limited involvement of the EP, and indirectly through national representation in the European Council and the Council.

It is true that, within the EU framework, the EP has been duly involved in those areas of EMU reform where the Community method has been used; namely, in financial regulation, and when it came to the initial creation of the framework for economic surveillance that is the European Semester.[50] However, when it comes to the process of economic coordination and enforcement itself, the EP has an ancillary role, at best: it may make use of the 'economic dialogue' instrument (expressly provided in five measures within the Six-Pack) to engage in discussion with other institutions or with national representatives at any point during the European Semester.[51] In the future, the Commission has proposed to enhance the EU political debate, and thus the EP's position, through presentation by all European political parties of their candidate for the post of Commission President at the EP elections.[52] In the longer term, the Commission's view is that, if further integration in economic and fiscal policy is pursued – to the point where a Treaty amendment is necessary – more democratic legitimacy will be needed at the EU level, and that this democratic legitimacy should be provided through direct means; that is, through the strengthening of the EP's role,[53] including by granting it certain budgetary control

---

[50] For further discussion of legislation adopted (both in relation to the European Semester and to financial regulation), see Hinarejos, *The Euro Area Crisis in Constitutional Perspective* (above n. 1), Chapter 3. The EP has also exerted an influence on 'road-map related deliberations' of the European Council concerning e.g. the evolution of the SSM: de Schoutheete and Micossi, 'On Political Union in Europe' (above n. 9), 10.

[51] On the genesis and nature of the economic dialogue, see Fasone, 'The Struggle of the European Parliament to Participate in the New Economic Governance' (above n. 11).

[52] 'Blueprint for a Deep and Genuine Economic and Monetary Union' (above n. 12), 37. See President Barroso's 2012 State of the Union Speech, http://ec.europa.eu/commission_2010–2014/president/news/archives/2012/09/20120912_1_en.htm.

[53] The Commission proposed, in the medium term, the merger of the Broad Economic Policy Guidelines and Employment Guidelines, and the adoption of this single instrument through the ordinary legislative procedure. Further proposals include that the potential decision to require a revision of a national budget be adopted through the ordinary legislative procedure, and that the ESM Treaty be integrated into the EU framework, so that the EP can be involved in scrutinising the ESM: ibid., 38. The Commission also proposed the strengthening of the EP's role by granting it normal budgetary control over the ECB's activity as banking supervisor: ibid., 39.

over the ECB,[54] and through possible institutional adaptations within the EP[55] and the Commission.[56]

Further reports have echoed the preference for action within the EU legal framework, and the need for more parliamentary involvement alongside further integration within the EU framework in the area, with varying degrees of detail: among them, the report produced by a group of foreign ministers led by Guido Westerwelle (the 'European Foreign Ministers' Future of Europe Group', or the 'Westerwelle group') in 2012,[57] the Four Presidents' Report (prepared by the President of the European Council, Herman Van Rompuy, together with the Presidents of the Commission, the Eurogroup and the ECB)[58], the EP's Resolution on the Four Presidents' Report,[59] Herman Van Rompuy's 2012 issues paper and,[60] most recently, the Five Presidents' Report (published by the Presidents of the Commission, the Euro Summit, the Eurogroup, the ECB, and the EP), which sets out an ambitious plan to complete EMU in three stages, and that would include the creation of a euro-area treasury.[61]

Overall, then, a very extended view – at least at the institutional level – is that further integration should take place within the EU legal framework, rather than without, and that existing mechanisms within that framework provide sufficient legitimacy and accountability for EU action as long as economic and fiscal coordination does not go beyond its current form;[62]

---

[54] Insofar as the ECB acts as a banking supervisor: ibid., 38. Further changes are proposed in order to improve the accountability of the SSM and agencies in the field of financial regulation: ibid.

[55] The creation of a 'euro committee' with special decision-making powers: ibid., 38.

[56] Possible formation of a structure akin to an EMU Treasury within the Commission: ibid., 38–9.

[57] 'Foreign Ministers Group on the Future of Europe: Chairman's Statement for an Interim Report', 15 June 2012, www.auswaertiges-amt.de/EN/Europa/Aktuell/120620_Zwischenbericht_Zukunftsgruppe.html?nn=479786.

[58] 'Towards a Genuine Economic and Monetary Union', Interim Report by President of the European Council Herman Van Rompuy, Brussels, 26 June 2012; Final Report by President of the European Council Herman Van Rompuy, Brussels, 5 December 2012.

[59] European Parliament Report with recommendations to the Commission on the report of the Presidents of the European Council, the European Commission, the ECB and the Eurogroup, 'Towards a Genuine Economic and Monetary Union' 24 October 2012 (2012/2151 INI).

[60] Herman Van Rompuy, Issues Paper on Completing the Economic and Monetary Union, September 2012.

[61] 'Completing Europe's Economic and Monetary Union', Report by Jean-Claude Junker, in close cooperation with Donald Tusk, Jeroen Dijsselbloem, Mario Draghi and Martin Schulz ('The Five Presidents' Report), June 2015.

[62] Again, this refers to the Commission's views set out in its 'Blueprint for a Deep and Genuine Economic and Monetary Union' (above n. 12), 36 et seq.; see also its Communications to

that is, as long as there is no Treaty amendment to increase the EU's powers in this regard. While the matters of democratic legitimacy and accountability are most problematic in relation to intergovernmental action outside the EU legal framework, it would be wrong to think that no such problems arise at all within that framework.

The generally positive institutional take on legitimacy and accountability within the current EMU framework seems to be premised on the idea that the economic coordination and surveillance orchestrated within the European Semester does not equate with dictating economic policy to Member States, to the extent that it is only a framework for coordination that relies primarily on soft-law elements. Yet the question is whether this still holds once we take into account the inclusion of hard-law elements for euro countries, and once we step away from the formal perspective to consider the effect that this central coordination has on national economic policies in practice. The issue becomes even more problematic when considering the situation of states in need of financial assistance that have submitted a macro-economic adjustment programme under the Two-Pack.[63] Moreover, as pointed out above, the strengthened role of technical actors within EMU continues to be a concern in this regard; the most obvious example is that of a 'disembedded' ECB.[64] Finally, there is a certain consensus that greater democratic legitimacy at the EU level will be necessary if the Treaty is amended to pursue further economic and fiscal integration.

The question of democratic legitimacy within the current EMU, as well as the proposals in order to enhance it in the future, merit a broader discussion beyond the scope of this chapter. For now, suffice it to say that a simple extension of the powers of the EP in this area would not solve all problems by itself: first, because this would not address the sociological aspect of the democratic deficit, the lack of an EU demos, or the lack of a sufficient degree of connection between EU citizens and the EU institutions that represent them. Second, a strengthened role for the current EP would make certain questions more pressing, namely the disproportionate representation of Member States and how to reconcile the composition

---

the EP and Council, 'Towards a Deep and Genuine Economic and Monetary Union: Ex ante Coordination of Plans for Major Economic Policy Reforms' (above n. 47), and 'Towards a Deep and Genuine Economic and Monetary Union: The Introduction of a Convergence and Competitiveness Instrument' (above n. 47). For examples of scholarly critique, see above n. 40.

[63] Hinarejos, *The Euro Area Crisis in Constitutional Perspective* (above n. 1), Chapter 3.

[64] Ibid.

of the Parliament – spanning all of the EU – with its stronger role in euro-area matters.[65]

VI   Executive Dominance and Judicial Control

Unsurprisingly, the fruits of executive dominance and intergovernmentalism have also managed to escape judicial control, to a large degree. For a start, judicial control is limited when it comes to the process of fiscal and economic coordination, or to the workings of the new financial supervision framework. Already in its 2012 Blueprint, the Commission proposed an extension of the jurisdiction of the Court of Justice if the Treaties were amended to confer further powers to the EU.[66] At the moment, however, the hybrid coordination framework that is the European Semester does not rely on the CJEU. Similarly, while the ECB has seen its role grow considerably and is set to acquire even more responsibilities in the management of financial markets, it will continue to be subject to limited judicial scrutiny.[67] Exceptionally, the legality of the ECB's Outright Monetary Transactions (OMT) programme was questioned in a reference before the Court of Justice; unsurprisingly, the Court of Justice adopted a cautious standard of review of the ECB's actions, given the latter technical expertise in the area.[68]

---

[65] On disproportionate representation: Fabbrini, 'After the Euro Crisis' (above n. 9), 4–5. Regarding the euro/non-euro cleavage, the proposals range from the creation of a new parliamentary organ, different from the EP, to the creation of a separate euro-committee with decision-making powers within the EP: see e.g., respectively, J. Piris, *The Future of Europe: Towards a Two-Speed EU?* (Cambridge University Press, 2011), 127 et seq., and the Commission's 'Blueprint for a Deep and Genuine Economic and Monetary Union' (above n. 12), 38–9.

[66] By deleting Article 126(10) TFEU (admitting infringement procedures against Member States) or by creating new competences and procedures, 'although one should not forget that some of the issues do not lend themselves to full judicial review': Commission's 'Blueprint for a Deep and Genuine Economic and Monetary Union' (above n. 12), 39.

[67] While, in principle, the actions of the ECB are subject to judicial review, the CJEU is only competent to review the validity of binding acts, and standing to bring an action for annulment is very limited (Article 263 TFEU). See further Eeckhout and Waibel, 'The United Kingdom' (above n.18), 641 et seq.

[68] The legality of the ECB's OMT Scheme was challenged before the German Constitutional Court: *Bundesverfassungsgericht*, Order of the Second Senate of 14 January 2014 – 2 BvR 2728/13 (*Gauweiler*). During the proceedings, the German Court asked the CJEU for a preliminary ruling on the legality of the scheme: Case C-62/14, *Gauweiler*, ECLI:EU:C:2015:400. This is the first – and up to the time of writing, only – time that the German Constitutional Court has asked for a preliminary ruling from the CJEU. The OMT scheme was considered lawful, as long as it complies with certain conditions. For comment, see e.g. D. Adamski, 'Economic Constitution of the Euro Area after the *Gauweiler*

As to the instruments created outside the EU legal framework, we have seen that the Court of Justice has been given limited jurisdiction under the TSCG to review national implementation of the 'golden rule'. Similarly, the Court has had to examine the conformity of the ESM Treaty with EU law,[69] and it is competent to adjudicate disputes between ESM members over the interpretation of the ESM Treaty, but there is no mention of judicial oversight of the day-to-day running of the ESM. This is a matter of importance because of involvement of EU institutions within the framework of the ESM, and because of the conditionality attached to ESM aid, which typically requires the receiving Member State to effect cutbacks that impact on citizens' social rights. These conditions are reflected in so-called 'memoranda of understanding' (MoU), or agreements negotiated between a country in need of financial assistance, and the institutions or entities that agree to provide this assistance on a conditional basis.[70]

Typically, these MoU impose harsh cutbacks on receiving states' budgets, and have an impact on their citizens' social rights. Compliance with these conditions is monitored by the Commission, the ECB and the IMF (the 'troika'). Given the impact of these MoU on citizens' social rights, questions have arisen as to the status of these documents, as well as to their justiciability and compatibility with EU law – more specifically, with the Charter of Fundamental Rights. So far, the Court has been asked on several occasions to provide a preliminary ruling on the legality of national measures adopted pursuant to an MoU (or, formally, to elaborate on whether EU law would preclude measures such as the ones at stake). So far the Court has denied the existence of a link to EU law in these cases, thus refusing to consider the compatibility, within the preliminary ruling procedure, of the national measures implementing MoUs, and by extension of the MoUs themselves, with EU law.[71] Recently, however, the Court

---

Preliminary Ruling' (2015) 52 *CML Rev* 1451; A. Hinarejos, '*Gauweiler* and the Outright Monetary Transactions Programme: The Mandate of the European Central Bank and the Changing Nature of Economic and Monetary Union' (2015) 11 *ECLR* 563–76; Editorial, 'On Courts of Last Resort and Lenders of Last Resort' (2015) 2 *ECLR* 1. On the German reference and its significance, see e.g. T. Beukers, 'The Bundesverfassungsgericht Preliminary Reference on the OMT Program: "In the ECB We Do Not Trust. What About You?"' (2014) 15 *GLJ* 343.

[69] In *Pringle*, Case C-370/12, *Pringle* v. *Ireland*, ECLI:EU:C:2012:756, judgment of the Court of Justice, 27 November 2012. See further Hinarejos, *The Euro Area Crisis in Constitutional Perspective* (above n. 1), Chapter 8.

[70] These MoUs have been or are adopted in the context of EFSF, EFSM and ESM assistance, as well as in the context of Balance of Payments Precautionary loans.

[71] For further discussion of the role of EU and national courts in the wake of the crisis: Hinarejos, *The Euro Area Crisis in Constitutional Perspective* (above n. 1), Chapter 8.

clarified that while ESM acts remain outside the scope of EU law, the involvement of EU institutions in the adoption of those acts may give rise to the Union's liability in damages, as EU institutions are always subject to EU law and the Charter, even when acting under the ESM. While this is a welcome development, it is limited in scope,[72] and it does not change the fact that judicial control continues to be notoriously limited in this area.

VII   Final Remarks

The crisis has resulted in an increased dominance of the executive at both national and supranational levels, including executive expert bodies such as the Commission and the ECB. This dominance of the executive – and, especially, of national executives – has manifested itself in several ways. In general, there has been a resurgence of intergovernmentalism, or the adoption of decisions by means other than the Community method. This chapter has analysed the causes and facets of this resurgence, focusing especially on the adoption of measures of international law outside the EU legal framework and on the use of EU institutions in this ambit as a means to improve credibility. Finally, the chapter has outlined the negative consequences of the preponderance of the executive and the resurgence of intergovernmentalism in the wake of the crisis with regard to democratic and judicial control.

---

[72] Thus, while the ESM acts themselves cannot be challenged through the action for annulment, individuals can try to get damages. This will still be very difficult, given the high threshold required. Joined Cases C-8–10/15 P, *Ledra Advertising*, ECLI:EU:C:2016:701.

15

EU Law and Global Environmental Challenges

LUDWIG KRÄMER

I Introduction

At the beginning of the twenty-first century, there are numerous environmental challenges of a global nature and opinions certainly differ which are the most relevant ones. For example, the World Economic Forum identified water crisis, failure of climate change mitigation and adaptation and greater incidence of extreme weather events as the three most relevant environmental challenges; however, this list referred to the year 2014 only.[1] This author considers that global warming, the loss of biodiversity, the omnipresence of chemicals, resource management and the fight against poverty are the most important challenges of the present. This selection is arbitrary: nuclear accidents or military activities with biological or other new weapons might confront the planet with challenges that are at present not seriously taken into consideration; water scarcity and its consequences for agriculture might create huge problems for specific areas; genetic manipulation or microbiological developments might generate new threats. Yet, as a choice of delimiting the topic must be made, this chapter will concentrate on four of the five challenges that were mentioned.

The chapter will not deal with the fight against poverty, though this appears to be globally the biggest threat to the environment. However, a discussion on the European Union's (EU) measures to eradicate poverty at a global level could, on the one hand, not remain limited to EU measures. Rather the policies, strategies and measures of the EU Member States would also have to be included, as foreign policy – of which development aid and the fight against poverty are parts – has very largely remained in

---

[1] World Economic Forum, 'Global Risks 2014: Understanding Systemic Risks in a Changing Global Environment', Geneva, 2014.

the hands of the Member States, though the Treaty on European Union (TEU) provides for a 'common foreign and security policy' of the EU. On the other hand, EU and national policies which aim at the eradication of poverty go far beyond environmental aspects; they also include trade, security, industrial, agricultural, fisheries and other policies; a presentation of these different policies would require much more space than is available for this contribution. For example, the EU agricultural policy, which gives third-country agricultural products access to the EU market only to a very limited extent, is considered by many as impeding economic progress in developing countries; yet others underline the social and economic aspects of the EU agricultural policy for EU farmers and consumers and find some justification in the present EU policy. It is impossible to present and weigh the pros and cons of the different arguments in just a few lines.

Therefore, it will have to be sufficient to point out that the EU's external action has the objective, among others, of fostering 'the sustainable economic, social and environmental development of developing countries, with the primary aim of eradicating poverty'.[2] The EU budget for 2016 provides for 'international cooperation and development' expenses of about €3 billion.[3] However, the budget chapters for agriculture, transport, research, maritime affairs, migration, foreign policy, environment, neighbourhood negotiations humanitarian aid, energy, climate action, justice and consumers also provide for expenses which directly or indirectly benefit developing countries. The concentration on development measures alone would therefore give a wrong picture.

II   Climate Change

The international discussion on global warming and climate change began in the mid-1980s. As the UK prominently participated in this discussion and supported the concept of anthropogenic greenhouse gas emissions being mainly responsible for the global warming, the UK government was, right from the beginning, favourable to EU measures in order to stop global warming. This attitude facilitated the EU policy which decided, already in 1990, to stabilise CO^2 emissions by the year 2000. In 1994, the EU adhered to the United Nations (UN) Climate Change Convention and signed, in 1997, the Kyoto Protocol. When the USA withdrew its signature

---

[2] Article 21(2)(d) TEU. The eradication of poverty is also mentioned in Article 3(5) TEU.
[3] OJ 2016, L 48, 1, section 21.

under this Protocol, the EU declared publicly that the Kyoto Protocol 'was not dead' and deployed a strong international diplomatic activity in order to have this Protocol enter into force. These efforts succeeded in 2005.

The EU which had ratified the Kyoto Protocol in 2002,[4] complied with the commitment to reduce its greenhouse gas emissions by 8 per cent in 2012, compared to 1990. It used the provision in the Kyoto Protocol which allowed several states to jointly comply with their reduction obligations and adopted a burden-sharing decision which differentiated the reduction obligations of Member States according to a rather opaque policy process.[5] In 2009, another burden-sharing decision was adopted, fixing the obligations of EU Member States until 2020.[6] The EU also concluded the Doha amendment, undertaking to reduce its greenhouse gas emissions by 2020 by 20 per cent.[7] By 2012, the reduction of greenhouse gas emissions had reached 19.2 per cent.[8]

Furthermore, the EU actively promoted the conclusion of a new international agreement on climate change and signed, in April 2016, the Paris Agreement on climate change. In anticipation of that Agreement, the EU committed itself to reduce its greenhouse gas emissions until 2030 by 40 per cent, compared to 1990, to ensure a share of renewable energies in the overall consumption of energy of 27 per cent and to improve its energy efficiency also by 27 per cent.[9]

The objective of limiting the global warming to 2°C beyond pre-industrial levels was inserted, since the mid-1990s, in several policy statements of the European Council and also, progressively, in legislative texts. Since 2009, the Treaty on the Functioning of the European Union (TFEU) which is, together with the TEU a sort of constitution of the EU, provides as one of the objectives of the EU environmental policy 'combating climate change' (Article 191 TFEU). Article 194 TFEU, also inserted in 2009, asks the EU to promote 'energy saving and the development of new and renewable sources of energy'. Legislative measures in both the environmental and the energy sector are normally adopted by majority decisions and are

---

[4] Decision 2002/358, OJ 2002, L 130, 1.

[5] Ibid.

[6] Decision 406/2009, OJ 2009, L 140, 136.

[7] Decision 2015/146, OJ 2015, L 26, 1.

[8] Commission, COM (2014) 689.

[9] European Council, meeting of 23–24 October 2014, document EUCO 169/14. See also European Commission, 'A Framework Strategy for a Resilient Energy Union with a Forward-Looking Climate Change Policy', COM (2015) 80. The European Council, consisting of the Heads of State or Government of the twenty-eight EU Member States, is the highest political institution of the EU. Its decisions are of political, not legal, nature.

then binding on all EU Member States. However, when a Member State's choice between different energy sources or the structure of its energy supply is affected or when ecotax decisions are to be taken, EU decisions require unanimity.[10]

Since 1988, the EU recommended Member States to better use renewable sources of energy. It supported such initiatives with (modest) financial means. In 2001, an EU Directive[11] fixed as objectives a share of 12 per cent of renewable energies in the total EU energy consumption, and a share of 22 per cent in the total electricity consumption; non-binding targets for electricity consumption were fixed for each Member State. Another Directive of 2003 tried to stimulate the use of biofuels in the transport sector.[12]

Both Directives were replaced by a Directive of 2009[13] which requested Member States to reach a share of renewable energies in the gross final energy consumption of 20 per cent by 2020; no targets for electricity consumption were fixed. Furthermore, each Member State had to cover, by 2020, its energy consumption in the transport sector by at least 10 per cent with renewable energies. Member States were requested to adopt binding action plans with annual timetables and submit them to the Commission; when progress was not sufficient, Member States had to amend their action plans. They had to report annually on progress achieved. The Directive also contained provisions on sustainability criteria for biofuels and bioliquids, produced within and outside the EU. The Commission was obliged to extensively report on the implementation of the Directive, including on the question of whether third countries which supplied biofuels to the EU complied with the sustainability criteria and respected specific international labour and environmental agreements.

The 2015 progress report of the Commission stated that the share of renewable energies in the EU in 2014 was 15.3 per cent and that it would be possible to reach a 20 per cent share by 2020.[14] The share of renewable energy in transport was 5.7 per cent in 2014, and the Commission raised doubts, whether the 10 per cent target for 2020 could be reached.[15] The

---

[10] See Articles 192(2)(c) and 194(2) TFEU. Until 2016, all EU climate change-related legislation was adopted by majority decisions.

[11] Directive 2001/77, OJ 2001, L 283, 33. Under EU law, Directives address the Member States and are binding as to the result to be reached, see Article 288 TFEU.

[12] Directive 2003/30, OJ 2003, L 123, 42.

[13] Directive 2009/28, OJ 2009, L 140, 16.

[14] Commission, COM (2015) 293.

[15] Ibid. Difficulties in reaching the target for 2020 existed, according to the Commission, in France, Malta, Luxembourg, Netherlands, UK, Belgium, Spain, Hungary and Poland.

discussion on the large-scale use of biofuels became controversial in the EU. The report was silent on third countries' compliance with labour and biodiversity agreements and on respecting the sustainability criteria.[16]

Also, in the energy efficiency sector, the EU started with financial support of voluntary national measures. A first Directive of 1993 asked Member States to establish programmes to improve energy efficiency and to report on their implementation.[17] It was replaced by a Directive of 2006 which asked Member States to establish binding action plans for energy efficiency; the objective was to reach, by 2015, an improvement of energy efficiency of 9 per cent.[18] Another Directive of 2005[19] constituted the framework for binding measures on the energy consumption of products which led to a large number of binding energy efficiency standards for products. A Directive of 2002, replaced in 2010, aimed at the improvement of energy efficiency for (new and renovated) buildings.[20]

A new Directive of 2012 asked Member States to set an indicative energy efficiency target in order to reach the EU objective of improving energy efficiency by 20 per cent until 2020.[21] It also established provisions on public procurement, building renovation, energy audits, metering, billing information and a number of other measures to promote energy efficiency. Member States had to adopt national energy efficiency action plans and report annually to the Commission. Specific sanctions for the case of non-compliance were not foreseen.

The Commission's progress report of 2015 indicated that Member States' measures added up to 17.6 per cent of energy efficiency improvement by 2020;[22] the Commission expressed the view that recent measures adopted by some states would allow the envisaged target to be reached.

It is remarkable that for both the measures on energy saving and energy efficiency, no enforcement measures against Member States were taken; the achievements were reached with the obligation to adopt and

---

[16] The only reference to this problem was made in a progress report of 2013 (COM (2013) 75, 12) where it was stated: 'Whilst most non EU countries have ratified the fundamental conventions, enforcement is lower than in the EU or in the US which has not ratified many such conventions.'

[17] Directive 93/76, OJ 1003, L 237, 28.

[18] Directive 2006/32, OJ 2006, L 114, 64.

[19] Directive 2005/32, OJ 2005, L 191, 29; this Directive was replaced by Directive 2009/125, OJ 2009, L 285, 10.

[20] Directive 2010/31 on the energy performance of buildings, OJ 2010 L 153, 13; this Directive replaced Directive 2002/91, OJ 2003 L 1, 65.

[21] Directive 2012/27, OJ 2012, L 315, 1.

[22] Commission, COM (2015) 574.

implement action plans and to annually report to the Commission (and to other Member States). This form of cooperative discussions, suggestions for amendments of national action plans and learning from the example of other Member States apparently was relatively successful in achieving the political results which had been fixed.

In 2003, the EU adopted a Directive on emission-allowance trading with greenhouse gases which concerned about 45 per cent of all greenhouse gas emissions in the EU.[23] Companies had to buy emission allowances; where they did not need them, they could sell them on the market. The Directive aimed at inciting companies to invest in clean technologies instead of acquiring expensive emission allowances. However, as the Member States which were responsible for attributing the allowances were rather generous in the attributions, too many allowances were issued; this led to low prices of the allowances and did thus not constitute an incentive to invest in clean technologies. Attempts of reducing the quantity of emission allowances were not yet very effective; as no minimum price for CO^2 was fixed, the market does not function well.

Other legislative measures of the EU concerned reporting requirements for CO^2,[24] CO^2 emissions of cars,[25] the capture and storage of CO^2,[26] measures to reduce the land-filling of waste,[27] labelling CO^2 emissions of cars,[28] fluorinated gases in appliances[29] and numerous measures in the area of agriculture, environment and research.

Overall, the EU reached, between 1990 and 2012, a reduction of greenhouse gas emissions of 19.2 per cent, while at the same time its gross domestic product increased by 45 per cent.[30] At the same time, global greenhouse gas emissions increased from 22.7 billion tonnes to 34.5 billion tonnes, thus by some 50 per cent.[31]

---

[23] Directive 2003/87, OJ 2003, L 275, 32.
[24] Decision 525/2013, OJ 2013, L 165, 13; this Decision replaced Decision 280/2004, OJ 2004, L 49, 1.
[25] Regulation 443/2009, OJ 2009, L 140, 1 (passenger cars); Regulation 510/2011, OJ 2011, L 145, 1 (light-duty vehicles). No limit value was fixed for trucks.
[26] Directive 1999/31, OJ 1999, L 182, 1.
[27] Directive 2009/31, OJ 2009, L 140, 114.
[28] Directive 1999/94, OJ 2000, L 12, 16.
[29] Regulation 517/2014, OJ 2014, L 150, 195; this Regulation replaced Regulation 842/2006, OJ 2006, L 161, 1.
[30] Commission, COM (2014) 689. The UN 'Greenhouse Gas Inventory Data for the Period 1990–2013' (unfccc.int/resource/docs/2015/sbi/eng/21.pdf) does not contain data for the EU, but only for Member States separately.
[31] Netherlands Environment Agency, Trends in Global CO^2 Emissions, 2013 Report, The Hague 2013.

One essential part of combating climate change is the transfer of financial resources from developed to developing countries.[32] In this regard, the EU is relatively passive. Indeed, EU Member States prefer to give financial support to developing countries themselves, rather than via the EU. For example, the agreement between the EU and seventy-eight states of Africa, the Caribbean and Asia (ACP-countries) provides for a sum of €31.5 billion which shall be made available to these countries between 2014 and 2020; one of the possible activities which may be financed, being climate change measures.[33] Some €29 billion are made available from the Member States, and only the rest from the EU.

The EU budget for 2016 foresees EU contributions of some €800.000 to international climate change conventions.[34] Furthermore, some €250 million are earmarked for measures on climate change, environment and sustainable energy in non-ACP developing countries.[35] The EU provided for provisions concerning the clean development mechanism under the Kyoto Protocol which favours common actions between developed and developing countries to reduce greenhouse gases.[36] However, implementation is again in the hands of the Member States; no cumulative data for the overall EU measures under this mechanism are available.

The Commission declared that the EU had undertaken, in the context of the EU Multiannual Financial Framework 2014–2020 to direct 20 per cent of its overall budget to climate-relevant projects and policies.[37] This policy commitment, which is not laid down in the Multiannual Financial Framework itself,[38] would mean that until 2020, about €14 billion would be spent annually for climate-related projects in developing countries.[39] In contrast, the considerable state aid for fossil fuels, which is granted by the EU and by its Member States[40] and which the Commission itself qualified

---

[32] See UN Framework Convention on Climate Change, Article 4(3)(c); Paris Agreement, Article 9.

[33] See Decision 1/2013, OJ 2013, L 173, 67.

[34] EU Budget for 2016, OJ 2016, L 48, 1, section 340251.

[35] Ibid., sections 21020701 and 21020702. The actual payments in previous years were much lower which seems to indicate that developing countries are not too eager to request the financing of climate change and sustainable energy measures.

[36] Directive 2004/101, OJ 2004, l 338, 18.

[37] Commission, Communication, 'The Road from Paris', COM (2016) 110, 8.

[38] Regulation 1311/2013 laying down the multiannual financial framework for the years 2014–2020, OJ 2013, L 347, 884.

[39] Commission, 'The Road from Paris' (above n. 37), 8.

[40] State aid to fossil fuels by the EU and Member States is estimated at €81 billion per year: Commission (Ecofys), 'Subsidies and Costs of EU Energy', 2014.

as the 'biggest obstacle to innovation in clean technology',[41] has not been tackled yet by the EU.[42]

Following the adoption of the Paris Agreement, the Commission announced that it would submit legislative proposals for putting into legal form the policy commitments of the European Council for 2030, which would include the ratifying of the Agreement, a new effort-sharing decision which extended until 2030, proposals on land use, land-use change and forestry (LULUCF), on a reliable and transparent governance mechanism streamlining planning and reporting requirements, and the revision of the legislation on energy efficiency and renewables.[43] It did not announce any specific measure to approach the 1.5°C target of the Paris Agreement.

In conclusion, the EU fully complied with its commitments under the Kyoto Protocol and is well on track to comply with its commitments under the Doha Protocol. It has started to further reduce greenhouse gas emissions by 2030. Thus, the European Commission is right in praising the EU's 'international leadership and climate diplomacy'.[44] The EU achieved more than comparable developed countries – USA, Canada, Japan, Australia – could claim. The big problem is whether these measures are sufficient. A Dutch court recently found that the EU did not do enough to bring its greenhouse gas emissions down;[45] such arguments appear to be well founded, as already in 2007, the EU offered to reduce its greenhouse gas emissions under certain conditions by 30 per cent by 2020.[46] Also with regard to developing countries, EU diplomacy might be able to do more than making financial resources available.

---

[41] Commission, 'The Road from Paris' (above n. 37), 7.

[42] See, however, Decision 2010/787 on state aid to facilitate the closure of uncompetitive coal mines, OJ 2010, L 336, 24. This Decision provides that state aid to coal mines shall stop on 31 December 2018. Whether this Decision will be fully applied, is doubtful. Germany has already signalled that, having decided to stop nuclear energy production, it could not, at the same time, stop coal mining. And the government in Poland, which came to power in 2015, intends to heavily support national coal production.

[43] Commission (above n. 14), 9.

[44] Ibid., 2.

[45] Rechtbank Den Haag, Case C/09/456689/HA ZA-13–1396, *Urgenda*, ECLI:NL:RBDHA: 2015:7196, judgment of 24 June 2015.

[46] See Decision 406/2009 (above n. 6), Recital 3: 'the European Council of March 2007 endorsed a Community objective of a 30% reduction of greenhouse gas emissions by 2020 compared to 1990 ... provided that other developed countries commit themselves to comparable emission reductions and economically more advanced developing countries commit themselves to contributing adequately according to their responsibilities and capabilities'.

III   Loss of Biodiversity

The loss of biodiversity is a generally recognised global phenomenon. The Convention on Biological Diversity noted in 1992 that 'biological diversity is being significantly reduced by human activities'.[47] The Global Biodiversity Outlooks 4 and 5, elaborated in 2010 and 2015 under the auspices of the United Nations Environmental Programme (UNEP), demonstrated that the loss of biodiversity continued at global level and had not come to a standstill;[48] it identified as the major causes habitat loss and degradation, climate change, excessive nutritional loads and other forms of pollution, over-exploitation and unsustainable use and invasive alien species.

The EU is a wealthy, densely populated area with high economic and leisure activities. Biodiversity is thus under constant pressure and though the EU adopted numerous measures on biodiversity conservation, the success is limited.

The EU adhered to the international conventions on migratory species, biological diversity, the protection of the Alps, the conservation of Antarctic marine living resources, combating desertification, the conservation of European wildlife and natural habitats, trade in endangered species and African-Eurasian water birds. However, monitoring and enforcement of international conventions does not take place in practice unless the EU has adopted specific EU legislation – a directive or a regulation – to transpose the provisions of the respective convention into EU law. With the exception of the Convention on International Trade in Endangered Species (CITES), such legislation was not adopted by the EU for any of the mentioned conventions, so that these agreements are not monitored in the EU territory.

There is no comprehensive EU legislation on the conservation of biodiversity. The EU did not adopt legislation on soil protection; such legislation only exists in some Member States. The EU did not adopt legislation on the protection of the landscape. In 2014, it adopted legislation to fight invasive alien species, though this has not yet become operational.[49] As regards legislation on biodiversity conservation, the EU relies almost entirely on

---

[47] Convention on Biological Diversity, Recital 6.
[48] UNEP, 'Global Environmental Outlook 3' (2010); 'Global Environmental Outlook 4' (2015).
[49] Regulation 1143/2014, OJ 2014, L 317, 35.

the Directive on the conservation of wild birds (Birds Directive),[50] which protects all wild living birds in Europe and grants special protection to some 190 threatened species; and on the Directive on the conservation of natural habitats and species of wild fauna and flora (Habitats Directive),[51] which ensures the conservation of rare, threatened or endemic species, including about 450 animals and 500 plants. Some 200 rare and characteristic habitat types are also targeted for conservation.

Under both Directives, the EU created a 'Natura 2000' network which assembles at present about 28,000 natural land and marine habitats with a surface area of around 1 million km². Member States identified the habitats that needed protection which the Commission then included in lists of habitats of EU interest. Following that, the Member States had to formally protect the habitat and provide for a management plan, in order to ensure a favourable conservation status.

Since the adoption of the first Birds Directive in 1979, the EU undertook a very considerable number of measures in order to protect the biological diversity within and outside the EU. Good information on these measures, which cannot be enumerated here in detail, is found in the five reports which the EU sent, between 1998 and 2014, to the Secretariat of the Convention on Biological Diversity,[52] and the national reports which the EU Member States sent to the Secretariat.

In 1998, the EU adopted a biodiversity strategy[53] which envisaged four principal areas of activity: the conservation and sustainable use of biological resources; the sharing of genetic resources; research, control and exchange of information; and education, training and sensitivisation. The objectives of the strategy were to be reached within the context of ongoing EU activities, but to a large extent also by Member States. In 2001, the Commission adopted a Biodiversity Action Plan, consisting of four sections: agriculture; conservation of natural resources; fisheries; and economic development cooperation.[54] Attempts to create, within the Commission, an integrated administrative structure for having environmental and nature conservation requirements considered in the activities

---

[50] Directive 2009/147 on the conservation of wild birds, OJ 2010, L 20, 7; this Directive replaced Directive 79/409, OJ 1979, L 103, 1 on the same subject.

[51] Directive 92/43 on the conservation of natural habitats and of wild fauna and flora, OJ 1992, L 206, 7.

[52] Convention on Biological Diversity, First report of the European Union to the Convention on Biological Diversity, 1998; Second EU Report 2002; Third EU Report 2005; Fourth EU Report 2009; Fifth EU Report 2014.

[53] Commission, COM (1998) 42.

[54] Commission, COM (2001) 162.

of the other EU policies (agriculture, fisheries etc),[55] failed, however, so that the Action Plan did not change the administrative and political reality. Following a policy commitment by the European Council, the Decision on the sixth EU environment action programme laid down, in a legally binding form, the objective of 'halting biodiversity decline with the aim to reach this objective by 2010'.[56] Subsequently, the Commission submitted an action plan for halting the loss of biodiversity.[57] It identified a number of measures in order to reach the deadline of 2010, though most of these measures were to be taken by the Member States individually, not by the EU itself. When it turned out, in 2010, that the loss of biodiversity had not been stopped, the Commission adopted a new strategy, on the basis of which the Council concluded that by 2020 the loss of biodiversity should be halted and by 2050 the EU biodiversity and the ecosystem services which it provided, would be fully protected.[58] No specific measures were suggested. An interim assessment in 2015[59] showed that the 2020 target would probably not be reached.

In 2010, the European Environment Agency published a first 'EU bio-diversity baseline' on the state of biodiversity in the EU.[60] It found that – twenty years after the setting up of the Natura 2000 network – 17 per cent of the habitats of that network had a favourable conservation status as requested by Directive 92/43, 65 per cent had an unfavourable conserva-tion status and for 18 per cent the status was unknown. As regards species, 17 per cent had a favourable conservation status, 52 per cent an unfavour-able status, and for 31 per cent the status was unknown. Twenty-five per cent of the EU marine mammals, 15 per cent of terrestrial mammals, 12 per cent of birds, 22 per cent of amphibians, 22 per cent of reptiles, 16 per cent of dragonflies and 7 per cent of butterflies were threatened with extinction. The principal pressure on habitats came from agriculture which led, together with other pressures, to fragmentation, degradation and destruction due to land-use change: EU 'ecosystems are literally cut

[55] See on these attempts the First EU Report (above n. 52), 22.
[56] Decision 2002/1600, OJ 2002, L 242, 1, Article 6(1).
[57] Commission, COM (2006) 216.
[58] Commission, COM (2011) 244; Council, Document 7536/10 of 16 March 2010; see also Commission, COM (2010) 4; and COM (2010) 548.
[59] Commission, COM (2015) 478; see also European Environment Agency, 'State of nature in Europe', Copenhagen, 2015, 141.
[60] European Environment Agency, 'EU 2010 Biodiversity Baseline (adapted to the MAES typology)', Copenhagen, 2010.

to pieces by urban sprawl, rapidly expanding transport infrastructure and energy networks.[61]

The Commission indicated that in 2012 only 58 per cent of the Natura 2000 habitats had management plans in operation or in development, that 30 per cent of all species were threatened by over-exploitation of forests, oceans, rivers, lakes and soils, and a further 26 per cent by pesticides and fertilisers; between 1990 and 2006, bird populations in the EU declined by 10 per cent (farmland birds by 25 per cent, forest birds by 18 per cent).[62] Between 1961 and 2003, the EU ecological footprint increased from three to four hectares per person.[63]

These data do not show that the EU successfully responded to the global challenge of biodiversity loss. Not without reason are EU agriculture and fisheries activities mainly blamed for this situation.[64]

Internationally, the EU adhered to the Convention on Biological Diversity, as well as to the Cartagena and the Nagoya Protocol. It adopted a regulation to ensure that timber-exporting countries adopt a licensing scheme[65] and tried to conclude partnership agreements with timber-exporting countries to make this legislation operational.[66] It also adopted a regulation to prohibit the import of illegally harvested timber and timber products.[67] Long before the EU was allowed, in 2013, to adhere to CITES, it adopted EU legislation which was aligned to that Convention and was even, in parts, more protective;[68] all decisions of CITES were transposed into EU legislation. There are import bans on whales and whale products,[69] as well as on seals and seal products.[70]

The EU is by far the largest donor for biodiversity measures at international level. Between 2003 and 2006, the yearly external assistance for biodiversity – EU and EU Member States – totalled €1.5 billion and was

[61] Ibid., 88, 14, 19 and 21. The data do not include data from Bulgaria, Romania and Croatia.
[62] Commission, COM (2015) 478, 6; Fourth EU Report (above n. 52), 3; Fifth EU Report (above n. 52), 10 and 11.
[63] Fifth EU Report (above n. 52), 38.
[64] Fourth EU Report (above n. 52), 80.
[65] Regulation 2173/2005, OJ 2005, L 347, 1.
[66] By March 2015, such agreements were concluded with Ghana, the Republic of Congo, Cameroon, Liberia, Central African Republic and Indonesia. Negotiations with about ten other countries are ongoing.
[67] Regulation 995/2010, OJ 2010, L 295, 23.
[68] Regulation 338/97, OJ 1997, L 61, 1; this Regulation replaced Regulation 3626/82 of 1982, OJ 192, L 384, 1.
[69] Regulation 348/81, OJ 1981, L 39, 1.
[70] Regulation 1007/2009, OJ 2009, L 286, 36.

raised to €1.7 billion between 2006 and 2010;[71] since then, it certainly has not diminished. 'Very few [developing] countries have identified biodiversity as a priority sector for cooperation in their country strategy papers. This is a major impediment to increasing EU funding for biodiversity in development cooperation.'[72]

In conclusion, despite very considerable efforts undertaken by the EU and its Member States, the EU measures are insufficient to halt the decline of biodiversity within the EU and at global level.

IV   The Omnipresence of Chemicals

Chemicals, as substances or as products, are indispensable in modern life. Yet, they have a very considerable impact on human health and on the environment. When in the preceding sections climate change and loss of biological diversity were discussed as global environmental challenges, it should not be overlooked that the principal source of global warming is the emission of chemicals – in the form of greenhouse gases or ozone-depleting substances; and 'agriculture' as the main pressure on the natural environment in the EU 'exercises' this pressure to a large extent through the use of pesticides and fertilisers or the discharge of nitrates and other pollutants. According to the Commission, air pollution – principally nitrogen oxides (NOx) and fine particulate matters (PM_{10} and $PM_{2.5}$) – cause more than 400,000 premature deaths per year in the EU.[73] Other forms of pollution of the air, water and soil are less visible but nonetheless dangerous to humans, animals and plants.

The EU does not have a consistent, coherent product policy. Article 191 TFEU states that environmental policy should be based on the principles of prevention and precaution, of the need to fight environmental impairment as a priority at source and of the polluter-pays-principle. In practice, though, these principles – with the exception of the precautionary principle – are not applied when the EU adopts legislation in the area of free trade (free circulation) of goods and services within the EU, in agriculture, fisheries, state aid, transport or energy measures.

There is no systematic EU attempt to eliminate chemical substances that are toxic, carcinogenic or mutagenic or otherwise dangerous to humans or to the environment, though there are numerous pieces of EU legislation

---

[71] Fourth EU Report (above n. 52), 58; Fifth EU Report (above n. 52), 37.
[72] Fourth EU Report (above n. 52), 76.
[73] Commission, COM (2013) 718, 5.

which limit or prohibit the presence of some of such substances, in particular heavy metals. Examples of such legislation is that on cars and electrical/electronic products, toys, packaging material, batteries or crystal glass. However, the elaboration or strengthening of each legislative measure is heavily contested by the specific vested-interest groups which all too often leads to derogation, exceptions or compromises that are, from the point of view of human health or the environment, unsatisfactory. The general EU Directive on product safety refers to the safety for consumers, but not for the environment.[74]

An EU strategy to phase out cadmium to the extent possible, failed completely.[75] Restrictions on cadmium, lead, chromium and mercury are limited to very specific products or uses.[76] With the exception of lead, no concentration value (quality objective) for the air was fixed;[77] for water such concentration values were fixed for cadmium, lead and mercury.[78] Enforcement of this legislation is frequently improvable.

A number of pesticides were restricted in use or prohibited as a follow-up of the Stockholm Convention on Persistent Organic Pollutants.[79] All active substances for pesticides and biocides need an EU authorisation which is, overall, generously granted.[80] An EU Directive on the sustainable use of pesticides[81] remained general: it enabled Member States which wanted to limit the use of pesticides to take action, but was not sharp enough to enforce restrictions and is insufficiently monitored. EU legislation for pesticide residues on and in food fixes maximum residue levels for each pesticide (about 700) and for each type of fruit or vegetable, a huge

---

[74] Directive 2001/95, OJ 2002, L 11, 4; see, however, Court of Justice, Case C-288/08, *Kemikalieinspektionen*, ECR 2009, I-11031.

[75] See Commission proposal for a strategy, COM (87) 165; Council Resolution, OJ 1988, C 30/1. A good example is cadmium in fertilisers, by far the most important source of cadmium impacts on soil and the food chain: as the EU could not agree to limit the cadmium content in fertilisers, it allows Sweden, Austria and Finland such a limitation – since 1995, more than twenty years; see e.g. Commission Decision 2006/347, OJ 2006, L 29, 19.

[76] See Regulation 1907/2006 on the registration, evaluation, authorisation and restriction of chemicals (REACH) OJ 2006, L 396, 1, Annex XVII, No. 23 (cadmium); Nos. 18 and 18a (mercury); Nos. 63, 16 and 17 (lead); and No. 47 (chromium VI).

[77] Directive 2008/50, OJ 2008, L 152, 1.

[78] Directives 2008/105, OJ 2008, L 348, 84 and 2013/39, OJ 2013, L 226, 1.

[79] Regulation 850/2004, OJ 2004, L 158, 7; this Regulation replaced the Directive on the prohibition of pesticides of 1979.

[80] Regulation 1107/2009, OJ 2009, L 309, 1 (pesticides); Regulation 538/2012, OJ 2012, L 167, 1 (biocides).

[81] Directive 2009/128, OJ 2009, L 309, 71.

challenge for monitoring authorities; the monitoring reports do not signal significant problems.[82]

EU legislation on genetically modified organisms (GMOs) is very restrictive on the release of GMOs: while the presence of GMOs is allowed in certain limits, the cultivation of GM plants is almost completely restricted, and recent legislation enabled Member States to altogether prohibit such cultivation on certain conditions.[83] Several Member States provide for such a prohibition already. Hormones or other growth promoters in meat have been prohibited since the mid-1980s.

The EU abandoned an early approach to fix limitations for emissions into the air and discharges into the water from industrial installations[84] and opted instead for concentration limits (quality objectives) in air and water, knowing that compliance with such quality objectives can hardly be monitored and enforced.[85] Large industrial installations are obliged to apply the best available technique to reduce emissions,[86] a formula which gives broad discretion to permitting authorities. Medium-size installations will be covered by this formula in future;[87] small installations are not covered by EU regulations.

Exceptionally, air emission limit values are fixed, for example for waste incinerators, or cars and trucks. Thanks to the Montreal Protocol, there are large and effective restrictions to the marketing and use of ozone-depleting substances which go beyond the international obligations.[88] In contrast, emission limit values for greenhouse gases only exist for passenger cars (CO^2).[89] Other car emissions are fixed by a regulation of 2007.[90] No emission limit values exist for aeroplanes and ships, though ships have

---

[82] European Food Safety Authority, 'The 2013 EU Report on Pesticide Residues in Food' (2015) 13(3) *EFSA Journal* 4038.

[83] Directive 2015/412, OJ 2015, L 68, 1.

[84] Directive 84/360, OJ 194, L 188, 20 (air emissions); Directive 76/464, OJ 1976, L 129, 23 (water discharges).

[85] A good example is that of air pollution in the UK: EU Directive 2008/50 (above n. 77) requires Member States to have complied with its quality objectives by 2010, and at the latest by 2015. Where a breach is found, the remediation shall take place 'as soon as possible'. The UK government keeps on arguing that it cannot comply with the EU values before 2025.

[86] Directive 2010/75, OJ 2010, L 334, 17.

[87] Directive 2015/2193, OJ 2015, L 313, 1.

[88] Regulation 1005/2009, OJ 2009, L 286, 1.

[89] Regulation 443/2009, OJ 2009, L 140, 1.

[90] Regulation 715/2007, OJ 2007, L 171, 1.

to limit their SO^2 emissions in some EU waters. Some, not too stringent, emission limit values exist for new non-road machinery.[91]

As regards discharges into water, the strategy to phase out, by 2020, the discharge of dangerous substances into water was abandoned and replaced by a quality-objective approach.[92] More effective was a Directive on urban waste water which required all agglomerations with more than 2,000 people to have waste-water collection systems and at least secondary treatment for such waters and which, furthermore, prohibited the discharge of sewage sludge into waters.[93] In contrast, a Directive on the limitation of nitrates in water from agricultural sources[94] was reduced in its effectiveness by generous derogations granted and lack of enforcement by the Commission.

EU Regulation 1907/2006 on chemicals introduced a procedure for limiting or prohibiting the use of dangerous chemicals.[95] However, the process is slow: by 2016, six new substances were inserted into the list of restrictions/prohibitions, since the Regulation was adopted in 2006, and some restrictions amended.[96]

Internationally, the EU followed the approach of the Rotterdam Convention on 'prior informed consent'.[97] It did not question this approach, though it appears that, in nine out of ten cases, a chemical that is prohibited within the EU because of its toxic, carcinogenic or mutagenic properties also constitutes a risk in third countries. Frequently, developing countries do not have the necessary, scientific, administrative and political infrastructure to correctly and completely assess the risk of a chemical. The 'prior informed consent' approach is thus favourable to developed countries, but less advantageous to developing countries. The EU prohibited the export of metallic mercury and its compounds[98] and of a number

---

[91] Directive 2004/26, OJ 2004, L 146, 1.
[92] See, on the one hand, Directive 2000/60, OJ 2000, L 327, 1, Article 16; and, on the other hand, Directive 2008/105 (above n 78).
[93] Directive 91/271, OJ 1991, L 135, 40.
[94] Directive 91/676, OJ 1991, L 376, 1.
[95] Regulation 1907/2006 (above n. 76).
[96] See last Commission Regulation 474/2014, OJ 2014, L 136, 19. Overall, Annex XVII of Regulation 1907/2006 which lists the restrictions and prohibitions, contains sixty-five substances. It should, however, be pointed out that restrictions which are inserted in other pieces of EU legislation – e.g. heavy metals in batteries (Directive 2006/66, OJ 2006, L 266, 1) – are not listed in Annex XVII.
[97] Regulation 649/2012, OJ 2012, L 201, 60. Annex I Part 1 of the Regulation lists some 170 substances which are subject to the 'prior informed consent' procedure, because they are banned or severely restricted in use within the EU.
[98] Regulation 1102/2008, OJ 2008, L 204, 75.

of ozone-depleting substances;[99] in both cases, it followed international agreements.

Air emissions for aeroplanes and ships are fixed by the International Civil Aviation Organisation (ICAO) and by the International Maritime Organisation (IMO) respectively and are taken over by the EU, though such provisions hardly exist or are very loose. Progress in these two organisations is disappointingly slow, as vested interests have too much influence there and unanimous decisions are the rule. In both organisations, environmental concerns do not rank high in the priority list.

In conclusion, the EU has equipped itself with a modern, progressive legislative instrument as regards the marketing of chemicals (REACH), based on the precautionary principle. Progress under this Regulation is slow, because of strong vested interests. The limitation of emissions from mobile and stationary sources – in particular from transport – does not match with the disastrous state of air pollution within the EU, specifically in urban agglomerations. Discharges into water have been reduced. Agricultural activities – pesticide, fertiliser use – continue to put strong pressure on soils and on the natural environment and no policy change is in view. The enforcement of the existing provisions – the greatest problem of environmental law – is particularly problematic in the area of chemical substances.

V   Resource Management

The EU policy and strategy on resource management is still in its infancy. For decades, general EU policy was oriented towards economic growth, the import of raw materials, if that was necessary, and the export of manufactured products. The slowly growing awareness that there were limits to growth, that economic development had to be sustainable and that the planetary resources were not inexhaustible – all such ideas coming from the environmental sector – were beginning, in these last ten years, to bring about new reflections. Sometimes, external factors had an influence: the exhaustion of fish stocks in European waters gave rise to consideration of a different EU fisheries policy. The growing dependency on imported fossil fuels accelerated reflections on a change of energy policy orientations within the EU. Also, quite simple examples favoured a rethinking: the weight of a mobile telephone is some 100 grams; however, to produce a mobile telephone, about 80 kilograms of raw materials are necessary. A

---

[99] Regulation1005/2009, OJ 2005, L 286, 1.

passenger car might weigh, on average, about 1 ton. In order to produce a car, about 60 tons of raw materials are required. In a world with 9 billion people – all needing food and shelter, energy and products – the recourse to raw materials will inevitably become more difficult.

The European Commission clarified, in several communications, that its approach to an integrated product policy – defined as 'an approach which seeks to reduce the life cycle environmental impacts of products from the mining of raw materials to production, distribution, use and waste management'[100] – favoured voluntary measures by economic operators and that it did not intend to suggest legislation.[101] This approach did not achieve tangible results also because of divergencies among economic operators.

The EU did not take up in any serious form the invitation from the Rio Conference 1992 to deal with issues of sustainable production and consumption. A Commission proposal for an action plan on sustainable consumption and production of 2008[102] again concentrated on energy question and voluntary measures by economic operators. It met with limited enthusiasm of the European Parliament (EP) and the Council and was not really put into operation. More successful was a Directive on the eco-design of energy-related products[103] which led to a very considerable number of binding regulations on the reduction of energy consumption of products, such as computers, TV sets, household appliances, water heating equipment etc. Though the legislation allowed general environmental performances to be regulated, in practice the EU gave strong priority to energy consumption, as this fitted into the EU policy to combat climate change. This was completed by a Directive on energy labelling and standard product information (noise, water consumption) of (mainly) household appliances and office equipment.[104]

EU waste policy favoured, since the 1970s, the recycling of waste materials and fixed, as a first priority of any waste management policy, the prevention of waste generation. When this objective was adopted, it was overlooked that materials, before they became waste, were products; thus, a waste prevention policy required measures affecting products. EU waste

---

[100] Commission, COM (2001) 68, 2.
[101] Ibid.; COM (2003) 302; COM (2010) 614.
[102] Commission, COM (2008) 397.
[103] Directive 2005/32, OJ 2005, L 191, 29; in 2009, this Directive was replaced by Directive 2009/125, OJ 2009, L 285, 10. The Directives did not apply to cars, aeroplanes and other means of transport.
[104] Directive 2010/30, OJ 2010, L 153, 1; this Directive replaced an earlier Directive of 1992.

legislation of 2008[105] required Member States to adopt waste prevention programmes and contained a number of measures to promote the recycling of waste materials.

When proposals were made, in 2013–2014, to increase the recycling and recovery targets for certain waste materials – glass and metal, paper and plastics – the newly installed Commission considered that such measures went contrary to the EU objective of deregulation and announced that it would repeal its proposals on waste recycling. However, this announcement raised a storm of protests from Member States governments, the EP, the recycling industry and the general public. On this, the Commission gave in and declared that it had repealed its proposals because they were not ambitious enough. In 2015, it then came out with a proposal for a circular economy[106] and some recycling proposals.

The Commission understood under a circular economy to be 'where the value of products, materials and resources is maintained in the economy as long as possible and the generation of waste minimised'.[107] It proposed to examine and regulate in future, in the context of the Eco-Design Directive, also the reparability, durability, upgradability and recyclability of products; promote repair, reuse and recycling; boost the market for secondary raw materials and water reuse; develop provisions for waste-based fertilisers; and adopt quality standards for secondary raw materials. Measures on plastics, food waste, critical raw materials, construction and demolition material and biomass would be dealt with by priority. Furthermore, the Commission suggested ambitious recycling rates for waste materials (glass, metals, paper, wood, plastics and construction and demolition waste) and a reduction of the landfilling of municipal waste.[108]

The EP and the Council generally welcomed the Commission proposal on the circular economy, but asked for concrete legislative proposals.[109] Until now, only cars must be recyclable or recoverable up to a certain percentage.[110] The Commission also proposed that Member States encourage the use of products 'that are resource efficient, durable, reparable and

---

[105] Directive 2008/98, OJ 2008, L 312, 3.

[106] Commission, 'Closing the Loop - a European Union Action Plan for the Circular Economy', COM (2015) 614. The term 'circular economy' was taken from German law, where legislation on circular economy existed since 1994 (Kreislaufwirtschaftsgesetz).

[107] Commission, COM (2015) 614, 2.

[108] Commission, COM (2015) 398; COM (2015) 596 (packaging and packaging waste); COM (2015) 595 (paper, metal, wood, glass and plastics) and COM (2015) 594 (landfills).

[109] European Parliament, Resolution of 9 July 2015, Document P8-TA-Prov (20150266); Council, Resolution of 18 April 2016, Document ST 8004 2016 INIT.

[110] Directive 2000/53, OJ 2000, L 269, 34.

recyclable', and that they reduce the generation of food waste and waste generated in processes related to industrial activities.[111] To what extent such proposals, even if they were adopted by the legislator, are able to change the economic reality and move towards a circular economy, remains more than doubtful.

As regards relations with third countries, the EU implemented the Basel Ban which prohibits the export of hazardous waste to countries not members of the Organisation for Economic Cooperation and Development (OECD), even when the material is to be recycled. For other hazardous wastes that may be exported under the Basel Convention, and for non-hazardous waste, the EU applies the 'prior informed consent' principle.

Particular problems arise in the export of end-of-life vehicles[112] and of electrical and electronic waste (WEEE). Cars, even when they are no longer capable of being used, are all too often exported from the EU as second-hand cars which allows the application of waste legislation to be avoided. The EU has not yet taken measures to stop such abuse, for example by requiring that any car which is to be exported, undergoes a test to check whether it is roadworthy. Somehow better is the situation with WEEE, where Directive 2012/19 requires that a person who intends to export electrical or electronic equipment which is not waste has to prove that 'every item in the consignment' is a product and thus capable of being used.[113] It is not known whether this provision is applied in practice and has stopped shipments to developing countries of, for example, computers which were 75 per cent or more unusable.

When ships belonging to an owner within the EU come to the end of their useful life, they are regularly sold, at sea or in a third country, in order to be dismantled in Bangladesh, Pakistan, India or – to a lesser extent – in China. The environmental and social conditions in these dismantling facilities are appalling. Anticipating the Hong Kong Convention on the safe and environmentally sound recycling of ships, which has not yet entered into force, the EU adopted legislation on this issue.[114] That legislation provides in particular the setting up of an EU register of dismantling facilities which comply with International Labour Organisation (ILO) and basic environmental requirements. Ships from the EU may only be dismantled in such registered facilities. Whether this legislation will stop the

[111] Commission, COM (2015) 595.
[112] Directive 2000/53 (above n. 110).
[113] Directive 2012/19, OJ 2012, L 192, 38, Article 10 and Annex VI.
[114] Regulation 1257/2013, OJ 2013, L 330, 1.

present abuses of (EU) ship dismantling is doubtful, as nothing prevents a third-country owner to have his ship dismantled in a substandard facility.

As can be seen from this sketchy overview, the approach to a circular economy of the EU is, at present, more a political wish than an economic and environmental reality. The EU has not yet fully appreciated the economic impact which a future scarcity of raw materials might have. It has no provisions which provide for the compulsory use of recycled materials in production. It has no eco-design standards yet on recyclability, durability and other environmental characteristics. The consumption of water of certain household appliances shall be indicated on the label, but is not in any way limited. The same applies to the use of raw materials or rare earth elements, the reparability of products or their durability. Only in the energy sector are there efforts to limit the energy consumption of products and buildings, as the adoption of legislation was induced by climate change considerations.

VI   Other Challenges

International or global negotiations on environmental issues normally pose a policy problem for the EU, as it is obliged to find a common position for such negotiations – which is not always easy for a group of twenty-eight EU Member States. When an international problem is already the subject of EU legislation, the EU position is relatively easy to determine, as both the EU institutions and the Member States are obliged, under EU law, to defend the EU *acquis*. However, it is not always clear, whether an EU position on a specific problem exists. For example, at the 2009 Copenhagen Summit on Climate Change, the EU Heads of State or Government negotiated on their own and for themselves, without trying to find and promote a common EU line, though there was an EU policy at that time. This was different during the negotiations on the Paris Agreement on Climate Change. In this case, there was a position adopted by the EU Heads of State or Government on the EU climate change policy and targets until 2030. This position was then successfully defended by the EU and the Member States during the negotiations in Paris, where the EU spoke with one voice.

The only sanction which the EU has at its disposal, when a Member State does not respect the EU solidarity and negotiates or votes for itself, is to bring that Member State before the Court of Justice for the EU (CJEU). The EU took such a step, when Sweden went on its own in discussions under the Persistent Organic Pollutants Convention.[115] However, it did not

---

[115] CJEU, Case C-246/07, *Commission v. Sweden*, ECR 2010, I-3317.

take such a step when Denmark, in 2013, voted differently from the other EU Member States on the question of whether the polar bear should be classified in Annex I to CITES.[116]

With regard to global governance, the EU itself is not member of the UN, and nothing indicates that this situation will change in future. Indeed, it would be difficult to avoid giving a seat to the EU in the Security Council, but France and the UK, both permanent members of the Security Council, would then have to step down – which is not really possible against their will and is politically excluded. The EU does not pursue the objective of becoming a member of the UN, but it is aware that the present situation has considerable impact on numerous decisions taken by the UN or by one of the UN's daughter organisations. The lack of formal representation in the UN also explains to some extent, why the EU only takes a limited amount of political or governance initiatives at international level, in the environmental sector or beyond. Anyway, the political dimension of this problem is not limited to the environmental sector and will therefore not be further discussed.

The EU had long been pleading for the creation of a UN Environmental Organisation, in parallel to the World Trade Organization or the ILO. Past initiatives in this direction were opposed in particular by the United States and Saudi Arabia and did not succeed in re-evaluating UNEP.

Initiatives such as a Rio Declaration on environmental principles, a Johannesburg Declaration on sustainable development or similar attempts to advance the policy and legal policy discussion on the planet's environment are almost never started from the EU. First, such an initiative would require a consensus of the twenty-eight Member States on a common proposal – and it would take years to hammer it out. Second, while 'general principles of law, recognised by civilised nations' constitute, according to Article 38 of the Statutes of the International Court of Justice, a source of international law, such principles do not have the same function within the EU: the European Court of Justice has to apply the law as it is laid down in the EU Treaties, in international agreements to which the EU has adhered and in the numerous pieces of secondary EU legislation. Only where the interpretation of this written law does not lead to results is it possible to think of the application of general principles of law. This strong reliance on the written, codified law practically excludes the recurrence to international environmental principles – and makes at the same time EU

[116] See L. Krämer, EU Negotiating and Voting under the Amended CITES Convention (2015) 12 *Journal for European Environment & Planning Law* 3.

initiatives at the international scene to defend or promote environmental principles most unlikely.

The EU actively supports international initiatives such as the attempts to improve access to water or to better protect forests. Its activities in this regard are embedded into its development and humanitarian aid policy and are thus perhaps less visible. However, for the reasons mentioned above, it would be unrealistic to expect that the EU ever would initiate or start, for example, a global initiative to tackle the problem of land being used for biofuel generation and no longer for food production.

This reluctance to take the lead in environmental matters goes even further: the EU prohibited hormones and growth promoters in meat, but does not try to obtain global rules in this regard. The EU adopted very strict rules on the authorisation and in particular the cultivation of GMOs, but does not go to the international level to have such restrictions generalised. The EU very actively promotes the large-scale use of renewable sources of energy, but does not pursue this policy at international level. The EU does not take the lead to stop the financial support – including from the European Investment Bank or the European Bank for Reconstruction and Development – of coal-fired plants worldwide. The EU imposes relatively strict emission standards on its cars – but does not do anything to have strict car emission standards for the export of cars at UN level. The EU adhered to the Aarhus Convention and adopted provisions on access to information, participation in decision-making and access to justice in environmental matters, but does not undertake efforts to have such basic governance rules applied in other parts of the world.

VII   Concluding Remarks

Overall, it may be concluded that the EU tries to respond to global environmental challenges within its own territory. The EU environmental policy in any area – air and water, biodiversity, noise, products, waste, industrial installations – need not be afraid of comparisons with other developed countries or regions, such as United States, Canada, Australia, New Zealand, Japan, Norway, Switzerland, the North American Free Trade Area (NAFTA), the Common Market of South America (MERCOSUR) or the Association of Southeast Asian Nations (ASEAN) regions. Many of its institutional or substantive solutions to deal with environmental issues are exemplary. Look at the role of the European Court of Justice, which delivered, between 1976 and mid-2016, almost 1,000 judgments in environmental matters – interfering with national law and decision-making processes, but meeting no or very little resistance in the name of national sovereignty; the role of the European Commission as instigator of environmental legislation; the participation in the legislative process of the EP as the elected representative of more than 500 million citizens.

Also with regard to substantive environmental law there are frequent innovative and progressive solutions to environmental problems obtained by the EU which stretch from waste water treatment to drinking water, from chemical substances handling (REACH) to the large application of the precautionary principle for pesticides, biocides, GMOs and other chemicals; from waste stream management (WEEE, cars, packaging waste) to landfilling; from the Natura2000 network to environmental impact assessments for plans, programmes and projects; and from the reduction of greenhouse gas emissions to renewable energies and energy efficiency measures. The enumeration could be continued. The EU could and should improve in ensuring the application of its environmental provisions all over the EU, should increase citizens' rights and do more on noise pollution, nature protection and the transition to a low carbon economy.

Internationally, the EU does not bring to bear its full weight and know-how of environmental issues. Global environmental initiatives by the EU will not be seen in the foreseeable future. The EU also adheres to the principle that €1 which is invested for example in Africa should bring a return of €3 to the European economy. A fundamental change of this policy approach is not in sight. It might only occur when the demographic pressure of 9 billion people, together with climate change consequences, will be such that environmental migration will become a more urgent issue than it appears to be today.

This leads back to the question which had already been formulated earlier in this chapter: the EU does a lot for the protection of the environment – but is that enough? It is a poor consolation that the measures taken elsewhere are not a sufficient response either to the challenges which this planet faces.

16

The Normative Foundations of European Criminal Law

VALSAMIS MITSILEGAS

I Introduction

European criminal law one of the fastest-growing areas of European Union (EU) law. Its evolution has proceeded along a rocky constitutional road, reflecting national concerns about the impact of Europeanisation in this sensitive field on state sovereignty and national legal diversity. European integration in criminal matters has thus begun, slowly and largely within the intergovernmental framework of the third pillar, to evolve and to move firmly into a supranational framework after the entry into force of the Lisbon Treaty. Reflecting the dominance of national governments in its shaping, the content of European criminal law has focused predominantly on the prioritisation of law enforcement needs and on the promotion of a security dimension. The entry into force of the Lisbon Treaty has contributed towards another shift in direction, namely from uncritical securitisation to a European criminal law which is more mindful of the requirement to protect fundamental rights. In the policy and academic debate thus far, European criminal law has been viewed largely from the perspective of these two dichotomies: Europeanisation versus state sovereignty; and securitisation versus the protection of fundamental rights. This chapter will attempt to cast light on these dichotomies by viewing European criminal law from a different perspective, by exploring its normative foundations. Three main questions will be asked: the 'why' question, or what have been the stated aims of European criminal law? The 'how' question, or what are the main forms of governance of European criminal law? And the 'for whom' question, a question identifying the subjects of European criminal law. This structure will enable the development of an analytical framework on the normative foundations of European criminal law and will highlight the shift from a European criminal law focused on security and effectiveness to the need to embrace the protection of fundamental rights as the key normative foundation in this field. The transformative potential of the entry into force of the Lisbon Treaty, including the constitutionalisation of the Charter of Fundamental Rights, are key developments in achieving this paradigmatic change.

II   The 'Why' Question: The Aims of European Criminal Law

A key step in casting light on the normative foundations of European criminal law is to attempt to answer the question of 'why European criminal law'? This section will attempt to give an answer, by highlighting the various justifications put forward by EU institutions for the need and development of European criminal law. Three main justifications have predominantly appeared in this context. The first justification involves unsurprisingly the quest for security: the granting to the Union of express criminal law competence and its subsequent evolution into an Area of Freedom, Security and Justice has been premised upon the claim that the Europeanisation of criminal law is necessary to enhance the security of the Member States, the Union and, as will be seen below, the globe. In addition to the security rationale of European criminal law however, two further – and perhaps not immediately evident – justifications have emerged. Both justifications involve the use of criminal law in order to achieve the effectiveness of Union law, under a functionalist paradigm of criminal law. On the one hand, criminal law is used to achieve the effectiveness of Union law, by contributing towards the achievement of Union objectives and the effectiveness of Union policies such as the protection of the environment and the achievement of free movement. On the other hand, and taking this logic a step further, the Europeanisation of criminal law has been justified as necessary in order to protect effectively interests which are viewed as being exclusively 'European', such as the protection of the budget of the EU.

A   Security

The key justification for the Europeanisation of criminal law has been the quest for security in an increasingly globalised arena and in an EU without internal frontiers. In this context, European criminal law was considered necessary to address two parallel trends: the process of securitisation, which highlighted the emergence of a number of perceived global,

transnational security threats the tackling of which requires a coordinated approach; and the emergence of the EU, gradually but steadily, as
an area without internal frontiers permeated by the Schengen logic and
model.[1] The securitisation process has emerged strongly at the end of the
Cold War. The shift from the emphasis on military threats to the securitisation of broader phenomena has been well documented early on by
international relations scholars.[2] In the EU and beyond, one element of
this securitisation shift has been the elevation of forms of criminality as
threats which require urgent and concerted response by governments.[3]
Security threats in this context have assumed a chameleon nature over the
years – from drug trafficking in the 1980s to organised crime in the 1990s
and terrorism in the 2000s.[4] At EU level, such securitisation of crime has
largely acted as a factor justifying further EU integration in criminal matters and led to the introduction of the third pillar in the Maastricht Treaty
and the adoption of a plethora of legal and policy initiatives in the field.
In this context, particular focus has been placed on the transnational elements of the perceived threats, which are deemed to require a common EU
approach with Member States not being able to address these challenges
solely at the national level. The need for Europeanisation has been justified
here not only by the transnational and serious nature of the new security
threats, but also by the evolution of the Union as an area without internal
frontiers. This link was already made to some extent by the Commission
in its 1985 White Paper on the completion of the internal market.[5] It was

---

[1] V. Mitsilegas et al., *The European Union and Internal Security* (Palgrave/Macmillan, 2003);
     V. Mitsilegas, *EU Criminal Law* (Hart, 2003), Chapter 1.
[2] See in particular B. Buzan, *People, States and Fear: An Agenda for International Security
     Studies in the Post-Cold War Era* (Harvester Wheatsheaf, 1991); B. Buzan, 'New Patterns
     of Global Security in the Twenty-First Century' (1999) 67(3) *International Affairs* 431–51;
     D. Bigo, *Polices en Réseaux. L'expériénce Européenne* (Presses de Sciences Po, 1996).
[3] On the securitisation process, see B. Buzan et al., *Security: A New Framework for
     Analysis* (Lynne Rienner, 1998); and O. Waever, 'Securitization and De-securitization' in
     R. D. Lipschutz (ed.), *On Security* (Columbia University Press, 1995), 46–86.
[4] On this changing focus in the context of the development of money laundering counter-
     measures, see V. Mitsilegas, 'Countering the Chameleon Threat of Dirty Money: "Hard" and
     "Soft" Law in the Emergence of a Global Regime against Money Laundering and Terrorist
     Finance' in A. Edwards and P. Gill (eds.), *Transnational Organised Crime: Perspectives on
     Global Security* (Routledge, 2003), 195–211.
[5] COM (85) 310, 14 June 1985. The Commission considered that matters such as the coor-
     dination of rules concerning extradition were essential for the removal of internal frontier
     controls. See P. A. Weber-Panariello, 'The Integration of Matters of Justice and Home Affairs
     into Title VI of the Treaty on European Union: A Step Towards More Democracy?', EUI
     Working Paper RSC No. 95/32, European University Institute, 5.

put forward more forcefully in the Palma document,[6] whose conclusions were endorsed by the Madrid European Council in 1989;[7] the document asserted that the achievement of an area without internal frontiers could involve, as necessary, the approximation of laws, adding that the abolition of internal borders affects a whole range of matters including combating terrorism, drug trafficking and other illicit trafficking; improved law enforcement cooperation; and judicial cooperation. In the latter context it was noted that judicial cooperation in criminal matters should be intensified in order to combat terrorism, drug trafficking, crime and other illicit trafficking and that harmonisation of certain provisions should be studied.[8] The rest is history: the Maastricht Treaty has introduced the third pillar which, for the first time, conferred on the Union express competence to adopt criminal law; the Amsterdam Treaty has integrated the Schengen *acquis* into the Union legal framework and has introduced the achievement of an Area of Freedom, Security and Justice as a Union objective; and the Treaty of Lisbon has largely 'normalised' criminal law by moving from an intergovernmental to a supranational model of EU action in the field. The quest for security has been key in all these stages and in contributing towards the constitutional maturity of European criminal law. In this process, 'internal' and 'external' dimensions of security have been inextricably linked: external aspects of security have influenced the adoption of internal EU law in the field, while the EU has emerged strongly as a global actor in the field of criminal law.[9]

---

[6] The Palma document was prepared by a Coordinators' Group set up by the European Council and composed of twelve high-ranking officials, a chairman and the Vice-President of the Commission to coordinate Member States' actions with regard to free movement. See Weber-Panariello, 'The Integration of Matters of Justice and Home Affairs into Title VI of the Treaty on European Union' (above n. 5), 8–9.

[7] Council Doc. 89/1, 27 June 1989, http://europa.eu/rapid/pressReleasesAction.do?reference= DOC/89/1&format=HTML.

[8] The Palma document is reproduced in E. Guild and J. Niessen, *The Developing Immigration and Asylum Policies in the EU* (Martinus Nijhoff, 1996), 443–8.

[9] See inter alia: V. Mitsilegas, 'The EU and the Rest of the World: Criminal Law and Policy Interconnections' in M. Evans and P. Koutrakos (eds.), *Beyond the Established Orders: Policy Interconnections between the EU and the Rest of the World* (Hart, 2011), 149–78; V. Mitsilegas, 'The EU and the Implementation of International Norms in Criminal Matters' in M. Cremona et al. (eds.), *The External Dimension of the Area of Freedom, Security and Justice* (Peter Lang, 2011), 239–72; V. Mitsilegas, 'The European Union and the Global Governance of Crime' in V. Mitsilegas et al. (eds.), *Globalisation, Criminal Law and Criminal Justice. Theoretical, Comparative and Transnational Perspectives* (Hart, 2015), 153–98.

B   *Effectiveness*

The quest for security has not however been the only justification for the development of European criminal law. A key role for criminal law, from the early stages of European integration, has been to ensure the effectiveness of EU law. This functionalist role of criminal law has been reflected at two levels: at the level of the influence of EU law on national criminal law; and at the level of the adoption of EU criminal law. In terms of the impact of EU law on national criminal law, the Court of Justice of the EU (CJEU) has confirmed in a consistent line of case law that Union law places limits on the application of national criminal law, if the latter would have the effect of limiting disproportionately rights established by Union law. As early as 1981, the Court stated in *Casati* that:

> In principle, criminal legislation and the rules of criminal procedure are matters for which the Member States are still responsible. However, it is clear from a consistent line of cases decided by the Court, that Community law also sets *certain limits* in that area as regards the control measures which it permits the Member States to maintain in connection with the free movement of goods and persons. The administrative measures or penalties must not go beyond what is strictly necessary, the control procedures must not be concerned in such a way as to restrict the freedom required by the Treaty and they must not be accompanied by a penalty which is so disproportionate to the gravity of the infringement that it becomes an obstacle to the exercise of that freedom.[10]

The Court has reiterated this case law on a number of occasions placing limits on national criminalisation when this would constitute a disproportionate infringement of free movement rights.[11] In a significant post-Lisbon development, the Court has extended its case law to include limiting national criminalisation on the grounds of ensuring the effectiveness of an instrument of immigration enforcement within the Area of Freedom, Security and Justice. In the case of *El-Dridi*,[12] which concerned the compatibility of national criminalisation of immigration offences with the EU returns Directive, the Court reiterated that although in principle criminal legislation and the rules of criminal procedure are matters for which the Member States are responsible, this branch of the law may nevertheless be affected by EU law.[13] The Court added that Member States may

---

[10] Case 203/80, ECR [1981] 2595, para. 27. Emphasis added.

[11] See, inter alia, Case C-193/94, *Skanavi and Chryssanthakopoulos*, ECR [1996] I-929 and Joint Cases C-338/04 and C-359–60/04, *Placanica, Palazzese and Sorricchio*, ECR [2007] I-1891. For an overview see Mitsilegas, *EU Criminal Law* (above, n. 1), Chapter 2.

[12] Case C-61/11 PPU, *El-Dridi*, ECR [2011] I-03015.

[13] Ibid., para. 53.

not apply rules, even criminal law rules, which are liable to jeopardise the achievement of the objectives pursued by a Directive and, therefore, deprive it of its effectiveness.[14] It also confirmed the applicability of the principle of loyal cooperation as expressed in Article 4(3) of the Treaty on European Union (TEU).[15] The Court's ruling in *El-Dridi* is significant as it marks a departure from earlier case law: while traditionally, in rulings like *Casati*, the CJEU has placed limits on national criminal law in order to achieve free movement objectives, limits to national criminalisation are justified in order to achieve the effectiveness of an *enforcement* measure, namely the EU returns Directive.[16] In this context, the decriminalisation potential of the application of the principle of effectiveness has increased considerably.[17]

The use of EU criminal law to ensure the effectiveness of EU law more generally, and in particular the achievement of EU law objectives, has been highlighted by the CJEU in the period between the rejection of the Constitutional Treaty and the entry into force of the Lisbon Treaty in the context of legal-basis litigation. In two separate cases, the European Commission challenged two instruments of third pillar law in the field of environmental crime (the Framework Decision on environmental crime and the Framework Decision on the criminalisation of ship-source pollution) on the grounds that these criminal law instruments should have correctly been adopted under first pillar legal bases on the grounds that they serve to ensure the effectiveness of EU law.[18] The CJEU ruled in favour of the Commission in finding in both cases that the effectiveness of Union – then European Community (EC) – law justified the adoption of criminal law under a first pillar legal basis.[19] As the CJEU confirmed in its environmental crime ruling, while, *as a general rule, neither criminal law nor the rules of criminal procedure fall within EC competence*, this does not prevent

---

[14] Ibid., para. 55.

[15] Ibid., para. 56.

[16] See V. Mitsilegas, 'The Changing Landscape of the Criminalisation of Migration in Europe: The Protective Function of European Union Law' in M. Guia et al. (eds.), *Social Control and Justice: Crimmigration in an Age of Fear* (Eleven International Publishing, 2012), 87–114; and V. Mitsilegas, *The Criminalisation of Migration in Europe. Challenges for Human Rights and the Rule of Law* (Springer, 2015), Chapter 3.

[17] See V. Mitsilegas, 'From Overcriminalisation to Decriminalisation: The Many Faces of Effectiveness in European Criminal Law' (2014) 5 *New Journal of European Criminal Law* 415–24.

[18] For further analysis, see Mitsilegas, *EU Criminal Law* (above, n. 1), Chapter 2.

[19] Case C0176/03, *Commission v. Council* (environmental crime ruling), ECR [2005] I-7879; Case C-440/05, *Commission v. Council* (ship-source pollution ruling), ECR [2007] I-9097.

the EC legislature, *when the application of effective, proportionate and dissuasive criminal penalties* by the competent national authorities is an *essential measure* for combating serious environmental offences, from taking measures which relate to the criminal law of the Member States which it considers *necessary* in order to ensure that the rules which it lays down on environmental protection *are fully effective.*[20] The Court reiterated in both cases that the use of criminal law under the first pillar was necessary to achieve the effectiveness of the protection of the environment, which was considered by the Court to be one of the essential objectives of the (then) Community.[21] The Court's rulings in the cases of environmental crime and pollution at sea are seminal in confirming a functionalist vision of criminal law: rather than treating criminal law as a stand-alone area of Union policy, the Court has treated criminal law as a means to an end towards achieving Union objectives and the effectiveness of Union law.[22] This functionalist vision of criminal law has had repercussions extending far beyond the field of environmental crime: as will be seen in the following section, functional criminalisation has been constitutionalised post-Lisbon by Article 83(2) of the Treaty on the Functioning of the European Union (TFEU).

C   Protection of 'European' Interests

The third justification for the adoption of European criminal law is related to the need to protect what are perceived to be European interests which are deemed to be distinct from national interests in the field of criminal justice. A key example in this context is the protection of the budget of the EU. Safeguarding the EU budget is perceived as an EU interest *par excellence*, and the drive in European criminal law has been for *national* systems to be able to protect this European interest effectively. Underlying calls for EU intervention in this context has been a perception that national authorities are unwilling or unable to protect European interests (and in particular the budget of the EU) in the same way or as effectively as they would protect national interests by the use of criminal law. These perceptions have led to calls for the use of criminal law by the EU to protect effectively the EU budget and tackle fraud in two main ways: by ensuring

---

[20] Environmental crime ruling, paras. 47–8. Emphasis added.
[21] Ibid., para. 41. Ship-source pollution ruling, para. 60.
[22] V. Mitsilegas, 'The Transformation of Criminal Law in the Area of Freedom, Security and Justice' (2007) 26 *YEL* 1–32; Mitsilegas, *EU Criminal Law* (above, n. 1), Chapter 2.

that national law provides effective protection of the EU interests at stake and by putting forward legislation at the EU level aiming to establish a substantive and institutional framework which would provide an effective response to fraud against the EU budget. These two courses of action have been developing in a complementary manner for more than two decades, with EU institutions playing a key part in leading initiatives in these fields. The first strand of EU action involved efforts to ensure that Member States provide an equivalent level of protection of EU interests to that provided for national interests in their domestic criminal justice systems. A leading actor in this context has been the CJEU, which developed in the late 1980s the principle of assimilation. In its ruling on the *Greek Maize* case,[23] the Court stated that:

> where Community legislation does not specifically provide any penalty for an infringement or refers for that purpose to national laws, regulations and administrative provisions, Article 5 of the Treaty requires the Member States to take all measures necessary to guarantee the application and effectiveness of Community law.
>
> For that purpose, whilst the choice of penalties remains within their discretion, they must ensure in particular that infringements of Community law are penalised under conditions, both procedural and substantive, which are *analogous* to those applicable to infringements of national law of a similar nature and importance and which, in any event, make the penalty effective, proportionate and dissuasive.
>
> Moreover, the national authorities must proceed, with respect to infringements of Community law, *with the same diligence* as that which they bring to bear in implementing corresponding national laws.[24]

Based on the principles of effectiveness and equivalence, the Court thus introduced the principle of assimilation: Community law must be 'assimilated' in national legal systems, and infringements of Community law must be treated in a manner analogous to the manner that breaches of similar domestic law are treated. In this manner, criminalisation may occur at national level even in cases where such criminalisation is not expressly required by EU law. The Court stated subsequently that effective national measures in this context 'may include criminal penalties even where the Community legislation only provides for civil sanctions'.[25]

The principle of assimilation has since been introduced in the EU Treaties and appears post-Lisbon, along with the principles of effectiveness

---

[23] Case 68/88, *Commission* v. *Greece*, ECR [1989] 2965.
[24] Paras. 23–5, emphasis added.
[25] Case C-186/98, *Nunes de Matos*, ECR [1999] 4883, para. 14.

and deterrence,[26] in Article 325 TFEU.[27] The Court has since used Article 325 TFEU to highlight the obligations incumbent upon national authorities to provide effective protection for the EU budget. In the case of *Taricco*,[28] the CJEU ruled that Article 325 TFEU itself obliges the Member States to counter illegal activities affecting the financial interests of the EU through effective deterrent measures and, in particular, obliges them to take the same measures to counter fraud affecting the financial interests of the EU as they take to counter fraud affecting their own interests – hence reiterating the importance of the principle of assimilation.[29] In the event that the national court concludes that the national provisions at issue do not satisfy the requirement of EU law that measures to counter fraud (in this case VAT evasion) be effective and dissuasive, the Court continued, the national court would have to ensure that EU law is given full effect, *if need be by disapplying* those provisions without having to request or await the prior repeal of those articles by way of legislation or any other constitutional procedure.[30] The Court stressed in this context that the Member States' obligation to counter illegal activities affecting the financial interests of the EU through dissuasive and effective measures, and their obligation to take the same measures to counter fraud affecting those interests as they take to counter fraud affecting their own financial interests, are obligations imposed, inter alia, *by EU primary law*, namely Article 325(1) and (2) TFEU.[31] Those provisions of EU primary law impose on Member States a precise obligation as to the result to be achieved that is not subject to any condition regarding application of the rule which they lay down.[32] The provisions of Article 325(1) and (2) TFEU therefore have the effect, in accordance with the principle of the precedence of EU law, in their relationship with the domestic law of the Member States, of rendering automatically inapplicable, merely by their entering into force, any conflicting provision of national law.[33] The ruling in *Taricco* is thus of fundamental importance, as the Court strengthens the enforcement of the principles of effectiveness, dissuasion and assimilation established in Articles 325(1)

---

[26] Article 325(1) TFEU.
[27] According to Article 325(2) TFEU, Member States must take the same measures to counter fraud affecting the financial interests of the Union as they take to tackle fraud affecting their own interests.
[28] Case C- 105/04, judgment of 8 September 2015.
[29] Ibid., para. 37.
[30] Ibid., para. 49. Emphasis added.
[31] Ibid., para. 50.
[32] Ibid., para. 51.
[33] Ibid., para. 52.

and (2) TFEU by confirming that Article 325 TFEU has direct effect and primacy over national law and non-compliance leads to the disapplication of conflicting national law.

The entry into force of the Treaty of Lisbon has thus been followed by a strong ruling by the CJEU interpreting the TFEU's 'fraud' legal basis, Article 325 TFEU, in a maximalist way, aiming to ensure a high level of protection of European interests – namely the EU budget – by national criminal justice systems. In addition to the considerable effect of EU law on national criminal law that *Taricco* entails, the Treaty of Lisbon has also provided opportunities to EU institutions to strengthen the *EU* framework for the protection of the EU budget. In addition to the possibilities offered by Article 325 TFEU in this context, which will be analysed in the next section, a key development has been the introduction in the TFEU, after a lengthy gestation period and a high degree of controversy, of an express legal basis – Article 86 TFEU – enabling the establishment of a European Public Prosecutor's Office (EPPO). The detail on the establishment of the EPPO will be analysed in the governance part in the next section of this chapter. Here it suffices to say that the EPPO project – at least for EU institutions such as the Commission – is the outcome of mistrust towards national efforts to tackle fraud and a belief that national systems do not have the capacity to tackle fraud effectively without the establishment of an EU agency with powers in the field. According to the Commission's Explanatory Memorandum to its proposal for a Regulation establishing the EPPO, 'as Member States' criminal investigation and prosecution authorities are currently unable to achieve an equivalent level of protection and enforcement, the Union not only has the competence but also the obligation to act'.[34] The EPPO Treaty basis is the culmination of a long process of advocacy of EU legislation in the field of fraud, which began by the academic study on the *Corpus Juris* funded by the European Commission in the 1990s: the drafters of the *Corpus Juris* put forward a highly centralised model of European criminal law related to the fight against fraud, a model which emanated from the belief that the budget is a unique, European interest. According to its Explanatory Memorandum, 'the Budget, defined as "the visible sign of a true patrimony common to citizens of the Union" …, is the supreme instrument of European policy. To say this emphasises the extreme seriousness of any crime which undermines this patrimony'.[35] As will be seen in the following section, the

---

[34] COM (2013) 534 final, 2.
[35] M. Delmas-Marty (ed.), *Corpus Juris* (Economica, 1997), 12.

uniqueness and commonality of the EU budget and the heightened need for its protection have not thus far led to a high degree of harmonisation or to unification of law at EU level.

III   The 'How' Question: The Governance of European Criminal Law

There are three main forms of governance which the EU legislator has employed in order to give effect to the aims of European criminal law analysed in the previous section. These forms of governance consist of harmonisation of substantive criminal law, judicial cooperation in criminal matters, in particular via the application of the principle of mutual recognition in criminal matters, and the establishment of specific EU bodies and agencies in the field of criminal justice. This section will examine how these forms of governance have evolved in the changing EU constitutional landscape, by focusing in particular on the impact of the entry into force of the Lisbon Treaty. The analysis will be informed by the two inherent tensions in the development of European criminal law, namely the tension between the Europeanisation of criminal law and safeguarding state sovereignty and national legal diversity in this sensitive field on the one hand, and the tension between achieving the stated aims of European criminal law and upholding key EU values, in particular the protection of fundamental rights, on the other. An analysis of how the governance of European criminal law has evolved over time must also be informed by the constitutional momentum provided by the entry into force of the Lisbon Treaty in the field. We are now witnessing the constitutionalisation of European criminal law, entailing in particular the full applicability of general and constitutional principles of EU law on European criminal law. These principles include the principles of effectiveness,[36] primacy[37] and direct effect[38] of Union law, which have been found by the CJEU – in addition to the pre-Lisbon finding of the applicability of indirect effect[39] – to apply to European criminal law, including third pillar law. The constitutionalisation of European criminal law is also inextricably linked to the

---

[36] See the case of *Taricco* above and the case law on the European Arrest Warrant discussed in section III.B.

[37] See the case of *Taricco* above and the case of *Melloni* discussed in section III.B.

[38] See *Taricco*, but see the limits set out to the principle of direct effect in the field of criminal law in the case of Joined Cases C-387/02, C-391/02 and C-403/02, *Berlusconi*, ECR [2005] I-3565.

[39] Case C-105/03, *Pupino*, ECR [2005] I-5285.

parallel post-Lisbon constitutionalisation of the Charter of Fundamental Rights. As will be seen in the following section, the Charter can have a drastic effect on the reconfiguration of the normative foundations of European criminal law after Lisbon.

A   Harmonisation of Substantive Criminal Law

One of the main strands of governance in European criminal law has centred on efforts to harmonise substantive criminal law. Harmonisation of substantive criminal law has addressed all three justifications for European criminal law analysed in section II above. Harmonisation has been put forward to address security concerns, resulting in the extension of criminalisation in response to major security threats such as terrorism[40] and organised crime,[41] largely in line with global security initiatives.[42] Harmonisation has also pursued functionalist aims, with the EU adopting substantive criminal law to protect Union policies such as the internal market[43] and the protection of the environment.[44] Finally, harmonisation of substantive criminal law has taken place to create a level playing field regarding the protection of the financial interests of the Union, most notably by harmonisation attempts in the fields of fraud and corruption.[45] In a number of cases, harmonisation of substantive criminal law has been justified as pursuing more than one objective: in the case of money laundering,

---

[40] C. Murphy, *EU Counter-Terrorism Law* (Hart, 2012). On the implementation of EU law in select Member States, see F. Galli, *The Law on Terrorism: The UK, France and Italy Compared* (Bruylant, 2015).

[41] V. Mitsilegas, 'Defining Organised Crime in the European Union: The Limits of European Criminal Law in an Area of Freedom, Security and Justice' (2001) 26 *EL Rev* 565–81; V. Mitsilegas, 'The Third Wave of Third Pillar Law: Which Direction for EU Criminal Justice?' (2009) 34 *EL Rev* 523–60.

[42] Mitsilegas, 'The EU and the Implementation of International Norms in Criminal Matters' (above n. 9); Mitsilegas, 'The European Union and the Global Governance of Crime' (above n. 9).

[43] V. Mitsilegas, *Money Laundering Counter-Measures in the European Union: A New Paradigm of Security Governance versus Fundamental Legal Principles* (Kluwer Law International, 2003); V. Mitsilegas and B. Gilmore, 'The EU Legislative Framework against Money Laundering and Terrorist Finance: A Critical Analysis in the Light of Evolving Global Standards' (2007) 56 *International and Comparative Law Quarterly* 119–41.

[44] V. Mitsilegas et al., 'The Relationship Between Environmental Law and EU Criminal Law' in V. Mitsilegas et al. (eds.), *Research Handbook on EU Criminal Law* (Edward Elgar, 2016), 272–94.

[45] V. Mitsilegas, 'The Aims and Limits of EU Anti-Corruption Law' in J. Horder and P. Alldridge (eds.), *Modern Bribery Law: Comparative Perspectives* (Cambridge University Press, 2013), 160–95.

EU substantive criminal law encompasses both security and functional objectives, while EU criminal law on corruption can be seen as addressing in one way or another all three justifications for the Europeanisation of criminal law analysed in the previous section.

This multifaceted approach to the harmonisation of substantive criminal law has been confirmed by the entry into force of the Lisbon Treaty. The move from the intergovernmentalism inherent in the third pillar to the supranationalism of Lisbon has led to efforts to define in a clear manner the Union's competence to adopt legislation defining criminal offences and imposing criminal sanctions. The main legal basis for EU substantive criminal law harmonisation, Article 83 TFEU, puts forward a dual model of EU action in the field by combining a model of securitised with a model of functional criminalisation.[46] The model of securitised criminalisation is introduced by Article 83(1) TFEU. EU competence to criminalise is justified as necessary to combat specified areas of criminality the majority of which have been elevated after the Cold War by the international community and the Union as global security threats.[47] The objective of Article 83(1) TFEU to address security threats is also confirmed by the requirement for harmonisation to apply only to areas of particularly serious crime. In an attempt to circumscribe EU competence in the field further, Article 83(1) TFEU contains an express enumeration of these areas of serious crimes and specifies that these areas must have a cross-border dimension resulting from the nature or impact of such offences or from a special need to combat them on a common basis. These areas of crime are the following: terrorism, trafficking in human beings and sexual exploitation of women and children, illicit drug trafficking, illicit arms trafficking, money laundering, corruption, counterfeiting of means of payment, computer crime and organised crime. The functional criminalisation model is put forward by Article 83(2) TFEU, which can be seen as an attempt to translate in Treaty terms the main elements of the Court's rulings in the cases of environmental crime and pollution at sea. Article 83(2) TFEU in the Treaty of Lisbon confirms a functionalist view of criminal law. Rather than assuming the status of a self-standing Union policy, criminal law is thus perceived as a means to an end, the end being the effective implementation

---

[46] V. Mitsilegas, 'EU Criminal Law Competence after Lisbon: From Securitised to Functional Criminalisation' in D. Acosta and C. Murphy (eds.), *EU Security and Justice Law* (Hart, 2014), 110–29.

[47] Mitsilegas, 'Countering the Chameleon Threat of Dirty Money' (above n. 4).

of other Union policies.[48] Criminal law is thus used as a tool to achieve the effectiveness of Union law.[49] This expansive constitutionalisation of the Court's functional criminalisation approach in Article 83(2) TFEU has raised concerns with regard to the extent of criminalisation powers conferred upon the EU by the Lisbon Treaty. The Treaty attempts to address concerns with regard to the extensive use of Article 83(2) by introducing two central requirements for the use of EU competence in the field: the requirement that measures are essential to achieve effectiveness and the requirement that measures are essential to ensure the effective implementation of a Union policy *in an area which has been subject to harmonisation measures*.[50] However, even under this wording, functional criminalisation may include EU action to address the third aim of European criminal law, namely the protection of the EU budget. For both securitised and functional criminalisation, the Treaty attempts to place limits on the impact of EU intervention upon national criminal justice systems by Article 83 TFEU allowing the EU to legislate only in the form of minimum standards and only in the form of Directives, which give a degree of discretion to national systems to adjust to the EU requirements.

Notwithstanding these attempts to define clearly and circumscribe the extent of the Union's competence to define criminal offences and impose criminal sanctions, the adoption of Article 83 TFEU – and in particular its functional criminalisation arm – has raised a number of questions on the potential of EU law post-Lisbon to lead to over-criminalisation, by bringing into the fore the key question of 'why criminalise?' Inextricably linked to this question is the extent to which European criminal law can impact on national criminal justice systems and national legal diversity. These questions have arisen in practice in cases involving legal basis choices and the relationship of Article 83 TFEU with other treaty provisions. The first example involves the relationship between Article 83(2) TFEU and Article 325(4) TFEU, which confers upon the Union competence to adopt 'the necessary measures in the fields of the prevention of and fight against fraud

---

[48] Mitsilegas, 'The Transformation of Criminal Law in the Area of Freedom, Security and Justice' (above n. 22).

[49] For a critical view, see M. Kaiafa, 'The Importance of Core Principles of Substantive Criminal Law for a European Criminal Policy Respecting Fundamental Rights and the Rule of Law' (2011) 1 *European Criminal Law Review* 7, 19, arguing that the unique identity of criminal law cannot allow it to be reduced to a mere tool for the implementation of any policy.

[50] Emphasis added. On the limits of Article 83(2) TFEU, see P. Asp, *The Substantive Criminal Law Competence of the EU* (Skrifter Utgivna av Juridiska Fakulteten vid Stockholms Universitet Nr 79, 2013).

affecting the financial interests of the Union with a view to affording effective and equivalent protection in the Member States and in all the Union's institutions, bodies, offices and agencies'. The European Commission has opted in favour of using exclusively Article 325 TFEU as a legal basis for its recent proposal for a Directive harmonising substantive criminal law on fraud.[51] The use of Article 325 TFEU would lead to a higher level of harmonisation as EU action is not limited to minimum standards and the emergency brake and opt-out possibilities accompanying Article 83(2) TFEU do not apply in Article 325 TFEU – however at the time of writing it appears that the co-legislators have settled upon Article 83(2) TFEU as the legal basis. The second example involves the relationship between criminal and administrative law, and the extent of the Union's competence to criminalise in the presence of parallel EU administrative law imposing on series of categories of conduct non-criminal sanctions. This relationship has been tested in the context of post-Lisbon legislation on market abuse, where two parallel instruments – one on administrative and one on criminal law – have been adopted.[52] Two issues arise in this context in terms of criminalisation powers: the first, as mentioned above, is whether Member States are constrained by the adoption of criminal offences and sanctions under Article 83(2) TFEU in terms of their criminalisation choices at national level; the second, and related point, is whether Member States are similarly constrained by their choices of what to treat as an administrative infraction under the Regulation adopted under a separate legal basis. The requirement to ensure the effectiveness of Union law militates in favour of limiting national powers to criminalise in both cases. In the case of the interplay between EU administrative law and national criminal law, the choice by the EU legislator to address harmful behaviour (in this case market abuse) via merely administrative – and not criminal – sanctions would mean that the effectiveness of the EU policy and measure in question would be jeopardised if Member States adopted a harsher, criminal law approach. National criminalisation would also be contrary to the principle of proportionality, as enshrined in Article 49(3) of the Charter.[53]

---

[51] COM (2012) 363 final, Brussels, 11 July 2012. Article 325(4) TFEU.

[52] Regulation (EU) No. 596/2014 of the European Parliament and of the Council of 16 April 2014 on market abuse (Market Abuse Regulation) and repealing Directive 2003/6/EC of the European Parliament and of the Council and Commission Directives 2003/124/EC, 2003/125/EC and 2004/72/EC, OJ L 173, 12 June 2014, 1; and Directive 2014/57/EU of the European Parliament and of the Council of 16 April 2014 on criminal sanctions for market abuse (Market Abuse Directive), OJ L 173, 12 June 2014, 179.

[53] V. Mitsilegas, *EU Criminal Law after Lisbon* (Hart, 2016).

Read in this manner, the interaction between criminal and administrative law would lead not to over- but rather to de-criminalisation.[54]

B   Mutual Recognition

While a key feature of the development of such an area is the abolition of internal borders between Member States and the creation thus of a single European area where freedom of movement is secured, this single area of movement is not accompanied by a single area of law. The law remains territorial, with Member States retaining to a great extent their sovereignty especially in the field of law enforcement. A key challenge for European integration in the field has thus been how to make *national* legal systems interact in the borderless Area of Freedom, Security and Justice. Member States have thus far not opted for unification or a high degree of harmonisation of law in Europe's criminal justice area. The focus has largely been on the development of systems of cooperation between Member State authorities, with the aim of extending national enforcement capacity throughout the Area of Freedom, Security and Justice in order to compensate for the abolition of internal border controls. The simplification of movement that the abolition of internal border controls entails has led under this compensatory logic to calls for a similar simplification in inter-state cooperation via automaticity and speed.[55] Following this logic, the construction of the Area of Freedom, Security and Justice as an area without internal frontiers intensifies and justifies automaticity in inter-state cooperation.[56] Automaticity in inter-state cooperation means that a *national* decision will be enforced beyond the territory of the issuing Member State by authorities in other EU Member States across the Area of Freedom, Security and Justice without many questions being asked and with the requested authority having at its disposal extremely limited – if any at all – grounds to refuse the request for cooperation. The method chosen to secure such automaticity has been the application of the principle of mutual recognition in the fields of judicial cooperation in criminal matters. The principle of mutual recognition has been applied to all stages

---

[54] Mitsilegas, 'From Overcriminalisation to Decriminalisation' (above n. 17).

[55] V. Mitsilegas, 'Mutual Recognition, Mutual Trust and Fundamental Rights after Lisbon' in V. Mitsilegas et al. (eds.), *Research Handbook on EU Criminal Law* (Edward Elgar, 2016), 148–68.

[56] V. Mitsilegas, 'The Limits of Mutual Trust in Europe's Area of Freedom, Security and Justice. From Automatic Inter-State Cooperation to the Slow Emergence of the Individual' (2012) 31 *YEL* 319–72.

of the criminal process, from the pre- to the post-trial stage, and covers a wide range of criminal activity which would embrace all three justifications put forward for the adoption of European criminal law analysed in the previous section of this chapter.[57]

Mutual recognition is attractive to Member States resisting further harmonisation or unification in European criminal law as it is a form of governance which is designed to enhance inter-state cooperation in criminal matters without Member States having to change their national laws to comply with EU harmonisation requirements.[58] Mutual recognition creates extraterritoriality:[59] in a borderless Area of Freedom, Security and Justice, the will of an authority in one Member State can be enforced beyond its territorial legal borders and across this area. The acceptance of such extraterritoriality requires a high level of mutual trust between the authorities which take part in the system. It is premised upon the acceptance that membership of the EU means that all EU Member States are fully compliant with fundamental rights norms. It is the acceptance of the high level of integration among EU Member States which has justified automaticity in inter-state cooperation and has led to the adoption of a series of EU instruments which in this context go beyond pre-existing, traditional forms of cooperation set out under public international law, which have afforded a greater degree of scrutiny to requests for cooperation. Membership of the EU *presumes* the full respect of fundamental rights by all Member States, creating mutual trust which, in turn, forms the basis of automaticity in inter-state cooperation in Europe's area of criminal justice. The best example of mutual recognition in these terms is the system introduced by the Framework Decision on the European Arrest Warrant.[60] Automaticity and speed are coupled with the inclusion of only limited grounds to refuse the recognition and execution of a Warrant. The Framework Decision includes only three, in their majority procedural, mandatory grounds for refusal[61] which are complemented by a series of

---

[57] For further details on the application of mutual recognition in the field of European criminal law, see Mitsilegas, *EU Criminal Law* (above, n. 1).

[58] V. Mitsilegas, 'The Constitutional Implications of Mutual Recognition in Criminal Matters in the EU' (2006) 43 *CML Rev* 1277–311.

[59] K. Nicolaidis and G. Shaffer, 'Transnational Mutual Recognition Regimes: Governance without Global Government' (2005) 68 *Law and Contemporary Problems* 263–317; K. Nicolaidis, 'Trusting the Poles? Constructing Europe through Mutual Recognition' (2007) 14 *JEPP* 682–98.

[60] Framework Decision 2002/584/JHA of 13 June 2002 on the European Arrest Warrant [2002] OJ L 190/1.

[61] Ibid., Article 3.

optional grounds for refusal[62] and provisions on guarantees underpinning the surrender process.[63] Non-compliance with fundamental rights is not however included as a ground to refuse to execute a European Arrest Warrant. This legislative choice reflects the view that cooperation can take place on the basis of a high level of mutual trust in the criminal justice systems of Member States, premised upon the presumption that fundamental rights are in principle respected fully across the EU.

In a consistent line of case law starting before the entry into force of the Lisbon Treaty, the CJEU has adopted a broad approach to mutual recognition, embracing a teleological interpretation and stressing the need to achieve the effectiveness of the Framework Decision by ensuring that in principle mutual recognition takes place in a speedy and simplified manner.[64] The entry into force of the Treaty of Lisbon has added a further dimension to the question of the extent to which fundamental rights concerns should be taken into account and form grounds of refusal in a system of mutual recognition based on mutual trust. The Lisbon Treaty has signified the constitutionalisation of the EU Charter of Fundamental Rights and it was only a matter of time before the CJEU would be asked to examine the compatibility of the system of mutual recognition with the Charter. The first major case in this context was the case of *Radu*,[65] in which the CJEU was asked for the first time in such a direct manner by a national court on whether mutual recognition could be refused on fundamental rights grounds. In the present case, the Court answered in the negative. The Court reaffirmed the adoption of a teleological interpretation reiterating the purpose of establishing a simplified and more effective system of surrender based on mutual recognition.[66] Such a system will contribute to the Union's objective of becoming an area of freedom, security and justice by basing itself on the high degree of confidence which should exist between the Member States.[67] On the basis of this presumption of mutual trust, the Court found that the observance of Articles 47 and 48 of the Charter does not require that a judicial authority of a Member State should be able to refuse to execute a European Arrest Warrant issued for the purposes of

---

[62] Ibid., Article 4.
[63] Ibid., Articles 5, 27 and 28.
[64] See, inter alia, Case C-303/05, *Advocaten voor de Wereld* [2007] ECR I-3633 para. 28; Case C-388/08 PPU, *Leymann and Pustovarov*, para. 42; Case C-192/12 PPU, *Melvin West*, para. 56; Case C-168/13 PPU, *Jeremy F.*, para. 35.
[65] Case C-396/11, *Radu*, judgment of 29 January 2013.
[66] Ibid., paras. 33 and 34.
[67] Ibid., para. 34.

conducting a criminal prosecution on the ground that the requested person was not heard by the issuing judicial authorities before that Warrant was issued.[68] *Radu* thus follows the Court's earlier case law in two respects: it confirms that it is satisfied with the provision of fundamental rights protection in one of the two states which take part in the cooperative mutual recognition system (here, it is the executing state which is under the duty to uphold the right to be heard); and it places the protection of fundamental rights within a clear framework of effectiveness of the enforcement cooperation system which is established by the Framework Decision on the European Arrest Warrant. Too extensive a protection of fundamental rights (in both the issuing and the executing state) would undermine the effectiveness of law enforcement cooperation in this context.[69]

The focus on the effective operation of mutual recognition was reiterated by the CJEU in the case of *Melloni*.[70] Here the Court effectively confirmed the primacy of third pillar law (the European Arrest Warrant Framework Decision as amended by the Framework Decision on judgments *in absentia*, interpreted in the light of the Charter) has primacy over national constitutional law providing a higher level of fundamental rights protection. The Court rejected an interpretation of Article 53 of the Charter as giving general authorisation to a Member State to apply the standard of protection of fundamental rights guaranteed by its constitution when that standard is higher than that derived from the Charter and, where necessary, to give it priority over the application of provisions of EU law.[71] That interpretation of Article 53 would undermine the principle of the primacy of EU law inasmuch as it would allow a Member State to disapply EU legal rules *which are fully in compliance with the Charter* where they infringe the fundamental rights guaranteed by that State's constitution.[72] Article 53 of the Charter provides freedom to national authorities to apply national human rights standards provided that the level of protection provided for by the Charter, as interpreted by the Court, and the *primacy, unity and effectiveness* of EU law are not thereby compromised.[73] Allowing a Member State to avail itself of Article 53 of the Charter to make the surrender of a person convicted *in absentia* conditional upon the conviction being open

---

[68] Ibid., para. 39.
[69] see V. Mitsilegas, 'The Symbiotic Relationship between Mutual Trust and Fundamental Rights in Europe's Area of Criminal Justice' (2015) 6(4) *New Journal of European Criminal Law* 460–85.
[70] Case C-399/11, *Melloni*, judgment of 26 February 2013.
[71] Ibid., paras. 56–7.
[72] Ibid., para. 58. Emphasis added.
[73] Ibid., para. 60. Emphasis added.

to review in the issuing Member State (in order to avoid an adverse effect on the right to a fair trial and the rights of the defence guaranteed by the constitution of the executing Member State, by casting doubt on the uniformity of the standard of protection of fundamental rights as defined in that framework decision) *would undermine the principles of mutual trust and recognition which that decision purports to uphold and would, therefore, compromise the efficacy of that framework decision.*[74]

In *Melloni*, once again the Court has given priority to the effectiveness of mutual recognition based on presumed mutual trust. Secondary pre-Lisbon third pillar law whose primary aim is to facilitate mutual recognition has primacy over national constitutional law. The emphasis of the Court of the need to uphold the validity of harmonised EU secondary law over primary constitutional law on human rights (at both national and EU level) constitutes a grave challenge for human rights protection.[75] It further reveals in the context of EU criminal law a strong focus by the Court on the need to uphold the validity of a system of quasi-automatic mutual recognition in criminal matters which will enhance inter-state cooperation and law enforcement effectiveness across the EU. The Court's emphasis on the centrality of mutual trust as a factor privileging the achievement of law enforcement objectives via mutual recognition over the protection of fundamental rights has been reiterated beyond EU criminal law in the broader context of the accession of the EU to the European Convention of Human Rights (ECHR). Opinion 2/13 has included a specific part dealing with mutual trust in EU law. The Court has distilled its current thinking on mutual trust stating that:

> it should be noted that the principle of mutual trust between the Member States is of fundamental importance in EU law, given that it allows an area without internal borders to be created and maintained. That principle requires, particularly with regard to the area of freedom, security and justice, each of those States, save in exceptional circumstances, to consider all the other Member States to be complying with EU law and particularly with the fundamental rights recognised by EU law.

and adding that:

> when implementing EU law, the Member States may, under EU law, be required to presume that fundamental rights have been observed by the other Member States, so that not only may they not demand a higher level

---

[74] Ibid., para. 63. Emphasis added.

[75] According to Besselink, attaching this importance to secondary legislation as 'harmonisation of EU fundamental rights' risks erasing the difference between the primary law nature of fundamental rights and secondary law as the subject of these rights. L. F. M. Besselink, 'The Parameters of Constitutional Conflict after Melloni' (2014) 39(4), *EL Rev* 531–52, 542.

of national protection of fundamental rights from another Member State than that provided by EU law, but, save in exceptional cases, they may not check whether that other Member State has actually, in a specific case, observed the fundamental rights guaranteed by the EU.[76]

From the perspective of the relationship between EU criminal law and fundamental rights, this passage is striking. It follows a series of comments on the role of Article 53 of the Charter in preserving the autonomy of EU law, with the Court citing the *Melloni* requirement for upholding the primacy, unity and effectiveness of EU law.[77] The Court then puts forward a rather extreme view of presumed mutual trust leading to automatic mutual recognition. It thus represents a significant challenge to our understanding of the EU constitutional order as a legal order underpinned by the protection of fundamental rights. The Court, almost out of the blue, elevates the inherently subjective concept of mutual trust to a fundamental principle of EU law and endorses a system whereby the protection of fundamental rights must be subsumed to the abstract requirements of upholding mutual trust.[78] In this manner, mutual trust –which is conceived exclusively as trust between Member States – is transformed by the Court into a normative foundation of European criminal law. This approach leads to the uncritical acceptance of presumed trust across the EU: not only are Member States not allowed to demand a higher national protection of fundamental rights than the one provided by EU law (thus echoing *Melloni*), but also, and remarkably, Member States are not allowed to check (save in exceptional circumstances) whether fundamental rights have been observed in other Member States in *specific* cases. This finding is striking as it disregards a number of developments in secondary EU criminal law aiming to grant executing authorities the opportunity to check whether execution of a judicial decision by authorities of another Member State would comply with fundamental rights.[79] It also represents a fundamental philosophical and substantive difference in the protection of fundamental

---

[76] Opinion 2/13, paras. 191–2.

[77] Ibid., para. 188.

[78] For an extensive analysis see Mitsilegas, 'The Symbiotic Relationship between Mutual Trust and Fundamental Rights in Europe's Area of Criminal Justice' (above n. 69).

[79] The post-Lisbon Directive on the European Investigation Order has introduced an optional ground for non-recognition or non-execution where there are substantial grounds to believe that the execution of the investigative measure indicated in the EIO would be incompatible with the executing state's obligations in accordance with Article 6 TEU and the Charter (Article 11(1)(f)). Directive 2014/41/EU of the European Parliament and of the Council of 3 April 2014 regarding the European Investigation Order in criminal matters, OJ L 130, 1 May 2014, 1.

rights between the Luxembourg and Strasbourg Courts. This difference has been highlighted in the Strasbourg ruling in *Tarakhel*,[80] a case involving transfers of asylum seekers under the Dublin system, where the Court stressed the obligation of states to carry out a *thorough and individualised* examination of the fundamental rights situation of the person concerned.[81] In *Tarakhel* the Strasbourg Court, rather than requiring a general finding of systemic deficiency in order to examine the compatibility of a state action with fundamental rights, reminds us that the presumption of compliance with fundamental rights is rebuttable[82] and that effective protection of fundamental rights always requires an assessment of the impact of a decision on the rights of the specific individual in the specific case before the Court.[83] In *Tarakhel*, this reasoning has resulted in a finding of a breach of the Convention with regard to specific individuals even in a case where generalised systemic deficiencies in the receiving state had not been ascertained.[84] This difference in approach raises the real prospect of a conflict between ECHR and EU law, especially in cases of inter-state cooperation between EU Member States under the principle of mutual recognition. Eeckhout has commented that Opinion 2/13 confirms a radical pluralist conception of the relationship between EU law and the ECHR.[85] In the case of mutual recognition, this 'outward-looking', external pluralist approach which can be seen as an attempt to preserve the autonomy of Union law is combined with the parallel strengthening of an internal, intra-EU pluralist approach which stresses the importance of mutual trust, which is elevated by the Court to a fundamental principle of EU law.[86] Both internal and external pluralist approaches undermine the position of the individual in Europe's area of criminal justice by limiting the judicial avenues of examination of the fundamental rights implications of quasi-automatic mutual recognition on a case-by-case basis.

---

[80] *Tarakhel* v. *Switzerland*, App. No. 29217/12.
[81] Ibid., para. 104, emphasis added.
[82] Ibid., para. 103.
[83] According to Halberstam, *Tarakhel* is a strong warning signal to Luxembourg that the CJEU's standard better comport either in words or in practice with what Strasbourg demands or else the Dublin system violates the Convention. D. Halberstam, '"It's the Autonomy, Stupid!" A Modest Defense of Opinion 2/13 on EU Accession to the ECHR, and the Way Forward' (2015) 16 *GLJ* 105.
[84] *Tarakhel* (above n. 80), para. 115.
[85] P. Eeckhout, 'Opinion 2/13 on EU Accession to the ECHR and Judicial Dialogue- Autonomy or Autarchy?', Jean Monnet Working Paper 01/15, 36.
[86] Mitsilegas, 'The Symbiotic Relationship' (above n. 78).

C   The Establishment of Criminal Justice Agencies

Another key form of governance of European criminal law has been the establishment of EU agencies in the field of criminal justice. The establishment of these agencies has been controversial with regard to their impact on state sovereignty in the field of criminal law, and thus far the debate over their evolving legal regime has been fraught with disagreements regarding their structure, mandate and powers. There are currently two major EU criminal justice agencies, one in the field of police cooperation (Europol) and one in the field of judicial cooperation in criminal matters (Eurojust). They have both been established in order to serve clear security purposes, namely to contribute to the fight against serious and organised crime, but their mandate includes areas of criminality which would also fall within the more functional justifications of European criminal law. Their legal regime has been evolving over time, with their founding legislation already being repealed or replaced pre-Lisbon by new third pillar Decisions, which are to be in turn replaced by Lisbonised instruments which are currently being negotiated in Brussels.[87] Member States' reluctance to allow significant inroads by these agencies to their domestic criminal justice systems have influenced the configuration of their structure and powers: Europol officers do not have the power to arrest persons on the streets of EU Member States, the main powers and added value of Europol lying rather in its intelligence work and the analysis it can generate and provide to Member States; Eurojust, on the other hand, is structured on the basis of a highly intergovernmental, collegiate model and does not have the power to coerce national authorities to initiate prosecutions; it has rather assumed a role of facilitator of judicial cooperation and of coordinator of Member States' prosecutorial efforts in transnational cases. Notwithstanding these limits to their powers, operations by Europol and Eurojust may have a considerable adverse impact for the protection of fundamental rights. The example of the role of Eurojust in determining outcomes in cases of conflicts of jurisdiction is characteristic here. Eurojust assumes a coordinating role, bringing together national authorities to take decisions on which jurisdiction should prosecute. However, these meetings take place on an informal basis, with no representation by the defence,

---

[87] Council Decision 2009/371/JHA of 6 April 2009 establishing the European Police Office, OJ L 121/37. Council Decision 2002/187/JHA of 28 February 2002 setting up Eurojust with a view to reinforcing the fight against serious crime, OJ L 63/1, as amended by Council Decision 2009/426/JHA, OJ L 138/14. For a background, see Mitsilegas, EU Criminal Law (above, n. 1), Chapter 4; Mitsilegas, 'The Third Wave of Third Pillar Law' (above n. 41).

and with no legally binding or challengeable criteria. A number of criteria for deciding on conflicts of jurisdiction are stated – in a non-hierarchical manner – in the Annex of Eurojust's 2003 Annual Report, while the subsequent Framework Decision on conflicts of jurisdiction does not include any binding criteria in the field.[88] This pragmatic approach may have the advantages of informality and speed but sits at odds with the requirement to provide individuals affected by EU law effective judicial protection.

The entry into force of the Lisbon Treaty has provided fresh impetus for the establishment of EU criminal justice agencies by including an express legal basis for the establishment of an EPPO (Article 86 TFEU). The EPPO is designed to tackle specifically fraud against the EU budget, but the Treaty provides the possibility of the extension of the Office's mandate to include serious crime having a cross-border dimension.[89] The conception of the establishment of a European prosecutor to defend a European interest *par excellence*, namely the protection of the EU budget, has been reflected in the model of European prosecution put forward by the European Commission in its proposal for a Regulation for the establishment of the EPPO.[90] The Commission has put forward a centralised, hierarchical and vertical model of European prosecution. In the Commission's vision, centralisation is synonymous with prosecutorial independence and is justified on the basis of a lack of trust towards the capacity or willingness of national authorities to combat effectively fraud against the budget of the Union: after all, the EPPO has been legitimised primarily on the grounds of the current lack of effectiveness in combating fraud across the EU.[91] Within this centralised structure, the Commission has introduced two strong federal elements in its vision of the EPPO: exclusive competence and European territoriality. By granting the EPPO exclusive competence, the Commission sent a strong signal to Member States that it is only the EPPO which is responsible and competent for the investigation and prosecution of the 'European Union' offences associated with fraud against the Union budget.[92] The powers of the EPPO in this context have been backed up by the application by the Commission of the principle of European territoriality. According to Article 25 of the Commission's draft, for the

---

[88] Mitsilegas, *EU Criminal Law after Lisbon* (above n. 53).
[89] Article 86(4) TFEU.
[90] COM (2013) 534 final, Brussels, 17 July 2013.
[91] The Commission's Explanatory Memorandum to the draft EPPO Regulation asserts that Member States' criminal investigation and prosecution authorities are currently unable to achieve an equivalent level of protection and enforcement – COM (2013) 534 final, 2.
[92] Article 11(4) of the Commission's proposal.

purpose of investigations and prosecutions conducted by the EPPO, the territory of the Union's Member States will be considered *a single legal area* in which the EPPO may exercise its competence.[93] The Commission's draft thus mirrors the approach taken by the drafters of the *Corpus Juris*.[94]

The federal model of prosecution introduced by the Commission based on centralisation, exclusive competence and European territoriality has been rejected by Member States in subsequent negotiations. The EPPO Regulation is still under negotiation at the time of writing, with the outcome of negotiations crucial in determining how many Member States will actually participate in the establishment of the Office, as the Treaty enables the adoption of the Regulation under enhanced cooperation. Member States have replaced the centralised model of prosecution put forward by the Commission with a multilayered collegiate model, at times reminiscent of the intergovernmental collegiate model adopted by Eurojust. Moreover, both the concepts of exclusivity and European territoriality have been rejected by the Council. Exclusive competence has been replaced by priority competence of the EPPO, backed up by a right to evocation, while the provision on European territoriality has been deleted from the text. Negotiations are ongoing to determine the powers of the EPPO and the applicable law in relation to the operation of the respective EPPO layers.[95] While there is a lot to be discussed on the establishment of the EPPO from the perspective of sovereignty – and indeed the impact of this agency on both state sovereignty and national legal diversity in the field of criminal justice has been at the heart of current negotiations in Brussels – this focus on sovereignty may serve to mask fundamental concerns regarding the impact of the EPPO on the rights of individuals. The need for a political compromise which at the same time will address the complex legal reality of adding an EU layer to the operation of domestic criminal justice systems may lead to lacunae in human rights protection. Nowhere is this clearer than in the field of judicial protection vis-à-vis the operations of the EPPO. In stark contrast to the Treaty provisions on the judicial control of agencies, and Article 47 of the Charter, the Commission's draft Regulation stated that judicial review of EPPO acts will take place only at the national

---

[93] Article 25(1) of the Commission's proposal.
[94] For a background to the *Corpus Juris*, see M. Delmas-Marty, 'Guest Editorial: Combatting Fraud – Necessity, Legitimacy and Feasibility of the *Corpus Juris*' (2000) 37 *CML Rev* 247–56.
[95] Mitsilegas, *EU Criminal Law after Lisbon* (above n. 53).

and not at the EU level.[96] While it appears that latest drafts envisage some degree of EU judicial scrutiny of certain EPPO acts, EU judicial control of the EPPO remains limited.[97] As in the case of the regulation of Eurojust's activities on conflicts of jurisdiction, this approach may lead to significant limits to the effective protection of fundamental rights in Europe at the same time when criminal justice agencies proliferate.

IV The 'For Whom' Question: The Subjects of European Criminal Law

The analysis thus far has demonstrated that the answers to the 'why' and the 'how' questions have led to a system of European criminal law focused predominantly on security and effectiveness. Little attention has been given to the place of the individual in this system. Yet this paradigm may change if one looks at the normative foundations of European criminal law from a different lens, from the perspective of the individual. This section will attempt to do exactly this, by focusing on the role and the potential of taking seriously the protection of fundamental rights in the evolving EU constitutional framework. By focusing in particular on the entry into force of the Treaty of Lisbon, this section will analyse the impact of fundamental rights on the development of European criminal law from three different but interrelated perspectives: the possibilities offered by the constitutonalisation of the Charter of Fundamental Rights; the role of fundamental rights as limitations to uncritical law enforcement cooperation under the principle of mutual recognition; and the transformative effect of EU action to legislate for human rights, by making use of the Lisbon possibilities to adopt secondary legislation in the field of the rights of the defendant.

A The Charter

A key development for a paradigm change regarding the normative foundations of European criminal law has been the constitutionalisation of the Charter of Fundamental Rights, which has the same legal value as the Treaties[98] and has been seen as contributing to reinforcing the centrality of

---

[96] V. Mitsilegas, 'The European Public Prosecutor before the Court of Justice: The Challenge of Effective Judicial Protection' in G. Giudicelli-Delage et al. (eds.), *Le Contrôle Judiciaire du Parquet Européen. Nécessité, Modèles, Enjeux* (Collection de l'UMR de Droit Comparé de Paris (Université Paris 1), Société de Législation Comparée, 2015), XXXVII, 67–87.

[97] Mitsilegas, *EU Criminal Law after Lisbon* (above n. 53).

[98] Article 6(1) TEU. See P. Craig, *The Lisbon Treaty: Law, Politics, and Treaty Reform* (Oxford University Press, 2010), 200.

fundamental rights in the EU legal order.[99] The Charter contains a whole Title, Title VI, on justice. Title VI enshrines key rights and principles for the development of EU criminal law including the right to an effective remedy and to a fair trial[100], the presumption of innocence and right of defence,[101] the principles of legality and proportionality of criminal offences and penalties[102] and the right not to be tried or punished twice in criminal proceedings for the same criminal offence.[103] Further Charter rights which are relevant to EU criminal law include rights and principles enshrined in Title I of the Charter on dignity (including the provisions on human dignity,[104] the right to life,[105] the right to the integrity of the person[106] and the prohibition of torture and inhuman or degrading treatment or punishment[107]), in Title II on freedoms (including the provisions on the right to liberty and security,[108] the respect for private and family life[109] and the protection of personal data[110] as well as the provisions on freedom of expression and information,[111] freedom of assembly and association,[112] right to property[113] and protection in the event of removal, expulsion or extradition[114]), in Title III on equality (most notably the provisions on equality before the law,[115] non-discrimination[116] and the rights of the child[117]) and in Title V on citizens' rights (including the right to good administration,[118] the right of access to documents[119] and freedom of

---

[99] See S. Iglesias Sanchez, 'The Court and the Charter: The Impact of the Entry into Force of the Lisbon Treaty on the ECJ's Approach to Fundamental Rights' (2012) 49 *CML Rev* 1565–612, 1582.

[100] Article 47.

[101] Article 48.

[102] Article 49.

[103] Article 50.

[104] Article 1.

[105] Article 2.

[106] Article 3.

[107] Article 4.

[108] Article 6.

[109] Article 7.

[110] Article 8.

[111] Article 11.

[112] Article 12.

[113] Article 17.

[114] Article 18.

[115] Article 20.

[116] Article 23.

[117] Article 24.

[118] Article 41.

[119] Article 42.

movement and of residence[120]). Thus a whole raft of Articles, the majority of the Charter provisions, are relevant and applicable in the implementation of EU criminal law.[121] Moreover, the CJEU has affirmed that the Charter provisions have a broad application. In the case of *Fransson*,[122] the CJEU adopted a broad interpretation of the application of the Charter, including in cases where national legislation does not implement expressly or directly an EU criminal law instrument. The Court found that domestic law on VAT fraud does fall within EU law since there is a direct link between the collection of VAT revenue in compliance with the EU law applicable and the availability to the EU budget of the corresponding VAT resources.[123] The CJEU developed its approach on the applicability of the Charter in *Siragusa*[124] where it ruled that the concept of 'implementing Union law', as referred to in Article 51 of the Charter, requires a certain degree of connection above and beyond the matters covered being closely related or one of those matters having an indirect impact on the other.[125] As will be seen in the section on implementation below, the Court's approach has the effect of including a wide range of national legislation and measures related to national criminal justice systems within the scope of the Charter. This view is reinforced by the Court's finding in *Siragusa* that it is important to consider the objective of protecting fundamental rights in EU law, which is to ensure that those rights are not infringed in areas of EU activity, whether through action at EU level or through the implementation of EU law by the Member States.[126]

This broad interpretation of the applicability of the Charter is significant not only in relation to the interpretation of European criminal law by courts, but also in relation to the enhanced scrutiny opportunities it provides to EU institutions when assessing Member States' compliance with European criminal law. The Court's case law on the applicability of the Charter, combined with the EU law requirement for Member States to ensure the effectiveness of EU law, generate the requirement that the scrutiny of implementation of EU criminal law by Member States is not limited to the scrutiny of the implementation of specific provisions set out

---

[120] Article 45.
[121] See V. Mitsilegas, 'The European Union, Criminal Law and Human Rights' in L. Weber et al. (eds.), *The Routledge Handbook on Criminology and Human Rights* (Routledge, 2016).
[122] Case C-617/10, *Åklagaren v. Hans Åkerberg Fransson*, judgment of 26 February 2013.
[123] Ibid., para. 26.
[124] Case C-206/13, *Siragusa*, judgment of 6 March 2014.
[125] Ibid., para. 24.
[126] Ibid., para. 31.

in Directives and Framework Decisions, but also includes a holistic scrutiny of domestic criminal justice systems to the extent that elements of the
latter have a degree of connection with the implementation of EU criminal
law along the lines of the Court's approach in *Siragusa*. To give two concrete examples of where such degree of connection may exist: in the case
of mutual recognition, the monitoring of the implementation of measures
such as the Framework Decisions on the European Arrest Warrant or on
the Transfer of Sentenced Persons cannot be complete without monitoring of prison conditions at EU level. Similarly, in the case of the European
Arrest Warrant, scrutiny of implementation must include scrutiny of pre-
trial detention length and conditions in Member States, as well as scrutiny of the duration of pre-trial periods. The second example involves the
implementation of the rights of the defendant in criminal proceedings. It
is submitted that effective implementation of the relevant Directives will
only be ensured if national criminal justice systems are scrutinised holisti-
cally from the police station to trial and if scrutiny also covers the levels
of resources Member States commit towards the effective implementation
of EU law.[127] The emphasis on implementation in this manner has the
potential – along with the content of EU law – to have a transformative
effect on national criminal justice systems.

B   Fundamental Rights as a Limit to Mutual Recognition

The maximalist approach to mutual recognition adopted in the European
Arrest Warrant Framework Decision has led to reactions in European and
national legislatures seeking ways of accommodating fundamental rights
considerations within the operation of the EU system of mutual recognition. There are three ways in which fundamental rights concerns have been
addressed in legislation: via the use of parallel mutual recognition instruments to alleviate the adverse fundamental rights consequences of automaticity in the execution of mutual recognition requests; via the insertion
of grounds of refusal on fundamental rights grounds in subsequent legislation; and via legislation addressing proportionality concerns.[128] In terms
of the use of parallel mutual recognition measures, fundamental rights
concerns can be addressed by the Framework Decision on the mutual
recognition of bail decisions (the European Supervision Order), which

---

[127] Mitsilegas, *EU Criminal Law after Lisbon* (above n. 53).
[128] Mitsilegas, 'Mutual Recognition, Mutual Trust and Fundamental Rights after Lisbon'
(above n. 55).

would enable an individual surrendered under a European Arrest Warrant to spend the pre-trial period under bail conditions in the executing, and not the issuing, Member State.[129] In terms of the use of fundamental rights as a limit to mutual recognition, a number of Member States added non-compliance of surrender with fundamental rights as an express ground of refusal in their national law implementing the European Arrest Warrant Framework Decision.[130] Moreover, the post-Lisbon Directive on the European Investigation Order (EIO)[131] expressly includes non-compliance with fundamental rights as a ground for refusal to recognise and execute an EIO.[132] The preamble to the Directive affirms that the presumption of compliance by Member States with fundamental rights is rebuttable.[133]

The third way in which legislators have addressed fundamental rights concerns in the operation of mutual recognition has been via the insertion of proportionality-check requirements in secondary law. The focus on proportionality has been triggered by concerns that the extensive scope of the Framework Decision on the European Arrest Warrant combined with the abolition of the requirement to verify dual criminality has led to warrants being issued for offences considered minor or trivial in the executing state resulting in considerable pressure on the criminal justice systems of executing Member States and disproportionate results for the requested individuals.[134] The need to address these proportionality concerns was acknowledged by the European Commission in its latest Report on the implementation of the Framework Decision.[135] The prevailing view

---

[129] The use of the European Supervision Order as a means of addressing lengthy periods of pre-trial detention following the execution of a European Arrest Warrant was discussed and promoted in Sir Scott Baker, 'A Review of the United Kingdom's Extradition Arrangements', presented to the Home Secretary on 30 September 2011.

[130] On the implementation of the Framework Decision on the European Arrest Warrant, see Gisèle van Tiggelen et al. eds., *The Future of Mutual Recognition in Criminal Matters* (Éditions de l'Université de Bruxelles, 2009); and V. Mitsilegas, 'The Area of Freedom, Security and Justice from Amsterdam to Lisbon: Challenges of Implementation, Constitutionality and Fundamental Rights' in Julia Laffranque (ed.), *The Area of Freedom, Security and Justice, Including Information Society Issues, Reports of the XXV FIDE Congress, Tallinn 2012*, 3 vols. (Tartu University Press, 2012), III, 21–142 and national Reports included therein.

[131] Directive 2014/41/EU of the European Parliament and of the Council of 3 April 2014 regarding the European Investigation Order in criminal matters, OJ L 130, 1 May 2014, 1.

[132] Ibid., Article 11(1)(f).

[133] Ibid., Recital 19.

[134] See Joint Committee on Human Rights, 'The Human Rights Implications of UK Extradition Policy', Fifteenth Report, session 2010–12, 40–3.

[135] Report from the Commission to the European Parliament and the Council on the implementation since 2007 of the Council Framework Decision of 13 June 2002 on the European

has thus far been for proportionality to be dealt with in the issuing and not in the executing Member State. This is the interpretative guidance given in the revised version of the European Handbook on how to issue a European Arrest Warrant.[136] The requirement to introduce a proportionality check in the issuing state has also been introduced at EU level in the Directive on the European Investigation Order, which stipulates that the issuing authority may only issue an EIO where necessary and proportionate and where the investigative measures indicated in the EIO could have been ordered under the same conditions in a similar domestic case.[137] The Directive thus links proportionality with the requirement to avoid abuse of law via the undertaking of 'fishing expeditions' by the authorities of the issuing state.

C   Fundamental Rights as a Foundation of Mutual Recognition: Legislating for Defence Rights

Fundamental rights can be used to regulate mutual recognition not only in a negative, but also in a positive manner. A key example is the move to accompany mutual recognition with harmonisation of national systems of criminal procedure, most notably by legislating for human rights. For the first time, the Lisbon Treaty confers upon the European Union express competence to adopt minimum rules on the rights of individuals in criminal procedure in Article 82(2) TFEU. On the basis of this provision, a number of measures on the rights of the individual in criminal procedure have been adopted. These are thus far a Directive on the right to interpretation and translation;[138] a Directive on the right to information;[139] and a Directive on the right to access to a lawyer.[140] The Commission has also published a Green Paper on the application of EU criminal justice

---

Arrest Warrant and the surrender procedures between Member States, COM (2011) 175 final, Brussels, 11 April 2011, 8.

[136]   Council Doc. 17195/1/10 REV 1, Brussels, 17 December 2010.

[137]   Article 6(1)(a) and (b) respectively.

[138]   Directive 2010/64/EU on the right to interpretation and translation in criminal proceedings, OJ L 280, 26 October 2010, 1.

[139]   Directive 2012/13/EU on the right to information in criminal proceedings, OJ L 142, 1 June 2012, 1.

[140]   Directive 2013/48/EU on the right of access to a lawyer in criminal proceedings and in European arrest warrant proceedings, and on the right to have a third party informed upon deprivation of liberty and to communicate with third persons and with consular authorities while deprived of liberty, OJ L 294, 6 November 2013, 1.

legislation in the field of detention[141] and, in November 2013, has tabled a number of draft Directives on legal aid,[142] procedural safeguards for children[143] and the presumption of innocence.[144] These proposals have been accompanied by Commission Recommendations on the right to legal aid[145] and on procedural safeguards for vulnerable persons.[146] The adoption of EU measures harmonising national law on the rights of the individual in criminal proceedings has a transformative effect.[147] It has far-reaching applicability, with measures applying not only to cross-border, but also to purely domestic cases, and applying not only in the context of mutual recognition, but also in other areas of European criminal law including the operation of the EPPO. The adoption of EU defence-rights measures signals a paradigm shift from a system focused primarily – if not solely – on promoting the interests of the state and of law enforcement under rules of quasi-automatic mutual recognition to a system where the rights of individuals affected by such rules are brought into the fore, protected by and enforced in EU law. There are four main ways in which the Directives on procedural rights in criminal procedure will enhance the protection of fundamental rights in EU Member States. First of all, a number of key provisions conferring rights in the Directives have direct effect. This means that, in a system of decentralised enforcement of EU law, individuals can evoke and claim rights directly before their national courts if the EU Directives have not been implemented or have been inadequately implemented. Direct effect means in practice that a suspect or accused person can derive a number of key rights – such as the right to an interpreter or the right to access to a lawyer – directly from EU law if national legislation has not made appropriate provision in conformity with it. Second, this avenue of decentralised enforcement is coupled with the high level of centralised enforcement of EU criminal law which has been 'normalised' after the entry into force of the Lisbon Treaty. The European Commission now has full powers to monitor the implementation of these Directives by Member States and has the power to introduce infringement proceedings before the CJEU when it considers that the

---

[141] COM (2011) 327 final, Brussels, 14 June 2011.
[142] COM (2013) 824 final, Brussels, 27 November 2013.
[143] COM (2013) 822 final, Brussels, 27 November 2013.
[144] COM (2013) 821 final, Brussels, 27 November 2013.
[145] OJ C 378/11, 24 December 2013.
[146] OJ C 378/8, 24 December 2013.
[147] V. Mitsilegas, 'Legislating for Human Rights After Lisbon: The Transformative Effect of EU Measures on the Rights of the Individual in Criminal Procedure' in M. Fletcher et al. (eds.), *The European Union as an Area of Freedom, Security and Justice* (Routledge, 2016).

Directives have not been implemented adequately. Third, national criminal procedural law must be applied and interpreted in compliance and conformity with the Directives. The procedural standards set out in the Directives will have an impact on a wide range of acts under national criminal procedure. Fourth, the implementation of the Directives must take place in compliance with the Charter of Fundamental Rights. The Charter will apply not only to national legislation which specifically implements the EU Directives on procedural rights, but also to all other elements of domestic criminal procedure which have a connection with EU law on procedural rights in criminal proceedings.[148]

V   Towards a Paradigm Change: Fundamental Rights as the Key Normative Foundation of European Criminal Law

European criminal law has emerged and developed to serve multiple objectives: in addition to the obvious security objective, the EU has intervened in criminal matters in order to uphold the effectiveness of EU law, including the protection of key Union policies, objectives and interests. This logic based on security and effectiveness has permeated the forms of governance the EU legislator has adopted in the field of European criminal law. From the harmonisation of substantive criminal law, to the application of the principle of mutual recognition in criminal matters, to the gradual establishment of a number of EU criminal justice agencies, the governance of European criminal law thus far could serve to justify the conclusion that the normative foundations of European criminal law are, indeed, centred on the dual need to achieve security and effectiveness with little, if any, space left for the consideration of the position of the individual within Europe's criminal justice architecture. This chapter has argued that this security and effectiveness-led paradigm of European criminal law is becoming increasingly inadequate, in particular after the entry into force of the Treaty of Lisbon. The inadequacy of this paradigm is revealed if one asks the question: 'who is European criminal law for?' By focusing on the individual as the subject of European criminal law, the chapter has highlighted the transformative effect of primary and secondary EU fundamental rights law for a new way of thinking regarding the normative foundations of European criminal law. The entry into force of the Lisbon Treaty provides ample tools to ensure the effective protection of

---

[148] Mitsilegas, 'The Symbiotic Relationship between Mutual Trust and Fundamental Rights in Europe's Area of Criminal Justice' (above n. 78).

fundamental rights on the ground in the evolution of European criminal law and has the potential, in particular, to ensure far-reaching scrutiny by national courts and EU institutions of the fundamental rights compliance of Member States when implementing European criminal law. The adoption of secondary law targeted specifically towards the very protection of fundamental rights in the field of criminal justice constitutes a turning point in the way we think about European criminal law: rather than security and effectiveness, it is the protection of fundamental rights which emerges as its key normative foundation.

Conclusion: After Globalisation

Engaging the 'Backlash'

MARTTI KOSKENNIEMI

Is it still possible to think about globalisation in the way it has been for the past twenty years? The implicit answer given by the above chapters is: 'Yes, mostly it is.' The texts discuss the effects and legitimacy of the global expansion of economic and technical governance, speculate about progress and problems, and suggest institutional reforms in the way we have come to be accustomed. The present 'backlash' – Brexit, Trump, the rise of neo-nationalism and 'alt-right' etc. – appears not to have essentially changed the context or ways in which experts should address it. People will continue to be ruled by economic and technical decision-making taking place far away from their *Lebenswelt* because the historical 'script' has not changed: most significant problems are 'global' (or 'European') in nature and need resolution in institutions and by systems of knowledge that are equally 'global' (or 'European'). Of course, criticisms about the details of the process are legitimate and welcome. But though the intensity of the backlash today may be greater than before, its anti-internationalism and its communitarian priorities are familiar from the past and invite reacting in familiar ways: by highlighting the benefits that will eventually trickle down to everyone. In any case, the best experts are working day and night to solve the (inevitable) problems that arise from a global and European dynamic and there is no reason to believe they would not succeed in the way previous generations have succeeded.

Something like this view underlies most of the chapters in this book. The view may be right. But it may also be the case that criticisms of global 'elites' today are actually more basic than assumed by academic studies such as the present. In this concluding chapter I have chosen to assume that this is indeed the case and that a wide rift has opened between the consciousness of the global professional class and the politics of the developed West. While the electorate in Europe and the United States reaped the fruit of global progress in the twentieth century, they now feel not only

453

threatened but defeated and subordinated by the liberal-internationalist 'elites'. Owing to the huge power of the West in global governance institutions, the transformations in Western mass democracy are bound to influence global and European institutions and the context of international and European law. I propose to react to the chapters in this book by assuming that Brexit, Trump, neo-nationalism and the alt-right are not a passing phenomenon but will have a profound and long-lasting effect on global governance. I will first reflect on one liberal-internationalist reaction, namely the intervention 'Building Global Community' by Mark Zuckerberg, the founder of Facebook, in early spring 2017.[1] I will suggest that despite its well-meaning purpose, this reaction remains oddly but significantly off the mark. After a brief overview of the way the chapters touch upon but avoid directly addressing themes that have inspired the backlash, I will end with a few suggestions regarding how to begin such engagement.

According to Zuckerberg, when Facebook started, the task of 'building a global community ... was not controversial'. But now it had been taken over by a 'movement for withdrawing from global connection'. Zuckerberg worries about that 'movement' and wants to react to it. But he also believes that many 'are reflecting on how we can have the most positive impact'. And he suggests that 'the most important thing' now is '*to develop the social infrastructure to give people the power to build a global community that works for all of us*'. The manifesto then breaks down into five proposals. What is needed is building supportive communities (enhancing tradition); ensuring the safety of those communities; working with information so as to inspire new ideas and develop common understandings; helping support civic activism; and building inclusiveness.

These are reasonable proposals. Support for local communities, diversity and encouragement of diverse information are important. I am especially in agreement with the call to 'help people see a more complete picture, not just alternate perspectives'. Opinions after all do not emerge randomly, like mushrooms after autumn rain. They emerge from structures and patterns; and it is through the operation of those structures and patterns that the same people tend to win, and the same ones to lose. Zuckerberg offers no suggestion as to what this 'complete picture' might consist of but he suggests that it can perhaps be identified by realising that 'across the world there are people left behind by globalization'. '*Left behind*'.

---

[1] Mark Zuckerberg, 'Building Global Community', available (also for non-Facebook users) at https://www.facebook.com/notes/mark-zuckerberg/building-global-community/10154544292806634.

Much data supports something like that. For instance, it is well-known that while some of the middle classes in developing countries as well as the richest of the rich in the developed West have benefited from twenty years of globalisation, the middle classes in the West have won nothing; on the contrary, their relative income in regard to those other groups has decreased significantly.[2]

The outrage felt by the latter – the source of the 'backlash' – is made invisible by Zuckerberg's use of the first-person plural, his easy reference to values 'we' all share. Like international lawyers, Zuckerberg employs the expression 'global community' to convey the image of everyone being in 'this' together. '[A]re we building the world we all want?' he asks, inviting his readers to share the warmth of 'community'. But I do not think the 'backlashers' feel this way. Community is wholly phenomenological, a projection each makes from their own standpoint, with regard to their own hopes and fears. Zuckerberg writes about 'our collective values and common humanity'. But as Yuval Harari wrote in his response in the *Financial Times* (25/26 March 2017), this is too easy. Would Zuckerberg dare to actually name a value without alienating part of his audience? I doubt that the invitation to share a sense of community can match the power of the widely reported data that the wealthiest 1 per cent in the world now earn over 50 per cent of global wealth, and that the wealth of the richest sixty-two people has risen by 44 per cent in the five years since 2010 – while at the same time, the wealth of the 'bottom half' fell by 41 per cent.[3]

Nobody suggests that globalisation would have treated everyone equally. Some have won, even greatly, while others have won nothing and their position in respect of their neighbours has declined. So, I wonder about the expression: 'left behind'. A better expression than 'left behind' might be *defeated*.[4] They have lost *because* others have won. The problem in Zuckerberg's analysis, and in my view in much of the liberal and professional response to Brexit, Trump etc., lies in the unproblematic use of the

---

[2] B. Milanovic, *Global Inequality: A New Approach for the Age of Globalization* (Harvard University Press, 2016).

[3] 'An Economy for the 1 per cent', Oxfam Briefing Paper 210 (18 January 2016). In November 2017, Credit Suisse reported that the wealthiest 1 per cent of world population owned 50.1 per cent of all the world's household wealth. See https://www.credit-suisse.com/corporate/en/articles/news-and-expertise/global-wealth-report-2017-201711.html. According to the report, while global wealth increased in the prior twelve months by 6.4 per cent (in Europe, from 73.3 to 79.6 billion USD), there was zero growth in Africa (where it stayed at about 2.5 billion).

[4] The theme is from D. Kennedy, *A World of Struggle: How Power, Law and Expertise Shape the Global Political Economy* (Princeton University Press, 2016).

pronoun 'we' – as if all people were automatically to agree with the liberal-professional analysis and receipt. A revealing passage appears at the end of the Zuckerberg manifesto:

> History has had many moments like today. As we've made great leaps from tribes to cities to nations, we have always had to build social infrastructure like communities, media and governments for us to thrive and reach the next level.

The 'next level'? Like in a computer game. History is a pre-established script, progress means finding what is *already there*. All that is needed is to pick up those left waiting on a lower 'level', a prior station, and bring them where 'we' already are. As if that were possible *in view of the very knowledge produced by the academic and political institutions that are always called upon to justify the latest austerity measures*. When did greed not coincide with hypocrisy?

But what if people do not feel 'left behind' but rather *crushed* by an adversary whose values, objectives and even ways of life are felt as unsupportable violence. What if the objective is not at all – as Zuckerberg suggests – to make a 'positive impact' but to dismantle or destroy the structures of authority that have invested in the 'global governance' project – structures such as the European Union (EU), the Paris climate treaty, sustainable development, development assistance, human rights, Facebook, the World Trade Organization (WTO), 'mainstream media', the academy and international finance, the whole complex sustaining the 'global elite'? What if 'free trade', 'human rights' and 'environment', etc. are experienced as obfuscating the conditions in which most people spend their lives? What if those expressions are felt as part of a process that seeks to create a global underclass to be eternally exploited by a global system of authority with a propaganda system celebrating the eternally postponed benefits of globalisation: fake science – fake news – fake authority.

Notice that I am not enquiring whether the 'global system of authority' has *really* created or is even vaguely responsible for the violations felt by the defeated. I am not suggesting further enquiries into the effects of globalisation on the lives of local communities or even whether such 'communities' have ever existed or had any meaningful 'control over their lives'. Brexit, the electoral victory of Donald Trump or the rise of alt-right in Europe and the United States are not about new facts that research has brought to light. The backlash has not been occasioned by new studies on the legitimacy deficit in the EU, on the effects of climate change or the WTO regime on underprivileged populations. It emerges from an *opinion* that invokes, above all, personal experience. But this is not an 'experience' articulated by the professional elites. It is an opinion that is given shape and power in daily encounters at the mall, on the street, in a bar or a community centre, and in the voluminous streams of consciousness traversing the social media. It is not based on research and invokes no new data. Instead, it thinks of the world of science and technology as inextricable from that 'elite' whose preferences are being rejected. What better sign than the constant public disagreement between economic, technological and legal experts, their appearance on all sides of the spectrum of conventional politics, that what they are saying is likewise just based on 'opinions'? It is time for *our* opinion now to be heard!

The debate cannot therefore be influenced by better analysis on the effects of World Bank activities, of EU Directives or of transformations of the global climate. Improved economic models or more detailed statistical reports merely add to indecipherable bureaucratic pulp. On the contrary, the production of such studies, in case they were to support an existing 'global system of authority' (and it is hard to see how they could *not* support it), would by that very fact condemn them as propaganda. Moreover, to address *opinion* by such studies (or assuming that they manifest anything beyond a contrary opinion) only confirms the utter alienation of 'the global system of authority' from 'real people'. It may even appear as yet another insult and a demonstration of the despair with which the elites cling to their privileges. What the backlash rejects is not only the system of global authority but also the scientific and technical – and legal – vocabularies through which it has been instituted and that continues to sustain it. 'Drain the swamp!'

The difficulty about the backlash is that it is not about what we know or do not know in ways that 'knowledge' is made to work in the institutions of global governance. An argument that 'Brexit' is actually harmful for British workers, that climate change is going to hit at interests in the rust belt area or that free trade will raise everyone's standard of living has no critical bite because the backlash is not about the better management of common affairs as much as about getting rid of a whole class of people – the 'global elite' – and the institutions through which they exercise power, including (perhaps above all) the hypocritical vocabularies through which they do this. If so, then it is not just a new move in the old game of postwar international policy-making but an effort to set up a wholly new game that would produce different winners and losers – though only after first extracting revenge.

When this volume was conceived, the backlash did not yet have the force with which it burst on the political stage in Western Europe and the United States. It can thus be excused if the ensuing chapters operate with the calm spirit of rational reflection in which German thinking has always excelled. One of the writers, Robert Schütze, derives that spirit from the days of European Enlightenment and especially the work of Immanuel Kant – the 'eighteenth century prince of international law philosophy'. The suggestion is that Kant had laid down the institutional alternatives for global governance but decreed that whichever will be chosen, the ensuing rulership must be public in character and constitutional in form. The Schütze chapter ends just where the backlash begins – in the 'remarkable revival of "cosmopolitan" ideas' in the second half of the twentieth century. In the same spirit, Jochen von Bernstorff celebrates the twentieth century's most brilliant international rationalist, Hans Kelsen, defending his attack on nationalism ('positivism of the State will') and what he sees as Kelsen's relentless refusal to join forces with jurists who grasped at the economic opportunities opened up by public law universalism. Kant and Kelsen appear here as innovative operators of abstract structures as well as symbols for a certain idea of liberal reason that has through the twentieth century offered a horizon of virtue from which resources have been gathered to meet the century's disasters.

The historical chapters provide the ground from which Philip Allott continues his explorations about how 'philosophy' might deal with what he has for the past thirty years suggested to us is a global 'existential crisis'.[5] Allott addresses the rise of 'populist democracy' but sees it as no more than the 'obverse of government-managed democracy', associating it with the rule of 'opinion' liable to 'unsettle' 'social structures'. He suggests that this 'cry of the oppressed' may paradoxically reveal the way 'existing social forms, not least democracy and capitalism … [fail] to respect the true interests and true aspirations of human beings'. Well, maybe, maybe not. As usual, Allott's chapter sounds like the 'wisdom of the ages' but (perhaps like any such wisdom) remains coy about what it actually requires of us (apart from reading Plato). Aoife O'Donoghue completes Part I by taking us back to the constitutional world, using the resources from thinkers of tyranny from Machiavelli to Arendt and Anghie to make the essentially 'German' point about the need of legal experts to police the boundaries of liberal legalism. Perhaps understandably, none of the chapters

[5] See, especially, P. Allott, *Eunomia: New Order for a New World* (Oxford University Press, 1980).

seeks a departure from what O'Donoghue calls the 'constitutional ethic' – but none asks the implicit backlash question, either, as to why anybody not already well-positioned in the global governance project would wish to carve its basic rules in stone as a 'constitution'. Why would the defeated want to sacralise the victor's regime in this way?

The four chapters on the 'substantive challenges' illustrate in different ways the difficulty of integrating the backlash in legal analyses. Mark Weller's constitutionalist perspective on the norms on the use of force accepts that pacifist (and liberal?) rationalism can go only so far in this regard – pacifism remains 'utopian', and force is still needed for 'the common interest'. But the reasons that obstruct what Weller calls 'the civilisational mission' still remain curiously abstract and procedural: there is no mention of Syria, the annexation of Crimea, the intensification of the arms race or the bloodshed inside so many states today. What is there to learn (if anything) from, say, the (illegal) war on Iraq or the disaster of Libya? The distance of the chapters from most people's experience emerge in the Hoekman/Mavroidis chapter on the fragmentation of trade law. Their rationalist calculation of the 'advantages and disadvantages' of multi- and plurilateral approaches to trade was composed at a moment when the Trans-Pacific Partnership (TPP) and Transatlantic Trade and Investment Partnership (TTIP) died in their original formulation. It seems today anything but obvious whether 'tariffs [will] gradually become a non-issue for international trade relations'. There is something in the very effort to analyse the pros and cons of technical solutions for trade deals that makes this highly competent chapter sound precisely like the elite talk in which backlash hears only the obfuscations of the enemy. It is not only that the question of winners and losers is not addressed in a clear way but what 'winning' and 'losing' might mean today can no longer be taken for granted.

In a parallel vein, Markus Gehring suggests that international environmental governance has finally come to grips with the substance of what is happening to the world around us and that, therefore 'the only real unresolved challenge in international environmental governance is the lack of integration between the different regimes'. How to make experts in the different sub-disciplines speak better together? For the rest of us, well, there does not seem much else to do than to admire the 'legal innovations' and 'strategic action plans' and sympathise with the efforts at bureaucratic coordination. As if power and inequality had become irrelevant in a new world of 'governance' (the section on climate change makes no mention of the US withdrawal from the Paris agreement). Olympia Bekou's discussion of the fifteen years' experience with the International Criminal Court raises similar kinds of questions. No other institution symbolises the victory of 1990s liberal universalism more powerfully. The difficulties – attack by the African states, the unbalanced geographic spectrum of the proceedings, the massacres in the war in Syria continuing under everyone's eyes – conflict with the author's confident view of the court today moving into 'routine'. It is natural for the participants in the international criminal law project to seek to depict yesterday's victories as today's business as usual. But that is unlikely to persuade others.

The chapters on European constitutionalism and the substance of European law exercise themes familiar from past debates. The problems are technical, the way ahead – integration – set by history. Bruno de Witte, for example, argues that the union 'has almost entirely replaced its Member States as an international actor in a number of policy fields'. Really – France, the UK and Germany have been 'almost entirely replaced'? That is like Nigel Farage speaking – and a prologue to the call for 'taking back control'. The effort to avoid examining the world behind the treaties was always whistling in the dark, terribly risky if it turned out that the forest was actually full of monsters. The relationship between Europe and the world has many dimensions, but focus on 'autonomy' presumes an identity to 'Europe' and European law that may not today be taken for granted: there are almost as many 'Europes' as there are parties in the parliaments of Member States. Ramses Wessel discusses the many pressures both inside and outside the Union that push for further integration of EU foreign policy. But instead of physical phenomena these 'pressures' arise from elite interpretations that presume a consensus of values and express a worry about the efficiency of their realisation when there may be no such consensus at all. What if you are a fundamentalist Irish or Polish Catholic faced with a foreign policy project to advance safe abortions as part of gender equality? Legitimacy and subsidiarity remain big themes, as discussed by Katarzyna Granat, that aim at softening the intensity of integration. But what if there is no wish to compromise, and pressure to do so is already felt as a violation? What if one's desire is precisely to avoid Europe becoming more 'legitimate'? Dimitry Kochenov's chapter connects European citizenship (rightly, it seems) with building a 'European federation'. Here there would clearly be some room to debate: how does the backlash view such citizenship? The debates about more or less intergovernmentalism, as pursued by Alicia Hinarejos, seems equally distant from present debates about Europe's direction: it does not matter how powers are distributed between Brussels institutions; they are *all* part of the problem!

The chapters on substantive EU law read like reports internal to Union institutions, taking official objectives for granted, seeking their efficient realisation. Ludwig Krämer celebrates the 'innovative' and 'progressive' solutions the EU has proposed to environmental problems. Here Brussels appears as a busy centre where experts are churning out legislation so as to deal with climate change, to stem the loss of biodiversity and to prepare complex chemical regulations. There are, it appears, more than 1,000 judgments on environmental matters by the European Court of Justice! While all this hurly-burly must be a genuine source of satisfaction to the insiders, I wonder how the backlashers see it. What about those who do not share the green ethos of EU experts and academic commentators? The two groups often appear indistinguishable, their members change places, thereby facilitating inside identification of 'progress' but further contributing to the alienation of the rest. And what about human rights? Valsamis Mitsilegas gives his readers an exposé of the justifications on EU action in criminal law and an overview of the legal and policy instruments. Then he suggests that we are in the presence of a 'paradigm change' from security to 'fundamental rights'. But surely, the wish is father to the thought. Is there any chance of a further turn to human rights in policy-making after all that we have learned about developments in Poland and Hungary and about the xenophobia triggered by the fluxes of asylum seekers across the continent? Nothing is less certain.

The above chapters, with the exception of Allott's, do not engage with the backlash. Instead, they mostly pursue the liberal-internationalist agendas of the 1990s, confidently whistling in the dark. Old themes and problem-settings remain as they have been. Is this an ivory-tower effect, or just the general slowness with which academic communities react to political events ('owl of Minerva')? It may also not be obvious what the appropriate legal response would be. Domestically, the backlash has often targeted legal hierarchies and especially higher courts and 'unelected judges' as illegitimately intervening against the 'will of the people'. Reading the German *Verfassungsblog*, for example, one gets a vibrant sense of the ideological distance between the legal elites and the more vocal parts of the backlash. To the extent that the attacks are aimed at political correctness and 'human rights fundamentalism', law and lawyers lend themselves as obvious targets. International and European law are esoteric projects whose influence on what appears as 'global governance' in the eyes of the backlash is hard to measure. Research institutions do produce reports on legal aspects of current affairs and academic experts routinely participate in the work of international governance bodies. No doubt, both disciplines appear as part of the groups of winners. Positions taken by international lawyers on immigration, human rights of minorities and women, free trade and

climate change are what the backlash rejects. But there has been no specific attack on international or European *law*. Even the Trump administration has paid it the backhanded compliment of ignoring it.

It is not clear what the lawyers' response should be. There is a tendency
to interpret the backlash as a psychological reaction to the speed of what is
presented as 'change' (but '*plus ça change ...* ') – and to fall back on the his-
toricist assumption about those 'left behind'. This suggests that the liberal
internationalists should continue doing what they have been doing this
far, but more thoroughly – let there be more legitimacy, more efficiency,
more transparency, more participation, better coordination and so on. But
this might only stand out as more noise to block the power of the outrage.
Responding in this way might be right if it could be expected that in the
end reason will prevail and that 'reason' coincides with the priorities of
global and European institutions and the relevant academic commentary.
'Reason', on this view, would be its own defence. But this is surely what
the backlash is questioning – that the elite vocabularies that have hegem-
onised debates on international 'reform' since the 1990s actually are the
'voice of reason' instead of propaganda for distributive choices that favour
the interests of those who speak it.

But how do you defend 'reason' if not by reason? The first thing to do
would be to step into the shoes of the critic and try to see just what the position is from which *my* reason appears as illegitimate obfuscation. I have
elsewhere discussed the difficulty that international criminal lawyers have
in seeing themselves as the enemy of somebody.[6] 'How', they despair, 'can
reason and truth appear as unreason and fake news?' In two decades of
intensifying international activity in Geneva, Brussels and Strasbourg, the
priorities and problem-setting entertained by international experts have
been entrenched as an unquestioned common sense. Human rights, free
trade and the fight against impunity: the challenge would now be to see
them as contestable (and actually contested) vocabularies and institutional solutions through which some people exercise power over others,
to redescribe professional and technical decision-making as the constant
reproduction of political and social hierarchies.[7] It is not obvious that
those languages – and the systems of knowledge and expertise that they
sustain – possess the kind of openness that this would require. This should

---

[6] M. Koskenniemi, 'A Trap to the Innocent ...' in Claus Kress and Stefan Barriaga (eds.), *The
   Crime of Aggression. A Commentary* (Cambridge University Press, 2016), 1359–85.
[7] A good place from which to start would be reading Kennedy, *A World of Struggle* (above
   n. 4).

not be impossible, for often the most experienced experts are also the most aware of the limits and fragility of what they know, and of the difficulty of drawing clear conclusions from that knowledge. In expert encounters, one constantly hears laments about the uncertainties of one's discipline, and the way its leading representatives disagree about the fundamentals, perhaps especially about the fundamentals. But this knowledge rarely leaves the professional conference or the pages of a technical journal. Humility is attractive when one is among one's peers: academics readily admit to each other that everything can be (and usually is) contested by respectable opinions on the other side. But it is very hard to do that in public, to respond to a journalist in an interview where one is invited to speak as a legal or technical expert – 'well, I have no idea' – or at least recognise that alongside *my* preferred view, there is also that *other* view and that the choice between them cannot really be made by the technical tools we have. But even if this might sound a healthy move in a democracy where 'politics' is in crisis, it is not clear that it would suffice.

In a recent essay, Alan Finlayson described what he called 'Brexitism' as the refusal to engage in a 'rational' debate on reform, inspired by a wholesale frustration about 'liberal intellectuals' unable to produce clear visions of the future – whether it is the economy, technology or the environment – and the 'more or less' responses of academic elites, translated in the context of the 'Brexit' vote into a conviction that 'they' simply have no clue. 'If you don't know everything – about climate change, the economy or the political trajectory of Slovenia – then you know nothing.'[8] The modest reason of the liberal (according to 'Brexitism') will only always turn to supporting the (liberal) *status quo*. It is therefore not a 'reason' at all; it is a *bias*. The point therefore cannot be – for the 'Brexiters' – to engage in those interminable debates but to change the people who rule us: 'Whatever it will be, it cannot be any worse.' Liberal activists have always been reluctant to see themselves and men and women of power in this way – as representatives of a 'bias'. A first step for engaging the backlash would be to provide that re-description. The 'reason' of the internationalist, or the expert, whatever else it is, would also appear as discursive power, disciplinary power, media power and power of expertise. This is what it would require to take seriously the backlash experience of not having been 'left behind' but 'defeated'.

It has not always been clear what the Left cliché that expertise and governance should be 'politicised' might mean (apart from a call to increasing

---

[8] Alan Finlayson, 'Brexitism', London Review of Books (18 May 2017), 22.

the number of Left experts in governance). The re-description of global governance as political, in the sense of consisting of a pattern of institutional decision-making where open-ended economic and technical (including legal) vocabularies are used to maintain or strengthen definite hierarchies and distributionary choices, might at least provide a starting point for understanding and possibly engaging with the backlash. Whom does global governance support? No doubt, there are risks in posing such questions, not least because it suggests some equivalence between expert reason and 'populist' priorities, 'scientific truth' and 'widespread opinion'. It is likely that such an effort would also challenge the hierarchies *inside* expert regimes: highlighting the open-endedness of legal vocabularies would weaken the consensus among legal institutions and strengthen contesting voices. 'Global governance' would probably not remain quite what it has been once expert debates are also viewed as struggles over political preferences. But the alternative is likely to be worse. Not to engage the backlash at all might lead to its militarisation (or at least the spectre of such) – with the consequent tightening of the disciplines of governance and security over all of us.

Epilogue

Elements of a Theory of Global Governance

DAVID HELD

I Introduction

The politicians who gathered from forty-five countries in San Francisco in 1945 were faced with the choice of either allowing the world to drift in the aftermath of World War II, or to begin a process of rebuilding the foundations of the international community. Addressing the gathering of leaders, US President Harry Truman warned that the world was at a crossroads:

> You members of this Conference are to be the architects of the better world. In your hands rests our future. By your labors at this Conference, we shall know if suffering humanity is to achieve a just and lasting peace ... With ever increasing brutality and destruction, modern warfare, if unchecked, would ultimately crush all civilization. We still have a choice between the alternatives: The continuation of international chaos, or the establishment of a world organization for the enforcement of peace.[1]

At the heart of the post-war security arrangements was, of course, the newly formed United Nations (UN) and, along with it, the development of a new legal and institutional framework for the maintenance of peace and security. Article I of the UN Charter explicitly states that the purpose of the UN is to 'maintain international peace and security and to that end: to take effective collective measures for the prevention and removal of threats to peace'.[2] Moreover, Article I goes on to stress that peace would be sought and protected through principles of international law. It concludes with the position that the UN is to be 'a centre for harmonizing the actions of nations in the attainment of these common ends'.

---

[1] Harry S. Truman, Address to the United Nations Conference in San Francisco, 25 April 1945.

[2] United Nations, Charter of the United Nations, 24 October 1945, 1 UNTS XVI.

With peace comes the prospect of stable and rising prosperity. While maintaining global peace and stability serves the obvious purpose of limiting violence, it is also a quintessential prerequisite for accelerating 'globalisation' across many domains of human activity: trade, finance and communication being the most prominent among them.

The titanic struggles of World War I and World War II led to a growing acknowledgement that the nature and process of global governance would have to change if the most extreme forms of violence against humanity were to be outlawed, and the growing interconnectedness and interdependence of all nations recognised. Slowly, the subject, scope and very sources of international law were all called into question. The image of international regulation projected by the UN Charter (and related documents) was one of 'states still jealously sovereign' but now linked together in a 'myriad of relations'; states would be under pressure to resolve disagreements by peaceful means and according to legal criteria; subject in principle to tight restrictions on the resort to force; and constrained to observe 'certain standards' with regard to the treatment of all persons in their territory, including their own citizens.[3]

At the heart of this development lies claims made on behalf not just of individual states, but on behalf of an alternative organising principle of world affairs: ultimately, a community of all states, with equal voting rights in the UN General Assembly, openly and collectively regulating international life while constrained to observe the UN Charter and a battery of human rights conventions.[4]

Yet, the promise of the UN was compromised almost from its inception by the Cold War – the ideological and geopolitical tensions that would shape the world for almost fifty years. These tensions stemmed from the political, economic and military rivalry between the Soviet Union and the United States, each bolstered by their respective allies. However, this standoff facilitated, somewhat paradoxically, a deepening of interdependence among world powers. It is difficult to imagine a more immediate form of interdependence than Mutually Assured Destruction (MAD). Once the world reached a point at which a small group of decision-makers could release weapons that could, literally, obliterate the rest of the world, it created a new recognition of shared vulnerability. This awareness demanded greater coordination among world powers. Thus, the nuclear standoff

3 A. Cassese, 'Violence, War and the Rule of Law in the International Community' in D. Held (ed.), *Political Theory Today* (Polity, 1991), 256.
4 D. Held, *Democracy and the Global Order* (Stanford University Press, 1995).

of the Cold War drew world powers closer together as a way to mitigate the threat and ensure that military posturing did not escalate into all-out nuclear confrontation.[5]

Thus, despite all its complexities and risks, the post-World War II UN system, including weapons of mass destruction and the threat of MAD, facilitated, in many respects, a new form of 'governed globalisation' that contributed to relative peace and prosperity across the world over several decades. The importance of this should not be underestimated. The period was marked by peace between the great powers, although there were, of course, many proxy wars fought out in the Global South. This relative stability created the conditions for what now can be regarded as an unprecedented period of prosperity that characterised the 1950s onward. While the economic record of the post-war years varies by country, and by region, many experienced significant economic growth and living standards rose rapidly across several parts of the world. By the late 1980s a variety of East Asian countries were beginning to grow at an unprecedented speed, and by the late 1990s countries such as China, India and Brazil had gained significant economic momentum, a process that continues to this day (although Brazil is faltering now).

Post-war multilateral institutions – not just the UN, but the Bretton Woods institutions as well – created conditions under which a multitude of actors could benefit from economic activity, forming corporations, investing abroad, developing global production chains and engaging with a plethora of other social and economic processes associated with globalisation. These conditions, combined with the expansionary logic of capitalism and basic technological innovation, changed the nature of the world economy, radically increasing dependence on people and countries from every corner of the world.

This is not to say that international institutions were the only cause of the dynamic form of globalisation experienced over the last few decades. However, economic globalisation, and everything associated with it, was allowed to thrive and develop because it took place in a relatively open, relatively peaceful, relatively liberal institutionalised world order. By preventing World War III and another Great Depression, the multilateral order arguably did just as much for interdependence as microprocessors

---

[5] It is worth noting that this sense of shared vulnerability can only be upheld if both parties believe the 'good life' lies in this world; in other words, if they are both more or less secular. If this association is no longer valid the idea of shared vulnerability on this earth breaks down.

or email.[6] From the late 1940s to the beginning of the twenty-first century, a densely complex interdependent world order emerged.

II   Gridlock

However, global interdependence has now progressed to the point where it has altered our ability to engage in further global cooperation; that is to say, economic and political shifts in large part attributable to the *successes* of the post-war multilateral order are now amongst the factors grinding that system into gridlock or deadlock. Because of the remarkable success of global cooperation in the post-war order, human interconnectedness weighs much more heavily on politics than it did in 1945. The need for international cooperation has never been higher. Yet, the 'supply' side of the equation, effective institutionalised multilateral cooperation, has stalled. In areas such as nuclear proliferation, the explosion of small-arms sales, terrorism, failed states, global economic imbalances, financial market instability, global poverty and inequality, biodiversity losses, water deficits and climate change, multilateral and transnational cooperation is now increasingly ineffective or threadbare. Gridlock is not unique to one issue domain but appears to be becoming a general feature of global governance. Why?

It is possible to identify four reasons for this blockage, four pathways to gridlock: rising multipolarity, harder problems, institutional inertia and institutional fragmentation.[7] Each pathway can be thought of as a growing trend that embodies a specific mix of causal mechanisms.

Growing multipolarity. The absolute number of states has increased by 300 per cent in the last seventy years. More importantly, the number of states that 'matter' on a given issue – that is, the states without whose cooperation a global problem cannot be adequately addressed – has expanded by similar proportions. At Bretton Woods in 1945, the rules of the world economy could essentially be written by the United States with some consultation with the UK and other European allies. In the aftermath of the 2008–9 crisis, the G-20 has become the principal forum for global economic management, not because the established powers desired to be more inclusive, but because they could not solve the problem on their own.

---

[6] J. Mueller, 'The Obsolescence of Major War' (1990) 21(3) *Security Dialogue* 321–8; J. O'Neal and B. Russett, 'The Classical Liberals Were Right: Democracy, Interdependence and Conflict, 1950–1985' (1997) 41(2) *International Studies Quarterly* 267–94.

[7] T. Hale et al., *Gridlock: Why Global Cooperation Is Failing When We Need It Most* (Polity, 2013).

However, a consequence of this progress is now that many more countries, representing a diverse range of interests, must agree in order for global cooperation to occur.

Harder problems. As interdependence has deepened, the types and scope of problems around which countries must cooperate has evolved. Problems are both now more extensive, crossing more countries, and intensive, penetrating deep into the domestic policy space and daily life of many countries. Consider the example of trade. For most of the post-war era, trade negotiations focused on reducing tariff levels on manufactured products traded between industrialised countries. Now, however, negotiating a trade agreement requires also discussing a host of social, environmental and cultural subjects – GMOs, intellectual property, health and environmental standards, biodiversity, labour standards – about which countries often disagree sharply. In the area of environmental change, a similar set of considerations applies.[8] To clean up industrial smog or address ozone depletion required fairly discrete actions from a small number of top polluters. By contrast, the threat of climate change and the efforts to mitigate it involve nearly all countries of the globe. Yet, the divergence of voice and interest within both the developed and developing worlds, along with the sheer complexity of the incentives needed to achieve a low-carbon economy, have made a global deal extremely difficult to achieve.

Institutional inertia. The post-war order succeeded, in part, because it incentivised great power involvement in key institutions. From the UN Security Council, to the Bretton Woods institutions, to the Non-Proliferation Treaty, key pillars of the global order explicitly granted special privileges to the countries that were wealthy and powerful at the time of their creation. This hierarchy, it could be argued, was necessary to secure the participation of the most important countries in global governance. Today, the gain from this trade-off has shrunk while the costs have grown. The architects of the post-war order did not, in most cases, design institutions that would organically adjust to fluctuations in national power. And it is very hard to change them; for example, numerous efforts to alter or reform the position of the permanent members of the Security Council have floundered.

Fragmentation. The institution builders of the 1940s began with, essentially, a blank canvas. But efforts to cooperate internationally today occur in a dense institutional ecosystem shaped by path dependency. The exponential rise in both multilateral and transnational organisations has

---

[8] Ibid., Chapter 3.

created a more complex multilevel and multi-actor system of global governance. Yet, within this dense web of institutions mandates can conflict, interventions are frequently uncoordinated, and all too typically scarce resources are subject to intense competition. For instance, there are many examples of aid failing to meet its targets in pressing humanitarian crises due to the fragmentation of efforts. There are also many cases in emerging global health crises where the international community has failed to coordinate its action in sufficient time to prevent the loss of life accelerating.[9]

The challenges now faced by the multilateral order are substantially different from those faced by the 1945 victors in the post-war settlement. They are second-order cooperation problems arising from previous phases of success in global coordination. Together, they now block and inhibit problem solving and reform at the global level, and create the risk of dangerous drift in the global order, punctuated by force and violence.

Since *Gridlock* was published, I, along with my *Gridlock* co-author Thomas Hale, have been exploring anomalies and exceptions to the somewhat grim diagnosis of contemporary multilateralism. Is global governance more adaptive and resilient than previously believed? It is important to address this question not only to enhance our understanding of world politics, but also, crucially, to help think through practical solutions to the very real dilemmas of governing interdependence in the twenty-first century.[10]

III   Pathways through Gridlock

Examining a range of instances in which gridlock has not prevented effective global governance from emerging, eight 'pathways' out of gridlock have been uncovered in detailed analysis.[11] The pathways can be thought of either as routes 'through' gridlock, meaning more short-term adaptations, responses or strategies for dealing with pressing needs, or roads 'beyond' gridlock, meaning longer-term transformations dealing with the potential to substantially reshape world politics. Routes through gridlock may, over time, evolve into more substantial changes. Given space limits, five pathways will be focused upon here.

---

[9] See G. W. Brown and D. Held, 'Gridlock and Beyond in Global Health' in T. Hale et al. (eds.), *Beyond Gridlock* (Polity, 2017).

[10] T. Hale et al. (eds.), *Beyond Gridlock* (Polity, 2017).

[11] Ibid.

Civil society coalitions with reformist governments. Some of the greatest successes in global governance in the 1990s came about from concerted civil society efforts. When activist groups have been able to partner with countries led by progressive governments, significant shifts have been possible, such as the Landmines Treaty, the creation of the International Criminal Court, the Responsibility to Protect doctrine, the Guiding Principles for Internal Displacement or the Framework Convention on Tobacco Control.

Gridlock has likely increased the barriers to success for such coalitions by making it easier for recalcitrant states to block would-be reformers. Nonetheless, the mobilisation of such coalitions still provides a meaningful way to achieve results in global governance. Civil society groups and social movements tend to be more successful in agenda-setting and policy impact if (a) they work with governments or states and (b) seek change that, while reformist, can be accommodated within existing structures and organisational principles, at least in the short to medium term. More structural transformations of who gets what, when and how tend, if and when successful, to be the outcome of longer-term struggles and exchange between civil society/social movements and structures of power. Such transformations have been all too rare since the foundation of the UN and European Union (EU), and both of these, of course, were founded against the backdrop of catastrophe.

Autonomous and adaptive international institutions. Gridlock argued that the past seventy years of international institution-building has had a profound effect on world politics, with many positive outcomes, but also a number of second-order cooperation problems (e.g. institutional inertia and fragmentation) that result from a denser institutional landscape. While it is of course recognised that, under some conditions, international institutions can become formidable autonomous actors in world politics, on average, we might expect gridlock to reduce the ability of international institutions to act proactively.[12]

But there may also be systematic ways in which international organisations can be more autonomous and adaptive than these trends suggest. First, some international institutions have not seen their mandates or capabilities reduced under gridlock. The International Energy Agency, for example, possesses significant autonomy to decide on fuel-reserve requirements, and its restrictive membership (to Organisation for Economic

---

[12] M. Barnett and M. Finnemore, *Rules for the World: International Organizations in Global Politics* (Cornell University Press, 2004).

Cooperation and Development (OECD) countries) has ensured that it has not been hamstrung by contestation among Member States.[13]

Additionally, some international institutions have been given unique capacities to adapt to emerging issues and shifting constellations of power and interests. This ability may be particularly strong for legal institutions, which may possess a 'generative' function; that is, the ability to decide new rules for situations not originally envisioned by states. For example, the World Trade Organization (WTO) Dispute Settlement Mechanism has been increasingly called upon to adjudicate cases for which WTO members have established no clear set of rules. Many of these controversial cases have even involved member states, such as China, that joined the WTO significantly after the treaty-making process had occurred, and which we might therefore expect to challenge existing rules. Despite this difficult circumstance, the WTO adjudicators have developed a careful, politically informed jurisprudence that has been able to resolve disputes over a number of issues beyond what the WTO's creators originally envisioned, and ensured a relatively high rate of compliance with these decisions.

Plurality and diversity of actors and agencies around common goals and norms. Gridlock focused on the negative effects of fragmentation in global governance, such as the increase in transaction costs that may result, or the way in which forum-shopping can undermine incentives for cooperation. However, there may also be ways in which fragmentation can represent an adaptive and effective response to the challenges of cooperation.

A proliferation of diverse organisations and institutions, for example, may be efficacious when common rules or principles give coherence to an otherwise fragmented institutional landscape. For example, transnational commercial arbitration represents a common set of practices and procedures for resolving disputes between commercial actors across borders. While it depends in part on international treaty law, the work of actually adjudicating disputes is carried out by hundreds of private legal organisations around the world, specialising in commercial dispute resolution. The decisions of these bodies are then given force through domestic courts under both international and domestic law.[14] The regime has proven highly resilient, enduring across geopolitical shifts, including gridlock, that have undermined more formalised institutions.

---

[13] A. Florini, 'Global Energy Policy' in T. Hale et al. (eds.), *Beyond Gridlock* (Polity, 2017).

[14] T. Hale, *Between Interests and Law: The Politics of Transnational Commercial Disputes* (Cambridge University Press, 2015).

Interventions to alter the preferences of states over time. Because growing multipolarity increases the number of states with a voice, and with varying preferences, *Gridlock* expects cooperation to stall. Some scholars have, however, emphasised the way in which the proliferation of global governance may shift states' interests in ways that promote cooperation, for example by 'socialising' states in cooperative patterns.[15] One such mechanism involves interactions between international or transnational institutions and domestic constituencies. Under certain conditions, such institutions are able to strengthen groups within countries that favour increased cooperation or more effective compliance with existing institutions. For example, various human rights institutions were created partly to strengthen the role of pro-law, pro-rights bodies within domestic politics by elevating their voice to the international level. A similar idea animates the new 'pledge and review' system for national climate policies that was created by the 2015 Paris Agreement: domestic groups are empowered to ensure states meet their internationally recognised climate pledges, and lobby against them if they fail, or challenge them to do better if they succeed.

Threats to major powers' core interests. It is a core tenet of international relations theory that when one or more great powers has a strong national interest in policies that could create a global public good, they will be willing and often able to provide that public good. Hard versions of Realist theory see this condition as the only setting in which global public goods are likely to be provided, and it has been advanced as a prominent explanation for post-war global order.[16] A central argument of *Gridlock* is that this mechanism has been decreasingly common in more recent decades, as growing multipolarity (a) increases the number of great powers that are required to act to provide a global public good in many issues domains; and (b) increases the heterogeneity of interests amongst the great powers. Both of these effects make it less likely for a sufficient coalition of major powers to come together to provide a public good. For example, preventing global financial contagion requires a much larger coalition of countries to act than in, say, the 1970s and those countries' preferences are shaped by very different domestic political economies.

---

[15] J. Ikenberry, *Liberal Leviathan: The Origins, Crisis, and Transformation of the American World* (Princeton University Press, 2011).

[16] R. Gilpin, *War and Change in World Politics* (Cambridge University Press, 1981).

But while gridlock has reduced the conditions under which major powers will be able to provide global public goods as a positive externality of their national interests, it still remains possible. Moreover, it may be the case that gridlock, by reducing the efficacy of multilateralism, generates exactly the kinds of crises that are most likely to bring together great powers, despite long-term trends to the contrary. Such dynamics can be seen in the (fragile) P5+1 coalition which negotiated with Iran; in transgovernmental networks like the Financial Action Task Force (focused on money laundering, especially when connected to terrorist networks); in efforts to counter piracy around the Horn of Africa; in the launching of a concerted effort to tackle Ebola in West Africa; and in other security-oriented fields. Though growing multipolarity has made it less possible for a great power (or coalition of powers) to provide global public goods unilaterally, it remains possible. For issues where (a) a great power (or sufficient coalition of powers) have a strong interest in solving a problem and (b) no other great powers are opposed, we can expect action to overcome gridlock. Such occasions typically arise in the face of incontrovertible security threats when the relevant powers can gain much more from cooperation than from conflict. Outside the area of security, threats from the global economy (such as during the 2008–9 global financial crisis) or from the environment (above all climate change) can mobilise collective action, although it is not always durable beyond the experience of the immediate threat.

IV   Conclusion

The pathways through, and beyond, gridlock outlined here are an attempt to identify the general mechanisms through which effective global governance can be achieved even in the presence of second-order cooperation problems. A number of additional points help provide a context for understanding their role and relevance.

First, as with the four gridlock trends, each pathway through gridlock does not apply in each sector. Rather, different pathways may manifest in different combinations in different areas.

Second, it is important to note that pathways through gridlock may only be partial, or may be more effective in certain settings than in others. None of the pathways elaborated here can be recognised as silver bullets or panaceas. The focus is instead on relative improvements in outcomes compared to, for instance, doing little or nothing at all.

Third, different pathways can interact or combine to produce distinct outcomes. Some of them may work in concert with each other in such a way that the net effect is greater than the sum of the parts. Or, it may also be the case that pathways counterbalance each other – with some leading a sector out of gridlock, and others exacerbating gridlock.

Fourth, while gridlock and pathways through it provide elements of a theory of global governance, one must be acutely aware that these dynamics are inextricably linked to and conditioned by domestic political forces, particularly those in the major powers. In *Gridlock*, it was noted how political challenges in several major powers makes gridlock increasingly entrenched. Regrettably, there is little evidence that the situation has improved in the intervening years. In the United States, increasing partisanship driven by the rise of the radical right within the Republican Party, has limited the country's ability to legislate on major issues.[17] It has also rendered all but impossible the ability of the US Senate to ratify international treaties, prompting the executive branch to take unprecedented measures to credibly commit to international cooperation. In Europe, the ongoing tension between economic and political integration remains unresolved, while challenges like migration from the Middle East are threatening to roll back hard-won integration. In China, the challenge of reforming the economy from a highly polluting investment- and export-led model to one that emphasises domestic consumption and human welfare, threatens to substantially distract the government from global affairs. Across these diverse jurisdictions, cross-cutting trends like growing (intra-country) inequality raise fundamental challenges that are likely to exacerbate gridlock. While these domestic-level dynamics fall outside the focus here, they can reinforce gridlock and therefore affect any consideration of pathways beyond it.

The account of gridlock and pathways through it should be understood in the context of realistic counterfactuals. Many of the pathways explored, singly or in combination, will not usher in imminently a radically more effective set of global governance arrangements. The concern, instead, is in identifying systematic mechanisms that can reasonably ameliorate or undo the more pernicious consequences of multilateral gridlock. The hope is that the analytic arguments advanced here, suitably elaborated and tested, will increase our understanding of which political strategies can best advance human welfare in a globalised, gridlocked world.

In the aftermath of World War II the institutional breakthroughs that occurred provided the momentum for decades of sustained economic growth and geopolitical stability sufficient for the transformation of the

---

[17] N. McCarty et al., *Polarized America: The Dance of Ideology and Unequal Riches* (MIT Press, 2006).

world economy, the shift from the Cold War to a multipolar order and the rise of new communication and network societies. However, what worked then does not work as well now, as gridlock freezes problem-solving capacity in global governance. The search for pathways through and beyond gridlock is a hugely significant task – nationally and globally – if global governance is to be once again effective, responsive and fit for purpose.

INDEX